T0331997

Billionaires
in World Politics

Billionaires in World Politics

PETER HÄGEL

OXFORD
UNIVERSITY PRESS

OXFORD
UNIVERSITY PRESS

Great Clarendon Street, Oxford, OX2 6DP,
United Kingdom

Oxford University Press is a department of the University of Oxford.
It furthers the University's objective of excellence in research, scholarship,
and education by publishing worldwide. Oxford is a registered trade mark of
Oxford University Press in the UK and in certain other countries

Published in the United States of America by Oxford University Press
198 Madison Avenue, New York, NY 10016, United States of America

British Library Cataloguing in Publication Data
Data available

Library of Congress Control Number: 2020931639

ISBN 978-0-19-885271-1

Printed and bound in Great Britain by
Clays Ltd, Elcograf S.p.A.

In memory of my father, from whom I learned to look at the big picture, and for Pauline, who has drawn my mind to people's stories.

Acknowledgments

Arriving at this stage has involved a long voyage, and many friends, family members, and colleagues have supported me throughout the process, for which I am deeply grateful.

I thank my supervisor Hans-Peter Müller, whose enthusiasm for my research has allowed me to turn it into a dissertation, and whose encouragement and advice have helped me to pull it off. He pointed me to Max Weber's thinking about prophets, which has proven to be a fruitful notion when contemplating the role of billionaires in today's world. In addition to Hans-Peter Müller, Wolfgang Merkel, Friedbert Rüb, Jochen Steinbicker, and Seongcheol Kim have constituted an excellent viva jury, whose comments have aided me in improving my manuscript for the book publication.

Jochen Steinbicker has also helped me a lot with the first publication of parts of my research, and his remarks during our conversations have contributed to clarifying and solidifying a number of points—thank you! Richard Beardsworth has been a keen advocate of my billionaires project from the first sketches to the final publication—I am much obliged. I have appreciated Anja Röcke's useful comments, as well as the ideas emerging out of my talks with Oliver Feltham, Geoff Gilbert, Dan Gunn, Jayson Harsin, Peter Hyll Larsen, Michelle Kuo, and Steve Sawyer. Celeste Schenck, as well as Renate Stauß, Simon Raiser, Björn Warkalla, Joke Haafkens, Caroline Juillard, and Henri Peretz never tired of urging me to finish—thank you for your trust and your assistance.

The participants of the "Bringing the Individual Back In—International Relations and the First Image" workshop at the *ECPR Joint Sessions* in St. Gallen, April 12–17, 2011, were among the first to provide feedback on my nascent research project—thank you for your comments, especially Bernd Bucher, who helped me to refine my understanding of agency. I have also benefitted from the feedback on my presentation at the "From the 'Passion for Equality' to the Struggle Against Inequalities: Realities and Representations" conference at *The American University of Paris*, hosted by the *Center for Critical Democracy Studies* and *The Tocqueville Society*, February 5/6, 2016. Likewise, I am grateful for the remarks at the symposium on "Soziale Ungleichheit der Lebensführung" at *Humboldt-Universität zu Berlin*, January 13/14, 2017, notably Ronald Hitzler's recommendation to look at how billionaires relate to Machiavelli's understanding of political action.

At Oxford University Press, Dominic Byatt has been a key supporter from the beginning to the end, Jayshree Thirumaran, Olivia Wells and Matthew Williams have ensured an incredibly smooth publishing process, and Phil Dines has been a very meticulous copy editor. Many thanks to all of them, and to the anonymous reviewer for her/his endorsement and the valuable comments, which have helped me to restructure and improve my manuscript. I have also been impressed by how OUP's design team turned my vague idea into a powerful cover image.

Over the years, Pauline's unwavering confidence and backing has been priceless—thank you for sharing your strength and your intellect with me. Ezra and Armin have made me happy and proud—keep it up! Last but not least, I thank my parents for all that they made possible, and my sisters for being by my side.

Contents

List of Figures and Tables

List of Abbreviations

AI	Amnesty International
AIPAC	American Israel Public Affairs Committee
BEPS	Base Erosion and Profit Shifting
BIS	Bank for International Settlements
BIT	Bilateral Investment Treaty
BMGF	Bill & Melinda Gates Foundation (also "Gates Foundation")
CEO	Chief Operating Officer
DAH	Development Assistance for Health
EU	European Union
EMS	European Monetary System
ERM	European Exchange Rate Mechanism
FATCA	Foreign Account Tax Compliance Act
FBI	Federal Bureau of Investigation
FDI	Foreign Direct Investment
FPA	Foreign Policy Analysis
FSB	Financial Stability Board
GAVI	Global Alliance for Vaccines and Immunization
GDP	Gross Domestic Product
GOP	Grand Old Party (nickname for Republican Party in the U.S.)
HNWIs	High-Net Worth Individuals
HRW	Human Rights Watch
HSS	Health System Strengthening
IAC	Israeli-American Council
ICSID	International Centre for Settlement of Investment Disputes
ICT	Information and Communication Technologies
IFPMA	International Federation of Pharmaceutical Manufacturers & Associations
IHME	Institute for Health Metrics and Evaluation
IMF	International Monetary Fund
IO	International Organization
IPCC	Intergovernmental Panel on Climate Change
IR	International Relations (as an academic discipline)
LTTE	Liberation Tigers of Tamil Eelam (official name of "Tamil Tigers")
LVS	Las Vegas Sands Corporation
MNC	Multinational Corporation
NAFTA	North American Free Trade Agreement
NDI	National Democratic Institute
NED	National Endowment for Democracy
NGO	Non-Governmental Organization
ODA	Official Development Assistance

OECD	Organization for Economic Co-operation and Development
OSCE	Organization for Security and Co-operation in Europe
OSF	Open Society Foundations
OSGF	Open Society Georgia Foundation
OSI	Open Society Institute
PAC	Political Action Committee
PEPFAR	President's Emergency Plan for AIDS Relief
PPP	Public–Private Partnership
PTA	Preferential Trade Agreement
RJC	Republican Jewish Coalition
SESA	Survey of Economically Successful Americans (study)
SWAs	System-Wide Approaches
TCC	Transnational Capitalist Class
TNAs	Transnational Actors
TRO	Tamil Rehabilitation Organization
UHNWIs	Ultra High-Net Worth Individuals
UK	United Kingdom
UN	United Nations
UNCITRAL	UN Commission on International Trade Law
UNCTAD	United Nations Conference on Trade and Development
UNICEF	United Nations International Children's Emergency Fund
U.S.	United States (of America)
USAID	United States Agency for International Development
ViD	Vermögen in Deutschland (study)
WHA	World Health Assembly
WHO	World Health Organization
WTO	World Trade Organization
WWII	World War II

1

Introduction

Forbes started its famous listing of the world's richest people in 1987, during the same month that saw the publication of Tom Wolfe's novel *The Bonfire of the Vanities*, whose main protagonist, Wall Street trader Sherman McCoy, sees himself as a "master of the universe" (Wolfe 1987). At the end of Reagan's and Thatcher's second terms, neoliberal normativity was bourgeoning, globalization was accelerating, and wealth and income inequalities were about to take off to new heights, especially in the U.S. (Piketty et al. 2018). In 1987, the global top 200 accounted for US$295 billion, in 2019, the number of billionaires worldwide had grown to 2,153, with US$8.7 trillion of wealth.[1] In many ways, billionaires can be seen as the exemplary prophets of the neoliberal age, those "who, by [their] personal example, demonstrat[e] to others the way to religious salvation," as Max Weber described the role of religious prophets in the not-yet-disenchanted world (Weber 1978: 447). The secular prophets' Bible is *Forbes*, which calls itself "the capitalist tool," and the way to salvation is entrepreneurship. While there is no doubt that they are makers and shakers in the business world, the main question of my study concerns whether billionaires can indeed be, not masters of the universe (which seems too exuberant), but masters in world politics. The interventions of billionaires raise fundamental questions about political agency, which, in modern times, is usually understood as a social, collective undertaking. The Bill and Melinda Gates Foundation's first guiding principle stated that it "is a family foundation driven by the interests and passions of the Gates family"; George Soros once said that "I do have a foreign policy, . . . [m]y goal is to become the conscience of the world" (Kaufman 2002: 293); interviewed about his politics, Sheldon Adelson replied that "all my life I have been a very strong believer in my own convictions. And I never want to give them up because somebody makes a demand."[2] Such self-understandings take the public out of politics, replacing it with private enterprise. This book aims to show how the privatization of politics assumes a new dimension when billionaires wield power in international affairs.

---

[1] See *Forbes*'s timeline: Keren Blankfeld and Michela Tindera, "The World's Billioanires List: Three Decades of Ten-Figure Fortunes," *Forbes India*, April 11, 2017, online: http://www.forbesindia.com/article/leaderboard/the-worlds-billionaires-list-three-decades-of-tenfigure-fortunes/46637/1 (accessed June 15, 2019), also Piketty 2014: 430–52 and Milanovic 2016: 36–45.

[2] Boaz Bismuth & Amos Regev, "'We have come to put an end to Noni Mozes' dictatorship'," *Israel Hayom*, May 9, 2014, online: https://web.archive.org/web/20180702000429/http://www.israelhayom.com/2014/05/09/we-have-come-to-put-an-end-to-noni-mozes-dictatorship/ (accessed June 19, 2019).

Billionaires in World Politics. Peter Hägel, Oxford University Press (2020). © Peter Hägel.
DOI: 10.1093/oso/9780198852711.001.0001

Billionaires have already transformed electoral politics in several countries, with cases such as Berlusconi in Italy, Thaksin in Thailand, Piñera in Chile, Ivanishvili in Georgia, or Babiš in the Czech Republic. And then Donald Trump became the 45th U.S. President, appointing the richest cabinet in U.S. history, with several billionaires in senior positions.[3] Apparently, many of those who fear globalization trust successful entrepreneurs, rather than professional politicians, to make America great again.[4] The ubiquitous Trump, however, has no place among my case studies, because his politics as a private citizen had remained at the national level, and his role in world politics is POTUS, a representative of the state. Whether he mixes private interests with international diplomacy needs investigation,[5] but it is outside the scope of this book, which concentrates on billionaires as transnational non-state actors. For the same reason, billionaire kleptocrats, which use their office to protect and expand their wealth (Cooley & Heathershaw 2017), will not be covered. Until quite recently, billionaires were largely absent from the study of U.S. politics, even in some of the foremost books on the politics of inequality. In Jacob Hacker and Paul Pierson's *Winner-Take-All Politics*, Charles and David Koch receive one sentence, just as other "wealthy conservative activists" of long standing (Hacker and Pierson 2010: 122, 283), and in Martin Gilens' *Affluence and Influence*, George Soros and the Koch brothers share one short paragraph (Gilens 2012: 241). To be fair, it was only in 2010 that the Supreme Court's Citizens United decision liberalized political finance in America, which then allowed billionaires like Sheldon Adelson or Thomas Steyer to spend hundreds of millions of dollars during subsequent election campaigns.[6] Since then, following up on Jeffrey Winters' pioneering examination of oligarchy (Winters & Page 2009, Winters 2011), social science has slowly woken up to the potential power of billionaires in America.[7] Tellingly, Theda Skocpol,

---

[3] Nina Burleigh, "Meet the Billionaires Who Run Trump's Government," *Newsweek*, April 5, 2017, online: http://www.newsweek.com/2017/04/14/donald-trump-cabinet-billionaires-washington-579084.html (accessed June 15, 2019).

[4] See the survey results for Trump vs. Clinton during the 2016 presidential election campaign in Greenberg Quinlan Rosner 2016: 25 and Hart Research Associates/Public Opinion Strategies 2016: 19.

[5] See the "Trump, Inc.: Exploring the Mysteries of the President's Businesses" series of investigations by ProPublica journalists, online: https://www.propublica.org/series/trump-inc# (accessed June 15, 2019).

[6] *Citizens United v. FEC* (January 21, 2010) was a revolutionary decision, because it lifted restrictions for expenditure on "electioneering communication" by corporations and other legal persons, such as trade unions, thus placing the protection of free speech in the U.S. constitution's first amendment over legislative restrictions of campaign financing. For billionaires that want to use their personal funds, the ensuing *speechNOW.org v. FEC* (March 26, 2010) decision is more important, as it abolished limitations on how much an individual can contribute to an "independent expenditure" organization. This lead the way to the creation of so-called "Super-PACs," which, unlike normal PACs (political action committees), are not allowed to coordinate directly with political candidates or parties; on the other hand, unlike PACs (which can receive only up to US$5,000 per individual donor), Super-PACs can receive unlimited amounts of money from natural and legal persons *and* engage in political communication, including advocacy for or against specific candidates; see Mutch 2014.

[7] See Page et al. 2013, Page et al. 2019, Hertel-Fernandez 2019, as well as the "Politics Symposium" on "Why Political Scientists Should Study Organized Philanthropy" (Skocpol 2016). Several

once known for the structuralist argument that "revolutions are not made, they come,"[8] came to reach the conclusion "that the Koch network is... sufficiently ramified and powerful to draw Republicans into policy stands at odds not only with popular views but also with certain business preferences" (Skocpol & Hertel-Fernandez 2016: 695).

None of this research extends its horizon to world politics, however, and within the study of International Relations (IR), billionaires are more or less absent. Only in the specialized subfield of global health governance, where the influence of the Rockefeller Foundation and the Bill & Melinda Gates Foundation (BMGF) is hard to ignore, have billionaires received critical attention.[9] Yet, as many billionaires have acquired their wealth in global business and finance, some of them have also entered world politics. Analyzing them requires, at the level of theory, a rethinking of individual agency in IR, as the discipline has largely been focusing on collective actors, be they states, international organizations, multinational corporations (MNCs), or social movements. Their status equips billionaires with capacities that turn them into singular individuals. Most obviously, their enormous wealth is a highly fungible power resource to pursue their goals. Having conquered the business world may also confer a sense of "anything is possible" to a billionaire's venture into politics. Especially through philanthropy, George Soros and Bill Gates have made bold attempts to transform the world's political and social configurations. Such activities bring us back to a central ontological problem in social science: the relationship between agency and structure (Giddens 1979, 1984, Archer 1988, 2000, Wight 2006). Are billionaires "super-actors" with extraordinary capacities to "change the world"? What structural constraints and opportunities shape their behavior?

The rise of billionaires since the 1980s can be linked to material, ideational, and institutional changes, which have created an enabling environment that has allowed more individuals to become ultra-rich. At the material level, during the first half of the twentieth century, the two World Wars and the Great Depression had wiped out much pre-existing wealth (Piketty 2014, Milanovic 2016). Globalization, which increased steadily since the 1950s and strongly after the 1980s, has amplified the benefits of those who succeed in "winner-take-all" markets (Rosen 1981, Frank & Cook 1995 [2010]), for the simple fact that it enlarges such markets, and thus the profits to be made. Consequently, owners of MNCs form one of the largest groups of billionaires on the *Forbes* list. Within

---

journalistic accounts of the new plutocracy had been published before, e.g. Frank 2007, Rothkopf 2008, Armstrong 2010, Freeland 2012, Mount 2012 or West 2014.

[8] The phrase is attributed to the American abolitionist Wendell Phillips; Skocpol cited him approvingly (Skocpol 1979: 17).
[9] See Youde 2013, Eckl 2014, Birn 2014, McGoey 2015, Harman 2016.

globalization, the re-emergence of global finance since the 1970s is particularly important for two reasons: as it links and integrates national capital markets, it facilitates the growth of corporations and their owners' wealth; and it offers superior opportunities for financial investors to become billionaires, which is again reflected by this profession's prominence on the *Forbes* list (Mallaby 2010, Harrington 2016). In the background, the peacefulness that developed countries have enjoyed since WWII has contributed greatly to the globalization bonanza. Not only because wars destroy assets and disrupt cross-border commerce (Scheidel 2017), but also because the sacrifices of the two World Wars had created strong egalitarian demands for taxing the affluent, which seem to weaken in times of peace (Scheve & Stasavage 2010).

Neoliberalism has provided the ideology behind globalizing markets, privatization, and deregulation, and David Harvey has defined it concisely:

> Neoliberalism is . . . a theory of political economic practices that proposes that human well-being can best be advanced by liberating individual entrepreneurial freedoms and skills within an institutional framework characterized by strong private property rights, free markets and free trade. The role of the state is to create and preserve an institutional framework appropriate to such practices.
>
> (Harvey 2005: 2, also Slobodian 2018: 2)

Clearly, such a set of ideas sits very well with billionaires, especially with those that are considered to be "self-made," which, according to *Forbes*, represent the majority.[10] Following the crisis of "embedded liberalism" during the 1970s (Ruggie 1982, Kirshner 1999), neoliberalism has become a hegemonic paradigm. While some see neoliberalism as a strategic "class project" of elites trying to advance their material interests (Harvey 2005, Crouch 2011), its ideas also engender broader normative change (Centeno & Cohen 2012, Dardot & Laval 2013, Barnes & Hall 2013, Ban 2016). If billionaires in politics receive more and more popular support, the neoliberal creed must have gained hold beyond elite circles.

At the institutional level, states have been highly involved in facilitating economic globalization, reducing, via deregulation, many barriers that curbed business before. Strict controls of finance, in particular, had restrained the accumulation of wealth post-WWII (Helleiner 1994, Frieden 2006), and progressive income taxation with high top marginal rates limited it further. Over the past decades, especially since the 1990s, many states have significantly reduced taxes on

---

[10] The editorial line of *Forbes* is itself closely associated with neoliberal thinking, and therefore tends to overemphasize the "self-made" character of the fortunes it reports on, neglecting the role of inherited privileges and the inequality of chances. But even a critical assessment of the role of inherited wealth among the American members of the *Forbes* list finds the majority to come from lower and middle class families (35 percent) or upper class families with less than US$1 million inheritance (22 percent), see United for a Fair Economy 2012.

high incomes and wealth (Roine et al. 2009, Hacker & Pierson 2010, Milanovic 2016: 103ff). This is related to the growth of tax havens, which have become key nodes for private capital flows since the 1970s, allowing skillful wealth managers to minimize their rich clients' tax bills (Palan et al. 2010, Shaxson 2016, Harrington 2016, Seabrooke & Wigan 2017). In combination, both taxation trends create an institutional environment that enhances the chances of some to become and to stay ultra-rich, because they face less redistribution by the state. Philip Cerny has described this transformation as a shift from the welfare to the competition state (1990, 1997): to stay ahead in an increasingly competitive global marketplace, states favor policies that attract the relevant factors of production, notably capital.

None of these structural conditions are uniform across countries, which continue to differ with regard to their integration into the global economy and the tax regimes they apply (Weiss 2003). Still, overall they create a global setting that is favorable for billionaires in their pursuit of wealth. Pierre Bourdieu has argued that economic capital can also be transformed into cultural, social, and symbolic capital (Bourdieu 1983, 1989). In this sense, their wealth can give billionaires a privileged social standing that facilitates their access to political actors and the public sphere. A prime example is the investor Warren Buffett, the so-called "sage from Omaha," and his widely received positions on public policy, e.g. on the 2008 U.S. bailout package or the taxation of the wealthy.[11] Still, not all billionaires seem to be willing or able to turn their financial assets into political power, shifting from being an economic to becoming a social or political entrepreneur. Their agency, if understood as the capacity to mobilize and to transpose resources from one context to another (Sewell 1992: 16–20), varies. This variation depends on the specific fields actors find themselves in, but also on people's social experience of, and their reflective engagement with, their own agentic capacities (Emirbayer & Mische 1998, Archer 2007). Sociological research in Germany and the U.S. has shown that wealthy individuals tend to exhibit stronger self-efficacy beliefs than the average middle-class citizen (Lauterbach & Tarvenkorn 2011, Grundmann 2011, Cook et al. 2014, Zitelmann 2017). The very experience of success in the business world may thus enhance the capacity for agency among billionaires, especially if the skills gained in business can also be applied in politics, which depends on the characteristics of the political system in which billionaires want to intervene.

Although notoriously difficult to assess, as they can be hidden and mixed, goals are essential for any understanding of agency—unless one reduces intentions to

---

[11] "Buffett warns Congress," *CNNMoney*, September 28, 2008, online: http://money.cnn.com/2008/09/28/news/economy/Buffett.bailout/; Warren Buffett, "A Minimum Tax for the Wealthy," *The New York Times*, November 25, 2012, online: http://www.nytimes.com/2012/11/26/opinion/buffett-a-minimum-tax-for-the-wealthy.html (both accessed July 10, 2019). I thank Steve Sawyer for pointing me towards Buffett's public role.

being structurally induced, e.g. by an anarchical state of nature. With regard to states as actors in world politics, the discussion in IR used to be limited to how they pursue relative security or absolute economic gains (Grieco 1988). Constructivist research has shown that states' objectives also depend on their identities and the prevailing (inter)national norms (Checkel 1998, Finnemore & Sikkink 1998, Wendt 1999). Richard Ned Lebow has integrated these constructivist insights into a cultural theory of IR, which is particularly useful here, because he distinguishes fundamental goals in politics that he assumes to exist at any level of agency, individual or collective (2008: 114–17). Besides security and wealth, he identifies esteem as a third goal in politics, which depends on obtaining honor or social standing (ibid.: 43–121, esp. 91). As a relational goal that requires recognition by others, esteem's precise meaning is cultural in the sense that it varies, depending on what is being recognized (and thus socially constructed) to bring honor. Since 2010, the so-called Giving Pledge, launched by Warren Buffett and Bill and Melinda Gates, appeals to billionaires' public esteem and urges them to make a "to commit more than half of their wealth to philanthropy or charitable causes."[12] In order to facilitate connections with the established concerns of IR, I structure my investigation of billionaires around these three goals: security, wealth, and esteem.[13]

Within Amartya Sen's (1999) understanding of agency, who sees it as the capability to effect change according to one's objectives, billionaires may indeed look like "super-actors," at least in comparison to most ordinary people. Yet, as for everybody else, their autonomy is bounded by the social environment they operate in. Challenges to billionaires' autonomy come from perspectives that stress actors' embeddedness in networks and institutions (Goddard 2009, Stone 2008, Teles 2016), or that their agency reflects the habitual enactment of practices (Guilhot 2007, Adler & Pouliot 2011, Fejerskov 2015). Moreover, their agency always takes place within pre-constituted fields, in which billionaires are not the only ones vying for power (Fligstein 2001, Fligstein & McAdam 2011, 2012). Ultimately, if one wants to get to the heart of individual agency, one would need to reconstitute how people actually "make their way through the world," as Margaret Archer has called it. She tracks people's "internal conversation," in which individuals reflect on their options in relation to their environment so as to make up their mind about how to act, via in-depth interviews (Archer 2003, 2007). Since most billionaires, just as ministers or presidents, will be reluctant to make themselves available for extensive interview sessions, an analysis of their political agency will also be an exercise in taxing the limits of social science. In his treatment of political judgment as a core element of political agency, Markus Kornprobst reaches the

---

[12] See https://givingpledge.org/About.aspx (accessed June 7, 2019).
[13] Other motives like love may play important roles (Rengger 2010: 457), too, and some billionaires may exhibit very idiosyncratic goals.

following conclusion: "judgement revolves around orientating oneself by subsuming particulars under universals. How agents subsume eludes ambitious theorizing. Subsuming is a creative endeavour that cannot be squeezed into neat scholarly boxes" (Kornprobst 2011: 97). Further analysis thus needs to take the specificities of a billionaire's transnational actions into account, which is why, in order to analyze billionaires' power, I resort to case studies in the empirical section of this book. Charting largely unknown territory in IR, my research is exploratory (Stebbins 2001).

Although this study began as an open investigation with no particular national focus, in the end, my two primary selection criteria—relevance for world politics and data availability—produced an American sample. U.S. billionaires form the largest and wealthiest national group on the *Forbes* list,[14] and, as the world's largest and often most innovative economy, the U.S. also lures entrepreneurs from abroad. Three of the billionaires I cover adopted U.S. citizenship only as adults, after having migrated and shifted their business focus to America (Rupert Murdoch, Raj Rajaratnam, and George Soros). This attraction also extends to politics: if one wants to change the world, the current superpower is arguably the best base, especially if one follows Samuel Huntington's argument that "transnationalism is the American mode of expansion" (1973: 344).

For many billionaires, very little information is publicly available, even if they are at the top of the *Forbes* list. Hardly anything is known, for example, about Germany's once-richest citizen, the late Aldi co-founder Karl Albrecht (ranked 18th on *Forbes* in 2013), or Amancio Ortega, the richest European (ranked 6th on *Forbes* in 2019). As a pioneering study of wealthy Americans' policy preferences has summarized the problem: "Most of them are very busy. Most zealously protect their privacy. They often surround themselves with professional gatekeepers whose job it is to fend off people like us. (One of our interviewers remarked that 'even their gatekeepers have gatekeepers.')" (Page et al. 2013: 53, also Zitelmann 2017: 127, Page et al. 2019: 3f).[15] Investigative journalists have nevertheless succeeded in tracing and detailing the political activities of several billionaires. Their work provides a key source of information for my research. This implies that billionaires from countries with a vibrant media, based on the freedom of speech, will receive more public attention than those from countries where journalists would need to fear for their lives if they dig too deep into powerful billionaires' affairs. Several potentially interesting cases dropped out of my sample due to this yardstick, especially billionaires from Russia (Hoffman

---

[14] In 2019, the U.S. housed more than 28 percent of the world's billionaires (607 out of 2,153); see Louisa Kroll & Kerry A. Dolan, "Billionaires: The Richest People in the World," *Forbes*, March 5, 2019, online: https://www.forbes.com/billionaires/#69215f20251c (accessed June 10, 2019).

[15] The relative success of this research project shows that, with a large enough research budget, data on the very wealthy can be gathered. The average wealth of Page et al.'s population was, however, with "only" US$14 million, far from the realm of billionaires. For further discussion, see Page et al. 2011.

2011), some of which seem to engage in politics across borders, particularly within the space of the former Soviet Union—but I could not find enough reliable information. Likewise, the late Saudi Arabian billionaire Khalid Bin Mahfouz, once accused of having been a sponsor of al-Qaeda (and officially cleared of these charges), might have made a fascinating case study; information scarcity lead me to not pursue this case.[16] In contrast, much more could be found out about Raj Rajaratnam in America. The availability of data in the U.S. is also a consequence of its legal framework, which is very permissive for billionaires that want to employ their money for political purposes. Since their actions are legal, billionaires feel less of a need to hide them;[17] at the same time, with legality often come transparency requirements, e.g. the obligation for American tax-exempt private foundations to publish their annual tax filings, which must indicate all the recipients of donations from the foundation. Another major source will be (auto)biographies, which are available for a good number of billionaires. These are mainly informative if the particular billionaire has an interest in telling his story—which means that they are more likely to be produced in societies in which wealth accumulation is a positive value. This explains why American billionaires appear more in the spotlight: they operate in a society in which Ayn Rand's novels remain bestsellers, and in which public coverage—and celebration, as in *Forbes*—of billionaires is greater than in many other countries (Hochschild 1995, Page & Jacobs 2009, Zitelmann 2019). In Europe, home to Albrecht and Ortega (Spain), and advanced welfare states, billionaires seem to prefer the shadows.

While my initial discussion of billionaires in world politics takes place at a more general level, the question of how the national context matters for a billionaire's political agency will be addressed further within the case studies, and especially in the analytical conclusion. There, I develop comparative insights responding to three major questions. A key issue is whether billionaires are part of a global "super-class" (Sklair 2001, Petras 2008, Rothkopf 2008). Pluralist critics of the "ruling elite model" would be skeptical, as they underline the diversity of privileged actors' ambitions: billionaires may be "super-actors," but competition among them would prevent them from ruling collectively (Dahl 1958). Another crucial question concerns how billionaires relate to the main actors in IR, especially states, which requires an assessment of billionaires' relative power. Are billionaires part

---

[16] Mahfouz sued against these allegations published by Rachel Ehrenfeld and won all the libel lawsuits; see Ehrenfeld 2005: xi–xiv for the allegations and the Mahfouz family's responses on their website in the Internet Archive: https://web.archive.org/web/20120304131208/http://www. binmahfouz.info/news_20050503.html (accessed July 10, 2019). The Mahfouz proceedings against Ehrenfeld ultimately lead to legal changes in New York (the seat of Ehrenfeld's publisher), which protected free speech in the U.S. better against libel litigation (Barbour 2010: 4), which underscores my point about data availability in the U.S.

[17] As Page et al. (2019) have shown, even in the U.S., most billionaires seem to prefer "stealth politics," politicking in ways that avoid public scrutiny. My argument here is relative: billionaires in the U.S. are more public in comparison to billionaires in other countries.

of a larger "power shift," in which private transnational actors take over policy-making functions that were once, under the paradigm of sovereignty, the exclusive domain of states (Keohane & Nye 1972, Mathews 1997, Hall & Biersteker 2002, Risse 2013)? Finally, I examine the political and normative implications of billionaires' power in a world that remains attached to liberal democratic ideals. For billionaires within domestic politics, Jeffrey Winters has argued that "civil oligarchy" represents a serious limitation of democracy, but that the two can coexist (Winters 2011). His focus is narrow, however, seeing oligarchs as primarily interested in wealth defense. As billionaires use their extraordinary resources to shape public policy beyond wealth defense, we may expect more fundamental challenges to democracy.

Delineating "Billionaires as Transnational Actors in World Politics"

Political influence comes in many forms, which requires some delineation of what I mean with "billionaires as transnational actors"; "world politics" will be understood in a very broad sense, involving both cross-border politics between states, and global governance. The term "billionaire" is, of course, merely a contemporary heuristic to designate the very few that own enormous wealth, as expressed in current U.S. dollars. In 1923, every German was a Mark-billionaire, and in 2008–9, most Zimbabweans have been trillionaires in Zimbabwean dollars, but this made none of them wealthy apart from owning many sheets of colorful paper. I am referring to the people on *Forbes*'s list of the world's richest people, measuring their wealth in the world's lead currency. *Forbes*'s methodology is simple at the level of definition: any person with individual assets valued at least one billion US\$ will enter its list, except for "royal family members or dictators who derive their fortunes entirely as a result of their position of power."[18] It is the assessment of individuals' net worth that is complicated, because the market value of assets sometimes has to be estimated (villas, yachts, art collections...) and, even if publicly available, is always fluctuating (e.g. holdings of shares and other traded securities). The annual reshuffling and turnover on the *Forbes* list—only fifty-two persons from the 1987 inaugural list were still on the list twenty years later[19]—indicates the volatility of many fortunes. To estimate these values, in 2019, *Forbes* relied on the quantitative and qualitative research of seventeen employees in its "Wealth Team," fifty-two reporters, as well as further reporters in ten regional

---

[18] http://www.forbes.com/sites/luisakroll/2013/03/04/inside-the-2013-billionaires-list-facts-and-fig ures/ (accessed June 10, 2019).
[19] http://www.forbes.com/free_forbes/2007/0326/170.html (accessed June 10, 2019).

offices.[20] Since *Forbes*'s "The World's Billionaires" is the oldest and most recognized publicly available list, it will be used to provide the reference population for my inquiry.[21]

For studying the role of personal wealth in politics, *Forbes*'s cut-off point of one billion is somewhat arbitrary. Like all resources of power, wealth is relative: in a small and poor country, a multi-millionaire may have more potential power than a billionaire in the U.S. Also, a person's net worth is not the same as her disposable wealth: someone with a hundred million dollars in cash has a greater power resource than someone who would need to sell his company, which may involve co-owners, in order to possess financial firepower. The analytical discussion in this book could therefore apply to many millionaires, too. Still, billions are the accounting unit for the budgets of states and MNCs, and billionaires are thus the only natural persons that play in the same financial league as large-scale legal persons. This is the reason why they have been singled out here: they constitute a growing group of individuals that, in terms of financial capacities, can rival the major collective actors in world politics. In 2018, for example, the Bill & Melinda Gates Foundation (BMGF) disbursed US$3.2 billion in grants on global health projects, which represented 8.3 percent of the worldwide spending on global health. Only two donor countries had a larger budget for global health, namely the U.S. (US$13.2 billion) and the UK (US$3.3 billion).[22] The World Health Organization (WHO) itself spent US$2.6 billion, of which US$363 million were a voluntary contribution from the BMGF, which was the second largest contribution to the WHO's General Fund, after the U.S.[23] Most developing countries' governments manage health budgets that are significantly smaller than that of the BMGF.[24] Clearly, in the policy area of global health, Bill and Melinda Gates have become one of the key global actors (Cohen 2002, Birn 2014, Harman 2016).

How can billionaires influence politics? Following Charles Lindblom's seminal exposition of the privileged position of business (1977: 170–88), one may argue

---

[20] For the Forbes list and its methodology, see: http://www.forbes.com/wealth/billionaires (accessed June 10, 2019).

[21] Two competitors to the *Forbes* list exist, but they are both more recent and thus provide less historical data: *Bloomberg*'s "Billionaires Index" (http://www.bloomberg.com/billionaires/, since 2012), which introduced "real time" updating of billionaires' estimated net worth, reflecting market fluctuations, a feature that *Forbes* has copied since; and *Wealth-X* (http://www.wealthx.com/), which is a for-profit "wealth intelligence" enterprise that offers some information for free, but access to most of its research is for subscribers only and quite costly.

[22] Data comes from the *Institute for Health Metrics and Evaluation*, which is itself sponsored by the BMGF, online: https://vizhub.healthdata.org/fgh/ (accessed June 19, 2019). The next five largest donors were: Germany (US$1.7 bn), Japan (US$1.2 bn), Canada (US$0.9 bn), France (US$0.8 bn), and Sweden (US$0.7 billion).

[23] In several prior years, the UK contributed slightly more to the WHO than the BMGF. Data comes from the *Institute for Health Metrics and Evaluation*, online: https://vizhub.healthdata.org/fgh/ (accessed June 19, 2019).

[24] See the WHO's health financing database online: http://apps.who.int/nha/database/Select/Indicators/en (accessed June 19, 2019) as well as WHO 2018.

that the political power of many billionaires rests mainly on the investment decisions taken by the firms they own. In political systems with private enterprise, governments depend on private investment to generate economic growth and employment, which gives business owners major influence over politics. In this role, however, the billionaires who own and head a corporation hold a similar position as the CEOs that are employees of a corporation owned by a variety of shareholders. The degree of autonomy may vary, but their behavior as CEOs will, to a large extent, be driven by the economic logic of the corporation as an institution that needs to make profits and respond to its share- and stakeholders. Thus, billionaires' business decisions may have political implications, but, in this respect, they are not categorically different from other investors. George Soros's famous gamble against the British Pound in 1992 may have had an impact on world politics, but so did the combined decisions of currency traders during the 1997 Asian crisis. The appropriately named Marc Rich, once the "king of oil" and founder of what became one of the world's largest commodity-trading and mining companies, Glencore, can serve as another illustration. He secretly arranged the continuation of oil deliveries from Iran to Israel post-1979, which was a matter of great economic and political importance for Israel, but also, judging by Rich's own account, first a business opportunity with high profits (Ammann 2009: 102ff). He had already set up a very similar deal in 1973, covertly exporting Iranian oil via a secret pipeline through Israel (ibid.: 64–72). In 1979, he managed the deal as the billionaire owner of his company, in 1973 he was still a trader employed by the New York-based firm Philipp Brothers.

In keeping with the above, the political power of billionaires as business investors will not be a priority of this study, which is more concerned with what makes billionaires unique transnational actors: their individual control of vast financial resources that can be used without being constrained by the institutional logic of firms. The head of Goldman Sachs' foreign exchange trading floor does not have the personal resources to try to create "open societies"; George Soros does. Of course, gray areas exist, especially when billionaires have full control over a firm, which would allow them to use it as a tool to pursue non-business objectives, even if these involve financial losses. The Koch brothers, majority owners of one of the world's largest private companies, Koch Industries, provide such an example (Schulman 2014). Another gray area emerges when political and business objectives overlap, as is often the case in the media sector. Whether Rupert Murdoch has used the News Corporation to advance conservative ideology worldwide, or whether he simply targets conservative audiences to generate profits is a debate that is not easy to resolve (Wolff 2010: 259–84). The links between a billionaire's business and his political endeavors will be explored further in the chapter on their political agency, as well as within the case studies; the political dimensions of their business investments, on the other hand, remain largely outside my study.

Outline of the Book

Following this introduction, chapter 2 reviews how IR scholarship has been treating individual agency. Various theoretical perspectives, such as the "levels-of-analysis" and the transnational relations approach, have reserved room for the analysis of individuals in world politics, but concerns about academic discipline formation and real-world relevance have led to a widespread neglect of individual actors. While James Rosenau's research and the recent integration of social theory into IR offer fruitful ways of thinking about individual agency,[25] they often overemphasize the structural situatedness of actors fulfilling social roles. Revisiting the structure–agency debate, I take inspiration from Margaret Archer's sociological insights in order to propose that agency should be analyzed as a variable that requires contextual specification. Chapter 3 describes how, over the past decades, structural changes within the material (globalization and peace), ideational (neoliberalism), and institutional ("competition states" and global governance) realms have expanded the opportunities for individuals to become extremely rich and to engage in politics. Oftentimes, it will be argued, the same structural transformations that promote opportunities for individual wealth accumulation also provide openings in world politics for individuals to exercise power. In chapter 4, I develop arguments and hypotheses about the political agency of billionaires, in terms of capacities, goals, and power. While all billionaires control vast amounts of money, only few of them venture into world politics. A billionaire's motivation to act transnationally may stem from material interests or a sociopolitical identity whose commitments reach across national borders. Wealth can be a highly fungible power resource, but its activation depends on what can be purchased, which is regulated by laws and norms. Entrepreneurial success in business can foster self-efficacy beliefs as well as social and cultural capital, yet whether this can be put to use in politics is contingent upon the political field that a billionaire is trying to enter. Further analysis thus needs to take the specificities of a billionaire's transnational actions into account, which is happening in the case studies organized around three goals that are commonly assumed to drive the international behavior of states: security, wealth, and esteem. For each of these goals, I analyze two billionaires pursuing them. I have selected potentially powerful billionaires, because IR has ignored private individuals as political actors so far, implicitly adhering to a theory that claims: "in world politics, only collective actors matter." I want to test this theory.

Regarding security (chapter 5), I analyze the U.S. casino mogul Sheldon Adelson's interventions in the Israel–Palestine conflict, which ran counter to President Obama's foreign policy. Adelson has reportedly spent over US$200

---

[25] See Rosenau 1990, 2003, 2008, Wendt 1987, 1999, Cerny 1990, 2000, Wight 2006, Albert et al. 2013.

million on publishing a free newspaper, *Israel Hayom*, which has become the most widely read daily in Israel, staunchly supporting Benjamin Netanyahu and the "entrenchment-expansionism" position vis-à-vis Palestine. I also study claims about the hedge fund billionaire Raj Rajaratnam's alleged relationship with the LTTE ("Tamil Tigers") in his former home state Sri Lanka. While the case once produced spectacular headlines, upon closer inspection, the political agency of Rajaratnam appears as very limited or non-existent. For wealth and the economy (chapter 6), I look at how Charles and David Koch have tried to limit climate change mitigation in order to protect the fossil fuel–based business interests of their conglomerate Koch Industries. The Koch brothers spread climate change skepticism via the funding of think tanks and public advocacy, and they finance campaigns boosting politicians that oppose climate change mitigation. In Rupert Murdoch's case, his News Corporation has been his main political resource. He has used the opinion-shaping power of his media empire to extract favors from politicians abroad, especially in the UK, but also in Australia, by offering support (or threatening hostility) during election times. Concerning esteem and social entrepreneurship (chapter 7), I examine how billionaires use philanthropy to promote social change in foreign countries. Through the massive funding of research and public–private partnerships, Bill Gates, via his foundation, has advanced international vaccination programs to fight communicable diseases. His influence on agenda-setting and policy implementation in the governance of global health can be seen in the World Health Organization's declaration of a "Decade of Vaccines." George Soros's attempts to build open societies as a "stateless statesman" are extremely wide-ranging. I focus on his efforts to promote human rights and democracy, putting the spotlight on his role in regime change during the so-called "Rose Revolution" in Georgia. My case studies are geared towards identifying whether and how billionaires exercise power as transnational actors.

In the analytical conclusion of chapter 8, I evaluate my prior findings in order to address three major questions. First, is it more appropriate to see billionaires as "super-actors," or as a global "super-class"? I find substantial evidence of individual agency, and only limited applicability of the "transnational capitalist class" concept. Another challenge of billionaires' agency comes from institutional approaches, but institutional logics appear as relatively weak within the political organizations created by billionaires, because these institutions are so dependent on the volatile resources provided by their sponsors. Second, what is the relative power of billionaires within the international system? I highlight how states continue to set the legal framework for transnational politics. Yet, as outsiders coming from abroad and from business, billionaires can gain power via disruptive innovation and flexible alliance-building, using their wealth and their entrepreneurial skills. Counterfactual reasoning leads me to attribute substantial capacities for "making a difference" in world politics to most of the billionaires in my case studies. Finally, what does the power of billionaires mean for the liberal norms of legitimate political order? With billionaires as transnational actors, I argue that the tensions inherent in modern liberalism get magnified: individual freedom clashes with collective self-determination, private property subverts the public sphere, and territorially bounded conceptions of the demos conflict with cosmopolitan ideals. Billionaires like to see their actions in terms of output legitimacy, but this cannot make up for a basic lack of accountability. In line with the tenets of neoliberal normativity, billionaires benefit from and espouse "negative liberty." As these individuals become more powerful, however, the "positive liberty" associated with democratic political equality is diminishing.

2

Individuals in International Relations

Unless one subsumes them a priori into some collective entity, for example a transnational capitalist class (Sklair 2001), exploring billionaires in world politics requires looking at specific persons. Within the discipline of International Relations (IR), however, the role of individuals as political actors on the global stage has been largely relegated to the subfield of foreign policy analysis. Outside this niche, there is almost total neglect of the role of individuals in IR, no matter whether one studies bestselling textbooks (Baylis et al. 2016, Frieden et al. 2018, Goldstein & Pevehouse 2016, Kinsella et al. 2013), widely used readers (Art & Jervis 2016, Handler 2013, Mingst et al. 2019), the main academic handbooks and encyclopedia (Denemark 2010, Reus-Smit & Snidal 2008, Carlsnaes et al. 2013), or major theoretical treatises (Keohane 1984, Mearsheimer 2001, Russett & Oneal 2001, Wallerstein 2004, Waltz 1979, Wendt 1999).

In the manuals that initiate legions of undergraduate students to the study of IR, individuals usually feature briefly in the methodological section on the so-called "levels of analysis," but they disappear once it comes to analyzing global politics, both theoretically and empirically. *World Politics: The Menu for Choice* (Kinsella et al. 2013) provides a typical example. It treats individual "decision makers" on one page in the beginning (13f), yet when it introduces "Global Actors: States and Other Players on the World Stage" (43–66), the "other players" are "Humans in Groups: Nationalism and the Nation" and institutional nonstate actors like international organizations (IOs), nongovernmental organizations (NGOs), and multinational corporations (MNCs). Only within the section on foreign policy decision-making does the individual reappear on a few pages (146–54). In Karen Mingst, Jack Snyder, and Heather Elko McKibben's widely used reader of *Essential Readings in World Politics* (2019), merely three texts deal with the individual in IR, which all concern the decision-making of political leaders. In Scott P. Handler's collection (2013), as well as in the one by Robert Art and Robert Jervis (2016), there is not even one such text. The situation is very similar within the handbooks that try to synthesize the academic discipline's state of the art research. The single entry in the *Oxford Handbook of International Relations*, which somewhat covers individuals' roles, is the one on the foreign policy decision-making subfield (Stuart 2008). Likewise, in the SAGE handbook (Carlsnaes et al. 2013), when one reaches the "Structures and Processes of International Relations" section, individuals only surface in the entries on "Foreign Policy" (Carlsnaes 2013) and "Negotiation and Bargaining" (Odell

Billionaires in World Politics. Peter Hägel, Oxford University Press (2020). © Peter Hägel.
DOI: 10.1093/oso/9780198852711.001.0001

2013);[1] the twelve-volume "International Studies Encyclopedia" (Denmark 2010) contains no entry on individual actors.

Reasons for the Disregard of Individuals in IR

At least four reasons may account for the overall neglect of individuals in IR: the academic politics of discipline-formation, methodological and theoretical choices, empirically motivated judgments about relevance, and practical considerations of doing research. Working in an emerging and initially very interdisciplinary academic field, IR scholars felt a need to emancipate and distinguish their discipline from its parents, mainly, politics, history, and law (Guilhot 2008, Kaplan 1961, Schmidt 1998), which could be advanced by the claim to study a realm—the international—that has its own unique properties and logics. Much of the academic groundwork happened during the 1950s, when the impact of the two World Wars and the tensions of the Cold War provided further impetus for a focus on the international. Few books have been more influential in the formation of IR than Kenneth Waltz's *Man, the State and War* (1959), in which he distinguishes three "images" of international relations, each prioritizing a different sphere to explain the sources of war. The "first image" perspective concentrates on the individual (human nature), the second on the state (regime type), and the third on the structure of the international system (anarchy). When he finally argued that "the first and second images describe the forces in world politics, but without the third image it is impossible to assess their importance or predict their results" (238), Waltz had established a basis for privileging the international system in the study of world politics. Trying to justify why IR is a distinct academic discipline, Morten Kaplan came to the same conclusion, "that the system is subsystem dominant" (1961: 472). In an explicit attempt to promote a scientific model for the study of IR, J. David Singer then reframed Waltz's "images" as the "level-of-analysis problem" in his seminal article (1961, also 1960).[2] To develop a more analytical way of thinking about causality in world politics, he encouraged IR scholars to clarify how and why they explain international phenomena either at the level of the international system or via the level of the nation-state. For Singer, "the problem is really not one of deciding which level is most valuable to the discipline as a whole.... Rather, it is one of realizing that there is this preliminary conceptual issue and that it must be temporarily resolved prior to any given research undertaking" (1961: 90). Although Singer

---

[1] Janice Gross Stein's chapter on "Psychological Explanations of International Decision Making and Collective Behavior" also examines the role of individuals, but, again, mainly within the framework of foreign policy analysis, and also with regard to ethnic conflict (2013).
[2] See Onuf 1995 for a review of how conceptualizing world politics in terms of "levels" corresponds to a project of building a positivist science of IR.

expressed no principled preference for any particular level of analysis and allowed for other levels that could be "even more fruitful" (ibid.), in his own discussion, the level of the individual dropped out completely. Reviewing the legacy of the "level-of-analysis" perspective during the 1990s, Barry Buzan reckoned that "[w]hat might be called the Waltz-Singer dyadic approach to levels of analysis, focusing mainly on system/structure and unit/state is unquestionably still the dominant one in the field, despite much unhappiness with its severe simplification" (1995: 206).

Indeed, major theoretical disputes in IR have been and continue to be organized around the question of whether the state- or the system-level carries more explanatory power. Structural realists (Waltz 1979, Mearsheimer 2001) and world-systems theorists (Wallerstein 1974, 2004) contend that the properties of the international system shape the behavior of states. Waltz turned his previous insights into a fully-fledged *Theory of International Politics*, famously arguing against "reductionist" accounts of world politics, and for the primacy of the systemic level and its "ordering principles" (Waltz 1979: 60–101). For structural realists, the anarchical nature of international politics and the resulting security dilemma are determinant: "the structure of the international system forces states which seek only to be secure nonetheless to act aggressively toward each other" (Mearsheimer 2001: 3).[3] Although far from ignoring states' power and their security concerns, for Immanuel Wallerstein, the modern world-system is first and foremost defined by the logic of capitalism:

> If we say that a system "gives priority" to such endless accumulation [of capital], it means that there exist structural mechanisms by which those who act with other motivations are penalized in some way, and are eventually eliminated from the social scene, whereas those who act with the appropriate motivations are rewarded and, if successful, enriched.   (2004: 24)

Liberal theories of IR take the opposite viewpoint: their starting point is the unit, the level of the state, whose characteristics, configured via domestic politics, forecast its behavior (Moravcsik 1997). The most prominent statement resulting from this perspective is the democratic peace theory, which claims that democratic regimes do not go to war with each other (Doyle 1986). Economic interdependence (Rummel 1983, Rosecrance 1986, Schneider & Gleditsch 2010) and mutually beneficial cooperation via international institutions (Keohane 1984) do matter at the level of the system, but they stay linked to the presence of liberally constituted states (Russett & Oneal 2001). Alexander Wendt developed his constructivist approach against the materialism (security/prosperity interests) of the

---

[3] "The enduring anarchic character of international politics accounts for the striking sameness in the quality of international life through the millennia" (Waltz 1979: 66).

above theories, shifting the focus to ideational structures or culture, because he sees intersubjective frameworks of meaning as central to an understanding of world politics. His *Social Theory of International Politics* takes ontological questions very seriously and elaborates a sophisticated understanding of the relationship between actors and structures (1999: 139–90). Nevertheless, he explicitly treats states as actors (193–245), and concentrates on the construction of meaning and identity as they emerge out of interactions among states (313–69), distinguishing "three cultures of anarchy" rather than one materially determined form of anarchy (246–312). Overall, the initial methodological step to differentiate levels of analysis is continuing to permeate thinking about world politics and has de facto lead to a widespread privileging of interstate relations as the main object of inquiry within the dominant IR theories.

Criticism of the system-unit framing of world politics has primarily been directed at this state-centrism, or what John Agnew has called "the territorial trap" of IR (Agnew 1994, Walker 1993). A conceptual lens that reduces IR to relations between states will miss all kinds of global affairs that happen outside and beyond the organizational unit of the state. The study of such non-governmental interactions across state borders falls under what has been termed transnational politics (Kaiser 1969/1972), or transnational relations (Keohane & Nye 1972). Raymond Aron had been one of the first to introduce "transnational society" into IR, and his assumption that it "flourishes in proportion to the freedom of exchange, migration or communication" remains prescient (Aron 1966 [2003]: 105). Aron himself did not give transnational relations much further consideration, but when globalization intensified during the 1970s, "transnational actors" became an innovative research area. One would think that the role of individuals deserves some attention in such a framework, and many billionaires would seem to fit this category of "actors [that] are particularly successful in liberating themselves from the bonds of geography and represent the catalysts of transnational societies" (Kaiser 1969/1972: 809). And, in fact, in their introduction to the volume that linked transnational relations to a "world politics paradigm," trying to supplant the state-centric IR perspective, Joseph Nye and Robert Keohane do provide a definition that creates conceptual space for individual global action:

> [W]e define world politics as all political interactions between significant actors in a world system in which a significant actor is any somewhat autonomous individual or organization that controls substantial resources and participates in political relationships with other actors across state lines.   (1971a: 344f)

However, the contributions to their edited volume were exclusively concerned with collective actors and processes. They examined the growing relevance of private cross-border exchanges and highlighted multinational corporations in particular, but also other transnational groups such as the Ford Foundation, revolutionary movements, and labor unions (Keohane & Nye 1972). Even the article on the Catholic Church portrays it as an organizational structure in which the role of the pope clearly matters, but the actual persons occupying the highest seat are hardly being discussed (Vallier 1971). What guided the new transnational relations research was an emphasis on transnational actors as organizations or "units" that could be posited alongside states and international organizations, either acting in opposition to or in cooperation with them (Nye & Keohane 1971b: 729–34). A more sociological examination of how transnational organizations are being constituted as collective actors, or how individuals interact within and through them, did not take place. In their conclusion, Nye and Keohane were aware that "we still need to specify when an actor is behaving 'as a unit' and when its subunits possess significant autonomy" (1971b: 733).[4] The "subunits," ultimately, are individual human beings. Billionaires that influence politics across borders clearly fall into the category of transnational actors, but, so far, the transnational relations research agenda has largely ignored the role of individuals.

The reason behind this omission had a lot to do with concerns over "real-world" relevance, or "significance," as in Keohane and Nye's above definition of world politics. In one of the pioneering articles on "The Actors in World Politics," Arnold Wolfers, after discussing nonstate actors and individual decision-makers quite extensively, had assigned them a residual place. Their study may be useful to explain "deviations," when events in world politics do not conform to the competitive logic of the states-system (1959: 93, 95, 103–6), but "it would be dangerous for theorists to divert their primary attention from the nation-state and multi-state systems which continue to occupy most of the stage of contemporary world politics" (ibid.: 106). How much could individuals matter in a world apparently shaped by the balance of power between the United States and the Soviet Union? Nye and Keohane had anticipated this killer argument of the proponents of state-centric IR research, which

> have deliberately excluded transnational relations from the interstate system on the grounds that their direct political importance is small and that their indirect effects enter, along with domestic factors, into the formation of national foreign policies.... [T]his conclusion ... does contain a solid core of insight. States have been and remain the most important actors in world affairs.
>
> (Nye & Keohane 1971a: 343f)

---

[4] They suggested that the "bureaucratic politics" approach, pioneered by Graham Allison for the study of states' foreign policy decision-making (Allison 1969, 1971), could also be used to analyze the internal functioning of transnational organizations (Nye & Keohane 1971b: 731).

Against this backdrop, introducing large-scale non-governmental organizations like MNCs or the Catholic Church must have seemed daring enough, and scaling the level of analysis further down like a reductionist step too far. In Nye and Keohane's volume, Robert Gilpin had already advanced the realist outlook on transnational business as an expression and extension of American power: "it is closer to the truth to argue that the role of the nation-state in economic as well as in political life is increasing and that the multinational corporation is actually a stimulant to the further extension of state power in the economic realm" (1971: 419, also 1987, Starrs 2013). The empirical evaluation that, ultimately, interstate relations dominate world politics, carried the day, and, after a brief blossoming, the study of transnational relations in IR laid largely dormant until the end of the Cold War (Risse-Kappen 1995, Risse 2013: 429f).

This question of relevance pervades not only the critique of the transnational relations perspective; it can also explain why key IR scholars, which have been fairly attentive to the role of individuals (Waltz 1959, Keohane & Nye 1972, Wendt 1987), end up privileging the state and the state system in their theories of IR (Waltz 1979, Keohane 1984, Wendt 1999 and 2004). Alexander Wendt has put it nicely:

> It may be that non-state actors are becoming more important than states as initiators of change, but system change ultimately happens through states. In that sense states still are at the center of the international system, and as such it makes no more sense to criticize a theory of international politics as "state-centric" than it does to criticize a theory of forests for being "tree-centric".   (1999: 9)

The *Oxford Handbook of International Relations'* entry on "moral agency" thus expresses a broad consensus when it justifies focusing mostly on collective actors with the argument that "[i]ndividual human beings on their own lack the power, coordination, and resources necessary to achieve many espoused goals" (Erskine 2008: 701, similarly Hoover 2012). This may be true for most inhabitants of planet Earth, but it is simply wrong when billionaires control financial resources that rival many states' budgets.

Yet, if, given the question of relevance, one limits the study of individuals in world politics to the high and mighty, another set of problems appears, which concerns practical considerations of doing research. The whole research agenda is inconsequential unless, empirically, one expects to find something interesting about individual persons. Hence, taking individuals seriously will necessarily lead the researcher to the disciplines of psychology and sociology, and their various intersections, which have elaborated methods to study how people interact with each other, and how they relate to their environment. Unfortunately, many of the established methods will not be applicable when the object of research are persons that shield themselves against intrusion, including observation, either because they are too busy, or to protect themselves and their privileged position in society. As Margaret Hermann remarked in her psychological study of how the personal characteristics of political leaders affect foreign policy: "[P]olitical leaders like heads of government... are virtually inaccessible for personality testing or clinical interviewing" (1980: 14). The same applies to billionaires, as mentioned in the introduction. Commonly used techniques of social research, be they quantitative, such as surveys, or qualitative methods like participant observation, will also usually not be available if one examines the population of the *Forbes* lists. Proponents of political psychology in IR have nevertheless found methods to investigate international leaders "at distance," such as content analysis of public statements, observer ratings, or case studies (Levy 2013, McDermott 2004: 21–44). And, to put things into perspective, the challenges of empirically examining something as abstract and complex as the power of states appear at least as daunting as trying to get into the minds of powerful individuals.[5] Still, the practical difficulties of analyzing individuals, which are far removed from the reach of most researchers, have certainly contributed to turning this perspective into a niche.

Individuals in Recent IR Scholarship

Despite overall neglect, some renewed attention to Waltz's "first image" has occurred within all the major IR theories after the end of the Cold War. Ironically, while liberalism could be expected to be *the* approach predestined to address the first image, given the focus of its classical thinkers, such as John Locke, Immanuel Kant, or Adam Smith, on individual freedom and choice (Berlin 1969, Coleman 1996, Fleischacker 1999), liberal IR theory has remained the most silent about individuals in world politics. Following neoliberal institutionalism's engagement with structural realism (Keohane 1984, Baldwin 1993), the reorganization of liberal theory since the 1990s has emphasized the importance of societal preferences that shape states' foreign policies (Moravcsik 1997: 517f).[6] While much of this research gives priority to organized interests and collective actors, such a perspective also drives studies of how individuals' attributes and preferences impact on states' foreign policies. Thus, one line of research investigates what

[5] One of the most widely used quantitative indicators of "state power" in IR, the National Material Capabilities indicator (v5.0) from the "Correlates of War" research project, is made up of merely six values: total population, urban population, iron and steel production, energy consumption, military personnel, and military expenditure. See online: http://www.correlatesofwar.org/data-sets/national-material-capabilities (accessed June 26, 2019). Unsurprisingly, it has received much critique. On the problems of measuring power in IR, see Baldwin, D. 2016, Guzzini 2009, Treverton & Jones 2005.

[6] Moravcsik, in reviewing European integration studies, also examined high-level EU officials as individuals that may be seen as supranational entrepreneurs, but he accords them significant agency only under rare circumstances Moravcsik 1999).

kind of people support or oppose openness or closure in the international political economy; for example, how higher levels of education lead to more support for free trade (Hainmueller & Hiscox 2006, 2010, Mansfield & Mutz 2009, 2013). A similar research agenda examines so-called "audience costs," the consequences of disapproval that political leaders face if their foreign policies disappoint domestic audiences (Fearon 1994, Tomz 2007, Weeks 2008, Potter & Baum 2014). Although individual citizens do herewith enter into the explanation of international politics, they are being taken into account only as aggregates, at the level of public opinion, or as the median voter.

Realist approaches remain wedded to state power and its international distribution, but the rediscovery of "great statesmen" picks up on classical realists' concerns with leadership (Byman & Pollack 2001). Agreeing on anarchy and competition as the overarching features of the international system still leaves plenty of room for varieties of realism, which take diverging positions on the questions of whether states are more concerned about power (Waltz 1979) or threats (Walt 1987), about defending the status quo (Jervis 1978) or aggressively increasing their power (Mearsheimer 2001). "[S]tate intentions are a critical factor in international relations and, to the extent that individual personalities shape those intentions, they too must be considered important" (Byman & Pollack 2001: 114). Even if one believes that intentions are in large part structurally imposed by the security dilemma, the assessment of threats and risks involves processes of "perception and misperception in international politics," as Robert Jervis titled his book, which introduced the findings of cognitive psychology into IR (1976). He, like other realists that focus on the "first image," highlights that under certain conditions, especially those where "decision-makers are faced with a large number of competing values, highly complex situations, and very ambiguous information" (ibid.: 31), individual agency becomes significant and needs to be studied in order to explain outcomes. For those realists that open the black box of the state (Rose 1998, Barkin 2009, Jervis 2013), the precondition for individuals to make a difference is, however, their institutional position as leaders, or at least as highly placed officials, of powerful states. Daniel Byman and Kenneth Pollack's opening question of their "Let us now praise great men" article makes this clear: "How can we explain twentieth-century history without reference to Adolf Hitler, Joseph Stalin, Vladimir Lenin, Franklin Roosevelt, Winston Churchill, Mahatma Gandhi, or Mao Zedong?" (2001: 107).

In many ways, this realist bias has also shaped Foreign Policy Analysis (FPA), the IR subfield that concentrates on foreign policy decision-making and, as such, claims to

> develo[p] the actor-specific theory required to engage the ground of IR. With its assumption that human decision makers acting singly and in groups are the ground of all that happens in international relations and that such decision

makers are not best approximated as unitary rational actors equivalent to the state, FPA is positioned to provide the concrete theory that can reinvigorate the connection between IR ... and its social science foundation.   (Hudson 2005: 2)[7]

The best research in FPA is very attentive to the agency–structure problem (Snyder et al. 1962, Sprout & Sprout 1965, Carlsnaes 1992, 2013, Stein 2013), of how the participants in decision-making processes are situated in social and organizational contexts, e.g. when it looks at group dynamics and so-called bureaucratic politics (Allison 1969). While this certainly distances FPA from structural realism, the influence of the realist paradigm shows in that during much of its intellectual history, FPA has been "focusing mainly on diplomacy and security issues" (Carlsnaes 2013: 299). In the twenty-first century, this is no longer the case, as FPA has turned into a vibrant research area since the 1990s, in which the full diversity of theoretical IR approaches is engaged, and "foreign policy" now covers most international issue areas, not just security (Hudson 2005, 2007, Carlsnaes 2013). Yet, FPA continues to concentrate almost exclusively on state officials as relevant decision-makers. Its foundational text has been very explicit about one of its "most important methodological assumptions ... [,] that *only* those who are government officials are to be viewed as decision-makers or actors. In other words, no private citizen—no matter how powerful—can be a member of the analytical unit *unless* he temporarily holds a federal office" (Snyder et al. 1962: 99, emphasis in original). In a more recent definition of FPA, which appeared in the inaugural article of the new *Foreign Policy Analysis* journal, this state-centrism has been relaxed:

> The explanandum of foreign policy analysis includes the process and resultants of human decision making with reference to or having known consequences for foreign entities. Typically, the horizon of interest is delimited to decision making performed by those with the authority to commit resources, usually but not always the legitimate authorities of nation-states.   (Hudson 2005: 2)

While their "authority" would be less official than that of states, the "not always" would seem to cover billionaires like George Soros, who sees himself as a foreign policy actor on the global stage. Still, the original state-centrism remains pervasive: since its founding, almost all the research articles published in *Foreign Policy*

---

[7] "A 'ground' means the conceptualization of the fundamental or foundational level at which phenomena in the field of study occur .... (IR) as a field of study has a ground, as well. All that occurs between nations and across nations is grounded in human decision makers acting singly or in groups. In a sense, the ground of IR is thus the same ground of all the social sciences" (Hudson 2005: 1). There is sometimes confusion about the distinction between FPA and Foreign Policy as subfields of IR. As Carlsnaes explains, FPA is the approach more specifically focusing on decision-making, whereas Foreign Policy covers broader processes (Carlsnaes 2013).

Analysis have been exclusively investigating foreign policy decision-making by state officials. The same preoccupation manifests itself in the leading Foreign Policy textbook (Smith et al. 2016).

Despite the ongoing fixation on diplomacy and state officials, some important insights from FPA may also be valid for nonstate actors, in particular those that have adapted broader findings from psychology, neuroscience, and behavioral economics to political decision-making processes (Goldgeier & Tetlock 2001, Stein 2013, Mercer 2010, Holmes 2013, 2014, Renshon 2015, Hafner-Burton et al. 2017). One needs to be cautious, tough. The theories of cognitive consistency, heuristics, and biases (Kahneman 2011, Ariely 2008), for example, draw wide-ranging conclusions about the limitations of rationality in human decision-making and behavior. Yet, the generality of their claims does not hold up:

> A small but growing number of experimental studies done mainly in the last two decades suggests that experienced elites act differently from the population of less experienced university students who have been the mainstay of research in political psychology, behavioral economics and related scholarship on the psychology of decision-making.   (Hafner-Burton et al. 2013: 368)

These studies find, for example, that "experienced elites are less prone to loss aversion" and "more prone to overconfidence" (ibid.: 370, 372, also Sears 1986, Mintz et al. 2006, Sheffer et al. 2018). If one follows this reasoning further, one may also ask whether "elites" is itself too broad a category to generalize—would a hypothetical finding about overconfidence among senior diplomats also apply to billionaires? Without comparative empirical research on elite subgroups, which is very difficult to accomplish, any such knowledge transfer must remain speculative.

The extent to which the insights from social psychology approaches, which have examined the roles of national leaders within their "psychosocial milieus" (Hudson 2005: 12f), also pertain to private actors, is even more questionable. Given the state-centric nature of FPA, this research explores mainly how national culture affects the identities and the actions of state officials (Holsti 1970, Harnisch et al. 2011, Thies & Breuning 2012). Elected or appointed state officials are institutionally required to conform to certain role expectations, be it because of public opinion and questions of legitimacy, or because of formal and informal rules, codes and operating procedures that govern their function. Individuals that have no institutional affiliation (beyond their citizenship) with the state are under no such constraints, and their relevant milieus and role conceptions will therefore be, in all likelihood, much more idiosyncratic. Maybe a role conception of billionaires is the "Davos Man" (Huntington 2004); sociological studies of cosmopolitan elites will be interesting in this context (Sklair 2001, Davidson et al. 2009), and will be discussed further in my analytical conclusion. The basic question of social psychology approaches in FPA—how decision-making involves intersubjective frameworks of meaning (Kelman 1970: 5ff, Breuning 2011)—is certainly pertinent for any kind of individual actor in world politics, but the answers that FPA scholars have found for state officials are only of limited use for nonstate actors. This evaluation applies also to the organizational process/bureaucratic politics perspectives within FPA. Most of this research has been centered on top-level state bureaucracies, often in the U.S. executive (Allison 1969, Bendor & Hammond 1992, Halperin 1974, Halperin & Clapp 2006, Jones 2010). To be sure, whenever individuals establish organizations, be it states, firms, or NGOs, administrative procedures and internal coordination problems will matter for all the actors within them.[8] Nevertheless, the recruitment into and the hierarchical logic within state bureaucracies, especially in the field of diplomacy, would seem to constitute forms of social relations with special characteristics that are unlikely to operate in a similar way among individuals in the private sector. The persons that create, head, and sustain their own organizations—as is the case with many billionaire philanthropists and their foundations—will face challenges of organizational process and bureaucratic politics quite differently than the state officials working in an impersonal corporate structure. In fact, one study of wealthy entrepreneurs in Germany found that, very often, aversion to the limitations of organizational structures was a key motivation for becoming self-employed (Zitelmann 2017: 204–25).

Overall, the treatment of individuals in IR has been revived during the past two decades, but it is still largely confined to the viewpoints that had emerged during the earlier discussions of individuals in world politics. In 1959, Arnold Wolfers had identified the "minds-of-men" and the "decision-making" approaches as supplements to state-centric theorizing (Wolfers 1959: 84ff). "Minds of men" strongly resembles the liberal focus on public opinion, while "decision-making" resembles the FPA agenda, behavioral approaches, and the realist focus on state leaders. Herbert Kelman, in 1970, also emphasized exactly those two perspectives when discussing the role of the individual in IR (Kelman 1970). He added to it, as a minor point, "personal interaction across national boundaries" (ibid.: 14ff), the potential of intensifying cross-border relations to shift people's loyalties from the nation-state to more cosmopolitan values. While Wolfers and Kelman both judged interstate relations to remain paramount, Oran Young made the transnational relations perspective the cornerstone of his argument that world politics is moving towards a mixed-actor system, in which states are no longer dominant (1972). In this context, he observed that, "[t]o begin with, the human individual is slowly acquiring ... independent influence in world politics .... Then, ... there is the growing assortment of transnational organizations" (ibid.: 132). Afterwards, unfortunately, the study of individual actors in IR and the research on

---

[8] As Max Weber observed, in modernity, the logic of rational administration is to be found in the organization of the state as much as in business administration (Weber 1921–22 [1980]: 825).

transnational relations rarely cross-fertilized. Both the FPA and the "transnational relations" research agendas have thrived since the end of the Cold War, but they hardly ever met. To ascertain their respective relevance in IR, most research on foreign policy decision-making restricted itself to top-level state officials, and transnational relations research concentrated mostly on collective actors and organizations.[9]

Taking Individuals Seriously: James Rosenau's IR Theorizing

A noteworthy and rather solitary exception to the above status quo is the work of James Rosenau, who, among the Western scholars that have shaped the discipline of IR, has made individuals a key element in his framework for analysis. Coming from "the scientific study of foreign policy" (1971, 1974), in which he had focused on the influence of public opinion (1961, 1968) and domestic-foreign interrelations (1969, 1997), he turned increasingly dissatisfied with the state-centric model of IR (1980, Czempiel & Rosenau 1989). With the end of the Cold War, Rosenau became convinced that world politics is entering a period of "turbulence" (1990), in which contradictory trends, especially regarding globalization and localization, fragmentation and integration (1997: 99–117, 2003), make world politics more complex, disorderly, and "postinternational." Consequently, he saw it as his priority to conceptualize global change, which required linking transformations at the macro-level with those at the micro-level, an intellectual undertaking he pursued more thoroughly than most other IR scholars (1990: 141–77, 2003: 18–49). Instead of relying on the common levels-of-analysis methodology, when Rosenau discusses the relevant actors in world politics, he distinguishes individuals and collectivities, the latter as varying "levels of aggregation" (1990: 152ff). This allows him a very flexible typology of macro actors, including transnational organizations and movements. With regard to individuals, he identifies three ideal types, which, given their originality in IR theory, merit lengthier citations:

> The first...is the individual who belongs to macro collectivities and...is a *citizen* or organization *member* subject to aggregation, mobilization, and control. The second is the individual who leads macro collectivities..., the public official or organization leader who does the aggregating, mobilizing, and controlling of citizens or members. The third is the *private* actor, the individual who, quite

---

[9] The study of transnational relations has had a strong renaissance, in which the questions have moved from whether transnational actors matter in IR towards "the *conditions* under which...effects are achieved" (Risse 2013: 431). While new collective actors, especially NGOs and social movements, have been added to the older focus on MNCs and religious organizations, individuals still figure only very occasionally (Risse-Kappen 1995, Tarrow 2001, 2005, Price 2003, Orenstein & Schmitz 2006, Risse 2013).

apart from his or her membership in or leadership of collectivities, either is unintentionally drawn into the cascades of world politics . . . or who is able, by dint of special circumstances, to carry out independent actions in the global arena that may be consequential for the course of events.

(ibid.: 118, emphasis in original)

While the first two types correspond closely to the focus of FPA and liberal thinking about how public opinion influences states' foreign policies, Rosenau's third type opens an analytical category that was absent in IR theorizing before. He himself provides anecdotal examples of business executives and—very briefly—a Saudi billionaire that became entangled in U.S. foreign affairs (ibid.: 118ff). But many other cases would seem to fit into this category as well, such as celebrity activists for international causes like the rock star Bono (Busby 2007) or the movie actors Mia Farrow and George Clooney (Huliaras & Tzifakis 2010, 2012, also Tsaliki et al. 2011). Under conditions of turbulence in world politics, Rosenau assumes that private actors will enjoy greater opportunities to make a difference:

[T]he private actor's conduct is not so immediately bound up by the rules and requirements that collectivities demand of those who occupy roles in them. Hence . . . private actors are likely to be much more venturesome and capable of engaging in greater variety of behaviors than are leaders and members . . . . To understand the role of private actors, one has to look to both the macro and micro levels, the former to understand how circumstances may provide opportunities for the initiatives of private actors and the latter to probe how and why some such actors seize the moment and exploit the opportunities.

(Rosenau 1990. 119f)

These preliminary hypotheses and questions about private individuals in world politics, including billionaires, constitute very useful starting points. Unfortunately, Rosenau's terminology of how individuals relate to their environment—roles, role scenarios, and habits (1990: 210–42)—suggests rather high degrees of social determination in which "there is little meaningful left over as the quintessentially unique person" (ibid.: 117). But at the same time, matching his awareness of turbulence and change, he frequently highlights how "at such times, . . . individuals are most free, if not compelled, to make choices that previously might have been made for them through their links to macro structures and processes" (ibid.: 150, also 2003: 27). What Rosenau is struggling with is human *agency*—a term he never employs, despite its critical importance in social science discussions of the questions that concern him. Instead of trying to connect with sociology here, he comes up with his own concept of "habdaptive individuals," which tries to integrate habitual behavior and adaptive learning (1990: 228). In this, people's ability to shift from habit to creative adaptation is seen as a variable that is shaped by both micro and macro factors. Individual skills and capacities matter, in particular "analytic skills" and "cathetic capacity" (ibid.: 238f).[10] At the macro level, he sees a broad and powerful expansion of such skills among people, linked to rising education and urbanization levels and the information technology revolution (1990: 239, 333–387, 2003: 233–255, 2008: 13–23). He also notices frequently that some private actors exhibit greater faculties than others to be creative, innovative, entrepreneurial, or venturesome (1990: 120, 149f; 2003: 27). But why this is so remains largely unconsidered. Curiously, although he is aware of the uneven distribution of access to the resources that promote individuals' skills (2008: 14), he does not make social stratification and the control of material resources a factor in his framework.

To be fair, when Rosenau first developed his framework in 1990, substantial linkages between social theory and IR had only started to emerge (Wendt 1987, Dessler 1989, Onuf 1989), and his intuitive observations, hypotheses, and typologies did break major new ground for the study of individuals in IR. More regrettable is the fact that he stuck to this framework for analysis and did not develop it significantly in later publications. Rosenau's last book, with the promising title of *People Count! Networked Individuals in Global Politics* (2008), is even a step back. In it, he explicitly rejects looking into people's personal characteristics and histories, sidelining what most social scientists would term agency and what he calls "individual discretion" (2008: 8–10). Instead, he only focuses on the "social roles" individuals play, "the orientations and conduct of individuals that derive from the expectations of the roles they occupy in the systems that sustain one or another aspect of public affairs" (ibid.: 10). Accordingly, the book features twenty roles into which people may be fitted, from artists, bloggers, and citizens to soldiers and terrorists. The (very) wealthy are absent as a role, although Bill Gates, George Soros, and Ted Turner receive two sentences in the category of "business executives," mentioned "as exemplars of responsible business executives" because of "[t]heir contribution of significant amounts of their wealth to charity" (ibid.: 91). What could have been a fascinating examination of why and how people, due to their differing types of agency, count, remains fixated on how society's role expectations and the specifics of a given situation shape individual behavior. Ultimately, Rosenau's perspective is downplaying agency and privileging structure. As Alexander Wendt has pointed out: "Most IR scholarship assumes that roles are unit-level properties with no place in structural theory. I believe this misunderstands the nature of roles, which are properties of structures, not agents" (1999: 251). It is to the controversies over such questions that we now turn, because a better understanding of agency is a prerequisite for analyzing billionaires as individual actors in world politics.

---

[10] With "cathetic" he means "the capacity to attach emotion to issues and care about a preferred solution" (1990: 239).

The Structure–Agency Conundrum in Social Science

What is nowadays called the structure–agency puzzle has, in all likelihood, been discussed as long as human beings have tried to theorize their relationships with their environment. It is closely linked to controversies over holism versus methodological individualism (List & Spiekerman 2013) as well as the so-called micro-macro link (Collins 1981, 1992, Alexander et al. 1987). Although the academic discussion may appear increasingly arcane, the basic concerns of the structure-agency problem are very straightforward. Karl Marx has put them well in a much-quoted passage from his "18th Brumaire" analysis of the 1851 coup of Louis Napoleon in France:

> Men make their own history, but they do not make it as they please; they do not make it under self-selected circumstances, but under circumstances existing already, given and transmitted from the past. The tradition of all dead generations weighs like a nightmare on the brains of the living.[11]

With "[m]en make their own history," he introduces agency, the "circumstances existing already, given and transmitted" refer to structures, and he also highlights the crucial role of temporality. In his social theory, Marx is usually seen to be a structuralist when he stresses how the material context—production systems and the accompanying social relations—shape the human experience.[12] But it can also be argued, that, at least as a political activist for the communist cause, he very much believed in the possibility of agency, as his final thesis on Feuerbach (another popular quotation) indicates.[13]

Some of the most thorough and influential attempts to conceptualize the relationships between individuals and their social environment appear in the works of Pierre Bourdieu and Anthony Giddens. While their theories differ in many respects, they share, besides an affinity for convoluted phrasings, the goal of developing a dynamic understanding of the structure–agent relationship in which neither structures nor agents are being essentialized (Bourdieu 1977, Giddens 1979 and 1984). For Bourdieu, *habitus* is responsible for the (re)production of *practices* that structure individual behavior:

---

[11] See online: https://www.marxists.org/archive/marx/works/1852/18th-brumaire/ch01.htm (accessed July 10, 2019).
[12] See his 1859 "Preface to a Contribution to the Critique of Political Economy," online: https://www.marxists.org/archive/marx/works/1859/critique-pol-economy/preface.htm (accessed November 25, 2019).
[13] Written in 1845, it says that "The philosophers have only interpreted the world, in various ways; the point is to change it." His sixth thesis, however, emphasizes the social grounding of human agency: "the human essence is no abstraction inherent in each single individual. In its reality it is the ensemble of the social relations." Online: https://www.marxists.org/archive/marx/works/1845/theses/theses.htm (accessed November 25, 2019).

The habitus, the durably installed generative principle of regulated improvisa-
tions, produces practices which tend to reproduce the regularities immanent in
the objective conditions of the production of their generative principle, while
adjusting to the demands inscribed as objective potentialities in the situation, as
defined by the cognitive and motivating structures making up the habitus.

(1977: 78)[14]

Giddens also highlights the importance of "practical consciousness" in his "structuration" theory, arguing that "structures" should be seen as "structural properties" that manifest themselves in the practices and the memories of human beings
(1984: 17). Where Bourdieu sees a "dialectical relationship between the structure
and the dispositions making up the habitus" (1977: 84), Giddens conceives of the
"duality of structure":

The constitution of agents and structures are not two independently given sets of
phenomena, a dualism, but represent a duality ... [;] the structural properties of
social systems are both medium and outcome of the practices they recursively
organize ....Structure ... is always both constraining and enabling.

(1984: 25)

The insight that we should not objectify structure as some rigid external context
that predetermines behavior, but rather think of it as internalized dispositions that
depend on people's (re-)enactment of practices, remains widely accepted and goes
a long way to avoid any reification of "structures." Likewise, the observation,
especially in Giddens (1984: 17–25), that a specific structural arrangement of rules
and resources is not only setting the limits, but is also providing the opportunities
for individual action, has significantly enriched the social scientific understanding
of structure.

The potential of agency, on the other hand, is being relegated to the sidelines—
less by Giddens than by Bourdieu—as William Sewell (Sewell 1992) and Margaret
Archer (Archer 1982, 1988, 2000) have shown in trenchant critiques of Giddens's
and Bourdieu's theories. Sewell rejects Giddens's understanding of structures as
"virtual," since the concept contains both cultural or ideational "schemas," and
material resources. Against Bourdieu, Sewell argues that structures can be much
less stable and less prone to reproduction, and that there are many more possibilities for structural change,

"because structures are multiple and intersecting, because schemas are transpos-
able, and because resources are polysemic and accumulate unpredictably ... As

---

[14] *Habitus* and *practices*, for Bourdieu, are always specific to a *field*, social configurations with
particular distributions of power, forms of capital and *doxa*, taken-for-granted rules (1990).

I see it, agents are empowered to act with and against others by structures: they have knowledge of the schemas that inform social life and have access to some measure of human and nonhuman resources. Agency arises from the actor's knowledge of schemas, which means the ability to apply them to new contexts. Or, to put the same thing the other way around, agency arises from the actor's control of resources, which means the capacity to reinterpret or mobilize an array of resources in terms of schemas other than those that constituted the array."

(ibid.: 19f)

Different schemas and resources matter in different contexts, and the capacities to employ and control schemas and resources can vary enormously across persons. For Sewell, the extent of a person's agency depends mainly on her social position in a given set of cultural and material structures (ibid.: 20f). These insights fit billionaires in politics quite well: whether they can move from the business to the political world depends on their capacities to transpose cultural schemas, such as business practices, and resources, such as money, from one context to the other.

Archer shares Sewell's view that two types of structure, material and cultural, should be distinguished, and like him, she views structures, especially culture, as much less coherent and rigid than sometimes assumed in the social sciences (1988). But her main critique is methodological and more substantial than Sewell's. She argues against analytical conceptualizations that see agents and structures as mutually constituted; for her, the "duality of structure" in concepts of *habitus* or *structuration* theory, amounts to the fallacy of "central conflation":

[T]he difficulty is that [duality] ... effectively precludes a specification of when there will be "more Voluntarism" or "more Determinism".... Rather than transcending the voluntarism/determinism dichotomy, the two sides of the "duality of culture" embody them respectively: they are simply clamped together in a conceptual vice. This ... derives from Giddens not answering "when" questions–when can actors be transformative (which involves specification of degrees of freedom) and when are they trapped into replication (which involves specification of the stringency of constraints)? ... Since nothing could be much less helpful than a conceptualization of change as permanently imminent yet defiantly unpredictable, it is important to see that this is a direct consequence of the "duality" approach itself.   (1988: 86f)[15]

Why only some billionaires venture into global politics, while most stick, literally, to business as usual, does indeed seem to require some specification of individual

---

[15] In her 1988 book, Archer concentrated on culture as distinct from material structure, but her argument here against the "duality of culture" extends also to the "duality of structure" more generally, as exposed in her later books (Archer 1995 and 2000).

agency. Archer's "morphogenetic" counterproposal, grounded in the philosophy of science of critical realism (Bhaskar 1975 [1995], Archer 1995), embraces analytical (not philosophical) dualism instead, in which structure and agency are held separate in order to examine their interplay over time (1982, 1988: xii). For research purposes, it is more fruitful to characterize the relationship between structure and agents as "co-determination" rather than "mutual constitution." The crucial mediating factor between structure and agency is the process of "reflexive deliberation," which Archer has explored empirically as people's "internal conversation" (Archer 2003, 2007).

The agency–structure debate found its way from sociology into IR relatively early on, mostly via an adoption of Giddens's structuration theory (Wendt 1987, Dessler 1989, Cerny 1990, 2000).[16] Since then, IR has witnessed a major reconnection with social theory, following the emergence of constructivism as one of the dominant theoretical approaches, which, after all, is properly called social constructivism (Berger & Luckmann 1966, Adler 1997, 2002). Most constructivist research has concentrated on how intersubjective frameworks of meaning, especially norms, and culture more generally, affect the conduct of international affairs, and how they constitute the identities and interests of states (Katzenstein 1996, Keck & Sikkink 1998, Finnemore & Sikkink 1998). In line with the direction taken by Alexander Wendt, the paradigm's *spiritus rector*, the embeddedness of states in an international society has been at the center of attention (Wendt 1992, 1999, 2004).[17] Consequently, and despite constructivism's attachment to structurationist thinking—or, given the downplaying of agency in Giddens's theorizing, maybe also because of it—"agency has fallen through the ontological cracks for constructivists" (Checkel 1998: 341, also Bucher 2014). This can be observed in the choice of social theorists whose thinking has recently been integrated into IR, in order to elaborate how "social construction" works:[18] Pierre Bourdieu's *practices* (Pouliot 2008, Adler & Pouliot 2011, Bigo & Madsen 2011, Bigo 2011), Michel Foucault's *governmentality* (Merlingen 2003, Albert & Lenco 2008, Shani & Chandler 2010), Bruno Latour's *actor-network theory* (Best & Walters 2013), and Norbert Elias's *figurational thinking* (Linklater 2010, Linklater & Liston 2012). While all these approaches certainly have much to offer for IR,[19] as different as they are, they all share an emphasis on strictly relational social

---

[16] See Carlsnaes 1992 for a first adoption of Archer's theory for foreign policy analysis. More recently, Colin Wight (Wight 2006) has developed the most comprehensive discussion of agency–structure in IR, heavily relying on Archer's work (also Wight 2013 and 2014).

[17] In this, constructivism shares much with the English School of IR (Wight 1977, Bull 1977, Reus-Smit 2002, Buzan 2014).

[18] As has been argued by Stefan Guzzini, constructivism in IR is best seen as a meta-theory that can accommodate various social theories (Guzzini 2000).

[19] Another way of linking IR with social theory that has recently been advanced consists in building a fully social account of world politics as a "social whole" (Buzan & Albert 2010, Albert & Buzan 2013, Albert, Buzan, and Zürn 2013); agency is not a main concern here, either.

theorizing in which the structuring effects of social interactions predominate and individual agency recedes from the researcher's view.[20]

A representative example of this relational/structural bias in IR constructivism comes from the study of transnational activists and entrepreneurs—actor categories that would seem to be closely associated with agency. Yet, in their pathbreaking analysis, Margaret Keck and Kathryn Sikkink start with the following assumption: "When we ask who creates [advocacy] networks and how, we are inquiring about them as structures—as patterns of interactions among organizations and individuals" (1998: 5). Likewise, in her attempt to theorize the political entrepreneurs that "broker change" in world politics, Stacie Goddard ends up with "analyzing entrepreneurship—what is fundamentally an 'agentic' concept—with a theory that is profoundly structural, that sees entrepreneurial action as dependent on network position" (Goddard 2009: 257).[21] Treatments of elite organizations in global governance, from the study of epistemic communities (Adler & Haas 1992) to the various fora and clubs of business elites, such as the G–30 Consultative Group on International Economic and Monetary Affairs (Tsingou 2015), also tend to emphasize the social dynamics of the group, such as reputation-building, rather than individual agency. It is hence not surprising that the very few IR-related treatments of billionaires in world politics heavily depersonalize their analysis. Diane Stone has argued that the decentralized structure of George Soros's Open Society Foundations leads to institutional logics becoming more important, rather than Soros being the individual decision-maker (2008). In another examination of Soros, Nicolas Guilhot posits that Soros's endeavors are akin to performing philanthropic practices that perpetuate the existing capitalist order (Guilhot 2007).[22] Constructivism's negligence of agency also reveals itself in two otherwise fine studies of the Jewish diaspora in the U.S. and its relation to the Israel–Palestine conflict. Sheldon Adelson, who, as I will argue in chapter 6, is a major actor in this field, is completely ignored in Jonathan Rynhold's book (2015), and receives just one brief mention in Michael Barnett's (2016: 200).

---

[20] Confirming this assessment is Ted Hopf's introduction of the notion of habit into IR, where he complains that Pouliot's appropriation of Bourdieu's theory of practice (Pouliot 2008) "privileges Bourdieu's treatment of agency, while eliding his deep structuralism, thereby expecting much more potential for change and reflection than the logic of habit would permit" (Hopf 2010: 545). His broader claim that constructivism has "privileged agency over constraining structures" (ibid.: 540), however, seems wrong, and Hopf fails to substantiate it with any evidence. See Bucher 2014 for an opposing analysis that is more convincing.

[21] The notion of "norm entrepreneurs" has appeared frequently in constructivist accounts of epistemic/normative change (Adler & Haas 1992, Keck & Sikkink 1998, Klotz 2002), but without substantial theorization (Bucher 2014: 744ff). In their focus on professional networks in transnational governance, Leonard Seabrooke and Lasse Folke Henriksen allow more analytical space for individual agency (2017a, 2017b: 12).

[22] Although Guilhot's interpretation appears strongly influenced by Bourdieu's theory of practice, he does not refer to it explicitly.

Then again, the overall discounting of individual agency in IR constructivism does connect well with the upsurge—and radicalization (Powell & Dépelteau 2013)—of relational sociology (Elias 1991, Emirbayer 1997, White 2008, Latour 2005).[23] In this context, serious challenges have been launched against theories that focus on agency. Archer's framework in particular has been targeted by critics who contest her analytical dualism and, instead, advocate for a perspective that, not unlike Giddens's and Bourdieu's, sees structure and agency as inextricably linked, due to the inherently relational reality of human life as social life (Dépelteau 2008, Piiroinen 2014). The charge that Archer neglects the prevalence of social relations in a person's life, including the formation of a person's identity, appears to be a mere question of degree, as "the social" is central to what Archer considers "being human" (Archer 2000: 253–305, Donati & Archer 2015). The focus on agency is more decisive and divisive. For the critics, the question of "the individual contribution" to social processes and outcomes is ultimately a Kantian or Modernist obsession with the freedom of the individual, which is considered as unnecessary for sociological inquiry (Collins 1992, Loyal & Barnes 2001, Dépelteau 2008: 69, Piiroinen 2014: 85–8). In its most polemical expression, this leads to a complete rejection of agency as an appropriate research subject for the social sciences:

> Agency theorizing has led nowhere and has not even solved its own basic enigmata, including intention, will, decision, and the like.... "Agency" is a residual, consisting of that portion of variance unaccounted for by social struc-ture. Agency is not the cause, but the effect, of failures at prediction.
>
> (Fuchs 2001: 30, 34)

Analyzing Varieties of Agency

Although good reasons clearly exist for research that limits itself to the study of social relations, at least three arguments can be made in favor of studying agency, too. The first and most common is, ironically, a structural argument about the breakdown of routines and the rise of individualism in modernity, accelerating in late modernity. Archer has advanced it herself, as she sees, *contra* Bourdieu, a demise of routinization (2007: 38–48, 2010), with contemporary societies on a morphogenetic trajectory, in which structural conditioning becomes weaker and opportunities for choice multiply (2013a, 2014, 2017). But the general observation

---

[23] Since social relations are at the heart of sociology, what "relational sociology" consists of is highly contested. Margaret Archer and Pierpaolo Donati maintain that their own sociological theorizing is fundamentally relational (Donati & Archer 2015). Much of the controversy centers on questions of individual agency and subjectivity.

is also prominent among other social theorists that share little with Archer's methodology (Beck & Beck-Gernsheim 1994, Bauman 2000, Inglehart & Welzel 2005). If we are hence studying times in which the structuring of structure, to use Bourdieu's terms, diminishes (without disappearing), the "residual" of agency becomes all the more relevant.

The second argument is that only with a concept of agency can we link power with individual responsibility (Wight 2006: 205ff). Of course, this is, at first, essentially a moral standpoint, and it only becomes an analytical argument if we consider it the task of social science to uncover and explain power in human relations. Such a stance may come more naturally to political scientists than to relational sociologists, some of whom advocate to concentrate on "what happens in networks of people, where people in relation to each other together give normative power to one another but none of them alone have any (social scientifically interesting) power" (Piiroinen 2014: 89, also Fuchs 2001). Yet an emphasis on the social construction of norms can actually support the study of individual agency, once we observe ourselves to be living in societies with a culture that accords responsibility to individuals for their actions and the consequences these generate. Barry Barnes has developed a "relational" reading of agency that highlights precisely this social basis of "responsible agents":

> First, they act toward each other as agents capable of giving an intelligible account of what they are doing and why; and often this is much the same thing as stating why what they are doing is right and justified.... Secondly, they act toward each other as agents sensitive to symbolically conveyed evaluations of their actions and potentially responsive to them. Susceptibility in this sense is necessary for the co-ordination of actions and their coherent ordering around collectively agreed goals.... Social life as we know it requires responsible agents who may be held accountable, and to whom it makes a difference that they have been so held.   (2000: 74)

Thus, even someone like Barnes, who rejects the assumption of the *existence* of individual autonomy, recognizes that the *concept* of individual autonomy is the key to the moral order of (late) modern societies.[24] Within international politics, probably the best demonstration of the continuing prevalence of this moral order is the establishment of the International Criminal Court (ICC), which, since 2002, can prosecute individual political leaders for crimes against humanity (Roach

---

[24] Barnes develops his "fully social" perspective explicitly against social theories like Archer's that defend analytical dualism. Whether his naturalist philosophy of science or Archer's scientific realism is more suitable for the conduct of social science need not be of concern here, as they both end up providing strong arguments as to why agency should be studied. See Jackson 2010 for an overview of different philosophy of science standpoints in IR, and Monteiro & Ruby 2009 for a strong argument as to why different positions should not preclude dialogue among them.

2009, Hoover 2012). Seen from this angle, the argument turns into another structural cultural one: given a modern culture that has individual responsibility as its foundational norm, it would be analytically irresponsible to neglect agency.

Finally, the concept of agency, *contra* Fuchs, can be used in much more social scientifically useful ways than simply serving as the residual category for ultimately unexplainable individual thinking and doing. For this argument to be convincing, it will be necessary to further examine what is meant by "agency," and to show that interesting insights can be generated about it.[25] Doing so requires understanding agency as a variable, or, more precisely, two variables, as the concept comprises two different dimensions, which we find, for example, in Anthony Giddens, when he associates agency with the notion that "the individual could...have acted differently" (1984: 9), and also with the "capability to 'make a difference'" (ibid.: 14). Colin Campbell has shown how these two aspects permeate the discussion of agency in social theory, and he categorizes them as the "power of agency," the potential ("capacity") of a person for "performing self-conscious willed actions" (type 1), and the "agentic power," the individual potential of "acting independently of social structures" and "bringing about change in the world" (type 2) (Campbell 2009: 410). Often, confusion in the discussion of agency rests on the error to conflate both dimensions, the intrasubjective and the intersubjective, despite the fact that they do not necessarily correlate in a linear fashion; both types of agency vary, "over time, between individuals, and according to circumstances" (ibid.: 415). While the "power of agency" has much in common with reflexivity and self-efficacy, as examined in social-psychological studies (Bandura 1997, Elder-Vass 2007, Hitlin & Elder 2007: 177, 182ff), "agentic power" is closely related with the control of relevant resources and cultural schemas, which is shaped by one's position within social relations (Giddens 1984: 15f, 256–62, Sewell 1992). Margaret Archer's discussion of agency, though more complex in its elaboration of the psychological and social processes involved (2000), reflects a similar distinction. For her, it is at the level of the "person" where individuals develop a sense of "self" and of being an "actor" with relative autonomy, expressed in the reflective choice of commitments and the potential of creativity in the enactment of social roles.[26] At the same time, the structural context prearranges the menu of choice:

> [O]ur "social selves"...emerge respectively through our involuntary embroil-
> ment in society's distribution of resources and our voluntary involvement in
> society's role-array. However, they are themselves dependent upon the prior

---

[25] For extensive reviews of the use of "agency" in social theory, see Emirbayer & Mische 1998, Barnes 2000, Archer 2000, and—with a somewhat distinct focus on the "creativity" of action—Joas 1996.

[26] "Another way of putting these same two points about creativity and commitment is that the subject, thanks to his or her personal powers, has that which is needful for personal autonomy" (Archer 2000: 297).

emergence of a continuous sense of self and are co-dependent with the emergence of personal identity, which reflectively balances its social concerns with those embedded in the natural and practical orders of reality. The emergence of our "social selves" is something which occurs at the interface of "structure and agency". It is therefore necessarily relational, and for it to be properly so, then independent properties and powers have to be granted to both "structures" and to "agents." (ibid.: 254f)[27]

The variation in individuals' "power of agency" and "agentic power" also has an important temporal component, which is part of all the theorizing mentioned above, and which comes to the fore in Mustafa Emirbayer and Ann Mische's conceptualization:

> We define [human agency] as *the temporally constructed engagement by actors of different structural environments—the temporal-relational contexts of action—which, through the interplay of habit, imagination, and judgment, both reproduces and transforms those structures in interactive response to the problems posed by changing historical situations.*
> (Emirbayer & Mische 1998: 970, emphasis in original)[28]

Judgment as the "practical-evaluative" dimension of agency that "responds to the demands and contingencies of the present" (ibid.: 994–1002), and imagination as the "projective" dimension of agency that constructs possible futures (ibid.: 983–93) make immediate sense. In contrast, the inclusion of habit, the iterative dimension of agency that engages with the past (ibid.: 975–83), into a definition of agency may seem odd but only if one takes habit to mean an unreflected form of behavior, a mechanical response to structural exigencies. Bourdieu's *habitus* is sometimes seen as approaching such an understanding, despite the fact that Bourdieu does leave room for creativity in how people apply and adapt *habitus* to specific, contingent situations (Bourdieu & Wacquant 1992, Elder-Vass 2007). For Emirbayer and Mische, it is precisely the choices and the "maneuvering among repertoires" in relating past experiences to expectations about the present and the future that constitute agency in its iterative dimension (Emirbayer &

---

[27] In his appropriation of Archer's understanding for the study of IR, Colin Wight has labeled the different types agency₁, agency₂, and agency₃ (2006: 177–215), where agency₁ refers to the "freedom of subjectivity" (what Campbell calls "power of agency"), agency₂ refers to how individuals become agents of "the socio-cultural system...into which persons are born...[, and the] groups with which they identify," and agency₃ to "the social actor" as people occupy roles (ibid.: 213).

[28] Their definition neglects Campbell's distinction, as "engagement by actors" remains very vague, but when they talk about "agentic capacity" (Emirbayer & Mische 1998: 1005f), it appears as if they mean exactly Campbell's "power of agency," while reserving "agency" for the more action-oriented "agentic power." For another categorization of different temporalities of agency, see Hitlin & Elder 2007.

Mische 1998: 978ff). Once the different types and temporal dimensions of agency have been categorized, the empirical questions about the causes of variation become more precise:

1. *How do different temporal-relational contexts support (or conduce to) particular agentic orientations?*
2. *How do changes in agentic orientations allow actors to exercise different forms of mediation over their contexts of action?*
3. *How do actors reconstruct their agentic orientations and thereby alter their own structuring relationships to the contexts of action?.*
   (Emirbayer & Mische 1998: 1005, 1008, 1010, emphases in original)

Using Campbell's typology, the first question is about how structural conditions shape both the "power of agency" and the "agentic power" of differently situated individuals. The second question is about how differences in the "power of agency" relate to different forms of "agentic power." And the third question concerns the potential for reflexivity and changing one's own sense of the "power of agency." In her empirical research about how people are "making their way through the world," Margaret Archer has addressed these kinds of questions to identify different types or qualities of reflexivity, and how these are "forged from the interplay between subjects' natal social contexts and their ultimate personal concerns" (2007: 145, also 2003). I will later try to develop some hypotheses about the agency of billionaires in world politics, where chapter 3 starts with an analysis of the structural changes that provide opportunities for billionaires to operate as transnational actors. Chapter 4 will then specify billionaires' agency in its two dimensions, and when and why billionaires can be seen as "super-actors." Before moving to concrete cases, though, we still need to disentangle agency and power.

Agency and Power

As has been noted before (Giddens 1979: 88–95, Sewell 1992: 9ff, Campbell 2009: 409), agency is intimately linked with power, another concept notoriously difficult to define, despite its central role in political and social analysis. The objective here will not be to review the complex debates over the meaning of power,[29] but rather to extract those elements that are key to an understanding of agency, in order to clarify the relationship between the two. The main differences among theories of power concern three dichotomies that are best seen as each establishing a

---

[29] For comprehensive and illuminating treatments, see Morriss 1987, Haugaard 2002, Strecker 2012, and Baldwin, D. 2016.

continuum, on which specific approaches can be placed: analytical/evaluative, conflictual/cooperative, and strategic/structural. What unites most theorists of power is an understanding of it as a relational concept, although it remains to be seen whether the colloquial expression of "someone holding power" carries analytical meaning, too (Morriss 1987).

The first dichotomy concerns the basic question of whether power is primarily an analytical concept or essentially a moral and evaluative one that cannot be dissociated from normative standpoints.[30] The analytical stance is very common in political science (Dahl 1957), especially among Realist theorists in IR (Carr (1939) [2001], Morgenthau 1947), but also in social theory (Parsons 1963, Giddens 1979, 1984, Mann 1986). While the normative aspects of power are the natural domain of political theory and philosophy, strong arguments have been developed as to why *any* analysis of power will be faced with normative judgments (Lukes 1974, Guzzini 1993, 2005, Hayward & Lukes 2008, Strecker 2012). In the English language, the second dichotomy is reflected in the difference between "power over" and "power to," or a conflictual versus a cooperative understanding of power. The conflictual perspective emphasizes, in what is seen as the Weberian tradition, relationships of domination (Weber 1918 [2004] and 1978), whereas the cooperative or consensual viewpoint insists on power as empowerment to achieve outcomes (Parsons 1963, Arendt 1970).[31] Strategic understandings of power see it as being expressed in goal-oriented decision-making and actions, where actor "*A* has power over *B* to the extent that he can get *B* to do something that *B* would not otherwise do" (Dahl 1957 [1969]: 80). Yet, as Peter Bachrach and Morton Baratz have pointed out, decision-making always takes place in contexts, where the "mobilization of bias" may be institutionalized in such a way that the decision-making agenda is restricted (1962). The analysis of such structural conditions, which shape actors' options, must therefore, it has been argued, be part of the study of power (Lukes 1974, Foucault 1975, Bourdieu 1977, Hayward 2000). For example, the Supreme Court's Citizens United decision to liberalize the financing of political speech introduced a legal bias in favor of "freedom of speech," and against "political equality," which empowers billionaires.

The parallels in the discussions of power and agency with regard to the strategic/structural dichotomy are by now obvious, but whether all agency involves power, and vice versa, is far from clear. The voluminous *Encyclopedia of Power*, for example, has an insightful entry on "agency," but the author makes

---

[30] The distinction between moral and evaluative refers to whether one judges a specific actor's exercise of power according to moral criteria, or whether one evaluates a constellation of power among different actors in a given social system according to normative values like equality or freedom (Morriss 1987: 36–42, Lukes 2005: 60–9).

[31] Historically, it seems that the usage of the term power has been more associated with "power to" than with "power over," and its being mostly tied to notions of domination happened only during the twentieth century (Carroll 1972, Morriss 1987: 32ff).

no attempt to spell out its relationship with power (Dowding 2011). The conceptual confusion is best exhibited in Giddens, who tries to overcome the dichotomy by treating power "in the context of the duality of structure" (Giddens 1979: 91). For him, power is a "sub-category of 'transformative capacity', to refer to interaction where transformative capacity *is harnessed to actors' attempts to get others to comply with their* **wants**" (ibid.: 93, italics in original, bold emphasis added). Yet he also claims that power has nothing inherently to do with intention, will, or interests (ibid.: 90, 92), while simultaneously maintaining that interests are "logically connected with wants," as "interest concerns not the wants as such, but the possible modes of their realisation in given sets of circumstances" (ibid.: 189). Altogether, this sounds contradictory: How can power be about the realization of wants if it has nothing to do with interests? It becomes more logical once Giddens's understanding of wants enters the picture: "what people actually want in a given time and place . . . [is] conditioned and confined by the nature of the society of which an individual is a member" (ibid.: 190). Now the statements turn circular: Structure (society) instills wants in individuals, who then exercise power to make others comply with their wants. Giddens's refusal to link power to intentions at the individual level makes him again liable to the "central conflation" critique that has already been directed at his concept of agency: "Since the two aspects of power, the institutionalized and the strategic, become inseparably intertwined, it also becomes impossible to understand their *independent variation*" (Archer 1988: 93, emphasis in original).[32]

   With his notion that "capacity is harnessed," Giddens nevertheless captures a key insight, which has been elaborated most systematically by Peter Morriss, namely that power is essentially a dispositional concept: power usually becomes observable in its exercise, and its exercise always involves vehicles (or means) such as resources, but power should neither be reduced to its exercise, nor to being a vehicle.[33] Rather, at least when we talk about human life, power is a conditional disposition, a capacity to produce effects ("effecting outcomes") in which intention and hence choice are crucial (Morriss 1987: 14–28). It is an actor's property,

---

[32] Here, other, more radical proponents of "central conflation" and relational sociology are at least consistent when they reject both agency and power as meaningful categories for social theory (see Latour 1986, Fuchs 2001, Piironen 2014).

[33] Michel Foucault's notion that power is "an action upon an action" (Foucault 1982: 789) can therefore only be useful for studying the exercise of power, but it is wrong as a conceptual definition of power itself. Similarly, Dowding's critique of Morriss seems to concern only the exercise of power (Dowding 2008). For him, coming from a rational choice/game theory perspective, actors' intentions appear as fixed—and then what matters alone is the control of resources in strategic interaction with other actors. This is closely linked to his claim that social science is mainly interested in explaining "types" of actors, not in "token individuals" (ibid.: 251ff). He thus misses the argument of Morriss that, analytically, the study of the exercise of power comes after the study of power as a disposition, which involves intention.

but always relational in both its meaning and its exercise.[34] Seen in this way, however, power is more or less synonymous with the understanding of agency as developed by Campbell or Archer. Indeed, similar definitions of power, for example Bertrand Russell's "production of intended effects" (Russell 1938: 35), Rudolph Rummel's "vector-towards-manifestation" (1976: 165), or Arendt's "human ability not just to act but to act in concert" (Arendt 1970: 44), could just as well be taken as definitions of (collective) agency.[35] Morriss noticed himself that Amartya Sen's celebrated "capabilities approach" to human development (Sen 1985, 1999) has much in common with his own take on power (Morriss 2002: xxii–xxv)—except that Sen is mostly discussing "agency," avoiding the term "power." To minimize confusion, at least for the social sciences, it seems therefore useful to return to Max Weber's definition of power (*Macht*) as the "probability that one actor within a social relationship will be in a position to carry out his own will despite resistance, regardless of the basis on which this probability exists" (1978: 53). Like Morriss, he emphasizes the dispositional nature and the intentionality of power, but he specifies that it is directed towards others, in a social relation.[36] Does this imply reducing power to conflict and "power over"? Weber's subsequent concentration on *Herrschaft* (domination/authority) as a special form of *Macht* (power) has doubtless contributed to such a view, but his definition is actually more open. The English translators have suppressed the word "also" before "despite resistance," thus making the imposition of one's will always conflictual, whereas in the original German phrasing, this was only one modality among possible others.[37] As such, the concept can also accommodate modes of carrying out one's will that are cooperative, e.g. persuasion, or, in IR terminology, it encompasses both "soft" and "hard" power (Nye 2004). The billionaire that finances projects to encourage "open societies" and the billionaire that sponsors armed rebel groups or terrorist organizations are both exercising power, using money as the vehicle or means of power. "Their" power itself, however, is the capacity to produce outcomes vis-à-vis others, which is tied to their potential for

---

[34] Morriss distinguishes further between ability as a more general capacity and ableness as the concrete capacity given specific circumstances, where the latter is usually the domain of social and political power analysis, which requires taking the empirical distribution of power potentials and mobilizable resources into account (Morriss 1987: 80–97).

[35] All three authors do, however, then go on to differentiate more specific forms of power, with Arendt delineating her understanding of power from other concepts such as violence, authority, force, or strength.

[36] In the original German, *Chance*, which would translate better as "opportunity" or "prospect" instead of "probability," denotes the dispositional understanding of Weber better.

[37] "Macht bedeutet jede Chance, innerhalb einer sozialen Beziehung den eigenen Willen auch gegen Widerstreben durchzusetzen, gleichviel worauf diese Chance beruht." (Weber (1921–22) [1980], Kapitel 1, § 16). Weber himself found power to be "sociologically amorphous," which is why he opted not to engage with this concept further and focus on *Herrschaft* instead—but the social sciences have not followed him in this move (Müller 2007: 121, see there also for the relevant secondary literature). Giddens also keeps the more "open" reading of Weber's definition of power as something that may often involve conflict, but not inherently so (1979: 90–4).

agency, including their intentions. "Wealth is not political power ..., since, whilst some people use their wealth to collect politicians, others can only collect paintings" (Morriss 1987: 18).

Structural Power?

Ignoring individual intentions creates another shortcoming that is linked to Giddens's one-dimensional understanding of agency and power as "transformative capacity" (Giddens 1979: 92ff, 1984: 14f), which is also found among many other theorists (Campbell 2009). In his discussion of "political agency in a globalizing world," for example, Philip Cerny distinguishes between "transformational" and "structure-bound" actors, with the latter being seen as "passive" and with "limited opportunities" (2000: 438). But why would only the transformation of structures be an expression of agency and power, and not the "mobilization of bias" (Schattschneider 1960, Bachrach & Baratz 1962), the endeavors to stabilize or maintain structures? If the billionaire Koch brothers make efforts to maintain the status quo of societies relying on fossil fuels, funding a climate change countermovement to prevent the transformation of government policies towards promoting renewable energy sources (Greenpeace 2010), is this not an exercise of power? As Archer, once more, has noted in her critique of Giddens: "the capacity to introduce change does not necessarily involve power ..., while the use of power is no guarantee of change" (1988: 92). In her discussion of agency, she is hence careful to allow for both "defensive" and "promotive" agent projects (2000: 267–80). Of course, this requires opening the Pandora's box of consciousness and intention, because deeply habitual behavior that is simply conforming to (and thus reproducing) structural conditions is usually not associated with agentic power. This brings us back to the question of structural power: should we consider the structural context, which conditions people's choices, in terms of power? Steven Lukes, whose thinking about power is very attentive to institutionalized biases (1974), nevertheless felt the need to draw a sharp line:

> [P]ower ... presupposes human agency .... [A]lthough the agents operate within structurally determined limits, they none the less have a certain relative autonomy and could have acted differently. [I]n a world characterised by total structural determinism ... there would be no place for power .... [T]he notion of a power structure becomes a self-contradiction.   (1977: 6, 7, 9)

Here, the previously mentioned conceptualization of structure by Giddens, as rephrased by Sewell, does connect well with the understanding of power as a dispositional concept: a given structural context provides rules and resources, which are both constraining and enabling media of power, to agents; the asymmetries with regard to different actors' access to and control over rules and resources reflect the exercise of power in the past (Giddens 1979: 91ff, Sewell 1992).[38] It is therefore always necessary to examine structures when one studies power, but rather than speaking of "structural power," it is conceptually more consistent to refer to how structural properties affect both the capacities and the exercise of power. In a highly cited reappraisal of power in international politics, Michael Barnett and Raymond Duvall insist on differentiating "structural power," but their definition only takes "central conflation" towards new heights of circular reasoning:

> Structural power concerns the structures—or, more precisely, the co-constitutive, internal relations of structural positions—that define what kinds of social beings actors are. It produces the very social capacities of structural, or subject, positions in direct relation to one another, and the associated interests, that underlie and dispose action.   (2005: 52f)[39]

If structures produce actors' capacities, positions, and interests, we are really talking about determinism. Stefano Guzzini's earlier attempt to rework the concept of power in IR is more coherent, as he introduces "governance" to replace "structural power" as a term for impersonal, structural conditions: "The word 'power' will be reserved as an agent concept, and the term 'governance' will represent effects not due to a particular agent, whether individual or collective" (1993: 443).[40] If the Koch brothers are purposefully fostering libertarian think tanks in order to promote free enterprise without government interference (Schulman 2014), it makes sense to speak about them exercising power; "neo-liberalism," on the other hand, is better discussed in terms of a governing ideology, an ideational structure, as will be discussed in chapter 3.

One tricky question, which is directly related to the discussion above, remains: how should we treat the "unintended consequences" of actors' power? These can be observed in two different ways, the first of which rests entirely on power as a capacity, while the second is tied to the exercise of power. Thus, the mere presence of power inequalities may produce effects, because the exercise of power is being anticipated by others. For example, global health actors may refrain from criticizing the Bill & Melinda Gates Foundation, because they fear the potential loss of

---

[38] Archer (1988) and Lukes (Hayward & Lukes 2008), their many theoretical and methodological disagreements with Giddens notwithstanding, seem to adopt a similar perspective on structure and power.

[39] Their general definition of power is equally flawed: "Power is the production, in and through social relations, of effects on actors that shape their capacity to control their fate" Barnett & Duvall 2005: 45). In addition to committing the "exercise fallacy" (Morriss 1987: 15–18), their conceptualization lumps agency, structure, and power all into one concept.

[40] Though he makes no reference to her work, his graph on the agent–structure relationship closely resembles Archer's dualist understanding (Guzzini 1993: 472).

future funding from it. Alternatively, power may be exercised in the pursuit of one objective, but also produce other unintended consequences (Merton 1936, Giddens 1984: 9–14). When Bill and Melinda Gates put billions into the setting-up of private charter schools, state schools may experience their best students leaving the public education system, whose performance statistics then decline.[41] Likewise, the Gates Foundation's prioritizing of global health in their funding of research has led to significant adjustments among public agencies, e.g. U.S. in the pdf, the U.S. is here divided by a line break, which looks odd national health institutes, that finance health research (Matthews & Ho 2008, Olopade 2010). Often, such unintended consequences of power, linked as they are to underlying inequalities in the control over resources, have been emphasized in studies that argue in favor of some notion of "structural power" (Hayward 2000, Bates 2010). However, the analytical move to treat such cases as instances of power, rather than "structural conditioning," is in itself meaningful. As Stefano Guzzini has argued in his reading of Susan Strange's analysis of the structural power of the U.S. (Strange 1988): "By making actors also aware of the unintended effects of their action, they are asked to take this into account next time" (Guzzini 2005: 514). Clarissa Hayward, despite and because of her emphasis on "structural power" (2000), is very self-aware of the critical purpose of her focus: "students of power . . . should hold responsible those agents who, through their action or inaction, create significant, predictable, and avoidable constraints on the fields of action of others" (Hayward & Lukes 2008: 16). Yet, in assuming that an actor could and/or should have considered the unintended consequences of her power, and that she could have acted differently, we are back at agency with its key components of reflexivity and intention. In other words, we are transforming structural constraints into power as a specific form of agency, namely the one that pursues objectives vis-à-vis others. "[A]ttributing a function of power to an issue imports it into the public realm where action (or non-action) is asked to justify itself" (Guzzini 2005: 511). From this meta-theoretical perspective, which is shared by several theorists of power (Morriss 1987, Lukes 2005, Strecker 2012), asking questions about the "power" of billionaires in world politics is not only an analytical enterprise; it also involves assumptions about the unequal distribution of resources, the accompanying potential for power, the assigning of responsibility for consequences, and the need for justifications (Green 2013).

To sum up, in social science, structure and agency are key concepts used to problematize the engagement of human beings with their social, cultural, and material environment. Individual agency as the capacity to produce intended outcomes is analytically distinguishable, but empirically always linked to structural properties, such as the distribution of resources and cultural schemas, as well

---

[41] See Barkan 2011 and Kovacs 2011 for extended surveys of the impact of billionaire philanthropy on the U.S. education system.

as an actor's position within stratified social relations, which enable and limit the options a reflective actor can pursue. Power is a subcategory of agency, referring to political agency as the capacity of an actor to carry out her intentions vis-à-vis others. The very act of designating agency as "power" is a political move in that it stresses the potential for domination when one actor's capacities are having effects on the agency of others. To be clear: highlighting reflexivity and intentionality in human agency should not imply prioritizing these aspects a priori. Whether human agency is driven more by the unconscious, the habitual, or intentions has to be discussed in relation to specific cases and contexts. This is precisely the advantage of seeing agency as a variable. IR theories that take the agency–structure *problematique* seriously, notably variants of the constructivist approach, have mostly concentrated on the structural and habitual aspects of agency. Such an emphasis may prove to be fruitful as long as it concerns the study of actors that are constituted via formal institutions, for example diplomats in the enactment of states' foreign policies, or officials working in international organizations (Pouliot 2016, Hopf 2010, Adler & Pouliot 2011). Whether it is also the most suitable starting point for the study of individuals that personally control vast resources and build their own institutions seems more doubtful. Still, the structural outlook is indispensable to understand what conditions have facilitated the emergence of billionaires as transnational actors in world politics.

3

The Structural Context for Billionaires

Billionaires in the sense of the very few who control enormous financial resources have existed in many societies throughout the ages. But more often than not, control of wealth and politics have been directly linked—the legendarily rich Solomon and Croesus were kings, after all. In the modern age, with the rise of capitalism and liberal democracies, political authority and economic control could come to coexist as distinct realms.[1] In his sweeping review of different types of oligarchy, which for him means "the politics of wealth defense by materially endowed actors" (2011: 7), Jeffrey Winters has called this latest type "civil oligarchy," "the single most important transformation in the history of oligarchy" (ibid.: 208). According to him, oligarchs' objectives change as the rule of law converts property claims into property rights, enforced by the state. Oligarchs then no longer need to worry about (or resort to) violence when it comes to defending their wealth, which is their preoccupation when there is no protection of property rights. Instead, it is now mainly their income that needs to be shielded against taxation by the state (ibid.: 1–39, 208–74).[2] This transformation is closely linked with industrialization and the shift from wealth based on agricultural land towards wealth based on (increasingly urban) housing and investments in infrastructure, machinery, and financial assets, which, for the early industrializing countries such as Britain and France, happened mostly between 1700 and 1914 (Piketty 2014: 113–63).[3]

[1] Extremely rich royals as well as dictators continue to exist in modern times, and a few of them own wealth that would put them high on the *Forbes* global rich list, but *Forbes*, by its own definition, does not include them (see chapter 1). Occasionally, *Forbes* publishes data on "the world's richest royals," the last time in 2011, which showed the king of Thailand with US$30 billion on top, the sultan of Brunei with at least US$20 billion next, followed by the king of Saudi Arabia (US$18bn), the emirs of Abu Dhabi (US$15 bn) and Dubai (US$4bn), and then the first European, the prince of Liechtenstein (US$4 bn). See online: http://www.forbes.com/sites/investopedia/2011/04/29/the-worlds-richest-royals/ (accessed June 20, 2019). Since their wealth is intimately linked with their title and their institutional position (and/or its occupation by their families in the past), they will not be considered here, as our focus is on private actors. The same applies to dictators (for an analysis of Indonesia under Suharto and the Philippines under Marcos, see Winters 2011: 135–207).

[2] Winters uses a broad definition of income that sees not only capital gains taxes, but also inheritance taxes as taxation of income, because inheritance is understood as a transfer of property from the deceased to the heir, and thus as a form of income to the heir (2011: 208f). See Hägel 2012 for a critique of Winters' concept of oligarchy.

[3] Daron Acemoglu and James Robinson have made the interesting argument that mass democracy becomes more likely not just once urbanization and industrialization lead to an empowerment of the masses, but also when it becomes more acceptable to elites whose fortunes shift from immobile

Billionaires in World Politics. Peter Hägel, Oxford University Press (2020). © Peter Hägel.
DOI: 10.1093/oso/9780198852711.001.0001

The nineteenth century also saw the first so-called Gilded Age, during which individuals like John D. Rockefeller, Andrew Carnegie, or Cornelius Vanderbilt in the U.S. (Josephson 1934), or the Rothschild family in Europe, acquired fortunes that dwarfed those of most kings and queens, and would put them, adjusted for inflation, at the top of today's *Forbes* list. Hence, one structural prerequisite for the rise of billionaires, and one Karl Marx and neoclassical economists can agree upon, is the existence of a socioeconomic system that guarantees property rights in a "private sector" that is legally established by, but separate from, the public realm of politics (Rosenberg 1992). Given *Forbes*'s exclusive focus on "private" billionaires, this necessary condition is somewhat tautological. Whether it also forms a sufficient condition is more controversial, as this concerns the connection between capitalism and inequality: do market economies breed billionaires?

If we take the U.S. as the country with the most undiluted history of capitalism, without aristocratic legacies and socialist or dictatorial disruptions,[4] the answer is not straightforward. The Gilded Age came to an end, the "robber barons" passed away, and it took almost half a century until family names like Gates, Buffett, or Walton came to have a familiar sound like Carnegie or Rockefeller again. In between, during the middle of the twentieth century, the economist Simon Kuznets claimed in a highly influential paper that capitalism increases inequalities in its initial stages, which then decline again as capitalism matures—the famous "Kuznets curve" about the relationship between economic growth and income inequality showed an inverted U-shape (1953, 1955, also Milanovic 2016: 46–117). Although his observation relied only on data from the years 1913 to 1948, it was taken as pro-capitalist evidence when the Cold War grew hotter, and the socio-economic development of Western countries during the first two post-WWII decades seemed to confirm Kuznets' thesis. With substantial economic growth, the middle classes' fortunes did indeed expand, and only few people worried about oligarchy. C. Wright Mills' "the power elite" was one of the most critical concepts introduced at the time to discuss inequalities, but it focused on "those political, economic, and military circles which as an intricate set of overlapping cliques share decisions having at least national consequences" (1956: 18, also 269–7)— and not on oligarchs. Even this broad notion of elites was countered by those who saw a still greater diffusion of power (Dahl 1958, 1961), in which top decision-makers represented a functional, performance-based elite (Dahrendorf 1961, Keller 1963). Summarizing a widespread perception of the time, the first section

---

resources to more mobile ones, which are less exposed to the risk of redistribution via taxes (2006: 287–348).

[4] The main exception here is the pre–civil war slave-based economy of the Southern states of the U.S. (Piketty 2014: 158–63).

of Dahl's "*Who Governs?*" book was called "from oligarchy to pluralism" (Dahl 1961).

Yet, over recent decades, Kuznets' curve appears to be bending in the wrong direction, as rising inequalities within developed countries have officially been noticed (OECD 2008, 2011a, 2015), and pundits fret about a "superclass" (Rothkopf 2008), "plutocrats" (Freeland 2012), "the new few" (Mount 2012), and "the upper crust" (West 2014). Based on their painstaking construction of historical income and inheritance statistics, the economists Anthony Atkinson, Thomas Piketty, and Emmanuel Saez have been at the forefront of providing a long-term perspective on wealth and income inequalities (Atkinson & Piketty 2007, 2010, Atkinson et al. 2011, Piketty 2014). Their data show that while the arguments of Kuznets and the pluralists had good empirical evidence for the time period 1910–70, the chances for oligarchy have been growing afterwards (Piketty & Saez 2014, Alvaredo et al. 2018, Zucman 2019). Income and wealth inequalities are not yet back to the levels of the Gilded Age, except in the U.S. (Piketty et al. 2018), but a slow-moving trend towards nineteenth-century-like forms of stratification is visible in many developed and developing countries, despite significant differences among them. If no major disruptions happen, Thomas Piketty expects the twenty-first century, in terms of inequalities, to resemble the nineteenth century in the end (2014: 315–50). The world's billionaires have already been making huge steps upwards:

Figure 3.1 clearly shows that compared to the very slow and linear growth of the world's wealth, billionaires have seen much steeper increases (Milanovic 2016: 44). Most strikingly, in terms of distribution, Oxfam has calculated that, in 2018, the twenty-six richest billionaires owned as much wealth as the poorest half of the world's population, which comprised 3.8 billion people (2019: 12). Using similar data,[5] Piketty sees the different wealth growth rates as an enormous "force for divergence"—if these different wealth growth rates continue throughout the twenty-first century, the large majority of the world's wealth will be owned by a very small group of billionaires in 2100 (2014: 434–9, 623 fn5). Piketty is right to view this divergence trend as being "structural." The clear patterns we see in the evolution of inequalities, including billionaires' fortunes, do seem to indicate changing contexts that affect the chances to get very rich. Or, it is very unlikely that individual level variables like entrepreneurial talent decreased systematically during the middle of the twentieth century, and then reappeared from 1980 onwards. But Piketty's explanation takes an overly mechanistic tone: "Once a fortune is established, the capital grows according to a dynamic of its own, and it

---

[5] He uses a slightly different method to estimate global household wealth, which comes up with a sum about 20 percent higher than Credit Suisse 2013; see Thomas Piketty, "Annexe technique du livre « Le capital au 21e siècle »," online: http://piketty.pse.ens.fr/files/capital21c/Piketty2013AnnexeTechnique.pdf, page 72ff (accessed July 9, 2019). Oxfam's wealth data is based on Credit Suisse 2018. None of these estimates are "hard science."

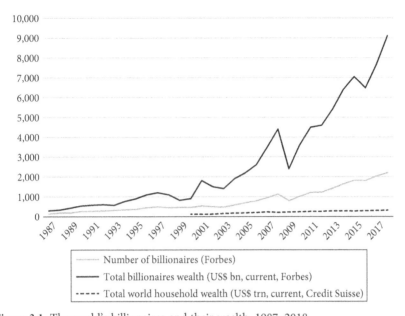

Figure 3.1 The world's billionaires and their wealth, 1987–2018

Sources: Forbes, various years for number of billionaires and their wealth, Credit Suisse 2018 for world household wealth.[6]

can continue to grow at a rapid pace for decades simply because of its size" (ibid.: 440). He assumes that access to professional wealth management and economies of scale, essentially due to the possibility of larger fortunes to better diversify their investment portfolio in terms of risks, provides higher returns (ibid.: 430f, also Harrington 2016). This is being illustrated with persuasive data on the return on investment rates of private U.S. university endowments, which do in fact increase with size (Piketty 2014: 447–50). Wealth concentration gets further amplified in time periods where economic growth stays below the average rate of return on capital (ibid.: 25–7, 199–234, 439). All of this may be correct, and Piketty's account of the long-term trends in capital/income shares and inequalities within countries does largely make sense.[7] Yet, his economic "laws" alone cannot explain

---

[6] Piketty notes that *Forbes* most likely underestimates the number and the wealth of billionaires, especially when it comes to "entry level" billionaires whose wealth is mostly based on inheritance and diversified investment portfolios, which are very hard to track for journalists (Piketty 2014: 441ff). Indeed, in all editions of its annual "Billionaire Census," Wealth-X came up with more billionaires than in the annual *Forbes* list: 2,604 in 2018 according to Wealth-X (2019: 5) versus 2,208 according to *Forbes*. Since Wealth-X provides no historical records pre-2012, their data is, however, not useful for a longer-term perspective. Credit Suisse's estimates of global household wealth only reach back to 2000 (2018).

[7] Much of Piketty's explanation rests on the evolution of growth rates, as real growth in the economy serves to counteract the expansion of previously accumulated wealth. Indeed, the ebb and flow of economic growth does correlate quite well with the evolution of inequalities in the long run. However, the average rate of return on capital that he computes, which is the second key variable in his

why billionaires à la Rockefeller had faded away during the middle of the twentieth century, and why they have had such a comeback since the 1980s.[8] In the following, I will try to outline the main structural changes that have created an environment for billionaires to flourish.

Although websites and books on how to become a billionaire are ever more popular, their authors rarely achieve what they preach themselves.[9] Obviously, there is no stringent formula to follow, and becoming a billionaire must have something to do with individual agency. But, as the previous section has shown, the patterns of rise and fall, and rise again, of extreme wealth throughout the past two centuries do point to shifts in the structural setting that either favors or hinders individuals in becoming ultra-rich. As the phenomenon of interest concerns the recent rise of billionaires, we need to pin down the structural conditions that have limited the emergence of billionaires pre-1980, and how these have become transformed into circumstances that are more conducive to getting immensely rich. Besides the economic aspect, we also need to inquire what allows billionaires to engage in global politics. Against the backdrop of IR's traditional state-centeredness, can we identify structural changes that grant resourceful individuals greater access to international affairs? Oftentimes, it will be argued, the same structural transformations that promote opportunities for individual wealth accumulation also provide openings in world politics for individuals to exercise power.

When studying structures, we initially return to Giddens's understanding of structural properties as specific configurations of resources and rules, formed via past practices, which provide a context for actors that is both enabling and

---

framework, appears contradictory to his argument: In Britain and France, the rates of return were much higher exactly during the period that saw the decline of inequalities, from WWI until 1960, with rates consistently over 6 percent instead of an average around 5 percent for the nineteenth and twentieth centuries overall (2014: 202). He tries to accommodate this by introducing—quite arbitrarily and without further explanation—a discounted "pure" rate of return to capital (ibid.: 205f), but even this does not make the contradiction go away. For a substantial critique of Piketty's work, especially his understanding of "capital," which merges two different variables of economic analysis—"wealth" as financial assets and "capital" as a factor of production—see Galbraith 2014, also Rognlie 2015 for the convincing critique that the growing capital share may be largely due to rising prices in real estate.

[8] Piketty does provide a number of social and political explanations throughout his book, which are often in line with the analysis presented here—but he musters them ad hoc. For his broader argument, he relies mainly on the purely economic logic. In his "policy implications" section (2014: 493–539), the role of taxation is being taken very seriously. But the index to his book shows just one entry on globalization, and none on neoliberalism.

[9] A particularly amusing example is the evangelical "prosperity preacher" Tom Anderson, who had a bestseller with "Becoming a Millionaire God's Way" in 2004, and then filed for bankruptcy just when his son, also a pastor in his father's church, published "Think Like a Billionaire, Become a Billionaire: As a Man Thinks, So Is He" in 2012. See Anderson 2004 and Anderson 2012 as well as online: Tammy Leitner, "Former church members question AZ pastor's financial advice," CBS 5, November 2, 2012, online: https://web.archive.org/web/20130214193806/http://www.kpho.com/story/19989878/former-church-members-question-az-pastors-financial-advice (accessed July 10, 2019).

constraining (Giddens 1979, 1984). If we differentiate further, following Sewell's critique of Giddens (Sewell 1992), between rules that are formalized and the less codified cultural frameworks of meaning—what Sewell calls schemas—we arrive at a distinction between material, ideational (culture), and institutional (rules) structures that shape the environment in which actors operate.[10] Since our phenomenon appears across the globe, we will look for changes occurring globally. Within the material realm, globalization and the decline of interstate war stand out. At the level of ideas, the progress of neoliberalism and the waning of alternative ideologies has been noted (Fukuyama 1989, Harvey 2005). Concerning institutions, at the level of the state, it is the shift from the welfare to the competition state, exhibited most notably in tax laws, but also through privatization and deregulation, which has marked recent decades. At the international level, the increasing complexity of world politics, which is no longer reducible to interstate affairs, will bring us back to transnational relations and global governance.

Distinguishing the material, the ideational, and the institutional does not imply that these realms are separate in the real world. On the contrary, they are evidently interconnected, as when the ideology of neoliberalism promotes economic globalization, which in turn prompts states to change their laws in efforts to improve their competitiveness, while those who benefit from competition will tend to embrace neoliberalism (Bell 2012, Centeno & Cohen 2012). Nevertheless, the analytic distinction between these realms follows standard social science practice in the search for causal explanations (Sil 2000), and is also being reflected in the different preoccupations of the three major IR theories. Realist theories focus on structure as the distribution of power in terms of control over material resources that can be used by a state to impose its will or to defend itself vis-à-vis others (Waltz 1979: 97–9, 129–93, Mearsheimer 2001). Constructivist scholars in turn claim that "that the most important structures in which states are embedded are made of ideas" (Wendt 1999: 309), as they shape actors' identities and interests. And liberal institutionalists concentrate on the impact of institutional design on

---

[10] Giddens discusses "interpretative schemes" as the modality of interaction that relates to structures of signification (1979: 81–5, 1984: 28–33), and thus ends up with a similar trinity of structural properties. However, his discussion of signification is limited to language/linguistics and is not well integrated into his treatment of structures as rule-resource sets. For Giddens, culture as a symbolic order, and especially ideology, belong to the intersection between communication and domination (1979: 165–19, 1984: 32f); his distinctions between culture, ideology, and norms are not fully consistent and convincing. To take an example of direct relevance for this study: certain aspects of the modern culture of individualism may be linked to institutions of domination, e.g. when we think about economic theory in the tradition of Adam Smith and how it constitutes the self-interested *homo economicus* (Hirschman 1977, Cohen 2014). But it would seem far-fetched to correlate the whole body of ideas from Kant and Descartes to Sartre, which continues to shape modern individualism, with a system of domination.

state behavior (Keohane 1984, Russett & Oneal 2001).[11] Serving as heuristic devices, the different structural realms highlight the distinct aspects of an enabling context that has facilitated the rise of billionaires in world politics. They also allow for better differentiation between countries: while structural transformations can be observed at the global level, national contexts continue to vary with regards to how states are integrated into the global economy, how dominant neoliberalism is, or how public policy and laws affect the distribution of resources (Weiss 2003, Soederberg et al. 2005).

A similar logic lies behind the separate analysis of structural conditions and billionaires' agency. Of course, every structural constellation is to an important extent based on the results of prior actions (Wight 2013), and some billionaires have at times contributed to establishing the structures we will study. As entrepreneurs and investors, many billionaires advance economic globalization. The Koch brothers have played a non-negligible part in spreading neoliberal ideology, via founding and financing various libertarian think tanks, such as the Cato Institute (Schulman 2014: 89–116). Other billionaires have lobbied politicians for privatization and deregulation policies from which they expected to profit. And George Soros's promotion of open societies, for example when his money empowers NGOs like Human Rights Watch (Neier 2003: 289ff), is contributing to a "power shift" in world politics, towards transnational societal actors (Mathews 1997). In order to pursue causal explanations of the interplay between actors and structures, we can separate them analytically, so as to assess the relative impact of the one on the other. Structures can exhibit emergent properties that are more than the sum of their parts (Archer 1995: 60–92, 163–246, List & Spiekermann 2013), and that can have autonomous effects upon actors. For example, while we may identify specific actions that have reestablished the free movement of capital post-WWII (Johns 1983, Johns & Le Marchant 1993, Helleiner 1994, Burn 2006), at least since the 1990s, a system of global finance is in place, held stable via competitive dynamics based on the institution of sovereignty and "offshore" legal constructs. This can usefully be seen as an emergent property that exercises strong structural constraints upon states and their tax administrations on the one hand, and which offers great opportunities for individual wealth accumulation on the other hand (Andrews 1994, Palan 1998, 2002, Palan et al. 2010).

Current attempts to revitalize and reconfigure structural theorizing in IR, which explicitly assimilate IR to social theory, have emphasized the need to take a systemic perspective that makes statements about the "social whole" of IR and how specific features of it—such as differentiation and stratification—determine the behavior of actors (Donnelly 2012, Albert & Buzan 2013, Albert et al. 2013). Unfortunately, they have a tendency to sidestep the complexities of the structure-

---

[11] For a fine analysis of the limitations of structural reasoning in both Waltz and Wendt, see Donnelly 2009 and 2012.

agency discussion and to fall back on understandings of systems and structures that border on reification, as in Jack Donnelly's standpoint: "for the purposes of structural analysis there is much to be said for treating actors as occupants of structural positions rather than subjects or the targets of system effects—and treating structures as structures of systems (of which actors are parts) rather than as external influences on agents" (2012: 632). Such a stance will be resisted here, because it discards agency (despite Donnelly's claim to the contrary, ibid.), which is crucial for an analysis of individuals in world politics. The emergent properties of material, cultural, and institutional structures can bring strong forces to bear on actors, but the responses they engender "cannot be 'automatic' but [are] necessarily mediated by human reflexivity" (Archer 2013b: 8). In the following sections, the task will be to highlight those structural properties that are most relevant for billionaires as transnational actors in world politics.

Material Changes: Globalization and Peace

Thinking about the material context of action is not an exercise in naturalism. While world politics is certainly shaped by some hard-to-change natural "givens" of geography, e.g. if one looks at the political implications of landlocked or island states (Hintze 1906, Mearsheimer 2001, Kaplan 2012), in the Anthropocene, much of what is usually being associated with material structures is the result of human interaction with the environment, which depends on the available techniques of manipulation. Emphasizing the human-made aspect of material conditions does not, however, detract from the fact that existing geography and technology together do affect the ways in which human beings satisfy material needs and wants, how they experience time and space, and how they interact with each other. Even Wendt (1999: 109–13, 130–5), who privileges ideational structures otherwise, concedes a "rump materialism," according to which "the distribution and composition of material capabilities at any given moment help define the possibilities of our action" (ibid.: 112). Archer shares a similar understanding of material structures (1995). Within IR, Daniel Deudney has developed the most systematic discussion of how the material context, or what he calls "geo-technics" (2007: 39), matters.[12] In his critique of neorealism's focus on the distribution of material resources for the exercise of power, he usefully distinguishes between the

---

[12] His positioning within the structure–agency discussion also fits with the perspective I have adopted previously: "The material environment composed of the interaction of geography and technology are for human *practical* purposes effectively revelations of natural possibilities not primarily constructed by humans. But which arrangements humans actually arrive upon can be impeded or facilitated by material contexts (along with numerous other factors) but are not fully determined by them" (2007: 59, emphasis in original). Deudney's understanding of technology is noteworthy, as he distinguishes "between technology (knowledge of how to manipulate nature) and technics (tangible artifacts). Major technological inventions, such as nuclear weapons, rest upon technological discoveries

composition and the distribution of material capability (Deudney 1993, 2000a). What interests us here is precisely how changes in the composition of material structures have contributed to the changes in the distribution of material resources that we see with the rise of billionaires. The first Gilded Age coincided with what has been termed the "first" globalization from the nineteenth century until 1914, whereas the trend towards a new Gilded Age follows the intensification of the "second" globalization since the 1980s.[13] The period of declining inequalities is marked by the two World Wars and the relative collapse of economic interdependence associated with them. Can we go beyond this temporal correlation and posit causal mechanisms that would explain the distributional changes—the (re-)emergence of extreme wealth—by linking them to transformations in the composition of material structures?

Globalization is commonly defined as a process or a set of processes that generate a "widening, deepening and speeding up of worldwide interconnectedness" (Held et al. 2006: 5), leading to "time-space compression" (Giddens 1990, Harvey 1990) and—the aspect that is most contested—a shift from the national to the global with regard to consciousness and social relations, including culture, economics, and politics (Featherstone et al. 1995).[14] To an important extent, changes in the composition of material infrastructures are underpinning globalization. When it comes to the movement of resources, goods, and people, new transportation technologies have facilitated interconnectedness. During the first globalization, railroads and steamboats made transportation across long distances and continents faster, cheaper, and more reliable (Harley 1988, Estevadeordal et al. 2003). Since the 1950s, similar progress has been made possible with the advent of jet engine aviation and container shipping (Levinson 2006, Hummels 2007). During both periods, simultaneous innovations in communication technologies—the telegraph, the telephone, and transoceanic cables during the first; satellites, wireless broadcasting, fiber-optic cables, and the internet during the second globalization (Castells 1996, Deibert 1997, Hanson 2008)—further contributed to the strengthening of global ties. Global communication concerns the exchange of information-based services as well as the possibility of monitoring

---

of possibilities given by nature and revealed by science" (ibid.: 296 fn46). Wendt's "rump materialism" is built upon Deudney's work.

[13] Arguably, antecedents of globalization can be found much earlier, and, in qualitative terms, the explorations around 1500 and the ensuing colonial empires can be seen as the true beginnings of globalization. As O'Rourke & Williamson show, however, the volume of economic cross-border exchanges and the extent of global integration increased dramatically during the nineteenth century, especially after 1850, marking a "dramatic structural break," at least for Europe (2005: 25, also 1999, 2002, 2004, Rosenberg 2012, Iriye 2014, Baldwin, R. 2016).

[14] For reviews of conceptualizations of globalization that arrive at similar definitions, see Caselli 2012: 1–17, Martell 2010: 1–17, and Scholte 2005. Much disagreement concerns the questions whether increasing interconnectedness will lead simply to more intense interactions or also to forms of global integration.

and controlling complex cross-border operations. Here, the digital revolution (Negroponte 1996), which allows for the processing of massive amounts of data and the worldwide dissemination of digital content almost instantly with next to no transaction costs, thus fusing information and communication technologies (ICT), is a new development genuine to the second globalization. ICT lies behind the qualitative change from inter-industry exchanges during the nineteenth century to the intra-industry exchanges that dominate the second globalization (Keohane & Milner 1996, Schiller 1999, Thun 2017). In terms of business and economics, the most basic consequences of globalization are much larger potential markets. This concerns not only selling goods and services to more customers around the world, but also opportunities to increase profit margins by making production processes more efficient via access to cheaper resources and labor (Milanovic 2016). The new material infrastructure makes it possible to set up worldwide production networks or value chains, relying on outsourcing, offshoring, and subcontracting while maintaining centralized control thanks to the use of ICT (Brooks 2005, Thun 2017). In this global geo-technical space, so-called global cities form the hubs through which flows of goods, services, information, and people are being channeled, and where the key players managing these flows operate (Sassen 1991, Knox & Taylor 1995, Taylor et al. 2011).

Micro-economic research has examined the conditions under which a few "superstar" actors can dominate so-called "winner-take-all" markets (Rosen 1981, Frank & Cook 1995 [2010]). This can happen in truly oligopolistic or monopolistic markets (here one can think of the oil, gas, and other natural resources billionaires), but also in highly competitive markets, when extraordinary achievement is coupled with extraordinary rewards (the paradigmatic examples being entertainment or sports superstars).[15] Confirmation for this comes from statistical analysis that finds billionaires overrepresented in countries with high corruption scores, but also in countries with high economic freedom scores (Neumayer 2004, Torgler & Piatti 2013). In his review of billionaires' wealth, the doyen of economic inequality research, Anthony Atkinson, supports this perspective: "Consideration of the origins of such fortunes suggests that many are made in 'winner take all' markets (as is evidenced by the fact that I am writing this paper using Microsoft Word, not WordPerfect which I used ten years ago)" (Atkinson 2006: 25, also Rothkopf 2008: 29–33). Whether Bill Gates's worth has grown exponentially because he exploited a monopoly, or whether Microsoft turned into a "natural" monopoly because it produced outstanding network effects, belongs to the morality of wealth and need not disturb us for now.[16] In

---

[15] For a treatment of possible sources of winner-take-all markets, see Frank & Cook 1995 [2010]: 32–44.

[16] See Piketty (2014: 443–47) for an argument about how the social reality of extreme wealth needs more consideration than the morality of it. Within economics, the related debate has mostly focused on CEO's incomes rather than entrepreneurs' wealth increases. One line of research emphasizes the rentier

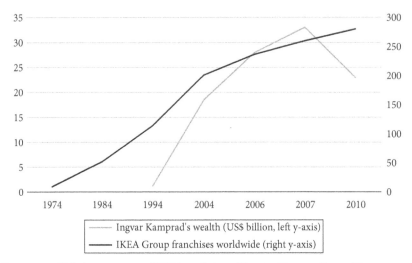

Figure 3.2 Global expansion of IKEA and rise of Ingvar Kamprad's wealth

Sources: The Economist, ("The secret of IKEA's success," 24 February 2011), for the IKEA franchises, *Forbes*, various years, for Kaprad's wealth estimates[17]

any case, the logic of "winner-take-all markets" is not about literal monopolies, but about "those-near-the-top-get-a-disproportionate-share markets" (Frank & Cook 1995 [2010]: 3).[18] Globalization increases the size of such markets, and economic superstars may thus become billionaires rather than "merely" multimillionaires. A prototypical illustration of this logic is the expansion of IKEA (Jonsson & Foss 2011). Besides homogenizing interior decoration around the world, it has also seen its founder Ingvar Kamprad leap into the top ten of the Forbes list once IKEA went global (Figure 3.2).

Broader empirical support for the connection between global markets and the rise of billionaires comes from statistical analysis that finds billionaires disproportionately concentrated—once level of development, country size and other alternative variables have been controlled for—in states that are more globally integrated (Torgler & Piatti 2013). The recently established "Billionaires Census," based on the extensive database of the private for-profit company Wealth-X, provides further indications of how billionaires take advantage of globalization.

---

aspect of CEO's pay explosion (Bebchuk & Fried 2004), while others underline the impact of globalization and how the growth of CEO paychecks correlates with the size of their firm relative to their competitors (Gabaix & Landier 2008, Gersbach & Schmutzler 2014).

[17] After 2010, *Forbes* revised the fortune of the Kamprad family down to US$3 billion, because Ingvar Kamprad presented evidence that large parts of the IKEA corporate structure had been transferred to a foundation (Stenebo 2010: 193–210).

[18] In his seminal article, Sherwin Rosen summarized it this way: "first, a close connection between personal reward and the size of one's own market; and second, a strong tendency for both market size and reward to be skewed toward the most talented people in the activity" (1981: 845).

It reports for 2018 that almost 30 percent of the world's billionaires had their primary residence in just fifteen global cities (Wealth-X 2019: 14, also Hay 2013). Moreover, no matter whether they inherited it from their family or created it themselves, in 2014, 63 percent of all billionaires were categorized as being primarily engaged in one private—not publicly listed—company. "This distinct preference for private ownership is indicative of billionaires' active participation in guiding their primary business' [sic] strategy" (Wealth-X 2014: 26). Although a deeper examination of the more or less global reach of these companies would be necessary, this data does suggest that many billionaires are well situated to make the most of global winner-take-all markets. This applies to all kinds of markets, from retailing (e.g. Aldi, Amazon, Walmart), textiles (e.g. H&M, Inditex), and luxury goods (e.g. LVMH, Kering) to software (e.g. Alphabet/Google, Facebook, Oracle) and media (e.g. News Corp, CNN). One "primary industry," however, stands out: according to Wealth-X, "finance, banking and investment" is the main business activity for around 20 percent of billionaires (2019: 18). Finance is also particularly well suited to gain from a world connected via ICT, as it allows for the processing of highly intricate data in the quest for investment opportunities worldwide. At the same time, the architecture of global finance—which includes very material ICT networks like payments and financial messaging services, such as SWIFT (Hägel 2009)—is itself advancing globalization. It links and integrates national capital markets, which provides companies with more options to finance their global business strategies (Bryant 1987, Frieden 1991, 2006).

The process of both the first and the second globalization, and with it the rise of billionaires, experienced one major interruption during the twentieth century, which is delimited by the two World Wars and the Great Depression in between. Obviously, major war can be a devastating force for wealth, not only when it destroys physical capital, but also in its capacity to disrupt cross-border commerce and to damage business and investor confidence, which makes markets plummet (Scheidel 2017). The absence of war—which is the common negative definition of peace (Boulding 1964, Cortright 2008)—is, in return, a structural material condition that is very favorable for wealth accumulation. After 1945, even though the number of conflicts has increased, if measured in terms of battle deaths, war has seen a sharp decline (Gat 2006, Pinker 2011, Gleditsch et al. 2013, Human Security Research Group 2014), see Figure 3.3.[19]

Two significant changes in the composition of material conditions have been associated with this trend. The first refers to the transformation of warfare that comes with the availability of nuclear weapons of mass destruction and intercontinental ballistic missiles. As Daniel Deudney has shown, the radical implications

---

[19] While major inter-state war has become rare, "new wars" have come to account for most violent conflicts (Münkler 2002, Kaldor 2012). The battle deaths of these new wars, most of which take place in the less developed world, are included in figure Figure 3.1.

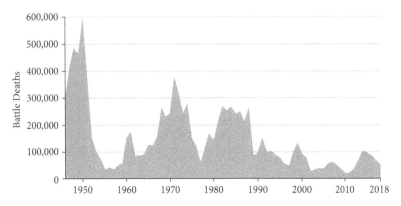

Figure 3.3 Trends in armed conflict, 1946–2018
Source: CC BY Strand et al. 2019: 2/PRIO

of nuclear missiles for the parameters of the security dilemma had been noted by leading realist IR thinkers (Herz 1960, Morgenthau 1964, Waltz 1990), but they neglected to revise their theories (Deudney 1993, 2000a, 2000b). The relationship between anarchy and security varies in relation to the materially shaped "violence interaction capacity,"[20] a concept that allows comparison of different geopolitical historical eras. While the industrial era (1850s–1950s) saw violence interaction capacity grow rapidly, horrendously evidenced by the death toll of the two World Wars, the nuclear bomb pitched it to a new level of mutually assured destruction that brought a fearful, yet relatively peaceful Cold War based on nuclear deterrence (Waltz 1990).[21]

The second change is linked to what has been called the "capitalist peace" theory (Schumpeter 1919, Gartzke 2007, Mousseau 2009, Schneider & Gleditsch 2010). Though it also emphasizes institutional structures—property rights, free trade, and investment arrangements[22]—key arguments concern the material basis of industrial and post-industrial capitalism, which tends to make war less, and peace more profitable. This has to do, first, with industrial development: "Development can alter [the] incentives [for war] if modern production processes de-emphasize land, minerals, and rooted labor in favor of intellectual and financial capital... the rents from conquest decline, even as occupation costs increase"

---

[20] Deudney defines it as "an aggregate factor composed of *violence density* and *violence proximity*. Violence density is determined by dividing the volume of violence by habitable territory; violence proximity is determined by dividing the velocity of violence by the size of the terrain" (Deudney 2000a: 26, emphases in original).

[21] For a revisionist argument why the impact of nuclear weapons may be overstated, see Mueller 2010. According to him, the pre-nuclear devastation of WWI and WWII, via advanced conventional weapons, served as a sufficient deterrent for further large-scale war.

[22] On this, the capitalist peace theory is in a major struggle with democratic peace theory, which highlights the political, rather than the economic institutions of modern liberal states (Doyle 1986, Russett & Oneal 2001).

(Gartzke 2007: 172). And, secondly, relating back to globalization, growing inter-dependence between countries makes war more costly (in terms of opportunity costs), and offers substitutes for conquest: foreign investment and trade (Gartzke 2007: 173, Gat 2013: 153). Both logics already applied during the nineteenth century, which, with the onset of the industrial-commercial revolution during the first globalization, also witnessed long periods of peace among the developed nations (1815–54, 1870–1914)—a novelty compared to previous history (Gat 2013: 152). Of course, none of this "capitalist peace" prevented the two World Wars, as Norman Angell, the most prominent early proponent of the theory (Angell 1910), had to realize in hindsight. Still, Stephen Brooks takes the distin-guishing feature of the second globalization—the deeper cross-border intertwine-ment of production processes via multinational corporations' trade and investments—to argue that war is even more costly, relative to peace, today (Brooks 1999, 2005, 2013):

> [T]he globalization of production has made it structurally easier for many highly advanced states to rely on MNCs to secure needed external resources and supplies. Among the most economically advanced states, not only have the costs of war greatly increased during the post-World War II era, but it also appears that the potential benefits of conquest have greatly declined during this period.   (Brooks 1999: 667)

As all structural forces, neither globalization nor peace function in a deterministic fashion. Their effects are both probabilistic and conditional. They are probabilistic in the sense that they represent structural properties—larger markets, greater investment opportunities, less harm to commerce and wealth—that increase the possibilities to become and to stay ultra-rich. The consequences for any aspiring individual billionaire depend on the specific composition of his business and her fortune. Globalization can be a boon or a bane, depending on whether larger markets imply competitive pressures or chances for growth. In capital-scarce countries, becoming integrated into global markets may well weaken local oli-garchs (Frieden 1991). And although war hurts many people, there have always been war profiteers that know how to benefit from violent conflict, even if their number is currently declining (Brooks 2013). Nonetheless, the arguments pre-sented above can partially explain why changes in the composition of the material context coincide with the renewed rise of billionaires. While the nineteenth century had seen similar transformations, new transportation technologies, the digital revolution, and the nuclear/capitalist peace constitute an environment, post-1945, that is even more conducive to those who win in global markets (Milanovic 2016). To be sure, other forces drive globalization and the decline of interstate war, too, and the material conditions are often linked with ideational and institutional structures. For example, Kenneth Scheve and David Stasavage have demonstrated how the sacrifices of the twentieth century's two World Wars had created strong egalitarian demands for taxing the affluent—which appear to decrease in times of peace (Scheve & Stasavage 2010, 2012). But this does not detract from the value of singling out the particular contributions that material structures make to the rise of billionaires.

It now remains to be seen whether globalization and peace also provide increasing opportunities for individuals to make their mark in world politics. Here, the research on transnational relations provides some clues again. The most straightforward observation is that the very same infrastructure of globalization that allows commercial interactions may equally be used for social and political engagement across borders (Rosenau 1980, 1990, Deibert 1997, Florini 2000, O'Brien et al. 2000, Cerny 2010). Jessica Mathews has turned this into the widely noticed claim that a "power shift" is underway, in which the technologies of globalization turn the balance in favor of global civil society, and against states (1997). One empirical indicator is the growing number of international nongovernmental organizations, a trend that transcends the twentieth century, but has intensified after 1945 (Boli & Thomas 1999). This refers back to Raymond Aron's insight about how transnational society thrives in proportion to the density of transnational exchanges. Karl Kaiser, in his exposition of transnational politics, argued similarly:

> The weapons revolution has broken the "hard shell" of the territorial state; the revolution in communication and transportation, the rise of an advanced industrial society which inherently expands social interaction, and the growing impact of a perception of interdependence have broken the "hard shell" of the social state.   (Kaiser 1969/1972: 810)[23]

However, both Kaiser and Aron immediately went on to highlight that it is the legal systems of states and the international treaties they sign that determine individuals' activities in their territories, and both mention the Soviet Union's iron curtains for illustration (ibid.: 811, Aron 1966 [2003]: 105–7). Institutional factors thus seem to trump material possibilities, or, put more subtly: globalization and peace do provide a hospitable environment for transnational political actors, including billionaires, but access to the political realm depends on authorization by the established political institutions (Risse-Kappen 1995, Tarrow 2001, 2005: 1–34).[24] This argument is persuasive with regard to politics in the public sphere, and will be discussed further in the following chapters. When the governments of

---

[23] With "social state," Kaiser refers to the nation as the social community within the state.

[24] Similarly, in his early critique of the transnational relations framework, Samuel Huntington acknowledged the impact of material changes for the rise of transnational actors post-1945 (1973: 339–44), yet remained skeptical about their autonomy, which he saw as conditioned by states (ibid.: 356).

Russia, Kazakhstan, and Uzbekistan felt threatened by Soros's open society foundations, they tightened their laws to restrict the operation of externally funded organizations (Berg 2006). On the other hand, as the literature on the clandestine and illicit aspects of globalization demonstrates, the sheer magnitude and complexity of global transactions does make it increasingly difficult for state institutions to control what crosses their borders (Nordstrom 2007, Birtchnell et al. 2015, Shelley 2018). Notwithstanding the fact that powerful states like China or the U.S. may erect "great firewalls" and wide-ranging surveillance apparatuses (Lyon 2015, Griffiths 2019), the twenty-first century's global space of flows does appear harder to scrutinize than in times of less interdependence. Billionaires that prefer to stay out of the public eye find a formidable infrastructure to channel resources around the world, for business as well as for political influence.

Ideational Changes: The Rise of Neoliberalism

Highlighting the ideational structures that shape action is not an exercise in phenomenology, although it shares a number of problems with the philosophy of consciousness, notably the difficulties to distinguish the material from the mental experience. In social theory, the question about the causal role of ideas has often juxtaposed the Marxist perspective of ideas and culture as part of an epiphenomenal superstructure (Marx 1859 [2002]) with Max Weber's greater emphasis on the causal force of culture (Weber 1904 [2002]). In the tradition of this great debate, William Sewell and Theda Skocpol have argued over the influence of ideology (Sewell 1985, Skocpol 1985). Largely structuralist in her understanding of social revolutions (Skocpol 1979), when it comes to ideas, Skocpol defends an agency-centered approach: "I prefer to reserve the term 'ideology' for idea systems deployed as selfconscious political arguments by identifiable political actors" (ibid.: 91). Her logic behind this position is one that is often used to discount the structural properties of ideas: culture is never fixed, there are always many ideas floating around, allowing actors to pick and choose. In contrast, Sewell sees ideology

> as an anonymous and collective, but transformable, structure, constitutive of the social order .... Ideology must be seen neither as the mere reflex of material class relations nor as mere "ideas" which "intellectuals" hold about society. Rather, ideologies inform the structure of institutions, the nature of social cooperation and conflict, and the attitudes and predispositions of the population   (1985: 61).

Within the dialectic of agency and structure, the question is not whether one or the other perspective is always right, but whether one can identify, for given time periods, the emergence of relatively stable frameworks of meaning that condition the possibilities of action in particular ways (Archer 1988, Gofas & Hay 2010b: 40–7). Ideas originate with specific actors, but they can acquire structural properties if they turn into widely accepted norms and values that are being held stable via cultural processes of reproduction, for example education, or via institutionalization, especially in law.[25]

Across the social sciences, ideational research had been relegated to the sidelines during most of the second half of the twentieth century, but it has seen much renewed interest since then (Gofas & Hay 2010a, Béland & Cox 2011a). In IR, the return of ideas as explanatory variables is closely associated with the rise of social constructivism since the 1980s (Kratochwil & Ruggie 1986, Onuf 1989, Katzenstein 1996, Checkel 1998, Ruggie 1998, Abdelal et al. 2010).[26] Alexander Wendt in particular has promoted a "structural idealism" according to which culture as collective "knowledge structures held by groups…generate[s] macro-level patterns in individual behavior over time" (1999: 161f). These "have effects that cannot be reduced to agents and their interactions. Among these effects is the shaping of identities and interests, which are conditioned by discursive formations—by the *distribution* of ideas in the system" (ibid.: 138, emphasis in original). Changes of ideational structures will always depend on actors upholding or modifying their beliefs and values. Since this involves causal beliefs about how the world and people hang together (Béland & Cox 2011b: 4), ideational change will usually emerge in relation to transformations in the material and institutional context.[27] Yet, this should not be seen as an automatic process of triggers and results, because it involves reflexivity on the part of human actors (Hay 2011). Moreover, change may occur due to a "pure" reflexive and discursive engagement with ideational structures—the favorite activity of philosophers and theorists of all stripes. Ideologies usually combine values and beliefs in ways that contain inherent tensions, which stimulates further discussion. Liberalism, which, with individual freedom as its founding value (Mill 1859 [1974]), would seem to be ideally situated for being billionaires' preferred ideology, is a case in point. As Isaiah Berlin has highlighted, its central value, liberty, has at least two sides, the negative liberty of non-intervention, and the positive liberty of "self-mastery" and "collective self-direction" (Berlin 1969). Seen in this light, ideational shifts in liberal societies can be interpreted as moves to embrace the one or the other side more.

---

[25] In the following, I will subscribe to "the core definition of ideology as a *coherent and relatively stable set of beliefs or values*" (Knight 2006: 625, emphasis in original), which is very similar to what Mehta calls "public philosophies or zeitgeist" (2011: 25), or what Goldstein and Keohane distinguish as "worldviews" (1993b: 8f). See also Berman 2011.

[26] An older tradition of taking perceptions and frameworks of meaning seriously exists in the FPA subfield, see Jervis 1976, also Goldstein & Keohane 1993a.

[27] The specification of why and how ideational structures change is among the least theorized aspects of ideas in politics (Berman 2011: 106f and 123, Mehta 2011). In his study of the adoption of Keynesianism in different countries, Peter Hall usefully distinguished the policy viability, administrative viability, and political viability of new ideas, but these criteria focus exclusively on how ideas fit into existing institutional structures (Hall 1989).

One of the early and most influential applications of ideational theorizing, pre-Wendt, has been John Ruggie's analysis of how the multilateral "Bretton Woods" economic order post-WWII was built on collective values, what he called "social purpose," that constituted "embedded liberalism" (Ruggie 1982). This term borrows the notion of embeddedness from Karl Polanyi, who, simultaneously analyzing and expressing the *zeitgeist* of the interwar years, had argued that people will oppose the imperatives of a market society. In his famous "double movement," the logic of the nineteenth century, which saw the market economy increasingly disembedded from social relations, is being reversed (Polanyi 1944 [1957]). For Ruggie, the construction of the "Bretton Woods" order represented the broader normative consensus that Polanyi had identified. It combined a refusal of laissez-faire principles, which had guided the era of the gold standard during the late nineteenth and early twentieth century, with an acceptance of the need for substantial national autonomy. The latter was seen to be necessary for the kind of macroeconomic policies that Keynes had promoted (1933, 1936), and also for the functioning of the expanding welfare state (Marshall 1950).[28] As such, "embedded liberalism" expressed both ideas about the proper role of the state and the accompanying international economic order (Ikenberry 1993). "[T]hat multilateralism and the quest for domestic stability were coupled and even conditioned by one another reflected the shared legitimacy of a set of social objectives to which the industrial world had moved, unevenly but 'as a single entity'" (Ruggie 1982: 398). The key institutional expressions of these collective ideas were the explicit authorization of capital controls, exemptions from free trade, and fixed yet adjustable exchange rates.

Though embedded, the main idea was still liberalism, and in this sense, the values of the international economic order were not against getting rich per se. In its overall support for trade and exchange rate stability, the Bretton Woods order was clearly business-friendly. But the ideological endorsement of national autonomy had at least two implications that could limit the possibilities of wealth accumulation. First, it explicitly foresaw state intervention in the economy, which—depending on the particular national regime in power—could mean extensive redistribution, via nationalization of business or progressive taxation and welfare transfers. In the Keynesian framework, high inequalities were to be avoided for economic and political reasons, because they could undercut economic growth and destabilize capitalism itself (Kirshner 1999: 327). And second, in legitimizing the limitation of international capital flows, it restrained the material opportunities to benefit from global markets. This can explain how the ideational structure of "embedded liberalism" contributed to the decline in

---

[28] Although the "Keynesian welfare state" is a popular term, Keynes, both as economic theorist and as politician, had only indirect influence on the development of welfare states (Marcuzzo 2010).

inequalities during the 1950s and 1960s: it provided rationales for the kind of institutions that discouraged the accumulation of extreme wealth.

The following decade, however, saw a deep crisis of "embedded liberalism," which is largely associated with material and institutional changes: the abandonment of fixed exchange rates in 1971, the oil price shocks of 1973 and 1979, and the "stagflation" combination of high inflation and economic stagnation in many developed countries during the 1970s, which ran counter to Keynesian assumptions about macroeconomic policymaking (Bruno & Sachs 1985, Kirshner 1999, Eichengreen 2008: 134–84, Evans & Sewell 2013: 40–3). Soon after, neoliberalism would replace "embedded liberalism" as the dominant paradigm for the world economy. Several analyses of the rise of neoliberalism view it as a strategic scheme of capitalist elites, which gained political power with the elections of Margaret Thatcher in Great Britain in 1979 and Ronald Reagan in the U.S. in 1980, and then turned into a global, imperialist project (Cafruny & Ryner 2003, Duménil & Lévy 2004, Saad Filho & Johnston 2005).[29] David Harvey is the most explicit representative of this interpretation, which is often based on Marxian historical materialism and Gramscian frameworks of hegemony, and, as such, downplays the independent role of ideas:

> We can...interpret neoliberalization either as a *utopian* project to realize a theoretical design for the reorganization of international capitalism or as a *political* project to re-establish the conditions for capital accumulation and to restore the power of economic elites.... I shall argue that the second of these objectives has in practice dominated.   (2005: 19, emphases in original)

Much of Harvey's reasoning is convincing and well supported by empirical evidence, as far as it concerns neoliberalism's rise to dominance during the 1980s and 1990s. For the process of shifting from "embedded liberalism" to neoliberalism during the 1970s, on the other hand, Harvey's story is analytically flawed. The new entrepreneurial and financial actors, which he claims to have been the main self-interested promoters of neoliberalism, including various billionaires (ibid.: 31–8), were not yet that influential during the transformation period of the 1970s. By definition, a new elite cannot have been the old elite, and if it was not so powerful in the past, then we have to rely on something else than "class power" to explain its rise. Neither will a simple reference to the material crisis do. If periods of crisis involve uncertainty, then "what constitutes an economic crisis *as a crisis* is not...self-apparent.... Given this, the set of available ideas with which to interpret the environment, reduce uncertainty, and make

---

[29] For an equally critical but analytically much more subtle analysis, see Plehwe, Walpen, and Neunhöffer 2006a.

purposeful collective action possible becomes crucially important" (Blyth 2002: 9f, emphasis in original; also Hay 1999).

This is precisely the purchase of an ideational analysis: it can trace the construction of new ideologies and how these gain traction. The study of the origins of neoliberal thinking has recently produced a number of in-depth historical accounts, which all, including those closer to a Gramscian perspective (Walpen 2004, Mirowski & Plehwe 2009), demonstrate that during its formative years, neoliberalism was first and foremost an intellectual project (Burgin 2012, Jones 2012). At its center was the Mont Pèlerin Society, founded by Friedrich August von Hayek in 1947 and presided by Milton Friedman between 1970 and 1972, which served as a transnational community of liberal thinkers, mostly economists, who shared a commitment to reviving liberalism.[30]

> [T]hey perceived their roles as public intellectuals to be one of precipitating long-term ideological change, and they thereby rebelled forcefully against institutional structures that risked sacrificing the mantle of academic objectivity in favor of more immediate political aims.   (Burgin 2012: 57)

The notion "neoliberal" was initially meant to distinguish the renewal of liberalism from the "laissez-faire" principles of the nineteenth century.[31] But instead of advocating for a management of markets via government intervention, as Keynes had done in his "end of laissez-faire" (Keynes 1927), for Hayek, this meant a strong role for the state insofar as it provides and enforces the rules that make competition in markets flourish (Hayek 1944 [1994]: 21, also Burgin 2012: 56, Jones 2012: 6f). This fundamental belief in the superiority of markets to organize exchange, together with the recognition of the importance of the rule of law, especially to protect private property, defines the essence of neoliberalism since its beginnings (Harvey 2005: 2, Plehwe & Walpen 2006: 27, Turner 2008: 4f). Especially among the European thinkers of neoliberalism, the primacy of the rule of law, isolated from the vagaries of democracy, also extended to the global sphere and the construction of international institutions (Slobodian 2018). On many other questions, such as monopolies, the merits of individualism, or the provision of welfare, there were differing viewpoints and vigorous debates among the participants of the Mont Pèlerin Society during its first two decades (Burgin 2012: 55–122, Jones 2012: 30–133). Only during the 1960s, and with the growing

---

[30] Unsurprisingly, financial support for the Mont Pèlerin Society and its activities mostly came from a variety of businessmen and pro-business organizations, but Hayek guarded its intellectual autonomy, and, in its funding, the Mont Pèlerin Society did not have extraordinary resources (Burgin 2012: 97ff and 126ff).

[31] Initially defining their approach as "neoliberal" during the 1950s, Milton Friedman and other proponents later abandoned the idiom, due to the terminological confusion, especially in the U.S., around the term "liberal" (Burgin 2012: 170, 175ff).

prominence of the "Chicago School" economists, in particular Milton Friedman, did the contours of neoliberal ideology become sharper.

Friedman himself had narrowed his views, which became condensed in his bestselling "Capitalism and Freedom" (Friedman 1962). "If *The Road to Serfdom* had presented a defensive manifesto for an ideology in a state of retreat and disarray, *Capitalism and Freedom* provided a platform for a movement that was prepared for an aggressive offense" (Burgin 2012: 174). The main thrust now was to limit the role of government to a minimum in order to extend the logic of markets to as many realms as possible. Building on their prior academic work, which was often empirically and theoretically sophisticated, the Chicago members of the Mont Pèlerin Society could command scientific respectability.[32] The legal scholar Aaron Director and the economist George Stigler had developed strong arguments against state regulation of the economy, including antitrust (Stigler 1975). James Buchanan, who had received his PhD from Chicago, was one of the founders of the "public choice" school in political economy that questions the rationality of democratic governments (Buchanan & Tullock 1962). During the 1960s, neoliberalism thus came to develop strong tenets in favor of privatization and deregulation, and against taxation and public services, including welfare. Despite the focus on competition, in its endorsement of free enterprise "Chicago neoliberalism" went as far as relativizing the threat of monopolies, because state intervention was seen as more dangerous (Crouch 2011: 16f, 52–62, Burgin 2012: 170ff, 180, Wu 2018: 83–118). The rule of law—constitutionalism—was to safeguard the neoliberal order against potential encroachments, even if these emanated from democratic majorities (Burgin 2012: 119f, Turner 2008: 167–91, Slobodian 2018). Besides establishing these general principles, the Chicago economists also applied their neoliberal framework to a range of economic policy issues. Milton Friedman in particular had worked on questions of exchange rates, inflation, and unemployment, and his empirical and theoretical analyses, popularized in *Capitalism and Freedom*, regular *Newsweek* columns, and television appearances, attacked the very basis of the post-war Keynesian consensus of "embedded liberalism" (Burgin 2012: 178ff). When stagflation materialized afterwards, neoliberal thinkers could claim to have foreseen the troubles, which made their proposed solutions—both their general principles and more concrete policies like monetarism and flexible exchange rates—all the more attractive (Blyth 2002: 139–51, Crouch 2011: 8–23). At this point, neoliberalism had evolved into a coherent framework with which to make sense of the 1970s crisis and with causal beliefs about how to progress. In other words, it could serve both as a general ideology and as a "policy paradigm" (Hall 1993, also Berman 2013). Its later rise to

---

[32] Hayek received the Nobel prize in Economics in 1974, Friedman in 1976, Stigler in 1982, Buchanan in 1986 (Horn, Mirowski, and Stapleford 2011, Burgin 2012: 159–213, Evans & Sewell 2013: 36f).

hegemony, both at the global level and in many countries, is much more inter-twined with political struggles, in which actors often used the ideology strategic-ally, to advance their economic interests (Duménil & Lévy 2004, Harvey 2005, Plehwe et al. 2006a, Hall & Lamont 2013a, Ban 2016).[33] At the global level, key tenets of neoliberalism came to be condensed into the so-called "Washington Consensus" (Williamson 1990, Babb 2013), endorsed by the U.S., the IMF, and the World Bank in their relations with developing countries, which replaced the "embedded liberalism" consensus of the original Bretton-Woods order (Babb 2013, Slobodian 2018). The accompanying institutionalization of the neoliberal state and a neoliberal international economic order will be discussed in chapter 4.

For now, we still need to spell out how neoliberalism represents a new idea-tional structure that is much more favorable for billionaires than the "embedded liberalism" it replaced. With regard to wealth accumulation, it is not very difficult to see how an ideology built on free enterprise and the protection of private property suits wannabe billionaires of the entrepreneurial kind. Deregulation as the reduction of barriers for and limitations of commerce, be it tariffs, taxes or other restrictions, and the extension of private property into new realms of commodification, notably intellectual property rights, obviously benefits success-ful businessmen and -women.[34] An ideology that aims to limit the state and embraces private initiative also legitimizes "civil society" to take over functions previously reserved for public policymaking (Plehwe et al. 2006b: 10–17, Munck 2005: 65f, Jaeger 2007). This is not to say that any nonstate initiative is a neoliberal project, as it is clearly too simple to reduce the complexity of "civil society" to privatization (Kaldor 2003, Powell 2007). Still, neoliberal ideology does favor leaving as much as possible to the "voluntary exchange" among individuals, without worrying much about the power differentials that come with unequal control over material resources (Friedman 1962: 22–36). As such, it lends support to private standard-setting and other forms of private authority within national and global governance (Cutler 2003, Potoski & Prakash 2009, Vogel 2009, Green 2014).

At a more general level, economic sociologists and anthropologists have emphasized cultural changes in the very understanding of subjectivity since the 1980s (Bröckling 2007, Boltanski & Chiapello 2007, Greenhouse 2010, Dardot & Laval 2013). Thus, Peter Hall and Michèle Lamont observe that "neoliberalism inspired changes in the dominant scripts of personhood toward ones more

---

[33] In their typology of mechanisms that lead to the global diffusion of neoliberal policies, Beth Simmons, Frank Dobbin, and Geoffrey Garrett distinguish coercion, competition, learning, and emulation—the latter two would involve the impact of the ideational structure of neoliberalism (2008b).

[34] It has been noted that deregulation in practice actually relies on re-regulation, since the opening and functioning of markets always requires rules (Vogel 1996). Yet this does not detract from the fact that market-making regulation encourages business.

focused on a person's individuality and productivity" (Hall & Lamont 2013b: 5).[35] Pierre Dardot and Christian Laval are among those who push this line of thinking furthest, claiming that beyond ideology and policy prescriptions, neoliberalism has become the "existential norm" or "new global rationality," based on the "generalization of the enterprise-form":

> This norm enjoins everyone to live in a world of generalized competition; it calls upon wage-earning classes and populations to engage in economic struggle against one another; it aligns social relations with the model of the market; it promotes the justification of ever greater inequalities; it even transforms the individual, now called on to conceive and conduct him- or herself as an enterprise.... [I]t is "world-wide" in that it obtains on a world scale; and, far from being confined to the economic sphere, it tends to totalize—that is, create a world in its own image through its power to integrate *all* dimensions of human existence.   (Dardot & Laval 2013: 3, emphasis in original)

Alas, Dardot and Laval, like many other critics of neoliberal ideology, remain mostly at the theoretical level and rely mainly on anecdotal evidence of policy changes that reflect the neoliberal spirit. Hence, they have little empirical material to respond to critics like Harvey and Skocpol, who see ideology primarily as a tool for actors to advance their material and political interests. A strong argument is hidden in a footnote: one of the most powerful neoliberal decision-makers, Alan Greenspan, the chairman of the U.S. Federal Reserve from 1987 to 2006 and an explicit admirer of Milton Friedman's work, admitted publicly after the 2008 financial crisis that, in his policymaking, he had been misguided by his ideology (ibid.: 223 fn17, also Burgin 2012: 215f).[36] Since he had retired by then, it is hard to count this as a strategic defense. Lucy Barnes and Peter Hall have made the effort to trace ideological changes at the macro level, and do find significant support for a cultural shift toward neoliberalism from the 1980s onwards: Across the OECD countries, political parties on the left increasingly embraced neoliberal positions (Barnes & Hall 2013: 212f); and results from the World Values Survey indicate rising support for "payment by ability," even among low-income groups (ibid.: 214f).[37] If those who stand to gain the least from neoliberal ideas—and,

---

[35] "[H]owever, these changes cannot be understood as the imposition of neoliberal modes of thinking on entirely plastic individuals. People respond to neoliberal values with varying degrees of enthusiasm and resistance" (ibid.).

[36] Likewise, Sewell's strongest argument in favor of the autonomous force of ideology appears when he shows how the French revolutionaries' adherence to ideology (insisting on the clergy swearing an oath of allegiance to the state) ran counter to their material and political interests, inciting the Vendée counterrevolution (1985: 79ff).

[37] At the same time, values attached to redistribution and the welfare state did not decline. "Although market-oriented ideas have left their mark on the popular imagination, they do not seem

empirically, have gained the least (ibid.: 215ff)—adopt them nevertheless, one can be confident that changes in ideational structures have exercised causal force.

In one of the most discussed ideational interpretations of recent history, Francis Fukuyama captured the important notion that with the end of the Cold War, in the realm of ideology, liberalism had no more serious contenders (Fukuyama 1989). Yet, in declaring liberalism victorious, he ignored the inherent tensions of an ideology that builds its order on individual freedom, and the very different varieties of liberalism these tensions can engender. Returning to Isaiah Berlin's concept of negative and positive liberty, one can see the period from 1930 to 1970 as one in which the balance shifted towards the positive liberty of "collective self-mastery," in the form of trade unions, mass democracy, and expanding welfare states—the framework of Ruggie's "embedded liberalism." Since the 1980s, the pendulum has swung in the other direction, celebrating the negative liberty of unrestrained individualism. As the new entrepreneurial form of subjectivity becomes dominant, it creates not only tolerance for billionaires, but admiration. This is being reflected by the fact that a search for "billionaires" in online bookstores mainly turns out three types of literature: heroic biographies, how-to-become-a-billionaire manuals, and erotic fantasies with billionaires as the objects of desire. Billionaires can be seen as the prophets of the neoliberal age, in which competition, entrepreneurship, and success form the secular trinity. Some of them are what Max Weber has called an "ethical prophet," who acts as "an instrument for the proclamation of a god and his will, be this a concrete command or an abstract norm. Preaching as one who has received a commission from god, he demands obedience as an ethical duty" (Weber 1978: 447). The founder of Virgin, Richard Branson, markets his bestselling *Screw It, Let's Do It: Lessons in Life and Business* in his own publishing house (Branson 2006). Charles Koch, who is almost religiously libertarian, is spreading *The Science of Success* (2007) and *Good Profit* (2015). All the self-made billionaires on the *Forbes* list, embodying the triumph of entrepreneurship, serve as "exemplary prophets," "who, by [their] personal example, demonstrate[e] to others the way to religious salvation" (Weber 1978: 447).[38] Whereas, under the more equality-oriented "embedded liberalism," billionaires would attract disapproval, in a world governed by a neoliberal spirit, they become role models. Fukuyama himself has expressed deep worries over rising inequalities, because he fears that they will undermine democracy (Fukuyama 2012). But he, like others (Crouch 2011), notes that despite the 2008–9 financial crisis and its ensuing "Great Recession," no mass-mobilizing

---

to have eroded feelings of social solidarity or the belief of a majority of citizens in most OECD countries that governments bear responsibility for securing it" (Barnes & Hall 2013: 215).

[38] In his sociology of religion, Weber portrays prophets as charismatic leaders, whose missions have strongly shaped civilizations, not just by promoting coherent world views, but even more so in affecting how people conduct their lives, see Riesebrodt 2001: 199, Adair-Toteff 2014.

alternative has appeared on the ideological horizon. What has been rising in many countries is the new old face of nationalism in various populist guises, which may work against the further liberalization of global commerce. But, as Trump's election in 2016 demonstrated, nationalism can be compatible with the entrepreneurial spirit of neoliberalism. In most countries and most years that have been surveyed for the Edelman Trust Barometer between 2001 and 2018, people trusted "NGOs" and "business" significantly more than "government."[39] It is this favoring of private initiative over public policy that remains the central legacy of neoliberalism, empowering billionaires. While the apparent resilience of neoliberalism in the face of crisis and criticism has certainly much to do with the weakness of ideological contenders, it is equally related to its strong institutionalization, to which we will turn now. In Quinn Slobodian's account of the "Geneva school of neoliberalism," which focuses more on the Austrian and German neoliberal thinkers than on the Chicago school, "at the root of the neoliberal idea of international order is the notion of so-called competitive federalism, with the possibility of capital following opportunities across borders wherever they arise" (2018: 267).

Institutional Changes: The Competition State and Global Governance

Examining the institutional context that has facilitated the rise of billionaires is not an exercise in legalism, although the formalization of rules via institutions is a key aspect that distinguishes institutional analysis from the ideational realm.[40] "Institutional thinking emphasizes the part played by institutional structures in imposing elements of order on a potentially inchoate world" (March & Olsen 1984: 743). Institutions react to and reflect material and ideational processes, and evolve through political struggles and bargaining. They reduce uncertainty and affect expectations in specifying what kinds of behavior will be encouraged (incentives) or discouraged (sanctions). As such, in IR, international institutions are often analyzed from a rationalist perspective, which sees them as functional

---

[39] These surveys started small in 2001 and have expanded over the years; at the end of 2018, they surveyed twenty-seven countries and revealed, on average, 69 percent trust in NGOs, 68 percent trust in business, and 58 percent trust in government among the "informed public," and rates around 10 percent lower for each institution among the "general public." Online: https://www.edelman.com/research/edelman-trust-barometer-archive (accessed July 20, 2019).

[40] This distinction is not always clear. Some authors see formalized rules, particularly those enforced by governments, as part of the material environment (e.g., Sewell 1992: 8, Inda & Rosaldo 2008: 29), while others reduce institutions to the ideas they embody (e.g. Searle 2005, 2010, Chwieroth & Sinclair 2013). Douglass North's ubiquitous definition of institutions as both formal and informal North 1990: 4), while usefully extending the economic research agenda, arguably contributed much to blurring the distinction between the roles of ideas/culture and legal institutions. See Blyth 2003: 695ff, Lieberman 2002 for general discussion and Voigt 2013 for a plea to limit institutions to formal rules.

responses to problems of cooperation and coordination in the absence of centralized authority (Keohane 1984, Martin & Simmons 1998, Koremenos et al. 2001). In this light, any structuring that institutions do is reducible to the interests of the institution-builders. Yet, in fixing the rules of the game over time (North 1990), institutions can also embody structural properties of their own that shape action afterward.[41] The constellation of actors involved in establishing an institution may be different from the constellation required to modify or abolish it, as is often the case with political constitutions. Once in place, institutions can acquire autonomy from those who created them (Barnett & Finnemore 1999). Owing to their durability, they may produce unintended consequences not foreseen by the actors that created them. Due to the logic of path dependence, based on the mechanisms of increasing returns, self-reinforcement, positive feedbacks, or lock-in, institutions can structure behavior and outcomes in the long run (Mahoney 2000, Pierson 2000, 2004, Page 2006).

When and how such path dependence can be broken in order to allow for institutional change is a crucial question, especially in relation to agency (Crouch & Farrell 2004, Beyer 2005). Often, scholars have relied on exogenous shocks or other contingent factors, but the notions of ruptures and settled and unsettled times (Swidler 1986, Sewell 1996) have been treated more systematically with the concept of critical junctures which denotes "*relatively* short periods of time during which there is a *substantially* heightened probability that agents' choices will affect the outcome of interest" (Capoccia & Kelemen 2007: 348, emphases in original, also Soifer 2012, Rinscheid et al. 2019). From a structural perspective, this is frequently the case when frictions between different structural realms appear, e.g. between the institutional and the material or ideational (Sewell 1992: 16ff, Lieberman 2002, Peters et al. 2005). But institutional change can just as well happen gradually and incrementally (Pierson 2004: 79–102, Streeck & Thelen 2005), because institutional arrangements are usually the result of compromises that contain in-built tensions, which get amplified when the distribution of power among the institution-supporting actors is shifting (Mahoney & Thelen 2010).

Despite much progress in the conceptualization of institutional change, distinguishing a critical juncture or significant gradual change from continuity in institutional structures is often only possible in hindsight. In 1982, Ruggie still had confidence that the institutional nexus of "embedded liberalism" would last (1982: 412–15), whereas by now the historical evidence suggests that the 1970s mark both a critical juncture and the beginning of momentous gradual change in the global political economy. Ruggie had been right in foreseeing continuity in one

---

[41] Accordingly, the main branches of the "new institutionalism" in the social sciences, associated with rational choice, historical, and sociological institutionalism, differ with regard to which functions of institutions they emphasize, as well as with regard to their explanations of institutional change. See Hall & Taylor 1996, Immergut 1998, Kingston & Caballero 2009. An attempt to bridge rationalist and historical institutionalist analysis via the concept of bounded rationality is Jupille et al. 2013.

international institution: the global trade regime. However, the multilateral institutionalization of free trade had been the more "liberal" part of "embedded liberalism," and, as such, it corresponded very well with the intensification of the second globalization and neoliberalism's rise to dominance.[42] Indeed, with the creation of the World Trade Organization (WTO) in 1995, the legalization of free trade via the establishment of the dispute settlement mechanism represents a depoliticization of trade issues that is fully in line with the neoliberal preference for the rule of law (Schuyler 1997, Joseph 2013: 56–90, Slobodian 2018: 23–5, 263–86). Moreover, at the regional level, especially within the EU, the liberalization of trade has gone much further, leading to a common market with very little barriers to and even stronger constitutionalization of free trade (Ravenhill 2017).[43] The growing reach—both geographically and in terms of legal protection—of trade-promoting organizations has consolidated an institutional structure that enables billionaires and their companies to benefit from trade in global markets. Although some statistical analyses have questioned whether trade institutions have a strong effect on actual trade volumes (Rose 2004), research that treats WTO participation more comprehensively, as a set of interlocking national, regional, and international institutions that promote trade together, does show that the institutions stimulate the growth of commercial exchange (Goldstein et al. 2007, Johnson et al. 2013, Goldberg & Pavcnik 2016).

More drastic institutional change happened with regard to the mobility of capital, which is of crucial concern for billionaires' finances. The explicit reliance on state controls over the cross-border movement of capital had been the "illiberal" part of the Bretton Woods framework, as the freedom of finance to operate across borders was being subordinated to the imperatives of stability and national autonomy. Post-WWII, capital controls were deemed necessary for the pursuit of economic reconstruction via Keynesian macroeconomic policymaking, and to protect the stability of the Dollar/Gold-pegged exchange rate system. (Helleiner 1994: 3–6, 25–80, Abdelal 2007: 43–53, Chwieroth 2010: 105–120). However, the IMF's role in maintaining the Bretton Woods system was relatively weak, as both the maintenance of the dollar-gold convertibility, the pegged exchange rates, and the use of capital controls ultimately hinged on the participating states, especially the U.S. as the economic and political hegemon. Institutional stability was therefore subject to U.S. support, which weakened once the expenses of the Vietnam

---

[42] However, conforming to "embedded liberalism," free trade under WTO rules is still neither absolute, nor does it cover all areas of commerce. Several of the exceptions that Ruggie had identified as protecting national autonomy and "social purpose"—in agriculture, and environmental, health, and labor protections—persist, and further trade liberalization has stalled since 2001 within the WTO framework (Kim 2012).

[43] A related institutional component behind the expansion of global trade consists of preferential trade agreements (PTAs), which do include regional PTAs like the EU or NAFTA, but also their extensions, for example the EU–Mexico PTA, and purely bilateral PTAs like those between Japan and several of its Asian neighbors (Büthe & Milner 2008, 2014, Manger 2009).

War and the Great Society program in combination with a growing current account deficit made the maintenance of the dollar-gold convertibility exceedingly costly. The unilateral dissolution of the US-Dollar convertibility into gold by President Nixon in 1971 lead to the collapse of the pegged exchange rate system in 1973, and since then the developed states have kept their currencies floating at the global level (Eichengreen 2008: 91–141).

This move towards floating exchange rates represents a critical juncture, because of two important consequences: it eliminated one of the key purposes of capital controls, and it created a more volatile and complex international monetary system, which then encouraged the use of financial instruments, such as the trading of currency derivatives, to offset exchange rate risks—an effect Hayek had foreseen early on (Hayek 1937: 54–72). In combination with rising trade volumes, it became increasingly difficult for states and their bureaucrats to use capital controls for distinguishing between trade- and investment-related financial flows, which were welcome, and speculative financial flows, which used to be restricted. "For governments, the utility of controls declined as their perceived costs thereby increased" (Goodman & Pauly 1993: 51). The U.S. (in 1974) and the United Kingdom (in 1979) were the first developed countries to abolish capital controls, and during the 1980s and early 1990s, most other OECD member states followed suit (Helleiner 1994: 123–68). Around the same time, the IMF started to promote capital account liberalization and made it part of its demands in negotiations over IMF loans (Chwieroth 2010). Likewise, in 1988, the EU issued a directive on implementing the free movement of capital, and one year later, the OECD crafted its Code of Liberalization of Capital Movements. These new legal instruments "exerted their most profound effect in negotiations with prospective members[, t]he privileges of membership being contingent on meeting the liberal standards articulated in the rules" (Abdelal 2007: 12). Here, the end of the Cold War needs to be emphasized as a second critical juncture that concerns the geopolitical reach of (neo-)liberal institutions. Beyond erasing the appeal of liberalism's main ideological rival (Fukuyama 1989), the break-up of the Soviet Union and the demise of the planned economies in the Communist countries also removed many political barriers to the institutionalization of neoliberal policies. Newly independent states could liberalize domestically and join the IOs that promoted liberal standards, such as the IMF, the WTO, or the EU, and within the IOs where the Soviet bloc countries had already been members, mainly the UN system, Cold War blockages waned (Tallberg et al. 2013: 15).

The disappearance of capital controls among the developed (and also many developing) countries evolved in tandem with the re-emergence of global finance, which simultaneously undermined capital controls and benefited from their subsequent loosening. Clearly, as already discussed, the global ICT infrastructure and neoliberal ideas played an important role in this transformation (Bryant 1987, Goodman & Pauly 1993: 57, Abdelal 2007, Chwieroth 2010). And little would have happened without the policy choices of specific governmental actors in allowing financial service providers greater freedom, which involves both deregulation and new "market-making" regulations. Various choices in the United Kingdom, all geared towards strengthening the City of London as a global financial center, were especially relevant: the Bank of England's early endorsement of the unregulated Euromarkets (Burn 2006); the ongoing support of offshore finance in the outskirts of the British colonial empire (Johns 1983, Johns & Le Marchant 1993, Palan et al. 2010: 124–49); and the Thatcher government's "Big Bang" reform of the London stock exchange in 1986. Similar steps were taken by the U.S., the other prime mover (Helleiner 1994: 147ff). These two countries' decisions had enormous weight, because their financial sectors dominate world financial markets (Simmons 2001: 592ff). The precise contribution of each factor—political agency, material and ideational structures—is hard to measure, which is not my objective here. The re-emergence of global finance with largely free movement of capital is a story of gradual institutional change in key countries, from the late 1970s onwards. Overall, however, around the 1990s, a new institutional framework was in place that is exerting strong structural properties since, and which is very favorable to wealth accumulation (Andrews 1994).

At the international level, it is marked by the absence of supranational global institutions that control capital flows. To be sure, a few international regimes exist that attempt to control security-related financial flows, notably with regard to money laundering and terrorist financing, such as the Financial Action Task Force (Hägel 2009); and various international standards have been established, often by private regulators, that aim to harmonize best practices, for example with regard to capital adequacy requirements for banks, accounting standards, or financial reporting (Simmons 2001, Singer 2007, Büthe & Mattli 2011, Drezner 2014). But apart from these market-protecting regulations, at least since the second half of the 1990s, most cross-border movements of capital are free, as endorsed by the rules of the IMF, the OCED, and the EU. For prospective billionaires, this has opened up a world of opportunities. Of course, once inside a country's jurisdiction, national laws continue to affect how businesses can operate—most importantly, how capital is being taxed. Yet, given free movement, states are in competition with each other to attract and keep mobile capital, in the hopes of benefiting from investments and boosting their financial sector. The exercise of sovereignty in making national laws has therefore to be considered in relation to what other states are doing. Philip Cerny was one of the first to identify this shift from the welfare to the competition state: "the state itself is having to act more and more like a market player, that shapes its policies to promote, control, and maximize returns from market forces in an international setting" (1990: 230). This has led to vigorous debates over convergence and "races to the bottom," in which research initially showed that the path dependency of established welfare states produced more resilience than expected by the "competition state" hypothesis (Pierson 1996, Garrett 1998, Swank 2002), and that national varieties of capitalism could endure due to comparative institutional advantage (Hall & Soskice 2001, Weiss 2003). More recent empirical research, however, seems to indicate that while the transformation of state institutions under globalization is complex, both the relative shrinking of the welfare state and the increasing institutionalization of "competition state" features have become realities. Wolfgang Streeck, in particular, has convincingly argued that the maintenance of welfare states in advanced capitalist countries since the 1970s has largely been "bought," or better: "borrowed," via rising public debt—a strategy that appears to reach its limits after the 2008–9 financial crisis (Streeck 2013, also Genschel 2004, Horsfall 2011, Swank 2016).[44]

As a consequence of the "competition state" logic, key institutional structures that favor billionaires have been established at the national level.[45] The most obvious changes happened in the realm of taxation. Taxes on income, property, and economic activity naturally affect the bottom line calculations of actors, and if labor, capital, and businesses are mobile, they may choose to exit, in order to move to jurisdictions where less taxation allows them to accumulate more wealth (Hirschman 1970). The exercise of mobility clearly depends on other place-specific factors, too, such as the availability of infrastructure, proximity to consumers, or specialized labor markets, and it may be legally restricted, as is often the case for labor migration (much more so during the second than during the first globalization of the nineteenth century). By now, the empirical evidence is plain: Although some significant national differences persist, convergence towards lower taxation levels for mobile tax bases has been taking place among the developed countries since the 1980s.

> [I]nternational tax arbitrage is a major factor in corporate taxation and presumably also in capital income taxation. It is of minor relevance in labour income or consumption taxation where only very selected parts of the tax base, such as high-income professionals and highly excised goods, are sensitive to cross-national tax differentials.
>
> (Genschel & Schwarz 2011: 351, also Overesch & Rincke 2009, Swank 2006, 2016)

---

[44] This reliance on debt-financing is often being ignored, for example in Colin Hay's argument that, despite global competition, there remains much room for state action (Hay 2017). See Fougner 2006 for a review of the "competition state" discourse.

[45] For in-depth analyses of the role of the state in neoliberal ideology, see Turner 2008 and Plant 2010. For comparative studies of how specific states have implemented neoliberal policy prescriptions in line with the logic of the competition state, see Fourcade-Gourinchas & Babb 2002, Cafruny & Ryner 2003, Soederberg et al. 2005, Hacker & Pierson 2010.

In Table 3.1, only the official tax rates have been taken into account. For rich individuals that receive and keep their income and assets in their home country, redistribution via taxation has strongly declined, making wealth accumulation easier. Even greater opportunities arise from the use of strategic tax planning and tax evasion that involves so-called tax havens or offshore financial centers, which have proliferated since the 1970s (Hampton 1996, Palan 2003, Palan et al. 2010). These approximately fifty to sixty entities, of which Switzerland has historically been the most important, but which also include special legal constructs in the U.S., Luxembourg, or the United Kingdom, represent the spearhead of global tax competition, because they offer very low or even no taxation of assets held in their jurisdiction (Palan et al. 2010: 17–105, Zucman 2013: 17–42). As individuals, billionaires can choose to take residence or citizenship in tax havens, in order to avoid paying capital income or wealth taxes, which, while significantly declining over the past decades, still exist in many countries. The 2014 Wealth-X "Billionaires Census" had identified the top ten jurisdictions with the highest billionaires per capita density, and the first six were tax havens: Liechtenstein (5 billionaires), Bermuda (7), Luxembourg (17), Hong Kong (82), Switzerland (86), and Singapore (32) (Wealth-X 2014: 38).[46] Overall, however, only a small fraction of the world's billionaires emigrates to tax havens. Analyzing the *Forbes*

Table 3.1 Statutory tax rates, 1985–2009

	Sample	1985	1996	2005	2009
General tax rates					
VAT standard rate	OECD-20	16	18	18	18
	CEEC-10	NA[a]	NA	20	21
Excises on cigarettes[b]	OECD-20	40[c]	41	37	40
	CEEC-10	NA	NA	NA	25
Top individual income tax rate	OECD-20	65	52	47	46
	CEEC-10	NA	NA	29	23
Corporate tax rate	OECD 20	44	36	31	29
	CEEC-10	NA	31	17	13
Targeted tax rates					
(Top) interest income tax	OECD-20	59	39	34	33
rate—residents	CEEC-10	NA	NA	NA	18
Withholding tax rate on	OECD-20	13	8	7	8
interest income—non-residents	CEEC-10	NA	NA	7	6

Source: Genschel & Schwarz 2011: 356, by permission of Oxford University Press/Society for the Advancement of Socio-Economics.

[46] The next four countries were the oil producers United Arab Emirates (46), Qatar (9), Kuwait (12) and Norway (15). What the data does not show is for how many billionaires the tax haven is their country of origin—as is Liechtenstein for its billionaire monarch Hans-Adam II.

billionaires from 1996 to 2010, Tino Sanandaji found that only 13 percent of them have emigrated from their country of origin. Of these, a mere third moved to a tax haven (Sanandaji 2012: 5).[47]

The relative absence of billionaires' naturalization in tax havens, just like the relative infrequency of corporate headquarters in tax havens, is not really surprising, because rich individuals and corporations can take advantage of tax havens without giving up the benefits of citizenship and residency in their home countries. Transnationally organized companies gain from tax havens via strategic tax planning that remains completely legal. It only requires making the most profitable business components formally reside in tax havens, which is relatively easy to do if these are based on immaterial services or intellectual property rights, such as trademarks, copyrights, or patents that can earn license fees no matter where they are located. The non- or less profit-making business lines may then remain in high-tax states (Desai 2009, Gravelle 2013, OECD 2013). For billionaires that own their private companies, which are the majority, circumventing corporate taxes in this way increases their capital tied to their firm(s). The late Ingvar Kamprad's IKEA operates like this, as it has been split into the IKEA Group and Inter IKEA Systems, where individual IKEA stores pay an annual franchise fee of 3 percent of their turnover for the use of the IKEA brand to Inter IKEA Systems, which itself is owned and managed through a complex and shifting web of trusts and foundations based in various tax havens (Stenebo 2010: 193–210, Genschel & Schwarz 2011: 346f). Many other firms of billionaires have been reported to engage in similar profit-shifting and tax avoidance schemes, which have become part and parcel of professional wealth management, organized within so-called global wealth chains (Harrington 2016, Shaxson 2016, Seabrooke & Wigan 2017).

Personal wealth and the income derived from it are more difficult to enjoy legally without taxation, as states like the U.S. tax the global income of their citizens, and people cannot subdivide themselves into separate legal persons in the same manner as businesses.[48] People can, though, channel their wealth through tax havens, and hide their ownership, with the aid of instruments such as special forms of trusts and foundations, anonymous property titles, or secret bank accounts (Palan et al. 2010: 77–106). Undeclared to their home countries, such practices may constitute tax evasion or fraud, which are illegal—and therefore difficult to measure. "Guesstimates" of the amounts of money thus concealed have come up with staggering figures, from US$12 trillion in 2007 (Palan et al. 2010: 5) to US$21 and 32 trillion in 2010 (Henry 2012). Gabriel Zucman has provided the most systematic analysis of how much private wealth is being hidden in tax

---

[47] More generally, of those who migrated, 70 percent moved from a country with a higher to one with lower capital income taxation (ibid.).

[48] To avoid double taxation by both home country and country of residence/business, most countries have established systems of bilateral treaties. See Rixen 2011 on how this treaty system, as an unintended consequence, has contributed to tax competition and tax havens.

havens, via studying the "black holes" in countries' official capital account statistics. He comes up with US$7.5 trillion in 2013, considered to be a solid estimate of the minimum amount, which nevertheless represents 8 percent of the total private wealth worldwide, or around 10 percent of the world's GDP (2013: 43–53). Since, to be effective, tax avoidance through tax havens entails the use of what Jeffrey Winters has called the "income defense industry" of specialized law firms, accountants, and asset managers (2011: 213ff, Harrington 2016), whose services are very costly, it is safe to assume that much of these US$7.5 trillion belongs to the richest people on Earth (Zucman 2014: 141, Alstadsæter et al. 2018, 2019). The US$2.26 trillion, which billionaires were reportedly holding in cash or highly liquid cash-equivalent assets in 2018 (Wealth-X 2019: 16), fit into this sum, although it is of course impossible to know where exactly all the billionaires keep their personal fortunes. What is sure is that tax havens offer tremendous opportunities to get around income- and wealth-decreasing taxation, and in doing so, they also exert strong pressures on other states to decrease or even to abandon the taxation of wealth. The best example is the poster child of social democracy, Sweden, which had developed high taxation of wealth and inheritance during the middle of the twentieth century, then gradually lowered these taxes from the 1970s onward, especially after 1990, until it gave up the taxation of inheritance in 2004, and that of wealth in 2007 (Henrekson & Du Rietz 2014, Henrekson & Waldenström 2014).

Whereas taxation determines how much individuals can keep of their income and wealth, several other institutional changes affect the very generation of it. They concern privatization and competition law, deregulation, and investment protection. All of them correspond to neoliberal ideas about the proper roles of private property, markets, and the state, but they also represent adjustments to the new international reality of increasing competition for mobile capital.[49] Once more, national diversity persists in all these policy domains, reflecting the path dependencies of country-specific institutional arrangements and the effects of varying partisan politics. Still, as with taxation, comparative research has demonstrated clear trends across countries, which are all associated with the rise of competition states since the 1980s.

The privatization of previously state-owned enterprises or public services extends the market logic to new realms and, in doing so, opens up new business opportunities. To a large degree, governments have pursued this institutional change in the expectation of raising revenues and increasing the efficiency of privatized businesses, in order to improve their fiscal position and to attract

[49] In terms of causal forces, several studies have shown that, during the 1980s and early 1990s, the shift towards "neoliberal" policies were correlated with right-wing governments, indicating a strong influence of ideology and partisanship, but since then they have become more generally adopted, also by left-wing governments, indicating a greater influence of globalization and the logic of the competition state (Schneider et al. 2005, Busemeyer 2009).

capital (Schneider et al. 2005, Schneider & Häge 2008, Busemeyer 2009). A comprehensive review of the OECD countries shows major privatization over three decades: "While in 1980, about 5.5% of GDP was on average provided by public enterprises, this share dropped to 2.6% in 2007" (Obinger et al. 2014: 1301).[50] In previously planned economies like in Eastern Europe, where the large majority of business had been state-owned, the transformation from socialism to capitalism has occasioned the most profound privatization. This can be particularly billionaire-friendly when the formerly state-owned enterprises represented monopolies, as has often been the case, notably in public utilities and services like water provision, transportation, or telecommunications. If the privatization process is set up in such a way that the original monopoly or dominance of the public enterprise continues in its privatized form, the result will be the kind of "winner-take-all market" that has been identified as producing extraordinary wealth (Crouch 2011: 79–96, Petras 2008).[51] The most striking examples of such an outcome are the rise of the billionaire oligarchs in the former Soviet Union (Guriev & Rachinsky 2005, Fortescue 2006, Hoffman 2011), and the world's fifth-richest man in 2019, Carlos Helu Slim, whose wealth derives in large parts from his stake in the privatized Mexican telecommunications market (MacLeod 2004: 99f, Winter 2007, Manzetti 2010). In Europe, Silvio Berlusconi's media empire would not have been possible without the prior privatization of TV broadcasting in Italy (Stille 2006: 52–73).[52] Obviously, the concentration of private ownership is not only related to whether a market tends towards natural monopoly (Baumol 1977), but equally by the legal antitrust framework in place. Since the 1980s, in line with the neoliberal ideas of the Chicago School (Turner 2008: 206–12), antitrust law in the U.S. (Pitofsky 2008), and later also in Europe, came to tolerate market-dominating firms much more than in the past.[53] A key argument behind this legal evolution was that, in the context of growing international competition, the size and position of a firm should no longer be judged in national terms alone (Crouch 2011: 52–66). No doubt, such a reformulation of competition law has helped many billionaires to keep their companies intact even when they reached

---

[50] Here, public enterprise does not refer to public services, but for-profit companies that used to be state-owned.

[51] There are various ways of privatizing state-owned assets, which can either discourage or encourage concentrated private ownership. For overviews, see Roland 2008.

[52] The distinction between privatization and liberalization can be blurred, as, substantially, there is not much difference between a state selling its formerly public telecommunications sector and a state that simply sells (or auctions off) licenses to new entrants into a liberalized telecommunications market. In each case, a new market for private firms is being created.

[53] On the one hand, a strong global trend towards establishing independent antitrust agencies has taken place since the late 1980s, in order to ensure competitive markets without political interference Djelic 2005, Gerber 2012). On the other hand, a more contested and less universal trend has consisted in reformulating the rationale of competition policy and jurisprudence along the lines of the "Chicago School," which focuses more on the economic effects of dominant firms and less on domination per se (Bailleux & Vauchez 2014, Wu 2018).

dimensions that would previously have been considered monopolistic, or at least oligopolistic. Prime examples are Bill Gates's Microsoft, Mark Zuckerberg's social media triad of Facebook/Instagram/WhatsApp, Sergey Brin and Larry Page's Alphabet/Google, which, despite several legal challenges and a few cutbacks they had to suffer, have not been forced to give up their market-dominating positions (Page & Lopatka 2007, Gavil & First 2014, Wu 2018: 119–26).

It has been argued that, as a consequence of privatization and the growing complexity of business and technology, developed countries have turned towards the model of the regulatory state, in which quasi-autonomous regulatory agencies set and enforce the technical rules in specific business areas (Majone 1994, Lodge 2008). Frequently, especially at the global level, this involves new forms of private self-regulation or mixtures of public–private rule-making, which often tend to be business-friendly, in the worst case leading to "regulatory capture" where the regulatory agency embodies business interests (Mattli & Woods 2009, Büthe & Mattli 2011, Young 2012). Yet it would be wrong to claim that the decades since the 1970s have been an era of general deregulation. Even under conditions of global competition, states with large markets have substantial leeway to set high regulatory standards, for example related to health and security, because companies will comply in order to have access to the customers and the resources of these markets.[54] The logic of the competition state can, however, lead to less regulation in sectors where both the companies and the customers are materially or virtually mobile. The most important sector is financial services, especially those catering to so-called "ultra high-net worth individuals" (UHNWIs).

Whereas the threat of moving business to tax havens, which often boast less regulation in addition to low taxation, is not very credible for mass-market banking, it carries weight for financial services such as hedge funds, which attract mainly institutional investors and UHNWIs. Not incidentally, and despite the fact that their business model is based on highly leveraged speculation, hedge funds have remained largely unregulated for most of their existence, and markedly so during their time of rapid expansion since the 1990s (Fioretos 2010, Woll 2011). Many hedge fund managers such as George Soros, Steve Cohen, or John Paulson are amongst the billionaires with the highest annual earnings, which can vary between US$1 billion and US$4 billion in good years (Mallaby 2010).[55] The UHNWIs that invest their money in hedge funds equally benefit from soaring rates of returns on their investment (Harrington 2016), which are possible due to

---

[54] Even in an area that has traditionally been associated with "race to the bottom" competition, the shipping business with its "flags of convenience," significant re-regulation has happened (Barrows 2009). For the diverse dynamics of private regulation, see Vogel 2009.

[55] Until 2018, in the U.S., hedge funds managers also benefited from a tax code aberration that allowed them to count their management fees as "carried interest," subject to a capital income tax rate between 15 and 20 percent, rather than as ordinary income with a top rate of 35–37 percent (Winters & Page 2009: 741).

limited prudential regulation. The same applies to several other financial services, which often involve securitization and high leverage and are summarized as the "shadow banking system" (Financial Stability Board 2014, Thiemann 2018). Strictly speaking, the term deregulation is only appropriate for measures that end previously existing regulations, for example, in U.S. finance, the abolishment of interest rate ceilings and the repeal of the separation between commercial and investment banks, which happened during the 1980s and 1990s. At least as important is the non-regulation of newly emerging practices, instruments, and business entities in finance, which has been the favored approach towards hedge funds and the shadow banking system.[56] Analyzing income inequalities in the U.S., comprehensive studies have demonstrated that the enormous rise in financial income is strongly correlated with non- and deregulation and the associated trend of financialization post-1980 (Hacker & Pierson 2010: 66ff, Philippon & Reshef 2012, Lin & Tomaskovic-Devey 2013). The OECD asserts similar effects of deregulation more broadly across its member states (OECD 2011a: 32). As the 2008 financial crisis has shown, in case risky speculation goes wrong, the consequences fall back onto the state, which feels obliged to bail out failing financial institutions in order to safeguard the stability of the economic system. Thus, financial non- and deregulation are predisposed towards privatizing profits and socializing risks (Admati & Hellwig 2013, Tooze 2018). While benefits accrue to all people that derive parts of their income from finance, they are being magnified in the case of billionaire investors.

One more institutional innovation that exhibits the logic of the competition state needs to be emphasized in order to explain how billionaires can benefit from globalization: the protection of foreign direct investments (FDI). Under the principles of sovereignty, when foreign individuals or companies invest in a country, they expose their capital to the rules of that state. This involves the risk that changing legislation may alter the conditions present at the moment of the initial investment, which may degenerate due to new regulations and taxes, or, in the worst case, expropriation. If their assets are mobile, transnational investors that anticipate less favorable rules can, of course, withdraw from a country. However, not all assets are always immediately mobile—they may be tied up in complicated contracts or in immobile factories. Therefore, to attract long-term FDI under conditions of global competition for capital, states have deemed it

---

[56] Neoliberal, pro-business publications like to point out that finance is in fact a highly regulated sector of the economy (Allison 2013), which is true. Such a view, however, downplays the non-regulation of activities in the shadow banking sector, which receives most of its funding from regulated financial services such as banks, which use it to circumvent the regulations that apply to them. At the international level, some agreements, especially the Basel accords (starting in 1988), have attempted to harmonize financial risk management, with limited success (Kapstein 1992, Simmons 2001, Singer 2007, Lall 2012, Thiemann 2014). In the EU, at least until the mid-2000s, liberalizing the common market for financial services took priority over prudential regulation (Abdelal 2007, Posner & Véron 2010, Mügge 2013).

necessary to devise a system of investor protection (Elkins et al. 2006, Blake 2013).[57] At its core are bilateral investment treaties (BITs) that establish legal protections for the investors of the capital-exporting state vis-à-vis the capital-importing state.[58] Much of their effectiveness relies on the delegation of dispute resolution—to varying degrees (Allee & Peinhardt 2014)—to private arbitration panels, whose procedures are usually stipulated via reference to the World Bank's International Centre for Settlement of Investment Disputes (ICSID) or the UN's Commission on International Trade Law (UNCITRAL). Through linkages to the United Nations Convention on the Recognition and Enforcement of Foreign Arbitral Awards, which counted 161 signatory states in 2019, damages awarded to private investors can be enforced around the globe (van Harten 2005, Schneiderman 2008). In other words, capital-importing countries surrender their sovereign rights to a private authority.

> The treaties grant foreign investors a right to file international arbitration claims directly against governments without first needing to exhaust local remedies. If governments refuse to participate in the proceedings or chose not to comply with an arbitral award, investors are allowed to confiscate their commercial property in most corners of the world, with only limited options for courts in the enforcing states to refuse execution. Combined with their wide scope of administrative review, this dispute-settlement mechanism makes BITs uniquely powerful in the context of international law.   (Poulsen & Aisbett 2013: 273)

Pioneered by Germany, Switzerland, and the Netherlands during the 1960s, the international network of BITs has expanded rapidly since the 1990s, and with it the number of arbitration cases (Elkins et al. 2006: 814–19, Simmons 2014: 31, UNCTAD 2018: 92):

Not only does this system constitute a formidable protection of international investments, it also tends to lock in the results of privatization and deregulation, because states have to fear litigation by foreign investors in case they are tempted to roll back earlier concessions that attracted foreign investments. Although the precise impact of BITs on FDI is difficult to establish, it seems clear that BITs have played a major role in the explosion of global FDI over the past decades (Sauvant & Sachs 2009, Milner 2014), especially when it comes to FDI in developing

---

[57] While the competition logic is overarching, the power of capital-exporting states during bilateral investment treaty (BIT) negotiations with developing capital-importing states also matters strongly (Allee & Peinhardt 2014).

[58] Attempts during the 1990s to establish a multilateral agreement on investments famously failed (Walter 2000). More recently, initiatives by the EU and within the WTO framework have advanced investor protection via multilateral treaties, but the global network of BITs remains the backbone of the investor protection system (Schill 2009). Preferential trade agreements (PTAs) also serve investment protection via specific clauses that can have similar consequences as BITs (Büthe & Milner 2008, 2014, Manger 2009).

countries that, traditionally, have had less extensive defenses of property rights than developed countries (De Soto 2000, North et al. 2009, Acemoglu & Robinson 2012). The international investment protection system hence provides the legal underpinnings for billionaires and their multinational corporations to take advantage of worldwide investment opportunities. "No other category of private individuals—not traders (who do not invest), not human beings in their capacity as human rights holders, not even national investors in their home state—is given such expansive rights in international law as are private actors investing across borders" (Simmons 2014: 42). Unsurprisingly, one of the most spectacular and controversial BIT-related arbitration results accrued to a billionaire, Ronald Lauder, heir of the Estée Lauder cosmetics empire and worth US$3.5 billion according to the 2017 *Forbes* list. In 2003, his company, CME, was awarded US$353 million in damages to be paid by the Czech Republic, because the majority of the arbitrators found CME's investment in the privatized Czech television market to have been harmed by new legislation that required quotas for domestic programming content.[59] Such cases, which seem to leave hardly any regulatory options for national governments, have become less likely. The second generation of international investment agreements, following a reform process during the second decade of the twenty-first century, usually grants states much more policy space than the first generation of treaties (UNCTAD 2018: 95–103). In general, as can be seen in Figure 3.4, the number of new BITs has been decreasing after 2001, and 2017 was the first year in which the number of terminated treaties (22) exceeded the number of new international investment agreements (18) (ibid.: 88). Still, "[t]he more than 3,000 first-generation treaties in existence today [represent] some 90 per cent of the [international investment agreements] universe" (ibid.: 103). Hence most of the investor-friendly legal infrastructure remains in place.

To sum up, privatization and deregulation offer new business opportunities, the global network of BITs protects investments, and lower taxation allows prospective billionaires to keep more of their profits. Beginning in the 1980s, and increasingly so since the 1990s, these features mark a world of competition states that try to attract mobile capital, thus constituting an institutional environment that is much more favorable to wealth accumulation than during the middle of the twentieth century, the heyday of welfare states. In the wake of the 2008–9 financial crisis and the ensuing worries over escalating levels of public debt, several national

---

[59] The case has stirred controversy not simply because of the (at the time) unprecedented size of the damages, but mainly because the damages were awarded to Lauder's company, domiciled in the Netherlands, under the Dutch–Czech BIT, whereas Lauder as an individual U.S. citizen had lost the very same case under the U.S.–Czech BIT only ten days earlier. The possibility to pursue the same legal action multiple times under different frameworks, which constitutes "forum shopping," is usually not possible in domestic law (van Harten 2005: 600ff, Sacerdoti 2008). Recently, it appears that developing countries are becoming more reluctant to renew or to comply with BITs (Simmons 2014: 42f).

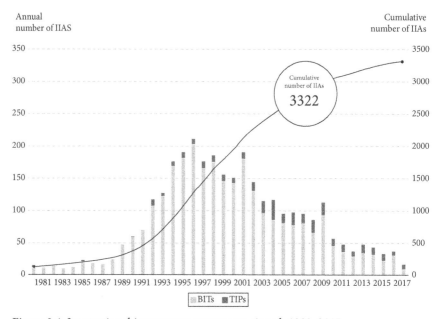

Figure 3.4 International investment agreements signed, 1980–2017
Source: UNCTAD 2018: 89; BIT=bilateral investment treaty; IIA=international investment agreement; TIP=treaty with investment provision

and international initiatives have been launched that might undo some of these institutional features. Stricter prudential rules attempt to limit risk-taking (and, as a consequence, profits) in the financial sector, via national, regional (EU), and international re-regulation. This has been a priority of recent G20 meetings and the specialized international bodies, the Financial Stability Board (FSB) and the Bank for International Settlements (BIS), which has adopted more demanding capital adequacy standards in its Basel III agreement. While some scholars judge the re-regulation efforts to be an overall success (Drezner 2014), more analysts remain highly skeptical whether much has changed (Boone & Johnson 2010, Lall 2012, Admati & Hellwig 2013, Donnelly 2014, Helleiner 2014). New initiatives to limit harmful tax competition are also under way. Individual countries, especially the U.S. with its "Foreign Account Tax Compliance Act" (FATCA, since 2010), have become more aggressive in pursuing tax evasion by their citizens, and push tax havens to cooperate bilaterally (Sharman 2006, Palan et al. 2010: 203–35, Palan & Wigan 2014, Zucman 2014: 142ff). At the international level, the OECD "Base Erosion and Profit Shifting" (BEPS) initiative is at the forefront of establishing standards for automated information exchange in tax matters between countries, and, for the corporate sector, addressing aggressive tax planning (OECD 2011b, 2014, 2019). The effectiveness of all these new measures still has to be evaluated once they have been implemented for a few years, but several experts on tax competition doubt that they will fundamentally reverse the dynamic of tax havens (Findley et al. 2014, Johannesen & Zucman 2014, Knobel & Meinzer 2014). After all, the basic features behind the logic of the competition state stay in place: globalization, the free movement of capital, and the basic institutional structure of world politics—sovereignty.[60] It is for this reason—the expectation that there will always be jurisdictions that try to attract business by undercutting the rules of other jurisdictions—that some of the remedies proposed by tax policy specialists involve important reconfigurations of state sovereignty and the establishment of stronger supranational enforcement schemes, such as heavy trade sanctions on non-cooperating countries, a world financial registry, or a global tax on capital (Zucman 2013: 97–108, Piketty 2014: 515–30). Regarding such steps, there appears to be insufficient agreement at the international level for the moment.[61]

Finally, does the new institutional context, which is so conducive to getting and staying very rich, also allow wealthy individuals greater impact in world politics? The question is closely connected with the broader IR discussion of transnational actors and the rise of private authority in global governance. While few doubt that states remain the primary actors, nonstate actors are seen as becoming more and more involved in governing global affairs (Rosenau & Czempiel 1992, Cutler et al. 1999, Hall & Biersteker 2002, Wight 2013, 2014, Zürn 2018).[62] Transnationally, when a billionaire wants to intervene in the politics of another country, the same institutional frameworks that permit entrepreneurs to pursue business opportunities often facilitate political engagement across borders, too. For example, as will be seen in the case studies of Sheldon Adelson and Rupert Murdoch, investments in the news media can be used to influence public opinion abroad. Unless there are specific restrictions, billionaires can take advantage of the free movement of capital to channel funds to NGOs, think tanks, lobbying firms, social movements, research institutes, etc., to affect political dynamics in foreign countries. Empowered by the institutional frameworks of liberalization and privatization,

---

[60] Rationalist explanations of the absence of tax cooperation (Genschel & Plümper 1997, Dehejia & Genschel 1999, Holzinger 2003) therefore only make sense against the backdrop of a competitive states system and the insulation of the state in law, which only happened during the late nineteenth century (Palan 2002).

[61] Even if countries sign an international convention, its implementation in practice is hard to verify unless outsiders can control it—which implies a major surrender of national sovereignty. The robust pressure of the U.S. to make foreign jurisdictions help them in the taxation of U.S. citizens does, however, indicate a unilateral step in this direction (Palan & Wigan 2014). The U.S. had already pursued such a strategy in combating terrorist financing, as, post-9/11, the CIA gained access to the data of the private financial messaging service SWIFT (Hägel 2009: 368–71).

[62] "Governance is the sum of many ways individuals and institutions, public and private, manage their common affairs. It is a continuing process through which conflicting or diverse interests may be accommodated and co-operative action taken. It includes formal institutions and regimes empowered to enforce compliance, as well as informal arrangements that people and institutions either have agreed to or perceive to be in their interest" (Commission on Global Governance 1995: 4).

billionaires as transnational actors could be interpreted in relation to a "retreat of the state" (Strange 1996) or a "power shift" towards civil society (Mathews 1997).

More recent research, however, questions such a zero-sum logic, persuasively arguing that states have often been complicit when it comes to the rise of private authority and public–private partnerships in transnational and global governance (Cohen 2006, Drezner 2007, Abbott & Snidal 2009, Green 2014). Most of this research is focusing exclusively on collective actors such as NGOs or MNCs, and the roles of individuals can therefore not be deduced directly from these analyses.[63] Insofar as billionaires can operate through the companies that they own, or via the foundations and NGOs that they create or support, the observations are nevertheless pertinent. Human Rights Watch, for example, a leading voice in the global human rights field, has been financed by George Soros to a large extent. Several surveys show a multiplication of opportunities for private actors in global governance since the 1990s, even if the influence of nonstate actors varies strongly across policy areas.[64] Within this field, Jessica Green makes the useful distinction between entrepreneurial and delegated private authority. In the first case, private actors create rules in the absence of state-made international regulations; in the second, states explicitly mandate private actors with certain functions (Green 2014: 10–14, 33–6).[65] Tim Büthe and Walter Mattli have analyzed key examples of the first category, the politics of private standard-setting at the global level (2011). Jonas Tallberg and his colleagues have scrutinized the second category, how transnational actors (TNAs) have gained access to the policymaking processes of international organizations (Tallberg et al. 2013). They have tried to cover the entire universe of international NGOs (INGOs) over time, and their research documents a real leap in the importance of private actors in global governance after 1990 (Figure 3.5).

This trend includes the Bill and Melinda Gates Foundation (BMGF), which is part of the UN Global Compact and an official partner of the International Health Partnership, which is administered by the WHO and the World Bank. In fact, in the International Health Partnership, it is the only private partner among a group otherwise constituted of countries and international organizations.[66] Green

---

[63] Ultimately, all rules are being made by specific actors. But the current state-of-the-art surveys of private authority in world politics, in general, do not differentiate between individuals acting alone or in concert. In fact, implicitly, they concentrate only on organized private actors, such as firms, NGOs, private regulatory and standard-setting bodies, etc. See Büthe & Mattli 2011, Tallberg et al. 2013, Roger & Dauvergne 2016, and Green 2014, who, despite her subtitle mentioning "agents and entrepreneurs," is also only examining collective private actors.

[64] "IOs are consistently most open in the area of human rights, in the policy function of monitoring and enforcement, and in the western hemisphere, while least open in security, decision-making, and the southern hemisphere" (Tallberg et al. 2013: 3).

[65] Green's empirical research concentrates only on global environmental governance, but her theoretical framework is intended to be general.

[66] Two other partners are themselves alliances with public and private partners: the Global Alliance for Vaccines and Immunization (GAVI, www.gavi.org) and The Global Fund to Fight AIDS,

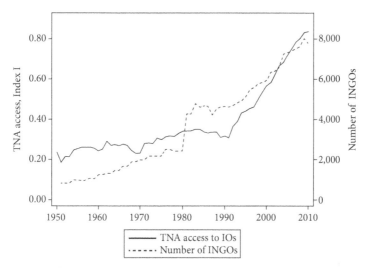

Figure 3.5 Number of INGOs and level of access by TNAs to IOs, 1950–2010
Source: Tallberg et al. 2013: 6, reproduced with permission of Cambridge University Press through PLSclear.

documents a similar trend in global environmental governance, both for delegated and entrepreneurial private authority; for the latter, she found only eleven private environmental regulations created during the period from 1950 to 1989, but 107 new ones from 1990 to 2009 (Green 2014: 72, 92). When trying to explain why private actors acquire regulatory authority or gain access to international organizations, all the authors rely on notions of demand and supply, in which the resources, especially the expertise, of transnational actors are seen as crucial.

> This simultaneous privatization and internationalization of governance is driven, in part, by governments' lack of requisite technical expertise, financial resources, or flexibility to deal expeditiously with ever more complex and urgent regulatory tasks. Firms and other private actors also often push for private governance, which they see as leading to more cost-effective rules more efficiently than government regulation
>
> (Büthe & Mattli 2011: 5, also Tallberg et al. 2013: 12ff, Green 2014: 31ff).[67]

Tuberculosis and Malaria (www.theglobalfund.org). The BMGF is again an official partner in both alliances.

[67] Tallberg et al. also find that the expansion of democratic norms among the member states of international organizations after the Cold War, the end of which they view as a critical juncture, has contributed much to allowing TNAs greater access to IOs (2013: 14ff, 34ff, 40ff).

In Ranjit Lall's analysis, nonstate actors help international organizations to pursue their mandate more effectively, especially when they are faced with member states that prioritize their national over the collective interest (2017). Confirmation of this argument comes from the independent performance assessments of global governance institutions, the so-called MOPAN surveys, which have given the public–private partnerships of The Global Fund and GAVI better institutional effectiveness ratings than the WHO.[68] If billionaires offer effective problem-solving, the institutional context of global governance is often welcoming them with open arms.

What the performance perspective neglects is where the perceived lack of expertise, and hence governing capacity, of national governments is coming from, and why this has changed so much after 1990. In this regard, Green briefly mentions globalization and neoliberalism as structural explanations of the rise of private authority (Green 2014: 37f), which would merit deeper analysis (Bartley 2007, Rushton & Williams 2012). Global production networks within MNCs evidently make national oversight more difficult. Privatization and de- or non-regulation directly entail a shift from public to private authority, as governments leave decision-making in the affected sectors to market actors. And neoliberal thinking legitimizes private self-regulation, considered to be superior to state intervention. The rise of private authority in global governance is thus also linked, both temporally and causally, with the other structural transformations at the material and ideational level presented before. None of these favorable structural conditions is uniform across countries, which continue to differ with regard to their level of integration into the global economy and the legal regimes they apply. Still, overall, a global context has emerged that empowers billionaires in their pursuit of wealth and politics.

Starting with the so-called "Battle of Seattle" in 1999 (Slobodian 2018: 273–86), and gaining momentum in the aftermath of the 2008 financial crisis, resistance against globalization, neoliberalism, and global governance has been rising. Various forms of populism, both on the left (Gerbaudo 2017), and, more so, on the right (Eichengreen 2018), attract voters that fear being left behind, economically or culturally, as exemplified in the ethno-nationalist and anti–free trade agenda of Donald Trump and the 2016 Brexit referendum in the UK. Some key indicators of economic globalization have also exhibited downward trends since 2016: global FDI inflows declined 3 percent from 2015 to 2016, and 23 percent from 2016 to 2017 (UNCTAD 2018: 184); in the face of mounting U.S. tariffs and trade tensions, world trade grew less than expected in 2018 (WTO 2019). In parallel, the number of the world's billionaires on *Forbes*'s list saw a rare drop, from 2,208 (2018) to 2,153 (2019), which shows once more how the generation of

---

[68] See MOPAN 2012, 2013, 2017. I thank the anonymous reviewer of my manuscript for pointing me to this argument.

extreme wealth is linked to global markets. If the anti-global trends persist, the opportunities for billionaires in world politics, which have been widening over the past decades, may shrink. Yet, it remains unclear whether opposition is merely causing a slowdown of globalization, or whether it will provoke a reversal. Michael Zürn sees the growing contestation of globalization and global governance as part of a process of politicization, which can go both ways (2018: 138–69). Under attack, the institutions of global governance may be pushed to adopt measures that strengthen their legitimacy, which could ultimately render them more robust.

4

The Political Agency of Billionaires

As chapter 3 has shown, billionaires' rise to wealth and their appearance in global affairs are tied to favorable conditions generated by structural changes since the 1980s. Yet, so far, only a few thousand individuals have managed to actually become billionaires, and even fewer of them have made their mark in world politics. This brings us back to questions of agency, its components and varieties, as well as its relevance. The goal will be to develop a more systematic understanding of billionaires as transnational actors in IR and to ask whether billionaires can be seen as "super-actors." I will not try to uncover why somebody becomes a billionaire, because my focus is on politics. However, since the accumulation of wealth usually precedes their entrance into politics, this very experience can be assumed to affect billionaires' political agency. What concerns us here is, first, the "agentic power" of billionaires, which is obviously linked to their financial capital, but also to associated forms of social and cultural capital. Secondly, the "power of agency" will be discussed, whether billionaires exhibit particularly strong notions of self-efficacy. In this respect, an interesting distinction can be drawn between billionaires that inherited their wealth and those that are "self-made." Once we have studied the sources of billionaires' agency, we will need to look at their goals, linking capacities with intentions. Clearly, people have many different objectives, making this a potentially unworkable exercise. In order to structure this sphere and to allow for a closer connection with established IR scholarship, three main goals will be highlighted: security, wealth, and esteem. These goals are conventionally being seen as driving the behavior of states in world politics. Thinking about how billionaires stand in relation to them and other collective actors will finally bring us to power as a special type of agency. What are the chances of billionaires to impose their will on others? Here, we will necessarily return to structural conditions, as the power of billionaires does not only depend on their dispositions. Indeed, the analytical dualism endorsed earlier (chapter 2) will inform all of the following discussion—theorizing billionaires' agency is about relative autonomy, and therefore must always include its social constitution and its limits, too.

Billionaires in World Politics. Peter Hägel, Oxford University Press (2020). © Peter Hägel.
DOI: 10.1093/oso/9780198852711.001.0001

Capacities: Capital and Entrepreneurship

When discussing political agency, both Margaret Archer and Albert Bandura, who are among the social scientists that highlight individual agency the most, reserve the term for collective endeavors (Bandura 1997: 482–502, Archer 2000: 253–82). In their discussions of "political agency in a globalizing world," Philip Cerny (2000) and Ronald Bleiker (2000) do the same. Their assumption seems to be that, in the realm of politics, what matters most is the ability "to act in concert" (Arendt 1970: 44), to be able to overcome collective action problems (Olson 1965). "Corporate Agency . . . cannot be rendered by any formula of the sort 'individuals plus resources'. Its typical powers are capacities for articulating shared interests, organizing for collective action, generating social movements and exercising corporate influence in decision-making" (Archer 2000: 266). For Archer, it is in aligning themselves with others that persons turn into political agents capable of structural transformation. Billionaires, however, do control resources that make them much less dependent on fellow citizens. They are able, single-handedly, to instigate political action, both collective and individual, via their capital. To the extent that money matters (which will be discussed later), the agentic power of billionaires is immense.

While much of their fortune is usually tied up in their businesses, many billionaires could follow Bill Gates's example and transform shares in their companies into capital to be used for other purposes. But even without such radical shifts, billionaires do control vast financial resources that can be used flexibly. According to Wealth-X's "Billionaires Census," in 2014, the world's billionaires held, on average, over "19% of their wealth in cash from previous salaries and investment exits, which has mostly been reinvested in highly liquid, diversified securities. This amounts to [an average of] US$600 million per individual—a sum that is higher than the GDP of Dominica" (Wealth-X 2014: 17). Since 2012, billionaires have increased the liquid assets component of their wealth steadily, so that in 2018, it made up over a quarter of their wealth, with an average of around US$868 million in liquidity (Wealth-X 2019: 16). Such figures also rival important budget lines in larger and more developed states, as the example of global health has already shown in the introduction. According to the OECD, in 2018, nine of its member states had official development aid (ODA) expenditures below US$800 million.[1] The overall campaign expenditures for the 2013 and 2017 parliamentary elections in Germany amounted to less than €60 million for all the major political parties together.[2] A German billionaire thus

---

[1] These were, in ascending order according to ODA expenditure, Iceland, Slovenia, Slovak Republic, Greece, Czech Republic, Portugal, Luxembourg, New Zealand, and Poland, see online: http://www.compareyourcountry.org/oda?cr=oecd&lg=en# (accessed June 22, 2019).

[2] See "SPD gönnt sich größtes Wahlkampf-Budget," *Spiegel Online*, June 12, 2013, online: http://www.spiegel.de/politik/deutschland/millionen-aufwand-spd-goennt-sich-groesstes-wahlkampf-budget-

could attempt to heavily influence elections, but none has done so for now, at least not in a legal way that requires the publication of donations to political parties above €50,000. In fact, the largest individual German donor since 2000 has been a mining engineer, Michael May, who has given almost €2.8 million, the majority of his family inheritance, to the Marxist-Leninist Party of Germany.[3] This stands out against recent elections in the U.S., where many billionaires have injected huge amounts into various campaigns, topped by the Koch brothers' network, which reportedly spent over US$400 million in 2012, and casino mogul Sheldon Adelson, who alone spent over US$90 million in 2012 and over US$122 million in 2018 on boosting Republican candidates (Vogel 2014, Mayer 2016).[4] Apparently, there is great variation in billionaires' involvement in politics, which brings us to the question of their power of agency. Recent sociological studies of the wealthy in Germany emphasize exactly this difference between the purely material capabilities that wealth offers (*Reichtum*) and the capacity of individuals to use their wealth for something else than just wealth generation (*Vermögen*).[5] In order to qualify as "super-actors," billionaires would need to exhibit not only extraordinary agentic power, but also an exceptional power of agency in world politics.

Why do people engage in politics? Attempts to provide general answers to this question often look at political participation in democratic polities, and the research frameworks and findings reproduce the tension between agency and structure. On the one hand are studies that emphasize structural features like a civic culture in determining participation (Almond & Verba 1963, Putnam 1993, 2000, Anderson 2010), on the other hand there are those that focus on individual characteristics (Gerber et al. 2011). Consequently, political efficacy as a key concept in the study of political participation comprises "two separate components:

---

a-905334.html and Mathias Brandt, "Das kostet der Bundestagswahlkampf," *Statista*, November 20, 2017, online: https://de.statista.com/infografik/8805/kosten-des-bundestagswahlkampfes/ (both accessed June 22, 2019).

[3] The next largest donors are billionaires, the majority shareholders of BMW, Susanne Klatten and her brother Stefan Quandt, who have each donated over €1.5 million to the CDU and FDP parties between 2000 and 2018. See Robert Roßmann, "2,5 Millionen Euro für den 'echten Sozialismus'," *Süddeutsche Zeitung*, December 12, 2008, online: http://www.sueddeutsche.de/politik/parteispender-millionen-euro-fuer-den-echten-sozialismus-1.784731, https://lobbypedia.de/wiki/Spezial:Abfrage_ausf%C3%BChren/Parteispenden and http://parteispenden.unklarheiten.de/?seite=auswertung_max imum (both accessed June 22, 2019).

[4] Since 2014, billionaires Thomas Steyer and Michael Bloomberg have given similar sums as Adelson to pro-Democrats campaigns, see the top donors database online: https://www.opensecrets. org/outsidespending/summ.php?disp=D (accessed June 22, 2019). The striking contrast between billionaires' involvement in German and U.S. elections cannot be explained by law—in both countries, there are no limits to how much individuals can spend on political campaigns, and only minor variations exist with regard to transparency and tax deductibility rules.

[5] In German, both *Reichtum* and *Vermögen* mean "wealth," but *vermögen* is also a verb that means "being able to do something." See Druyen 2011 and el Sehity & Schor-Tschudnowskaja 2011.

(1) internal efficacy, referring to beliefs about one's own competence to understand, and to participate effectively in, politics, and (2) external efficacy referring to beliefs about the responsiveness of governmental authorities and institutions to citizen demands" (Niemi et al. 1991: 1407f). Clearly, the two are interrelated, but exactly how remains a matter of much discussion. David Lassen and Søren Serritzlew, for example, have shown that individuals' beliefs about their internal political efficacy decreases when the size of the polity increases (2011). This (not very surprising) finding can explain why most individuals refrain from entering world politics: they probably expect their potential to make a difference to be rather low, because of the higher complexity and greater distance of global governance. Focusing on the micro level instead, Klemmensen and colleagues find evidence, based on twin research, which suggests that heritable traits play a significant part in political participation, too (2012, also Fowler & Dawes 2008). Genetic conditioning is, of course, also a structural form of explanation, because it reduces behavior to individual traits that are biologically given. Both bio- and macro-factors seem to influence the probability of political participation, but they are far from determining. To a large extent, people's power of agency emerges from their reflexive engagement with their social environment. This is the process that Archer describes as the construction of the social self (Archer 2000: 253–305). Studying it requires, at the micro level, attention to individuals' biography, and, at the macro level, "locat[ing] which sorts of social-structural, cultural, and socialpsychological contexts are more conducive to developing the different modalities of agency" (Emirbayer & Mische 1998: 1005).

To develop general insights about when and why billionaires engage in (world) politics, one would need comparative individual-level data, for example on personality traits, skills, biographical details, etc., which does not exist so far, and which appears most difficult to establish. Only very few studies have tried to understand wealthy individuals, either qualitatively via interviews (Mäder et al. 2010, Zitelmann 2017), or in a mix of quantitative and qualitative analysis based on surveys (Schervish & Havens 2001, Lauterbach et al. 2011, Page et al. 2013, 2019). These studies are not representative according to strict social science standards, and they admit as much.[6] They also do not capture billionaires, as their respondents' mean wealth is very much below the ten-digit range. The mean

---

[6] The qualitative study on how wealthy people "think and steer" in Switzerland interviewed over one hundred persons, selected rather randomly via personal contacts and a "snowball system," where one contact lead to the next; interviews were not standardized (Mäder et al. 2010: 13f, 167ff); Rainer Zitelmann proceeded similarly, interviewing forty-five very wealthy persons (2017: 126–8). The "Vermögen in Deutschland" (ViD—"Wealth in Germany") study tried harder to be representative and is based on 472 standardized paper-and-pencil interviews, but the researchers are aware of its limitations (Kortmann 2011, Lauterbach et al. 2011). Key problems are, first, to identify the wealth of households, and then, to get a representative sample to agree to be interviewed. The same problems affected the SESA pilot study, which is based on eighty-three standardized interviews with respondents from the Chicago area (Page et al. 2011, 2013, Cook et al. 2014: 385–8).

household wealth in the German "Vermögen in Deutschland" (ViD—"Wealth in Germany") study was €2.4 million, with the wealthiest household among the 472 respondents owning around €50 million (Lauterbach et al. 2011: 47f); in the Chicago-based "Survey of Economically Successful Americans" (SESA), mean wealth was US$14 million, with six of the 83 respondents owning more than US $40 million (Cook et al. 2014: 388, Page et al. 2013). Nevertheless, these studies provide the most systematic insights into the top 1 percent wealthiest households so far, and they do indicate remarkable differences between the wealthy and the average middle-class citizen with regard to self-efficacy. Trying to develop hypotheses about billionaires by relying on the characteristics of multi-millionaires is certainly somewhat questionable.[7] But, to advance comparison, some descriptive data on billionaires exists in the form of Wealth-X's "Billionaires Census" (various years), and hypotheses can be strengthened if we build them on the basis of broader theoretical and empirical insights on (political) self-efficacy.

The ViD study, which correlated people's wealth levels with socio-structural characteristics, such as education and professional status, and personality traits,[8] came to the following conclusion: compared to the middle class, "[r]ich people are especially open-minded towards the new, they are strongly extroverted, and they assume that they can determine their lives themselves" (Lauterbach & Tarvenkorn 2011: 80, author's translation). Among the wealthy, the richest subgroup of HNWIs revealed attributes that distinguish it further in a number of areas. Notably, they exhibited the highest values with regard to internal and external self-efficacy.[9] They were also the most open-minded towards the new, and the share of entrepreneurs that run their own business was much higher among HNWIs: 64.6 percent, vis-à-vis 7,5 percent among the middle class, 43.3 percent among the "prosperous," and 37.8 percent among the "affluent." This corresponds with Wealth-X's assertion that 63 percent of billionaires' primary businesses are privately held companies.[10] Further similarities concern age and education: the

---

[7] Rainer Zitelmann's qualitative study reached much higher wealth levels, including three billionaires, but with strong overrepresentation of individuals from the real estate sector. His findings about personality traits largely confirm the findings of ViD and other studies of wealthy people with lower average wealth levels (2017: 128, 132, 330f).

[8] To assess personality traits, ViD investigated internal and external efficacy and the often used so-called Big Five traits (conscientiousness, agreeableness, extraversion, openness, neuroticism). See Bandura 2012 for a discussion of the Big Five in contrast to self-efficacy measures.

[9] Among the rich, ViD distinguished a "prosperous" subgroup with liquid capital between €200,000 and €500,000; "affluents" with liquid capital between €500,000 and €1,000,000; and HNWIs with more than 1,000,000€. Most indicators of the characteristics of the groups in comparison to the middle class showed significant differences, but also among the three subgroups. In Zitelmann's study of the super-wealthy, optimism about self-efficacy was the personality trait that was the most uniformly pronounced (2017: 284f).

[10] Wealth-X 2014: 26; in terms of their wealth portfolio, private business holdings constituted, on average, almost 47 percent of billionaires' wealth. This share has declined significantly since 2014: 46 percent in 2015, 38.7 percent in 2016, 33.3 percent in 2017, representing a "marked shift in favor of public holdings, driven by the robust upturn in world equity markets ... and the strong growth in Asia's billionaire class, many of whom favor stock market listings over private ownership (in contrast to

average German HNWI in 2009 was sixty-one years old, the average billionaire in 2018 counted sixty-three years; the HNWIs in ViD stood out with 51.3 percent of them having a university degree, compared to 25.2 percent in the middle class; among billionaires, in 2015, 70.1 percent had a university degree (Lauterbach & Tarvenkorn 2011: 62, 72, 78ff, 89, Wealth-X 2019: 20, Wealth-X 2016a: 24). That high wealth levels tend to go together with higher education, successful entrepreneurship, and advanced age is not very groundbreaking, but it becomes more interesting once we relate it to social and political engagement.

An analysis of the extent of social engagement among Germany's wealthy households showed levels high above the German average (36 percent versus 82 percent among the wealthy), but also much heterogeneity in terms of who is engaged how much in what. Among the rich, two factors have been singled out that seem to affect social engagement: the extent of a sense of responsibility, and the source of one's wealth—people that had acquired their wealth via their own work tended to be significantly more engaged than those that became rich via inheritance, financial investments, or real estate (Ströing & Kramer 2011: 103–9). That self-made wealth leads more often to social engagement is also being supported by a statistical analysis of those billionaires that have signed the philanthropic "Giving Pledge": "self-made" billionaires were 20 percent more likely to have signed the "Giving Pledge" than billionaires that had inherited large parts of their fortunes (Sadeh et al. 2014: 5–7). Similarly, in Wealth-X's study of major donors (those who had given more than US$1 million) among the world's UHNWIs, individuals with self-made fortunes were overrepresented whereas those with inherited wealth were underrepresented (Wealth-X 2016b: 11). These observations are in line with Albert Bandura's finding that self-efficacy beliefs build up through mastery experiences in the course of people's lives, especially if mastering tasks and exercising control over one's environment involves overcoming obstacles (Bandura 1997: 80–5).[11] We can therefore hypothesize that the experience of success in business may lead entrepreneurs to develop stronger beliefs about their self-efficacy in social and political affairs. Further differences may derive from the specific business sector in which billionaires have prospered, for example whether they require more or less risk-taking and innovation. Paul Schervish, for example, finds wealthy individuals from the high-tech sector to be particularly engaged when they shift their activities to

trends in the US and Europe)" (Wealth-X 2018: 19, also Wealth-X 2017: 22). In 2018, private business holdings accounted for 35 percent of billionaires' wealth (Wealth-X 2019: 16f).

[11] At the individual level, he equally emphasizes physical and emotional states, the relative absence of anxiety and depression, which also finds support in the ViD study, where the wealthy showed much lower levels of personality traits associated with "neuroticism." For men, "neuroticism" decreased robustly with wealth: among HNWIs, only 7.4 percent exhibited strong "neuroticism" traits, compared to 16.7 percent among the middle class (Lauterbach & Tarvenkorn 2011: 74–9, 90).

philanthropy (Schervish 2014b). Such a connection is far from straightforward, however, because Bandura's research also shows that "people's beliefs in their capabilities vary across activity domains and situational conditions rather than manifest uniformly across tasks and contexts in the likeness of a general trait" (Bandura 2012: 13). Whereas Silvio Berlusconi used to come across as someone with high beliefs in his power of agency across many life domains, be it business, politics, romance, or entertainment, most billionaires seem to stick to their business, or at least that is what we know about them publicly.

Yet, self-efficacy beliefs can become more generalized if an activity domain requires and fosters skills that are useful in other activity domains, too. The mastery experience in one domain may then translate into beliefs about one's self-efficacy in other domains (Bandura 1997: 50–4). Clearly, whether entrepreneurial skills can be valuable in politics will depend on the political system in question—it will probably be much less the case in a theocracy than in a neoliberal state with "entrepreneurial government" (Dardot & Laval 2013: 215–54). The question of transposability is, moreover, closely linked to the societal context, where Bandura sees two further sources of self-efficacy beliefs operating: social modeling, "[s]eeing people similar to oneself succeed by perseverant effort," and social persuasion, the dis- or encouragement received by others, which involves social norms (Bandura 2012: 13).[12] Differences in societal contexts come to the fore if we take a comparative look at the political agency of the wealthy in Germany and the U.S.

Unfortunately, the ViD study concentrated mainly on social engagement and did not put a specific focus on political participation, which has only been captured in very broad categories of time and money spent on "politics/society" and political parties (Ströing & Kramer 2011: 119–40).[13] Nevertheless, in Germany, the ViD population displays stronger political engagement than the common citizen: 6.36 percent of the respondents said that they were active members in a political party, which is almost three times as high as the average party membership quota among voting-age Germans (2.25 percent, of which around a third are deemed inactive).[14] Although the wealthy Germans appear as much more politically engaged than their compatriots, their participation, as established by ViD, pales in comparison to the findings of the SESA study of wealthy Americans, which focused more explicitly on political engagement (Table 4.1).

---

[12] For a more extensive treatment, see Bandura 1997: 79–115.

[13] This choice of priorities reflects the overall rather uncritical approach of the ViD study, which appears as being mainly concerned with whether the rich use their wealth responsibly, avoiding questions about inequalities in political power.

[14] For overall party membership in Germany, see Schmidt 2011, for activity levels in 2009, see Spier 2011: 99.

Table 4.1 Percentages of wealthy Americans and the general public engaged in political activities

Percentages of Wealthy Americans and the General Public Engaged in Political Activities

Political Activity	Percentage (%) Participating						
	Total Public (Pew & ANES)	Public by Income					Wealthy (SESA)
		< $30,000	$30,000–$49,999	$50,000–$74,999	$75,000–$149,999	$150,000+	
Voted in 2008	78	73	73	84	83	84	99
Talk politics every day	19	14	19	19	26	32	42
Attended political meetings, rallies, speeches, or dinners[1]	12	8	10	15	14	22	41
Contributed money	18	10	14	19	27	44	60
Helped solicit or bundle contributions							21
Attend to politics "most of the time"	26	21	24	26	31	38	84
Belong to political organization	15	10	12	20	24	26	23
Volunteer for political organization	8	6	6	9	10	15	29
N[2]	2,251	509	337	296	488	127	83

[1] Survey of general public asked only about attending a political rally or speech.

[2] Number of respondents provided for the general public from the Pew survey. All general public questions come from the Pew survey except "Voted in 2008" and "Attend to politics most of the time" which are taken from the American National Election Studies.

Source: Cook et al. 2014: 389, John Wiley And Sons.

Political engagement is consistently increasing with higher income levels, but when it comes to "attending to politics" and active participation (attending meetings, giving money, volunteering), millionaires surpass their co-citizens by large margins. Active volunteering for a political organization stood at 29 percent in the U.S., over four times as much as the wealthy's engagement in political parties in Germany.[15] Whereas just about 6 percent of the rich Germans said that they had given money for political causes (Ströing & Kramer 2011: 140), it was 60 percent of the wealthy Americans. Among the one hundred richest billionaires in the U.S., political financing is even more prevalent: over 90 percent of them made reportable contributions to political organizations, and 36 percent of them acted as bundlers or fundraisers for political campaigns (Page et al. 2019: 43). The differences between the ViD study in Germany and the SESA findings in the U.S. may therefore be partly due to the fact that the U.S. survey reached wealthier households—in the German sample, political activity also appears to increase with rising wealth (Ströing & Kramer 2011: 118ff). The magnitude of the disparities, however, points to overarching differences between the political systems.

Unlike politics in Germany, which remains characterized by centralized political parties that are largely financed by the state and their party members, in the U.S., electoral politics are candidate-centered, and very capital-intensive campaigns require extensive private fundraising.[16] This allows wealthy individuals much greater influence over elections in the U.S., either via supporting favored politicians, as mentioned earlier, or by running for office themselves. It also affects the transposability of skills: fundraising obviously requires skills that belong much more to the repertoire of wealthy entrepreneurs than, for example, oratory or compromise-building at party conventions, the "slow, powerful drilling through hard boards" (Weber 1918 [2004]: 93). Largely self-financed candidates like the late billionaires Ross Perot (presidential election 1992: 18.9 percent of the votes; 1996: 8.4 percent) and Michael Bloomberg (Mayor of New York, 2001–13) are not unusual in U.S. politics, but hard to imagine in Germany. Other important institutional differences concern the political economy and the respective variety of capitalism, where the coordinated market economy of Germany contrasts with the liberal market economy of the U.S. (Hall & Soskice 2001). In this regard, Iain McMenamin has shown how political financing by individual firms is much less prevalent in Germany, with its corporatist tradition, than in liberal market economies like the U.S., because German firms can count on relatively effective representation via centralized business associations (McMenamin 2013). The varieties of capitalism also affect what sectors of a national economy produce billionaires. The U.S., with its comparative institutional advantage in "radical

---

[15] "Membership in a political organization" tends to be high in the U.S., because it frequently starts with being registered with one of the main parties, in order to be able to vote in these parties' primaries.
[16] For comprehensive comparisons, see Jesse & Sturm 2003, Lijphart 2012, McMenamin 2013.

innovation," has been particularly strong in finance and high-tech, while German "incremental innovation" favors high-quality industry (Hall & Soskice 2001). Globally, and especially in the U.S., most billionaires come from the finance/banking/investment sector (Wealth-X 2017: 23); in Germany, most come from industry, retailing, and consumer goods. In 2017, *Forbes* counted only three out of 114 German billionaires coming from the finance and investment sectors. The nature of a billionaire's business can be expected to have consequences for his politics. Billionaires whose wealth depends on consumer markets risk alienating customers if they express political positions publicly (Page et al. 2019: 20–2, 32, 41, 91); hedge fund managers don't have to worry about this. This can explain in part why we rarely hear about German billionaires meddling in politics, in comparison to the many politically active billionaires in the U.S.

The distinct political opportunity structures in Germany and the U.S. go hand in hand with differences in social norms and political culture. Wealthy U.S. citizens can look towards a great variety of past and current billionaires that openly compete to make their mark in politics. Tellingly, an evaluation of billionaires' influence in U.S. politics, published by the center-left Brookings Institution, mainly takes issue with transparency, but otherwise accepts the state of affairs: "It is perfectly reasonable for rich people to express their views, lobby Congress, and attempt to influence elections as long as others are aware of what they are doing and can organize accordingly" (West 2014: 15). German billionaires, on the other hand, have hardly any role models to inspire their own political self-efficacy beliefs. The only recent case, where the billionaire owner of the Mövenpick hotel and restaurant group, August von Finck, arranged €1.1 million of campaign financing for the liberal democrats (FDP) in 2009, presumably in return for tax breaks for hotels once the FDP was in government, caused major indignation and, arguably, contributed much to the eviction of the FDP from the Bundestag during the following election in 2013.[17]

The political agency of billionaires is thus never simply a consequence of their financial resources, nor is it a mere extension of the self-efficacy beliefs cultivated by their triumphs as entrepreneurs. It is also shaped by the social and political contexts that define the opportunity structures for wealthy individuals, as the contrast between the U.S. and Germany demonstrates. The question remains whether we can extend any of the above insights from national to world politics.

---

[17] See Florian Gathmann & Veit Medick, "Hohn und Spott für die 'Mövenpick-Partei'," *Spiegel Online*, January 19, 2010, online: http://www.spiegel.de/politik/deutschland/debatte-um-fdp-spende-hohn-und-spott-fuer-die-moevenpick-partei-a-672756.html; more recently, Finck has been suspected to finance campaigns for the new populist right party Alternative für Deutschland in Germany, but despite many indicators, hard evidence is missing so far, see Melanie Amann, Sven Becker & Sven Röbel, "A Billionaire Backer and the Murky Finances of the AfD," *Spiegel Online*, November 30, 2018, online: https://www.spiegel.de/international/germany/billionaire-backing-may-have-helped-launch-afd-a-1241029.html (accessed July 2, 2019). The other prominent political financing case in Germany, the so-called "Flick affair," dates back to the 1970s, see Kilz & Preuß 1983.

No prior studies or surveys exist about billionaires as transnational actors, and therefore I will limit myself to two tentative hypotheses, derived from the previous discussion: (1) *Billionaires will be more likely to enter world politics the more they have gained self-efficacy beliefs as entrepreneurs in international business.* Doing global business would expose billionaires to politics in different countries as well as to the institutions of global governance; their mastery experience of successful entrepreneurship would also immediately have a global dimension. However, whether this mastery experience can actually be transposed from global business to global politics appears to be highly contingent, depending not only on the individual billionaire, but also on the political issue and arena in question. (2) *Billionaires will be more likely to enter world politics if they live in a country where private "foreign affairs" are tolerated or even encouraged.* This refers to the social modeling and persuasion aspects of self-efficacy beliefs and to the political opportunity structure, which will be discussed further when we examine billionaires' power. It assumes that an individual's political socialization still happens first and foremost in their country of residence, which seems reasonable, but, in the case of billionaires, may be questioned by notions of a global ruling class or the "Davos Man," which will be analyzed further in the analytical conclusion (chapter 8).

Goals: Security, Wealth, and Esteem

For a full account of agency, as has been argued in chapter 2, it is necessary to link capacities with intentions or goals.[18] Those who generally question the concept of agency find this to be an impossible task. "There are many persons with many unknown intentions. The vast majority of these intentions are completely inaccessible to sociology, or indeed to any observer, short of an omniscientist [*sic*] God" (Fuchs 2001: 27, also Loyal & Barnes 2001). Such censure points to the problems of distinguishing reasons or goals from causes, and of establishing verifiable links between mental states (intentions) and effects in the material world (Pleasants 1999: 107ff, Azevedo 1997: 148–80). Behind much of this criticism seems to lie a disappointed hope, which somehow expects the social sciences to produce causal laws similar to the natural sciences, for example in Newtonian physics. Intentions, as they are being formed through reflective processes, are hard to pin down, especially if one is aiming to distinguish apparent from ulterior motives. However, the natural sciences are facing very similar

---

[18] Within social psychology, the notion of intentions covers a wider spectrum, whereas "goals" are usually more narrowly defined as "*a cognitive representation of a desired end-point that impacts evaluations, emotions and behaviors*" (Fishbach & Ferguson 2007: 491, emphasis in original, also Gollwitzer 1993).

problems when trying to identify the particles and forces that move the world within quantum physics, where theories of causality have moved away from mechanical towards probabilistic models. Indeed, as Alexander Wendt has been proposing, insights from quantum physics may also be used to conceptualize human intentionality in more fruitful ways than if one relies on mechanical notions of efficient causation (Wendt 2015: 63–5, 174–88, 287f). The intricacies of the philosophical debates around quantum ontology need not concern us here, but they do provide strong arguments for treating intentions as causes in the probabilistic sense: they should be seen as affecting the likelihood of outcomes.

Regarding states as actors in world politics, the discussion in IR has usually considered the goals of states as something exogenously given. Much of the debate between realists and liberals concerns whether and when states pursue relative security or absolute economic gains (Grieco 1988). For realists, the primacy of relative security derives from the anarchic structure of the international system.

> When faced with the possibility of cooperating for mutual gains, states that feel insecure must ask how the gain will be divided. They are compelled to ask not "Will both of us gain?" but "Who will gain more?" If an expected gain is to be divided, say, in the ratio of two to one, one state may use its disproportionate gain to implement a policy intended to damage or destroy the other.
>
> (Waltz 1979: 105)

For liberals, the primacy of prosperity arises from domestic politics: economic development, free markets, and democratic institutions are assumed to orient states towards cooperation via international institutions and law, at least when it comes to relations among liberal states, in order to realize mutual benefits for their citizens (Doyle 1986, Gartzke 2007). James March and Johan Olsen have grouped both the pursuits of security and economic well-being under a "logic of expected consequences," which they contrast with a "logic of appropriateness" (1998). The latter emphasizes that states' objectives also depend on their identities and the prevailing (inter)national norms, which is at the heart of constructivist research (Checkel 1998, Finnemore & Sikkink 1998). Richard Ned Lebow has integrated these constructivist concerns into what he calls a cultural theory of IR, which is particularly useful here, because he distinguishes fundamental motives and goals in politics that he assumes to exist at any level of agency, individual or collective (2008: 114–17). Besides security and material well-being (what he calls "satiation"), which entail the acquisition of power and wealth, he identifies esteem as a third goal in politics, which depends on obtaining honor or standing (ibid.: 43–121, esp. 91). As a relational goal that requires recognition by others, esteem's meaning is cultural in the sense that it varies across time and societies, depending on what is being recognized to bring honor. Lebow is aware that these three goals do not exhaust the universe of possible human goals, but he argues that they are the most relevant in world politics (Lebow 2010: 486, Rengger 2010: 457f). This seems plausible enough for collective actors like states, even though affective goals like friendship may also play a minor role for them (Koschut & Oelsner 2014). For individual actors, affective goals can be more important, and there are possibly intriguing stories yet to be uncovered, of billionaires that try to intervene in world politics to impress their loved ones.[19] Yet, in order to allow for more immediate connections with established IR scholarship, this study will mainly focus on billionaires' agency in their pursuit of the three fundamental goals that appear to drive states' behavior in world politics.

These goals of states, however, as the term "exogenously given" indicates, have often been treated as being structurally induced—by the anarchic structure of world politics (realism), the social and political structures of domestic politics (liberalism), or ideational/normative structures (constructivism). In his critique of this structural determinism in IR, Markus Kornprobst has recently proposed to pay greater attention to political judgment as a notion that captures the agency aspect within the pursuit of goals:

[J]udging is practical reasoning by subsuming particulars under universals. Universals are the taken-for-granted ideas that individuals employ to make sense of political life such as causal and constitutive relationships, ideas of belonging and positioning vis-à-vis others, and standards of behaviour.... For the most part, universals are more or less widely shared across communities. Yet there are also some idiosyncratic universals that an individual acquires during his or her peculiar socialization process.... Universals tend to be multivocal, that is, they are interpreted differently by different actors.... Taken together, universals make up the "tool kit"...from which individuals draw to make sense of the world.   (Kornprobst 2011: 78)

This perspective connects well with Margaret Archer's framework,[20] in which the reflective development of commitments, first and foremost to oneself, character-izes human agency: "It is we human beings who determine our priorities and define our personal identities in terms of what we care about. Therefore we are quintes-sentially evaluative beings" (Archer 2000: 318).[21] Amartya Sen's understanding of

---

[19] David McKnight, for example, recounts how Rupert Murdoch changed his mind on climate change due to his son James; this, however, seems to have produced relatively little effect on the climate change skepticism among many of the news media owned by Murdoch (McKnight 2013: 202ff, also Folkenflik 2013: 92ff).

[20] Kornprobst does not reference Archer, but his own model of political judgments within "co-configurative cycles" comes very close to Archer's morphogenetic approach; compare Kornprobst 2011: 84–7 with Archer 1995, 2013b.

[21] While Wendt finds Archer's critical realism to large extents compatible with quantum ontology, he prefers Giddens's "mutual constitution" to Archer's "co-determination" conceptualization of the relationship between structures and agents (Wendt 2015: 243–66, esp. 260). However, in doing so, he is

agency similarly highlights the freedom to pursue objectives (1985: 203ff). At the same time, choices about goals do not take place in some vacuum of "free will"— they always emerge out of people's engagement with the natural, practical, and social orders of reality (Archer 2000: 283–305). Within the dualism of structure and agency, this implies that structural properties shape people's goals, but people nonetheless exercise their own judgment in the selection and formulation of "their" goals.[22] When studying billionaires' goals, a problem emerges that Benjamin Page, Jason Seawright, and Matthew Lacombe have called "stealth politics" (2019: 7). They find that most U.S., billionaires, although often active in politics, are making very few public statements about their political goals, especially when it comes to specific policies. One way to deal with this is to derive billionaires' goals from their actions, which, like the funding of campaigns or think tanks, can indicate their political outlook. Sometimes, one can also rely on reports from investigative journalists; and some, e.g. Bill Gates or George Soros, are very transparent about their goals.

Billionaires do have to worry more about their personal security than ordinary citizens, because their wealth makes them tempting targets for extortion, as several high-profile kidnappings of billionaires (or their family members) have shown in the past.[23] But, from a political perspective, this is mostly a matter of internal security. Usually, billionaires can rely on protection by the states in which they reside, and they obviously have the funds to pay for supplementary private protection, so that fear for their personal security will rarely be a major concern when it comes to their involvement in world politics. They may, on the other hand, get involved in international security if they view security not only as an individual affair, and decide to finance war or peace efforts. This depends upon billionaires' sociopolitical identities, whether they see themselves as being part of a larger community to which they extend allegiance and solidarity. In the modern world, sociopolitical identity remains largely organized around nations, as people are integrated both culturally (ethnicity) and politically (citizenship) along national lines (Calhoun 2007, Gat and Yakobson 2012).[24] Within IR, nations

---

missing Archer's point: her disentanglement of agents and structures happens for analytical reasons, not as a philosophical assumption within ontology.

[22] Within realism, the question of judgment has entered the debate via the notion of "perceptions" (Jervis 1976), and its relevance can be seen in the opposition between "offensive" and "defensive" variants of realism, whether concerns over power or concerns over threats are more important for states (Walt 1987).
[23] Among the most famous cases are Theo Albrecht (1971), J. Paul Getty's grandson in 1973, Richard Oetker (1976), Freddy Heineken (1983), Hong-Kong tycoon Li Ka-shing's son in 1996, Walter Kwok in 1997, Eddie Lampert in 2003, and Jakob von Metzler (2002), but the list is much longer.
[24] Clearly, other sociopolitical identities also exist and matter, most notably class and religion— people have crossed borders to fight for Communism, as in the Spanish Civil War, or, as in Syria and Iraq, for an Islamic State. Billionaires may also exhibit very local sociopolitical identities, which would make an involvement in world politics unlikely. See Merton 1957 on the classical distinction between local and cosmopolitan identities.

and nationalism have almost exclusively been studied as collective identities—how, as social constructs, they shape the corporate agency of nation-states (Bloom 1993, Hall 1999). Whenever national communities spread across state borders, because of the (re-)drawing of territorial borders or migration, complex security constellations between homelands, diasporas, and their host states emerge (Brubaker 1996, Koslowski 2005, Sheffer 2003, Shain 2007), which can escalate into cross-border ethnic conflicts (Lake & Rothchild 1998, Saideman 2001, Smith & Stares 2007). With their financial firepower, billionaires may get involved in such transnational security issues. While social scientists can identify the dominant social norms that define a particular national identity, it is much harder to generalize about the extent to which it matters for specific individuals and their behavior. The roles associated with the adoption of a national identity are part of social structure, but whether and how people choose to enact these roles depends on their agency (Archer 2000: 295–305, McCrone & Bechhofer 2015: 26).

Sheldon Adelson, for example, the Zionist U.S. casino mogul, has made the security of Israel one of his main goals, and has massively intervened in U.S. and Israeli politics in order to "[oppose] a two-state solution or any accommodation of Palestinians" within the Israel–Palestine conflict (Ball 2012). In contrast, George Soros, despite descending from a Jewish family, has stated on several occasions that he did not see his Jewishness as "a sense of tribal loyalty that would have led me to support Israel. On the contrary, I took pride in being in the minority, an outsider who was capable of seeing the other point of view" (Soros 1991: 4, 1995: 240–2). Neither his business nor his philanthropic ventures exhibit any particular attention to Jewish causes. Instead, he describes himself as "hav[ing] a very big ego…. I can find sufficient scope for it only by identifying with humanity…. I aspire to make the world a better place" (Soros 2011: 37f). Ulrich Beck (2004), Kwame Anthony Appiah (2006), David Held (2010), Martha Nussbaum (2019), and others have defined such a social identity as cosmopolitan, and Soros's commitment to it can be seen in the geographic diversity of his projects, which span the globe (Sudetic 2011, Porter 2015). Although Adelson and Soros are both Jewish U.S. citizens, the choices of their political loyalties and transnational activism represent very different stances: an ethnonational identity in Adelson's case, a cosmopolitan identity in the case of Soros. Exactly how a person's socio-political identity emerges and evolves is a matter of biography.[25] At a more general level, we can nevertheless hypothesize that *billionaires will be more likely to intervene in international security affairs if they have developed a sociopolitical identity whose sense of belonging has a transnational dimension.*

Billionaires can also engage in world politics to advance their material well-being, which, as a goal, is easier to locate at the individual level than security, even

---

[25] See Tarrow 2005: 35–58 for a discussion of varying forms of (rooted) cosmopolitanism in practice.

though its precise meaning is less obvious than it might seem. The very fact that they have accumulated enormous fortunes indicates that wealth is a priority for billionaires, at least for those that are "self-made." What exactly material well-being denotes varies from one person to another—for some, it is a vast property in a privileged location; for others, living surrounded by a collection of rare artefacts. Whether increasing one's material wealth is actually improving one's experience of well-being is more complicated. Research that tries to measure "well-being," either for states (Stiglitz et al. 2010, Allin & Hand 2014, Philipsen 2015) or for individuals (Tatzel 2013), indicates that there is no linear correlation between measures of material possessions and well-being (Kahnemann & Deaton 2010). In fact, materialistic goals seem to lower people's well-being (Dittmar et al. 2014). However, for the purposes of our study, this does not matter, as long as, from the actor's point of view, the pursuit of material wealth appears as a worthwhile goal. Groucho Marx once put it nicely: "While money can't buy happiness, it certainly lets you choose your own form of misery." Of course, the meaning of this goal is at the same time socially constructed. As Thorstein Veblen (1899), Joseph Schumpeter (1912: 135ff), Axel Honneth (2004), and others have argued, especially in capitalist societies, entrepreneurial success, material rewards, and conspicuous consumption also serve as expressions of social status and recognition. Obtaining wealth is therefore both about material well-being and the social standing attached to it. Moreover, in market economies with high degrees of commodification, money is a very flexible tool that can be used for the satisfaction of material desires, but for other purposes, too. In this sense, it is difficult to assess whether the quest for wealth is an ultimate goal, or whether it simply serves as an intermediate objective in the pursuit of something else. While we may never have certainty about the position of material well-being in a particular billionaire's set of goals, we can still study how billionaires intervene in world politics in order to increase their wealth at the time, without wondering whether there is an ulterior motive for the future.

The most common examples of transnational interventions by billionaires are lobbying endeavors vis-à-vis governments and international organizations, in order to advance their business interests. From lobbying, it is only a small yet legally significant step towards corruption, the direct bribing of foreign officials and politicians in order to obtain outcomes in one's favor. Since this practice has been made illegal in most countries over the past two decades, especially via the OECD's Anti-Bribery Convention from 1997, it is harder to detect (Abbott & Snidal 2002). More indirect are attempts to influence public policy by shaping public opinion across borders, as when David and Charles Koch sponsor think tanks and foundations that intervene with skepticism in the global climate change debate (Greenpeace 2010). The Kochs' business empire is truly global, with operations in around sixty countries. At a general level, one should expect that

billionaires will be more likely to engage in transnational political activism if their pursuit of wealth depends on political decisions abroad.
While political interventions to increase one's wealth will frequently be hidden and hence difficult to research, billionaires' pursuit of esteem is an easier goal to study, because honor depends on public recognition. As Richard Ned Lebow argues, honor as the means to achieve esteem is related to one's social standing, and honor societies therefore tend to be highly stratified (Lebow 2008: 63–72, 162–4). Esteem should thus be of growing importance in the contemporary world, where the inequalities between those at the very top and the rest have been widening over the past decades (Alvaredo et al. 2018). Its intersubjective nature makes it tempting to view esteem as a goal that is instilled by society, leaving little room for agency.[26] In modern societies with complex social relations and normative claims, however, a large array of opportunities for acquiring esteem exists (Honneth 1994: 197–210), and individuals can choose their commitments and exercise judgment when pursuing esteem. This is being captured by the distinction between self-esteem and esteem. What brings public esteem is being elaborated at the level of society, but people can develop their own understandings of self-esteem.[27]

For billionaires, the politically most relevant channel of competition for honor in today's world appears to be philanthropy, at least in the Anglo-American cultural setting (Friedman & McGarvie 2003, Adloff 2010, Zunz 2012, Reich 2018). Going back to Greek mythology (Aeschylus recounting the Titan Prometheus' *philanthropos* as he gave fire to humans), the original meaning of philanthropy refers to a love for humanity that manifests itself in serving others, and, as such, is closely linked to morality. Robert Payton and Michael Moody define philanthropy as "moral action," used by individuals to "implement their moral imagination" and to "interven[e] in other people's lives ... to do them good and to advance the public good" (2008: 96).[28] Such an agency-centered interpretation can capture the altruistic individual, helping anonymously, only concerned about his or her self-esteem. It cannot, however, explain why philanthropy is being pursued to a greater or lesser extent, during different time periods, in different societies. Neither can it help us to understand the social processes

---

[26] Lebow mentions ancient Sparta as an example that comes close to the ideal type of a highly integrated "honor society" (2008: 70ff).
[27] Lebow, who emphasizes the cultural/structural component in the pursuit of esteem (2008: 122–51), acknowledges: "Motives are cultural and personal. Culture defines and shapes the hierarchy of individual motives, channels them toward specific forms of expression and goals, and teaches people to respond when their goals are achieved or stymied. People nevertheless have choices and are never automatons in behavior or feelings. To understand foreign policy and international relations, we must understand the motives, goals, and emotions of relevant actors. There is simply no such thing as a universal strategic logic or hierarchy of motives that we can take for granted and use to model behavior" (2010: 487).
[28] Paul Schervish, a leading scholar of philanthropy in the U.S., expresses a very similar understanding of philanthropy being linked to individuals' "moral biography" (2006 and 2014a).

when the philanthropy of a large variety of individuals is converging around a very limited number of issues. Based on her fieldwork among American philanthropists, Francie Ostrower arrives at a definition that emphasizes the socially constructed aspect of philanthropy. She sees philanthropy as

> a mark of class status that contributes to defining and maintaining the culture and organizational boundaries of elite life...[, which] takes on meaning in the context of a cultural emphasis on individualism and private initiative and a mistrust of governmental power and large-scale bureaucracies.   (1995: 6, 8)

In his comparison of philanthropic foundations in Germany and the U.S., Frank Adloff similarly highlights the importance of social relations, status and honor, and the institutional embeddedness of philanthropy. To this, he adds the mortality-transcending role of institutionalized philanthropy—via foundations that carry their name, individuals can hope to garner esteem beyond their own death (2010: 59–79, 161–7, 407–17).[29] Whether individuals' philanthropy mainly conforms to the expectations of society and peers, in order to gain public esteem, or whether it is a more personal action through which billionaires realize their self-esteem, requires empirical investigation.[30]

George Soros, for example, initially developed his international philanthropy during the 1980s almost without public notice; in fact, he did not appear in *Who's Who* until 1994 (Kaufman 2002: 157, 179f, 201). His venture into philanthropy happened largely as trial and error, and in response to a midlife crisis, when Soros was searching for new goals that could bring meaning and self-esteem to his life (ibid.: 152–7, 163–72, Soros 1995: 112f). Only during the 1990s can we discern a greater concern with public recognition and esteem, not least evidenced by the number of books and articles Soros has been publishing since then.[31] The so-called Giving Pledge, officially launched in June 2010 by America's wealthiest individuals, Warren Buffett and Bill and Melinda Gates, also illustrates both sides of philanthropy. It invited American billionaires to make a public "moral

---

[29] Adloff's reliance on Marcel Mauss' gift theory (Adloff 2010: 34–55), which stresses norms of reciprocity within the exchange of gifts (Mauss 1967), does, however, seem inappropriate for large-scale philanthropic endeavors where the givers rarely meet the recipients.

[30] Friedman's historical analysis of American philanthropy captures as much: "[P]hilanthropy has had much to do with a specific person who has intended at least some measure of charitable benevolence towards others.... To a greater or lesser extent, the philanthropist has imposed his/her vision of a good society...on others.... Yet, the individual philanthropist has never...been separable from the institutional context of his/her behavior" (2003: 9).

[31] Soros himself has claimed that he started to nurture his public celebrity status only instrumentally, in order to be better able to promote his ideas and his philanthropy (1991: 141–4, Kaufman 2002: 240f); later, he has acknowledged that he has "learned to accept gratitude" and public recognition for his accomplishments (1995: 249), but he still maintains that "[s]ince my philanthropy is a source of ego satisfaction, I feel I do not deserve any thanks for it" (2011: 38).

commitment to give ... the majority of their wealth to ... philanthropic causes";[32] 204 pledges had been made by mid-2019. On the one hand, the Giving Pledge can be seen as reviving a tradition from America's first Gilded Age, expressed by steel-baron Andrew Carnegie in his "Gospel of Wealth":

> This, then, is held to be the duty of the man of Wealth: ... to consider all surplus revenues which come to him simply as trust funds, which he is called upon to administer, and strictly bound as a matter of duty to administer in the manner which, in his judgment, is best calculated to produce the most beneficial results for the community—the man of wealth thus becoming the mere agent and trustee for his poorer brethren, bringing to their service his superior wisdom, experience, and ability to administer, doing for them better than they would or could do for themselves.... Such, in my opinion, is the true Gospel concerning Wealth, obedience to which is destined some day to solve the problem of the Rich and the Poor, and to bring "Peace on earth, among men Good-Will."
>
> (1889: 661f, 664)

Although the explicit paternalism of the nineteenth century is missing in the twenty-first century, a sense of moral duty and peer pressure pervades the Giving Pledge as much as Carnegie's *Gospel of Wealth*. The fact that most of the pledges address causes that have long been identified as the typical recipients of philanthropy—health, education, arts and culture, and human services—points further towards the socially constructed nature of philanthropic goals.[33] Until 2005, the Bill & Melinda Gates Foundation matched this profile, mainly investing in health and education.

On the other hand, several scholars have argued that the contemporary ultra-wealthy, especially those that are "self-made," take an entrepreneurial approach to philanthropy that marks a departure from prior charitable giving as a more passive exercise of moral duty (Adloff 2010: 337–48, Harvey et al. 2011, Taylor et al. 2014, West 2014: 73–91). Variants of this new approach have been called "social entrepreneurship" (Bornstein 2004), "venture philanthropy" (Moody

---

[32] See https://givingpledge.org/About.aspx. Since then, the official website of the Giving Pledge has modified its phrasing, addressing itself not only to Americans, but to "the world's wealthiest individuals and families." Initial attempts by Buffett and Gates to persuade billionaires in China and India to join or emulate the initiative yielded hardly any results, but in 2019 there were forty-six Giving Pledge participants residing outside the United States (See "Buffett and Gates Prod India's Wealthy to Be More Philanthropic," *The New York Times*, March 24, 2011: http://www.nytimes.com/2011/03/25/business/global/25rupee.html and http://glasspockets.org/philanthropy-in-focus/eye-on-the-giving-pledge/a-closer-look) (all accessed July 7, 2019).

[33] See http://glasspockets.org/philanthropy-in-focus/eye-on-the-giving-pledge/a-closer-look for an analysis of the causes supported by billionaires that have joined the "Giving Pledge." For a broader analysis of the causes that receive the most attention by philanthropists, see Lloyd & Breeze 2013: 107–16, Goss 2016 as well as the annual reports on philanthropy in the U.S. published by http://givingusa.org/ (all accessed July 7, 2019).

2008), "philanthrocapitalism" (Bishop & Green 2008), or "hyperagency" (Schervish 2003). Some national survey- and interview-based evidence, mostly among multi-millionaires, seems to confirm the growing prevalence of this strategic outlook (Schervish 2014b, Lloyd & Breeze 2013). A quantitative content analysis of the 122 pledges of the billionaires that had joined the Giving Pledge by 2013 found that by far the largest motivation is "impact": "billionaires talk mostly about what kind of changes they want to achieve" (Sadeh et al. 2014: 11).[34] Bill Gates and George Soros fit into this picture perfectly. Both first achieved market-leader positions with their companies: Gates with founding Microsoft (Wallace & Erickson 1993), Soros with founding the Quantum fund, for many years the most profitable hedge fund (Kaufman 2002: 134–46). And both transferred their material and entrepreneurial capacities into their philanthropy, which is global and results-oriented like their businesses. From this perspective, Bill Gates's decisions to give most of his wealth to philanthropy, to shift his entrepreneurship from Microsoft to his foundation, and to initiate the Giving Pledge, can be seen as deliberate attempts to transform the meaning and practice of philanthropy, thus providing a new role model for his fellow billionaires.[35]

The Gates Foundation has also been at the forefront of another transformation that makes philanthropy highly relevant for world politics: the increase in international philanthropy, which has happened in parallel with the rise of globalization (Curti 1963, Lloyd & Breeze 2013: 33). In 1987, international philanthropy represented only 1.8 percent of American charitable giving; in 2012, it made up 6.4 percent (Giving USA 2013), and has stayed around this level since.[36] According to the Gates Foundation's annual reports, right from the beginning, in 1999, near to half of its US$2.4 billion in grants expenditure concerned "Global Health" (Bill & Melinda Gates Foundation 2000: 15); in 2017, 86.2 percent of its US$4.7 billion in grants went to international projects ("Global Development": 37.6 percent, "Global Health": 26.8 percent, "Global Growth & Opportunity": 13.7

---

[34] Motivations that indicate a more habitual quest for esteem, coded as "Legacy," "Received Example," and "Values," also figured prominently among the pledgers, but altogether only about half as strongly as "Impact" (Sadeh et al. 2014: 12; for similar findings, see Lloyd & Breeze 2013: 76ff).

[35] This is precisely how Margaret Archer understands the interplay between personal and social identity for individuals: "In living out the initial role(s), which they have found good reason to occupy, they bring to it or them their singular manner of personifying it or them and this, in turn, has consequences over time. What it does creatively, is to introduce a continuous stream of unscripted role performances, which also over time can cumulatively transform the role expectations. These creative acts are thus transformative of society's very normativity, which is often most clearly spelt out in the norms attaching to specific roles." (2000: 296)

[36] For 2017, see https://givingusa.org/see-the-numbers-giving-usa-2017-infographic/ (accessed July 2, 2019), which reports that 6 percent of all U.S. philanthropy went to "international affairs." These figures may underestimate the extent of international philanthropy—whereas Giving USA estimates a rise from around US$3 billion in 1987 to US$19 billion in 2012, the Hudson Institute comes up with US$12 billion in 1988 and US$39 billion in 2011 (Hudson Institute 2006, 2010, 2013). However, the Hudson Institute's calculation includes corporate giving, the financial value of volunteer time, and U.S. universities and colleges' scholarship grants to students from developing countries studying in the U.S.

percent, "Global Policy & Advocacy": 8.1 percent).[37] While most of their co-citizens continue to practice philanthropy at the national level, Bill and Melinda Gates, following in the footsteps of John D. Rockefeller (Birn 2014), have become global players that affect public policies both at the level of the UN and, trans-nationally, in many developing countries. George Soros had moved into world politics at least twenty years before Bill Gates, at a time when no role model of the "stateless statesman" existed. His overarching cause—building open societies—also does not fit well into the customary boxes of philanthropic causes. And he deliberately does not want to join the Giving Pledge, just as he has long been very skeptical of institutionalized philanthropy (Kaufman 2002: 163–9; Soros 2011: 39ff). Both billionaire philanthropists have already been nominated numerous times for the Nobel Peace Prize, but whereas Gates appears to be driven more by public esteem, Soros's philanthropy seems to be determined by more idiosyncratic definitions of self-esteem. With regard to the pursuit of public esteem, we can expect *billionaires to be more likely to engage in transnational philanthropy if they belong to a social community in which international philanthropy is being honored.* If billionaires' philanthropy is mostly about self-esteem, we can hypothesize, in a similar vein as for security, that *they will be more likely to pursue international philanthropy if they have developed a self-identity that values transnational solidarity.*[38]

Power: Individual Freedom and Its Limits

Wealth, as Mr. Hobbes says, is power. But the person who either acquires, or succeeds to a great fortune, does not necessarily acquire or succeed to any political power, either civil or military. His fortune may, perhaps, afford him the means of acquiring both, but the mere possession of that fortune does not necessarily convey to him either. The power which that possession immediately and directly conveys to him, is the power of purchasing.
(Adam Smith, *The Wealth of Nations*, Book 1, "On the Real and Nominal Price of Commodities, or their Price in Labour, and their Price in Money")

The above observation by Adam Smith captures the essence of the question regarding the political power of billionaires. Wealth is merely a vehicle that

---

[37] For 2015, see online: https://www.gatesfoundation.org/Who-We-Are/Resources-and-Media/Annual-Reports/Annual-Report-2017 (accessed July 5, 2019).

[38] If one extends the concept of security to "human security" (UNDP 1994, Paris 2001), the boundary between security concerns and philanthropy becomes blurry. In theory, a distinction can be made between goals that derive from a person's sense of belonging (sociopolitical identity) and those that derive from a person's achievements (self-esteem). In practice, motivations and goals are often mixed, and the person that tries to help others because she sees herself as belonging to them may simultaneously boost her self-esteem.

provides, first and foremost, the capacity to purchase whatever is available for purchasing. The German sociologist Hans Jürgen Krysmanski seems to think that almost anything can be bought. He has advanced a rather crude Marxist interpretation of "the empire of billionaires," in which the super-rich form the inner circle of power, because of their "money-power," and all the other elites, including the political elite, only serve as instruments of the super-rich (Krysmanski 2012: 36–41, 62–9).[39] Anna Porter's journalistic appraisal of George Soros's accomplishments comes to the opposite conclusion: "So, after spending more than $12 billion over thirty years to make the world a better place, what is Soros's legacy? Despite his gargantuan efforts, 'open society' or liberal democracy is in worldwide decline" (Porter 2015: 201). Whereas Krysmanski simply equates wealth with power, Porter sees one of the biggest transnational paymasters as ultimately powerless, because he has not accomplished his overarching goal. A more careful assessment of billionaires' power in world politics needs to take the relational character of the exercise of power seriously, which requires that it be considered case by case. Whether wealth can be turned into power depends (to specify Adam Smith's "may, perhaps") both on billionaires' political agency and on the relevant political context.

As the preceding two sections have argued, billionaires' agency in world politics is about individual capacities, choices, and judgments regarding commitments and goals, but also about billionaires' sociopolitical identities and the cultural contexts in which they live. All billionaires possess enormous material resources, yet not every billionaire turns into a transnational political actor. Other things being equal, they are more likely to do so if they have developed capacities, in terms of self-efficacy beliefs and experience, as international business entrepreneurs, if their identities comprise transnational ties of belonging and solidarity, and if transnational engagement is being encouraged, or at least valued, within the society of their country of residence. As transnational political actors, their exercise of power then depends on who or what they are trying to affect. Power, as discussed earlier, refers to the capacity of an actor to carry out one's will vis-à-vis others; its exercise is therefore necessarily relational, and the study of it needs to take the "other" into account (Dahl 1957, Foucault 1982: 752ff). For the purposes of my investigation, this other is, first and foremost, a state, not necessarily because billionaires want to use their power against it, but because states set the boundaries of what is allowed to happen across their borders. If billionaires

---

[39] However, his analysis contains several contradictory statements: when Krysmanski talks about "global command" at the level of world politics, it is the U.S. and the G8—powerful nation-states—that matter most (2012: 89), and when he criticizes the Giving Pledge, he notes that the US$600 billion initially pledged amounted only to two years of U.S. official development assistance (ibid.: 135). He is also unable to differentiate between highly impersonal multinational corporations owned by a variety of stockholders, and billionaires, which, for the most part, became rich as owners of private enterprises (ibid.: 77, 100ff, 212–21).

target other actors abroad in their transnational endeavors, for example political parties, social movements, rebel groups, or a subnational government, states will normally be involved.

In the modern world, nation-states are the holders of sovereign power, and individuals are tied to them via citizenship; international politics denotes relations between states and the international institutions they create, and a key question of the "transnational politics" paradigm concerns the extent to which nonstate actors gain political power vis-à-vis states (Keohane & Nye 1972, Mathews 1997, Risse 2013). Such a power shift need not be a conflictual zero-sum game. In fact, with regard to billionaires as transnational actors, we should expect it to happen often in a cooperative manner: billionaires have financial resources to offer, and states may grant them access to public policymaking in exchange.[40] Under conditions of neoliberal globalization, where states compete for capital and the privatization of public services is seen as beneficial, opportunities for such deals multiply. The global context, as presented in chapter 3, has become favorable for transnational billionaires. A significant example is the spreading practice of "citizenship for sale." More and more states have established legal avenues for foreigners to acquire residency permits and/or citizenship in return for an investment or a payment. For many rich people, diversifying their passport portfolio is primarily a matter of mobility, as "golden" (Portugal) or even "platinum" (Australia) visas expand their range of hassle-free travel, for example within Europe's Schengen area.[41] That the branding of some of these visa arrangements is identical to the products of a major credit card company is no accident. It represents the commodification of the relationship between the members of a political community and their collective organization. Something you used to be born with, in the world of nation-states, is turning into something that can be purchased (Shachar 2009, 2014). This increases the opportunities to turn wealth into power, since, apart from mobility rights, citizenship is also regulating political access to government. In all states, citizens are privileged over foreigners when it comes to participating in public policymaking.[42] As a naturalized U.S. citizen, George Soros

---

[40] To be sure, there may also be offers that are very hard to refuse, such as the meal offered to a starving man or the credit offered to a bankrupt state, which blur the analytic distinction between coercion and cooperation, but this needs to be evaluated case by case.

[41] Provisions vary in whether they require specific investments, for example in employment-generating businesses, real estate or government bonds, or one-off payments. Most states offer temporary residency permits at first, which transform into permanent resident and/or citizen status after a few (often five) years. The size of the required investment/payment varies, too, with smaller states like Dominica or Latvia requiring less than US$250,000, and larger states like Australia or France requiring several million. In Europe, notably in Portugal, Malta, and Cyprus, states offered "citizenship for sale" in response to the financial and sovereign debt crises post-2008. See Shachar & Bauböck 2014, Sumption & Hooper 2014, Transparency International & Global Witness 2018, European Commission 2019.

[42] The "Migrant Integration Policy Index" surveys the political participation rights of migrants: http://www.mipex.eu/political-participation (accessed July 3, 2019). See also Migration Policy Group 2013 and Falguera et al. 2014.

can vote in U.S. elections; more importantly (for a billionaire), post–Citizens United,[43] he can also spend unlimited amounts of his money on super-PACs during U.S. election campaigns (Vogel 2014, West 2014: 33–72). Non-U.S. citizens face many more restrictions, even though there are a few legal ways for them to influence U.S. elections. Not only are they barred from voting and running for office, they are also forbidden from financing campaigns and severely curbed in their rights to engage in lobbying and to own media outlets (Teachout 2009, Freeman 2012).[44]

Outside the U.S., as a foreigner, Soros is much more limited as an individual non-citizen, but also when he is working through his foundations. "[States] enact and enforce the rules under which NGOs emerge, operate, use resources, and survive; govern NGOs' physical access to territories and populations; and grant NGOs permission to operate in specific issue areas" (Dupuy et al. 2015: 422). The ups and downs of Soros's engagements in Russia illustrate the range of opportunities: from 1987 until 2000, during the unstable transformation years under Gorbachev and Yeltsin, Soros and his foundations could work relatively unrestrained; under Putin, their operations were first restricted and finally outlawed (Lanskoy & Suthers 2013, Porter 2015: 107–16, Daucé 2015). Such increases in state control over civil society organizations, and foreign ones in particular, have happened in many other countries, too (Figure 4.1).

This trend can be seen as a reaction to the rise of NGOs as transnational actors since the 1990s. It is more prevalent in autocracies than in democracies (Dupuy et al. 2015: 422), and, among democracies, states with pluralist forms of interest representation appear to be more permissive than those with corporatist traditions (Bloodgood et al. 2014). Further generalizations along those lines have been attempted within thinking about political opportunity structures, as it has been developed by the study of social movements and contentious politics (Eisinger 1973, Kitschelt 1986, McAdam 1996).[45] However, leading scholars in this research tradition have themselves argued that while political opportunity structures

---

[43] See chapter 1, fn6.

[44] "Prohibitions against foreign office holding, and foreign gifts to public officers, are found in the Constitution. Direct contributions by foreigners to elections are now prohibited by the Federal Election Commission ('FEC'), and have been federally prohibited for the past half century. Foreign ownership of media is prohibited by the Federal Communications Commission ('FCC'), and foreign lobbying is regulated by the Foreign Agents Registration Act ('FARA')" (Teachout 2009: 6). Rupert Murdoch, for example, had to give up his Australian citizenship and become a naturalized U.S. citizen in 1985 before he could build his Fox network (Wolff 2010: 189).

[45] One of the classic definitions sees political opportunity structures as "consistent—but not necessarily formal or permanent—dimensions of the political environment that provide incentives for people to undertake collective action by affecting their expectations for success or failure" (Tarrow 1994:85). Of course, the value of the insights to be gained from these research agendas is limited by the fact that they concern the conditions that facilitate collective action—the formation, organization, and mobilization of individuals as a collective actor, whereas our focus on billionaires is about individual political agency. Still, the features of political opportunity structures selected here do appear relevant for both collective and individual action.

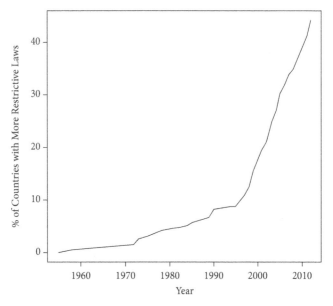

Figure 4.1 Percentage of countries that have passed more restrictive NGO laws worldwide (cumulative), 1955–2012

"Between 1955 and 1994, 17 out of 195 countries passed more restrictive laws regarding the operations of foreign NGOs and foreign funding flows. Between 1995 and 2012, 69 additional countries worldwide did so. Currently, 44% of countries (86 of 195) worldwide have adopted legislation that specifically restricts foreign NGOs and/or foreign funding flows."

Source: Dupuy et al. 2015: 423. Taylor & Francis Ltd., https://www.tandfonline.com/toc/rrip20/current.

clearly matter, it is more promising to move "away from the search for general models . . . and toward the analysis of smaller-scale causal mechanisms" (Tarrow & Tilly 2007: 445f). This reflects an awareness that political action is often more dynamic and diverse than what can be captured by concentrating solely on political opportunity structures (McAdam et al. 2001, Tilly & Tarrow 2006). In other words, for the study of power relations, the interplay between structure and agency requires more case-specific analysis.

Promising attempts to conceptualize political action integrate structural (institutional) features, actor-specific features (such as skills and resources), and strategic interaction. Giddens's "strategic conduct analysis" and Bourdieu's "field analysis" are prominent examples (Giddens 1979: 80ff, 1984: 288ff, Stones 1991, Bourdieu & Wacquant 1992: 94–114); more recently, Neil Fligstein and Doug McAdam have presented their theory of "strategic action fields" (Fligstein 2001, Fligstein and McAdam 2011 and 2012).[46] All field theories are based on

---

[46] The earlier social movement literature had also focused on the distribution of other political actors, in terms of their heterogeneity and their power, within a state, and on the dynamic features of a political regime, whether it is prone to change, stable, or unstable (Tilly & Tarrow 2006: 57);

assumptions about spheres of action that have their own rules and logics (Bourdieu's *doxa*), and in which actors know, more or less, those rules and their position within a specific field (Bourdieu & Wacquant 1992: 97–100, Martin 2003: 28–45, Fligstein & McAdam 2012: 181). This assumption about actors' acquaintance with the rules of the game may need relaxation for billionaires in world politics. Since, in politics, many strategic action fields remain chiefly organized along national lines, billionaires as transnational actors will usually be external actors in a two-fold sense: they come from abroad, and from a different field (business). Hence, both the billionaires in question and the actors with which they engage in power relations will, at least initially, find themselves in situations that are out of the ordinary and that will therefore require improvisation, trial and error, and innovation. Fligstein and McAdam recognize this potential of external actors to be disruptive:

> Outside challengers often make the most effective adversaries because they are not bound by the conventions of the strategic action field and instead are free to bring new definitions of the situation and new forms of action to the field. Their ability to be successful in this effort will depend on a number of factors: the strength of the field incumbents, the defection of challengers to the side of the invader, and, in the modern period, the attitude of relevant state actors toward the invading group.   (2012: 99f)

Further specifications must take the characteristics of the respective field into account. It seems likely, for example, that state actors guard their autonomy the most in the security field.[47] In the following case studies of billionaires in world politics, it will therefore be important to identify the political field in which they attempt to intervene, vis-à-vis those actors with whom they try to exercise power, and which posture the relevant state actors and institutions are taking. And, of course, we will need to analyze whether and how billionaires' resources can be used to pursue their goals: what wealth can purchase (or not). This is not simply a

---

conceptually, however, this is misleading, since such features emerge out of the interplay between agents and structures (as Tilly and Tarrow notice themselves)—they are, strictly speaking, not a part of the properties of political opportunity structures.

Margaret Archer's theory is not so much concerned with power, but her conceptualization of collective ("corporate," in her terminology) agency (2000: 265–82) has a lot in common with Fligstein and McAdam's view of strategic interaction within fields. However, Archer remains at the very macro level of differentiating epochs of morphostasis and morphogenesis; she does not specify fields within epochs.

[47] This has also been found in the study of the openness of international organizations (IOs) vis-à-vis nonstate actors: "IOs are consistently most open in the area of human rights, in the policy function of monitoring and enforcement, and in the western hemisphere, while least open in security, decision-making, and the southern hemisphere" (Tallberg et al. 2013: 3).

financial question, but also one of transferable skills, precisely because it is geared towards the transformation of financial resources into political power.[48]

How to choose individual cases from the *Forbes* list? My final selection of cases is based on three criteria. The first is theory-driven: I wanted to have cases for the three different goals that I have identified as pertinent (security, wealth, and esteem). The second is pragmatic: I wanted to study cases for which sufficient information was publicly available, which is the main reason why my selection is biased towards U.S. billionaires. The third is relevance: I wanted to choose billionaires that held the promise of making a difference in world politics. Several billionaires that had been mentioned in non-academic books or news articles (Frank 2007, Rothkopf 2008, Armstrong 2010, Mount 2012), turned out, upon closer inspection, to be only minor players on the global stage, e.g. Marc Rich (Ammann 2009) or Chuck Feeney (O'Clery 2007). Some of these will be addressed briefly here and there as examples, but they did not merit to be treated as cases. As elaborated in chapter 2, the study of IR appears to adhere to a hypothesis that claims: "in world politics, only collective actors matter." My selection of potentially powerful billionaires is, then, not a selection bias (Geddes 1990), but an attempt to question one of the underlying assumptions of IR.[49] This does not imply that my ultimate findings were preordained. In all of my case studies, I have tried to engage in process-tracing, "to trace the links between possible causes and observed outcomes" (George & Bennett 2005: 6), leaving it open to investigation whether the actions of the billionaire constitute individual power in world politics or not. In fact, the billionaire in my second case study, Raj Rajaratnam, despite having been the subject of bold and accusatory headlines, comes out as an individual with very limited political agency. The assessment of the billionaires' power in my other case studies is also rarely clear-cut.

[48] Here, it helps to recall Morriss's understanding of power as a dispositional concept wherein "ableness" designates the concrete capacity given specific circumstances (Morriss 1987: 80–97). Building upon the literature on transnational social movements, Fligstein and McAdam emphasize the need for "social skills" within strategic action fields (2012: 34–56, 178–83). This seems appropriate for collective actors whose very power derives primarily from the capacity to mobilize and coordinate many individuals. For billionaires, this may be less crucial if their resources (money) can be used as incentives for coordination and cooperation.

[49] Since my cases are not "crucial cases" in the established methodological sense of most/least likely cases, even if my cases show that "billionaires matter," they cannot be seen as disconfirming the "only collective actors matter in world politics" hypothesis in a definitive sense. Social theory, including IR on this specific question, is usually making probabilistic statements, which cannot be disconfirmed by a few case studies unless these are crucial cases (Eckstein 1975, Gerring 2007: 237f).

5

Security

Security is the goal that is at the center of the study of IR in modern times (Morgenthau 1947, Waltz 1959). "[S]ecurity, in an objective sense, measures the absence of threats to acquired values, in a subjective sense, the absence of fear that such values will be attacked" (Wolfers 1952: 485). Of course, what exactly counts as a value that needs "security" is already contested, and constructivist scholarship has put great efforts into understanding the social construction, the "securitization," of both "security" and perceived threats to it (Wendt 1992, McSweeney 1999, Wæver 2011). Most scholars agree that, in IR, security refers to survival and existential threats to it (Buzan et al. 1998: 21, Huysmans 1998: 234, Ciutǎ 2009). Usually, international security is about the survival of states vis-à-vis potential aggressors, either internally (civil war) or externally (interstate war); nonstate actors play a role in this in the form of transnational violence, e.g. in cases of terrorism, piracy, mercenaries, or cross-border insurgency (Singer 2007, Abrahamsen & Williams 2010). Without denying the importance of broader concepts of security and securitization, e.g. "human security," which involves environmental and health threats (UNDP 1994, Paris 2001), I will mainly look at how billionaires engage with the security of states, in order to keep my analysis closer to the mainstream concerns of IR.

In theory, security should be expected to be the policy area in which billionaires are least likely to make a difference, since it is often considered to be the *domaine réservé* of states (Morgenthau 1951). And indeed, international security is where Andrew Carnegie encountered the limits of his political agency. Carnegie was probably the modern billionaire who controlled the most financial capital (equivalent to 2 percent of U.S. GDP in 1901),[1] and also the most social capital, but after selling his Carnegie Steel Company in 1901, he set his goal in a field that was hard to conquer.

> [H]is last years were consumed with...world peace....[H]e campaigned for naval disarmament, then an international court, a league of peace, and treaties of arbitration between the nations of Europe and the United States....As the European nations, followed closely by the United States, entered into an escalating naval arms race, he inserted himself into the diplomatic mix as an insider

[1] Jacob Davidson, "The 10 Richest People of All Time," *Money*, July 30, 2015, online: http://time.com/money/3977798/the-10-richest-people-of-all-time/ (accessed July 7, 2019).

with access to the White House and Westminster. He would spend the rest of his days as an outspoken "apostle of peace," commuting back and forth between his homes in New York and Scotland, and the world's capitals. Only at age eighty, in the second year of the Great War, did he recognize that his efforts had been in vain. He spent his last years in silence, ... his optimism shattered.

(Nasaw 2006: xv, also 641–775, esp. 724–56)

In Carnegie's case, the heads of states at the time were not willing to let the billionaire spoil their pursuits of national security, no matter how doomed these appear in hindsight.

Among contemporary billionaires, there are several cases that have made news media headlines but, like Carnegie, did not pass my "relevance" selection criteria in order to be considered for an in-depth case study on international security. Ted Turner, the founder of the global news channel *CNN* and a self-declared fan of the UN, embarrassed by the billion dollar debt the U.S. owed to the UN in membership dues, had the idea to pay the arrears with his own money. He then found out that international law did not allow individuals to purchase a government's debt, nor to make direct contributions to the UN. So, instead, he spent almost US $1 billion to create the United Nations Foundation,[2] which supports UN programs in different areas, many of which relate to "human security" (Turner & Burke 2008: 345ff). However, a direct impact on international security is hard to discern. In his memoirs of *A Life in War and Peace* (2013), Kofi Annan, the UN General Secretary at the time when Turner made his gift, did not mention the billionaire.

Unlike Turner, who remembers vividly the "incredible amount of pride" that the "ovations" gave him when he publicly announced his gift to the UN,[3] Chuck Cheeney is remarkable for having given away most of his wealth (over a billion US$) without any public notice. An Irish American who had made his fortune with building the global retailer Duty Free Shoppers, Feeney gave money to boost the peace process in Northern Ireland during the 1990s. He was part of a small group of Irish Americans that tried to convince Gerry Adams, the leader of Sinn Féin, the political arm of the Irish Republican Army (IRA), to call a ceasefire and start peace negotiations, intermediated by the U.S. under its new President Bill Clinton. During the peace negotiations, Feeney spent around US$720,000 on

---

[2] See online in the Internet Archive: https://web.archive.org/web/20110104224723/http://www. unfoundation.org/press-center/press-releases/2006/ret-new-committment-another-1-billion.html (accessed July 2, 2019).

[3] Turner & Burke 2008: 347f. Since public recognition has been so important for Turner, his UN gift seems to fit better into my philanthropy/esteem type of political agency; in this category, though, the billionaires that I have selected, George Soros and Bill Gates, are more relevant than Turner. Even according to his own account, Turner does not appear to take a very active role in the foundation, delegating most of the initiatives to the foundation's executives (ibid.: 349f). He is, however, chairman of the foundation's board, which also included Kofi Annan, see online: https://unfoundation.org/who-we-are/our-board/ (accessed July 2, 2019).

providing Sinn Féin with representative offices in Washington, D.C. When the peace process became a reality, Feeney funded various projects aimed at reconstruction and reconciliation in Northern Ireland, spending US$30 million (O'Clery 2007: 184–94). Although Gerry Adams mentions Chuck Cheeney very warmly, briefly, in his memoirs (2003: 156f), both the billionaire's and the politician's accounts indicate that Feeney's role in the peace negotiations was largely that of a supportive, yet passive financial backer.

While Turner's and Cheeney's impacts on international security seem limited, both confirm my assumption that billionaires' transnational political activism tend to be linked to a global outlook in business. This also characterizes the two billionaires that I will now investigate further: Sheldon Adelson receives most of his income from his company's casinos in Macao and Singapore, and Raj Rajaratnam made his money as a hedge fund manager in global finance. Unlike Carnegie and Turner, who can be seen as embracing cosmopolitan "world peace" identities, Rajaratnam's and Adelson's transnational security concerns have been motivated by ethnonationalist allegiances. In both cases, the security goals go beyond the bolstering of "their" group's identity claims and involve very concrete matters of territory and survival.

Electioneering Security: Sheldon Adelson and Israel–Palestine

Sheldon Adelson (*1933) is best known for his financial largesse in supporting Republican candidates in U.S. elections (Vogel 2014: 77–98, Zengerle 2015), but he is equally, if not more politically involved in Israel, mainly via financing a free daily newspaper, *Israel Hayom* ("Israel Today"), which many observers see as a pro-Netanyahu propaganda vehicle. In fact, both sides of his political engagement form a coherent whole, situated within the field of Jewish diaspora politics, in which Adelson, as the once self-declared "richest Jew in the world,"[4] aims to play a decisive role. While he has largely been silent about his tactics and strategies, which have to be deduced from his actions,[5] Adelson has expressed his primary goal rather bluntly. Interviewed by his own newspaper in 2014, responding to the question of "[h]ow much of [your] money are you willing to put for the protection of the people of Israel, the Jews and Israel?," Adelson replied:

Whatever it takes. I don't do anything half way. I am not a politician. I am a man of values. You cannot believe in values and make compromises on everything in

---

[4] In the terms of the *Forbes* estimates, this statement was only true in 2007. In most of the other years of the twenty-first century, *Oracle*-founder Larry Ellison has captured this title.

[5] Adelson himself has stated that "when it comes to political issues, or my personal issues, or my philanthropic issues, ... I never talk about what I'm going to do to anybody. All I just do is do." (Vogel 2014: 80)

order to be political. . . . [A]ll my life I have been a very strong believer in my own convictions. And I never want to give them up because somebody makes a demand. I am not a half Zionist. I am a full Zionist.[6]

In taking this stance, Adelson positions himself in what is one of the most critical issues of international security, the enduring conflict between Israel and the Palestinians. At its heart lie competing nationalist claims over territory and its political control, as well as the question of Palestinian refugees (and their off-spring), which fled their homes in the wake of the fighting that led to the establishment of the Israeli state in 1948. For the Palestinian side, the conflict is primarily about self-determination and justice, whereas for the Israeli side, security is the overriding concern. Proposals for how to find a settlement that could reconcile both sides differ widely, but the objective to have separate states for Israel and the Palestinians, the so-called "two-state solution," has been the focal point of peace negotiations, from Oslo in 1993 to the 2013–14 talks. The main sticking points have been where the borders between Israel and Palestine would run, whether Jerusalem would be a divided capital, what would happen to Jewish settlers in the occupied territories, and whether Palestinian refugees would have a "right of return" (Smith 2013, Gelvin 2014). Among the Israeli side, highly divergent perspectives exist as to what it means to be a Zionist and to protect the security and the survival of the Israeli state. While variants of the idea of one common state for the Palestinians and the Jewish people emerge from time to time, both as anti-Zionist (Hussein 2015) and as very robust Zionist projects (Glick 2014), the principal distinctions within Israel's contemporary political landscape, as summarized by Toby Greene, reflect three positions. On the center-left, one finds "proactive two-statism," which seeks peace either via nego-tiations or (further to the left) unilateral concessions to the Palestinian side. On the center-right, the "preservation of the status quo" takes priority over an increasingly nominal commitment to the two-state solution. Further towards the right, often based on religious-nationalist sentiments, politicians seek "entrenchment–annexationism," aimed at expanding Israel and the territory it controls, mainly via settlements and their protection by the state (Greene 2015). Attitudes are similarly divided when it comes to Israel's relations with its neigh-bors, where the possibility of Iran becoming a nuclear power is seen as the most urgent and serious threat. Regarding how to deal with Iran, politicians more on the right, for example Prime Minister Benjamin Netanyahu, have advocated

---

[6] Boaz Bismuth & Amos Regev, " 'We have come to put an end to Noni Mozes' dictatorship'," *Israel Hayom*, 9 May 2014, online: https://web.archive.org/web/20180702000429/http://www.israelhayom.com/2014/05/09/we-have-come-to-put-an-end-to-noni-mozes-dictatorship/ (accessed June 19, 2019).

preventive military action (if necessary unilaterally), while politicians further to the left, notably former President Shimon Peres, have opposed such moves.[7]

In interviews, publications, and speeches, Sheldon Adelson has made it clear where he stands on Israel's security. In an op-ed published in 2012, in which he harshly criticized Obama's foreign policy vis-à-vis Israel, he explained the reasons for his preoccupation with Israel's security:

> Not since 1967 has Israel's safety been more precarious. Iran is now racing for a nuclear bomb while bragging they only need "24 hours and an excuse" to destroy the Jewish state. Egypt is lost to the Muslim Brotherhood. Hezbollah is armed to the teeth in Lebanon. Turkey's government is more foe than friend. The Gulf States use enormous petroleum wealth to fund global anti-Israel propaganda. The "Arab Spring" continues to usher extremists into power. And Hamas rules Gaza.[8]

More specifically, Adelson is opposed to a two-state solution, both in principle, because he doubts the legitimacy of Palestinian nationalism, and for security reasons. At a conference panel at New York's Yeshiva University, in 2013, he claimed that "[t]here's no such thing as a Palestinian. Do you know what they are? They call themselves southern Syrians.... To go and allow a Palestinian state is to play Russian roulette."[9] He confirmed his impression a year later at a panel of the Israeli-American Council: "The purpose of the existence of Palestinians is to destroy Israel."[10] Moreover, Adelson is financing the hardline Zionist Organization of America, which maintains a strong stance against limitations of Jewish settlements on the West Bank. In 2014, he pledged to give US$25 million to Ariel University, which is located beyond the Green Line in the West Bank Israeli settlement of Ariel, saying that "[t]he donation to Ariel University is about building a Zionist wall in place of the crack. I hope that the city of Ariel, the capital of Samaria, will grow and flourish in wake of the university's expansion."[11]

---

[7] The political divisions regarding Iran have been more complicated, as Netanyahu's then Defence Minister Ehud Barak, a former Labor Party leader, who had left his party in 2011, supported Netanyahu's line in 2012; major opponents of a unilateral military strike came from the security and intelligence apparatuses, most prominently the former head of the Mossad, Meir Dagan, who has no clear political affiliation. See Ben Meir 2013 and Lupovici 2016.

[8] Sheldon Adelson, "Don't risk Israel's security on Obama's words," *JNS.org*, October 11, 2012, online: http://www.jns.org/latest-articles/2012/10/11/dont-risk-israels-security-on-obamas-words.html#.ViZcy34rK70 (accessed June 19, 2019).

[9] Josh Nathan-Kazis, "Sheldon Adelson Wants Nuclear Strike on Iran–Says Two-States 'Russian Roulette'," *The Forward*, October 23, 2013, online: http://forward.com/news/186079/sheldon-adelson-wants-nuclear-strike-on-iran-say/ (accessed June 19, 2019).

[10] "Sheldon Adelson: Palestinians Are Made-up Nation That Exists Only to Destroy Israel," *Haaretz*, November 9, 2014, online: http://www.haaretz.com/jewish-world/jewish-world-news/1.625542 (accessed June 19, 2019).

[11] See Chaim Levinson, "Sheldon Adelson to Give $25m to Ariel University," *Haaretz*, June 23, 2014, online: http://www.haaretz.com/israel-news/.premium-1.600746, and Josh Nathan-Kazis, "From

All of this aligns him with the "entrenchment–annexationism" position that is widespread among the radical right in Israel, whose growing influence has been thoroughly expounded (Pedahzur 2012: 6f). Adelson's closeness to Israel's radical right also shows up in his attitude towards democracy, which he sees as expendable in the face of security concerns: "So Israel won't be a democratic state, so what?," he asked in 2014, "adding that democracy, after all, is not mentioned in the Torah."[12] Despite this reference to the Torah, there are no indicators that Adelson's political stance is primarily rooted in religious convictions. This differentiates him from many other people among Israel's far right, which often adhere to orthodox versions of Judaism (ibid.: 61–80). Various figures of speech—particularly Adelson's recurring use of the image of building a wall around Israel—suggest that he is instead inspired by Revisionist Zionism, the founding ideology of the secular right in Israel.[13] With regard to foreign policy, Adelson takes right-wing views, too. Thus, he proposed that an effective way to prevent Iran from developing nuclear weapons would be for the U.S. to threaten the country with a nuclear attack, by detonating a nuclear missile in the Iranian desert, and then warning that "the next one is in the middle of Teheran," unless Iran gives up its nuclear weapons program.[14]

The determination expressed in his political statements reflects Adelson's experience as a rags-to-riches entrepreneur who accumulated his wealth through a series of bold large-scale investment decisions (Bruck 2008, Vogel 2014: 77–98, Zengerle 2015). Born in 1933 in the U.S. as the son of a Lithuanian immigrant cabdriver, after several ups and downs in various business ventures, Adelson became wealthy by launching the computer trade show Comdex in Las Vegas in 1979. He then entered the billionaire league by building a series of so-called integrated resorts centered on gaming, starting with the opening of the Venetian in Las Vegas in 1999, then the world's largest casino, which has been surpassed by the Venetian in Macao in 2007; in 2010, the Marina Bay Sands in Singapore

---

the Right: ZOA Faithful Challenge Israelis on Freeze," *The Forward*, December 16, 2009, online: http://forward.com/news/121180/from-the-right-zoa-faithful-challenge-israelis-on/sthash.lyeu1mzY.dpuf. The "Dr. Miriam and Sheldon G. Adelson Medical School" at Ariel University was inaugurated in 2018, see https://www.ariel.ac.il/wp/med/en/ (accessed June 19, 2019).

[12] "Sheldon Adelson: Palestinians Are Made-up Nation That Exists Only to Destroy Israel," *Haaretz*, November 9, 2014, online: http://www.haaretz.com/jewish-world/jewish-world-news/1. 625542, Marc Fisher, "Sheldon Adelson: Casino magnate, mega-donor is a man of many motives," *The Washington Post*, October 23, 2012, online: https://www.washingtonpost.com/politics/dec ision2012/sheldon-adelson-casino-magnate-mega-donor-is-a-man-of-many-motives/2012/10/23/ 926d031e-0744-11e2-858a-5311df86ab04_story.html (both accessed June 19, 2019).

[13] One of the most famous pamphlets of Ze'ev Jabotinsky, the original ideologue of Revisionist Zionism, is called "The Iron Wall" (1923) and argues for Jewish colonization of Israel by force. See Rynhold & Waxman 2008 and Shlaim 2014.

[14] The statements have been captured on video, see https://www.youtube.com/watch?v= ScRRh6bCAiM (accessed June 19, 2019).

became the third pillar. These casinos—as well as several other resorts, three of them in Macao—are ultimately owned by the Las Vegas Sands Corporation (LVS), a publicly listed Fortune 500 company of which Sheldon Adelson is chairman of the board, treasurer, and CEO, as well as, if one includes his family and trusts, the majority stockholder.[15] An indicator of the sheer size of Adelson's projects is the fact that four of these resorts rank among the world's twenty-five largest buildings in terms of floor space.[16] Since 2010, extraordinary growth in Macau and Singapore has multiplied revenues and overall profits for LVS. In 2014, around 92 percent of the corporation's US$5.4 billion operating income (Adjusted Property EBITDA)[17] derived from its operations in Macao and Singapore, most of it from gaming; in 2018, Macao's and Singapore's share was 90 percent of US $5.3 billion (Las Vegas Sands Corporation 2015: 42–69, esp. 50, 2019: 126). This implies that Adelson can engage in U.S. and Israeli politics without having to worry much about whether his politics may negatively impact his business interests, since these are largely located in third countries. In 2019, *Forbes* listed Adelson as number 24 on its global ranking, with an estimated wealth of US$35.1 billion, largely based on his stockholdings in LVS. Most of this wealth is not liquid as long as Adelson wants to maintain a majority share in the corporation, but LVS has been practicing a generous dividends policy since 2012, providing the billion-aire and his wife with enormous financial liquidity, over US$7.7 billion, pre-tax, up until 2018 (Table 5.1).

One of the most in-depth portraits available cites Adelson asserting, in 2008, how "[i]n my sixty-three years in business, in over fifty different businesses, I've broken the mold and changed the status quo," and describes him as someone who "takes pride in being an outsider, who has suffered rejection and ridicule but has avenged every slight, many times over" (Bruck 2008). It appears as if Adelson's staggering mastery experiences in business have equipped him with an extraor-dinary sense of self-efficacy: "I have a belief to stand up for what you believe in, even if you have to stand alone." This also expresses itself in the suggestive detail that when he is reflecting, Adelson refers to himself as "Self—that's what I call myself" (Allen 2012). Since the early 1990s and the marriage to his second wife Miriam, who, unlike her husband, does hold Israeli citizenship, Adelson's agency

---

[15] "Mr. Adelson, his family members and trusts and other entities established for the benefit of Mr. Adelson and/or his family members (Mr. Adelson, individually our 'Principal Stockholder,' and the group, collectively our 'Principal Stockholder and his family') beneficially own approximately 56% of our outstanding common stock as of December 31, 2018. Accordingly, Mr. Adelson exercises signifi-cant influence over our business policies and affairs" (Las Vegas Sands Corporation 2019: 27).

[16] See online: https://en.wikipedia.org/wiki/List_of_largest_buildings_in_the_world#Largest_area (accessed May 4, 2019).

[17] Adjusted Property EBITDA is not a corporation's net income, but it measures the operating profitability of a company's different segments before non-operating expenses are being deducted. The total net income declared by LVS was US$1.9bn in 2012, US$3bn in 2013, US$3.6bn in 2014, US$2.4bn in 2015, US$2bn in 2016, US$3.3bn in 2017 and US$2.9bn in 2018 (Las Vegas Sands Corporation 2017: 45, 54, 2019: 46).

Table 5.1 Income from cash dividends for Sheldon & Miriam Adelson, 2012–18

Year	No. of common stock LVS shares held by Sheldon & Miriam Adelson	Cash dividends p.a. per common share declared by LVS (US$)	Total cash from LVS dividends for Sheldon & Miriam Adelson (US$)
2012	436,585,274	3.75	1,637,194,778
2013	433,351,888	1.40	606,692,643
2014	419,230,258	2.00	838,460,516
2015	407,542,132	2.60	1,059,609,543
2016	407,157,140	2.88	1,172,612,563
2017	405,912,099	2.92	1,185,263,329
2018	409,400,106	3.00	1,228,200,318
Total			7,728,033,690

Source: LVS Annual Reports and Proxy Statements, various years[18]

has been extending into the political realm. By then, he had switched his political allegiance from the Democrats to the Republicans, and, reportedly influenced by Miriam, developed a strong concern for Israel (Bruck 2008). But it was only after 2000 and the massive expansion of his fortune—he entered the *Forbes* list in 2001—that Adelson had the financial resources to become a major philanthropist and political operator. Just as he has ensured that his business would remain firmly under his control, people who have worked with him on U.S. politics affirm that "[w]ith Sheldon, there's no process, no system, no team, no bureaucracy, no nothing. It's just him and his wife . . . . Sheldon's the rare person who can afford to

[18] On the homepage of the *Las Vegas Sands Corporation*, the relevant information can be accessed under "Annual Reports" (https://investor.sands.com/financial-reports/Annual-Reports/default.aspx), "Dividend History" (https://investor.sands.com/financial-reports/Dividend-History/default.aspx); the share distributions are being reported annually in April within the "Proxy Statements" under "SEC filings" (https://investor.sands.com/financial-reports/SEC-Filings/default.aspx) (accessed June 6, 2019).
  Since 2009, Adelson has shifted large parts of his personal shareholdings to his wife Miriam, who is twelve years younger than him and, in 2019, owned 42.7 percent of the LVS shares, while Sheldon owned over 10.3 percent. Further 11.4 percent each are held by the "General Trust under the Sheldon G. Adelson 2007 Remainder Trust" and the "General Trust under the Sheldon G. Adelson 2007 Friends and Family Trust," which I have not included in my dividend calculations in Table 5.1. From 2008 to 2012, LVS only paid dividends to preferred stock (mostly owned by the Adelsons), less than US$100 million per year (Las Vegas Sands Corporation 2012: 46).
  In the U.S., qualified dividends are taxed as capital gains, the tax rate of which was 15 percent between 2008 and 2012, and 20 percent since 2013 (to which, since 2010, a 3.8 percent net investment income tax has to be added for high earners such as the Adelsons); on the other hand, if reinvested, the dividends will earn capital income afterwards. Various donations, such as the US$364 million that the Adelsons put into the Dr. Miriam and Sheldon G. Adelson Charitable Trust in 2012, are, moreover, tax deductible (see Ade Adeniji, "What Are Sheldon and Miriam Up To? Eight Things to Know About Adelson Philanthropy," *Inside Philanthropy*, May 29, 2014, online: http://www.insidephilanthropy.com/home/2014/5/29/what-are-sheldon-and-miriam-up-to-eight-things-to-know-about.html, accessed June 19, 2019).

make a $100 million mistake.... Anything about Sheldon is because he can"
(Zengerle 2015).[19]

One part of Adelson's political activities appears to serve his economic well-being: he has expressed strong views against progressive taxation, as well as against trade unions, which used to be powerful in the Las Vegas hotel and casino business until Adelson pushed hard to have his first resort, the Venetian, union-free (Bruck 2008). This aligns him with the Republican Party, which, during the past decades, has championed policies that reduce progressive taxation and limit the rights of trade unions (Hacker & Pierson 2010). His partisanship in supporting Republican candidates in their election campaigns therefore entails a substantial degree of material self-interest. At the same level lie Adelson's lobbying efforts against Internet gambling, which can be seen as attempts to protect his brick-and-mortar casinos. He has also been using his extensive contacts among Republican lawmakers in the U.S. in order to support his business interests abroad, notably when he was trying to win his first casino licenses in Macao and Japan.[20] While business interests thus play a vital role in Adelson's politics, his Zionist goals appear to take center stage, at least when it comes to his political engagements in the U.S. and in Israel. In fact,

Adelson's political network grew in part through the trips that he and his wife took to Israel with lawmakers through the American Israel Public Affairs Committee [AIPAC]. "I've accompanied 205 congressmen and senators to Israel," he recalled. "So, I spend a week with each one of 'em. So, you must know that I have a lot of friends".   (Allen 2012)

[19] Whether the Adelson couple is making decisions together, or whether Sheldon is taking the lead, is unclear, since they often appear to act jointly. Over the years, Sheldon has not only transferred most of his LVS shares to his wife, in 2018, she also became the publisher of Sheldon's newspaper, *Israel Hayom*. See Yonatan Kitain, "Miriam Adelson takes reins at Israel Hayom," *Globes*, May 17, 2018, online: https://en.globes.co.il/en/article-miriam-adelson-takes-reins-at-israel-hayom-1001236852 and Christina Binkley, "Meet Dr Miriam Adelson: the record-breaking Republican donor driving Trump's Israel policy," *The Guardian*, January 7, 2019, online: https://www.theguardian.com/us-news/2019/jan/07/meet-dr-miriam-adelson-the-record-breaking-republican-donor-driving-trumps-israel-policy (all accessed June 19, 2019).

[20] See Bruck 2008, Peter Wallsten and Tom Hamburger, "Sheldon Adelson, top 2012 donor, launching campaign against Internet gambling," *The Washington Post*, November 17, 2013, online: https://www.washingtonpost.com/politics/sheldon-adelson-top-2012-donor-launching-campaign-against-internet-gambling/2013/11/17/d70054f6-4e40-11e3-be6b-d3d28122e6d4_story.html, Nathan Vardi, "Sheldon Adelson Is Winning His War Against Online Gambling," *Forbes*, June 3, 2014, online: http://www.forbes.com/sites/nathanvardi/2014/06/03/sheldon-adelson-is-winning-his-war-against-online-gambling/, Dustin Volz, "GOP Presidential Hopefuls Introduce Sheldon Adelson-Backed Bill to Ban Online Gambling," *National Journal*, June 24, 2015, online: http://www.nationaljournal.com/s/25134/gop-presidential-hopefuls-introduce-sheldon-adelson-backed-bill-ban-online-gambling, and Rachel M. Cohen "Sheldon Adelson Got a Surprise Gift in the Middle of the Government Shutdown," *The Intercept*, February 8, 2019, online: https://theintercept.com/2019/02/08/sheldon-adelson-online-gambling/ (all accessed June 19, 2019), See Justin Elliott, "Trump's Patron-in-Chief," *ProPublica*, October 10, 2018, online: https://features.propublica.org/trump-inc-podcast/sheldon-adelson-casino-magnate-trump-macau-and-japan/ (accessed June 16, 2019).

With his participation in AIPAC, for which he has been the largest individual donor over many years, including US$10 million to finance its new office building, opened in 2008 in Washington, D.C. (Zengerle 2015), Adelson has been at the heart of Jewish diaspora politics. The Jewish diaspora forms one of the paradigmatic cases of an ethnonationalist diaspora that remains attached, despite and because of thousands of years in exile across the world, to its homeland—since 1948, the state of Israel (Sheffer 2003: 8ff, 36ff). This, of course, does not mean that all Jewish people see themselves as part of the Jewish diaspora, or as Zionists; their social identities are also shaped by their, often longstanding, integration into the countries where they are resident citizens (Cohen & Horenczyk 1999). Beyond the unifying factors of kinship and the collective memory of the Holocaust, Jewish people differ widely with regard to the languages they speak, whether they are religious or not, and what kind of attachment (if any) they maintain towards Israel. Within this complex scene, the relationship between Israel and American Jews is by far the most crucial one: first, because the U.S. and Israel host about the same number of people that define themselves as Jewish, with each country counting around 5.6 million, which together represented more than 80 percent of the Jewish population worldwide in 2010.[21] Second, as a global military superpower, U.S. foreign policy is highly relevant for Israel. And, third, because the Jewish diaspora in the U.S. is particularly affluent, on average (Pew Research Center 2013: 42), and at the top: in 2013, the Israeli edition of *Forbes* reported that among that year's 1,426 billionaires in the world, 167 or 12 percent were Jewish, seventeen of them Israeli, and 108 American citizens.[22] This combines with the tradition among American Jewry of giving generously to Jewish causes and Israel, which had been institutionalized in the United Jewish Appeal (since 1999: United Jewish Communities). The positions taken within the American Jewish diaspora therefore have the potential to greatly influence politics in Israel, either by shaping the foreign policy of the U.S., or via direct interventions in Israeli politics through the funding of specific causes, organizations, and politicians (Barnett 2016). With his money, Sheldon Adelson pursues distinctive tactics at each level—the American Jewish diaspora, U.S. foreign policy, and Israeli politics—in order to advance his overall strategic goal, the security of Israel and its Jewish people.

While support by the American Jewish diaspora for the homeland reaches as far back as the 1830s, the extent, cohesiveness and direction of it has varied substantially. Yossi Shain, who has pioneered the study of the roles of diasporas in IR, summarizes the evolution after the founding of the Israeli state as follows:

---

[21] "There are about 14 million Jews around the world.... This estimate is based on the number of people who self-identify as Jewish when asked about their religion on national censuses and large-scale surveys. However, the worldwide figure could be larger if a broader definition (such as having a Jewish grandparent) or smaller if a tighter definition (such as an unbroken line of matrilineal Jewish descent) were imposed." (Pew Research Center 2012: 42ff).

[22] See online: http://www.forbes.co.il/rating/list.aspx?en6v0tVq=FK (accessed June 19, 2019).

[T]he period between the late 1960s and the late 1980s can generally be seen as the Israelization phase of the Jewish-American diaspora, characterized by uncritical support of the state and the embrace of secular Zionism as a major feature of Jewish-American identity and culture.... However, as Israel's existence as a state appeared more secure, controversial topics, previously suppressed by the exigencies of survival, began to force themselves onto the national agenda..., especially after the signing of the 1993 Oslo accords.... Overall, the new divergence of public postures found expression in shifting patterns of diasporic monetary support of homeland causes, and hence in changing and less monolithic influences on components of homeland security.... Thus diasporic sponsors have exercised considerable leverage in promoting the implementation of their own values in Israeli society and in shaping aspects of national identity in a manner consistent with their worldview.   (Shain 2007: 56ff)[23]

The changing status of AIPAC within the American Jewish diaspora reflects the shifts outlined by Shain. Post-WWII, AIPAC has been the establishment pro-Israel Jewish diaspora organization in the U.S., which, especially since the 1980s, is wielding strong bipartisan influence in Congress, via an extremely well-organized nationwide network of activists, effective fundraising, and highly professional lobbying. Throughout its history, AIPAC has defended positions more or less in line with the Israeli government in power, although it has at times been closer to the policies of the center-right Likud Party when a center-left coalition governed (Mearsheimer & Walt 2007: 115ff, Sasson 2014: 26–8, Bruck 2014).

In the twenty-first century, however, AIPAC's leading role among American Jewry is being challenged. In 2008, the more liberal lobbying organization J Street has been founded, which explicitly aims to provide critical perspectives on U.S. and Israeli politics (Ben-Ami 2011, Shain & Rogachevsky 2014).[24] Around the same time, Sheldon Adelson broke with AIPAC, apparently because he was upset about the organization's endorsement of more U.S. economic aid for the Palestinian Authority, as well as its official support for a two-state solution to the Israel–Palestine conflict.[25] Instead, he increased his funding of Jewish diaspora organizations further to the right, such as the Zionist Organization of America, which received at least US$2.7 million between 2006 and 2015 from him, or One Jerusalem, which has advocated for a united Jerusalem within Israel.[26] Adelson has also become the main backer of the Israeli-American Council (IAC), which

---

[23] For similar assessments, see Waxman 2016 and Sasson 2014: 13–30.

[24] The mission statement of J Street declares support for a two-state solution, see: https://jstreet.org/about-us/mission-principles/ (accessed July 2, 2019).

[25] Ron Kampeas, "AIPAC stance irks donors," *JTA*, November 16, 2007, online: http://www.jta.org/2007/11/16/news-opinion/politics/aipac-stance-irks-donors (accessed July 2, 2019).

[26] See the tax filings of the Adelson Family Foundation online: https://projects.propublica.org/nonprofits/organizations/47024330, also http://www.publicintegrity.org/2013/02/06/12145/super-pac-patron-sheldon-adelson-pours-riches-pro-israel-groups (both accessed July 2, 2019).

may turn into a nationwide alternative to AIPAC. In 2007, it started out in Los Angeles as a small regional cultural organization for Israeli expats living in the U.S., but has since expanded rapidly, thanks in large part to major gifts from Adelson—between 2013 and 2018, over US$63 million. "Spokespersons for the IAC vehemently deny any political bent or intent, despite the fact that the group recently participated in the campaign against the Iran deal, calling on its members, AIPAC-style, to lobby their local Congress members."[27] Whether Adelson will propel the IAC into becoming a true rival of AIPAC remains to be seen: the IAC's first annual conference, with over 750 delegates in 2014, has been much smaller than AIPAC's flagship "Policy Conference," which drew 14,000 delegates in 2015—but by 2018, the IAC National Summit counted over 3,000 participants, including Vice President Mike Pence, Senate Democratic Leader Chuck Schumer, and House Democratic Leader Nancy Pelosi.[28] At the very least, the IAC provides Adelson with a forum in which he can publicize his political perspective—at all IAC annual conferences, he has been one of the keynote speakers. In 2014, he used the occasion to air his controversial views on the Palestinians and Israeli democracy; in 2015, Adelson discussed the then much more consensual Taglit-Birthright Israel program, which is the other major diaspora project financed by him.

During the same period that has seen increasing diversification among Jewish diaspora organizations, a debate over distancing between Israel and American Jews, especially those belonging to younger generations, has emerged. Surveys have provided evidence—using indicators like intermarriage, religious and cultural practices, and self-identification—that, since the 1990s, younger American Jews may be becoming less attached to their religious culture and to Israel (Cohen & Kelman 2007, Pew Research Center 2013). While some of these findings have been questioned by other researchers (Heilman 2010, Sasson 2014), the Taglit-Birthright Israel program is making concrete efforts to counter any risks of distancing or alienation. "Birthright Israel seeks to ensure the future of the Jewish people by strengthening Jewish identity, Jewish communities, and connection with Israel via a trip to Israel for the majority of Jewish young adults from around the world."[29] These trips are being organized as educational journeys where small groups with trained tour guides follow an itinerary that mixes some

---

[27] See Chemi Shalev, "Adelson's IAC: American-Israeli Expat Society, AIPAC Foil or Both?," *Haaretz*, October 20, 2015, online: -http://www.haaretz.com/israel-news/.premium-1.681329, also "Adelson family contributes $13 million to Israeli-American Council," *Jewish News Syndicate*, March 19, 2018, online: https://www.jns.org/sheldon-adelson-donates-13-million-to-israeli-american-coun cil/ and Josh Nathan-Kazis, "Breaking With Script, Adelson Portrays IAC as a Hardline AIPAC Alternative," November 5, 2017, online: https://forward.com/news/386949/breaking-with-scrip-adelson-says-iac-is-a-hardline-aipac-alternative/ (accessed July 2, 2019).

[28] See Ron Kampeas, "When Israeli Americans meet, there's politics, partying, and pride," *The Times of Israel*, December 5, 2018, online: https://www.timesofisrael.com/when-israeli-americans-meet-theres-politics-partying-and-pride/ (accessed July 2, 2019).

[29] The program's vision statement online: https://www.birthrightisrael.com/about_us_inner/52? scroll=art_2 (accessed June 19, 2019).

personal flexibility with a coherent core of site visits and encounters (*taglit* means discovery in Hebrew), all geared towards forging strong bonds between the participants and Jewish life in Israel (Saxe & Chazan 2008, Kelner 2010, Abramson 2017, 2019). Expenses for the Birthright trip, including international flights and accommodation, are almost entirely being paid for by the Taglit-Birthright Israel program. From its launch in 1999 until 2018, over 700,000 Jewish adults between eighteen and twenty-six years have taken part in such trips, the large majority of which has come from the American diaspora.[30] These trips are obviously very costly—the Birthright Israel Foundation's 2018 annual report states US$96.5 million expenses for program and supporting services in 2018 (Birthright Israel Foundation 2019: 47). While Sheldon Adelson was not involved in the founding of Taglit-Birthright Israel, since 2007, when he donated US$36.1 million, he has become by far its largest individual donor, altogether contributing over US$410 million to the Birthright Israel Foundation until 2018 (Birthright Israel Foundation 2019: 37).[31] Adelson's gifts made it possible to expand Birthright to over 40,000 participants per year, whereas it had only around 10,000 to 20,000 trip-takers in the years prior to 2007 (Kelner 2010: 5f).

Is his funding giving the billionaire any sway over the content of the program? Since Adelson is making his donations on a short-term basis, usually year to year, the possibility of funding cuts, even if never pronounced, is certainly looming over Taglit-Birthright Israel. In 2014, one of Adelson's closest associates, Michael Leven, has become the Chairman of the Planning Committee at the Birthright Israel Foundation after retiring from Las Vegas Sands, where he had served as president between 2009 and 2014.[32] In 2017, Sheldon and Miriam Adelson

---

[30] By 2013, more than two thirds of all Birthright participants had been from the U.S. (Saxe et al. 2013: 3).

[31] Taglit-Birthright Israel has been initiated by other billionaires, Charles Bronfman, Michael Steinhardt, and Lynn Schusterman, whose net worth (between US$1 billion and US$4 billion) is much smaller than Adelson's. From the beginning, the Israeli government has been a substantial co-sponsor of the project, financing it at a similar level as Adelson: around US$100 million overall up to 2010, and another US$100 million committed from 2011 to 2013, see Josh Nathan-Kazis, "Government of Israel to Give More to Birthright Program," *Forward*, January 12, 2011, online: http://forward.com/news/134636/government-of-israel-to-give-more-to-birthright-pr/#ixzz3uUeBbyot (accessed November 20, 2015). In 2019, the Birthright Israel Foundation indicated 28 percent of its funding as coming from the Israeli government, see online: https://birthrightisrael.foundation/supporters. For a detailed analysis of the origins and the evolution of the Taglit-Birthright Israel program, see Kelner 2010. Adelson's yearly donations are being reported in the Adelson Family Foundation's tax filings (990-PF forms, available online: https://projects.propublica.org/nonprofits/organizations/47024330 (all accessed June 19, 2019).

[32] See Nathan Guttman, "Sheldon Adelson Is a Philanthropist Like No Other," *Forward*, November 3, 2014, online: http://forward.com/news/israel/208220/sheldon-adelson-is-a-philanthropist-like-no-other/, Judy Maltz, "Adelson Crony to Fill Key Policy-making Role at Birthright," *Haaretz*, June 5, 2014, online: http://www.haaretz.com/jewish-world/.premium-1.597140, and Anthony Weiss, "Sheldon Adelson's No. 2 Michael Leven Steps Out of Shadows," *Forward*, December 22, 2014, online: http://forward.com/news/breaking-news/211435/sheldon-adelsons-no-2-michael-leven-steps-out-of-s/ (all accessed June 20, 2019).

became members of the new Honorary Board of the Birthright Israel Foundation, and they were at the center of the foundation's eighteenth anniversary gala in 2018, where they received the Guardians of the Jewish Future Award and announced a new US$70 million gift (Birthright Israel Foundation 2019: 37). These close ties between the far-right billionaire and Birthright have fostered criticism of the Birthright program among liberal Jewish groups, especially once certain changes to the program were revealed. In 2017, the more liberal tour operator URJ Kesher, associated with the Reform Movement in the U.S., was excluded from the Birthright program, and a two-year experiment of integrating encounters with Arab Israelis in the schedule of the trips was terminated.[33] Whether any of these decisions are due to Adelson's influence is, however, of secondary interest, because the Birthright trips have been an ethnonationalist project from the beginning, and the program's sidelining of the problems with the Israeli-occupied territories also preceded Adelson's involvement.

Adelson reportedly examined the whole Taglit-Birthright Israel project in detail before starting his giving in 2007, and he must have liked what he saw (Bruck 2008). While Birthright claims to be nonpartisan and without a political stance on the Israel–Palestine conflict, which has been confirmed by survey analysis (Kelner 2010: 193f, Sasson et al. 2014), its basic mission and its outcomes clearly correspond with Adelson's goals.[34] Research on Birthright trips demonstrates short- and long-term effects on participants' attitudes, particularly if they used to be distant from Jewish culture. Surveys show that the Birthright trips' "greatest impact is observed on connection to Israel, where participants were 2.5 times as likely to feel 'very much' connected to Israel," in comparison with similar nonparticipants; long-term studies confirm that this effect persists over time (Saxe et al. 2013: 13, Saxe et al. 2017: 10).[35] Based on extensive fieldwork and participant observation,

---

[33] See "Birthright cuts out encounters with Arab Israelis," *The Times of Israel*, November 3, 2017, online: https://www.timesofisrael.com/birthright-cuts-out-encounters-with-arab-israelis/, Judy Maltz, "How Orthodox Groups Are Taking Over Birthright, and Using It to Target Young U.S. Jews," Haaretz, November 26, 2017, online: https://www.haaretz.com/israel-news/MAGAZINE-how-orthodox-groups-are-taking-over-birthright-targeting-young-u-s-jews-1.5626920, Allison Kaplan Sommer, "Between Adelson and BDS, Birthright Has Become a Political Battlefield," *Haaretz*, July 3, 2018, online: https://www.haaretz.com/israel-news/.premium-how-birthright-became-a-political-football-1.6224433, Cathryn J. Prince "J Street launches Birthright-style trip to Israel that will include Palestinians, *The Times of Israel*, March 14, 2019, online: https://www.timesofisrael.com/j-street-launches-birthright-style-trip-to-israel-that-will-include-palestinians/, as well as the activist campaign https://www.notjustafreetrip.com/ (all accessed June 19, 2019).

[34] For Adelson's own views on Birthright, see his interview with: Boaz Bismuth & Amos Regev, "'We have come to put an end to Noni Mozes' dictatorship'," *Israel Hayom*, May 9, 2014, online: https://web.archive.org/web/20180702000429/http://www.israelhayom.com/2014/05/09/we-have-come-to-put-an-end-to-noni-mozes-dictatorship/ (accessed June 19, 2019).

[35] See also Cohen & Kelman 2007: 16–18, Saxe et al. 2009: 16, Volodarsky et al. 2019. Most of the academic research on Birthright outcomes has taken place at the Steinhardt Social Research Institute at Brandeis University and has been supported by the Birthright Israel program and the Andrea and Charles Bronfman Philanthropies. Charles Bronfman and Michael Steinhardt have been two of the founders of Birthright Israel. Still, the social science methodologies of this research seem sound, and

Saul Kelner has built a careful analysis of how Birthright achieves its political outcomes without having to rely on crude propaganda:

Limited to discursive presentations that are framed as the Other's narrative and that are filtered through the voices of Israeli guides, Arab nationalist narratives command little if any emotional weight on the tours. By contrast, [Birthright] tourists will not only hear Israel's ashes to redemption story but also experience it through sensation, dialogue, drama, display, and more. In addition, they will be guided through processes of self-exploration that will enable them to link their personal stories to collective Jewish narratives, which they can thereby embrace as their own. The fundamental asymmetry in the experience of Arab and Jewish narratives helps to accomplish the important ideological work of the tours in securing diaspora Jewish support for Zionism's claim of a right to Jewish self-determination in the ancestral land. By making these claims subjectively compelling and experientially self-evident, the tours work to win Jewish hearts and minds in the face of global campaigns to delegitimize Jewish assertions of national rights in Israel   (Kelner 2010: 194f).

By allowing more young Jewish adults to go on a Birthright trip, thanks to his funding, Adelson is thus strengthening the diaspora's attachment to Israeli territory as the Jewish homeland (Abramson 2017). While this mission of Birthright used to be fairly uncontroversial among American Jewry, the recent politicization of the trips reflects not only opposition against Adelson, but also deepening rifts within the Jewish community with regard to the Israel–Palestine conflict and the role of the U.S. (Barnett 2016, Waxman 2016).

In general, U.S. foreign policy has been treating Israel favorably, for moral reasons, which include support for "the only democracy in the Middle East" as well as "redress for historic suffering" (the Holocaust), and for strategic reasons, because it is seen as an important ally in the Middle East, with which the U.S. is sharing intelligence and military cooperation (Weinberg 2014: 63f, also Freedman 2012). Pro-Israel lobbying efforts (Mearsheimer & Walt 2007), especially those that, like AIPAC's, emanate from the Jewish diaspora (Waxman 2012), but also from Evangelical Christian groups (Rubin 2012), solidify and enhance the very special relationship between the two countries. Yet, just as there are sharp political divisions within Israel, what "being pro-Israel" concretely entails is a highly contested question within the U.S. (Shain & Rogachevsky 2014, Rynhold 2015, Waxman 2016). Solid majorities or pluralities among American Jewry believe in a two-state solution for the Israel–Palestine conflict, think that Jewish settlements on the West Bank hurt Israel's security, and have supported Obama's efforts to

---

other research on Birthright Israel without ties to it is largely confirming the findings (Kelner 2010, Abramson 2017, 2019, Ben Hagai et al. 2018).

reach a nuclear agreement with Iran (Pew Research Center 2013: 81–100, Waxman 2017). Such views are largely in line with those held by the Democratic Party's constituency.[36] And since 1924, American Jewry has consistently been loyal to the Democrats, preferring its presidential candidate over the Republicans' candidate, usually with more than two thirds of its votes (Maisel & Forman 2004, Mellman et al. 2012, Weisberg 2014). Adelson has himself been part of this traditional pro-Democrats Jewish political culture until the early 1990s, when he shifted his allegiance to the Republicans. Initially, his switch seems to have been motivated by economic self-interest with regard to policies on taxation and trade unions (which still matter for him today). However, his interventions in the most recent presidential campaigns appear to prioritize U.S. foreign policy and the security of Israel.[37]

While Adelson had already been a significant contributor to Republican causes before, his funding became truly outstanding once he became a multi-billionaire (Bruck 2008), and once the U.S. Supreme Court decisions removed limitations on individual campaign contributions in 2010. Since then, he has been spending large amounts of his personal fortune on promoting his favorite candidates during Republican primary and presidential elections, as well as on campaigning against their opponents, especially Barack Obama.[38]

In 2012, Adelson spent $20 million supporting Newt Gingrich, single-handedly keeping him afloat during the primaries and doing great damage to Mitt Romney in the process; then, after Gingrich finally fell, Adelson shelled out $30 million to plump up Romney. All told, Adelson reportedly spent $100 million against Obama in 2012. In 2016, says one prominent Republican operative, "every candidate thinks, *I can either be the Gingrich of the cycle,* meaning Sheldon could give me oxygen, or *I don't want to be on the opposite side of who his Gingrich is this cycle.* They want to benefit from Sheldon's largesse or make sure no one else benefits from it" (Zengerle 2015, emphasis in original).[39]

---

[36] However, since the breakdown of the Oslo peace process, political opinions among American Jewry regarding Israel have become increasingly divided, with more and more Jewish Americans slowly shifting towards the right on these issues; in contrast, Democratic Party voters have generally moved further towards the left, criticizing Israel and showing sympathy for the Palestinians (Rynhold 2015: 58–91, 139–80).

[37] Sheldon G. Adelson, "I Didn't Leave the Democrats. They Left Me," *The Wall Street Journal,* November 4, 2012, online: http://www.wsj.com/articles/SB10001424052970204712904578092670469140316 (accessed July 5, 2019).

[38] For his negative evaluation of Obama's Israel policy, see Sheldon Adelson, "Don't risk Israel's security on Obama's words," *Jewish News Syndicate,* October 11, 2012, online: http://www.jns.org/latest-articles/2012/10/11/dont-risk-israels-security-on-obamas-words.html#.ViZcy34rK70 (accessed July 2, 2019).

[39] Reports that include non-public campaign expenditure put Adelson's overall spending during the 2012 election cycle at US$150 million. See Peter Stone, "Sheldon Adelson Spent Far More On Campaign Than Previously Known," *Huffpost,* https://www.huffpost.com/entry/sheldon-adelson-2012-election_n_2223589 (accessed July 2, 2019).

Consequently, the so-called "Adelson primaries" have become a noteworthy part of U.S. politics. Republican presidential hopefuls that want Adelson's money are keeping him updated on their political endeavors, especially those relating to Israel, and come to visit him in Las Vegas, which often coincides with the annual Spring Leadership Meeting of the Republican Jewish Coalition (RJC) in Las Vegas, of which Adelson is a board member and funder. "Those who receive money from Adelson typically do so only after meeting with him personally, and he has been known to abruptly and capriciously cut off funding for an offense as minor as a quote in a newspaper article that he didn't like" (ibid., also Bruck 2012, Vogel 2014: 77–98).

If one merely looks at election outcomes, Adelson's campaign financing, for many years, can be judged a failure. In the eyes of most pundits, his initial 2012 favorite, Newt Gingrich, never had a real chance of becoming elected, and Mitt Romney was unsuccessful in ousting Obama. At the level of agenda-setting, however, Adelson's spending seems to be contributing to a much fiercer pro-Israel foreign policy stance among Republican politicians. This has already been observed in 2012:

> Gingrich went from Middle East moderate to saber-rattling hawk after Sheldon Adelson's millions began flowing into the candidate's coffers.... Compared to the views he expresses now, which are a full-blown echo of Adelson's, the Gingrich of six years ago was a moderate, endorsing Obama-like policies he now condemns.[40]

Similarly, New Jersey governor Chris Christie, another Republican at times deemed to have high potential for the 2016 presidency, aligned his views on Israel and Middle East foreign policy with Adelson's. For example, he expressed increasingly aggressive positions on U.S. policy vis-à-vis Iran and Muslims. It has also been reported that he apologized in person to Adelson after having referred to the "occupied territories" in a speech before the RJC. He claimed that his use of the term, which is considered to be insufficiently pro-Israel among conservative Zionists, had been an accident.[41] Jeb Bush, governor of Florida and another

---

[40] Wayne Barrett, "Is Gingrich's Hard Line on Palestine Paid for by Sheldon Adelson?," *The Daily Beast*, January 18, 2012, online: http://www.thedailybeast.com/articles/2012/01/18/is-gingrich-s-hard-line-on-palestine-paid-for-by-sheldon-adelson.html (accessed July 2, 2019). In a 2005 policy paper, Gingrich had advocated that "[i]t is vital to our credibility in the entire Middle East that we insist on an end to Israeli expansionism" and that "the U.S. government should actively support a democratic Palestinian state" (Gingrich 2005).

[41] See Terrence Dopp, "Chris Christie and Ted Cruz Slam Iran at Adelson Event," *Bloomberg*, March 29, 2015, online: http://www.bloomberg.com/politics/articles/2015-05-29/christie-joins-cruz-in-courting-republican-benefactor-adelson, Eli Clifton, "Christie Pivots to Islamophobia and toward Adelson," *LobeLog*, December 2, 2015, online: https://lobelog.com/christie-pivots-to-islamophobia-and-toward-adelson/, Kenneth P. Vogel, "Christie apologizes for 'occupied territories'," *Politico*, March 29, 2014, online: http://www.politico.com/story/2014/03/chris-christie-occupied-territories-

presidential hopeful in 2016, came under fire from Adelson as soon as he published his list of twenty-one foreign policy advisors, which included the former secretary of State James Baker. Baker, who had served under Jeb's father George H. W. Bush during the 1990s and who is considered to represent, in IR terms, a realist outlook on foreign policy, with no special concern for Israel. When Baker was scheduled to give a speech at J Street (in which he eventually did criticize the Netanyahu government's policies), Adelson,

> [w]orking with other Jewish Republicans, . . . began lobbying the Bush campaign to disown Baker as an adviser or, at a minimum, force him to cancel the speech . . . . Bush did not budge . . . . "Sheldon basically said Jeb is dead to him," recalls one prominent Republican to whom Adelson vented   (Zengerle 2015).

The ways in which Jeb Bush later tried to reconcile with Adelson, which included his public distancing from Baker and his brother George W. Bush offering a self-made painting of the mogul's Singapore casino to Adelson, indicate how seriously Republican candidates are taking the unofficial primaries in Las Vegas.

Exactly how much influence Sheldon Adelson is having over the Republican Party's pro-Israel stance is hard to gauge. For once, while Adelson has become by far the most lavish donor with a vigorous pro-Israel agenda, the Republicans also have some other major pro-Israel donors, such as the New York hedge fund billionaire Paul Singer, whose much smaller fortune (*Forbes*: US$3.2 billion in 2019) is partially compensated for by his extensive social network (Zengerle 2015). And besides individuals, one needs to take broader ideological and political changes into account, too. In his analysis of the Arab–Israeli conflict in American political culture, Jonathan Rynhold identifies three dynamics behind the surge in Republican support for Israel (Rynhold 2015: 31–57, 95–115). First, the growing influence of evangelical or fundamentalist Christian beliefs among Republican voters, for which support for Israel is in line with the Bible's predictions about Israel as God's chosen people and the end of times (dispensationalism). Secondly, the rise of a neoconservative intellectual elite among right-leaning media and policy circles, for whom support for Israel is a strategic imperative in the global struggle of democracy against totalitarian forces.[42] Both ideational trends have, thirdly, been reinforced in the wake of the 9/11 terrorist attacks, as Israel came to

---

apology-105169, and Alec Macgillis, "The Time Chris Christie Stood Up to Sheldon Adelson," *New Republic*, March 31, 2014, online: https://newrepublic.com/article/117207/christies-apology-adelson-occupied-territories-shift (all accessed July 6, 2019).

[42] In their much-discussed analysis of the pro-Israel lobby in the U.S., realist IR scholars John Mearsheimer and Stephen Walt (2007) are aware of these broad support bases, but they underestimate the religiously based backing of Israel, and they overemphasize the role of Jewish thinkers among the neoconservative movement.

be seen as a stalwart against Islamism, and thus a key ally of the U.S. Importantly, this overall shift to a more determined pro-Israel stance among Republicans happened not only at the level of intellectual and political elites, but equally among the Republican electorate. Especially post-9/11, a large majority among Republican voters is viewing Israel as a strategic ally and strongly favors it over the Palestinians.[43] The neoconservative editor of the now defunct Weekly Standard, William Kristol, sees it as a central issue of Republican political identity today: "People stand up and say that they're pro-life, pro-gun, anti-tax, and pro-Israel" (Zengerle 2015).

Notwithstanding these structural developments, it would be inappropriate to ignore the personal impact of Sheldon Adelson. As the above examples have shown, Adelson's campaign contributions go a long way in explaining why Republican politicians' stances have become not simply pro-Israel, but also more hawkish on specific issues. A highly visible manifestation of Adelson's clout in Republican politics happened in 2015 around the negotiations of the Joint Comprehensive Plan of Action Iran deal in Congress. "It was understood by the Republican presidential candidates that strong opposition to the deal was a possible route to big campaign contributions from Adelson" (Drew 2015). Although proof is lacking, several critics have suggested Adelson was involved in setting up the controversial speech of Israeli Prime Minister Benjamin Netanyahu before Congress, in which he strongly criticized the Obama adminis-tration's efforts to reach a deal with Iran regarding that country's nuclear pro-gram.[44] "For the first time in US history, the opposition party thumbed its nose at the president by inviting the head of another nation—Netanyahu—to address Congress to urge rejection of an international measure the president supported" (ibid.). During the speech, Sheldon and Miriam Adelson were sitting in the front row of the Congress balcony for visitors. Before and after the speech, groups and individuals that received substantial funding from Adelson (or from PACs he is financing) have been torpedoing Obama's Iran deal persistently.[45] When the Iran

---

[43] On the questions of a Palestinian state and Israeli settlements in the West Bank, however, Republican voters have remained divided in their opinions (Rynhold 2015: 52ff), and are thus less in line with Adelson's positions.

[44] Jonathan Lis and Nati Tucker, "Livni: Netanyahu, Adelson destroying Israel-U.S. ties," *Haaretz*, March 4, 2015, online: http://www.haaretz.com/news/israel-election-2015/.premium-1.645204, DeWayne Wickham, "Wickham: Adelson behind Israel flap?," *USA Today*, January 26, 2015, online: http://www.usatoday.com/story/opinion/2015/01/26/adelson-netanyahu-iran-obama-sanctions-spending-news-influence-israel-wickham/22319523/. For more details about the organization of Netanyahu's Congress speech and the role played by the Israeli ambassador to the U.S., Ron Dermer, a Netanyahu appointee, see Dylan Scott, "Meet the Man at the Center of the Unprecedented US-Israel Rift," *Talkingpointsmemo*, February 13, 2015, online: http://talkingpointsmemo.com/dc/ron-dermer-netanyahu-speech-boehner-obama (all accessed July 2, 2019).

[45] See Peter Stone, "Casino Tycoon Sheldon Adelson Takes $100 Million Gamble on GOP Senate," *The Daily Beast*, March 9, 2014, online: http://www.thedailybeast.com/articles/2014/09/03/casino-tycoon-sheldon-adelson-takes-100-million-gamble-on-gop-senate.html?utm_medium=referral&utm_source=pulsenews, Kenneth P. Vogel, "Adelson opens checkbook for GOP," *Politico*, September 17,

deal finally came to a vote before the Senate in September 2015, all Republican senators voted against it as a united front. Still, they failed to reach the blocking threshold of sixty votes. As during the 2012 presidential elections, Adelson's plans did not succeed in the short run. In the country where he is a citizen, Adelson's wealth helped to make the Republican Party a more aggressive defender of Israel's security. But as long as Obama remained president, who made the nuclear agreement with Iran one of his foreign policy priorities, Adelson's impact at home was limited.

This changed with the election of Donald Trump as president in 2016. During the early months of the 2015/16 campaigning season, Adelson had been hesitant. While Trump had opposed the Iran nuclear deal from the beginning, his position on the Israel–Palestine conflict appeared as less pro-Israel than the Republican Party mainstream. But in 2016, at AIPAC's annual policy conference in March, Trump delivered a staunchly pro-Israel speech, including the promise to move the U.S. embassy to Jerusalem. In early May, he accepted the expansion of Israeli settlements in the West Bank. Ten days later, on May 13, 2016, Adelson endorsed Trump for president in an op-ed for *The Washington Post*. Several meetings between the two billionaires preceded this rapprochement.[46] Together with his wife Miriam, Adelson then donated over US$82 million to Republican Party funds and candidates, including US$20 million to the anti-Clinton Super-PAC "Future45," for the 2016 presidential and congressional elections. With US$5 million, Adelson was also the largest contributor to Trump's inauguration celebration.[47] Even more money followed during the 2018 congressional elections

---

2014, online: http://www.politico.com/story/2014/09/sheldon-adelson-republican-fundraising-111088, Paul Blumenthal, "Republicans And Iran Deal Opponents Are Funded By The Same Mega-Donors," *The Huffington Post*, March 10, 2015, online: https://www.huffpost.com/entry/iran-deal-republicans_n_6841976, Eric Lipton, "G.O.P.'s Israel Support Deepens as Political Contributions Shift," *The New York Times*, April 4, 2015, online: http://www.nytimes.com/2015/04/05/us/politics/gops-israel-support-deepens-as-political-contributions-shift.html?_r=0 (all accessed July 6, 2019).

[46] See Brian Schaefer, "Where Does Donald Trump Stand on Israel?," *Haaretz*, November 10, 2016, online: https://www.haaretz.com/world-news/MAGAZINE-where-does-donald-trump-stand-on-israel-1.5384623 (accessed May 15, 2019); Sarah Begley, "Read Donald Trump's Speech to AIPAC," *TIME*, March 21, 2016, online: https://time.com/4267058/donald-trump-aipac-speech-transcript/; David Martosko and Geoff Earle, "EXCLUSIVE: Trump insists Israel should keep building West Bank settlements as he says Netanyahu should 'keep moving forward' because Palestinians fired 'thousands of missiles' at Jewish state," *Daily Mail*, May 3, 2016, online: https://www.dailymail.co.uk/news/article-3571403/Trump-insists-Israel-building-West-Bank-settlements-says-Netanyahu-moving-forward-Palestinians-fired-thousands-missiles-Jewish-state.html. Sheldon G. Adelson, "Sheldon Adelson: I endorse Donald Trump for President," *The Washington Post*, May 13, 2016, online: https://www.washingtonpost.com/opinions/sheldon-adelson-i-endorse-donald-trump-for-president/2016/05/12/ea89d7f0-17a0-11e6-aa55-670cabef46e0_story.html; Justin Elliott, "Trump's Patron-in-Chief," *ProPublica*, October 10, 2018, online: https://features.propublica.org/trump-inc-podcast/sheldon-adelson-casino-magnate-trump-macau-and-japan/ (all accessed June 18, 2019).

[47] See "Trump 2017 Inauguration Donors," *OpenSecrets.org*, online: https://www.opensecrets.org/trump/inauguration-donors (accessed May 18, 2019).

cycle, when the Adelson couple shelled out over US$123 million for Republican Party funds and candidates. In both 2016 and 2018, as back in 2012, they were by far the largest donor for the GOP, contributing more than three times as much as the next individual pro-Republican donor.[48] With Trump in the White House, Adelson has seen several policy changes that coincide with his interests, both on the business front, where Las Vegas Sands is seen to benefit from new tax and gambling regulations,[49] and with regard to U.S. foreign policy in the Middle East. Several sources confirm that

> Mr. Adelson in particular enjoys a direct line to the president. In private in-person meetings and phone conversations, which occur between the two men about once a month, he has used his access to push the president to move the United States embassy in Israel to Jerusalem and, more recently, cut aid to the Palestinians.[50]

In 2018, the choice of John Bolton as the President's new National Security Advisor, and Trump's withdrawal from the Iran nuclear deal were two other decisions in line with Adelson's goals.[51]

Sheldon Adelson's transnational investments in Israeli politics have been more consistently fruitful. The focus of his support in Israel is Benjamin "Bibi" Netanyahu, with whom he is friendly at a personal level and in agreement about Israel's security. Adelson has described Netanyahu as "not a political person. [His] wind blows in the direction of his ideology, and his deep and unwavering support and love for the Jewish people and the state of Israel. I am absolutely convinced

[48] See the contributions calculations on *OpenSecrets.org*, for 2016: https://www.opensecrets.org/overview/topindivs.php?cycle=2016&view=fc, and for 2018: https://www.opensecrets.org/overview/topindivs.php?cycle=2018&view=fc (accessed May 18, 2019).

[49] Special provisions in the 2017 "Tax Cuts and Jobs Act" resulted in almost US$1.2 billion benefits for *Las Vegas Sands*, and Trump has reportedly been promoting Adelson's bid to gain a casino licence in Japan. See Justin Elliott, "Trump's Patron-in-Chief," *ProPublica*, October 10, 2018, online: https://features.propublica.org/trump-inc-podcast/sheldon-adelson-casino-magnate-trump-macau-and-japan/. In January 2019, a U.S. Justice Department decision restricted internet gambling in the U.S., which is something Adelson and *Las Vegas Sands* had been lobbying for. See Edvard Pettersson, "U.S. Online Gambling Reversal Puts 'Chill' on Industry," Bloomberg, January 15, 2019, online: https://www.bloomberg.com/news/articles/2019-01-15/u-s-now-says-all-online-gambling-illegal-not-just-sports-bets (both accessed June 16, 2019).

[50] Jeremy W. Peters, "Sheldon Adelson Sees a Lot to Like in Trump's Washington," *The New York Times*, September 22, 2018, online: https://www.nytimes.com/2018/09/22/us/politics/adelson-trump-republican-donor.html. In a separate investigation, it was reported that "'He just calls the president all the time. Donald Trump takes Sheldon Adelson's calls,' said Alan Dershowitz, who has done legal work for Adelson and advised Trump." See Justin Elliott, "Trump's Patron-in-Chief," *ProPublica*, October 10, 2018, online: https://features.propublica.org/trump-inc-podcast/sheldon-adelson-casino-magnate-trump-macau-and-japan/ (both accessed June 16, 2019).

[51] See Chris McGreal, "Sheldon Adelson: The Casino Mogul Driving Trump's Middle East policy," *The Guardian*, June 8, 2018, online: https://www.theguardian.com/us-news/2018/jun/08/sheldon-adelson-trump-middle-east-policy; Eli Clifton & Jim Lobe, "Trump's Choice of Bolton Satisfies His Biggest Donor," *Lobe Log*, March 24, 2018, https://lobelog.com/trumps-choice-of-bolton-satisfies-his-biggest-donor/ (both accessed July 16, 2018).

that Bibi says what he means, means what he says."[52] Netanyahu is seen as inspired by Revisionist Zionism, already propagated by his father, which has shaped the ideological roots of the Likud, the party that he has been leading between 1996 and 1999, and again since 2005, and with which he became prime minister of Israel for the fourth time in 2015. Both in regard to the broader security situation of Israel (its precariousness in a hostile world) and more specific issues such as a Palestinian state (no), settlements (yes), Jerusalem (undivided) or Iran (preventive strikes if necessary), Adelson and Netanyahu largely see eye to eye. While, as a politician, Netanyahu has sometimes been making tactical concessions that go against his ideology, in general he seems to stick to his convictions (Netanyahu 1993, Aronoff 2014: 43–77). Under diplomatic pressure from the first Obama administration in 2009, for example, Netanyahu did acknowledge the possibility—subject to severe conditions—of a Palestinian state, and ordered a ten-months settlement freeze on the West Bank (Pedahzur 2012: 201ff). Later, though, he returned to endorsing settlement consolidation and expansion, and, during the 2015 Knesset elections, he questioned the prospect of Palestinian statehood.[53] Overall, like Adelson, Netanyahu appears close to the "entrenchment–annexationism" position in Israeli politics, which also shows in his choice of political partners, as his last three government coalitions have included the radical right party Habayit Hayehudi ("The Jewish Home"). From Adelson's perspective, backing Bibi therefore makes a lot of sense. Direct funding in the same way as in the U.S., however, is not an option.

Israel's political financing laws are very restrictive and forbid foreign citizens and corporate entities to make financial contributions to political parties or candidates. Political parties and election campaigns in Israel are mainly publicly financed, with austere limitations on private contributions, so that even Sheldon's wife Miriam, with her Israeli citizenship, could not engage in directly funding Netanyahu in a meaningful way.[54] Newspaper ownership by foreigners, on the

---

[52] Josh Nathan-Kazis, "Sheldon Adelson Wants Nuclear Strike on Iran—Says Two-States 'Russian Roulette'," *The Forward*, October 23, 2013, online: http://forward.com/news/186079/sheldon-adelson-wants-nuclear-strike-on-iran-say/. See also Zengerle 2015 and Raviv Drucker, "The Real Connection Between Netanyahu and Adelson's Israel Hayom," *Haaretz*, June 13, 2015, online: http://www.haaretz.com/opinion/.premium-1.660914 (all accessed July 2, 2019).

[53] See "Full Text of Netanyahu's Foreign Policy Speech at Bar Ilan," *Haaretz*, June 14, 2009, online: http://www.haaretz.com/news/full-text-of-netanyahu-s-foreign-policy-speech-at-bar-ilan-1.277922, Jodi Rudoren, "Netanyahu's History on Palestinian Statehood," *The New York Times*, March 20, 2015, online: http://www.nytimes.com/interactive/2015/03/20/world/middleeast/netanyahu-two-state-solution.html?_r=0, Raphael Ahren, "Why Netanyahu won't approve a Palestinian state," *The Times of Israel*, October 28, 2015, online: http://www.timesofisrael.com/why-netanyahu-wont-approve-a-palestinian-state/, Isabel Kershner, "Israel Approves First New Settlement in Decades," *The New York Times*, March 30, 2017, online: https://www.nytimes.com/2017/03/30/world/middleeast/israeli-settlements-netanyahu.html (all accessed July 2, 2019).

[54] The only exception are foreign donations to primary elections, which are allowed up to NIS 50,000. See the online overview of Israel's political finance regulations: https://www.idea.int/data-tools/country-view/144/55 (accessed July 3, 2019).

other hand, is unregulated in Israel, and this is where Adelson saw an opportunity for boosting his friend by financing a pro-Netanyahu daily. When attempts to take over the existing newspapers *Israeli* and *Maariv* had not worked out,[55] Adelson launched a new daily tabloid, *Israel Hayom*; its first issue was published on July 30, 2007, with 150,000 copies distributed across Israel. Besides being visually attractive, professionally edited, and hosting a number of experienced and well-known journalists, *Israel Hayom*'s main "selling point" has been that it is being distributed for free across Israel.[56] Before Sheldon Adelson's intrusion, the Israeli newspaper market had been dominated by two mainstream tabloids: *Yedioth Ahronoth* and *Maariv*. Between 1995 and 2007, *Yedioth Ahronoth* had the highest exposure rate among newspaper readers, which declined from 54.5 percent to 38.4 percent, while *Maariv* maintained the second place with an exposure rate moving from 23.9 percent to 17 percent (Gilboa 2008). After 2007, very swiftly, *Israel Hayom* became the most widely read newspaper. With an exposure rate of 20.2 percent in 2008, it immediately surpassed *Maariv*, and then kept on catching more and more readers: 26.9 percent in 2009 and 35.8 percent in 2010, the first year where it narrowly surpassed *Yedioth Ahronoth*. Since then, it has been solidifying its number one status: 38.1 percent in 2011, 39.3 percent in 2012, 38.6 percent in 2013, 39.2 percent in 2014, and 39.5 percent in 2015 (*Yedioth Ahronoth*: 35.4 percent).[57] After 2016, when both *Maariv* and *Yedioth Ahronoth* started to distribute free versions of their newspaper as well, *Israel Hayom*'s share has been declining to around 29 percent in 2018, but keeping its "most read" status.[58] How much money Adelson put into *Israel Hayom* remained unknown for a long time,

---

[55] Ronny Koren-Dinar, "World's Richest Jew Buys Half of Free Israeli Daily," *Haaretz*, April 24, 2006, online: https://www.haaretz.com/1.4902558, Shlomi Sheffer, "Adelson Accuses Israeli Partner of Embezzling From Freebie Paper Yisraeli," *Haaretz*, November 9, 2006, online: https://www.haaretz.com/1.4930574, Ronny Koren-Dinar and Shlomi Sheffer, "Sheldon Adelson May Buy Maariv After All," *Haaretz*, March 14, 2007, online: https://www.haaretz.com/1.4810864 (all accessed July 2, 2019).
[56] Asaf Carmel, "A Newspaper With an Agenda," *Haaretz*, July 31, 2007, online: https://www.haaretz.com/israel-news/culture/1.4957138 (accessed July 2, 2019).
[57] The survey-based data on readership (exposure rate) has been established via surveys by the private company TGI. See Ayala Tsoref, "Yisrael Hayom Overtakes Maariv," *Haaretz*, July 29, 2008, online: https://www.haaretz.com/1.5008760, Ora Coren and Ophir Bar-Zohar, "Yedioth No Longer a Monopoly, Anti-Trust Authority Rules," *Haaretz*, January 4, 2010, online: https://www.haaretz.com/1.5081556, Ophir Bar-Zohar, "Israel Hayom Pulls Ahead of Yedioth," *Haaretz*, January 19, 2011, online: https://www.haaretz.com/israel-news/business/1.5109963, Nati Tucker, "Israel Hayom Ups Market Share," *Haaretz*, January 31, 2013, online: https://www.haaretz.com/israel-news/business/.premium-israel-hayom-ups-market-share-1.5227664, Nati Tucker, "Israeli Newspapers Join Global Industry's Downward Trend," *Haaretz*, January 22, 2014, online: https://www.haaretz.com/.premium-israeli-newspapers-join-downtrend-1.5313718, "Israel Hayom Remains Israel's Widest-Read Daily Newspaper, Report Says," the algemeiner, January 27, 2016, online: http://www.algemeiner.com/2016/01/27/israel-hayom-remains-israels-widest-read-daily-newspaper-report-says/ (all accessed July 2, 2019).
[58] See Nati Tucker, "Excess of Free Newspapers, Led by Adelson's Israel Hayom, Choking Israel's Print Media," Haaretz, January 25, 2017, online: https://www.haaretz.com/israel-news/business/excess-of-free-newspapers-choking-israels-print-media-1.5490749, and "TGI survey: Israel Hayom leads in weekday readership," Israel hayom, January 31, 2019, online: https://www.israelhayom.com/2019/01/31/tgi-survey-israel-hayom-leads-in-weekday-readership/ (all accessed July 2, 2019).

because, as a private company, the newspaper has no obligation to make its financials public. In 2017, the journalist Uri Blau, who had gained access to internal *Israel Hayom* documents, revealed that the "cumulative losses between the founding of the freebie and 2014 were 730 million shekels ($190 million)."[59]

Adelson has made it very clear that his principal goal has been to change the political balance among Israeli media. According to him, when he started investing in Israel, the publisher of *Yedioth Ahronoth*, Arnon "Noni" Mozes, begged him not to put him out of business, to which Adelson responded: "I won't start on the condition that you move your paper from the far Left to the middle. To the center of the political spectrum." In the same interview, Adelson also stated that "[m]y wife and I wanted to start the newspaper because I came to realize that the existing media at that time was deceitful to the Israeli public.... I don't need the money."[60] Apparently, Adelson made his move in close consultation with Netanyahu, whose appointments calendar indicates that both met six times before *Israel Hayom*'s launch and three more times during the five months afterwards. Netanyahu's calendar also shows that he had dozens of meetings with Amos Regev, who became *Israel Hayom*'s editor-in-chief, and Natan Eshel, a later vice-president at *Israel Hayom*.[61]

> "There is no question about it, Bibi was involved up to his neck in the process of establishing the new newspaper," says someone who has discussed the subject with Netanyahu. "He talks about this rather freely.... After all, it's impossible to have any conversation with Bibi without him mentioning how frustrated he is with the media's conduct when it comes to him.... He says that the difference between Noni Mozes...and Adelson is that Mozes wants to influence and to make a profit at the same time, while Adelson just wants to influence the public with his newspaper."[62]

Although Adelson and *Israel Hayom* deny it,[63] many observers see *Israel Hayom* as a propaganda vehicle, which, in its reporting and in its choice of coverage and

---

[59] Uri Blau, "Adelson's pro-Netanyahu Free Daily Newspaper Lost $190 Million in Seven Years," *Haaretz*, January 9, 2017, online: http://www.haaretz.com/israel-news/1.763975 (accessed July 3, 2019).

[60] Boaz Bismuth & Amos Regev, "'We have come to put an end to Noni Mozes' dictatorship'," *Israel Hayom*, May 9, 2014, online: https://web.archive.org/web/20180702000429/http://www.israelhayom.com/2014/05/09/we-have-come-to-put-an-end-to-noni-mozes-dictatorship/ (accessed June 19, 2019).

[61] After the revelations, the Prime Minister's office declined to make meetings between Netanyahu and Adelson or Regev public under Isarel's "freedom of information" regulations, because they are claimed to be "personal friends" of the prime minister. See Raviv Drucker, "The Real Connection Between Netanyahu and Adelson's Israel Hayom," *Haaretz*, June 13, 2015, online: https://www.haaretz.com/opinion/.premium-the-real-connection-between-bibi-and-israel-hayom-1.5371408, and Nati Tucker, "Israel's Channel 10 Reports on pro-Netanyahu Slant at Israel Hayom Daily Newspaper," *Haaretz*, February 5, 2013, online: https://www.haaretz.com/.premium-ch-10-adelson-paper-has-pro-bibi-bias-1.5228358 (both accessed July 2, 2019).

[62] Asaf Carmel, "A Newspaper With an Agenda," *Haaretz*, July 31, 2007, online: https://www.haaretz.com/israel-news/culture/1.4957138 (accessed July 2, 2019).

[63] Boaz Bismuth & Amos Regev, "'We have come to put an end to Noni Mozes' dictatorship'," *Israel Hayom*, May 9, 2014, online: https://web.archive.org/web/20180702000429/http://www.israelhayom.com/2014/05/09/we-have-come-to-put-an-end-to-noni-mozes-dictatorship/ (accessed June 19, 2019).

headlines, is promoting Netanyahu and his policies (Dahan & Bentham 2017). It has been conveyed that the in-house rules at *Israel Hayom* "state that when unflattering information about the prime minister and his wife is revealed, the report should be relatively modest, with a headline that stresses the response of the Prime Minister's Office and should include criticism of the interests that led to [the information's] publication in the first place."[64] Amos Regev supposedly "intervenes in the content produced by reporters and slants it to provide more positive coverage of Prime Minister Benjamin Netanyahu."[65] And according to the *Economist*, the link between *Israel Hayom* and Netanyahu is so close that "[i]ts headlines are routinely approved by the prime minister's office."[66] Under such circumstances, it comes as no surprise that during the 2015 Knesset elections, *Israel Hayom* "was filled with headlines that repeated Likud campaign themes and generous quotes by Netanyahu while heaping abuse on the other parties."[67] All of these allegations received strong empirical support when, following a legal battle and an order by the Israeli Supreme Court, in August 2017, Netanyahu had to open his phone log. This revealed, on average, around 0.75 phone calls per week between Adelson and the prime minister from 2012 to 2015, and twice as many conversations between Netanyahu and the *Israel Hayom* editor Regev. "In the days following the calls between Netanyahu and Regev, the newspaper featured additional headlines matching the prime minister's messages."[68] With the above in mind, one understands why, in Israel, many people call *Israel Hayom* "Bibiton," merging Netanyahu's nickname with "iton," the Hebrew word for "newspaper."

Of course, the crucial question is what impact Adelson's Bibiton, having become the leading newspaper read by around 30–40 percent of Israel's adult population, is

---

[64] Nati Tucker and Amir Teig, "The Watchdogs' Watchdog: 'Balanced' Journalism Is a Recipe for Corruption," *Haaretz*, August 26, 2014, online: https://www.haaretz.com/israel-news/business/.premium-balanced-journalism-door-to-corruption-1.5261252, also Emilie Grunzweig, "Israel Hayom Censors Suicide Note of Israeli Protester Who Set Himself on Fire," *Haaretz*, July 15, 2012, online: https://www.haaretz.com/israel-hayom-edits-protester-s-suicide-note-1.5266590, and Barak Ravid, "Israel Hayom Buries Top Pundit for Criticizing Netanyahu," *Haaretz*, January 21, 2013, online: https://www.haaretz.com/.premium-israel-hayom-buries-top-pundit-1.5225542 (all accessed July 2, 2019).

[65] Nati Tucker, "Israel's Channel 10 Reports on pro-Netanyahu Slant at Israel Hayom Daily Newspaper," *Haaretz*, February 5, 2013, online: https://www.haaretz.com/.premium-ch-10-adelson-paper-has-pro-bibi-bias-1.5228358, also Anshel Pfeffer, "How Sheldon Adelson Is Changing the Face of Israeli Media," *Haaretz*, April 8, 2014, online: https://www.haaretz.com/.premium-adelson-is-changing-israeli-media-1.5244407 (both accessed July 2, 2019).

[66] "A tough deal to swallow," *Economist*, April 8, 2015, online: http://www.economist.com/news/middle-east-and-africa/21647937-first-political-ramifications-agreement-iran-may-be-felt-israel-tough-deal (accessed May 2, 2019).

[67] Nati Tucker, "Israeli media asking itself how it got the election so wrong," *Haaretz*, March 22, 2015, online: https://www.haaretz.com/.premium-israeli-media-asking-itself-how-it-got-the-election-so-wrong-1.5340097 (accessed July 2, 2019).

[68] Nati Tucker, "Late-night phone logs suggest Netanyahu influenced headlines in Israel's most-read paper," *Haaretz*, September 3, 2017, online: https://www.haaretz.com/israel-news/phone-logs-suggest-netanyahu-influenced-headlines-israel-s-most-read-paper-1.5447954 and Raoul Wootliff, "Forced by court order, Netanyahu reveals 230 calls to Israel Hayom editor," *The Times of Israel*, August 31, 2017, online: https://www.timesofisrael.com/forced-by-court-order-netanyahu-reveals-almost-weekly-phone-calls-with-adelson/ (both accessed July 2, 2019).

having on politics in Israel. On the surface, the conclusion seems easy: out of office since 1999, after *Israel Hayom*'s launch in 2007, Netanyahu has become prime minister at every election. In 2006, the Likud, already under Netanyahu's leadership, received only 9 percent of the votes at the Knesset elections—afterwards, it has steadily increased its share, in 2009: 21.6 percent, in 2013: 23.3 percent, in 2015: 23.4 percent, in 2019: 26.5 percent.[69] However, many other events and processes have also affected Israeli politics during this time period. For example, the Likud's low score in 2006 has to be related to Ariel Sharon, Likud's leader in 2005, founding the new party Kadima, which was later headed by Ehud Olmert, another former Likud politician, after Sharon was incapacitated by a stroke on January 4, 2006. Olmert faced mounting corruption charges, with an indictment served in 2009. Likud's high score in 2013, on the other hand, was achieved in a joint list with the Yisrael Beitenu party (Gerstenfeld 2015). Moreover, many Israelis came to view Sharon and Olmert's 2005 disengagement from Gaza, which Netanyahu opposed (as well as the Second Lebanon War in 2006), as a failure, since Hamas won the 2006 Palestinian legislative election and later took control of Gaza by force, from where thousands of rockets have been fired at Israel, especially between 2006 and 2009. This changing security environment has certainly played a crucial role in shifting Israel's public opinion and election outcomes towards the right (Pedahzur 2012: 189ff, Perliger & Zaidise 2015, Roth 2015). Demographic trends, particularly due to immigration from the former Soviet Union and high birth rates among the orthodox Jewish population, are also contributing to a rightward swing in Israeli politics (Cincotta & Kaufmann 2010, Acosta 2014). In such an unstable political environment, neatly isolating the framing effects of newspaper consumption on political attitudes and behavior, which is complex to start with (Druckman 2004, Chong & Druckman 2007), is becoming very difficult. Existing political communication studies do, nonetheless, demonstrate that consumption of partisan media outlets is influencing political polarization and partisan mobilization in Israel.[70]

The best evidence of *Israel Hayom*'s bearing upon election outcomes can be detected in the reactions of Netanyahu's competitors, which have tried three times to pass legislation that would outlaw the way in which *Israel Hayom* is being published. A first challenge was launched in 2009, when nineteen Knesset members from eight different parties submitted a bill that would have made it a requirement for anybody who holds more than 50 percent of the controlling interest in an Israeli newspaper to be an Israeli citizen and a resident of the country. Sheldon Adelson's ownership of *Israel Hayom* would thus have become

---

[69] For the official election results, see online: https://main.knesset.gov.il/en/mk/pages/elections.aspx (accessed July 4, 2019).

[70] While Tsfati & Chotiner 2016, which finds evidence that selective media exposure is increasing political polarization in Israel, did not study readers of *Israel Hayom*, Dvir-Gvirsman et al. 2015, which finds evidence that partisan media is mobilizing voters in Israel, did include readers of *Israel Hayom*. Unfortunately, no study concentrating specifically on *Israel Hayom* readers could be found.

illegal, but the bill never passed.[71] In 2010, another bill sought to ban the "free distribution of a newspaper for a period of more than a year, with the exception of institutional subscriptions."[72] With Netanyahu enforcing coalition discipline among the Knesset members belonging to his government coalition, he managed to get sixty-one to fourteen votes against the bill during its first reading. The third legislative challenge came during fall 2014 with a "law for the advancement and protection of written journalism in Israel" that would have required *Israel Hayom* to

> charge its readers at least half the price of its cheapest competitor....The law [was] being sponsored by members of rival parties to Netanyahu's Likud, from the right and left, both coalition and opposition members. Even Netanyahu's senior ministers have attacked the paper; Foreign Minister Avigdor Lieberman called it "Pravda" and Economics Minister Naftali Bennett described it as "a mouthpiece of one man."[73]

On November 12, 2014, a forty-three to twenty-three majority, including several parliamentarians from three of Netanyahu's coalition partners, voted for this third "anti-*Israel Hayom*" bill at its preliminary reading. Three weeks later, Netanyahu dissolved the Knesset, which, under Israeli law, implies that bills that have not gone beyond their first reading are being shelved. While there had been other substantial disagreements within his government coalition, especially over the budget and a basic law proposal that aimed at fortifying the character of Israel as a Jewish nation-state, the potential loss of *Israel Hayom* seems to have been a major motivation for the prime minister.[74] For the subsequent elections in 2015, Netanyahu could thus continue to count on *Israel Hayom*'s espousal of his

---

[71] Zvi Zrahiya, "'Anti-Adelson' Bill Would Bar Foreigners From Owning Israeli Newspapers," *Haaretz*, December 18, 2009, online: https://www.haaretz.com/1.4899571, and Haaretz Service and Mazal Mualem, "MKs Look to Ban U.S. Jewish Billionaire From Owning Newspaper," *Haaretz*, December 12, 2009, online: https://www.haaretz.com/1.4965420 (both accessed July 2, 2019).

[72] Zvi Zrahiya, "Knesset Rejects 'Israel Hayom' Law," *Haaretz*, June 3, 2010, online: https://www.haaretz.com/1.5128693, and Zvi Zrahiya, "Agents of PM Scramble to Quash Anti-freebie Law," *Haaretz*, May 30, 2010, online: https://www.haaretz.com/1.5126764 (both accessed July 2, 2019).

[73] Anshel Pfeffer, "Everything You Need to Know About the Israel Hayom (Or anti-Sheldon Adelson) Law," *Haaretz*, November 12, 2014, online: https://www.haaretz.com/.premium-a-primer-on-the-israel-hayom-law-1.5327699, also: Jonathan Lis, "Knesset Advances Bill to Curb Free Distribution of pro-Netanyahu Daily," *Haaretz*, November 12, 2014, online: https://www.haaretz.com/israel-hayom-law-passes-knesset-reading-1.5327681, Jonathan Lis, "Ministers Back Free Vote Over Bill to Ban Free Distribution of Israel Hayom," *Haaretz*, November 2, 2014, online: https://www.haaretz.com/.premium-panel-backs-free-vote-on-free-newspaper-bill-1.5323475 (all accessed July 2, 2019).

[74] Yossi Verter, "Knesset's Dissolution: A Sure Win for One Man," *Haaretz*, December 4, 2014, online: https://www.haaretz.com/.premium-knesset-s-dissolution-sure-win-for-one-man-1.5340934 (accessed July 2, 2019). For an analysis of how control of the media had already been a key focus of Netanyahu during the 1990s, see Peri 2004: 180ff.

candidacy. In the weeks just before the elections, for example, the press run of *Israel Hayom*'s weekend edition was raised from 400,000 to 550,000 copies.[75]

How much Adelson's newspaper has contributed to Netanyahu's victory on March 17, 2015 is again very hard to quantify, not least because anti-Netanyahu campaigns exercised significant countervailing influence.[76] Some of these, notably the V15 campaign, also received funding from abroad, including money from the Jewish-American billionaire S. Daniel Abraham.[77] However, no other Israeli politician has received foreign support as substantial and persistent as Netanyahu has through Sheldon Adelson's financing of *Israel Hayom*. The repeated battles in the Knesset over this relationship show how seriously this has been taken by Israel's parties across the political spectrum. Structural changes in Israel's demography and security environment may account for the broader shift towards the right in Israeli politics, but in and of themselves they cannot explain which political actors on the right would benefit. In Israel's highly fragmented and volatile party system, several candidates could be seen as potentially gaining from more conservative public opinion (Perliger & Zaidise 2015, Roth 2015). But, since 2007, only one of them has had such a massive propaganda machine as *Israel Hayom* behind him: Benjamin Netanyahu.[78] One can therefore conclude that Adelson's investments in Israeli politics have succeeded in helping to keep a politician in power who shares his outlook on Israel's security.

That Adelson's political agency should, overall, be greater transnationally than in the country where he is a citizen is surprising only at first sight. In addition to differing political contexts, where, post-2007, Israel's political climate has been closer to Adelson's positions than in the U.S., the relative size of Adelson's funding varies, too. Between 2007 and 2014, the casino tycoon's campaign expenditure in the U.S. was roughly similar, in absolute monetary terms, to his bankrolling of *Israel Hayom*. Yet, in the U.S., with its much larger electorate, his US$100–150 million for the Republicans have to be contrasted with the total US$7 billion that

---

[75] Nati Tucker, "Israel Hayom Boosts Print Run Ahead of Election," *Haaretz*, March 4, 2015, online: https://www.haaretz.com/israel-news/business/.premium-israel-hayom-boosts-print-run-ahead-of-election-1.5331818 (accessed October 2, 2015).

[76] Thus, the editorial line of *Israel Hayom*'s main competitor, *Yedioth Ahronoth*, expressed strong criticism of Netanyahu throughout the election campaign, see Yossi Verter, "Israel election's biggest battle being fought by newspaper tycoons," *Haaretz*, February 10, 2015, online: https://www.haaretz.com/premium-the-sheldononi-war-of-2015-1.5304251 (accessed July 2, 2019).

[77] Nathan Guttman, "Is V15 a Conduit for American Funds to Benjamin Netanyahu's Opponents?," *Forward*, February 6, 2015, online: http://forward.com/news/israel/214246/is-v15-a-conduit-for-american-funds-to-benjamin-ne/#ixzz3yMEsfZko, "Billionaire backing anti-Netanyahu NGO V15 wishes Labor leader were 'stronger'," *Haaretz*, February 7, 2015, online: https://www.haaretz.com/.premium-v15-backer-wishes-herzog-were-stronger-1.5302991, Glenn Kessler, "Netanyahu's claim that 'tens of millions' in foreign money was aimed against him," *The Washington Post*, March 20, 2015, online: https://www.washingtonpost.com/news/fact-checker/wp/2015/03/20/netanyahus-claim-that-tens-of-millions-in-foreign-money-was-aimed-against-him/ (all accessed July 2, 2019).

[78] Within a context of increasing personalization of politics, as it has been diagnosed for Israel (Balmas et al. 2014), the effect of a leading newspaper endorsing one particular candidate can be expected to particularly strong.

have, at a minimum, been spent on the 2012 presidential election. In the end, despite Adelson's pro-Republican largesse, Obama raised more campaign money than Romney (Vogel 2014: 181ff, West 2014: 40ff). In 2018, when the Democrats regained the House, the Adelsons were the number one donors for the Republican Party, with over US$122 million, but the next largest donors, Michael Bloomberg (US$95 million) and Thomas Steyer (over US$72 million), together gave more to the Democrats.[79] In Israel, a far smaller country where direct campaign financing is highly restrained by law, the multi-billionaire faced much less competition, and his intervention thus had better chances of making a difference. In the U.S., where many other billionaires try to influence politics, Sheldon Adelson has seen both victories, with Trump's Israel policy, and losses, during Obama's presidency. In Israel, he has been helping Netanyahu to stay in power since 2009.

Funding Insurgency? Raj Rajaratnam and the Tamil Tigers

The costs of contemporary conventional warfare—where state-of-the-art fighter jets sell for more than US$100 million and U.S. expenditure on the Iraq and Afghanistan wars calculates in the trillions[80]—seem so high that individuals, even billionaires, are unlikely to make a difference in interstate war. Funding insurgencies or terrorism in asymmetrical conflicts, on the other hand, appears as much more accessible,[81] and, within today's world, increasingly relevant. While interstate war has been declining, political violence related to the so-called "new wars" has become more prevalent. The key characteristic of these new conflicts is the heavy involvement of nonstate actors, such as irredentist nationalities, rebel groups, warlords, mercenaries, or terrorist organizations (van Creveld 1991, Münkler 2002, Kaldor 2012). While allegiances in the new wars are often complex, mobilization around ethnic group identities are a frequent feature, especially in multiethnic states where the government has been pursuing politics of exclusion

---

[79] See online: https://www.opensecrets.org/outsidespending/summ.php?cycle=2018&disp=D&type=V&superonly=N (accessed July 2, 2019).
[80] See the "Costs of War" project at the Watson Institute for International and Public Affairs at Brown University (http://watson.brown.edu/costsofwar/), and Crawford 2014 for a summary. In less developed regions, however, conventional warfare, if it does not involve air force or navy, can be much less costly. Historically, post-WWII, around 56 percent of insurgencies used a guerrilla strategy, and 32 percent a conventional strategy, but in the twenty-first century, guerilla campaigns predominate by far (Jones & Johnston 2013: 5–7).
[81] Seth Jones and Patrick Johnston from the RAND Corporation give the example of the Taliban, whose annual revenues, estimated at US$100 to US$200 million, compared to the annual U.S. war expenditure in Afghanistan with a ratio of 1:500. They define insurgency as "a protracted political–military activity directed toward subverting or displacing the legitimacy of a constituted government and completely or partially controlling the resources of a country through the use of irregular military forces and illegal political organizations" (Jones & Johnston 2013: 1).

and discrimination along ethnic lines (Horowitz 2000, Wolff 2005).[82] If billion-aires have developed a sociopolitical identity that ties them to groups experiencing violent conflict, they may want to intervene in order to advance "their" group's security. Since insurgent groups usually lack the traditional financing mechanisms of state actors (taxes and loans or bonds), they need to find alternative forms of funding:

> Resources are tightly intertwined with insurgency. Although many accounts of insurgency focus on the voluntary provision of resources by peasants and ordinary people, these contributions are often insufficient to fuel organized violence, particularly in situations with a strong counterinsurgent state, regions lacking significant economic wealth, or intense competition among militant groups. Insurgents frequently look to states, diasporas, and a variety of illicit economic activities for the material underpinnings of their rebellion
>
> (Staniland 2012: 145).[83]

The hedge fund billionaire Raj Rajaratnam (*1957), a naturalized U.S. citizen born in Sri Lanka (keeping dual citizenship), and the insurgency of the so-called Tamil Tigers, the Liberation Tigers of Tamil Eelam (LTTE), fit squarely into this framework, as Rajaratnam has been charged with having been a major funding source for the Tigers. The final defeat of the LTTE by the Sri Lankan army on May 19, 2009, after twenty-six years of armed insurgency, and the arrest of Rajaratnam for insider trading in the U.S. on October 16, 2009, for which he has been convicted and sentenced to eleven years in prison on October 13, 2011, have allowed information to surface in order to analyze the billionaire's role in the conflict.

Most scholars agree that the insurgency in Sri Lanka can be seen as an ethnic conflict in which the country's Tamil minority, which represented almost 13 percent of the population in 1981, reacted against various forms of discrimination and exclusion instituted by the post-independence national government, which privileged the Sinhalese majority (74 percent in 1981).[84]

---

[82] This is not to say that ethnic rivalries are the source of conflicts—cross-national quantitative analysis suggests otherwise, pointing to weak state capacity as the main reason for the outbreak of insurgencies (Fearon & Laitin 2003).

[83] During the Cold War, much external funding came from states, as both the U.S. and the Soviet Union supported insurgencies that they expected to be either anti- or pro-Communist; such funding declined massively during the 1990s. While cross-national quantitative analysis indicates that external support for insurgents makes civil wars last longer, exactly how (much) external support aids insur-gencies is unclear and seems to depend on the specifics of the insurgency, notably the type of its organizational structure (Staniland 2012, Testerman 2015).

[84] The 2001 government census, less encompassing than the prior census from 1981, reported 4.3 percent Sri Lankan Tamils, which attests to the high rate of emigration, and also the lives lost, during the war years (DeVotta 2009: 1024). While the Sri Lanka Tamils are largely Hindu, the Sinhalese are

When the government refused to accommodate demands for Tamil autonomy, many Tamil youths became disillusioned with conventional politics and began to argue for the creation of a separate Tamil state, called Eelam. In the wake of the 1972 Constitution that replaced the one created by the British and recognised Buddhism as the state religion, reaffirmed the primacy of the Sinhalese language, and removed formal safeguards for minorities, the Tamil political parties began to articulate a secessionist agenda.... In brief, Tamil nationalism matured in several stages, beginning at the time of Ceylonese independence. As Tamil demands for political power were thwarted, ethnic consciousness turned into a full-fledged secessionist movement (Wayland 2004: 412f).

In 1983, the struggle deteriorated into a civil war, in which the LTTE, under its leader Vellupillai Prabhakaran, became the dominant force fighting for an independent Eelam. By the 1990s, it had won important military victories, held large parts of Sri Lanka's North and East, and had built up a "Black Tigers" squad of suicide bombers to spread terror, which assassinated a former prime minister of India (1991) and a Sri Lankan president (1993). Between 2002 and 2006, peace negotiations took place during an unstable ceasefire, which broke down, and then the fighting resumed until the crushing of the Tigers. In its course, the conflict has claimed at least 100,000 victims and displaced over 1 million people, around half internally, while the other half has sought asylum in India and Western countries, expanding the Tamil diaspora there (DeVotta 2009: 1046f).[85]

In order to maintain the military force to resist the much larger Sri Lankan state, the LTTE required substantial external funding.[86] Most of it—several reports claim up to 80 percent of the annual income the LTTE handled during the 2000s (Fair 2005: 140, Human Rights Watch 2006: 11)—was sourced from the Tamil diaspora. By far the richest member of the Tamil diaspora (in fact, the wealthiest Sri Lanka-born person) has been Raj Rajaratnam, whose family had emigrated to England in 1971, and who later moved to the U.S. for an MBA at Wharton Business School and a career in finance. While his father had been a senior management executive, Rajaratnam built his fortune on his own as a hedge fund manager, first for the bank Needham & Co, from 1997 onwards as founder of the Galleon fund, which had a peak value of US$7 billion in 2008, the year when

mostly Buddhists; their languages also differ strongly. For general overviews of the conflict, see DeVotta 2004 and Jeyaratnam 2000.

[85] In 2009, the largest Tamil diasporas were "in Canada (over 250,000), the United Kingdom (around 150,000), India (over 100,000), Germany (over 50,000), and France, Australia, and Switzerland (around 50,000 each)" (DeVotta 2009: 1023).

[86] "At its apogee between the mid-1990s and 2006, the LTTE controlled nearly one-quarter of Sri Lanka's territory; comprised an army of over 20,000...; commanded a navy with speedboats and nearly a dozen ships for ferrying weapons and supplies,... and operated a nascent air force" (DeVotta 2009: 1023). See also Stokke 2006.

Rajaratnam entered the Forbes list of the 400 richest Americans with an estimated fortune of US$1.8 billion.[87] Coinciding with Raj Rajaratnam's arrest in October 2009, the *Financial Times* reported that a spokesperson for the Sri Lankan Defence Ministry "alleged that Mr Rajaratnam had sponsored the Tamil Tigers for several years with 'many millions of US dollars'."[88] The accused has been denying these charges, which is unsurprising, considering that the U.S. had already designated the LTTE as a "foreign terrorist organization" back in 1997, and given that he is currently facing a civil lawsuit in which LTTE victims from Sri Lanka demand compensation from him.[89] Rajaratnam argues that he has only ever donated money for philanthropic causes like orphanages or emergency relief after the 2004 tsunami in Sri Lanka. U.S. tax records for 2005 and 2006 show that the billionaire's charity Tsunami Relief Inc. donated around US$7 million, half of which went to the Tamil Rehabilitation Organization (TRO).[90] This organization is widely believed to have served—among other channels—as a fundraising conduit and the "development wing" of the LTTE (Human Rights Watch 2006: 11, also Gerharz 2014: 49, 103f). "TRO's efforts worldwide reportedly have allowed the LTTE to use humanitarian aid, which TRO collected from the international community after the December 2004 tsunami, to launch new campaigns to strengthen LTTE military capacity." For this reason, in November 2007, the U.S. Department of the Treasury, using Executive Order 13224, designated the TRO "as a front to facilitate fundraising and procurement for the LTTE," making donations to it illegal.[91]

The tax filings of the Rajaratnam Family Foundation, for which Raj served as the treasurer and his father as president, show donations to the TRO that add up

---

[87] Online: https://web.archive.org/web/20081022145948/http://www.forbes.com/lists/2008/54/400list08_Raj-Rajaratnam_RUQ2.html (accessed July 4, 2019).

[88] James Fontanella-Khan, "Sri Lanka claims Rajaratnam gave Tamil Tigers 'millions'," *Financial Times*, October 18, 2009, online: http://www.ft.com/cms/s/0/9629749a-bc17-11de-9426-00144feab49a.html?dbk#axzz3goOeGSjM (accessed July 4, 2019).

[89] See the case on the law firm's website: https://www.motleyrice.com/article/rajaratnam-us-judge-terror-finance. The case has been judged admissible on April 28, 2014, despite the fact that the plaintiffs suffered their injuries during terrorist attacks in Sri Lanka, because the alleged crime of terrorist financing is being claimed to have happened in the U.S. See: KRISHANTHI et al v. RAJARATNAM et al, No. 2:2009cv05395—Document 161 (D.N.J. 2014), online: http://law.justia.com/cases/federal/district-courts/new-jersey/njdce/2:2009cv05395/233958/161/ (accessed July 2, 2019).

[90] US$2.5 million went directly to the TRO in Colombo, US$1 million went to the U.S. franchise of the TRO. It is not clear how much of these amounts have been Rajaratnam's personal donations, because "Tsunami Relief Inc." also held fundraising events at which many other people donated.

[91] See "Treasury Targets Charity Covertly Supporting Violence in Sri Lanka," *U.S. Department of the Treasury*, November 15, 2007, online: https://www.treasury.gov/press-center/press-releases/Pages/hp683.aspx. The plaintiffs against Rajaratnam claim that he knowingly sponsored terrorism through his donations to the TRO, see KRISHANTHI et al v. RAJARATNAM et al, No. 2:2009cv05395—Document 161 (D.N.J. 2014), online: http://law.justia.com/cases/federal/district-courts/new-jersey/njdce/2:2009cv05395/233958/161/ (accessed July 2, 2019). See also Michael J. de la Merced, "Rajaratnam and the Tamil Tigers Connection," *The New York Times*, October 18, 2009, online (including links to the public tax statements): http://dealbook.nytimes.com/2009/10/18/rajaratnams-donations-and-the-tamil-tigers-connection/?_r=0 (all accessed July 7, 2019).

to over US$6 million between 2003 and 2005.[92] Altogether, the organizations linked to Rajaratnam thus gave almost US$10 million to the TRO between 2003 and 2006, and more than half of it before the tsunami disaster on December 26, 2004. This largely matches the content of a cable from October 13, 2006 by James R. Moore, the deputy chief of the U.S. Embassy in Colombo. In it, he summarized insights from secret reports on LTTE financing between 2003 and 2006, which Sri Lankan government officials had shared with him. If we follow this document, the donations linked to Rajaratnam represented about half of all the donations that the TRO in Sri Lanka received from the U.S., and almost 20 percent of worldwide donations to the TRO in Colombo.[93]

At first sight, the above could suggest that Raj Rajaratnam was indirectly involved in the funding of the LTTE insurgency. A deeper analysis of his role, however, needs to situate Rajaratnam within the field of Tamil diaspora politics. Extensive research, often based on fieldwork, depicts the Tamil community as a uniquely structured field, in which the LTTE in Sri Lanka and the diaspora abroad remained very tightly linked across borders (Fair 2005, Wayland 2004, Radtke 2009, Gerharz 2009, Sriskandarajah 2005). In its elimination, often by force, of rival Tamil liberation movements during the 1980s, and in its military and terrorist campaigns against the government during the 1990s, the LTTE exhibited a highly effective organizational structure, based on strong discipline and hierarchy, with Prabhakaran as the undisputed military and political leader (Staniland 2014: 141–77). This mode spread from warfare to governing when, at the height of its power, from around 2000 to 2004, the LTTE ruled almost half of Sri Lanka's North and East provinces, with total control of the Mullaitivu and Kilinochchi districts (Moorcraft 2012: 32–42, 102f). For this time period at least, it is more fitting to consider the LTTE as an authoritarian proto-government than as a rebel movement (Stokke 2006).

[A]nyone thought to undermine the organization was considered a traitor and was targeted for assassination. The group instituted a pass system to prevent people from exiting its areas. It ruthlessly taxed the civilian population, required each family residing in its areas of control to supply a member for its fighting units, and drafted civilians for manual labor. Whenever the LTTE was short of cadres, children (and sometimes even elderly Tamils) were conscripted

[92] The largest donation—US$5 million to the TRO in LTTE-controlled Northern Sri Lanka (Kilinochchi)—took place in 2003. The public tax filings of the foundation can be found online: https://projects.propublica.org/nonprofits/organizations/226866723 (accessed July 7, 2019).
[93] In this calculation, Rajaratnam donations to the TRO offices in the U.S. and in Colombo have been added together. The US$5 million donation from 2003 to the TRO in Kilinochchi (see prior footnote) does not appear in the embassy cable. See the cable online: https://wikileaks.org/plusd/cables/06COLOMBO1679_a.html (accessed July 7, 2019).

forcibly.... The LTTE's...tactics extended to the Tamil diaspora, with many coerced to contribute toward the separatist cause. (DeVotta 2009: 1032)

Among many Tamils in the diaspora, particularly those, the majority, who left Sri Lanka since the 1970s in reaction to discrimination and the civil war, support for Tamil liberation and emotional attachment to Eelam have been high.[94] The LTTE fostered and channeled this support strategically, by implanting its members in leadership positions at many diaspora organizations.[95] In terms of culture, major festivities in the diaspora revolved around the Tamil Tigers, for example the Martyr's Day and the Heroes Day, which regularly involved broadcastings from Prabhakaran. Usually, such gatherings also served as fundraising occasions. Besides special events, the LTTE employed large numbers of expatriate Tamils that were responsible for collecting donations among the diaspora on a regular basis. This fundraising happened in a highly systematic manner and frequently involved intense psychological pressure, and sometimes extortion and violence, which Human Rights Watch has called a "culture of fear" (Human Rights Watch 2006: 14).

In the late 1980s, Prabhakaran devised a strategy to manipulate these sentiments to financially and politically promote his goals by establishing networks of LTTE cadres within the diaspora. For example, it was a well-known secret among Tamils that LTTE cadre monopolized positions as interpreters within the immigration bureaucracies of Canada, Norway and Switzerland. Since the LTTE saw itself as the ultimate voice of Tamils—and given its use of violence against those who did not—its activity was something that all exiles were forced to take a stand on. Most chose the path of least resistance.... The LTTE's manipulation of many diaspora Tamils has made it almost impossible to determine the true level of the support for militancy. (International Crisis Group 2010: 5)

The reputation of the LTTE as an uncompromising force certainly helped. A credible threat that could not be dealt with by the host states' police or courts was linked to the LTTE's control of Tamil territories in Sri Lanka: they could claim that visits to these areas, as well as the well-being of family members still living there, would depend on the diaspora members' financial support for the LTTE

---

[94] "Because most of the members of the Sri Lankan Tamil diaspora still have family members in Sri Lanka and because most have at least one family member (however near or remote) killed, raped, or tortured in the war, the diasporan Tamils have a strong distrust of Colombo" (Fair 2005: 139, also Pragasam 2012).

[95] This does not imply that the Tamil diaspora communities in the various host states formed one monolithic bloc. In several areas, especially culture and development, but also regarding the peace process between 2002 and 2006, diaspora groupings had their own ideas and projects regarding the future of Tamil Eelam that differed from the LTTE's vision, and sometimes helped to shape the LTTE's agenda (Fair 2005: 144ff, Gerharz 2014). Still, there is scholarly consensus that the Tamil Tigers dominated the cultural and political life of the diaspora.

and its front organizations. Katrin Radtke therefore seems right in her analysis of the moral economy of the Tamil diaspora when she depicts the changing nature of LTTE-support in the diaspora during the 1990s as shifting from "donation to taxation" (Radtke 2009: 203, also Chalk 2008, Fair 2005, Human Rights Watch 2006, La 2004, Solomon & Tan 2007, Wayland 2004).

Any assessment of individual participation in the Tamil liberation struggle thus needs to take the transnational authority of the LTTE into account, which extended far beyond North-Eastern Sri Lanka, deep into the Tamil diaspora communities in Western Europe and North America. At the same time, the internal constitution of diasporas has to be contrasted with the policies of their host states (Wayland 2004, Hägel & Peretz 2005, Shain 2007). In this regard, the 9/11 terror attacks on the U.S. represent a critical juncture, which lead to fundamental change in most of the countries that hosted large Tamil communities. Before 9/11, the political systems of Western liberal democracies offered a very enabling environment for Tamil activists, which could use expansive political and civil rights to advocate for an independent Tamil Eelam (Chalk 2008, Sriskandarajah 2005). As counterterrorism turned into a high priority for Western states, support for the LTTE and many of its affiliate organizations became illegal in key host countries (Chapin 2011). While India (1992), the U.S. (1997), and the UK (2001) had been forerunners in banning the LTTE, Canada and the EU followed suit in 2006; around 2007, LTTE-related NGOs like the TRO, as well as donations to them, also became proscribed. These developments have been reported to make LTTE-fundraising among the diaspora more difficult, also because it gave Tamils in the diaspora better excuses for not donating (Solomon & Tan 2007, International Crisis Group 2010: 6). Nonetheless, the LTTE apparently managed to extract increasing amounts from the diaspora in order to finance its "final war" after 2005.[96]

In light of the features that have characterized the field of Tamil diaspora politics, Rajaratnam's relationship to the LTTE appears much less significant than the headlines have made it look. The civil law suit against Rajaratnam may turn out new findings, however, the available evidence points to a much more limited involvement. To be sure, various details from Rajaratnam's biography indicate that he has been committed to the Tiger's ultimate aims (Raghavan 2013: 88, 107, 317).[97] But such sentiments have been very widespread among

---

[96] Christine Fair claims that the changed environment post-9/11 also allowed members of the diaspora to make more demands vis-à-vis the LTTE, especially with regard to pursuing a political solution in the peace process between 2002 and 2004, but this assessment is not being shared by other studies (Fair 2005: 144ff). Paul Moorcraft reports, on the basis of Sri Lankan intelligence estimates, that the LTTE's annual income from the diaspora more than doubled during 2002–2008, compared to the period 1993–2002, to over US$200 million (Moorcraft 2012: 106). A Human Rights Watch report similarly states that "[i]n late 2005, the escalation of LTTE attacks on Sri Lankan forces... coincided with a massive LTTE fundraising drive among the Tamil diaspora" (Human Rights Watch 2006: 25).

[97] But it appears very unlikely that Rajaratnam or his family had forged ties with the liberation movement in Sri Lanka before their emigration, because Raj (in 1969, off to boarding school, then

members of the Tamil diaspora, and, to a large extent, they can be seen as the outcome of strategic socialization efforts by the LTTE, as its transnational bridge-heads shaped the cultural and political life in the diaspora. "With these activities impinging upon their daily lives in an almost unavoidable fashion, diaspora members have been constantly reminded of their obligation to support the fight for Tamil Eelam" (Gerharz 2014: 50, also Staniland 2014: 157f, 168ff). Despite Rajaratnam's extraordinary status as the world's richest Sri Lankan, his actual level of involvement appears quite ordinary, in proportional terms even low.[98] The amounts he donated to the TRO are, relative to income, smaller than the dona-tions the Tamil Tigers expected from the average diaspora member. Various reports indicate that the LTTE asked, per year, for around 10 percent of the median household income per family in the diaspora communities of France, Canada, and the United Kingdom. If one assumes that Rajaratnam must have earned income from his hedge fund in the range of US$100–200 million annually, then the known contributions of US$10 million to the TRO over the course of four years represent merely a 1.25 percent to 2.5 percent "tax" rate.[99] The annual income of the LTTE has been estimated to have been, during the mid-2000s, within a similar range: US$100–200 million (Fair 2005: 140, Solomon & Tan 2007: 16, International Crisis Group 2010: 6, Moorcraft 2012: 106).

This means that Rajaratnam definitely would have had the financial capacity to boost the Tamil Tiger's resources in a major way.[100] But his known contributions to the TRO represented only a small fraction of the LTTE's total revenues. As soon as donations to the TRO became illegal in the U.S., in 2007, Rajaratnam stopped

eleven years old) and his family (in 1971) had left Sri Lanka for England before the very founding of the Tamil Tigers in 1972 (Mehta 2011).

[98] It is highly unlikely that Rajaratnam used the informal money transfer system undiyal, highly popular among the Sri Lankan Tamil diaspora for remittances, for secret transfers. However, undiyal service providers usually only handled smaller amounts of money up to the five-digit range, and, post-9/11, undiyal also became subject to strict identification and registration regulations (Aiken & Cheran 2005).

[99] These are only rough estimates. Nothing is known about whether the average Tamil household had income above or (more likely) below the national median. The OECD reports the following median household disposable incomes for 2007: US$20,000 in France, US$25,000 in Canada and the UK (OECD 2011c: 43); LTTE fundraisers reportedly asked individual Tamil families to donate around €2,000 in France, between Cdn$2,500 and Cdn$5,000 in Canada, and around £2,000 in the UK (Human Right Watch 2006: 25, Solomon & Tan 2007: 19). Hedge funds typically charge their clients according to the formula "2 + 20": a 2 percent management and a 20 percent performance fee. At its height, Rajaratnam's Galleon Group managed around US$7 billion and posted a return on investment of 25.69 percent in 2006 and 12.2 percent in 2007, which, according to "2 + 20," would have generated income of around US$500 million in 2006 and US$300 million in 2007 for Galleon, from which would need to be deducted taxes and expenses (Raghavan 2013: 106ff, 266, also Mallaby 2010: 381ff). Rajaratnam's *Forbes*-estimated wealth of US$1.8 billion in 2007 also indicates income between US $100 million and US$200 million per year, on average, since 1997, the founding year of the Galleon Group.

[100] Whether more money actually would have improved the LTTE's chances in the war is questionable—when the LTTE was crushed in 2009, its funds were far from depleted (International Crisis Group 2010: 7f, Moorcraft 2012: 106).

giving. In any case, his political behavior appears to have been largely in conformity with the social norms that shaped the field of Tamil diaspora politics.[101] We have no indications that, apart from his donations, Rajaratnam tried to influence the conflict in Sri Lanka in any other way, e.g. by making his financial contributions conditional upon specific political decisions, for example regarding the peace negotiations. Analytically speaking, there is little to suggest that he exercised significant political agency within Tamil diaspora politics beyond following the rules of the game.

---

[101] In general, the biographical information gathered by Anita Raghavan (2013) paints a picture of Raj Rajaratnam as being someone primarily driven by material ambitions, which adds to the impression that exercising political agency was less important for him than his business success.

6

Economy

The pursuit of wealth is the most trivial goal that makes billionaires enter world politics. Few people will be surprised to learn that some individuals who have dedicated their lives to wealth accumulation are sometimes trying to intervene in politics across borders to advance their material interests. It's what we would expect from billionaires with a global business outlook. The political pursuit of wealth can happen legally, via the lobbying of foreign governments, or illegally (Abbot & Snidal 2002), when it involves the bribing of foreign officials (Elliott 1997, Rose-Ackerman & Palifka 2016). Examples of both are not hard to find. A case in point is the Indian steel-magnate Lakshmi Mittal, with his efforts to lobby British, U.S., and EU politicians in order to boost the business prospects of his company ArcelorMittal, the world's largest steel-maker. He apparently wants to make more money to be able to continue buying the most expensive homes in the world, and to finance the most extravagant parties.[1] In late 2016, the Israeli billionaire Beny Steinmetz, whose company Beny Steinmetz Group Resources is active in natural resource extraction in Africa, was put under house arrest in relation to "claims that he paid millions of dollars in bribes to secure mineral assets in one of the world's poorest nations," Guinea.[2] In 2019, Steinmetz reached a deal, mediated by the former president of France, Nicolas Sarkozy, in which the Guinean government dropped its corruption charges against him.

Instances of lobbying and corruption in the pursuit of wealth also concern several of the billionaires that I study in other contexts. Thus, in 2016, Sheldon

---

[1] See: "Glimpsing a fairytale wedding," BBC News, June 22, 2004, online: http://news.bbc.co.uk/2/hi/south_asia/3830009.stm; "Mittal 'outraged' by Steelgate row," BBC News, February 22, 2002, online: http://news.bbc.co.uk/2/hi/uk_news/politics/1834776.stm; "LN Mittal spent $470,000 lobbying with US on China," *The Economic Times*, May 7, 2009, online: https://economictimes.indiatimes.com/news/international/ln-mittal-spent-470000-lobbying-with-us-on-china/articleshow/4493659.cms?from=mdr; Jonathan Leake and Bojan Pancevski, "Carbon credits bring Lakshmi Mittal £1bn bonanza," *The Sunday Times*, December 6, 2009, online: https://www.thetimes.co.uk/article/carbon-credits-bring-lakshmi-mittal-pound1bn-bonanza-wdlf29x5vf8 (all accessed July 7, 2019).

[2] See Ian Cobain and Peter Beaumont, "Israeli tycoon Beny Steinmetz arrested over Guinea bribery claims," *The Guardian*, December 19, 2016, online: https://www.theguardian.com/world/2016/dec/19/israeli-tycoon-beny-steinmetz-arrested-over-guinea-bribery-claims, also Patrick Radden Keefe, "Buried Secrets: How an Israeli billionaire wrested control of one of Africa's biggest prizes," *The New Yorker*, July 8, 2013, online: http://www.newyorker.com/magazine/2013/07/08/buried-secrets, and Franz Wild and Thomas Biesheuvel, "Mining Billionaire Ends Bitter Guinea Dispute After Months of Secret Negotiations," Bloomberg, February 25, 2019, online: https://www.bloomberg.com/news/articles/2019-02-25/steinmetz-stages-guinea-comeback-in-sarkozy-brokered-deal (all accessed July 7, 2019).

Billionaires in World Politics. Peter Hägel, Oxford University Press (2020). © Peter Hägel.
DOI: 10.1093/oso/9780198852711.001.0001

Adelson's Las Vegas Sands Corporation "agreed to pay $9 million to end the Securities and Exchange Commission's more than five-year probe into whether it violated a federal anti-bribery law by paying a consultant to help it do business in China and Macau."[3] When Bill Gates was the CEO of Microsoft, the software giant lobbied hard to avoid antitrust rulings in the U.S., the EU, and other countries (Auletta 2001, Gavil & First 2014: 185–234). Yet, most multinational corporations that are not controlled by a billionaire engage in lobbying, too, and some, e.g. Siemens, have also been condemned for their bribery of foreign officials.[4] Oftentimes, such lobbying or corruption do not have a major influence on world politics, because they are mainly about winning local favors in countries where a company wants to increase its profits. In order to emphasize the relevance for world politics, I have therefore tried to find cases where the billionaire's pursuit of wealth has larger implications. As the Koch brothers try to guard their fossil fuel–related business, their interventions in U.S. politics can affect global climate change mitigation. And when Rupert Murdoch attempts to boost his global media empire, elections in foreign countries can be at stake.

Protecting Fossil Fuels: The Koch Brothers and Climate Change

Charles Koch (*1935) and David Koch (1940–2019) have co-owned Koch Industries, their stakes in which *Forbes* estimated to be worth US$50.5 billion for each of them in 2019, which made them share the eleventh rank on the list of the world's richest people. Until 2018, the brothers usually acted together, in business as in politics.[5] David then retreated, for health reasons, in June 2018, and passed away in August 2019. How much of their wealth is fungible is hard to know—since Koch Industries is a privately held company (the second largest in the U.S.), it is not required to publish annual reports and financial statements, which makes it difficult to specify profit generation. The company claims to have, historically, reinvested 90 percent of its earnings, and to have almost 120,000 employees in fifty countries in 2019.[6] The brothers inherited the firm from their father in 1967, when it had "650 employees and a value of about $50 million"

---

[3] "GOP Donor Sheldon Adelson's Company to Pay $9 million in Bribery Case," *Fortune*, April 7, 2016, online: http://fortune.com/2016/04/07/sheldon-adelson-sec-bribery/ (accessed July 10, 2017).

[4] David Gow, "Record US fine ends Siemens bribery scandal," *The Guardian*, December 16, 2008, online: https://www.theguardian.com/business/2008/dec/16/regulation-siemens-scandal-bribery (accessed June 9, 2019).

[5] See Mayer 2016: 53, Schulman 2014: 4ff, 89ff, 96, 244, 365 and John McCormick and Bill Allison, "David Koch Steps Down From Family Business, Political Work," Bloomberg, June 5, 2018, online: https://www.bloomberg.com/news/articles/2018-06-05/david-koch-stepping-down-from-business-and-political-activities (accessed June 9, 2019).

[6] Online: https://www.kochind.com/about (accessed June 9, 2019).

(Schulman 2014: 81, also 7–88). Charles has been chairman and CEO of Koch Industries since then, David joined later, and together they bought out their two other brothers, Frederick and Bill, in 1981. Koch Industries has grown into a conglomerate that had, until the mid-2000s, "labored largely as a middleman in the oil and petrochemical industries" (ibid.: 242), operating petroleum refineries and pipelines, as well as providing related engineering, trading, and financial services, which also include other commodities such as minerals and nitrogen (Koch 2007, 2015). The company diversified with the purchases of Invista (2004), a synthetic-textiles producer, and Georgia-Pacific (2005), a pulp and paper company (Schulman 2014: 240ff). Still, fossil fuels have long been at the heart of Koch Industries, which, in 2015, was among the largest lease-holders of tar sands in Canada, and, with the Pine Bend refinery in Rosemount, Minnesota, owned one of the major refineries of Canadian heavy crude oil in the U.S.[7]

Politically, the Koch brothers have been self-declared libertarians for most of their lives. Their father, Fred Koch, had been one of the founding members of the John Birch Society (1958), a radical anti-communist group that promotes laissez-faire capitalism and is against government intervention, taxation, and redistribution (Schulman 2014: 40–56, Mayer 2016: 38ff). While much of this seems to have taken root in their convictions, Charles and David moved away from communist conspiracy theories and were drawn to libertarian thinkers and groups. In economics, the Austrian school, especially the ideas of Ludwig von Mises and Friedrich von Hayek, have strongly influenced the brothers' beliefs. In the late 1970s, Charles described his view on government as "[i]t is to serve as a night watchman, to protect individuals and property from outside threat, including fraud. That is the maximum"; his position has hardly changed since.[8] Within Koch Industries, Charles has advanced a (copyrighted) "Market-Based Management" style that tries to apply the logics of entrepreneurship and creative

---

[7] The exact calculation of Koch Industries' holdings in Canada is difficult, because the registration process for tar leases (including joint ventures and intermediaries) is not fully transparent, see David Sassoon, "Koch Brothers' Political Activism Protects Their 50-Year Stake in Canadian Heavy Oils," *InsideClimateNews*, May 10, 2012, online: https://insideclimatenews.org/news/20120510/koch-indus tries-brothers-tar-sands-bitumen-heavy-oil-flint-pipelines-refinery-alberta-canada, Steven Mufson, "Does Koch Industries hold most Canadian oil sands leases? It's complicated," *Washington Post*, April 7, 2014, online: https://www.washingtonpost.com/business/economy/does-koch-industries-hold-most-canadian-oil-sands-leases-its-complicated/2014/04/07/2470e5e4-be70–11e3-b574-f874887 1856a_story.html?utm_term=.564b63284c25 and Bruce Livesey, "How Canada made the Koch brothers rich," National Observer, May 5, 2015, online: http://www.nationalobserver.com/2015/05/04/news/ how-canada-made-koch-brothers-rich (all accessed June 9, 2019). Historically, the Pine Bend refinery has been one of the most profitable assets within the Koch empire. Koch Industries' petroleum-related activities are gathered within its subsidiary Flint Hills Resources, which owns two other major refineries in Corpus Christi, Texas.

[8] See Schulman 2014: 106 and Koch Industries' own website of "Kochfacts," where more recent statements of Charles Koch are being collected, e.g. his 2012 "Perspectives on Economic Freedom," in which he argues that "big governments are inherently inefficient and harmful" (online: http://web.archive. org/web/20120828054037/http://www.kochfacts.com/kf/perspectiveseconomicfreedom/(accessed June 12, 2019).

destruction to the inner workings of the conglomerate (Koch 2007, 2015, Schulman 2014: 240–55). Unlike conservative billionaires, such as Rupert Murdoch, whose libertarian principles are largely limited to the economic realm, the Koch brothers' belief in maximizing individual freedom seems to apply more broadly. They spoke out against the Vietnam War, they cofounded (and funded) the Cato Institute, a think tank that is promoting libertarian positions also when it comes to civil liberties and foreign policy, and Koch Industries has started to advocate for criminal justice reform in the U.S. to reduce mass incarceration.[9]

Nonetheless, the Koch brothers' primary concern has been economic freedom, which clearly coincides with their business interests. They have, for example, repeatedly supported Republican politicians who share their economic agenda even if these were championing conservative positions on social issues (Schulman 2014: 309, 351, 362, Mayer 2016: 4, 88, Skocpol & Hertel-Fernandez 2016: 689f). At the most basic level, for billionaires, minimizing the role of the state promises to reduce their tax burden—the less a government spends and the less it redistributes, the less revenues it will have to raise in taxes, which allows people to keep more of their income and wealth.[10] Richard Fink, Executive Vice President responsible for public affairs at Koch Industries back then, put it succinctly during a confidential meeting at one of the Koch brothers' seminars in 2014: "We want to decrease regulations. Why? It's because we can make more profit, O.K.? Yeah, and cut government spending so we don't have to pay so much taxes."[11] A key threat to the Koch brothers' wealth are environmental regulations, since Koch Industries is so deeply invested in the petro-chemical business. Environmental protection laws are the epitome of regulations that aim to limit or sanction business externalities, such as pollution, thereby increasing the costs of doing business (Coase 1960, Regan 1972). Be it filter systems for factories and refineries, or safety standards for toxic substances, much environmental legislation has strong effects on Koch Industries' profit margins. According to official data aggregated by the Political Economy Research Institute at the University of Massachusetts Amherst,

[9] Schulman 2014: 96ff, 103ff and Koch Industries online: http://news.kochind.com/feature-stories/ and-justice-for-all (accessed June 12, 2019).

[10] The Koch brothers themselves have argued that it would be easier for them to lobby for government favors, such as subsidies, instead of promoting freedom, see Matthew Continetti, "The Paranoid Style in Liberal Politics," *Weekly Standard*, April 4, 2011, online: http://www.weeklystandard. com/paranoid-style-liberal-politics/article/555525?page=3 (accessed June 12, 2019).

[11] Citation based on the transcript of an audio recording obtained from an anonymous attendee of the political strategy seminar, organized by the Koch brothers, on June 15, 2014. In his talk, Fink emphasized how, in order to reach more people, his audience (presumably mostly wealthy donors) needs to develop a freedom narrative that goes beyond self-interest and can offer something to society's "middle." See Lauren Windsor, "Top Koch Strategist Argues The Minimum Wage Leads Directly To Fascism," *Huffpost*, September 3, 2014, online: https://www.huffpost.com/entry/koch-brothers-record ing_n_5757592, as well as the full transcript: http://web.archive.org/web/20141009182614/https:// ladylibertine.net/2014/09/02/road/ (accessed June 12, 2019).

in 2014, Koch Industries ranked as number eight among the top one hundred air polluters in the U.S.[12] Indeed, as the company grew during the 1980s and 1990s, it had several run-ins with the law, which all boiled down to insufficient compliance with costly environmental and safety regulations:

> In 1995, the Justice Department sued Koch for lying about leaking millions of gallons of oil from its pipelines and storage facilities in six different states. . . . Koch industries agreed to pay a $30 million fine, which was the biggest in history at that point, for violations of the Clean Water Act. . . . [In a wrongful death lawsuit, in] 1999, [a jury] found Koch Industries guilty not just of negligence but of malice, too, because it had known about the extreme hazards its decaying pipeline had posed. . . . The jury . . . imposed a fine . . . demanding Koch Industries pay . . . $296 million. At the time, it was the largest wrongful death award on record.[13]

After these expensive verdicts, which had shown that trying to cut corners in the pursuit of profits can be financially damaging, Charles Koch shifted his company's behavior towards maximum compliance with the existing legal framework. At the same time, the legal brawls made the Koch brothers even more aware of how much politics can affect their company's fortune (Schulman 2014: 229f, Mayer 2016: 138). An ongoing worry for the future of Koch Industries concerns the policy debate over how to respond to climate change. If governments decide to intervene in the economy in ways that make the use of fossil fuels (and their derivative products) more expensive, or if they subsidize competitors (alternative energy sources), substantial parts of the Koch brothers' business empire would be threatened. While most of the other policy issues relevant to the Koch brothers fall mainly within U.S. domestic politics, climate change obviously has a global dimension.

---

[12] Political Economy Research Institute (University of Massachusetts Amherst), "Toxic 100 Air Polluters Index (2016 Report, based on 2014 Data)," online: https://www.peri.umass.edu/toxic-100-air-polluters-index-2016-report-based-on-2014-data; on their "Greenhouse 100 Polluters Index (2016 Report, based on 2014 Data)," *Koch Industries* ranked 22nd, emitting 0.42 percent of all U.S. greenhouse gases (online: https://www.peri.umass.edu/greenhouse-100-polluters-index); on their "Toxic 100 Water Polluters Index: (2016 Report, based on 2014 Data)," it ranked 11th. Koch Industries has pointed out that what the Political Economy Research Institute calls pollution are legally permitted emissions, online: http://web.archive.org/web/20150411150514/http://www.kochfacts.com/kf/kochs-position-on-climate-changegreenpeace-distortions/ (all accessed June 12, 2019).

[13] Mayer 2016: 126–30. See also Schulman 2014: 211–28, and Asjylan Loder and David Evans, "Koch brothers flout law getting richer with secret Iran sales," *Bloomberg Markets*, October 3, 2011, online: https://www.bloomberg.com/news/articles/2011-10-02/koch-brothers-flout-law-getting-richer-with-secret-iran-sales as well as the response by Koch Industries, "Koch General Counsel Mark Holden Responds to Bloomberg Markets Magazine," October 27, 2011, online: http://web.archive.org/web/20120416072727/http://www.kochfacts.com/kf/koch-general-counsel-mark-holden-responds-to-bloomberg-markets-magazine/. Daniel Indiviglio argues that Koch Industries' track record is not much different from other major corporations in similar sectors, but he neglects to take the magnitudes of the damage and the fines into account ("Bloomberg's Exposé on Koch Industries Reveals . . . What Exactly?," *The Atlantic*, October 4, 2011,   online: https://www.theatlantic.com/business/archive/2011/10/bloombergs-expos-on-koch-industries-reveals-what-exactly/246154/) (all accessed June 12, 2019).

Given their strong libertarian beliefs, their material interests, and their run-ins with the law, it is not surprising that the Koch brothers entered politics. The extent and the determination of their political involvement, however, continues to stun observers. Technically, almost all of their efforts take place in the form of philanthropy, by creating, funding, and controlling organizations that, under the U.S. tax code, are considered as nonprofit, which can make contributions to them tax-deductible.[14] The evolution of the Koch brothers' political behavior can be divided into four stages. At first, from the late 1960s until 1980, the brothers, mainly Charles, funded various libertarian groups and projects, many of which were located at the fringe of U.S. politics. But a larger goal existed already. "Charles began in institution building.... To Charles, libertarianism wasn't just theoretical. He wanted action. Wholesale political and social change" (Schulman 2014: 99, 102). The most important legacies from this period are the research and education initiatives, the Institute for Humane Studies and the Cato Institute,[15] which develop and spread the libertarian message and provide policy advice. While the Koch brothers have built all their ideological and political projects in coalitions with other like-minded people, from the beginning, "the Kochs exerted unusually tight personal control over their philanthropic endeavors" (Mayer 2016: 148, 162, also Schulman 2014: 312ff). The capstone of this period was David Koch's running as the vice-presidential nominee of the Libertarian Party during the 1980 presidential election. The nationwide campaign was largely sponsored by David himself, and brought the party over 1 percent of the national vote. Afterward, the Koch brothers realized that they had to reach beyond the libertarian movement in order to gain more political influence (ibid.: 109–16).

During the second period, which covers the 1980s and 1990s, the Koch brothers, while maintaining their promotion of libertarian ideas, spent more efforts on influencing public policy at the federal level. Daniel Schulman has noted how closely their political plan resembled their company: "Their plan for

---

[14] Not all nonprofit organizations gain a status that makes contributions to them tax-deductible. For example, today's centerpiece of the Koch brothers' political machine, Americans For Prosperity, is a 501(c)(4) social welfare organization under the IRS tax code; it is itself tax-exempt, but donations to it are not tax-deductible. However, tax-deductible donations can be channeled to other eligible foundations first, e.g. the Americans For Prosperity Foundation, which can then donate to Americans For Prosperity, which ends up achieving the same tax deduction for the original donor. The Koch brothers appear to have been channeling money using this method, see Mayer 2016: 163, Joanna Smith, "Big money fuels health care battle," *The Star*, August 1, 2009, online: https://www.thestar.com/life/health_wellness/2009/08/01/big_money_fuels_health_care_battle.html, and Rick Cohen, "The Starfish and the Tea Party, Part II," *Nonprofit Quarterly*, September 15, 2010, online: https://nonprofitquarterly.org/2010/09/15/the-cohen-report-the-starfish-and-the-tea-party-part-ii/ (all accessed June 12, 2019).

[15] The Institute for Humane Studies had been founded in 1961 by Baldy Harper. Since his death in 1973, the Koch brothers have played a leading role in the institute, see Chris Young, "Koch-funded think tank offers schools course in libertarianism," *Center for Public Integrity*, September 11, 2014, online: https://www.publicintegrity.org/2014/08/26/15387/koch-funded-think-tank-offers-schools-course-libertarianism (accessed June 12, 2019). For their control over the Cato Institute, see Schulman 2014: 103ff, 314–24, also Mayer 2016: 148ff.

bringing about a free-market epoch and Koch Industries' business model—gathering raw materials and refining them into more valuable products consumers desire—were basically one and the same" (Schulman 2014: 264). Accordingly, the brothers have often relied on corporate executives, which had proven themselves within Koch Industries, when staffing their political outfits—as was the case with Richard Fink, who has served as Charles Koch's chief political strategist since the 1980s.[16] If they couldn't find the appropriate human resources in-house, the Koch brothers hired external professionals. In 1981, the Cato Institute moved from California to Washington, D.C., in order to be at the heart of politics, and a new think tank, which later came to be called the Mercatus Center, was being created nearby, with Koch money and under Fink's direction, at George Mason University (in Fairfax, Virginia). While the think tanks generated research and policy proposals, in 1984, the Kochs and Fink launched Citizens for a Sound Economy as an advocacy and lobbying group that directly engaged with the legislative process in the capital. It was made to look like a consumer grassroots organization, but actually represented corporate interests, a tactic that would later be repeated in other Koch-funded campaigns. "What we needed was a sales force that participated in political campaigns or town hall meetings, in rallies, to communicate to the public at large much of the information that these think tanks were creating," David Koch reminisced.[17] Citizens for a Sound Economy advocated for privatization and less taxation, and cultivated close ties with the Reagan administration. During the 1990s, Citizens for a Sound Economy fought, with success, the Clinton administration's healthcare reform, which would have made it mandatory for employers to offer health insurance for their employees, as well as a proposed new energy tax, which would have made the use of nonrenewable energy more expensive, potentially hurting Koch Industries.[18]

The beginning of the third stage in the evolution of the Kochs' politics came in 2003. It would turn their various outfits into a highly professional political machine, operating nationwide and integrating many other like-minded donors and activists, several of which are also billionaires. That year, Charles and David organized the first of what would become twice-yearly secret "seminars," to which they invite wealthy individuals, in order to raise funds and to coordinate political action. Starting very small, by 2010, the Koch seminars had over two hundred

---

[16] Daniel Schulman, "Charles Koch's Brain," *Politico*, September/October 2014, online: http://www.politico.com/magazine/politico50/2014/charles-kochs-brain.html#.WUFQRIx9670 (accessed June 12, 2019).

[17] Matthew Continetti, "The Paranoid Style in Liberal Politics," *Weekly Standard*, April 4, 2011, online: http://www.weeklystandard.com/paranoid-style-liberal-politics/article/555525?page=3 (accessed June 12, 2019).

[18] Both the healthcare reform and the energy tax (the so-called BTU tax) had many more opponents than just the Koch brothers, hence it is difficult to single out their contribution via Citizens for a Sound Economy. In the case of the BTU tax, however, local pressure (via targeted rallies and ads) arranged by Citizens for a Sound Economy appears to have played a major role in swinging key Democratic legislators against Clinton's proposal. See Schulman 2014: 266–70 and Erlandson 1994.

attendants, and more than five hundred in 2016. Since 2012, the seminars have become institutionalized under the helm of the Freedom Partners Chamber of Commerce, which, according to *Politico*, acts as "the Koch brothers' secret bank," gathering money from members and seminar attendants, and distributing it to advocacy groups, politicians, and political organizations that promote the "economic freedom" agenda.[19] Beyond political discussions and fundraising, the seminars also fulfill an important social function, to "build and leverage social solidarity—weaving ties among wealthy donors and between donors and other political players" (Sclar et al. 2016: 16). The most important recipient of Koch-gathered funds has become Americans for Prosperity, which also began in 2003, after Citizens for a Sound Economy disintegrated, following internal disagreements between the Koch brothers and the organization's chairman, Dick Armey, who left to form FreedomWorks. The Koch brothers set up Americans for Prosperity as a "general-purpose advocacy and constituency mobilization federation,...which deploys a combination of advertising, lobbying and grassroots agitation during and between elections" (Skocpol & Hertel-Fernandez 2016: 686).

Regarding ideology and goals, the branching-out of the Koch brothers implied a narrowing of their libertarian agenda in politics, which became more than ever limited to "economic freedom." Potentially divisive questions such as social issues or foreign policy, on which fellow millionaires and billionaires are more likely to disagree, have largely been avoided. In analytical terms, the Kochs have answered Robert Dahl's challenge of the ruling class' "low potential for unity" by concentrating on what Jeffrey Winters sees as collective "income defense" by oligarchs (Dahl 1958: 465, Winters 2011: 208). Whereas, in the past, the Koch brothers wanted to create a libertarian alternative to the Republican Party, since the third stage of their politicking, most of their activism is geared towards making the Republican Party, in which they have never held an official position, adapt stances that match their own. This strategy came to the forefront during the 2008 and 2012 presidential elections, in the Koch brothers' fight against Barack Obama, but it has also been ongoing in many other elections, both at the federal level and within states. In 2012, post–Citizens United, organizations linked to the Koch brothers spent over US$400 million, and Americans for Prosperity claimed several hundred employees and over 2 million activists (Schulman 2014: 292, Mayer 2016: 314, Vogel 2014: 124ff). In their deep analysis of the relationship between the Koch brothers and the Republican Party, Theda Skocpol and Alexander Hertel-Fernandez conclude:

[19] Mike Allen & Jim Vandehei, "The Koch brothers' secret bank," *Politico*, September 11, 2013, online: http://www.politico.com/story/2013/09/behind-the-curtain-exclusive-the-koch-brothers-secret-bank-096669 (accessed June 12, 2019). The other main vehicle used by the Koch brothers to gather funds is the Center to Protect Patients' Rights, see Schulman 2014: 311ff and Mayer 2016: 188ff.

Americans for Prosperity...enforces its own highly disciplined policy agenda but at the same time is thoroughly intertwined with the Republican Party.... [T]he contemporary Koch operation has put in place a parallel federation that can discipline and leverage Republican politicians across multiple levels of government. (2016: 688, 696)

In many ways, the Kochs' network has taken on the functions of a political party, with Republican Party politicians being auditioned at the brothers' seminars, who, if they conform to the "economic freedom" agenda, receive extensive support, not just financially, but also in the form of actual voter mobilization efforts.[20] Although the Koch network looks like a complex web of separate organizations, several of which have no direct legal link to the Koch brothers or Koch Industries, the overall coordination of it appears to be centralized around the two billionaires. Many former and current senior executives of Koch Industries, presumably loyal to Charles and David, occupy key positions, such as Mark Holden, who is Chairman of the Board of the Freedom Partners Chamber of Commerce and Senior Vice President, as well as General Counsel, of Koch Industries.[21] Obviously, this does not mean that the Koch brothers control the donors in their network, or the Republican Party. Several of the billionaires that have cooperated with Charles and David, such as Sheldon Adelson, Paul Singer, Robert Mercer, or Betsy and Dick DeVos, have also created and worked with other conservative political ventures. Likewise, the Koch brothers have at times supported different free market think tanks and political advocacy groups like the American Enterprise Institute, the Club for Growth, the Heritage Foundation, or the Manhattan Institute for Policy Research, in which other billionaire patrons, e.g. Richard Mellon Scaife, have played bigger roles (Mayer 2016: 12–18, 77, 256). When it comes to the Tea Party movement, which, since 2009, has radicalized the Republican Party, the Koch brothers have been a major backer, but not as much as the organization of their former partner, Dick Armey's FreedomWorks (Skocpol & Williamson 2012, Vogel 2014: 134–44, Mayer 2016: 165–97). During the 2012 elections, while Koch-related spending was the largest financial

[20] Through the Freedom Partners Chamber of Commerce, the Kochs own parts of the political data analytics firm i360 (http://www.i-360.com/), which has merged with the brothers' earlier database of digital voter profiles, Themis. See Mike Allen & Kenneth P. Vogel, "Inside the Koch data mine," *Politico*, 8 December 2014, online: http://www.politico.com/story/2014/12/koch-brothers-rnc–113359 (accessed April 6, 2019), Mayer 2016: 368ff.

[21] Probably, the complexity of the Koch network is intentional, in order to exploit different legal statuses for different political activities, to reap various tax advantages, to be able to guarantee anonymity to donors, and to conceal the Koch brothers' overall strategy. The network has been visualized within the front and end covers of Mayer 2016, as well as by *opensecrets/Center for Responsive Politics* (https://www.opensecrets.org/news/2014/01/koch-network-a-cartological-guide/) and *ProPublica* (https://projects.propublica.org/graphics/koch). See Skocpol & Hertel-Fernandez 2016: 686, Mayer 2016: 148, 162, Schulman 2014: 312ff, Vogel 2014: 131 and https://freedompartners.org/about/ (all accessed June 6, 2019).

force, the more traditionally conservative super-PAC American Crossroads, cofounded by Karl Rove and other Republican Party insiders, did not trail far behind, spending over US$325 million (Vogel 2014: 168ff). In such a crowded conservative universe, where many resourceful individuals and organizations rival for influence over the Republican Party, it is hard to isolate the Koch brothers' impact, especially since their economic freedom agenda is often overlapping with the interests of corporate America and other wealthy individuals.[22] Moreover, if one only looks at the results of the presidential elections, the Koch brothers' political interventions have been failures: Obama was elected twice, despite their massive agitation against him, and in 2016, fellow billionaire Donald Trump won the elections without support from the Kochs, who had favored other Republican candidates, because several of Trump's economic stances, e.g. on trade and immigration, contradicted libertarian economics.[23] At the same time, the Koch brothers have certainly helped to shift the Republican Party further to the right on economic issues such as taxation, healthcare and social spending, regulation, and labor union rights, especially within state-level politics (Skocpol & Hertel-Fernandez 2016: 692–6). Apparently, in response to their disappointments at federal elections, and also in order to reduce the harmful publicity that has cast them as selfish radical villains, which reflected negatively on Koch Industries, Charles and David have adjusted their strategy once more after 2012. During this fourth stage, they now want to focus less on elections and concentrate more on policies, and they are engaged in a major "rebranding," putting greater efforts into public relations and training activists, with the goal to convince more people of free market values.[24] While much of the above is confined to domestic politics, climate change has remained at the core of the Koch brothers' politics for decades.

Anthropogenic climate change is the global public policy challenge par excellence—it affects the whole Earth, and it requires global cooperation and efforts in order to be mitigated effectively (Victor 2011, Keohane 2015). From

---

[22] In their comprehensive accounts of how U.S. politics has come to represent more and more the interests of the wealthy few, at the expense of the lower and middle classes, Martin Gilens never refers to the Koch brothers, and Jacob Hacker and Paul Pierson mention them only fleetingly (Gilens 2012, Hacker & Pierson 2010: 283f). While this constitutes a serious gap in their analysis, probably due to a lack of information about the Kochs at the time when their books were written, it also shows how the Koch brothers have been part of larger trend, driven by many powerful actors.

[23] "Full Transcript of Charles Koch's Interview with Fortune," *Fortune*, July 12, 2016, online: http://fortune.com/2016/07/12/transcript-charles-koch-fortune/ and Charles Koch, "Trump's policies must not benefit only big businesses like mine," *Washington Post*, April 27, 2017, online: https://www.washingtonpost.com/opinions/charles-koch-trumps-policies-must-not-benefit-only-big-businesses-like-mine/2017/04/27/aaed9d74-29ed-11e7-a616-d7c8a68c1a66_story.html?utm_term=.da064aebb708 (both accessed June 6, 2019).

[24] Ashley Parker and Maggie Haberman, "With Koch Brothers Academy, Conservatives Settle In for Long War," *The New York Times*, September 6, 2016, online: https://www.nytimes.com/2016/09/07/us/politics/kochs-republican-conservative.html, also Jane Mayer, "New Koch," *The New Yorker*, January 25, 2016, online: http://www.newyorker.com/magazine/2016/01/25/new-koch (both accessed June 6, 2017).

an IR perspective, the Koch brothers' interventions in the debate over climate change matter in two ways: if they take actions across borders, and, more importantly, if they affect the national and international climate change policies of the U.S., which represents a classic case of the domestic sources of foreign policy (Hiscox 2017). The changing position of the U.S. within global environmental politics is, indeed, a puzzling question. Up until the 1980s, the U.S. was a leader in this field, but from the 1990s onwards, the EU has taken over this role, and the U.S. has frequently acted as a laggard or even a spoiler when it comes to international environmental treaties, e.g., when it failed to ratify the 1997 Kyoto Protocol on climate change, or when it withdrew from the Paris Agreement on climate change in 2017. Several structural reasons have been put forward to explain this shift in global environmental politics. Economically, since the U.S. has much higher CO_2 emissions per capita than almost all EU member states (and also most other large developed countries), climate change mitigation tends to be more costly in the U.S. Politically, since the 1980s, the rise of green parties in European polities with proportional representation electoral systems has given environmental concerns a dedicated voice in political competition, parliaments, and (sometimes) governments. The American electoral system, on the other hand, inhibited similar developments, and "the influence of environmental lobbies in the United States steadily weakened beginning in the early 1990s" (Kelemen & Vogel 2010: 441, Vogel 2012). At the level of values and beliefs, majorities of Americans recognize climate change as a reality, are concerned about it, and support actions to mitigate climate change. But public opinion in the U.S. is more skeptical than in many other Western countries, when it comes to the politically important questions of how threatening climate change is, whether it is due to human activity, and whether climate change mitigation should be a political priority. Strikingly, despite the fact that the scientific evidence about man-made climate change has consolidated over the years (IPCC 2001, 2008, 2015), in 2016, only 48 percent of surveyed Americans believed that the Earth is warming due to human activity, and only 27 percent realized that the scientific community has reached a consensus.[25] This discrepancy between the scientifically established facts and U.S. public opinion has spurned a large amount of research, and it is precisely with regard to this question that the Koch brothers entered the debate, as Greenpeace claimed with a much publicized report on *Koch Industries Secretly Funding the Climate Denial Machine* (Greenpeace 2010).

Many factors may affect people's views on climate change, such as level of education (Lee et al. 2015), experience of weather events (Marquart-Pyatt et al.

---

[25] Pew Research Center 2016: 22, 26, Richard Wike, "What the world thinks about climate change in 7 charts," Pew Research Center, April 18, 2016, online: http://www.pewresearch.org/fact-tank/2016/04/18/what-the-world-thinks-about-climate-change-in-7-charts/ (accessed June 21, 2019), also Lorenzoni & Pidgeon 2006, Nisbet & Myers 2007, Painter & Ashe 2012, Capstick et al. 2015.

2014), or individual cost–benefit analysis (Ansolabehere & Konisky 2014), which may fluctuate with the business cycle (Scruggs & Benegal 2012). These correlates of climate change beliefs vary strongly across countries. Within the U.S., the most sophisticated studies conclude that, much more than in other countries, two factors stand out when it comes to explaining people's beliefs about climate change: political affiliation and trust in science.[26] In fact, the two are linked, as Americans' attitudes toward climate change have become sharply divided along partisan lines: in 2016, only 15 percent of conservative and 34 percent of moderate Republicans believed climate change to be due to human activity, in contrast to 63 percent of moderate and 79 percent of liberal Democrats; only 16 percent of conservative and 13 percent of moderate Republicans perceived that a scientific consensus about man-made climate change exists, in contrast to 29 percent of moderate and 55 percent of liberal Democrats; only 15 percent of conservative and 32 percent of moderate Republicans trusted climate scientists to provide full and accurate information, in contrast to 45 percent of moderate and 70 percent of liberal Democrats (Pew Research Center 2016: 31, 37f). Back in 1990, hardly any partisan divisions over environmental concerns in general and climate change in particular were observable; polarization then emerged during the 1990s and accelerated in the twenty-first century, especially after 2007 (McCright & Dunlap 2011, Guber 2013: 103, Marquart-Pyatt et al. 2014: 251). A similar polarization trend can be seen for Democrats' and Republicans' trust in science (Gauchat 2012: 175).

In trying to explain the growing polarization on climate change, researchers find strong support for the "elite cues" theory, according to which polarization is first happening among political and media elites, and then spreads among citizens:

New information on climate change (e.g., an IPCC report) is…unlikely to reduce the political divide. Instead, citizens' political orientations filter such learning opportunities in ways that magnify this divide. Political elites selectively interpret or ignore new climate change studies and news stories to promote their political agendas. Citizens, in turn, listen to their favored elites and media sources where global warming information is framed in a manner consistent with their pre-existing beliefs on the issue.

(McCright & Dunlap 2011: 177, also Brulle et al. 2012, Carmichael, et al. 2017)

---

[26] For comprehensive reviews of existing studies, see Marquart-Pyatt et al. 2014, Lee 2015: 1016f and Hornsey et al. 2016, for relevant individual studies on the determinants of climate change beliefs in the U.S., see McCright & Dunlap 2011, Gauchat 2012, Brewer 2012, Guber 2013, Lewandowsky et al. 2013, Hamilton et al. 2015, Pew Research Center 2016, and Mildenberger & Leiserowitz 2017. These studies employ statistical analyses in order to test the influence of other variables, such as weather events, education, and economic situation, and find that all other independent variables are trumped by beliefs about politics and/or science.

The nature of the news media in the U.S., where longstanding journalistic norms encourage reporters to present diverging sides of an argument, has facilitated this process, as, faced with what looks like a controversy, people tend to take sides according to their political affiliations.[27] The growth of partisan media, which gained traction in the online, radio, and cable TV segments of the news media, such as the right-leaning *Fox News*, has amplified polarization: these outlets act as "echo chambers" that consolidate people's partisan views on climate science and climate change (Feldman et al. 2011, Feldman et al. 2014, Hmielowski et al. 2014, Jang & Hart 2015, Jasny et al. 2015, Carmichael et al. 2017). While the Koch brothers do not own media outlets,[28] they have funded many of the elites whose views get represented in the media: think tanks and their experts, politicians, and even scientists that have a long track record of expressing views that question, criticize, or deny the mainstream scientific consensus about anthropogenic climate change.[29] At the Cato Institute, for example, policy papers with titles like "How Fossil Fuels Saved Humanity from Nature and Nature from Humanity" have been published regularly (Goklany 2012: 34), and the director of its Center for the Study of Science was the notorious climate change skeptic Patrick J. Michaels, a frequent columnist with print and TV media.[30]

Beyond plenty of anecdotal evidence, several studies have by now accumulated enough data to show the overall magnitude of the Koch brothers' funding of institutions that sow doubts about climate change. Greenpeace has gathered all the publicly available information on the donations of the four organizations that are directly controlled by Charles and David, the Charles Koch Foundation, the Charles Koch Institute, the David H. Koch Charitable Foundation, and the Claude R. Lambe Charitable Foundation (which was closed down in 2013).

---

[27] This "balance as bias" mechanism in the media coverage of climate change has been shown to operate throughout the 1990s until the early 2000s; after 2005, it became less prevalent in the print media (Schmid-Petri et al. 2017). Other journalistic norms in the U.S. that may promote giving extra room to contrarian viewpoints are personalization, dramatization, and novelty, see Antilla 2005, Boykoff & Boykoff 2007, Boykoff 2011.

[28] In 2013, the Koch brothers contemplated buying the Tribune company, which owned major newspapers such as the *Los Angeles Times* and the *Chicago Tribune*, but, faced with public resistance, they later backed down, see Amy Chozick, "Conservative Koch Brothers Turning Focus to Newspapers," *The New York Times*, April 20, 2013, online: http://www.nytimes.com/2013/04/21/business/media/koch-brothers-making-play-for-tribunes-newspapers.html?_r=1& (accessed June 26, 2019).

[29] While outright denial of man-made climate change dominated the discourse of right-leaning think tanks during the 1990s, in the twenty-first century, the critics (like the Koch brothers themselves) of the scientific climate change consensus focus more on climate change mitigation, trying to argue that the economic costs of climate change mitigation are too high in relation to potential benefits. Spreading doubt about the scientific consensus does, however, remain a key objective (McCright & Dunlap 2000, Boussalis & Coan 2016). See also "Full Transcript of Charles Koch's Interview with Fortune," *Fortune*, July 12, 2016, online: http://fortune.com/2016/07/12/transcript-charles-koch-fortune/ (accessed June 26, 2019).

[30] Online: https://www.cato.org/people/patrick-michaels, see also the critical survey of his work, his public appearances, and how much of it has been funded by fossil fuel firms: https://www.desmogblog.com/patrick-michaels (accessed June 26, 2019).

Between 1997 and 2017, their donations to climate change–skeptical think tanks and advocacy groups added up to almost US$150 million.[31] Of course, and this has been Koch Industries' official reply to Greenpeace,[32] these donations go to institutions that cover many other policy issues besides energy and climate change. It is, however, striking that the Koch brothers substantially increased their funding to the think tanks most active in questioning climate change in 1997, which was not an election year in the U.S., but the year the Kyoto Protocol was being negotiated and signed.[33] Comprehensive analyses of the climate change countermovement, using computational text and social network analysis, show that the institutions supported by the Koch brothers occupy central positions within the network of climate change contrarians, and thus "have greater influence over flows of resources, communication, and the production of contrarian information" (Farrell 2016b: 372). Post-2007, organizations receiving funding from the Koch foundations "produced discourse that was qualitatively different from organizations that did not receive such funding, and these differences tended to revolve around energy production, debates about the effects of CO_2, and questions about the scientific veracity of long-term climate change" (Farrell 2016a: 95f).[34] Such empirically observable shifts in the discourses of climate change contrarians indicate that a strategy has been pursued, but as long as the modalities of funding (whether it comes with instructions and conditions) remain secret, one cannot assess the extent of the Koch brothers' influence with certainty. Charles and David have also not been alone, since other corporations, notably major oil producers like ExxonMobil and coal mining companies, share the same interest in downplaying climate change (Coll 2012: 67–92, Banerjee et al. 2015). Still, around 2005, the Koch brothers had become the largest funder of the climate change countermovement in the U.S. After 2007, when public exposure and criticism of billionaire-funded climate change skepticism grew, two libertarian donor-advised funds, Donors Trust and Donors Capital Fund, which can guarantee anonymity to their donors, turned into the key "dark money" funding tool. By 2009, these funds accounted for over 20 percent of the money received by the

---

[31] All data available at: http://www.greenpeace.org/usa/global-warming/climate-deniers/koch-industries/ (accessed June 26, 2019).

[32] Koch Industries, "Koch's position on climate change/Greenpeace distortions," March 8, 2010, online: http://web.archive.org/web/20150411150514/http://www.kochfacts.com/kf/kochs-position-on-climate-changegreenpeace-distortions (accessed June 26, 2019).

[33] Koch funding for these five major climate change–skeptical think tanks increased sharply, from around US$700k in 1995 to almost US$2 million in 1997, then back down to US$900k in 1998: National Center for Policy Analysis, Competitive Enterprise Institute, Citizens for a Sound Economy Foundation, Heritage Foundation, Foundation for Research on Economics and the Environment. For analysis of the relevant think tanks and their mobilization against the Kyoto Protocol, see McCright & Dunlap 2000: 508 and McCright & Dunlap 2003, Koch donations data from: http://www.greenpeace.org/usa/global-warming/climate-deniers/koch-industries/ (accessed June 26, 2019).

[34] In his research, Justin Farrell analyzed all the texts produced by 164 organizations within the climate change countermovement between 1993 and 2013.

climate change countermovement (Greenpeace 2010: 19, Brulle 2014: Figures 3 and 4). Several facts hint at close links between the Koch brothers and Donors Trust and Donors Capital Fund, but their precise role cannot be established.[35]

During the same period in which the Koch brothers became central figures in the funding of the climate change countermovement, Americans for Prosperity took the lead in pressuring lawmakers in Congress to defy climate change mitigation. During the 2008 presidential race, both Obama and his Republican opponent John McCain had argued for measures to reverse global warming, and with Obama in office and a United Nations Climate Change Conference scheduled for 2009, the policy process was in a critical phase. Starting in 2008, Americans for Prosperity pushed members of Congress to sign a "No Climate Tax" pledge, which stated that "I will oppose any legislation relating to climate change that includes a net increase in government revenue." By 2012, 62 percent of all Republicans in the House, and 47 percent of Republicans in the Senate had signed onto the pledge, even though many of them represented constituencies where public opinion was not opposed to climate change mitigation (Skocpol & Hertel-Fernandez 2016: 693). Tim Phillips, who had been hired by the Koch brothers as the president of Americans for Prosperity, has been remarkably frank about their "No Climate Tax" strategy:

> Until 2010, some Republicans ran ads in House and Senate races showing their support for green energy. "After that, it disappeared from Republican ads," said Tim Phillips.... "Part of that was the polling, and part of it was the visceral example of what happened to their colleagues who had done that." What happened was clear. Republicans who asserted support for climate change legislation or the seriousness of the climate threat saw their money dry up or, worse, a primary challenger arise. "It told Republicans that we were serious," Mr. Phillips said, "that we would spend some serious money against them."[36]

---

[35] The founder and former director of both Donors Trust and Donors Capital Fund, Whitney Ball, had previously been development director at the Cato Institute, and participated in one of the secret Koch seminars in 2010; the later director, Lawson Bader, had been vice president of the Mercatus Center, another "Koch-tank." The Koch-directed Knowledge and Progress Fund gave a "general operating support" donation of almost US$5 million to Donors Trust, and Americans for Prosperity has been the largest recipient of grants (over US$20 million) from Donors Trust. Yet, the two funds received US$511 million between 2005 and 2012, only US$32 million of which are traceable to their donors. See Graham Readfearn, "Exclusive: Major Climate Denial Funders Donors Trust and Donors Capital Fund Handled $479 Million of Dark Money," *Desmog*, May 12, 2015, online: https://www.desmogblog.com/2015/05/12/exclusive-major-climate-science-denial-funders-donors-trust-and-donors-capital-fund-handled-479-million-untraceable (accessed June 26, 2019), also Brulle 2014, Mayer 2016: 206ff.

[36] Coral Davenport and Eric Lipton, "How G.O.P. Leaders Came to View Climate Change as Fake Science," *The New York Times*, June 3, 2017, online: https://www.nytimes.com/2017/06/03/us/politics/republican-leaders-climate-change.html (accessed June 6, 2019), also Mayer 2016: 163.

The plan seems to have worked. The American Clean Energy and Security Act, a bill which had still gained a majority in the House in 2009, never was put to a vote in the Senate, and no other major climate change mitigation bills have been passed since then. Among Republican congressmen, opposition to climate change mitigation has become part of their collective creed, exacerbating polarization, which had not yet been the case before 2009 (Fisher et al. 2013).

To be fair, the Koch brothers are far from being alone in preventing meaningful climate change mitigation at the national and international levels of U.S. politics. It was, for example, President Trump who withdrew from the Paris Agreement in 2017, and he had received much support from the coal industry, and none from Charles and David Koch; Trump's Secretary of State at the time, Rex W. Tillerson, was ExxonMobil's CEO before. As with the broader radicalization of the Republican Party mentioned earlier, separating the individual impact of the Koch brothers from other forces that have fostered U.S. opposition to climate change mitigation is difficult. Still, among the private actors wielding power in this field, the Kochs can at the very least be seen as *primus inter pares*. With regard to other billionaires and corporations that work with the Koch brothers, the question of power is secondary, since their cooperation is based on shared economic interests. When it comes to spreading climate change skepticism among the public and shifting politicians' stances on climate change, the concerted efforts of the Koch brothers and their allies have been successful. Many of the protagonists of the climate change countermovement have collaborated with the think tanks and advocacy groups for which the Koch brothers have been, overall, the major funder. Some of this climate change contrarianism has transnational links, for example the over US$500k of Koch money that went to the libertarian Fraser Institute in Canada, or "fake science" studies that were commissioned from Danish and Spanish researchers by Koch-supported think tanks.[37] Since ideas have no borders, the climate change skepticism of U.S. organizations may influence elites and public opinion abroad, but while this has not been studied in-depth so far, comparative evidence indicates that, among Western countries, contrarianism is nowhere as prevalent as in the U.S. (Painter & Ashe 2012, Capstick et al. 2015). There, climate change skepticism has coincided with the growing sway of the Koch brothers over the Republican Party, as their secret seminars have become focal events that attract more and more wealthy donors and Republican politicians. Their Americans for Prosperity, "[w]ith massive resources and a full array of political capacities,... has set up shop on the GOP right and become a powerful shaper of the careers of party operatives and the agendas of Republican politics"

---

[37] Greenpeace 2010: 9–13 and Alexis Stoymenoff, "'Charitable' Fraser Institute accepted $500k in foreign funding from Koch oil billionaires," *Vancouver Observer*, April 26, 2012, online: http://www.vancouverobserver.com/politics/2012/04/25/charitable-fraser-institute-accepted-500k-foreign-funding-oil-billionaires?page=0,1 (accessed June 6, 2019).

(Skocpol & Hertel-Fernandez 2016: 695). Over decades, the Koch brothers have used their wealth to build an intellectual and organizational infrastructure that is being deployed, within their larger "economic freedom" agenda, to block climate change mitigation policies in the U.S. This evidently has repercussions at the international level, where the UN Paris Agreement, like the Kyoto Protocol before, loses much of its effectiveness without U.S. participation, because the Koch brothers' home country is responsible for almost one fifth of global carbon emissions.[38] Charles and David may be genuine adherents of libertarianism, but there have been no major "stop the war on drugs," "legalize all immigrants," or "gay marriage now" campaigns sponsored by them until 2017. In contrast, Americans for Prosperity organized a "Hot Air Tour" with the slogan "Global Warming Alarmism: Lost Jobs, Higher Taxes, Less Freedom" in 2008, which sent a hot air balloon to rallies in forty U.S. cities, as well as, abroad, in Copenhagen (2009) and Cancun (2010), when UN climate conferences took place there.[39] Most of their political goals—minimal government, free markets, no climate change mitigation—have "dovetailed seamlessly with their personal financial interests" (Mayer 2016: 4), while the consequences, with climate change, risk affecting the whole Earth.

Valorizing Conservatism: Rupert Murdoch's Opinion-Shaping

All speakers, including individuals and the media, use money amassed from the economic marketplace to fund their speech, and the First Amendment protects the resulting speech.... [T]hey accumulate wealth with the help of their corporate form, may have aggregations of wealth, and may express views "hav[ing] little or no correlation to the public's support" for those views. *Differential treatment of media corporations and other corporations cannot be squared with the First Amendment*, and there is no support for the view that the Amendment's original meaning would permit suppressing media corporations' political speech.

(Citizens United v. Federal Election
Commission 558 U.S. 310, 314 (2010), emphasis added)[40]

---

[38] See Hovi et al. 2003 and James Mcbride, "The Consequences of Leaving the Paris Agreement," Foreign Affairs, June 1, 2017, online: https://www.cfr.org/backgrounder/consequences-leaving-paris-agreement (accessed June 6, 2019).
[39] See Mayer 2016: 216f and online: https://www.desmogblog.com/americans-for-prosperity. Even the brothers' financing of criminal justice initiatives has, until 2016, been mostly focusing on white collar crime, see Jane Mayer, "New Koch," *The New Yorker*, January 25, 2016, online: http://www.newyorker.com/magazine/2016/01/25/new-koch (accessed June 6, 2019).
[40] See online: https://www.supremecourt.gov/opinions/boundvolumes/558bv.pdf (accessed April 6, 2019).

Reading the above reasoning in the U.S. Supreme Court's (in)famous decision, which granted corporations the right to unlimited spending on "political speech," it is hard not to think of Rupert Murdoch (*1931).[41] Labeled "the SunKing" and "the man who owns the news," over several decades Murdoch has built "the last of the old media empires," worth over US$19.4 billion in 2019 according to *Forbes*, providing him with unprecedented opportunities to influence public opinion.[42] Unlike other renowned media moguls, who, like William Hearst or Silvio Berlusconi, made their mark primarily within their nation, Murdoch's conglomerate has global reach and has become a dominant player on three different continents. After inheriting his first newspapers from his father, the *News* and the *Sunday Mail* of Adelaide, Murdoch initially expanded at home, in Australia. His holdings there control the majority of the metropolitan newspaper market, including the leading national daily, *The Australian*, which he had founded in 1964. He then entered the British market with the purchases of *News of the World* (1968) and *The Sun* (1969), which he turned into the UK's daily with the largest circulation, as well as *The Times* and the *Sunday Times* (1981). Murdoch changed his citizenship from Australian to American in 1985, a move that was a legal prerequisite in order to be able to own U.S. television stations, which he was about to buy and turn into the *Fox Broadcasting Company* (1986). In 1996, he launched the *Fox News Channel*, which has grown into the most watched U. S. news channel. Murdoch's American media assets also include the *New York Post*, the *Weekly Standard* (founded in 1995, sold in 2009) and *The Wall Street Journal* (since 2007). These titles are only the politically most important media within Murdoch's empire. Many other smaller newspapers, publishing houses (HarperCollins) as well as major film and broadcasting companies (21st Century Fox, Sky, Star TV) are or have been part of his holdings (Kiernan 1986, Shawcross 1997, Page 2003, Wolff 2010, Folkenflik 2013). Until 2013, the publicly traded News Corporation integrated the different assets, with Murdoch and his family owning a decisive part of the voting shares, guaranteeing him executive control.[43] In the wake of the shattering UK phone-hacking scandal, which exposed a corrupt

---

[41] In his dissenting opinion, Justice Stevens highlighted that the case under consideration required no solution to the question of whether "the press" is different from other corporations; for him, this argument was introduced with the sole purpose of justifying the full deregulation of political speech legislation (Citizens United v. Federal Election Commission 558 U.S. 310, 473ff (2010)). See Hasen 1999 for an early legal investigation of this "Rupert Murdoch Problem."

[42] See Wolff 2010, Folkenflik 2013, and Andrew Neil, "Murdoch and Me," *Vanity Fair*, December 1996, online: http://www.vanityfair.com/news/1996/12/rupert-murdoch–199612 (accessed July 10, 2019).

[43] Dual-class stock structures, usually created at the formation of the corporation, are not uncommon in the media business. They allow the founders to own large parts of the preferred stock with voting rights while the publicly traded shares are primarily without voting rights. See Arsenault & Castells 2008: 491ff and Cynthia Littleton, "Control Issues: How Media Moguls Keep a Tight Grip on Their Empires," *Variety*, March 24, 2015, online: http://variety.com/2015/biz/features/dual-class-stock-structures-sumner-redstone-rupert-murdoch-comcast–1201459120/ (accessed April 6, 2019).

system where *News of the World* reporters illegally intruded into private phone systems, ignored by the police and politicians (Watson & Hickman 2012), Murdoch responded to shareholder concerns. In 2013, he split News Corporation into two separate entities: News Corp, which concentrates on newspapers and publishing, and 21st Century Fox, which gathered the broadcasting and film media; he also started to shift executive control to his sons Lachlan and James. In 2019, large parts of 21st Century Fox were sold to the Walt Disney Company, while the Murdoch family kept the Fox TV channels within the newly created Fox Corporation, with Lachlan Murdoch as CEO.[44]

"For better or worse, [News Corporation] is a reflection of my thinking, my character, my values," Murdoch said in 1996 (Shawcross 1997: 398), and this appears true in a fourfold sense, each time reflecting Murdoch's approach to both business and politics. Although his conglomerate contains several media titles considered as high-quality journalism (*Wall Street Journal, The Australian, The Times*), in the news business, he has been most successful with the tabloid format (Kiernan 1986, Page 2003), e.g. in print with *The Sun*, and in TV with *Fox News*. His biographers point out that his political views reflect this: "[w]hat is most striking is the crudity of his views, and his dismissive contempt for others" that don't share his perspective (Tiffen 2014: 97, also Wolff 2010: 282). Secondly, despite roaming among the high and mighty, Murdoch likes to see himself as an anti-establishment outsider. In his business, he has frequently made unexpected moves that went against the conceived wisdom of the time, for example when he set up a new printing and distribution platform in order to break the power of the highly unionized newspaper workers in London (Kiernan 1986: 309–17, Shawcross 1997: 223–37). "Murdoch is a pirate; he will cunningly circumvent rules, and sometimes principles, to get his way" (Auletta 1995, also Wolff 2010: 259ff, Chenoweth 2001: 43ff, McKnight 2013: 33ff, Watson & Hickman 2012). Thirdly, his biographers agree that Murdoch is extremely competitive, and that "winning" is his supreme value. This is perhaps best exemplified in Murdoch's old rivalry with Ted Turner and his various takeover battles, such as the one for the *Wall Street Journal* (Chenoweth 2001: 48–58, Shawcross 1997: 397ff, Wolff 2010: 2f, 261ff). Finally, just as his business empire is truly global, Murdoch appears to engage in politics without national attachments, which, in 1985, when he acquired U.S. citizenship, caused *The New York Times* columnist

---

[44] See Emily Steel, "21st Century Fox Announces New Murdoch Roles," *The New York Times*, June 16, 2015, online: https://www.nytimes.com/2015/06/17/business/media/21st-century-fox-announces-new-murdoch-roles.html, and Brooks Barnes, "Disney Moves From Behemoth to Colossus With Closing of Fox Deal," *The New York Times*, March 20, 2019, online: https://www.nytimes.com/2019/03/20/business/media/walt-disney-21st-century-fox-deal.html. In 2019, Rupert Murdoch was executive chairman of News Corp and chairman of Fox Corporation, his son Lachlan was co-chairman of News Corp and executive chairman and CEO of Fox Corporation, see online: http://newscorp.com/about/leadership/ and https://www.foxcorporation.com/management/executive-team/ (all accessed April 6, 2019).

William Safire to call him a "man without a country."[45] Strictly speaking, Murdoch's politics in Australia until 1985 as well as his engagement in U. S. politics from then on do not fall into the "transnational" category, whereas all his other activities, most notably those in the UK, do. At the same time, Murdoch does not embrace a liberal type of cosmopolitanism. He is strongly anti–European Union, and, overall, he promotes a neoconservative U.S.–UK alliance as the guarantor of free market capitalism (McKnight 2010, Daddow 2012, Tiffen 2014: 3, 137–143).

To feel unconstrained by existing rules and to subject everything to winning leads to opportunism. Indeed, Murdoch is well known for shifting alliances and dropping former partners throughout his career, whenever it promises advantages for his business (Chenoweth 2001: xiii–xvii, 18, 51, Tiffen 2014: 9ff, 103). Often, such flexibility has also characterized his relationships in politics. Like many people within what has become, since the 1970s, the neoconservative movement (Lind 2004, Vaïsse 2010), Murdoch first used to lean to the left side of the political spectrum. In the early 1950s, "during his Oxford years, he kept a bust of Lenin on his mantelpiece. For the next two decades, his political views ranged widely, often inconsistently, but from the mid-1970s he has consistently manifested a right-wing ideology—although sometimes tempered by commercial and political prag-matism" (Tiffen 2014: 90f). In his native Australia, Murdoch first massively supported the Labor Party's new leader, Gough Whitlam, to become prime minister in 1972, only to turn his newspapers against him three years later (Tiffen 2014: 107–20). In New York, while not yet a U.S. citizen, Murdoch made the *New York Post* boost the campaign of Edward Koch to become the Democratic Party's candidate and then the city's mayor in 1978 (Kiernan 1986: 206 9); during the 1990s, the billionaire supported the Republican Party's Rudolph Giuliani (Chenoweth 2001: 158ff). In the UK, between 1979 and 1995, Murdoch's media was staunchly behind the Tories, but for the 1997 election, he backed Tony Blair's Labour Party, and continued to do so during the elections in 2001 and 2005 (McKnight 2013: 60f, 84–105, 149–71).

In each of these cases, Murdoch congratulated himself publicly for his influ-ence, usually via his newspapers, most famously in the UK, where *The Sun*'s front page proclaimed after the 1992 election defeat of Labour "It's the Sun wot won it," and, after the 1997 Labour victory, "It's the Sun wot swung it" (McKnight 2013: 154, 162). When asked what gives him the most pleasure, Murdoch has answered "[b]eing involved with the editor of a paper in a day-to-day campaign. Trying to influence people" (Auletta 1995). Numerous accounts of how he is repeatedly exercising control over editorial lines, especially in his newspapers, fill all the Murdoch biographies; when employees stand in his way, he can threaten to

---

[45] William Safire, "Citizen of the world," *The New York Times*, May 16, 1985, online: http://www. nytimes.com/1985/05/16/opinion/essay-citizen-of-the-world.html (accessed May 22, 2019).

replace them (Kiernan 1986: 209, McKnight 2013: 89–99). Exactly how much power Murdoch can wield through his newspapers is difficult to assess, as we have already seen with Sheldon Adelson's *Israel Hayom* and its support for Benjamin Netanyahu. A particularly tricky question concerns whether the media is following or shaping public opinion. Potential persuasion effects of the media are very difficult to uncover in an environment where both public opinion and political behavior are influenced by a multitude of factors that are hard to isolate. Nevertheless, a few careful studies provide strong evidence that the positions taken by Murdoch's media have partially shifted their audience's political stances on key issues. Thus, in research that overcomes many of the problems in the study of media effects, Jonathan Ladd and Gabriel Lenz estimate that *The Sun*'s switch towards Blair during the 1997 election persuaded between 10 percent and 25 percent of its readers to vote for Labour (Ladd & Lenz 2009).[46] This finding has been largely confirmed by an even more detailed analysis of *The Sun*'s impact on its readers, which compares the elections of 1997 with 2010, when Murdoch's tabloid switched back to endorse the Tories.[47] Moreover, the unmeasurable counterfactual has to be taken into account as well—what might have happened if, instead of endorsing Blair, Murdoch would have orchestrated a damaging campaign against him, as he had done via *The Sun* during the 1992 election, which ended with a defeat of Labour's Neil Kinnock (McKnight 2013: 150ff). This aspect of "what would Rupert do?" relates to the "law of anticipated reactions" (Friedrich 1937: 16–18) and the "second face of power" elaborated by Bachrach and Baratz (1962). Since Murdoch has such great potential to influence public opinion, his non-decisions—not to attack someone or expose something—can be as important as the active exercise of his power. Anticipating the billionaire's power (as a disposition), politicians may consider it in their interest to conform to his preferences before Murdoch expresses any explicit demands; Tony Blair's government is often regarded as having internalized this mindset. Lance Price, one of Blair's spin doctors, recalls: "I have never met Mr Murdoch, but...he seemed like the 24th member of the Cabinet. His voice was rarely heard...but his presence was always felt" (Tiffen 2014: 156, also 179 and Page 2003: 2–7, 195f).

---

[46] Prior studies, notably Norris et al. 1999, whose analysis was more limited, had found no significant media effects during the 1997 election. By using panel data, which followed 1,382 respondents pre- and post-election, Ladd and Lenz are able to compare the group that read newspapers that switched their endorsement in 1996 with the control group whose preferred newspaper did not switch. Since they study the effect of all the newspapers that switched towards Labour, they do not isolate the influence of *The Sun*, but within their sample, it is by far the newspaper with the highest circulation (3.8 million in 1997, compared to a combined 1.2 million of the other newspapers that switched towards Labour, see Ladd & Lenz 2009: 397).

[47] "We find that The Sun's endorsements were associated with a significant increase in readers' support for Labour in 1997, approximately 525,000 votes, and its switch back was associated with about 550,000 extra votes for the Conservatives in 2010" (Reeves et al. 2016: 44, see also Brandenburg & van Egmond 2011).

Accordingly, even without exact calculations of media effects, many politicians have taken Murdoch's influence on their voters very seriously, and the media mogul is known to take advantage of this awareness in order to promote his business interests. Precisely because the media has influence over public opinion, it is usually subject to laws that go beyond a country's general antitrust policies. In Australia, media ownership and practices fall under the regulations issued by the Australian Communications and Media Authority (previously the Australian Broadcasting Tribunal); in the U.S., the Federal Communications Commission is in charge, and in the UK, the Office of Communications (since 2003). While all firms depend on governments to some extent (Lindblom 1977), media companies and politics are thus particularly intertwined. For Murdoch, friendly (or dependent) politicians have therefore been very valuable assets, especially from 1980 onwards, as his empire expanded across borders and different media. News Corporation's growth often happened via debt-financed takeovers, which, as debt accumulated, sometimes brought the conglomerate to the brink of insolvency. This made it ever more imperative for Murdoch to have political backing for his media business (Chenoweth 2001).[48] Amelia Arsenault and Manuel Castells see Murdoch's exploitation of the codependence between the media and politics as strategic:

> While many large media conglomerates exert political influence via financial contributions and through the editorial content of specific media platforms, Murdoch's vertical control allows NewsCorp to function as a more targeted political weapon in comparison to its peers. This political leverage facilitates NewsCorp's ability to expand its holdings through the granting of regulatory favors, leading to larger audience shares, which in turn expands its political clout, creating a cycle of influence.   (Arsenault & Castells 2008: 497)[49]

Although Murdoch himself denies having received political favors in his career (Page 2003: 1), the major instances are by now well documented. Again, British politics provides the best examples, first with Thatcher, then with Blair. Murdoch became an ardent admirer of Margaret Thatcher early on, and together with the

---

[48] "Murdoch became a giant in newspaper publishing without any special help from governments, and there were no important cases of governments assisting him before the 1980s" (Tiffen 2014: 156). See Page 2003: 122f for a small favor by Australia's deputy prime minister helping Murdoch to acquire the *News of the World* in the UK in 1968/69.

[49] Arsenault and Castells see this as a primary form of power in what Castells has called the "network society" in the "information age" (Castells 1996): "(1) the ability to program/reprogram the goals assigned to the network(s); and (2) the ability to connect different networks to ensure their cooperation by sharing common goals and increasing their resources" (Arsenault & Castells 2008: 489). Their emphasis on the specialness of this "switching power" seems overstated, however, since all modern news media contain this power potential—what distinguishes Murdoch is his personal centralized (vertical) control over the different media owned by News Corporation, his global reach, and the extent to which he has exercised this power.

newspaper's editor, Larry Lamb, he shifted *The Sun*, which had traditionally been more in favor of Labour, to support Thatcher during the 1979 election. "VOTE TORY THIS TIME. IT'S THE ONLY WAY TO STOP THE ROT," *The Sun's* front page shouted on Election Day. Twenty days after her victory, Thatcher finished a private letter to Lamb with "I owe you a great debt for the confidence you put in me. I hope to repay it over the next few years by the actions that I take."[50] This may have referred to her broader political program, but it certainly also came true in the more problematic sense of helping *The Sun's* owner personally. When Murdoch bought *The Times* and the *Sunday Times* in early 1981, the purchase was at risk of being stalled by the Monopolies and Mergers Commission, since Murdoch already owned *The Sun* and *News of The World*. Yet, according to various insiders, Thatcher heeded Murdoch's request to not refer the case to the antitrust agency. Similar regulatory favors from Thatcher's government to Murdoch's business happened in 1987, when Murdoch bought the daily *Today*, and in 1988 and 1990, when Murdoch sought to establish the *Sky* (later *BSkyB*) satellite television service (Kiernan 1986: 237–50, Tiffen 2014: 122–6, 157–67, McKnight 2013: 84–90, Page 2003: 253–78).

In financial terms, Murdoch's greatest return on investment from firmly backing Thatcher probably came in 1986. During the previous year, Murdoch had taken on enormous debt in order to buy half of the 20th Century-Fox film studio (for US$250 million) and the Metromedia TV stations (for US$1.55 billion) in the U.S., with the plan to establish a new TV channel, Fox. In order to finance the annual interest payments, he needed to get more cash out of his highly profitable newspapers in the UK. But existing labor arrangements, brought about and defended by the print workers' unions, ensured that much of the newspapers' surplus went into salaries. Therefore, Murdoch secretly built new computerized printing facilities outside London, in Wapping, to replace the labor-intensive mechanical print rooms; in 1985, he also sourced new workers from the less demanding electricians' union (Chenoweth 2001: 56–66, also Kiernan 1986: 310–22, Page 2003: 384–93). After Murdoch announced the move from London to Wapping, the printers and their unions predictably resisted. On January 24, 1986, the over 5,000 workers producing Murdoch's papers called for a strike, which allowed him to fire them, because Thatcher's government had put more restrictive trade union laws in place. Even more crucial

was the nightly presence of British police at the gates of the Wapping printing works to fight back thousands of protesting picketers trying to stop the

---

[50] Thatcher MSS (Churchill Archive Centre): THCR 2/4/1/10, May 24, 1979 "MT letter to Sun editor Larry Lamb," online: http://fc95d419f4478b3b6e5f-3f71d0fe2b653c4f00f32175760e96e7.r87.cf1.rackcdn.com/E72265A4FC5646B0B634FAEF86B433F2.pdf (accessed May 31, 2019). When Thatcher was the opposition leader from 1975 to 1979, Lamb had shifted support to her before Murdoch (McKnight 2013: 60).

newspapers from being driven from the plant. The protests continued for months, but in June 1986 support for Murdoch within the Conservative cabinet seemed to wobble, with a minister privately complaining... that six months of police support had cost £5 million. Murdoch shortly afterwards asked for and received a personal assurance from Thatcher that she would "squash" any weakening by her ministers.   (McKnight 2013: 87, also Auletta 1995)

While thousands of workers lost their jobs, Murdoch's publishing subsidiary in the UK, News International, saw its operating income jump from around £38 million in 1985 to over £150 million in 1987; the value of Murdoch's stockholding in his conglomerate, News Corporation, increased tenfold during the same period, from US$300 million to US$3 billion (Chenoweth 2001: 67f). Over all of Murdoch's career, it seems warranted to conclude that "[i]t was in the Murdoch-Thatcher relationship that the politics of mutual patronage reached its strongest expression" (Tiffen 2014: 157).

Only Murdoch's ties with Tony Blair may be put into the same league (McKnight 2013: 151). When preparing for the 1997 election, Blair had learned a lesson from eighteen years of Conservative government: it was hard to win an election against Murdoch's media in the UK. The extensive diaries of Blair's press secretary and close collaborator, Alastair Campbell (Campbell & Hagerty 2010, 2011a, 2011b), have provided clear evidence of how Blair sought Murdoch's support as early as 1994, travelling to Australia to deliver a keynote speech at the annual gathering of Murdoch's editors in 1995, and meeting with the billion-aire regularly in the run-up to the 1997 elections. While it is common knowledge that Blair's New Labour moved to the right, especially with regard to economic policy, in terms of broader ideology, the Tories were still closer to Murdoch. However, Thatcher's successor since 1992, John Major, was much less cooperative in his media policy than the Iron Lady. In 1995, his government had issued a report on media ownership and worked out a new broadcasting bill that would have put limits on the cross-ownership of newspaper and TV publishers, which threatened Murdoch's UK holdings. Blair, on the other hand, remained silent on the issue of media concentration and convinced Murdoch that he planned no media policies that would hurt News Corporation's interests. He would later admit that this had been a strategic decision in order to avoid having conflicts with the media.[51]

Hence, Murdoch had sound commercial reasons for switching to Labour, and that's what The Sun did on March 18, 1997, titling "The Sun Backs Blair" six weeks before his election victory and publishing another strong endorsement on Election

---

[51] See Chris Mullen, "Rupert Murdoch, Tony Blair, and me," The Guardian, August 25, 2011, online: https://www.theguardian.com/media/2011/aug/25/rupert-murdoch-tony-blair-chris-mullin (accessed April 6, 2019), Tiffen 2014: 178ff, McKnight 2013: 156ff, and Chenoweth 2001: 287ff.

Day.[52] While the billionaire's media did not produce the kind of unwavering support that they had provided during Thatcher's reign, Labour also did not satisfy all of Murdoch's policy demands. Still, throughout Blair's ten years in power, *The Sun* remained largely behind the prime minister, Murdoch had privileged access to Blair,[53] and harmful legislation was avoided. No tightening of antitrust laws happened (previously a Labour policy position), and proposals to limit "predatory pricing" for newspapers were squashed. Most importantly for Murdoch, whose News International had strongly lobbied for this, the new Communications Act of 2003 loosened the cross-ownership limitations introduced by the Major government, and also eliminated all existing restrictions on foreign ownership of British broadcasting (Tiffen 2014: 181f, McKnight 2013: 162ff, Barnett 2017).

Similar examples of political courtesies in exchange for sympathetic media coverage, or at least the hope not to get damaged by negative reporting, can also be found in other countries. In Australia, after Murdoch had given up his citizenship in 1985, the Labor government under Bob Hawke and Paul Keating felt that the Murdoch media would be more favorable to them than other Australian media groups. Over the course of 1986 and 1987, the government modified several regulations on media cross-holding, foreign ownership, and newspaper concentration in ways that were directly beneficial to Murdoch. They allowed him to sell his TV stakes with huge profits and to consolidate, through new takeovers, his control of the Australian newspaper market. Since then, Murdoch's papers dominate the Australian press (Tiffen 2014: 167–77, Page 2003: 404ff, Chenoweth 2001: 85–8). Under such conditions, Murdoch can count on his power's effects without having to exercise it. And when that fails, he can still mobilize his newspapers, as he did again during the 2013 elections in Australia. Having become frustrated by Labor, whose policies had boosted News Corporation's broadcasting competitors, the Murdoch press campaigned fervently against it during the election campaign, which was won by the former opposition, the Liberal–National coalition (Hobbs & McKnight 2014). In 2018, when the Murdoch-owned press turned against Prime Minister Malcolm Turnbull, and during the following elections in 2019, when it acted as a united front against

---

[52] From 1996 onwards, Blair also looked more and more likely to win against Major, which added the incentive of ensuring access to the winner to Murdoch's considerations for Blair.

[53] The close political relationship between Murdoch and Blair would eventually turn into friendship, as evidenced by Blair becoming the godfather of Murdoch's daughter with his third wife, Wendi Deng. The friendship reportedly broke apart when, later, Murdoch suspected Blair of having an affair with Deng. See "Tony Blair 'godfather to Rupert Murdoch's daughter'," *BBC News*, February 28, 2012, online: http://www.bbc.com/news/uk-politics–14785501 and "Life after power: The loneliness of Tony Blair," *The Economist*, December 17, 2014, online: http://www.economist.com/news/christmas-specials/21636603-celebrated-abroad-and-reviled-home-former-prime-minister-struggles-fulfil (both accessed April 6, 2019).

the Labor candidate Bill Shorten, Murdoch's dominance over Australia's news market was confirmed again.[54]

In China, the balance of power was reversed: Murdoch had to extend favors to the government in the hope of gaining market access. Trying to be allowed to expand his Star (and later Sky) satellite broadcasting into China, he dropped the BBC World Service from its programming in 1994, published the Deng Xiaoping biography by Deng's daughter with HarperCollins in 1995, and insisted on canceling HarperCollins's book contract with Hong Kong's last British governor, Chris Patten, in 1998 (Chenoweth 2001: 203f, 290–6, Tiffen 2014: 76–9, Auletta 1995). In the U.S., Murdoch's media power is much greater than in China, but more limited than in the UK or Australia, because competition with other media interests is more severe, and the larger division of power within the political system makes it harder to have key politicians one can count on. From the mid-1980s onwards, as his business interests in the U.S. broadcasting market increased sharply, Murdoch extracted several favors from politicians that, like New York's Mayor Giuliani or House Majority Leader Newt Gingrich, had benefited from Murdoch's media support. Most of this, however, took place after he had acquired U.S. citizenship, and thus falls into domestic politics. Pre-1985, while still being Australian, Murdoch already had his American newspapers promote New York mayor Ed Koch and President Reagan, but no direct business advantages seem to have been attached to these endorsements.[55]

Regarding the overall balance between politics and business, the vast majority of Murdoch's biographers comes to the conclusion, supported by the evidence presented so far, that "Murdoch's political affiliations move swiftly in accordance, not with political ideology, but with NewsCorp's bottom line" (Arsenault & Castells 2008: 497). According to this view, the media mogul may be an economic libertarian and a social conservative, but when these values conflict with the prospects of News Corporation, Murdoch puts profits over principles (Kiernan 1986, Auletta 1995, Shawcross 1997, Chenoweth 2001, Page 2003, Wolff 2010, Tiffen 2014). Political power is being accumulated primarily in order to transform it into economic benefit at opportune moments, when political intervention is required to protect and advance Murdoch's business. The fact that some of Murdoch's print titles have been consistently loss-making (e.g., *The Times, The*

---

[54] See Jonathan Mahler and Jim Rutenberg, "Part 3: The Future of Fox: An Even More Powerful Political Weapon," *The New York Times*, April 3, 2019, online: https://www.nytimes.com/interactive/2019/04/03/magazine/new-fox-corporation-disney-deal.html, and Bianca Hall "'Unrelentingly partisan': Did the Murdoch press sway the election?," *The Sydney Morning Herald*, May 25, 2019, online: https://www.smh.com.au/federal-election-2019/unrelentingly-partisan-did-the-murdoch-press-sway-the-election-20190522-p51q0s.html (accessed July 6, 2019).

[55] One major benefit of Reagan's presidency was radical deregulation of broadcasting in the U.S. under the Reagan-appointed chair of the Federal Communications Commission, Mark Fowler—yet this affected all broadcasting actors, not Murdoch specifically. See McKnight 2013: 62–83, Tiffen 2014: 103ff, 128ff + 183ff, Chenoweth 2001: 165–71, 199–215.

Australian, the *Weekly Standard*, and the *New York Post*),[56] which is sometimes used as an argument to demonstrate Murdoch's ideological commitments, can actually fit into this analysis. With a long-term perspective, which Murdoch has exhibited in many of his investments, a newspaper that loses US$20 million a year can make up for it via its opinion-shaping power that may produce political favors in the future (as long as other assets in his conglomerate provide profits). David McKnight doesn't deny that economic self-interest plays a major role in how Murdoch's media intervene in politics and public opinion. Still, his analysis emphasizes more how, since the 1980s, News Corporation has served as a vehicle to promote Murdoch's ideology (McKnight 2003, 2013: 18ff). In many instances, this claim is hard to prove, because Murdoch's ideology and commercial success have gone hand in hand. *Fox News*, for example, has been shown to have shifted significant numbers of U.S. voters and politicians further to the right of the political spectrum, thereby increasing polarization (DellaVigna & Kaplan 2007, Iyengar & Hahn 2009, Clinton & Enamorado 2014, Hopkins & Ladd 2014, Arceneaux et al. 2016). At the same time, it also exploited a gap in the TV news market and quickly turned into one of the most profitable assets in Murdoch's conglomerate (Tiffen 2014: 215–54, McKnight 2013: 127–48). Similarly, promoting neoliberal economic policy is obviously self-serving for a billionaire who does not want to be constrained by regulations and taxation (McKnight 2003). To a large extent, therefore, Murdoch's strategy since the 1980s can be summarized as "valorizing conservatism." Murdoch's media have often shaped public opinion and the political agenda in ways that promote conservative values (neoliberal economics and social conservatism) while simultaneously making profits from it, as exemplified by *The Sun* and *Fox News*. Once his stance was well established, Murdoch could extract further advantages from being flexible: any departure from conservative positions by his media—such as support for Labor—was a favor that Murdoch expected to be rewarded for.

The strongest arguments for seeing Murdoch as pushing a political agenda are also the ones most relevant for the study of IR, because they concern foreign policy. In this field, there are no direct commercial payoffs for Murdoch, apart from vague "support your commander-in-chief" considerations. Hence, one can assume a more autonomous role for ideological motivations. Since the 1980s, with regard to foreign policy, Murdoch has embraced neoconservative ideology, first within the context of Reagan's aggressive anti-Communism, and then more broadly as a framework for projecting U.S. military power to promote freedom and American national interests.[57] Within the *New York Post*, key neoconservative

---

[56] Sinclair 2016 and Colin Kruger, "Break-up could breathe new life into News," *The Syndey Morning Herald*, May 18, 2013, online: http://www.smh.com.au/business/breakup-could-breathe-new-life-into-news-20130517-2js2l.html (accessed April 6, 2019).

[57] U.S. neoconservatism is mainly a foreign policy paradigm—with regard to economics, it broadly supports capitalism and free markets, and, as such, is compatible with neoliberal economic ideology.

intellectuals, such as John Podhoretz, already received regular columns during the 1980s, and with the 1995 launch of the *Weekly Standard*, edited by Bill Kristol, Murdoch funded the most important mouthpiece of what Justin Vaïsse has called the third age of neoconservatism (Vaïsse 2010: 226ff, McKnight 2013: 72ff, 177ff). In doing so, Murdoch was one of the agenda-setters who helped to shift the foreign policy stance of the Republican Party to become closer in line with neoconservative objectives. The greatest impact of this manifested itself once George W. Bush became president, especially with the decision to invade Iraq in 2003. Murdoch's *Fox News* was an ardent and often unquestioning supporter of the Iraq War, more so than most other media, which reinforced pro-war attitudes among its viewers (Kull et al. 2003, Aday 2010). Within the U.S., however, many other actors and factors contributed to both the rise of the neoconservative movement and the Iraq invasion. In the post-9/11 climate, many Democratic Party politicians and mainstream media, such as *The New York Times* and the *Washington Post*, also expressed support for the attack on Iraq, at least initially (Kaufmann 2004, Gershkoff & Kushner 2005, Krebs & Lobasz 2007, Jacobson 2010).[58] The individual contribution of Murdoch is therefore hard to isolate in the U.S.

It is, once more, in the UK that one can see the "Murdoch effect" more strongly (Daddow 2012, also 2011). Since his early affection for Reagan and Thatcher, Murdoch's "most easily identifiable political cause was the strengthening of Britain's alliance with the United States" (McKnight 2013: 166, also 67ff). An enduring and crucial issue was Britain's role within Europe. Murdoch maintained a strong stance against European integration, and his UK media, especially the *Sunday Times* and *The Sun*, were the first newspapers with high national circulation to push a strong EU-skeptical agenda during the 1980s, thus setting the tone for what would later become a more widespread perspective of "destructive dissent" within UK reporting on Europe (Daddow 2012, Hawkins 2012). According to John Major,

[i]n the run-up to the 1997 election, ... [Murdoch] made it clear that he disliked my European policies which he wished me to change. If not, his papers could not and would not support the Conservative Government.... [H]e ... referred to all

---

[58] In their histories of neoconservatism, Justin Vaïsse and Jacob Heilbrunn both mention Murdoch only once, both designating him wrongly as "the Australian [*sic*] press mogul" and simply mentioning that he provided the funding of the *Weekly Standard* (Heilbrunn 2009: 213, Vaïsse 2010: 287). While this underestimates Murdoch's role, it is also true that, as intellectual projects, both *Fox News* and the *Weekly Standard* were largely shaped by their founding CEO/editor, Roger Ailes (*Fox News*) and Bill Kristol (*Weekly Standard*). In contrast to other media he has owned, Murdoch hardly intervened in the editorial lines of *Fox News* and the *Weekly Standard*. Still, the initiatives to found and fund a new conservative journal and a news channel came from Murdoch, and their editors seem to have been very closely aligned with Murdoch's own views. During its first fifteen years, the *Weekly Standard* "lost more than $30 million for News Corporation" (McKnight 2013: 177, also 138–44, and Tiffen 2014: 215–23).

his papers as "we". Both Mr Murdoch and I kept our word. I made no change in policy, and Mr Murdoch's titles did indeed oppose the Conservative Party.[59]

In favoring Blair over Major, which, as explained before, also involved compelling business interests, part of Murdoch's deal seems to have been that Blair convinced him that he would not draw the UK deeper into the EU, especially with regard to the euro. At the moments when Blair appeared to consider closer ties with the EU, Murdoch's newspapers immediately condemned such moves (Chenowth 2001: 287, Daddow 2012, McKnight 2013: 166ff).

Murdoch's anti-EU stance reached a climax during the 2016 Brexit referendum, the outcome of which Murdoch has called "wonderful," akin to a "prison break." While *The Times* maintained a neutral coverage of the Brexit campaign, *The Sun* aggressively supported Leave, spending over £96,000 on a "BeLEAVE in Britain" poster, "forcing its parent company, News Group Newspapers, to register as an official leave campaign group with the Electoral Commission."[60] In backing Leave, however, Murdoch was far from alone—the *Daily Express*, which had close ties to the UKIP party, and the *Daily Mail* were even more vigorously pro-Brexit; campaigns on social media played a significant role, too.[61] The independent effects of Murdoch's newspapers on Brexit is thus hard to establish, but many analysts agree that the long-term effects of decades of anti-EU reporting within Murdoch's media set the ground for the Leave victory (Rowinski 2017, Galpin & Trenz 2018). In part, Murdoch's opposition to Brussels may be motivated by the fear of regulation by a European superstate, as well as a general aversion to the tradition

---

[59] "Witness statement of Sir John Major to the Leveson Inquiry," May 14, 2012, online: http://webarchive.nationalarchives.gov.uk/20140122145147/http://www.levesoninquiry.org.uk/wp-content/uploads/2012/06/Witness-Statement-of-Sir-John-Major.pdf. In his own statements to the "Leveson Inquiry into the culture, practices and ethics of the press," which was set up in response to Murdoch's *News International* phone-hacking scandal, Murdoch himself claimed that he never asked any prime minister for anything. Frequently, he did not recall what had been discussed at a particular meeting, but, between 1988 and 2011, he counted seventy-two occasions where he had met, or had the possibility to meet, an acting British prime minister. See "Witness statement of Keith Rupert Murdoch," April 12, 2012, online: http://webarchive.nationalarchives.gov.uk/20140122145147/http://www.levesoninquiry. org.uk/wp-content/uploads/2012/04/Witness-Statement-of-Keith-Rupert-Murdoch2.pdf and "Exhibit-KRM-27," April 12, 2012, online: http://webarchive.nationalarchives.gov.uk/20140122145147/http://www.levesoninquiry.org.uk/wp-content/uploads/2012/04/Exhibit-KRM-27.pdf (all accessed June 6, 2019).

[60] See Jane Martinson, "Rupert Murdoch describes Brexit as 'wonderful'," *The Guardian*, June 28, 2016, online: https://www.theguardian.com/media/2016/jun/28/rupert-murdoch-brexit-wonderful-donald-trump, and Jasper Jackson, "The Sun spent £96,000 on poster backing Brexit," *The Guardian*, November 29, 2016, online: https://www.theguardian.com/media/2016/nov/29/the-sun-spending-poster-backing-brexit-leave-campaign, (accessed July 6, 2019).

[61] See David Deacon, Dominic Wring, Emily Harmer, John Downey, James Stanyer, "Hard Evidence: analysis shows extent of press bias towards Brexit," *The Conversation*, June 16, 2016, online: https://theconversation.com/hard-evidence-analysisshows-extent-of-press-bias-towards-brexit-61106, and Carole Cadwalladr, "The great British Brexit robbery: how our democracy was hijacked," *The Observer*, May 7, 2017, online: https://www.theguardian.com/technology/2017/may/07/the-great-british-brexit-robbery-hijacked-democracy?CMP=Share_iOSApp_Other (accessed June 6, 2019), also Levy et al. 2016, Gorrell et al. 2018.

of state interventionism on the European continent. When asked about why he opposes the EU so vigorously, Murdoch, who has denied making this statement, reportedly once said "[w]hen I go into Downing Street they do what I say; when I go to Brussels they take no notice."[62]

While Murdoch's anti-EU stance can therefore be seen as linked to the strategy of valorizing conservatism, his advocacy for the Iraq invasion in the UK, like in the U.S., revealed no business considerations. As with most of the 175 newspapers that News Corporation owned worldwide at the time, Murdoch threw the whole weight of his British media behind the Iraq campaign, before the decision to invade was taken, as well as afterwards.[63] In this, Blair, who had aligned himself with Bush and the decision for regime change in Baghdad early on, did not need persuasion (Bluth 2004). Murdoch's efforts were instead targeting public opinion, as a majority of British citizens opposed an Iraq invasion and withdrew their support from Blair. During the first months after the war had started in March 2003, public approval of it did indeed reach majorities. But much of this public backing evaporated soon, and, ultimately, the decision to attack Iraq—and allegations of deceiving Parliament over it—would, in 2007, lead to Blair's resignation, and has tarnished Blair's legacy since.[64]

The precise impact of Murdoch's anti-EU and pro–Iraq War stances on UK politics are again impossible to quantify. However, counterfactual thought experiments—what would have happened if Murdoch's media had pushed for deeper European integration and against the Iraq invasion?—indicate that the billionaire's power to shape public opinion and political agendas has consequences beyond simply helping him to win financially beneficial favors from politicians. Often, especially in the UK, Murdoch's transnational media power, both latent as a disposition and when exercised, has allowed him to valorize his conservative beliefs in ways that increased his wealth. In the process, Murdoch had, very self-consciously, significant influence on political outcomes, with regard to elections, foreign policy, and many lesser policy issues. According to one of his

---

[62] See Anthony Hilton, "Stay or go—the lack of solid facts means it's all a leap of faith," *Evening Standard*, February 25, 2016, online: http://www.standard.co.uk/comment/comment/anthony-hilton-stay-or-go-the-lack-of-solid-facts-means-it-s-all-a-leap-of-faith-a3189151.html, Robert Booth and Jane Martinson, "Rupert Murdoch: 'I've never asked any prime minister for anything'," *The Guardian*, December 19, 2016, online: https://www.theguardian.com/media/2016/dec/19/rupert-murdoch-ive-never-asked-any-prime-minister-for-anything (both accessed June 6, 2019). Murdoch has been shown to forget, deny, or contradict statements he has made in the past on many occasions (Tiffen 2014: 9ff).

[63] See Roy Greenslade, "Their master's voice," *The Guardian*, February 17, 2003, online: https://www.theguardian.com/media/2003/feb/17/mondaymediasection.iraq (accessed June 6,2019) and McKnight 2013: 169ff, McKnight & McNair 2012.

[64] See Clarke et al. 2009: 103–42, also Alan Travis and Ian Black, "Blair's popularity plummets," *The Guardian*, February 18, 2003, online: https://www.theguardian.com/uk/2003/feb/18/politics.iraq and the report of *The Iraq Inquiry* (also called "Chilcot Report"), the official investigation of the UK's participation in the Iraq invasion, launched by Prime Minister Gordon Brown in 2009, and published in 2016, online: http://www.iraqinquiry.org.uk/ (all accessed June 6, 2019).

former associates, Woodrow Wyatt, Murdoch had "megalomaniac moods [in which he] thinks he can choose the Prime Minister" (McKnight 2013: 157). Murdoch also likes to think of himself and his company as "change agents" (Wolff 2010: 2), which is certainly true with regard to how he has transformed the media landscape in Australia, the UK, and the U.S. (Kiernan 1986, Auletta 1995, Shawcross 1997, Chenoweth 2001). This also encapsulates the key aspect of his power. In his political endorsements, Murdoch, while known to be on the conservative side, has remained flexible, and it is precisely this flexibility that gives him power. Murdoch's wrath can be painful, and while his support can be hoped for, it cannot be taken for granted—it must be earned, all of which is helping him to extract favors from politicians. At the international level, probably no other media businessman has held more political power across borders than Rupert Murdoch.

7

Social Entrepreneurship

Whereas the pursuits of security and prosperity are the bread and butter of mainstream IR, the pursuit of esteem implicates broader conceptions of "self-interest." Social constructivists have been arguing that actors' interests derive from their identities, which emerge intersubjectively, in relation to prevailing social norms and values (Wendt 1999, Richard Ned Lebow 2008). With regard to governmental actors, a much discussed example is the EU, which has been interpreted as a "normative power" the behavior of which in world politics is not only about survival and prosperity, but also very much shaped by the identity that it has developed over the course of several decades of European integration and constitution-building (Manners 2002, Whitman 2011). In this reading, the EU wants to satisfy its self-esteem as an institution that is based on the rule of law, and it tries to gain public esteem within the international system as an actor that promotes cooperation through international law and organizations. If we scale this perspective down to the individual level, those billionaires whose interventions in world politics are not primarily driven by concerns for security and wealth are forming a broad, somewhat residual category. In Max Weber's famous distinction, such a billionaire would be living "for" politics in the sense of "feed[ing] his inner equilibrium and his self-esteem with the consciousness that by serving 'a cause' he gives his own life *meaning*" (Weber 1918 [2004]: 40, emphasis in original). Or, as George Soros has expressed it: "We all look for something that we value more than our own life, [. . .] [i]f we can find it, we are better off, we feel more satisfied" (Bruck 1995). To understand their goals, one has to examine each billionaire's conception of self-esteem, which may be grounded in his or her personal biography, and relate this to the cultural context, with its social construction of public esteem, in which (s)he resides. As discussed in Chapter 4, the channel through which billionaires are pursuing esteem, particularly within the U.S., is philanthropy.

While it has to be remembered that the largest volume of charitable donations, especially if one includes volunteer time, comes from ordinary citizens (Edwards 2010), philanthropy among the superrich is growing fast, and it is taking on new forms that are having visible impacts on public policy (Skocpol 2016, Collins et al. 2016, Callahan 2017, Reich 2018). Wealth-X estimates that there are over 200,000 "ultra high-net-worth individuals" (UHNWIs, with a net worth above US$30 million) in the world,

Billionaires in World Politics. Peter Hägel, Oxford University Press (2020). © Peter Hägel.
DOI: 10.1093/oso/9780198852711.001.0001

worth a total of US$30tn in 2015. Of these, 18,500 (8.7%) are estimated to be major donors—those who have made a significant gift of at least US$1m to philanthropic causes in their lifetime.... More than half (57%) of the world's major donors are based in the Americas, which reflects the longstanding tradition of public giving in the US.   (Wealth-X 2016b: 10)

Much of this philanthropy can be seen as habitual in the sense that it is part of an elite culture in which charitable giving is socially expected, promising to enhance a person's status and her social and cultural capital (Ostrower 1995, Adloff 2010). Wealth-X's data supports such an interpretation, as it shows that the typical concerns of education (47 percent), health (20 percent), and "arts, culture and humanities" (10 percent) make up the lion's share of giving by the superrich, whereas "public and social benefit" account for only 8 percent (Wealth-X 2016b: 12). Generous giving to one's alma mater, a local clinic, or a museum is not very interesting for IR. Among U.S. billionaires, however, the practice of philanthropy has been changing. Ted Turner's gift to the UN in 1997 may not have had a major impact on world peace, but his plan to change the social recognition game appears to have worked:

> After announcing my billion-dollar grant I challenged my fellow billionaires to do more. I realized many of them used their net worth as a way to keep score and they enjoyed seeing where they ranked on lists put out by magazines like Fortune and Forbes. Understanding how competitive most of these people are, I called on the media outlets to start publishing lists of these people who gave away the most. I figured that this would not only motivate people to try to get to the top of the philanthropy list, it could also shame some whose names didn't show up.
> (Turner & Burke 2008: 350, also McGoey 2015: 117)

As a follow-up, the Giving Pledge, initiated by Bill Gates and Warren Buffett in 2010, has revived Andrew Carnegie's call for total philanthropy, to donate the majority of one's wealth, and even *Forbes* has "top givers" lists since a few years. Kristin Goss has analyzed nearly two hundred of the most generous philanthropists in the U.S., the majority of which are billionaires, and she finds that "[m]ore than half of [them] ... have serious policy interests," with sixteen of them drawn to "international affairs and foreign policy" (Goss 2016: 445f, also Callahan 2017).

Such quantitative overviews demonstrate the growing significance of billionaire philanthropy in politics, but we still need to look at individual cases in order to determine their political agency in world politics. Oftentimes, billionaires are mainly giving money to existing organizations whose mission they share. Stanley and Fiona Druckenmiller, for example, are among the "most charitable" Americans, and Fiona Druckenmiller used to sit on the board of Human Rights Watch (HRW) and was in charge of the organization's first endowment-building fundraiser in 1999.[1] Yet this engagement seems to owe much to her husband's former Quantum fund collaboration with George Soros, who is HRW's major benefactor, and it looks as if she had no further influence on HRW beyond the fundraising. Three of America's foremost philanthropists, David Gelbaum, C. Frederick Taylor, and Andrew Shechtel, former associates at the TGS Management hedge fund, have committed around US$13 billion to philanthropy in secrecy (until revealed by an investigative journalist), with Taylor apparently being a major donor to human rights causes.[2] Whereas the Druckenmillers are prominent New York socialites who probably care a lot about public esteem, the three anonymous hedge fund donors must have been motivated purely by self-esteem. None of them, however, can be seen as a social entrepreneur, since their philanthropy seems to lack an active engagement with social and political change.

It is this last component that has been highlighted by various scholars who observe a distinct kind of "entrepreneurial philanthropy" among some contemporary billionaires:

[T]he true nature of entrepreneurial philanthropy . . . [lies in it being] *a world-making process through which already successful entrepreneurs use their power to accumulate more power, extend their social and political influence, and increase their capacity to shape society according to their will.*[3]

Billionaires in this vein represent what Max Weber has called politicians that live for politics, rather than off it. They have independent means to enter politics, not as professionals, but as individuals with a cause that gives their lives meaning in their own eyes, or in the eyes of their peers. Mairi Maclean and her colleagues have shown that, oftentimes, this step into philanthropy (and politics) involves a "break-through experience," a point at which the pursuit of wealth ceases to be satisfying, and new values and goals are being sought to provide meaning (Maclean et al. 2015). Bill Gates and George Soros have both recounted such moments in their lives, at which they shifted their entrepreneurship from business to trying to make the world—according to their own definitions—a better place.

---

[1] See Human Rights Watch, "Human Rights Watch Announces Landmark Endowment Campaign," September 14, 1999, online: https://www.hrw.org/news/1999/09/14/human-rights-watch-announces-landmark-endowment-campaign, and https://www.insidephilanthropy.com/wall-street-donors/stanley-druckenmiller.html (accessed June 23, 2019).

[2] Zachary Mider, "The $13 Billion Mystery Angels," May 14, 2014, *Bloomberg*, online: http://www.bloomberg.com/news/articles/2014-05-08/three-mysterious-philanthropists-fund-fourth-largest-u-dot-s-dot-charity#p2. Taylor channels his money through Wellspring Advisors, which describes itself as "coordinat[ing] grantmaking programs that advance the realization of human rights and social and economic justice for all people." Online: http://www.wellspringadvisors.com/our-mission/ (all accessed June 23, 2019).

[3] Harvey et al. 2011: 429, emphasis in original, also Schervish 2003: 13, 2014: 155ff, Maclean et al. 2015: 1625.

Fighting Diseases: Bill Gates and Global Health Governance

Bill Gates (*1955) is the most famous billionaire alive, and not only because *Forbes* has declared him "the world's richest person" during most years between 1995 and 2017; since 2018, he is behind Amazon's Jeff Bezos, but still number two with personal wealth estimated at US$96.5 billion.[4] He also represents the Schumpeterian archetype of the self-made entrepreneur (Schumpeter 1912: 131ff), and his philanthropy has reached unprecedented proportions. In 1986, Microsoft, the ubiquitous software corporation that he cofounded, went public, and for many years his shares in it constituted the main source of his wealth. But since the mid-1990s, executing a pre-set plan, he has gradually been selling nearly all of his stocks, using most of the proceeds to diversify his wealth via his privately owned investment firm, Cascade Investment LLC, thus outsourcing his wealth management to professionals. Another large part of these proceeds has been transferred to the Bill and Melinda Gates Foundation (BMGF), which, in 1999, merged the earlier William H. Gates Foundation (founded in 1994) and the Gates Library Foundation (1997), and received US$15.8 billion that year, immediately turning it into the world's largest philanthropic organization (Bill and Melinda Gates Foundation 2000). Overall, between 1994 and 2019, Bill Gates and his wife Melinda have given over US$35.8 billion worth of Microsoft stocks to their foundation.[5] In parallel to this shifting of funds, Bill Gates stepped down as Microsoft's CEO in 2000, and on June 15, 2006, Microsoft officially announced "that effective July 2008 Bill Gates, chairman, will transition out of a day-to-day role in the company to spend more time on his global health and education work at the Bill & Melinda Gates Foundation."[6]

That same month, the investor legend Warren Buffett publicized his decision to progressively donate 10 million (or around 83 percent) of his shares in Berkshire Hathaway, his holding company, to the BMGF in annual installments. Between 2006 and 2019, this has resulted in over US$27 billion worth of transfers to the Gates Foundation.[7] Combining the Gates and Buffett donations, in 2019, the BMGF had an endowment worth almost US$50 billion, and has, since its

---

[4] Gates, who has been among the *Forbes* global list since its beginning in 1987 (when he was thirty-one years old), has been the world's richest person in all years since 1995, except 2008 (no. 3) and 2010–13 (no. 2), see the historical data online: http://www.forbes.com/global/1999/0705/0213066a.html and https://stats.areppim.com/stats/links_billionairexlists.htm (both accessed June 6, 2019).

[5] Gates's personal Microsoft stock holdings have decreased to just over 1 percent of the company's shares, see http://www.forbes.com/profile/bill-gates/, also Anupreeta Das, "Breaking Down Bill Gates's Wealth," *Wall Street Journal*, September 19, 2014, online: http://blogs.wsj.com/moneybeat/2014/09/19/breaking-down-bill-gatess-wealth/ (both accessed June 6, 2019).

[6] See online: http://news.microsoft.com/2006/06/15/microsoft-announces-plans-for-july-2008-transition-for-bill-gates/#sm.0001jeiign4o8dpwtpu19w7yubmcc (accessed June 6, 2019).

[7] See Jonathan Stempel, "Warren Buffett donates $3.6 billion to Gates' and family charities," *Reuters*, online: online: https://www.reuters.com/article/us-buffett-charities/warren-buffett-donates-36-billion-to-gates-and-family-charities-idUSKCN1TW307 (accessed July 6, 2019).

inception, disbursed an almost equal amount of grants. These grants don't diminish its endowment, because the BMGF's investment manager, Michael Larson, who is simultaneously in charge of Gates's private fortune, "has delivered a compounded annual return of 11.1% on endowment-related investments."[8] Although Buffett has become one of the BMGF's trustees and advisors, he has repeatedly stated that he will not get involved in the foundation's operations and decision-making.[9] In this relationship, Buffett appears as a passive social investor, whereas Gates is acting in line with the model of social entrepreneurship (Bishop & Green 2008: 51–74). This corresponds closely with their different business experiences: Buffett has accumulated his wealth as a financial investor acquiring shares in existing companies expected to generate long-term value growth; the origin of Gates's wealth is entrepreneurial, based on innovation and aggressive strategies to turn Microsoft into a standard-setting and market-dominating company (Wallace & Erickson 1993, Isaacson 2014: 313–43).

When Bill Gates shifted his entrepreneurship from Microsoft to the BMGF, the foundation published "15 guiding principles" regarding "the Gates family's beliefs about the role of philanthropy and the impact they want this foundation to have":[10]

1. This is a family foundation driven by the interests and passions of the Gates family.
2. Philanthropy plays an important but limited role.
3. Science and technology have great potential to improve lives around the world.
4. We are funders and shapers—we rely on others to act and implement.
5. Our focus is clear—and limited—and prioritizes some of the most neglected issues.
6. We identify a specific point of intervention and apply our efforts against a theory of change.
7. We take risks, make big bets, and move with urgency. We are in it for the long haul.
8. We advocate—vigorously but responsibly—in our areas of focus.

[8] See Anupreeta Das, "Breaking Down Bill Gates's Wealth," *Wall Street Journal*, September 19, 2014, online: http://blogs.wsj.com/moneybeat/2014/09/19/breaking-down-bill-gatess-wealth/, and https://www.gatesfoundation.org/who-we-are/general-information/foundation-factsheet (accessed July 6, 2019).
[9] One of the conditions for the coming-through of Buffett's donations is that either Bill or Melinda Gates "must remain alive and active in the policy-setting and administration of BMG[F]"; see his letter announcing his donation online: http://www.berkshirehathaway.com/donate/bmgfltr.pdf (accessed June 6, 2019).
[10] The BMGF's homepages has stopped publishing these "15 guiding principles" several years ago, but the *Internet Archive* has the BMGF's older webpages with the "15 guiding principles" archived from 2007/2008: https://web.archive.org/web/20071011221455/http://www.gatesfoundation.org/AboutUs/OurValues/GuidingPrinciples/default.htm (accessed July 6, 2019).

9. We must be humble and mindful in our actions and words. We seek and heed the counsel of outside voices.
10. We treat our grantees as valued partners, and we treat the ultimate beneficiaries of our work with respect.
11. Delivering results with the resources we have been given is of the utmost importance—and we seek and share information about those results.
12. We demand ethical behavior of ourselves.
13. We treat each other as valued colleagues.
14. Meeting our mission—to increase opportunity and equity for those most in need—requires great stewardship of the money we have available.
15. We leave room for growth and change.

Many of these principles exhibit what Paul Shervish has identified as common features of how high-tech entrepreneurs approach philanthropy. Of these, the following stands out: "An idealistic and optimistic belief in the capacity of the individual to make a difference,... which comes from seeing the revolutionary effect that their problem-solving approach has had in business."[11] In a commercial environment marked by rapid and often fundamental change, many high-tech entrepreneurs have accumulated their wealth in a short amount of time by creating a product for a new and growing demand, and by being actively involved in the production process, like Gates with Microsoft's development of operating systems software for personal computers (Schervish 2003: 13, Isaacson 2014: 337, 358ff, 485). This can result in a sense of what Schervish calls "hyperagency": "the ability to be a producer and a creator of the organizational life of a society rather than simply a supporter and participant" (Shervish 2014b: 172). The BMGF's principles 1, 3, and 5–7, in particular, express exactly such a belief in Gates's ability to harness science and technology in creative ways to bring about positive change that improves other people's lives.

The "hyperagency" point of view, however, needs to be contrasted with perspectives that emphasize the structuring influence of social practices and context. Thus, Gates's move into philanthropy inscribes itself plainly into a U.S. culture of philanthropy that has been shaped during America's first Gilded Age by the tycoons which dominated that era's leading industries. Gates has reportedly studied Carnegie's *Gospel of Wealth* before launching his own philanthropy, and is also admiring the heritage of the oil baron John D. Rockefeller (McGoey 2015:

---

[11] The findings are based on surveys and interviews among twenty-eight wealthy U.S. entrepreneurs from the high-tech industry in 2000, two of whom were billionaires. The other, equally fitting features identified by Shervish are: "An insistence on research and 'due diligence' for the start of any new venture. A strategic-thinking approach that combines both a global view and a broad-systems approach. A strong belief in the centrality to success of teamwork, partnering and collaboration rather than competition.... A fundamental belief in the development and application of human capital as the basis for solving society's problems. A conviction that innovation, constant change and a reassessment of circumstances are crucial to progress" (Shervish 2014b: 157f).

111, Bishop & Green 2008: 13ff, 53f, 74, 169). Gates's library program, which at first sought to provide free Internet access for U.S. public libraries and has since expanded globally, obviously builds on the philanthropic mission of Carnegie, who established some 3,000 public libraries in the U.S. and abroad (Bishop & Green 2008: 53ff).[12] And Rockefeller made his philanthropic mark by having his foundation "virtually single-handedly popularize the concept of international health, [as] it was the major influence upon the field's 20th century agenda, approaches, and actions" (Birn 2014: 2, also Chernow 1998: 568ff). Gates's focus on education and global health can therefore be seen as straightforward updates of his predecessors' role models. Indeed, many of the features frequently associated with 21st century "philanthrocapitalism," such as its emulation of business management techniques or its focus on results and impact, had already characterized the philanthropy of the Gilded Age (Harvey et al. 2011, Eckl 2014, McGoey 2015: 40-62, Youde 2013). Still, one important difference does emerge: Gates has retired much earlier from his business. He transitioned into social entrepreneurship at mid-career, when he was in his forties, and made it his full-time occupation at age 53. For Carnegie and Rockefeller, the creation of their foundations happened when they were in their seventies, and it was geared towards the institutionalization of a philanthropic legacy. Gates, on the other hand, appears to be determined to see his foundation achieve its objectives during his lifetime, and to steer it in its course.[13] At the same time, the expansion of his foundation does itself embody a process of institutionalization, and it is operating in the highly structured fields of public education and international development cooperation (Fejerskov 2015). This is raising questions about the scope of Gates's agency, which will be discussed more at the end of this chapter. What seems clear, though, is that Bill Gates's turn towards philanthropy is very much about the pursuit of public esteem. Just before the BMGF's creation, Gates had been openly chided by other billionaires, such as Ted Turner, for not giving generously, and Microsoft was in the midst of threatening antitrust cases in the U.S. and the EU, which made Gates look like a greedy monopolist (Auletta 2001: 130ff, McGoey 2015: 117). From the beginning, Gates has put his name and his person at the center of his foundation, and every major

---

[12] See online: http://www.gatesfoundation.org/What-We-Do/Global-Development/Global-Libraries (accessed June 6, 2016).

[13] Although both had given generously throughout their lives, their major donations occurred when they set up the Carnegie Corporation (1911, when Carnegie was seventy-six years old) and the Rockefeller Foundation (1913, when Rockefeller was seventy-four years old). Carnegie had advocated for giving one's wealth away during one's lifetime in his *Gospel of Wealth* (1889), but, to his own regret, waited too long to accomplish this self-set goal (Nasaw 2006: xv, 766ff, Chernow 1998: 563ff). Whereas the Carnegie Corporation and the Rockefeller Foundation had relatively broad boards of trustees, the BMGF has only three trustees: Bill and Melinda Gates, and Warren Buffett. While Rockefeller was highly religious, both Carnegie and Gates were/are secular.

step is being announced in press releases. Since then, portraits of Gates as a great benefactor of humankind have replaced robber baron associations.[14]

Bill Gates claims that he had always planned to give his wealth "back to society," but that his decision to do so long before the usual retirement age has been driven by a realization of the scale and the urgency of global health problems during the mid-1990s.[15]

> When I first learned about world health, . . . I was kind of stunned. I half expected that the United States and other governments and foundations were really taking these low cost interventions and saying that the value of life is the same throughout the world and really focusing on that problem. And yet the more I learned about it the more I realized that there is a real market failure here. There's a failure of visibility; there's a failure of incentives; there's a failure of cooperation that has really led to a very disastrous situation.[16]

In Gates's eyes, private philanthropy needs to step in, because the logics of politics and markets operate in ways that neglect health problems in the Global South: "Rich governments are not fighting some of the world's most deadly diseases because rich countries don't have them. The private sector is not developing vaccines and medicines for these diseases, because developing countries can't buy them."[17] He is aware that most philanthropy maintains a local or national focus, and ascribes this to ignorance, due to a lack of media coverage. In contrast, and in line with his global business experience, Gates is expressing a cosmopolitan social identity, the values of which seem to draw upon both John Rawls's theory of justice and Peter Singer's moral philosophy:

> [B]efore you think about what giving makes sense you might . . . think of yourself as somebody who's going to be born to an arbitrary womb . . . —what changes would you want to make in the world [?]. And certainly taking that perspective, you'd step back and say wow, . . . the billion people in the rich countries have

---

[14] Rockefeller and Carnegie, too, had tarnished reputations because of monopoly accusations, and also because of violent suppressions of worker strikes (Chernow 1998: 571ff, Nasaw 2006: 405ff, 459ff).

[15] In the following, the BMGF's work on education will be ignored, because it is largely intervening at the national level within the U.S.; for critical analyses, see Kovacs 2011, Cody 2014, and Au & Lubienski 2016.

[16] Bill Gates, speech at World Economic Forum Annual Meeting 2001, January 29, 2001, online: http://www.gatesfoundation.org/Media-Center/Speeches/2001/01/Bill-Gates-2001-World-Economic-Forum (accessed June 22, 2019).

[17] Bill Gates, speech at 2005 World Health Assembly, May 16, 2005, online: http://www.gatesfoundation.org/Media-Center/Speeches/2005/05/Bill-Gates-2005-World-Health-Assembly (accessed June 22, 2019).

health and access to very basic things that a high percentage of the 5 billion do not, and that cause I think would rise above all others.[18]

Singer's utilitarian position, with its emphasis on effectiveness, efficiency, and measurability, has much in common with a business entrepreneur's thinking, except that it is substituting profit maximization with *The Most Good You Can Do* (Singer 2015). Accordingly, Gates's approach to global health is tailored towards realizing assessable objectives that improve poor people's health:

[H]ealth aid is very measurable, you can look at vaccination rates, you can look at advances in changing behaviors that'll stop the AIDS epidemic. There are breakthroughs coming, but even in the vaccines that we have today, we're not getting them out there.... There are 30 million children a year who don't get vaccines. There's a certain amount of money that would cause them to get those vaccines and that would save three million lives a year.[19]

Gates has also appropriated other experiences from his business success for his philanthropy—a belief in progress based on science and collaboration:

[M]y work at Microsoft had three magical elements: an opportunity for big breakthroughs; a chance to make a big contribution by building teams of people with different skill sets focused on tough problems; and work that let me engage with people who were smart and knew things I didn't. I have found—not surprisingly—that my job at the Bill & Melinda Gates Foundation meets these same criteria. The work of the foundation reflects the essential optimism that Melinda and I feel about the future, and our belief that a combination of scientific innovation and great partnerships with leaders who work on behalf of the world's poorest people can dramatically improve the human condition.[20]

---

[18] Bill Gates, "Global Foundation Address," September 12, 2000, online: http://www. gatesfoundation.org/Media-Center/Speeches/2000/09/Bill-Gates-Global-Foundation. Gates relates having been introduced to the "veil of ignorance" position by Warren Buffett, and makes no reference to the (anti-utilitarian) Rawls; he has, however, quoted Peter Singer on various occasions, and many of his considerations appear to correspond with Singer's. On the paperback edition of Singer's *The Life You Can Save* (Singer 2010), Bill and Melinda Gates's endorsement of the book features prominently on the front cover. See also Peter Singer, "What Should a Billionaire Give—and What Should You?," *New York Times Magazine*, December 17, 2006, online: http://www.nytimes.com/2006/12/17/maga zine/17charity.t.html?_r=0, and Richard Waters, "An exclusive interview with Bill Gates," *Financial Times Magazine*, November 1, 2013, online: http://www.ft.com/cms/s/2/dacd1f84-41bf-11e3-b064-00144feabdc0.html (all accessed June 22, 2019).

[19] Bill Gates, speech at the *2002 World Economic Forum*, February 2, 2002, online: http://www. gatesfoundation.org/Media-Center/Speeches/2002/02/Bill-Gates-2002-World-Economic-Forum (accessed June 22, 2019).

[20] Bill Gates, "Testimony Before the Senate Committee on Foreign Relations," March 10, 2010, online: http://www.gatesfoundation.org/Media-Center/Speeches/2010/03/2010-Senate-Testimony (accessed June 22, 2019).

The fact that the BMGF's first two CEOs came directly from Microsoft—Patty Stonesifer (1997–2007), former vice president, and Jeff Raikes (2007–14), former president of the Microsoft Business Division, manifests the continuity between Bill Gates's enterprises.[21] Most of the BMGF's expenditure on global health has been financing biomedical approaches, chiefly vaccine and drug development, in order to fight communicable diseases in developing countries. This has characterized the BMGF's first decade in particular, as Stonesifer recalls: "Bill, Melinda and I were a bunch of product-development people. . . . We assumed others would focus on getting the products we developed to those who needed them."[22] Only in 2006 did the BMGF add a "Global Development" program that also focuses on poverty and hunger, which, in 2011, lead to a significant shift, integrating the foundation's global health work closer with its development program, to provide "more holistic support to the people we serve" (BMGF 2012: 4, also BMGF 2008: 5–16, Birn 2014: 11).

As a grant-making institution, the BMGF, which declared 1,489 employees in 2019, is primarily channeling money to other actors, particularly scientific research and international health delivery organizations.[23] Given the multitude of the BMGF's funding of health-related projects over the past two decades, a comprehensive examination of its engagement in global health is beyond the scope of this book.[24] Nevertheless, several major funding programs have been maintained over time, and they characterize the BMGF's priorities: (1) The BMGF's first super-sized donation, US$750 million, in 1999, went to the Global Alliance for Vaccines and Immunization (GAVI), a public–private partnership (PPP) launched in 2000 to improve children's immunization against infectious diseases in developing countries (Muraskin 2002 and 2005). From 2000 until 2020, the BMGF has committed over US$4 billion to GAVI, making it the largest

---

[21] The BMGF's third CEO, Sue Desmond-Hellmann (since 2014), an oncologist with a career in the biomedical industry and former chancellor of the University of California San Francisco, is the first without a Microsoft background.

[22] "Bill Gates's other chief executive," *The Economist*, January 18, 2007, online: http://www.econo mist.com/node/8550607 (accessed June 22, 2016).

[23] See online: http://www.gatesfoundation.org/Who-We-Are/General-Information/Foundation-Factsheet (accessed June 22, 2019).

[24] In 2016, the BMGF's grants database counted almost 15,000 entries. Its search function is limited; for example, if one is looking for interesting keywords like "vaccine" or "drug," in order to assess the biomedical orientation of the BMGF, the results are capped after the first 1,000 results. The foundation does indicate its priorities and grants, and its annual reports publish funding by area, but the categorization of funding areas has changed over the years, making comparisons difficult. For example, while polio and other vaccination programs as well as "family health" figured under the BMGF's "Global Health" division until 2011, since then they fall under the "Global Development" division, whereas "Global Health" now contains principally biomedical research and development projects. As of 2015, the BMGF has stopped publishing detailed annual reports. Between 1999 and 2007, the BMGF's annual reports comprised thirty to seventy pages and provided broad overviews; the reports' volume shrunk continuously afterwards, as the foundation concentrated on its website, where it allows open access to its grants database, its financial data, and its research.

contributor for many years.[25] (2) At the 2003 World Economic Forum, Bill Gates announced the so-called "Grand Challenges in Global Health," a program that funds innovative science addressing predefined research questions (Varmus et al. 2003, Cohen 2005). Initially equipped with US$200 million, it later received additional US$250 million; another "Grand Challenges Explorations" program started in 2007 (US$100 million), and in 2014, the BMGF announced a further round of "Grand Challenges" (with no specified funding envelope). Since then, the research funding rounds have become smaller and more regular, and have spread out globally to include regional and national programs, often in collaboration with government institutions, e.g. in China, India, and Brazil.[26] (3) With huge grants to individual organizations, the BMGF invests in initiatives that combat specific diseases, mainly malaria, HIV/AIDS, polio, and tuberculosis. For descriptive overviews of the BMGF's financing, the Institute for Health Metrics and Evaluation (IHME), itself largely funded by the BMGF, is the best source, as it details funding sources, channels, and focus areas for all the major global health actors.[27] Figure 7.1 shows that the BMGF's funding priorities shifted very little between 2000 and 2015, except that malaria and maternal health received relatively less funding, while the residual "other" category grew (for the BMGF as well as for GAVI, "newborn and child health" covers primarily vaccines/immunization).

So far, only one study has attempted an in-depth analysis of the BMGF's global grant-making, covering the period 1998–2007 (McCoy et al. 2009), while several others have focused on specific areas such as the BMGF's work on combating Malaria (Eckl 2014) or Tuberculosis (van Dyck 2015), its role within GAVI (Storeng 2014), or the effects of its scientific research funding (Matthews & Ho 2008, Krestin 2010). For the purposes of this study, the BMGF's role in its interactions with private organizations—mainly, NGOs and other foundations—and within the scientific field will only be touched upon briefly, since my interest lies more with Bill Gates's influence in global health governance. Up until 2016,

[25] The UK government has become the largest GAVI contributor since 2015. For the 2000–20 period as a whole, the BMGF accounts for 17.53 percent of GAVI's donor contributions, behind the UK with 26.3 percent. See the GAVI's financing online: http://www.gavi.org/funding/donor-contributions-pledges/ and https://www.gavi.org/investing/funding/donor-profiles/bmgf/ (accessed June 22, 2019).

[26] See BMGF, "Bill & Melinda Gates Foundation and Grand Challenge Partners Commit to Innovation with New Investments in Breakthrough Science," October 7, 2014, online: http://www.gatesfoundation.org/Media-Center/Press-Releases/2014/10/Gates-Foundation-Grand-Challenges-Breakthrough-Science; the various programs together form the "Global Grand Challenges," see https://gcgh.grandchallenges.org/ (accessed June 22, 2019).

[27] The IHME at the University of Washington was founded in 2007 with an initial core grant of US $105 million from the BMGF, in line with the foundation's focus on measurability and assessment. In 2015, the IHME and the WHO signed a memorandum of understanding regarding their collaboration on global health data (online: http://www.healthdata.org/sites/default/files/files/MOU_IHME_WHO_050615.pdf), highlighting the status the IHME has acquired as the world's leading source of health statistics. IHME online: http://www.healthdata.org/, for historical trends and data visualizations: http://vizhub.healthdata.org/fgh/ (accessed June 22, 2019).

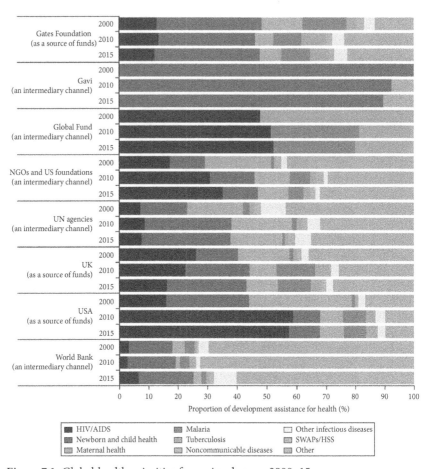

Figure 7.1 Global health priorities for major donors, 2000–15

Source: Reprinted from The Lancet, Dieleman et al. 2016: 2541, with permission from Elsevier.

the BMGF has, for example, given US$355 million to Rotary International to support polio eradication, and US$112 million to Save the Children to protect newborn lives.[28] Between 1998 and 2007, more than a third of the BMGF's total funding, or US$3.27 billion, "was allocated to research and development (mainly for vaccines and microbicides)" (McCoy et al. 2009: 1645). Such immense injections of money clearly have the potential to alter the priorities and behavior of NGOs, scientists, and universities. Ruth Krestin's study suggests that the BMGF's funding influx has encouraged the malaria research community to focus more on applied research and product development (Krestin 2010: 89ff). Via demonstration effects, the BMGF may contribute to overall increases in the funding of a

---
[28] BMGF Fact Sheet, online: http://www.gatesfoundation.org/Who-We-Are/General-Information/Foundation-Factsheet (accessed July 4, 2019).

specific area, if its initial investments attract others to follow suit. Alternatively, and more problematically, BMGF funding may produce crowding-out effects that displace other actors' investments. For malaria research, Krestin's results indicate that the BMGF's boost of applied research did not diminish basic research, as other funding sources, especially the U.S. National Institutes of Health and the British Wellcome Trust maintained their support of malaria-related basic research (Krestin 2010: 91). Gates's money seems to have expanded the field of malaria research, attracting new scientists to it, rather than displacing previously existing priorities. For scientific research on tuberculosis, Marcus van Dyck comes up with similar conclusions (van Dyck 2015: 69–90).[29] Besides influencing research priorities, the BMGF's involvement with the scientific community has another effect that augments its own role in global health. As it encourages and engages with innovative scientific projects, the BMGF is developing authority in the field, because it can back its positions and decisions with scientific expertise. Just as Bill Gates once prided himself with mastering most of the code produced by Microsoft programmers (Cringely 1996: 112ff), he is nowadays able to cite the latest research challenges and findings in biomedical science, which enhances his legitimacy within the global health field (Gates 2015, 2018).

Many critical questions can be posed about the BMGF's choices, whether too much of its science funding ends up in Western research institutions, "whether the foundation allocates its funding according to need, both in selection of diseases and health issues, and in the focus on vaccines and technology," and whether it is actually achieving its objectives (McCoy et al. 2009: 1652). As McCoy and his colleagues admit themselves, answers to such questions are very difficult to establish, both normatively and empirically, as they would need to take into account complicated cost–benefit analyses and the changing context in which the BMGF operates. Choices taken at one point due to a perceived need may look different later as a consequence of other actors' choices. A serious discussion, for example, concerns whether, after 2000, too much funding has gone into combating HIV/AIDS, at the expense of fighting other diseases (Rushton 2011). Yet, as can be seen in Figure 7.1, a huge amount of new funding appeared from 2003 onwards, dwarfing the BMGF's prior expenditure on HIV/AIDS, as a result of George W. Bush's decision to create the "President's Emergency Plan for AIDS Relief" (PEPFAR). Between 2004 and 2015, PEPFAR provided US$57 billion through bilateral HIV/AIDS programs alone.[30] The existing accounts of PEPFAR's origins mention absolutely no influence of Bill Gates and his foundation (Donnelly 2012, Goosby et al. 2012, Varmus 2013). Anthony Fauci, then

---

[29] Van Dyck wrongly claims that funding of tuberculosis-related basic research decreased between 2007 and 2013 when, in fact, his graph shows that it stagnated in absolute terms; only its relative share within an increasing pie shrunk (van Dyck 2015: 70).
[30] See online: http://www.pepfar.gov/funding/budget/index.htm (accessed July 4, 2019).

director of the National Institute of Allergy and Infectious Diseases and scientific leader of PEPFAR, has, however, acknowledged that "the Gates Foundation has transformed the whole issue of global health . . . , because it also galvanizes others to get involved."[31] In a related argument, Kirstin Matthews and Vivian Ho claim that Gates's "Grand Challenges in Global Health," via demonstration effects and advocacy, influenced the U.S. National Institutes of Health to shift more funding towards global health research (2008). With this, we are entering the political discussion of whether and how Bill Gates has affected the decisions of governmental actors and the broader agenda of global health governance.

Here, it has to be emphasized that Bill Gates entered the scene during a period in which the structural context was particularly favorable. As discussed in Chapter 3, during the 1990s, neoliberal ideas had gained broad dominance, welcoming the private sector to take over previously public functions, and calling for the public sector to emulate business practices; this also applied to global health (Chorev 2013, Rushton & Williams 2012). When the BMGF appeared in 1999, public sector global health initiatives, including international organizations such as the WHO, were emerging from a post–Cold War crisis (Brown et al. 2006, Lidén 2013: 14, Birn 2014: 8f). Despite—some say, because of (McCoy & McGoey 2011, Mitchell & Sparke 2016)—the advance of globalization, many poor countries, especially in sub-Saharan Africa, had experienced economic decline and a dramatic rise in health problems during the 1990s, epitomized by the spread of the HIV/AIDS pandemic with its high death toll. Yet, international development assistance had failed to follow suit, growing far slower than the actual disease burdens (Figure 7.2).

The appointment of Gro Harlem Brundtland as the WHO Director-General in 1998 marked a critical juncture, as she embodied the expectation to turn global health into a political priority again (Williams & Rushton 2011, Hanrieder 2015b: 95ff). Figure 7.2) shows that this did indeed happen—funding started to multiply in the wake of several high-level summits focused on global health (e.g., in 2000, the G8 summit in Okinawa, and the UN Millennium Summit). Prior to Bill Gates's entry, Gro Harlem Brundtland, in her inaugural address to the World Health Assembly, had already emphasized the importance of public–private partnerships and how the private sector "has an important role to play both in technology development and the provision of services." In this speech, she also

---

[31] "Interview with Anthony S. Fauci," *The Miller Center Foundation and the Edward M. Kennedy Institute for the United States Senate*, September 10, 2007, online: https://www.emkinstitute.org/resources/anthony-s-fauci. In their memoirs, the key political actors involved in instigating PEPFAR—Condoleeza Rice and George W. Bush—don't mention Bill Gates. Bush, however, grants that the rock music celebrity Bono helped to persuade him to launch PEPFAR (Bush 2010: 333–54). At the same time, Bono had received US$1 million of funding for his pro-Africa advocacy operation "DATA" from the BMGF (Tyrangiel 2005, James Traub, "The Statesman," *New York Times Magazine*, September 18, 2005, online: http://www.nytimes.com/2005/09/18/magazine/the-statesman.html?_r=0, all accessed July 4, 2019).

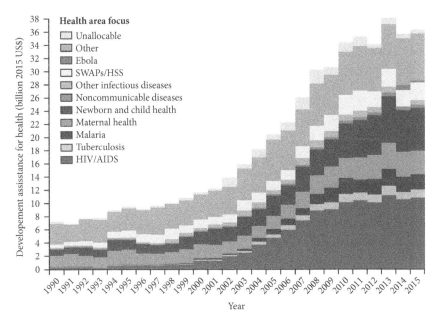

Figure 7.2 Development assistance for health by health focus area, 1990–2015

Source: Reprinted from The Lancet, Dieleman et al. 2016: 2538, with permission from Elsevier.

established a renewed priority for the "eradication and rolling back [of] diseases," especially malaria, and for better statistics and reporting, because "[h]ealth is pure and sound economics."[32] Much of what critics call the "Gates approach" (Birn 2005, 2014)—directing global health towards cost-effective biomedical interventions that promise measurable short-term results—had thus become common currency, even among center-left leaders such as Brundtland, Bill Clinton, and Tony Blair, *before* the founding of the BMGF (Cueto 2004, Brown, Cueto & Fee 2006, Storeng 2014: 873f).

While Bill Gates thus arrived at open doors, his announcements, in 1999, that he would massively increase the BMGF's endowment and make grants for global health a priority,[33] came as a surprise that had a momentous influence on turning the 2000s into the "grand decade for global health."

[32] Gro Harlem Brundtland, Speech to the Fifty-first World Health Assembly, Geneva, May 13, 1998, A51/DIV/6. Online: http://apps.who.int/gb/archive/pdf_files/WHA51/eadiv6.pdf (accessed July 4, 2019).

[33] "$50 million to the Malaria Vaccine Initiative (MVI) to accelerate the development of a new vaccine to prevent malaria; The Bill and Melinda Gates Children's Vaccine Program, a $100 million commitment to speed the delivery of life-saving vaccines to children in developing countries; Motherhood Mortality Reduction, a $50 million program administered by Columbia University to prevent maternal death in pregnancy and childbirth in the poorest countries; and a $25 million gift to the International AIDS Vaccine Initiative," see BMGF, "Gates Foundation Confirms Increase in Endowment," August 22, 1999, online: http://www.gatesfoundation.org/Media-Center/Press-Releases/1999/08/Bill-Melinda-Gates-Foundation, and BMGF, "Bill & Melinda Gates Foundation

The self-propelling effect of this money was dramatic. The fact that resources for health could get close to the 'b-word'—billion—in one simple stroke energized the global health community beyond anything ever seen before. It liberated the minds of those striving for global action and enabled them to think really big for the first time (Lidén 2013: 27, also Cohen 2002 and 2006, Youde 2013: 149).

Although this impact is impossible to quantify, almost all observers, including the BMGF's fiercest critics, agree on its importance. "Without question, the emergence of the Gates Foundation has contributed to the rise in global health spending and to a much needed injection of energy and political capital into global health over the past decade" (McCoy & McGoey 2011: 150, also People's Health Movement 2008: 256, Birn 2014: 10).

More controversial are assessments of the BMGF's power in shaping the policy agenda of global health, both directly and indirectly. Within the global health community, a longstanding divide concerns the relative merits of so-called horizontal versus vertical approaches (Cueto 2004, Brown et al. 2006, Garrett 2007, Ooms et al. 2008). On the one hand, horizontal or "health systems" approaches, which, historically, have been championed by European and especially Scandinavian development assistance, emphasize building and strengthening the infrastructure of national health systems as a precondition for improving people's health. Vertical approaches, on the other hand, concentrate on interventions that target specific health problems such as infectious diseases, and have often been at the center of U.S. development assistance, starting with the Rockefeller Foundation at the very origins of international health cooperation (Birn 2014). In practice, horizontal and vertical approaches matter both, and need to be integrated. Without functioning health systems, the prevention and treatment of specific diseases is impossible. At the very least, immunization, for example, requires a health infrastructure for the storing, distribution ("cool chains"), and dispensing (nurses and doctors) of vaccines (Hill 2011, Ooms et al. 2008). But the role of external donors in these approaches differs. Assisting in the development of national health systems is more complex and therefore makes external oversight as well as outcome assessment quite complicated. Vertical initiatives, in contrast, seem to offer less opportunities for the diversion of donors' resources, and their results, such as the number of vaccinations administered (and thus "lives saved"), are easier to quantify.[34] In the history of global health, both approaches have had their ups and downs.

Announces $750 Million Gift to Speed Delivery of Life-Saving Vaccines," November 23, 1999, http://www.gatesfoundation.org/Media-Center/Press-Releases/1999/11/Global-Alliance-for-Vaccines-and-Immunization (all accessed July 4, 2019).

[34] From a somewhat different normative "global public policy" angle, the influential "Global Health 2035" report makes a distinction between the "core" and the "supportive" functions of global health

The heyday of the horizontal perspective was during the 1970s, culminating in the 1978 International Conference on Primary Health Care in Alma-Ata with its stated goal of "Health for All by the Year 2000"; it became challenged during the 1980s, and increasingly sidelined during the 1990s (Cueto 2004, Brown et al. 2006, Moran & Stevenson 2013: 128). Vertical approaches have been at the heart of U.S. and WHO policies during the two decades after WWII, and have come back to dominate the global health agenda of the twenty-first century. The failure of the mid-twentieth-century attempt to eradicate malaria, which relied strongly on the insecticide DDT, often serves as a negative example of vertical approaches, while the eradication of smallpox, frequently cited by Bill Gates, is the most famous success story (Birn 2014). As the prior presentation of Bill Gates's thinking and funding makes clear, the BMGF has predominantly embraced vertical approaches to global health. Many insiders that have worked with Bill Gates on global health issues confirm his stance against horizontal approaches: "he is vehemently against health systems . . . he basically said it is a complete waste of money, that there is no evidence that it works, so I will not see a dollar or cent of my money go to the strengthening of health systems" (Storeng 2014: 868). The critical question then concerns whether Bill Gates can impose his preferences on other actors within the governance of global health.

In terms of annual budget, the BMGF has become, after the U.S. and U.K. governments, but before the WHO in most recent years, the third largest actor in global health (Birn 2014: 9). Still, Bill Gates is fully aware that the foundation's capacity is limited:

[I]t is important to note that the foundation's resources represent only a small part of the overall funding picture for fighting disease and improving health in developing countries. Our global health grants accounted for about 5 percent of total donor assistance for health in 2007.[35]

governance, where the "core" "addresses market failures caused by the crossnational interdependence of the global health system" and aims at the provision of global public goods, such as research and development to combat infectious diseases. The "supportive" functions address "government failures" and "largely coincide with traditional development aid—for example, providing assistance to developing countries where national health systems are underdeveloped and lack the resources to address national health challenges" (Blanchet et al. 2013: 5f, also Jamison, Summers et al. 2013: 1939f). Much of the "vertical" approaches would seem to fall into the "core," while much of the "horizontal" approaches would seem to fall into the "supportive" functions.

[35] Bill Gates, "Testimony Before the Senate Committee on Foreign Relations," =March 10, 2010, online: http://www.gatesfoundation.org/Media-Center/Speeches/2010/03/2010-Senate-Testimony (accessed June 22, 2016). In relation to the overall funding of global health during the 2000–13 period, as shown in Figure 7.3, the BMGF's share is 5.9 percent. See also Fejerskov 2015: 1109.

Figure 7.3, from a comprehensive survey of international health development assistance, illustrates Gates's assessment—the BMGF has become a major actor in global health, but, as so often in world politics, this is a crowded arena.

Many of the BMGF's initiatives therefore happen in cooperation with other donors, often in the form of PPPs, in which the BMGF frequently insists on "matching grants" as a condition for its own expenditure. It is in these instances that Bill Gates's capacity to influence public policy is coming to the fore, because his foundation's financial incentives—frequently, the BMGF has been the largest donor within the PPPs it supports—and its advocacy can shape the agenda and the direction of global health policymaking.

> Major IOs including the World Health Organisation (WHO) are now grantees, and the Foundation's principal donor status for many PPPs has assured it board-level representation and with this procedural influence within key organs of global health governance. Moreover, despite its lack of operational programmes and only a handful of field offices, experts formally affiliated with the Foundation are increasingly playing a lead role in international policy formation
> (Moran & Stevenson 2013: 118, also Birn 2014: 10ff, Eckl 2014: 107ff).

Between 2000 and 2007, the BMGF provided 1–5 percent of the WHO's annual budget; from 2008 to 2018, it provided 10–15 percent, usually being its second largest donor, surpassed only by the U.S. (and, in 2013 and 2015, by the UK).[36] My own analysis of the BMGF's nearly 270 grants to the WHO (1999–2015) reveals that almost all of these donations have been earmarked for specific purposes.[37] Of its US$2.5 billion given to the WHO, the BMGF assigned a large majority towards fighting infectious diseases (81.5 percent), within which polio has been the paramount concern (54.1 percent), followed by general vaccine delivery (8 percent), malaria (6.8 percent), HIV/AIDS (5.3 percent), and pneumonia (2.4 percent).[38] Some of the other funding categories could be seen as being part of a broader "health system strengthening" approach, especially the grants towards "family health" (6.6 percent) and "integrated delivery" of healthcare (2.9 percent), yet many of the largest grants in these categories also have clear biomedical or

---

[36] For data and visualization, see online: http://vizhub.healthdata.org/fgh/, my calculations.

[37] In doing so, the BMGF, although "earmarking" more than other WHO donors, is not alone: most of the WHO member states earmark large parts of their contributions as well, so that almost 80 percent of the WHO's budget has become earmarked (Birn 2014: 9).

[38] The other infectious diseases are: the so-called "neglected infectious diseases" (1.6 percent), enteric diseases (1.4 percent), tuberculosis (1.4 percent), dengue fever (0.2 percent), cholera (0.1 percent) and influenza (0.1 percent). Grants towards tobacco control (0.6 percent) have been the only ones targeting noncommunicable diseases. For my analysis, over 95 percent of the BMGF grants haven been straightforward to categorize, because they were highly targeted. Only a handful of smaller grants exhibited multiple objectives and had to be allocated more subjectively. Only grants above US $50k have been considered. All data from: http://www.gatesfoundation.org/How-We-Work/Quick-Links/Grants-Database, my calculations.

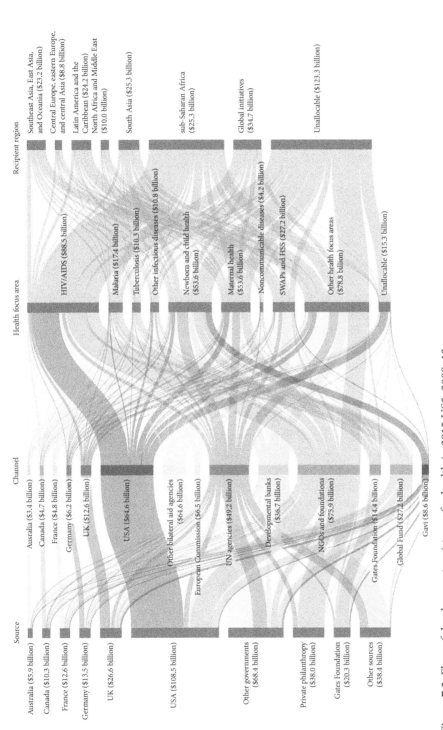

Figure 7.3 Flow of development assistance for health in 2015 US$, 2000–13

Source: Reprinted from The Lancet, Dieleman et al. 2016: 2540, with permission from Elsevier.

technocratic purposes. For example, a US$23 million "family health" grant went to "evaluate the efficacy of neonatal vitamin A supplementation in reducing infant mortality," and the lion's share of "integrated delivery" funding was a US$48 million grant "to support the Health Metrics Network."[39] Only 3.7 percent of the BMGF's grants served to support the general functioning of the WHO. This shows that Bill Gates has no intention to give blank checks to other global health actors—virtually all of his foundation's grants to the WHO serve objectives that are closely in line with his biomedical approach, which favors vaccines and drugs in fighting infectious diseases:

> The Gates family was...preoccupied with achieving impact. It considered the large, UN-led health efforts to be largely adrift and feared investing in existing efforts that would not be able to achieve tangible, measurable results. It also feared that, given its enormous economic clout, an investment by the Gates Foundation would simply replace public-sector funding   (Lidén 2013: 24).

Has Bill Gates managed to shift the WHO's global health agenda to correspond with his own objectives? If one stays at the macro level of funding distribution, the first impression is affirmative: between 1990 and 1999, the WHO allocated, on average, over 30 percent of its budget to horizontal approaches ("system-wide approaches/health system strengthening"—SWAs/HSS); in the 2000–15 period, this average was almost cut in half, to 17 percent. In contrast, vertical initiatives against infectious diseases received 16 percent of the WHO's budget in the 1990–99 period, and almost 20 percent in 2000–15.[40] Once Bill Gates's grants started arriving, the WHO's priorities seem to have become much more aligned with his. However, the decisive break in the WHO's support for horizontal approaches had already happened before the BMGF's entry—in 1998 and the years after, during the first directorship of Gro Harlem Brundtland, when the WHO budget's share of SWAs/HSS went from 35 percent in 1997 to 25 percent in 1998 and then to 19 percent in 2000. If one looks back at Figure 7.2, one sees that, overall, horizontal approaches had become marginalized throughout the 1990s,

---

[39] See   online: http://www.gatesfoundation.org/How-We-Work/Quick-Links/Grants-Database/ Grants/2009/09/OPPGH5297 and http://www.gatesfoundation.org/How-We-Work/Quick-Links/ Grants-Database/Grants/2004/12/OPP31044_01 (all accessed July 4, 2019).

The remaining funding categories–nutrition (2.1 percent), "integrated development" (1 percent), "family planning" (1 percent), "emergencies" (0.4 percent, mainly, in 2014, Ebola-related), and sanitation (0.1 percent)—may be seen as contributing to broader development assistance, but they make up less than 5 percent of all BMGF grants to the WHO.

[40] WHO budget allocation data according to http://vizhub.healthdata.org/fgh/, author's calculations during July 2016; the data categorization on this tool has been changed since then, and SWAs/HSS are now being displayed with much higher percentages. This seems mainly due to counting measures to eradicate polio among SWAs/HSS, which was not the case in 2016, and which seems inappropriate, given that it targets a specific communicable disease. Sometimes, SWA is also meant to stand for "sector-wide approaches," and HSS for "health sector support."

and they have remained more or less equally neglected since then. Development assistance for global health has multiplied since 2000, but this has predominantly happened through expanding vertical interventions against infectious diseases. In this sense, Bill Gates's approach has certainly reinforced this strategic direction, but he is far from being its sole instigator or promoter.[41]

Despite its immense donations, the BMGF naturally has no formal standing within the WHO, which is an intergovernmental international organization. But, in 2005, Bill Gates, as a private actor, was given the unprecedented privilege to address the World Health Assembly (WHA), the WHO's governing body that gathers its member states' ministers of health, as the keynote speaker. In his speech, he emphasized "science and technology" as the answers to the world's most pressing health problems, pointed to PPPs such as GAVI as the models for delivering health solutions, and encouraged WHO member states to provide more funding.[42] In 2011, he was invited for another keynote speech at the WHA, where he advocated for a "Decade of Vaccines," urging "[a]ll 193 member states[:] you must make vaccines a central focus of your health systems." Whereas in 2005, Bill Gates's rhetoric maintained a clear distinction between the BMGF's work and that of the WHO's member states, in 2011, his speech was full of "we" and "let us," seeing himself as part of the political leadership: "In January of last year, I called for the world to accelerate progress on vaccines. That was a moment, and now there is momentum. I'm excited that global health leaders are now collaborating to put a specific global vaccine action plan in place."[43] Evidently, Bill Gates was fully aware of his agenda-setting power, and took credit for it. He and his wife had indeed launched the "decade of vaccines" idea at the 2010 World Economic Forum, pledging US$10 billion to the effort. And one year after Gates's WHA speech, in 2012, the WHA delegates officially turned the "decade of vaccines" vision into a "Global Vaccine Action Plan 2011–2020." On the WHO website and in speeches by then WHO Director-General Margaret Chan, the BMGF's leadership regarding the "decade of vaccines" was openly acknowledged.[44] When, in 2014, Melinda Gates was invited to the WHA, several global health NGOs published a protest note stating that "[i]t is unacceptable that the WHO,

---

[41] Arguably, and often neglected by studies that focus critically on Gates (Brin 2014, McGoey 2015), the U.S. government's vast increase in global health funding, especially, via PEPFAR, to fight HIV/AIDS, is at least as much behind the biomedical turn as the BMGF.

[42] Bill Gates, speech on May 25, 2005 at the 58th World Health Assembly, online: http://www.gatesfoundation.org/Media-Center/Speeches/2005/05/Bill-Gates-2005-World-Health-Assembly (accessed July 4, 2019), also Birn 2014: 11.

[43] Bill Gates, speech on May 17, 2011 at the 64th World Health Assembly, online: http://www.gatesfoundation.org/Media-Center/Speeches/2005/05/Bill-Gates-2005-World-Health-Assembly (accessed July 4, 2019).

[44] See BMGF, "Bill and Melinda Gates Pledge $10 Billion in Call for Decade of Vaccines," January 29, 2010, online: http://www.gatesfoundation.org/Media-Center/Press-Releases/2010/01/Bill-and-Melinda-Gates-Pledge-$10-Billion-in-Call-for-Decade-of-Vaccines, and http://www.who.int/immunization/global_vaccine_action_plan/DoV_GVAP_2012_2020/en/ (all accessed July 4, 2019).

supposedly governed by sovereign nation states, should countenance that at its annual global conference, the keynote address would be delivered thrice in ten years by individuals from the same private organization, and from the same family."[45]

Case studies of WHO policymaking on malaria suggest that the BMGF is also shaping decisions very concretely, even within disease-specific areas. In February 2008, *The New York Times* reported that the WHO's then-malaria chief, Dr. Arata Kochi, had circulated a memorandum in which he warned of how the BMGF and malaria scientists sponsored by the foundation were influencing the WHO's policy on malaria.[46] His worry was mainly about the BMGF's authority, that it had created a "malaria cartel" with a dominant expert consensus, which stifled other perspectives on malaria. Julian Eckl has further argued that it was Bill and Melinda Gates that shifted the WHO's malaria strategy from "Roll Back Malaria" (initiated by Brundtland in 1998) towards the more ambitious and controversial "Eradicate Malaria" (Eckl 2014: 108f). Whether one deems malaria eradication to be possible depends largely on how much hope one puts into the future provision of an effective malaria vaccine.[47] The Gates's move towards malaria eradication happened during the 2007 Malaria Forum, which had been hosted by the BMGF, outside the WHO framework, but with participation of the WHO Director-General Margaret Chan, who embraced the Gates's opening call to eradicate malaria:

> Come on. Let's be brave. And I want to thank both of you [Bill and Melinda Gates] for taking that very brave step forward and challenge us. We have to make it work in the interest of humanity. I [for] one, pledge WHO's commitment to move forward with all of you.   (cited in Eckl 2014: 109)

---

[45] Melinda Gates, speech on May 20, 2014 at the 67th World Health Assembly, online: http://www.who.int/mediacentre/events/2014/Melinda-Gates_WHA-remarks.pdf, "Melinda Gates addresses the World Health Assembly: Civil Society registers its protest," online: https://web.archive.org/web/20161007012034/http://www.phmovement.org/en/node/9397 (accessed July 4, 2019).

[46] Donald G. McNeil Jr., "Gates Foundation's Influence Criticized," *The New York Times*, 16 February 2008, online: http://www.nytimes.com/2008/02/16/science/16malaria.html?_r=0, also Robert Fortner, "Malaria eradication: How the Gates Foundation sets global health policy," November 5, 2012, online: http://robertfortner.posthaven.com/malaria-eradication-how-the-gates-foundation (all accessed July 4, 2019).

[47] The most promising malaria vaccine candidate has been "RTS,S" (trade name: Mosquirix), developed by GlaxoSmithKline within the PPP "RTS,S Malaria Vaccine Candidate." Mosquirix has been approved by EU regulators, and, in 2019, pilot implementation started in Malawi. It promises an efficiency rate of up to 40 percent among children. The BMGF has provided over US$200 million to PATH, a nonprofit research partner of GlaxoSmithKline in the PATH Malaria Vaccine Initiative, for this project. See Amy Maxmen, "First proven malaria vaccine rolled out in Africa–but doubts linger," *Nature*, April 25, 2019, online: https://www.nature.com/articles/d41586-019-01342-z (accessed July 4, 2019).

During discussion at the Malaria Forum, when asked what he would do if not everybody wanted to sign onto malaria eradication, Bill Gates responded that "hopefully we find other players to step in and take their place" (ibid.: 108). Here, the mechanisms of Gates's power come to the fore: first, he provides the forum, which allows him to set the agenda, and then he makes it clear that the BMGF is not dependent on any single collaborator, since, due to its financial resources, it can bypass uncooperative partners and find others. In the twenty-first century's global health universe, this flexibility in building coalitions has expanded greatly, because a multitude of new global health partnerships, primarily PPPs, has emerged, which take important roles next to the traditional international organizations and their member states.

A principal reason for PPPs in global health derives from the fact that many of the technical and scientific resources for producing vaccines or drugs are concentrated within the pharmaceutical private sector, but developing countries often lack the money to purchase biomedical commodities. Since the 1990s, a growing number of formally institutionalized PPPs bring the private and the public sector together, mainly pharmaceutical companies, donor governments, and international organizations like the WHO, but also nonprofit NGOs and foundations, in order to overcome market failures (Reich 2002, Abbott & Gartner 2012, Bartsch 2011). For supporters of PPPs, this is also seen as a way to circumvent political and bureaucratic struggles within the WHO or other international organizations, which have traditionally been heading global health initiatives (Barnes & Brown 2011). The rationale for PPPs had gained significant ground before the BMGF appeared, with crucial backing from the Rockefeller Foundation and the World Bank, which, during the 1990s, had started to address health as a critical issue for economic development. PPPs were a natural vehicle of choice for Bill Gates, himself coming from the private sector.

According to the International Federation of Pharmaceutical Manufacturers & Associations (IFPMA), which manages a database that aims to track all global health partnerships involving research-based pharmaceutical businesses, there are over 250 active PPPs of this kind.[48] In 2019, the BMGF was a partner in 35 different PPPs, only surpassed by the UN (61), the U.S. (55) and the WHO (51),[49] and long before the UK (14), the European Union (11) or—the next largest NGO—the Wellcome Trust (13). The size and scope of these PPPs vary

---

[48] Over the past years, the BMGF has been an official partner in many different PPPs, some of which have been temporary or barely institutionalized. A comprehensive overview is difficult, because the BMGF does not provide a centralized list of PPPs it is (or has been) participating in. The following data derives from the IFPMA online directory (https://globalhealthprogress.org/explore-our-collaborations/ accessed December 11, 2019), the BMGF's online grants database, and information on the PPPs' websites.

[49] Both the UN and the U.S. totals comprise several different agencies, such as UNICEF and UNDP for the UN, or USAID and the U.S. NIHs for the U.S. The largest pharmaceutical companies have even higher PPP participation rates: Sanofi (78), GlaxoSmithKline (74), Novartis (52).

considerably, as does the BMGF's role in them. Sometimes, drawing on its long-standing experience in this field, the BMGF is merely providing resources for impact assessment, as with the DREAMS "Stemming the Tide of HIV in Adolescent Girls" initiative, which is part of the U.S. government's PEPFAR program. Other BMGF-supported PPPs are very specific partnerships between the foundation and one pharmaceutical company, such as Merck, Novartis, or GlaxoSmithKline. Within many of the PPPs it is participating in, the BMGF has occupied seats on the partnership's governing or advisory boards. Within the largest global PPP, The Global Fund to Fight Aids, Tuberculosis and Malaria, to which the BMGF has given over US$2 billion, and pledged a further US$649 million (2017–19), it holds a permanent voting seat on the governing board.[50] In 2016, the situation was similar with AERAS, which developed a new tuberculosis vaccine (US$420 million from BMGF, four BMGF staff members on advisory boards);[51] the TB Alliance (almost US$500 million from BMGF, one BMGF staff member on governing board); the International AIDS Vaccine Initiative (around US$270 million from BMGF, one BMGF-associated governing board member and one staff member on advisory committee); the International Partnership for Microbicides (around US$164 million from BMGF, one BMGF staff member on governing board, one on scientific advisory board); the Roll Back Malaria Partnership (US$21 million from BMGF, one BMGF staff member on governing board); the Uniting to Combat Neglected Tropical Diseases (US$363 million pledged from BMGF, one BMGF staff member on "stakeholder working group"); and the Global Polio Eradication Initiative (one BMGF staff member on governing board). An analysis of the BMGF's work in all of these PPPs is beyond the scope of my research. Instead, the foundation's role within its first and most heavily funded PPP, the Global Alliance for Vaccines and Immunization (GAVI), which is the second largest global health PPP, shall serve as an illustration.[52]

Prior to GAVI, the Children's Vaccine Initiative PPP had already been developed, but disagreements over its funding, its relation to the WHO, and the private sector's influence had compromised its progress. Bill Gates's US$750 million donation in 1999 then turned the tables in setting GAVI up as an independent institution, as a careful reconstruction of GAVI's birth has shown: "the WHO

---

[50] See online: https://www.theglobalfund.org/en/private-ngo-partners/resource-mobilization/bill-melinda-gates-foundation/ (accessed July 6, 2019).

[51] AERAS closed down in 2019, after one of its tuberculosis vaccine candidates achieved a breakthrough in clinical tests in 2018; its assets have been transferred to the International AIDS Vaccine Initiative, another PPP with BMGF support. See "IAVI Acquires Aeras TB Vaccine Clinical Programs and Assets," October 1, 2018, online: https://www.iavi.org/newsroom/press-releases/2018/iavi-acquires-aeras-tb-vaccine-clinical-programs-and-assets (accessed July 6, 2019).

[52] The Global Fund is the largest global health PPP, but "[t]he Gates Foundation had taken a backseat role in the design of the new fund, feeling that this new institution was altogether too large, too complicated and too political to be one of its core investments" (Lidén 2013: 38, also Barnes & Brown 2011).

leadership was aware that the Gates Foundation was on the doorstep, and wanted to do the utmost to provide them with a platform for investing money in immunization" (Sandberg et al. 2010: 1354, also Muraskin 2002, 2005, Lidén 2013: 25). On GAVI's governing board, the BMGF is holding one of the four permanent seats, besides the WHO, UNICEF, and the World Bank; while donor and recipient governments hold five seats each, these are rotating, and no state has a permanent seat.[53] GAVI's mandate is "to optimise access to currently underused vaccines, to strengthen health and immunisation systems in countries, and to make innovative immunisation technology available" for children in developing countries (Hill 2011: 78). GAVI allows recipient countries to choose their own immunization priorities when applying for funding, and via "market shaping efforts" and innovative financing mechanisms, it is trying to overcome market failures. For existing vaccines, the GAVI partners are aggregating demand and procurement for vaccines, which lets them negotiate lower prices with pharmaceutical producers. With regard to new vaccines, the GAVI partners are effectively subsidizing the industry's vaccine development and production in exchange for price and provision guarantees.[54] The disbursement of GAVI funds to recipient countries is linked to eligibility criteria, performance monitoring, and, increasingly so since 2007, requirements to provide matching funds, which is intended to guarantee the long-term sustainability of national immunization programs.[55] Through its positive incentive—funding—and the ability to withhold this in the future (negative incentive), GAVI is clearly wielding power in shaping the national health systems, especially with regard to vaccination, of recipient developing countries (Hill 2011: 100ff, da Silva 2013: 85–104). Although anecdotal evidence seems to suggest that some GAVI-induced health spending may divert resources from other important causes (Starling et al. 2002: 33, Storeng 2014: 872), overall, GAVI is being credited with substantially improving vaccination rates (Gandhi 2015). GAVI itself claims that, between 2000 and 2018, it has contributed "to the immunisation of more than 700 million children" and "has helped developing countries to prevent more than 10 million future deaths through its support for

[53] The remaining "representative" seats are allocated to, one each, the vaccine industry of developing countries, the vaccine industry of industrialized countries, civil society organizations, and research and technical health institutes. The GAVI's CEO (nonvoting) and nine "independent individuals" complete the GAVI's twenty-eight-seat governing board, see online: http://www.gavi.org/about/govern ance/gavi-board/composition/ (accessed July 4, 2019). Before 2008, GAVI's board comprised only fifteen seats, but the four permanent seats were held by the same organizations (Starling et al. 2002: 5).

[54] As of 2006, GAVI's International Finance Facility for Immunisation is transforming long-term donor pledges into "vaccine bonds" that make financing more immediately available. Since 2009, GAVI's Advance Market Commitment, is incentivizing the development and the provision of new pneumococcal vaccines. See online: https://www.gavi.org/about/gavis-business-model/ and https://www.gavi.org/investing/innovative-financing/ (accessed July 4, 2019).

[55] See online: http://www.gavi.org/about/governance/programme-policies/co-financing/ (accessed July 4, 2019).

routine immunisation programmes and vaccination campaigns."[56] Bill Gates has considered GAVI the "best investment we've ever made" (Lidén 2013: 25). While GAVI is thus looking like the perfect embodiment of the "Gates approach" to global health, a considerable change in GAVI's strategy has put doubts on such an evaluation. Responding to shortcomings identified in prior evaluations of GAVI's achievements, in December 2005, the GAVI board voted narrowly in favor of extending its vaccine programs to include a "health systems strengthening" (HSS) component, which resulted in a new HSS plan in 2006. "The goal of HSS is to improve immunization coverage and other maternal-child health outcomes by strengthening the capacity of health systems to deliver high quality services" (Naimoli 2009). Apparently, this paradigm shift happened at the behest of GAVI's then-CEO (2004–10) Julian Lob-Levyt, a British doctor, with strong support from the UK and Norwegian governments, and against the explicit wishes of the U.S. and the BMGF (Storeng 2014: 868).[57] Some observers see this shift as an indicator of GAVI moving away from a narrow biomedical approach to a more integrated understanding of immunization, in line with recognition that vertical disease-oriented interventions rely on functioning health systems for their implementation. At the international level, this normative realignment had been expressed in the "Paris Declaration on Aid Effectiveness" in 2005, which has gained broad acceptance and whose principles have been endorsed by GAVI (Hill 2011: 80f). The WHO's 2010 World Health Report "Health Systems Financing: The Path to Global Coverage" and the International Health Partnership's movement towards "Universal Health Coverage 2030" denote further headway in this direction.[58] As mentioned before, over the years, the BMGF

---

[56] See online: http://www.gavi.org/about/mission/facts-and-figures/ (accessed July 4, 2019). The health impacts of specific interventions are notoriously difficult to measure, as many other socioeconomic factors also affect the prevalence of health problems (Cohen 2014). The BMGF is itself heavily funding impact studies, for example via financing the Center for Global Development, which held active BMGF grants worth US$37.6 million in 2019 (see online: http://www.cgdev.org/section/funding, accessed July 4, 2019) and has published the "Millions Saved" series that documents "Proven Success in Global Health" (Glassman & Temin 2016).

[57] The BMGF had already pledged its second US$750 million grant (over ten years) to GAVI at the beginning of 2005, and therefore could not exercise financial leverage. In its corresponding press release, the BMGF stated that its grant will also serve to "strengthen immunization services," but no mention of "health systems" was made, see "Gates Foundation, Norway Contribute $1 Billion to Increase Child Immunization in Developing Countries," January 24, 2005, online: http://www.gatesfoundation.org/Media-Center/Press-Releases/2005/01/Supporting-the-Global-Alliance-for-Vaccines-and-Immunization (accessed July 4, 2019).

[58] The International Health Partnership "IHP+" has been founded in 2007 as a forum to improve the coordination among the variety of donors and recipient countries, initially with a focus on the realization of the UN Millennium Development Goals. As these have been transformed into the Sustainable Development Goals in 2015, the IHP has turned itself into UHC2030. While the BMGF has been a founding member of IHP+, it has been conspicuously absent from the "UHC 2030" consultations during June 2016. See online: https://www.uhc2030.org/about-us/ and https://www.uhc2030.org/fileadmin/uploads/ihp/Documents/About_IHP_/mgt_arrangemts___docs/UHC_Alliance/List_of_participants_Final_4_7.pdf; the Paris Declaration: http://www.oecd.org/dac/effectiveness/34428351.pdf, and WHO 2010 (all accessed July 4, 2019).

also seems to have come around to a more holistic understanding of global health, for which the expansion of its "Global Development" division, especially since 2011, has been taken as an indicator (BMGF 2012: 4). For Adam Fejerskov, such moves represent a major transformation of the BGMF:

> [L]ending far less agency to the organization and its leadership, this process of homogenization through normative isomorphism may appear to have happened "behind the back" of those assumed to be in control of the organization's development. . . . [The BMGF is] increasingly engaged in structural and funda-mental issues of having to not just develop products but also to ensure their delivery in local contexts (with all that follows of political, social and cultural constraints). . . . [G]radual appropriation to the dominant logics and norms of the field of development cooperation should not necessarily be understood as a deliberate decision made by the foundation, but rather as a pathdependent consequence of engaging in issues of global development.   (2015: 1109)

This interpretation is highly overstating its case. In quantitative terms, as shown in Figure 7.1, while the BMGF has increased its funding for SWAs/HSS, in 2015, this budget line still represented less than 5 percent of the foundation's total expend-iture; in 2018, it had only moved to 5.51 percent.[59] Regarding the "Universal Health Coverage 2030" agenda in global health, Bill Gates has been reluctant to sign on to it, and when the BMGF finally became a partner, it was within the context of the Primary Health Care Performance Initiative (PHCPI). There, the BMGF is working with the World Bank and the WHO on "better measurement and knowledge-sharing" for the delivery of primary healthcare—and not on funding primary healthcare delivery.[60] If, in its own reporting, the BMGF's "Global Development" division has grown massively, this is largely due to reshuffling—polio eradication and vaccine delivery as well as family health and planning used to figure under "global health" until 2011, and have been moved to "Global Development" afterwards (BMGF 2012: 10, 2013: 6). In fact, all of the BMGF's contributions to GAVI now appear to count as part of its "Global Development" division.[61] Within GAVI, funding of HSS has very little to do with building comprehensive primary healthcare systems. Katerini Storeng's in-

---

[59] Data according to http://vizhub.healthdata.org/fgh/ (accessed July 4, 2019), which also shows that, in 2018, 14.35 percent of global health spending went to SWAs and HSS, a much higher percentage than the share within the BMGF's spending.

[60] See the BMGF's President for "Global Development": Chris Elias, "Strong Primary Health Care Systems are a Critical First Step to Achieving Universal Health Coverage," *Medium*, May 21, 2018, online: https://medium.com/@ChrisJElias/strong-primary-health-care-systems-are-a-critical-first-step-to-achieving-universal-health-coverage-f02e7f156fcd and "UHC2030 Welcomes PHCPI as a New Related Initiative," March 14, 2018, online: https://www.uhc2030.org/news-events/partner-insights/uhc2030-welcomes-phcpi-as-a-new-related-initiative-460892/ (accessed July 4, 2019).

[61] In Figure 7.1, the BMGF's funding of GAVI is figuring under "newborn and child health."

depth analysis of GAVI's approach to HSS is showing how most of it is specifically geared towards improving vaccine delivery:

> Within GAVI, HSS support has primarily come to signify a modality for achieving its primary aim, its vaccination goals. Indeed, critics often characterise it as veering towards immunisation strengthening support, rather than broader health systems support. It is 'cold chain-focused', said a former GAVI employee.
>
> (Storeng 2014: 871)

Indeed, whenever Bill Gates is talking about his involvement with GAVI, references to HSS, which are rare, are exclusively focused on vaccination. During the GAVI pledging conference in 2015, for example, his speech only mentioned "sustainable immunization systems," giving the example of "a 'super thermos' cooler that keeps vaccines at a safe and constant temperature for a month or more."[62] The BMGF's and GAVI's modest embrace of HSS is not so much an instance of conforming to the norms of horizontal global health approaches as it represents a targeted broadening of vertical immunization strategies. Bill Gates seems to have gone through a reflective learning process, during which he realized how critical healthcare delivery is: "Technology on its own won't improve vaccine equity or coverage. But it's exciting to see how health workers think differently and take the initiative when provided with new and better tools."[63] Some of this learning has probably emerged out of Gates's interactions with proponents of "health systems strengthening," yet for him, science and technology remain key and "health systems" matter only inasmuch as they bring the biomedical solution to the people.[64]

In summing up, it is tempting to declare Bill Gates as the unofficial minister of global health. Many experts on global health have concluded that the BMGF holds "prime sway at formal global health decision-making bodies" (Birn 2014: 12) and that it has turned into the "center of gravity" in global health, either "rivaling" (Lidén 2013: 49) or even "eclipsing" (House of Lords 2008: 57) the WHO.[65] To

---

[62] Bill Gates, "Address at the Gavi Pledging Conference," Berlin, January 27, 2015, online: http://www. gatesfoundation.org/Media-Center/Speeches/2015/01/Gavi-Pledging-Conference. Consequently, the global health funding data tool http://vizhub.healthdata.org/fgh/, indicates no SWAs/HSS funding for GAVI. The Gates's annual letters, published since 2009 (http://www.gatesfoundation.org/Who-We-Are/Resources-and-Media/Annual-Letters-List, all accessed July 4, 2019), also exhibit no conversion to HSS.

[63] Bill Gates, "Address at the Gavi Pledging Conference," Berlin, January 27, 2015, online: http:// www.gatesfoundation.org/Media-Center/Speeches/2015/01/Gavi-Pledging-Conference (accessed July 4, 2019). See also Gates 2015. A capacity for adaptive learning had already characterized Gates's management style at Microsoft (Wallace & Erickson 1993: 248).

[64] An independent review of the World Bank's relationship with GAVI concludes that "after 2008, GAVI's strategy was increasingly focused on the technology aspects of its mandate that is, accelerating the introduction of new (but also more costly) vaccines in developing countries.... This change in emphasis of GAVI's corporate goals has been supported by several of GAVI's major stakeholders, in particular the Gates Foundation" (Independent Evaluation Group/World Bank Group 2014: 41).

[65] Such assessments vary according to issue area. In the area of health aid—the largest area of global health—Tine Hanrieder also judges the BMGF to have become a more influential player than the

claim that Bill Gates has singlehandedly imposed his biomedical outlook on others would, nevertheless, be exaggerated. First, global health remains a vast field and different approaches, notably the "Universal Health Coverage 2030" platform, can thrive with support from other donors if the Gates Foundation is disinclined. Second, among the WHO and important donor governments, a willingness to engage the private sector, to emphasize cost-effective measures, and to focus on infectious diseases had already become prominent before the BMGF emerged. The U.S. government, in particular, has been an ardent supporter of similar ideas and practices, and since George W. Bush's PEPFAR initiative, it has become the primary source of funding for global health, accounting for more than a third of it in recent years. Under the Barack Obama administration, the two American heavyweights became closely aligned. In 2010, Obama appointed Rajiv Shah, who had worked for almost a decade on vaccines and agriculture at the BMGF before, as the director of the United States Agency for International Development (until 2015), and Nils Daulaire, who also had close connections with the BMGF, as the U.S. representative to the WHO executive board (until 2014).[66] Bill Gates has been able to make his experience from Microsoft, namely that innovation and partnerships are the key to dominate a market, work out in global health, too.

His great leap into philanthropy in 1999 incited other donors to follow suit, and his foundation is a financial octopus whose grant-making arms reach into almost all corners of the global health universe. The volume of the BMGF's expenditure has become larger than that of the WHO, and whereas most of the WHO director-general's money is nondiscretionary, Bill Gates can set his priorities freely. Through the massive funding of biomedical scientific research, the BMGF and its chairman have acquired expertise-based legitimacy within the field. At the BMGF's fifteenth anniversary in 2015, Bill and Melinda Gates felt confident enough to pronounce several "big bets" for the next fifteen years, such as cutting "the child death rate in half," "[w]iping polio and three other diseases off the face of the earth," "[f]inding the secret to the destruction of malaria," and "[f]orcing HIV to a tipping point."[67] Such ambitions reflect not only authority, but also a

WHO, but she still sees the WHO as a global health "orchestrator" in the area of epidemiologic surveillance (Hanrieder 2015a: 202ff).

[66] Daulaire had been CEO of the Global Health Council since 2000, which had received around 40 percent of its revenue from the BMGF, see: Robert Fortner, "Malaria eradication: How the Gates Foundation sets global health policy," November 5, 2012, online: http://robertfortner.posthaven.com/malaria-eradication-how-the-gates-foundation, Mark Landler, "Curing the Ills of America's Top Foreign Aid Agency," *The New York Times*, October 22, 2010, online: http://www.nytimes.com/2010/10/23/world/23shah.html?_r=0 and "Statement on Dr. Rajiv Shah, USAID Administrator-Designate," BMGF, November 19, 2009, http://www.gatesfoundation.org/Media-Center/Press-Releases/2009/11/Statement-on-Dr-Rajiv-Shah-USAID-AdministratorDesignate (all accessed July 14, 2019).

[67] See online: https://www.gatesnotes.com/2015-annual-letter?page=0&lang=en&WT.mc_id=01_21_2015_AL2015-GF_GFO_domain_Top_21 (accessed July 4, 2019).

businessman's perspective on measurable returns on investment, which has been characterizing Bill Gates's philanthropy from the start. Via large-scale grants to other organizations, especially PPPs such as GAVI, and the WHO itself, the BMGF is able to shape the global health agenda, by demanding matching grants and representation on governing boards. In addition, Bill Gates is spending large amounts on advocacy and media relations in order to raise awareness and to strengthen support for his agenda.[68] In all of this, his "vertical" approach to global health is concentrated on fighting infectious diseases, sidelining strategies that focus more on the socioeconomic determinants of health and the building of comprehensive primary healthcare systems. The WHO's declaration of the "The Decade of Vaccines" in 2012, following Bill Gates's agenda-setting, is the best example of how pervasive the "Gates approach" has become.

Building Open Societies: George Soros as "Stateless Statesman"

[I]f we wish to remain human, then there is only one way, the way into the open society. We must go into the unknown, courageously, using what reason we have, to plan for security *and* freedom.   (Popper 1945: 177, emphasis in original)

At a time when memories of Carnegie, Rockefeller, and other Gilded Age bene-factors were fading, and long before Bill Gates and the Giving Pledge had popularized ideas of "philanthrocapitalism," George Soros (*1930) acquired notoriety as the most generous and the most political transnational philanthropist, calling himself a "stateless statesman" (Soros 1991: 143, Kaufman 2002: 164). Unlike Bill Gates, whose philanthropic vocation exhibits a strong grounding in the American culture of giving, George Soros's endeavors emerge from a more idiosyncratic biography. Thus, he explicitly rejected conventional notions of charity and institutionalized giving during his first two decades as a philanthropist (Soros 1995: 147f, 2011: 39ff). Soros's liberal outlook has been strongly influenced by his experience of totalitarian Nazi and Stalinist rule while growing up in Hungary, and by his subsequent studies in exile with Karl Popper at the London

---

[68] In 2018, the BMGF spent US$501 million on "Global Policy and Advocacy", 12 percent of which went to "Global Program Advocacy & Communications" (see online: https://www.gatesfoundation. org/Who-We-Are/Resources-and-Media/Annual-Reports/Annual-Report-2018 accessed December 11, 2019). For in-depth portraits of the BMGF's influence in the coverage of global health issues among major media outlets, including *The New York Times, The Guardian, Der Spiegel*, and *Al Jazeera*, see Robert Fortner, "Why you might think like Bill Gates about global health," February 13, 2016, online: http://robertfortner.posthaven.com/why-you-might-think-like-bill-gates-about-global-health and Ian Graham, "Gates Foundation: The Rich Disruptor," *MediaPowerMonitor*, September 10, 2018, online: https://medium.com/mediapowermonitor/gates-foundation-the-rich-disruptor-be774b83493e (all accessed February 27, 2020).

School of Economics and Political Science (Kaufman 2002: 3–80). Popper is best known for his critical-rationalist stance within the philosophy of science (Popper 1935, 1963), which has informed Soros's thinking about reflexivity, a key element in both his worldview and his investment strategy (Soros 2013).[69] For Soros's political stance, Popper's *The Open Society and Its Enemies* has been more important. In it, Popper, opposing Plato, develops an anti-totalitarian argument based on the assumption of human fallibility in a constantly changing world, and presents critical discussion within "open societies" as the alternative to what he calls tribal, traditional, or "closed societies" (Popper 1945: 149–77). Popper's endorsement of political individualism and universal humanitarianism, "the demand that we should be rational, look after ourselves, and take immense responsibilities" (ibid.: 154), reads almost like a blueprint for Soros's later career. The billionaire's philanthropy has been driven by a cosmopolitan social identity and a deep belief in the potential of human agency to change the world's structures, with the ultimate objective to foster open societies (Soros 1991: 147–250).

Upon his arrival at Wall Street in 1956, Soros developed strong skills as an arbitrage trader, specializing in transatlantic deals where he could take advantage of his European background and connections. Becoming relatively rich, he simultaneously continued his philosophical pursuits (Kaufman 2002: 83–118). When managing his first large fund for the investment firm Arnhold & S. Bleichroeder in 1967, he started to apply his insights about reflexivity more systematically to finance, and in 1979, Soros would rename his own fund Quantum, in reference to Heisenberg's uncertainty principle, which has stimulated his ideas about reflexivity.

> [I]mperfect views can influence the situation to which they relate through the actions of the participants. For example, if investors believe that markets are efficient then that belief will change the way they invest, which in turn will change the nature of the markets in which they are participating (though not necessarily making them more efficient). That is the *principle of reflexivity*.
> (Soros 2013: 310, emphasis in original, also Soros 1987)

Within the growing hedge fund industry, in which Soros has been one of the legendary pioneers, his approach has been called macro-investing (Mallaby 2010:

---

[69] Soros's one major disagreement with Popper concerns the nature of the social sciences, which, for Soros, are categorically different from the natural sciences, due to human reflexivity (Soros 1991: 192, 2013: 316ff). Soros claims that his real ambition had been to become a philosopher, which shows in the amount of theoretical chapters published in his many books; he considers himself a failed philosopher, and most observers agree that he has had a hard time expressing his theoretical ideas (Soros 1995: 209–36, Kaufman 2002: 106–18, Porter 2015: 39–46). The best summary of his conceptual framework is Soros 2013.

83–108). It encompasses identifying broad social, economic, or political changes, investing early in financial instruments that are expected to rise in value due to these trends, and then selling once a booming market has driven up those values, before an eventual bust. In the 1970s, for example, Soros anticipated the energy crisis and the food crisis, and later his investments have frequently involved major political decisions relating to the international political economy. Such undertakings naturally cultivated a global perspective. "[M]ore than any other New York fund manager, Soros had a web of political contacts in Washington, Tokyo, and Europe" (ibid.: 93). In his dealings, he exploited the new instability after the collapse of the Bretton Woods system and was one of the protagonists of the reemergence of global finance, which I have discussed earlier as one of the structural transformations that have favored the rise of billionaires.[70]

> Soros was absorbed at any given time in complex scenarios related to global trading.... What Soros understood better than most were the cause-and-effect relationships in the world's economies.... Soros dealt with currencies and interest rates... [and] followed broad trends in the global financial markets.
> (Slater 2009: 60, also 45, 64, 71, 76f)

Thus, he reaped large profits from the devaluation of the US$ following the 1985 Plaza Agreement, and his most spectacular bet was against the British pound in 1992, which led to the UK devaluating its currency and leaving the European Exchange Rate Mechanism (ERM), which was the core of the European Monetary System (EMS), the precursor of the euro. This episode also highlights Soros's determination for calculated risk-taking. Once he spotted an opportunity, he often went full-in: he put almost US$10 billion against the pound, and earned around US$1 billion in profits from it (Kaufman 2002: 235–41). Besides reflexivity, Popper's notion of fallibility comes alive in Soros's investment strategy, too: "When George is wrong, he gets the hell out" (Slater 2009: 61). Over the years, Soros's funds have always been among the best-performing. Between 1970 and 1980, his first hedge fund, the Soros Fund, gained 3,365 percent, while the Standard & Poor's composite index grew only 47 percent (Slater 2009: 75). Until 2015, Quantum was the fund with the highest absolute profits, generating US$42.8 billion over its lifespan. Quantum, which, since 2011, is a private fund for Soros and his family only, is the main source of Soros's wealth, which, according to Forbes, stood at US$8.3 billion in 2019, much reduced from the almost US$25.2 billion in 2017. This drastic reduction is due to Soros shifting US$18 billion to his Open Society foundations in 2017, to build endowments for the future, and to

---

[70] Soros also took full and early advantage of tax havens, starting with his first Double Eagle hedge fund for Arnhold & S. Bleichroeder, which was set up in 1969 in Curacao, "where it escaped both SEC scrutiny and capital gains taxes" (Slater 2009: 70).

avoid taxation. Large parts of this wealth have been accumulated using legal loopholes in the U.S. tax code that allowed hedge fund managers to defer taxes on fees paid by clients (if those fees were reinvested in one's fund)—this loophole closed at the end of 2017.[71]

During the late 1970s, at a period when his wealth was rapidly reaching triple-digit million dollars, Soros went through a midlife crisis and started searching for meaningful goals (Kaufman 2002: 147–59): "I determined . . . that I had enough money . . . , that what really mattered to me was the concept of an open society, based on the recognition that we all act on the basis of imperfect understanding" (Soros 1995: 112f). In 1979, he set up the Open Society Fund; for several years, his venture into philanthropy was a process of trial and error. After donations to black students in South Africa, Amnesty International, and opposition movements in the Soviet bloc, such as Charta 77 in Czechoslovakia and Solidarność in Poland, he decided on his first major project in 1983, which would bring him back to his native Hungary, where a gradual liberalization of the economy had exposed cracks in the previously closed communist society. There, in 1984, Soros created his first foundation abroad, which officially promoted cultural and educational exchanges, but with the ulterior motive of introducing liberal ideas, intellectual discussion, and diversity. At the time, a few million dollars were able to achieve a lot, both politically—the foreign exchange-starved government of Hungary proved very accommodating—and practically. One of his operations with the greatest impact was to send several hundred Xerox machines to Hungarian cultural and educational institutions, which allowed citizens to spread the information they wanted, independent from the government (Kaufman 2002: 163–200).

As the Soviet Union crumbled and his fortune reached ten figures, Soros delegated more and more business to his associates and employees, and turned his philanthropy from private side projects into his main activity (Soros 1991). He set up an Open Society Foundation (OSF) network all over the former Soviet Union and Warsaw Pact countries, with the explicit goal to build open societies, funding a wide variety of educational projects, human rights associations, and independent media.[72] Between 1994 and 2000, Soros's personal contributions to his various foundations totaled more than US$2.5 billion (Kaufman 2002: 256). In the twenty-first century, the OSF network has expanded further in the U.S. and across the globe, especially in Africa, with a presence in thirty-nine countries in

---

[71] The tax loophole had been closed in 2008, and deferred taxes had to be paid by the end of 2017, see Nishant Kumar, "Bridgewater's Dalio Now Has the Most Profitable Hedge Fund," *Bloomberg*, January 26, 2016, online: http://www.bloomberg.com/news/articles/2016-01-26/bridgewater-s-dalio-trumps-soros-as-most-profitable-hedge-fund, and Katherine Burton and Peggy Collins, "George Soros Pours Billions Into Charity Ahead of Tax Deadline," *Bloomberg*, October 17, 2017, online: https://www.bloomberg.com/news/articles/2017-10-17/george-soros-pours-billions-into-charity-as-tax-deadline-looms (all accessed July 3, 2019).

[72] Until 2010, the central coordinating office in New York was called Open Society Institute, since then, its name is Open Society Foundations.

2019, over eight hundred employees, and annual expenditure around one billion US$. The overall money spent by Soros's foundations, from the beginnings in Hungary in 1984 to 2019, amounts to more than US$15 billion, making it by far the largest private philanthropic enterprise with a directly political mission.[73]

In fundamental ways, the characteristics of Soros's business have extended to his philanthropy: "he was directly involved in their operations; he took large risks, based, however, on his own careful analysis of situations; and he acted boldly and quickly to invest for gain and to retreat to cut losses" (Krisch 2009, also Kaufman 2002: 179). For example, when, during the late 1980s, his attempts to implant foundations in China and Czechoslovakia encountered too much local opposition, he closed them down quickly (Soros 1995: 126–35, Kaufman 2002: 213–21). The boldness of his investment decisions, both in finance and philanthropy, appear to derive from a pronounced sense of voluntarism, which he has expressed himself repeatedly:

> I was a confirmed egoist but I considered the pursuit of self-interest as too narrow a base for my rather inflated self. If truth be known, I carried some rather potent messianic fantasies with me from childhood which I felt I had to control, otherwise they might get me into trouble. But when I had made my way in the world I wanted to indulge in my fantasies to the extent that I could afford.
>
> (Soros 1991: 3, also 1995: 143, 2011: 37f)

Obviously, one person cannot oversee the workings of all the civil society organizations supported by the Open Society Foundations in so many different countries (Stone 2008, 2010). Soros has been fully aware of this challenge, and his approach to it has been the same as in his fund management: while he gives large degrees of autonomy to the people working with him, he remains in charge of making strategic decisions about investment priorities, magnitudes, when to leave, and where to go next (Soros 1995: 125, 141, 2011: 19, 42, Neier 2003: 294ff, 2011: 336ff). Although Soros has never relented his leadership, one can identify at least three stages within the development of the OSFs, all initiated by Soros, with deepening institutionalization at each step. (1) Until the mid-1990s, the OSF network consisted of a myriad of projects with Soros as the sole coordinator; no centralized budgets or annual reports existed. (2) The hiring of Aryeh Neier, previously the executive director of Human Rights Watch and a close collaborator of Soros, as the president of the Soros Foundations in 1993, marked a move towards increasing professionalization and harmonization; the first centralized

---

[73] See https://www.opensocietyfoundations.org/who-we-are (accessed July 3, 2019). The BMGF has become larger in financial terms, but much of its global health work, such as the funding of biomedical research and vaccination programs, does not have a direct political agenda.

annual report was published in 2000 (Soros 1995: 147ff, Soros Foundations Network 2000, Neier 2003: 289–302). (3) Around 2010, when he was entering his eighties, Soros changed his mind with regard to the longevity of his foundations; in 2012, the appointment of Christopher Stone to replace the retiring Aryeh Neier came with the expectation that the new president would streamline and unify the OSFs, in order to prepare for an eventual post–George Soros future.[74] Soros's "endowment" vehicle to fund operations, including his foundations in various countries, is the Foundation to Promote Open Society, which he created in 2008 and which held over US$10 billion in 2017, invested in the Quantum Endowment fund.[75]

The gradual institutionalization of Soros's philanthropy happened in parallel with a shift in his pursuit of esteem. Many of his projects during the 1980s happened under the radar of public attention, and Soros apparently did not seek broader social recognition back then (Kaufman 2002: 179ff, Slater 2009: 135–42). That none of the foundations or buildings financed by him, such as the Central European University, has the sponsor's name attached to it, is often taken as an indicator that for Soros, his cause—and hence, his self-esteem—is more important than prestige (Neier 2011: 292f, 296, 335). At the same time, the many books and articles he has published since 1987 do reveal a continuous struggle for public esteem (Soros 1987, 1991: esp. 139–44). His biographer recounts how Soros was being laughed at by the political establishment after advocating a Marshall Plan for Eastern Europe at a conference on European security in 1988 (Kaufman 2002: 228ff, 290ff, also Soros 2011: 21). This quasi-traumatic episode showed him the limits of moving from finance to politics, but four years later, his financial success helped him to overcome these. Soros's greatest investment feat gave him worldwide publicity as "the man who broke the Bank of England," and "[h]e made a conscious decision to exploit this new notoriety . . . to gain influence among world leaders" (Kaufman 2002: xiii, also 235–41 and Soros 2011: 26). Soros has reflected about the tension between self- and public esteem, and has rationalized his public role as helping to promote his cause of building open societies. Yet he has also

---

[74] Earlier, Soros had foreseen his philanthropy to come and go with him. In 2018, his son Alexander Soros became the Deputy Chair on the Global Board of the OSF, beside his father, hinting at dynastic succession. See Soros 2011: 41–6 and David Callahan, "Philanthropy vs. Tyranny: Inside the Open Society Foundations' Biggest Battle Yet," *Inside Philanthropy*, September 14, 2015, online: http://www.insidephilanthropy.com/home/2015/9/14/philanthropy-vs-tyranny-inside-the-open-society-foundations.html, accessed July 3, 2019.

[75] See online: https://pdf.guidestar.org/PDF_Images/2017/263/753/2017-263753801-10377dae-F.pdf. The Foundation to Promote Open Society is registered as a 501(c)3 private exempt foundation under U.S. law and has no website, but see online: https://projects.propublica.org/nonprofits/organizations/263753801; for the designation of chairmen and directors, see the first 990PF tax filing for 2008, in which George Soros appears the Chairman and Director: https://projects.propublica.org/nonprofits/download-filing?path=2009_12_PF%2F26-3753801_990PF_200812.pdf (all accessed July 9, 2019).

admitted that "I have had these illusions, or perhaps delusions, of grandeur and they have driven me" (quoted in Kaufman 2002: 292, also Soros 2011: 37f).

An objective as ambitious and abstract as "building open societies" poses serious problems for impact assessment. One could, like Anna Porter has been doing in one of only two overviews of Soros's philanthropy that have been published so far,[76] try to see whether the world has become a better place, in line with Soros's goals. For her, Soros has failed, because "liberal democracy is in worldwide decline . . . , there has been an overall decline in human rights during the last decade . . . [, t]he European Union . . . is in disarray . . . [, and] Africa is still a mess" (Porter 2015: 201f). If Soros would have solved all of these problems, he would be omnipotent. Yet, despite his childhood fantasies, he is no god. Precisely because Soros is aiming for structural change, an analysis of his political agency needs to take the dynamics of the political fields in which he is intervening into account. This also involves counterfactual reasoning—what might have happened if the billionaire had not acted? Clearly, this is complicated, as Soros would emphasize, by the reflexivity inherent in all social interactions. The effects of vaccination on child health are relatively easy to measure in comparison with the effects of funding human rights NGOs. Soros is fully aware of these difficulties, and it is the reason why he does not "believe in quantitative measures for evaluating programs. I . . . would find it difficult to spell out the value system I apply in deciding between various alternatives" (2011: 44). Still, one can look at specific outputs, link them to observed outcomes, and attempt to evaluate the relationship between them. Given the extraordinary breadth of Soros's activities over almost four decades, a comprehensive review is beyond the scope of these pages. Even at the aggregate level and looking only at the OSF, the variety of Soros's funding is impressive:

> Over the last 33 years, the Open Society Foundations had expenditures of more than $13 billion. Much of this spending has been directed at specific priority issues and regions for the Open Society Foundations such as:

> - **$1.6 billion on democratic development** in the countries of Eastern Europe and the former Soviet Union;
> - **$737 million for public health issues** such as HIV and AIDS, TB, palliative care, harm reduction, and patients' rights;
> - **$214 million to fight discrimination** and advance the rights of Roma communities in Europe;

---

[76] The other overview is Sudetic 2011, which has a foreword by Soros and an afterword by Neier, but is only looking at a selected number of OSF projects outside the former Soviet Union/Warsaw Pact region (except for one chapter on the "Rights of Roma"). The two major biographies of Soros do cover Soros's philanthropy as well, but not from an analytical perspective (Kaufman 2002, Slater 2009).

- **$2.9 billion to defend human rights**, particularly the rights of women, ethnic, racial, and religious minorities, and often marginalized groups such as drug users, sex workers, and LGBTQ communities;
- **$2.1 billion for education projects** ranging from preschool to higher education reform;
- **$1.5 billion to promote reform in the United States** on issues such as criminal justice, drugs, palliative care, education, immigration, equal rights, and democratic governance.[77]

Instead of a general review, I will briefly discuss Soros's promotion of human rights, because this has been a constant throughout his philanthropic career, as well as provide a closer analysis of his role in the so-called color revolutions, particularly in Georgia (2003), since this has attracted major international attention. Other interesting subjects would have been Soros's backing of the international campaign to ban landmines, the campaign to enhance transparency in natural resources extraction, or the campaign for the establishment of the International Criminal Court, because these campaigns all related to the creation of important international treaties or regimes (Neier 2003: 298ff, Sudetic 2011: 61–92, 102–15). I do not study these cases simply for reasons of limited space. They all merit deeper analysis of the billionaire's contribution, though one faces the same difficulty as with human rights and the color revolutions: besides Soros, many other actors have been involved.

For George Soros, promoting and protecting human rights is at the heart of the rule of law, which he sees as essential for open societies, and over the years he has been the greatest individual financier of international efforts to promote human rights.[78] Over the years, human rights have been a top, if not the top funding priority of Soros, as can be seen in Figure 7.4 detailing the OSF's 2018 program budget. The billionaire's first step into world politics was an apprenticeship with the U.S. Helsinki Watch Committee (the precursor of Human Rights Watch—HRW), the creation of which had been triggered by the signing of the Helsinki Final Act in 1975 (Kaufman 2002: 173ff, Soros 1995: 116). It was at Helsinki Watch that he met Aryeh Neier, who was the organization's cofounder and executive director before moving on to lead HRW and then to become the first

---

[77] Highlighting in original, online: https://web.archive.org/web/20170602033134/https://www.opensocietyfoundations.org/about/expenditures (accessed July 3, 2019).

[78] Earlier on, Soros had refused to define "open societies," which, within OSF mission statements, websites and publications, only happened under Aryeh Neier—but the rule of law has always been central (Soros 1995: 112ff, Porter 2015: 56). The first OSF annual report described "open societies" as follows: "At the most fundamental, philosophical level, the concept of open society is based on the recognition that people act on imperfect knowledge and that no one is in possession of the ultimate truth. In practice, an open society is characterized by the rule of law; respect for human rights, minorities, and minority opinions; the division of power; a market economy in which business and government are separate; and a thriving civil society. Broadly speaking, open society is a way to describe the positive aspects of democracy" (Soros Foundations Network 2000: 8).

president of Soros's foundations network and the Open Society Institute (Neier 2003: 289ff). Besides the multitude of human rights-related programs going on inside his own foundations, most of which happen at the country level, Soros has also become the principal sponsor of HRW, which has been called "the most powerful...Western human rights organization" by *The New York Times*.[79] HRW has around four hundred employees and counts as an authoritative source of reporting on human rights conditions across the world; based on its expertise, it pushes for policies to advance human rights. Soros has been one of HRW's main backers since its beginning, but the organization had—and has—several wealthy donors behind it. During HRW's first endowment fundraising in 1999, other donors gave as much or more than Soros, who gave US$5 million.[80] Since 2010, which is when he announced a US$100 million donation, to be disbursed over ten years, Soros is the largest benefactor of HRW.[81] Soros's approach is thus two-pronged, local and global. Through his own foundations, he is primarily empowering human rights advocacy within the forty states where his network has an office, or the 120 states where it supports programs. Via his funding of HRW, Soros helps to strengthen international human rights norms and to expose violations of them globally.

Within IR, research has shown that the nexus between international human rights norms and the empowerment of actors who fight for human rights within states is critical for the protection of human rights (Keck & Sikkink 1998, Finnemore & Sikkink 1998, Risse et al. 1999, 2013, Simmons 2009, Murdie 2014,

---

[79] David Rieff, "The Precarious Triumph of Human Rights," *The New York Times*, August 8, 1999, online: http://www.nytimes.com/1999/08/08/magazine/the-precarious-triumph-of-human-rights.html (accessed July 3, 2019).

[80] See Human Rights Watch, "Human Rights Watch Announces Landmark Endowment Campaign," September 14, 1999, online: https://www.hrw.org/news/1999/09/14/human-rights-watch-announces-landmark-endowment-campaign. Pre-2000, few 990PF tax filings are available for the Soros foundations, and HRW does not indicate the names of the major donors in its own 990 filings (which is legally not obligatory). In 1999, Soros had committed US$5 million to HRW for general support, to be spread out over five years. For 2000, the various donations to HRW indicated in the OSI 990PF tax filings add up to US$1,560,650. This sum also appears on HRW's filing for 2000, which made the OSI contribution the third largest in 2000, with one donation of around US$2 million and one of US$2.5 million above Soros's contribution. See the 990s online: https://projects. propublica.org/nonprofits/download-filing?path=2002_03_EO%2F13-2875808_990_200103.pdf (HRW) and https://projects.propublica.org/nonprofits/download-filing?path=2002_01_PF%2F13-7029285_ 990PF_200012.pdf (OSI 2000) and https://projects.propublica.org/nonprofits/download-filing? path=2002_11_PF%2F13-7029285_990PF_200112.pdf (OSI 2001). HRW's accountancy ran from January 2000 to April 2001 for 2000, hence OSI contributions from spring 2001 need to be included (all accessed July 3, 2019).

[81] Stephanie Strom, "Soros to Donate $100 Million to Rights Group," *The New York Times*, September 7, 2010, online: http://www.nytimes.com/2010/09/07/business/07gift.html?_r=0. On average, HRW received almost US$68 million per year in donations between 2011 and 2015; Soros's US$10 million thus represent around 15 percent of annual donations to HRW. See online: https://projects. propublica.org/nonprofits/organizations/132875808. Soros, however, was never a member of HRW's board of directors; he only serves as one of the thirty members of the advisory panel for HRW's Americas division, see online: https://www.hrw.org/about/people/advisory-committee/americas-division (all accessed July 10, 2019).

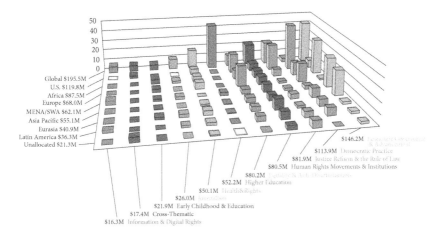

Figure 7.4 Open Society Foundations 2018 program budget by theme and region

The 2018 budget by programmatic theme includes the budget for each of the ten programmatic themes, plus the cross-thematic budget ($686.6 million). It excludes reserves ($93.6 million), program administration not specific to any particular theme ($64.4 million), foundation administration not specific to any particular theme ($36.7 million), and general administration ($124.5 million). The budget for the ten programmatic themes, plus the cross-thematic budget, includes direct program costs for those themes ($619.9 million), as well as program and foundation administrative costs ($13.1 million) where these have been categorized to a theme.

Source: CC BY Open Society Foundations, https://web.archive.org/web/20190515072637/https://www.opensocietyfoundations.org/about/expenditures-budget (accessed July 2, 2019).

Ron et al. 2016). While it is generally accepted that human rights have become core norms of the current global order, there is debate over whether the promotion of these norms actually leads to improvements in human rights conditions. At the level of specific cases, qualitative research has highlighted many instances where international human rights organizations such as HRW have had positive impact (Hafner-Burton & Ron 2009: 366–70). Quantitative comparative research used to be more skeptical, but by now a large number of studies also indicate that the actions of international human rights organizations have significant consequences. By exposing the human rights abuses of governments publicly, groups like HRW stimulate accountability within abusive states, and their "naming and shaming" can also lead external actors—other states, investors, importers, and exporters—to change their behavior, e.g. by imposing sanctions.[82]

The problem for our current question lies in the fact that Soros is not the only "Mr. Human Rights," and HRW is not the only international human rights organization. In fact, many of the quantitative assessments of human rights "shaming" are primarily using the reports of Amnesty International (AI) as an independent variable in their statistical analyses, and only some include HRW

---

[82] For quantitative studies, see: Murdie & Bhasin 2011, Davis et al. 2012, Barry et al. 2013, Murdie & Peksen 2013a, 2013b, Hendrix & Wong 2013, Ausderan 2014, Peterson et al. 2018.

next to it (Clark 2010, Clark & Sikkink 2013). AI has been at least as vital in the promotion of human rights as HRW and the Soros foundations, and in virtually all the states where Open Society Foundations or HRW operate, AI has a presence, too. AI relies much more on a vast multitude of donors, has many more members, and a larger budget than the Soros-affiliated institutions.[83] Besides AI, HRW, and Soros, plenty of other international and national NGOs promote human rights, too, as well as many states and international organizations (Guilhot 2005, Forsythe 2012). Trying to isolate Soros's contribution in this context is near impossible, precisely because his actions are part of a wide-ranging movement of structural change (Boli & Thomas 1999). One could try to analyze in detail where and how the human rights reporting and advocacy of the Soros-sponsored organizations differ from others,[84] but the more one looks into specifics, the more difficult it becomes to determine Soros's agency. He has acknowledged himself that, while he likes to make the broad strategic choices in his philanthropy, he also grants substantial leeway to his staff in how they run the various programs of his foundations (Soros 2011: 19, 36). A more in-depth investigation of the billionaire's power is hence more promising when it concerns a strategic choice, such as questions of regime change.

Soros's philanthropy within the so-called "color revolutions" is a critical case, because it continues his earliest priorities, the opening up of the "closed" systems of the former Soviet Union and its satellites. Unlike the end of the Cold War, however, which was too complex a process to try to single out the contribution of one billionaire (Lebow & Risse-Kappen 1994, Gaddis 2005, Service 2015), the color revolutions were more contained episodes in which the influence of Soros can be distilled better. Following the precedents of regime change in Slovakia (1998) and especially Serbia (2000), similar techniques of mobilizing opposition forces around fraudulent elections—each time involving a symbolic opposition color, hence the name—lead to the abdications of (semi-)authoritarian incumbent rulers in Georgia (2003), Ukraine (2004), and Kyrgyzstan (2005) and to the installation of—so it seemed, at least initially—more democratic governments (Beissinger 2007, Tucker 2007, Bunce & Wolchik 2010). This wave of regime changes provoked major controversies over external actors' meddling in coun- tries' internal affairs. On this question, when interviewed about his operations in foreign countries during the 1990s, Soros has been quite blunt: "Of course, what I do should be called meddling, because I want to promote an open society"; "I do

---

[83] In 2017, AI raised €295 million for human rights work, most of it coming from over two million small donations, with no donation above €1 million (https://www.amnesty.org/en/2017-global-financial-report/); in 2017, it had sections in over seventy countries and claimed to have over 7 million "supporters," combining members and donators (https://www.amnesty.org/en/about-us/how-were-run/structure-and-people/, accessed July 2, 2017).

[84] At least until 2000, one noticeable difference between AI and HRW has been that HRW focused more on so-called second-generation human rights (social and economic rights) than AI (Welch 2001). See also Bob 2002, Ron et al. 2005, Ron et al. 2016.

not accept the rules imposed by others" (1995: 138, 145). True to his "stateless statesman" self-image, he has also admitted that his concern for countries like Ukraine and Georgia involves strategic considerations, which reach back to his experience of Stalin's Soviet Union occupying Hungary while growing up there. Asked why he supported Ukraine so much during the 1990s, he answered: "As long as Ukraine prospers, there can be no imperialist Russia" (ibid.: 131). But he claimed at the same time that "I am categorically opposed to supporting political parties" (ibid.: 138). All of these issues would come to the fore during the color revolutions.

Assessing the impact of Soros—or, for that matter, any other foreign or domestic political actor—on the color revolutions remains complicated, because it concerns specific critical junctures within larger political processes. The literature on democratization and regime change has long been divided between approaches that emphasize underlying conditions such as socioeconomic development and state–society constellations (Lipset 1959, Therborn 1977, Inglehart & Welzel 2005) and those that focus more on the strategic behavior of political actors (Rustow 1970, Collier 1999). This question over whether structural features or political agency matter more has also been hotly debated with regard to the color revolutions. Some authors point to factors such as state capacity and the degree of dependence on the West when explaining the resilience or collapse of post-Soviet authoritarian regimes (Jones 2006, Way 2008, 2009, Levitsky & Way 2010). More agency-centered approaches acknowledge the necessity of enabling conditions, but they convincingly argue that the most striking characteristic of the color revolutions was the regional diffusion of a modular "electoral revolution" model, where successful examples could be emulated in other countries. They highlight the importance of political actors in determining the timing, the direction, and the nature of the color revolutions. "[T]he key issue posed . . . was less a matter of whether regimes were ready to depart than of whether the opposition was ready to defeat them" (Bunce & Wolchik 2010: 47, also Beissinger 2007, 2009, Bunce & Wolchik 2006, 2009, 2011).

When looking more closely at the role of external actors in democratization processes, the question of structure vs. agency reappears (Carothers 2009): is foreign "democracy promotion" assistance geared towards developing the socioeconomic conditions that increase the chances of democracy, or is it directly supporting the political actors that may push for transitions towards democracy? With regard to this discussion, George Soros's approach of "building open societies" is largely about promoting structural change. In fact, his support for independent media and civil society organizations, which was quite innovative during its early years (Carothers 1996), became part of the Western foreign policy mainstream during the 1990s, when the Zeitgeist proclaimed that liberal democracy had become the only game in town (Fukuyama 1989). As processes of democratization spread globally, especially in the post-Soviet space, support for them rose to the top of the development agenda in the West. While tried and trusted foreign aid efforts such as economic development, institution-building, and political education still played their parts, assistance to civil society became a new focus of Western democracy promotion (Ottaway & Carothers 2000, Plattner 2009, Bush 2015). This was backed by a strong current of neo-Tocquevillian theorizing about the crucial role of civil society in generating the social capital deemed necessary for "making democracy work" (Putnam 1993, 2000). It also concurred with the neoliberal paradigm, as it was geared towards boosting the private sector rather than sending money to potentially wasteful and corrupt governments (Kamat 2004, Guilhot 2005). Since then, billions of dollars from both private (e.g., besides Soros, the Ford or the MacArthur Foundations) and public (e.g., various EU or USAID programs) donors have been channeled to civil society organizations in democratizing countries, the merits of which have become very contested. Whereas some statistical analyses seem to indicate a positive correlation between foreign "democracy promotion" assistance and democratization (Finkel et al. 2007), others claim that foreign aid to civil society has no independent statistical effect (Spina & Raymond 2014). Strong theoretical arguments and fieldwork have raised serious doubts about what Sarah Henderson has been calling the "paradox of externally promoting democracy" (Henderson 2003, also Lutsevych 2013, Beichelt et al. 2014, Bush 2015). The main thrust of this critique points out how the dependence of local NGOs on foreign funding is likely to undermine the expectations of neo-Tocquevillian theories. Instead of fostering grassroots networks of civic engagement (Putnam 1993), foreign funding may keep local NGOs beholden to their external sponsors and detached from the society they operate in (Henderson 2003: 150–75). Within this critique of foreign civil society promotion, Soros's network of national OSFs has repeatedly been (partially) exempted. Its activities are seen as both more principled and more locally anchored than those civil society promotion endeavors that receive their funding from foreign governments (Carothers 1996, Stewart 2009: 807, Bush 2015: 152–7).

Trying to understand the impact of Soros within the color revolutions is being complicated by the fact that we are looking at transformation processes where, next to the domestic political leaders, several foreign actors participated. In addition, "both domestic and external actors . . . have reasons for either concealing or exaggerating their contributions" (Stewart 2009: 805, also Mitchell 2012: 86).[85]

---

[85] This observation extends to some of the most detailed scholarly accounts of Georgia's "Rose Revolution," which have been written by former participants. Thus, during 2003, Irakly Areshidze (2007) was the campaign manager for David Gamkrelidze and his pro-business New Rights Party, which opposed the "young reformers." From 2002 until 2004, Lincoln Mitchell (2004, 2009, 2012) was director of the Georgian branch of the U.S.-based National Democratic Institute, which was an important supporter of the efforts to have free and fair elections.

In the following, I will concentrate on Georgia's so-called Rose Revolution, because it was the first of the electoral revolution cases within the post-Soviet region, and because Soros's influence there was, arguably, the most pronounced. In financial terms, taking population size and level of development into account, the Open Society Georgia Foundation (OSGF) has received much more funding than the International Renaissance Foundation, Soros's vehicle in Ukraine.[86] Moreover, in Ukraine (Aslund & McFaul 2006, Karatnycky 2006), as well as in Kyrgyzstan (Radnitz 2010), local oligarchs were much more invested in the political maneuvers surrounding the Orange and the Tulip Revolutions than Soros. In the case of the Rose Revolution in Georgia, in contrast, Soros funding seems to have been a more important factor relative to the domestic scene.

During the second half of the 1990s, under President Eduard Shevardnadze, Georgia had developed a neo-patrimonial, competitive authoritarian regime, which remained relatively open with regard to civil liberties. Elections were rife with fraud, corruption within politics and public services was pervasive, but civil society and independent media could voice critique and opposition without fear of harsh repression (Broers 2005, Fairbanks 2004, Mitchell 2004). In 2001, Shevardnadze's Citizens' Union of Georgia (CUG) party disintegrated, as the so-called "young reformers" broke rank in order to form their own parties: Mikheil Saakashvili, former Minister of Justice, created the National Movement and Zurab Zhvania, former Chairman of the Parliament, founded the United Democrats, later joined by Nino Burjanadze. Consequently, the campaigns for parliamentary elections, scheduled for November 2, 2003, turned into a heated contest, as local elections in 2002 had exposed the weakness of the ruling party. Saakashvili and Zhvania–Burjanadze presented themselves as the pro-democracy, pro Western, and anticorruption alternatives to Shevardnadze, a profile they managed to sharpen by warning of election fraud and insisting on free and fair elections. This call was echoed and supported by some of the most prominent NGOs in Georgia as well as by Western organizations, such as the EU and the U.S. government. From spring 2003 onwards, a student movement called Kmara ("enough" in Georgian) agitated against Shevardnadze. The most popular private TV channel, *Rustavi-2*, relentlessly broadcasted anti-government attacks, exposing corruption scandals as well as showing, repeatedly, the documentary film *Bringing Down a Dictator*, which describes the success of the uprising against Milošević in Serbia (Anable 2006). Gradually, the election campaign developed into a highly charged standoff between Shevardnadze and the opposition around Saakashvili, Zhvania, and Burjanadze. When independent exit polls and parallel

[86] The IRF's budgets were around 50 percent larger than the OSGF's, but this corresponds to the different level of development (GDP per capita in PPP), which was also around 50 percent higher in Ukraine during the early 2000s, whereas Ukraine's population was more than ten times larger than Georgia's (2000: IRF US$9.3 million, OSGF US$6.1; 2005: IRF US$10.1 million, OSGF US$6.6 million, see Open Society Institute 2001 and 2006).

vote tabulations showed a clear majority for the opposition parties, exposing the official results as fraudulent, over two weeks of street protests in Tbilisi challenged Shevardnadze to recognize his coalition's defeat. In a final showdown on November 22, 2003, Saakashvili and his supporters stormed the parliament, brandishing roses as a sign of victory; the next day, Shevardnadze resigned, and in January 2004, Saakashvili was elected President of Georgia with a 96 percent majority (Karumidze & Wertsch 2005, Welt 2006, Mitchell 2009). What was Soros's involvement in this electoral revolution?

It seems clear that by mid-2002, Soros had become frustrated with the Shevardnadze government, which had been stalling on anticorruption initiatives supported by Soros's OSGF, and was contemplating a regime change. Thus, in June 2002, he personally awarded the annual Central European University's "Open Society Prize" to Mikheil Saakashvili and Zurab Zhvania, who had just emerged as Shevardnadze's major opponents. A month later, Soros said with regard to Georgia's upcoming elections that

> [i]t is necessary to mobilize civil society in order to assure free and fair elections because there are many forces that are determined to falsify or to prevent the elections being free and fair. This is what we did in Slovakia at the time of Mečiar, in Croatia at the time of Tudjman and in Yugoslavia at the time of Milošević.
>
> (MacKinnon 2007: 108)

Explicitly drawing on the prior experience of the "electoral revolution" model in other Eastern European countries, Soros's statement reveals an objective and a strategy. In order to implement it, he put Alexander "Kakha" Lomaia, who had been the Eurasia Foundation's country director in Georgia before, in charge.[87]

At first, Lomaia became the "Former Soviet Union" regional director of the Soros-sponsored "Democracy Coalition Project." In this function, he brought seven leading NGOs of Georgia together, who, in December 2002, collectively proposed seven measures for ensuring free and fair elections, stating that

> the forthcoming elections . . . give a chance to overcome the prolonged political crisis. How events develop in the future depends on how active the whole society will be. A determined and concerted effort of civic organisations is necessary to encourage wider public participation.[88]

---

[87] Lincoln Mitchell, who was directly involved with the preparations for the 2003 elections in Georgia as the Chief of Party of the *National Democratic Institute*'s Georgia office, and who has generally downplayed external (especially, Western) influences on the Rose Revolution, characterized Lomaia's role in the Rose Revolution as "important". . . . He was one of the people who . . . had a strategic sense of what the post-election scenario might look like" (interviewed in Angley 2010: 460).

[88] See "Statement of the Georgian Coalition for Democracy (Demcoalition)," December 19, 2002, online: https://web.archive.org/web/20040420053637/http://www.demcoalition.org/pdf/Statement% 20of%20the%20Georgian%20Demcoalition.pdf (accessed July 9, 2019). The seven NGOs were the

Irakly Areshidze, who participated in these NGO meetings during fall 2002, claims that from the beginning, the real goal was to "use the coalition to lay the groundwork for the removal of Eduard Shevardnadze after the November [2003 parliamentary] elections" (Areshidze 2007: 97). In 2003, Lomaia was promoted to lead the OSGF as its executive director, and, in direct contact with Soros, the OSGF "launched the Election Support Program, an effort by civil society activists, NGO leaders, international organizations, and intellectuals to ensure fair elections and full media coverage of the campaigns and voting" (Open Society Institute 2004: 30f).[89] Thus, OSGF financed an exit poll that, together with a parallel vote tabulation, was a key element in the "electoral revolution" model, since it revealed the victory of the opposition and the fraudulence of the official results (Welt 2006: 15ff, Bunce & Wolchik 2006, 2010). In order to challenge the government and its official results, political mobilization and supportive media coverage were necessary. As far as this concerns the OSGF's long-term support for Georgian civil society and independent media, Soros's helping hand is widely acknowledged. Soros had set up the OSGF already in 1994, and with yearly budgets around US $3–5 million, it has been a key player in the Western-funded "NGO-zation" of Georgia's civil society (Nodia 2005: 14). All studies of the role of Georgia's civil society organizations during the Rose Revolution emphasize that the leading NGOs constituted a close-knit community where personal connections, built over years of meeting and cooperating on many different projects, were vital (Angley 2013: 52f, Companjen 2010: 22–4, Hash-Gonzalez 2012: 51).

During 2003, however, the OSGF appears to have backed the opposition against Shevardnadze's regime in a much more direct way, namely by financing the student movement Kmara and the pro-opposition TV coverage of the main private channel, *Rustavi-2*. The details of this involvement are not fully clear and have led to some wild accusations, e.g. that "Soros spent $42 million ramping-up for the overthrow of Shevardnadze."[90] Such a figure seems highly unlikely, as it would be roughly ten times the amount the OSGF was spending annually in Georgia. Adjusted for level of development (GDP p.c. in PPP), which

"Caucasus Institute for Peace, Democracy, and Development," the "Georgian Young Lawyers' Association," and the "Liberty Institute," which all three had frequently worked with Soros's OSGF before, as well as the "International Society for Fair Elections and Democracy," the "Former Political Prisoners for Human Rights," the "Partnership for Social Initiatives," and the "Centre for Social Studies." See Open Society Institute 2003: 102f and Areshidze 2007: 97ff.

[89] While there are some doubts about the autonomy of Lomaia and the involvement of Soros (Areshidze 2007: 101, Angley 2010: 231), several reports and interviews confirm that Soros was directly monitoring the activities of his foundation in Georgia at the time. See MacKinnon 2007: 110f and "Die Revolutions-GmbH," *Der Spiegel*, November 14, 2005 (46/2005), online: http://magazin.spiegel.de/EpubDelivery/spiegel/pdf/43103188 (accessed July 5, 2019).

[90] This statement has been attributed to a "former member of the Georgian Parliament," cited by Richard W. Carlson, "Georgia on His Mind: George Soros's Potemkin Revolution," *The Weekly Standard*, May 24, 2004, online: http://www.weeklystandard.com/georgia-on-his-mind/article/5330 (accessed July 5, 2019), also Porter 2015: 101.

was over ten times higher than in Georgia, and population size, which was seventy times larger, it would be the equivalent of spending over US$32 billion on the 2004 presidential election in the U.S. In Georgia, much less money could make a big difference. The OSGF's 2003 annual report indicates spending US$332,179 on an Election Support Program, whose goal was "Support of Fair Elections: mobilizing Voters from various social groups to actively participate in elections; support of pre-election debates; informing voters on election procedures and importance of elections"; US$106,363 were allocated to the Mass Media Program, whose "main priority... for 2003 was fair coverage of parliamentary elections and media monitoring" (Open Society Georgia Foundation 2004).[91] Nowhere does the annual report mention support for Kmara. However, statements from direct participants in the elections as well as research based on interviews with former Kmara activists all mention that the OSGF was the main sponsor of Kmara (Angley 2013: 49, Areshidze 2007: 106f, 144, Duda 2010: 193, 249, Kandelaki & Meladze 2007: 111f). The OSGF's director, Lomaia, has also been cited during 2003 as acknowledging his organization's support for Kmara.[92]

Thus, the OSGF paid for a trip to Serbia so that future Kmara activists could meet with Otpor leaders that had contributed to ousting Milošević in 2000, and it also subsidized a training camp during June 2003 in Georgia where more than a thousand activists learned about nonviolent protest and civil disobedience tactics. Most of the OSGF's money, though, seems to have been used to finance Kmara's TV-ads on *Rustavi-2*, which, simultaneously, provided income for the pro-opposition TV station (Anable 2006, Areshidze 2007: 124f, 144, Duda 2010: 201ff, MacKinnon 2007: 112f). While Kmara's contribution to the Rose Revolution has sometimes been downplayed, most participants and analysts agree that the stance and the coverage of *Rustavi-2* was, in the words of Mikheil

---

[91] There are, however, significant sums whose spending is not being detailed. The central annual report of the Open Society Foundations network shows overall US$5.64 million expenses for Georgia in 2003 (Open Society Institute 2004: 103), in contrast to the US$2.25 million total in the OSGF's report. This appears quite normal, as the larger central budget includes the foundations' administrative overhead costs for Georgia (over US$600k in 2003, as in prior years) as well as expenses by programs that were being run from New York (over US$1 million); still, since no further expenditure details are being provided, it is possible that parts of this money was channeled towards supporting Kmara or other "Rose Revolution" activities. In OSGF's annual report, various programs also have "Contribution to Election Support Program" budget lines, which add up to US$300k, and it is unclear whether these sums constituted the "Election Support Program," or—which would be more in line with the reporting logic—whether they provided additional funds. It is, of course, also possible that Soros provided undocumented money to Georgia's opposition out of his own pocket, rather than through his foundation network.

[92] See "Is George Soros Funding Georgian Opposition?," *REF/RL Newsline*, May 23, 2003, online: http://www.rferl.org/a/1142915.html and Natalia Antelava, "How to stage a revolution," *BBC News*, December 4, 2003, online: http://news.bbc.co.uk/2/hi/europe/3288547.stm (both accessed July 5, 2019). The latter article cites Laura Silber, senior policy adviser for Soros's foundation, saying that none of the OSGF's "money went directly to Kmara," which keeps the possibility open that OSGF financed Kmara through intermediaries.

Saakashvili, "extremely important. It was really instrumental."[93] In fact, it is hard to disentangle the NGOs, Kmara, and *Rustavi-2*. Although quite small in its number of participants, which never surpassed 3,000 (Kandelaki 2006), Kmara's highly symbolic and provocative actions, such as marches, graffiti, or burning of flags, provided exactly the kind of visual material that helped to transmit, on TV, the impression of a citizen uprising. Much of this "revolution staging" had been strategically planned, as personal networks among senior actors linked the media with the student movement and the civil society organizations, and coordination between them was frequent (Areshidze 2007: 269ff, Angley 2010: 247ff, 440ff, Anable 2006: 18f, Duda 2010: 201ff). Funds from the OSGF went to most of the groups involved, and its director Lomaia belonged to the core group of civic leaders (Angley 2013: 52).

On the whole, it looks as if George Soros has been able to realize his goal in Georgia, at least in the short run. The "electoral revolution" model, which he had evoked in 2002, was consistently pursued during the following year by his OSGF, under the local leadership of Lomaia, who used Soros's money to finance civil society opposition forces that, ultimately, lead to Shevardnadze's resignation and to the victory of Soros's then friend, Mikheil Saakashvili. How close the relationship between Lomaia and Saakashvili was is best illustrated by the fact that during the final act of the Rose Revolution, when Saakashvili stormed the parliament on November 22, 2003, Lomaia was right next to him. And after the presidential elections in 2004, Lomaia became Saakashvili's Minister for Education and Science, and later, in 2007, his National Security Advisor.[94] A precise assessment of Soros's power in the case of Georgia's Rose Revolution is, however, more complicated, because other key actors had been working towards the same goal. First of all, Saakashvili and other leaders of the political opposition in Georgia obviously had their own interests—seizing the government—and could mobilize local forces (party members and supporters, campaign contributions from Georgian business, etc.) that, most studies agree, were at least as crucial as foreign backing. Especially during the two weeks after the fraudulent elections, Saakashvili's political leadership appears to have been decisive in bringing down Shevardnadze's government (Areshidze 2007, Welt 2006, Mitchell 2009). Still, the possibility of a sudden regime change was, according to most participants, not something that had been expected long in advance. Many saw a compromise solution with Shevardnadze and a more gradual transformation, leading up to the 2005 presidential elections, as more likely (Karumidze & Wertsch 2005). The "revolutionary" option emerged mainly out of the more radical civil society

---

[93] Saakashvili, interviewed in Karumidze & Wertsch 2005: 25. See also Anable 2006,
[94] See Lomaia's official biography from when he was Georgia's permanent representative to the United Nations: http://www.un.org/press/en/2009/bio4065.doc.htm as well as "Die Revolutions-GmbH," *Der Spiegel*, November 14, 2005 (46/2005), online: http://magazin.spiegel.de/EpubDelivery/spiegel/pdf/43103188 (both accessed July 5, 2019).

agitation, and the corresponding TV coverage (Areshidze 2007: 144ff, Broers 2005: 340f, Duda 2010: 213f, Mitchell 2009: 124). Soros's concerted support for the more radical NGOs, the student movement Kmara, and the TV-channel *Rustavi-2* can therefore be seen as having generated a critical juncture, opening a window of opportunity, which was then seized by Saakashvili.

Second, other foreign actors were promoting democratization in Georgia in similar ways as Soros. While European organizations, especially the EU and the OSCE, remained fairly neutral, largely limiting their role to standard international election monitoring, the U.S. was more actively involved. At the diplomatic level, the U.S. government offered little support to its long-time ally Shevardnadze.[95] U.S. development organizations—primarily the National Endowment for Democracy (NED) and USAID—had, like Soros, financed civil society organizations and independent media, including *Rustavi-2*, for many years prior to the Rose Revolution (Mitchell 2009: 115ff, ARD 2002).[96] And the National Democratic Institute (NDI), connected to the Democratic Party and publicly funded under the umbrella of NED, as well as, at the program level, via USAID, had cultivated close ties with some of the same NGOs as Soros's OSGF. In their attempts to foster collaboration among the different opposition parties and through their sponsorship of the parallel vote tabulation during the election, the NDI's country directors in Georgia, Mark Mullen and Lincoln Mitchell, also took sides against Shevardnadze (Areshidze 2007: 99–104, Mitchell 2009: 123, Angley 2010: 449–58, MacKinnon 2007: 114f). However, most of these decisions and activities opposed Shevardnadze only insofar as they pressed him to ensure free and fair elections. This was certainly the tenor of the official U.S. envoys—former Secretary of State James Baker, and Senator John McCain—who visited Georgia during 2003. Retrospectively, Lincoln Mitchell may be downplaying his own (and the NDI's) role too much, but the thrust of his analysis fits the accounts of many other observers:

The more radical civic leaders who consistently articulated a very strong anti-Shevardnadze view . . . worked for NGOs funded by OSI [Open Society Institute],

---

[95] MacKinnon has linked this to U.S. geopolitical interests (2007: 94–115), especially the construction of the Baku–Tbilisi–Ceyhan pipeline, which transports Caspian Sea oil to the Mediterranean, bypassing Russia. During 2003, Shevardnadze's government seemed to be turning away from its Western allies, as it announced the opening of its energy sector to Russia's Gazprom. While energy independence from Russia certainly was part of U.S. interests in Georgia, the timing of events speaks against MacKinnon's interpretation. Shevardnadze's overtures towards Russia happened during the summer of 2003, long after Western organizations had called for free and fair elections and started to support opposition forces. Hence, Shevardnadze's turn towards Russia looks like a reaction to, not a cause for U.S. support for the Georgian opposition.

[96] The U.S. funding of democracy promotion in Georgia was significantly higher than that of Soros—USAID counted US$91 million between 1994 and 2004, whereas the OSGF spent a total (all programs, not only those related to democracy promotion) of US$80 million between 1994 and 2014 (USAID 2005: 5–7, Open Society Georgia Foundation 2014: 3).

rather than by European or American governmental sources. In general, OSI was more aggressive in their approach to the 2003 election and had a far keener sense of the need to push for democratic reform during these elections. . . . In this respect, while . . . this organization may have pursued the foundation of what has become the electoral, or color, revolution strategy, it is critical to bear in mind that this view was . . . [not] shared by the broader democracy assistance and diplomatic communities in Georgia in 2003.   (Mitchell 2009: 124)

While U.S. interests and actions coincided considerably with those of Soros,[97] it was the billionaire's funding strategy that was most geared towards regime change during Georgia's election year.

Soros's own reflections on his role in the Rose Revolution are ambiguous. On the one hand, in a 2004 interview, he said that "I'm delighted by what happened in Georgia, and I take great pride in having contributed to it."[98] On the other hand, he and OSI spokespersons have repeatedly emphasized that, like other Western actors, they only tried to support free and fair elections.[99] Once one takes the aftermath of the Rose Revolution into account, it looks as if Soros's public modesty is a tactical move to protect his foundation network. Within Russia and other post-Soviet authoritarian regimes, such as Uzbekistan and Kazakhstan, the color revolutions produced strong fears of Western intervention in their domestic affairs, which led to legal restrictions and repression of foreign NGOs operating in these countries. Several of these measures, particularly in Russia and Hungary, have targeted Soros's foundations specifically, as nationalist politicians, sometimes using anti-Semitic and xenophobic rhetoric, see the billionaire as an easy target in order to score points with their electorate (Berg 2006, Ambrosio 2007, Koesel & Bunce 2013, Carothers & Brechenmacher 2014).

Moreover, Georgia itself did not turn into a beacon of democracy after the Rose Revolution. Upon taking power, Saakashvili's government took various actions that curtailed the influence of independent media, the rule of law, and the influence of civil society, justifying these moves as necessary for modernizing the country and fighting corruption. And, in 2008, Saakashvili lead Georgia into a hazardous and ultimately doomed military conflict with Russia over South Ossetia

---

[97] The coherence of "the U.S." is, in the case of the Rose Revolution, uncertain, because people like the local staff of the NDI seem to have often acted on their own, without clear instructions from Washington (Areshidze 2007: 101, Mitchell 2009: 120–6). Soros and the OSGF may have collaborated with U.S. political actors in specific instances, such as organizing the exit polls, but a broader strategic cooperation is unlikely, not least since Soros was, in 2003, deeply opposed to the domestic and foreign policies of George W. Bush's government, spending dozens of millions US$ to counteract them (Open Society Institute 2004: 9–13, 166–85, Soros 2004).

[98] David Holley, "Soros Invests in His Democratic Passion," Los Angeles Times, July 5, 2004, online: http://articles.latimes.com/2004/jul/05/world/fg-soros5 (accessed October 5, 2016).

[99] See the "letter to the editor" by Deborah Koeppel (Regional Director, Caucasus & Central Asia, Open Society Institute), The Globe and Mail, November 28, 2003, also Soros 2006a: 62 and Open Society Institute 2004: 30f.

(Isrotiuli Memkvidreoba 2009, Muskhelishvili & Jorjoliani 2009, Monson 2009, Halbach 2013). Soros himself is very much aware of the negative consequences that came out of his association with the Rose Revolution:

> One of the reasons why President Putin came to regard me as a personal enemy was my support for Mikheil Saakashvili in Georgia. That is a truly sad story as far as I am concerned.... Saakashvili in power turned out to be much less of a paragon of open society than when he was in opposition. In the meantime, I was accused by the Russian media of being Saakashvili's pay master, and Putin advised the rulers of the Central Asian republics to close down my foundations.... This painful lesson taught me to keep a greater distance from the internal politics of the countries where I have my foundations.
>
> (Soros 2011: 33f)

In the same pages, Soros again only admits to financing exit polls in Georgia, awarding the Open Society prize to Saakashvili, and donations to the new government in 2004.[100] Yet, in a nonpublic document from the *Open Society Foundations* network, which was leaked during summer 2016, probably by Russian hackers, the reconstruction of OSGF's past sounds different:

> From its earliest days, OSGF made a profound impact on the political and civic life of Georgia, demonstrated by the events of 2003's peaceful Rose Revolution. Several NGOs that had been nurtured and backed by OSGF played central roles in the peaceful protests that ended the rule of Eduard Shevardnadze, and, following the transfer of power to Mikheil Saakashvili..., many senior OSGF staff members left to take up positions inside the new government.[101]

Even though it does not address the specific role of Soros, this internal assessment comes very close to the analysis developed above. Overall, via his funding and his local lieutenant, Alexander Lomaia, Soros was one of the key actors that turned Georgia's election year into a critical juncture that made a regime change possible. With hindsight, some have concluded, like Anna Porter does, that Soros's (as well as those of the EU and the U.S. government) attempts at democracy promotion in

---

[100] Soros gave several million U.S. dollars "to a capacity-building fund set up by the United Nations Development Program, which paid supplementary salaries of a thousand dollars a month to members of Saakashvili's cabinet and a hundred dollars a month to personnel of the police force" (Soros 2011: 33f).

[101] "Open Society Georgia Foundation Strategy for 2014–2017," online: https://web.archive.org/web/20160814233104/http://soros.dcleaks.com/download/?f=/Caucasus%20and%20Central%20Asia/2014%202017%20national%20foundation%20strategies/2014%20strategy%20georgia.pdf&t=eurasia; the public OSGF strategy for 2014–2016 did not feature this background information, online: https://web.archive.org/web/20140725045238/http://www.osgf.ge/index.php?lang_id=ENG&sec_id=179 (accessed October 5, 2016).

the post-Soviet region have failed (Porter 2015: 105ff, 201ff). Such a view is clearly exaggerated, not least since Georgia remains among the most liberal post-Soviet countries, with relatively free and fair recent elections. Still, as Soros regrets, the hopes put into Saakashvili did not materialize as expected. In terms of agency, however, we have to distinguish purposive action from unanticipated consequences (Merton 1936). Later turns of events do not detract from the fact that during 2003, Soros exercised pivotal power in Georgia.

8

Analytical Conclusion

Taking a step back from the case studies presented in the previous chapters, what can we conclude about billionaires as transnational actors in world politics? As mentioned at the outset, a sample size of only six case studies does not lend itself to generalizations. To build typologies or even theories with regard to the political agency of billionaires would require a much more comprehensive analysis of the billionaire population, which I will leave to future research. My goal was to examine whether the usually implicit and sometimes explicit assumption in IR, namely that "[i]ndividual human beings on their own lack the power, coordination, and resources necessary to achieve many espoused goals" (Erskine 2008: 701), stands up to scrutiny in the case of billionaires. Drawing on the insights from my case studies, I will pursue three lines of analysis.

"Individuals" is a problematic term. Large parts of social theory contest the notion that human beings act autonomously, which is at the center of the structure–agency debate. My first concluding question will therefore address billionaires' agency—with all that their money can buy, should we think about them as "super-actors," or are they nonetheless bound up in social structures that shape the way they act? A strong reproach of billionaires' agency that I want to address comes from neo-Marxist theories about the transnational capitalist class; another challenge arises from institutional approaches. My second query extends the agency *problematique* to IR—can billionaires make a difference in a world dominated by states and other collective actors? This will also necessitate a discussion of billionaires' power. Finally, I want to reflect on the normative implications—if billionaires do wield power in world politics, what does this imply for the liberal values that have informed much modern thinking about political order? In a world of states and global governance, the analytical and normative issues raised by billionaires are twofold: how do their transnational activities affect self-determination within states, and what is their contribution— positive or negative—at the supranational level? In these interrogations, I hope to connect my findings with broader discussions and highlight avenues for further research.

Billionaires in World Politics. Peter Hägel, Oxford University Press (2020). © Peter Hägel.
DOI: 10.1093/oso/9780198852711.001.0001

Billionaires as "Super-Actors" or a Global "Super-Class"?

[T]hose princes can stand alone who have sufficient manpower or money to assemble an army equal to an encounter with any aggressor.... And so he should have a flexible disposition, varying as fortune and circumstances dictate.

(Machiavelli 1531 [2004]: 45+76)

In purely financial terms, the billionaires studied here are "super-actors," all having figured among the top hundred of *Forbes*'s global wealth list, except Raj Rajaratnam, who, in several ways, besides serving a prison term for insider trading, is the odd man out among my case studies. True to their name, the billionaires' liquid assets comprise billions of dollars,[1] which gives them unrestricted budgets that surpass those of most other political actors, including many small or poor states. But it is not just money that equips these billionaires with agentic power. All of them have accumulated their fortunes themselves, sometimes starting from zero (Sheldon Adelson and George Soros), sometimes coming from privileged yet not superrich families (Bill Gates, Rupert Murdoch, Raj Rajaratnam), or, like the Koch brothers, turning a multi-million family company into a multi-billion conglomerate. All of them have excelled as entrepreneurs, creating businesses that count among (or are) the dominant player(s) in their industry, such as Microsoft or News Corp. Four of Sheldon Adelson's casinos are among the world's twenty-five largest buildings, and George Soros managed the best-performing hedge fund for several decades. Beyond financials and the development of entrepreneurial skills, their business feats have also turned these billionaires into "super-actors" by providing them with mastery experiences and strong self-efficacy beliefs. Adelson calls himself "Self," and Soros has admitted to having held messianic fantasies. Yet, like all of us, as Aristotle would emphasize, they remain social beings, and thinking about the billionaires' individual agency has to confront some serious challenges emanating from the social scientific study of class and institutions.

When David Rothkopf popularized the notion of the global superclass, positing that each of its 6,000 members "has the ability to regularly influence the lives of millions of people in multiple countries worldwide" (Rothkopf 2008: xviii), social scientists were delighted by his insider acumen, but criticized his understanding of social class. A list that comprises heads of state, CEOs, religious leaders, military commanders and billionaires, among others, is hardly apt to fit the category "class," no matter whether one defines it in sociocultural or socioeconomic terms. What Rothkopf seemed to be getting at, in line with his main sociological

---

[1] For the Koch brothers, we have no data on their liquidity, but, given their company's estimated worth and their annual expenditure on politics, it can't be low. In Murdoch's case, his media companies are the relevant political asset.

reference, C. Wright Mills' "power elite" (Mills 1956), was "being powerful" as the common trait uniting the members of the "superclass." Yet, as had already been a key critique of Mills, such a trait alone is insufficient to form an integrated group that would be powerful collectively. More often than not, powerful individuals have rival interests and are in conflict with each other (Dahl 1958, Keller 1963). In his analytical framework of oligarchy, Jeffrey Winters counters this pluralist argument by emphasizing how, in capitalist societies with institutionalized private property, a common interest in wealth and income defense may unify the ultra-rich in their opposition to taxation, as we have seen with the political alliances built by the Koch brothers in the U.S. (2011: 208–74, esp. 224ff). However, Winters finds it hard to imagine how this logic could apply to the realm of world politics (ibid.: xvii).

Addressing this issue, neo-Marxist scholarship has advanced the idea that a new class formation is emerging out of (as well as propelling) globalization. In this perspective, as much economic activity, especially production and investment, has shifted from international exchange to integrated global processes, a transnational capitalist class (TCC) is superseding the nation-state-based bourgeoisie (Robinson & Harris 2000, Sklair 1995, 2001). The rise of multinational corporations and global finance is seen as providing the structural context for the formation of the TCC as a class-in-itself, comprised largely of transnational corporate elites and global investors, accompanied by the political elites of global governance (Robinson & Harris 2000: 21ff). The TCC has also developed as a class-for-itself, bonding around neoliberal ideology and a global, often cosmopolitan conscious-ness, which both get articulated and spread within institutionalized social spaces such as the Trilateral Commission, the OECD's various forums, or the World Economic Forum in Davos (Gill 1990, van der Pijl 1998, Graz 2003). Empirical research, which is mostly analyzing the connections between members of the TCC, e.g. across corporate boards and global policy forums, has found substantial evidence of network integration, especially within the European and transatlantic context (Carroll 2010, Carroll & Sapinski 2010, 2016, Dreiling & Darves 2016, Heemskerk & Takes 2016). In the TCC research framework, billionaires receive no special attention, as it is mainly concentrating on the senior executives of multi-national corporations. Billionaires as businessmen that individually control global companies can fit into the TCC paradigm, but such corporations represent only a small part of the leading stock market indices, whose blue chip companies usually don't have a single majority stockholder; hence it makes sense for TCC theory to not single out billionaires. Are billionaires thus simply the wealthiest members of the TCC?

For those billionaires that engage in politics primarily in order to advance their economic interests, the TCC framework appears compelling. The Koch brothers and Rupert Murdoch have a proven track record of expanding their business globally and curbing the power of organized labor (Schulman 2014: 298f,

McKnight 2013: 59f, 86ff).[2] Both are also among the most outspoken proponents of neoliberal economic policies—the Koch brothers have spent enormous sums on spreading pro-free market ideology; in Murdoch's case, it is part of his media empire's DNA (Mayer 2016, Wolff 2010: 262). With their support for privatization and global markets, their values correspond significantly with what is seen as the TCC agenda. However, neither the Koch brothers nor Murdoch seem to share the purported cultural values of the TCC—they support decidedly national approaches to politics and exhibit little attachment to globalist or cosmopolitan social visions.[3] The Koch brothers have never attended the World Economic Forum; Murdoch has been a regular Davos participant until 2011, but, through his media and in his own statements, he has consistently agitated against the EU and other supranational initiatives (McKnight 2013: 155, 166f, Wolff 2010: 262f). In both cases, this corresponds with their strong (economic) libertarian values, which are against state intervention in the economy per se, and even more categorically against any kind of world government. At the same time, it is also an expression of their individual agency. Instead of joining the transnational elite circuits that foster globalization and global governance, Murdoch and the Koch brothers have preferred to build and control their own opinion-shaping schemes—Murdoch's media empire and the Koch network of foundations, think tanks, and super-PACs. These allow them to influence public opinion according to their personal values, which are not always part of the mainstream TCC consensus, such as the Koch brothers' climate change skepticism or Murdoch's anti-EU stance.

How billionaires engaged in transnational security issues could fit into the TCC framework is less obvious, because security interests may or may not coincide with economic interests. At the systemic level, there is of course the longstanding discussion about the liaison between capitalism, democracy, and the "liberal" peace (Angell 1910, Doyle 1986, Brooks 2005, 2013, Gartzke 2007). In this context, peace can be seen as a fundamental element in the TCC's purported concern for "securing the political stability of the system . . . to build a stable and regulated environment for global accumulation" (Robinson & Harris 2000: 43). The US$1 billion donation by Ted Turner, the founder of CNN, to the UN seems to have been motivated by such considerations:

---

[2] In 2017, according to the Koch Industries website, of the conglomerate's almost 130,000 employees worldwide, around half (67,000) were employed in the U.S., see: http://www.kochind.com/locations/ (accessed July 10, 2019).

[3] Initially, Robinson and Harris saw three fractions within the TCC, and both the Koch brothers and Murdoch might fit into the "free-market conservatives" fraction, which "call[s] for a complete global laissez-faire based on an undiluted version of the Washington consensus" (Robinson & Harris 2000: 43). How this would relate to a transnational class consciousness remained unclear, though; in later writings, this fraction disappeared from the TCC framework (Robinson 2012).

The United Nations has long been one of my favorite organizations. It's vitally important for the world to have a place where leaders can get together and try to solve global problems, and I've always believed that as long as countries are talking, they don't go to war with each other.   (Turner & Burke 2008: 345)

An unexpected collaboration between George Soros and Charles Koch, who have been funding opposite candidates and policies in U.S. politics over many years, also fits the "capitalist peace" bill. In 2019, they announced their co-sponsorship of a new think tank in Washington, D.C., The Quincy Institute, which "promotes ideas that move U.S. foreign policy away from endless war and toward vigorous diplomacy in the pursuit of international peace."[4] The billionaires that I have been studying more in-depth, however, exhibit little concern for "securing global accumulation" when pursuing their transnational security goals. There may be some overlap, e.g., when Sheldon Adelson is supporting Benjamin Netanyahu, he is partnering with a politician who endorses neoliberal economic policy (Filc 2010: 62ff). But Adelson's transnational backing of Netanyahu is not about his business interests, which lie outside Israel. Both Adelson's engagement in Israel and Rajaratnam's in Sri Lanka have been tied to ethnonationalist allegiances and projects, not capitalist schemes. Neither have the two billionaires ever attended Davos, nor have they expressed any cosmopolitan values publicly. It can even be argued that both Adelson and Rajaratnam have acted against the collective interests of the TCC. Being for the expansion of West Bank settlements and against a two-state solution in Israel, or being for an independent Tamil state in Sri Lanka, are missions that risk destabilizing the concerned regions.[5] As such, they run counter to the logic of the capitalist peace (Gartzke 2007). While Adelson's and Rajaratnam's transnational security interventions can thus not be captured by a global "superclass" perspective, they do not necessarily turn them into "super-actors," either. In the case of Rajaratnam, much of his support for the Tamil cause seems to have taken place in conformity with strong social norms, which had been imposed on the Tamil diaspora via the LTTE's transnational operations. The political agency of Sheldon Adelson, in contrast, has been running counter to the majority consensus of American Jewry and, during the Obama presidency, official U.S. foreign policy. From what we know, he is organizing his promotion of Netanyahu and settlement expansion in Israel largely on his own, together with his wife.

---

[4] See online https://quincyinst.org/ and Stephen Kinzer, "In an astonishing turn, George Soros and Charles Koch team up to end US 'forever war' policy," *The Boston Globe*, June 30, 2019, online: https://www.bostonglobe.com/opinion/2019/06/30/soros-and-koch-brothers-team-end-forever-war-policy/WhyENwjhG0vfo9Um6Zl0JO/story.htmlThe?fbclid=IwAR0FSvtCg0Gu3RBxalbh0DD9OIj2h2NS-3uSoCG3uiQi9wYnJ7qi3RX9Sqk (accessed July 4, 2019).

[5] The UN Security Council Resolution 2334 (2016) condemning Israel's settlement expansion, which passed with 14–0 votes, affirmed the broad global consensus on the issue, online: https://www.un.org/webcast/pdfs/SRES2334-2016.pdf (accessed July 4, 2019).

The philanthropy of Bill Gates and George Soros further demonstrates the limits of the TCC perspective. At first sight, the biographies of both billionaires exhibit features that would designate them as prime members of the TCC. Both made their fortunes in global business, both embrace cosmopolitan identities and values, both have participated in Bilderberg conferences at least once (Bill Gates in 2010, George Soros in 1996),[6] and both are longstanding participants at the annual Davos meetings. Consequently, Gates and Soros have each been singled out as individual examples within descriptions of the TCC (Robinson & Harris 2000: 43, Sklair 2006: 33). In his approach to global health, Gates is lauding private enterprise and market mechanisms, e.g. when he is partnering with leading pharmaceutical corporations in vaccine development and production (McGoey 2014, 2015: 216ff, Mitchell & Sparke 2016). Yet his main rationale for intervening in global health is to compensate for what he sees as market failures. Soros, while viewing markets as superior to central planning, is very critical of laissez-faire capitalism. Although Soros has articulated this position consistently throughout his career (1987: 325ff, 2006b: 199–249), it surprised Kees van der Pijl, one of the key neo-Marxist thinkers about transnational classes in IR: "on the eve of the 1997 meeting [in Davos,] ... Soros, unexpectedly denounced 'the destruction of those values which do not produce commercial return' and 'the totalitarian tendency of unregulated market capitalism'" (1998: 135). Within the TCC framework, as in Marxist thought more generally, dealing with the varieties of capitalism usually involves identifying how the capitalist class is fractured according to where and how capitalists earn their profits, and whether they need to make compromises with other social classes. In this vein, Soros is seen as belonging to the "structuralist" TCC faction, which is supposed to have an interest in strengthening global governance in order to maintain the stability of the global system (Robinson & Harris 2000: 43, Guilhot 2007). However, such an analysis simply does not correspond with the economic interests of Soros: as a hedge fund manager specialized in arbitrage and macro-investing, his business has typically benefited from international turmoil, as when he contributed to push the UK out of the European Exchange Rate Mechanism in 1992. Soros's concern for global governance thus has little material base; neither do his concerns for human rights, minorities, or open societies. For Bill Gates, it is also difficult to construct a link between his economic self-interest and his philanthropy. Back in the 1990s, when he was still the CEO of Microsoft and his company was embroiled in antitrust litigation, Gates's philanthropy may have looked like a fig leaf or "consciencelaundering."[7] Microsoft may also have hoped to benefit from "healthier" emerging

---

[6] See online: https://en.wikipedia.org/wiki/List_of_Bilderberg_participants (accessed July 4, 2019).
[7] Harvey 2014: 286 and Randall Smith, "As His Foundation Has Grown, Gates Has Slowed His Donations," *The New York Times*, May 26, 2014, online: https://dealbook.nytimes.com/2014/05/26/as-his-foundation-has-grown-gates-has-slowed-his-donations/?_php=true&_type=blogs&_r=0 (accessed July 4, 2019).

markets—but in the twenty-first century, Gates has largely divested himself from Microsoft, and his and the BMGF's fortune, like Soros's, is based on diversified financial assets. In fact, this quality of their wealth, namely that it is diversified, not attached to one company's fortune, and highly liquid, adds much to their capacity of being a super-actor.

Departing from orthodox Marxism and drawing more on Gramsci and Bourdieu (Berman 1983, Morvaridi 2012: 1193ff), one could interpret the philanthropy of TCC members as sophisticated efforts to gain social and symbolic capital, which in return allows them to secure their dominant economic status (Harvey et al. 2011: 432). In such analyses, Gates and Soros would use global capitalism to expand their fortunes, and their philanthropy is at best a Band-Aid for the wounds inflicted by capitalism, or, more fundamentally, simply a tool "to perpetuate the new socioeconomic order" (Guilhot 2007: 447, also Žižek 2006). Parts of Soros's and Gates's philanthropy fall into this framework, e.g. when their funding of private sector educational initiatives involves the promotion of neoliberal values (Guilhot 2007, Kovacs 2011, McGoey 2015: 113–47, van der Pijl 1998: 130f). Also, a few of their financial investments have overlapped with their philanthropy, creating potential conflicts of interest in the sense that the success of some of their philanthropic endeavors may have impacts on their profits or their foundations' endowments (Birn 2014: 14, McGoey 2015: 207–28, Soros 1995: 142ff). Still, most of their wealth and income derive from financial investments that have no direct connections with their philanthropy, which is mainly targeting regions that lie at the margins of global finance. While the Koch brothers' policy interventions against climate change mitigation are tied to their business interests, Gates and Soros would also be earning double-digit annual profit rates in the absence of their philanthropy. In a fundamental sense, their shift from business to philanthropy marks a departure from the capitalist logic of accumulation, which is central to the TCC paradigm, in line with its reliance on Marxist political economy. It is probably for this reason that Slavoj Žižek becomes so spiteful when he denounces Soros and Gates as "liberal communists":

Soros's daily routine is a lie embodied: half of his working time is devoted to financial speculation, the other half to "humanitarian" activities . . . which work against the effects of his own speculations. The two faces of Bill Gates are exactly like the two faces of Soros: on the one hand, a cruel businessman, destroying or buying out competitors, aiming at a virtual monopoly; on the other, the great philanthropist who makes a point of saying: "What does it serve to have computers if people do not have enough to eat?" (Žižek 2006)

While it is true that the annual earnings of Gates and Soros, and hence also their philanthropy, depend on profit-making, their actions are transforming the logic of capitalism. In the unlikely case where all capitalists would follow Carnegie's *Gospel of Wealth* or the Giving Pledge, capitalism would cease to be merely a system of accumulation, and would turn into a system of redistribution. When critics of Gates and Soros reason that philanthropists give with one hand what the other hand has taken before (Žižek 2006, Guilhot 2007, Birn 2014: 15f, McGoey 2015: 8ff), they neglect the fact that the two processes often concern very different groups of people. The British Pound's depreciation after Soros's speculative attacks against it certainly created winners and losers among foreign exchange traders and British citizens. But it probably had few effects on people in the former Soviet Union, which is where most of his philanthropy went during the early 1990s. Likewise, Microsoft's profits were not extracted from the people in the least developed countries, which is where the Gates Foundation is primarily active. To be sure, this has nothing to do with socialism, as it is a privatized form of redistribution, in which billionaires command the modes and the objectives of redistribution (Callahan 2017, Giridharadas 2018). Problems of power inequalities and accountability remain, as will be discussed further in the last chapter. Still, giving-it-all-away philanthropy does not fit into the TCC framework.

Overall, there appears to be limited value in using (super-)class analysis for understanding the billionaires that I have studied here. Their political interventions do not converge around economic class interests. Especially those billionaires that pursue goals related to security and social change exhibit no direct alignment with what the TCC is supposed to stand for. This does not mean that the TCC framework is inappropriate for other members of the *Forbes* list—only a more comprehensive study of billionaires can find this out. Nor does it imply that billionaires should be seen as "super-actors" in terms of being heroic individuals free from social constraints, what Margaret Archer has called the "Modernity's Man" fallacy (2000: 51–85). As far as we can know, in his transnational relations, Raj Rajaratnam was not an agent of capitalism, but an agent of the Tamil diaspora. Regarding the other billionaires, their choices of normative commitments appear less socially determined, but they are nonetheless shaped by the social norms and relations that form part of their biographies: Adelson and Revisionist Zionism, the Koch brothers and American libertarianism, Murdoch and neoconservativism, Soros and his studies with Karl Popper, Gates and the U.S. culture of philanthropy. At the micro level, the social relations within the billionaires' families also seem relevant, with interesting gender dynamics: Sheldon Adelson's turn towards Zionist politics is intertwined with his second marriage to Miriam (Bruck 2008), just as George Soros's seeking of greater public esteem coincided with his second marriage to Susan (Kaufman 2002: 206, 306). And the legacy of their fathers appears to affect both Rupert Murdoch and Charles Koch (Chenoweth 2001: 37f, 46f, Koch 2015: 5–12). However, pending the publication of the billionaires' personal diaries and correspondence, an investigation of friends and family crosses the frontiers of social science and risks entering the domain of Murdoch's tabloids.

A further challenge to the "super-actor" hypothesis comes in the form of institutional analysis. Rajaratnam seems to have been enmeshed in the standard transnational organization of the Tamil diaspora, subject to its norms and how they were enforced. Among the other billionaires in my case studies, Adelson is the only one operating without any kind of formal institution, although the recipients of his money, like the Israeli-American Council, Taglit-Birthright Israel, and *Israel Hayom*, are organizations. All the other billionaires have built specific organizations to pursue their goals, such as the Kochs' Americans for Prosperity, Soros's Open Society Foundations, the Gates Foundation, or Murdoch's News Corp. All of these organizations have more than a thousand employees, which means that principal–agent problems of delegation, oversight and control (Jensen & Meckling 1976), as well as the imperatives of organizational culture (Dobbin 1994), need to be considered (Teles 2016). Thus, Diane Stone has claimed that institutional logics may be more important in the functioning of the Open Society Foundations than George Soros as an individual (2008), and Adam Fejerskov has tried to make a similar point about Bill Gates and the BMGF (2015: 1109). This brings us back to the structure–agency debate within institutional analysis, where the discussion has focused on the possibilities of "institutional entrepreneurship" and its role in institutional change (DiMaggio 1988, Christensen et al. 1997, Leca et al. 2008). In this literature, social status and control over resources have been identified as enabling conditions for entrepreneurial agency within organizations. In line with the arguments developed by resource dependence theory, these conditions get amplified immensely when the actor is not an employee within an institution, but a billionaire who creates an organization that depends on his or her financial backing in order to survive.[8]

The evidence deriving from my case studies suggests little institutional takeover and high levels of power held and exercised by the billionaire founders and funders. Murdoch has consistently owned enough voting shares in his corporations to safeguard his executive control. *Israel Hayom* depends entirely on Adelson's money, just as the Open Society Foundations do on Soros's. Gates only has Warren Buffett as funding associate, who appears to be a consenting "silent investor." With Americans for Prosperity, the pool of funders is less transparent, but the Koch brothers seem to have been firmly in charge. Typically, the billionaires fill executive positions with people they can trust, because they have collaborated with them for a long time, as was the case when Soros hired Aryeh Neier to become the first president of his Open Society Foundations. Oftentimes, most visibly within the Koch's network and the Gates

---

[8] In their classic statement of resource dependence theory with regard to the external control of organizations, Jeffrey Pfeffer and Gerald Salancik stated ten conditions that "affect the extent to which an organization will comply with control attempts," almost all of which seem to be satisfied in the case of billionaire founders and funders of organizations (1978: 44).

Foundation, when staffing their political organizations, the billionaires rely on personnel that previously earned its credentials within their business ventures. If employees nevertheless disappoint the trust put into them, their position at the top of the organization's hierarchy allows the billionaires to apply sanctions. Soros has acknowledged that he "cannot give a proper accounting of the far-reaching and varied activities going on inside [my foundations network] because I am not aware of all of them," and that he has often "deferred to the judgement of the local boards." Yet, "if I seriously disagreed with their judgments, I changed the board" (2011: 19, 36).

When the billionaires invest in other pre-existing organizations, they often do so with sums that make them the principal donor, as was the case with Adelson and the Israeli-American Council and Taglit-Birthright Israel, or Soros and Human Rights Watch, or Gates and GAVI and even the WHO.[9] Moreover, their donations to other organizations are usually earmarked for targeted purposes and on a short-term basis, so that the renewal of their donations becomes subject to performance evaluation. If the recipient fails to meet the donor's expectations, the donations risk going to more accommodating grantees (Teles 2016: 458). In all of this, the billionaires heed Machiavelli's advice "to have a flexible disposition," which is something they must have already learned while succeeding with their businesses in competitive markets. They watch out not to be constrained by permanent entanglements, building and choosing their allies as they see fit to achieve their objectives. It is therefore not only their wealth, but the strategic use of it that can turn billionaires into "super-actors" who can pursue their goals with greater autonomy than other political actors, most of which depend more on collective action and which operate under financial constraints that make them more dependent on others.

This is not to deny that, as the billionaires' organizations grow and persist over time, institutional dynamics and the professional norms of the fields in which these organizations operate may eventually play a larger role. In particular, organizational logics can be expected to become more important once the founding entrepreneurs retire and pass their leadership on. Such shifts have been well documented for the foundations of earlier billionaires, for example the Rockefeller Foundation and the Ford Foundation (Macdonald 1956, Parmar 2012). In 2019, George Soros and Rupert Murdoch were eighty-eight years old, Sheldon Adelson eighty-six, and Charles Koch eighty-four. In their planning for posterity, it is not clear whether their businesses and their political organizations will see a dynastic succession, or whether they will be turned into impersonal foundations, trusts, or

---

[9] Regarding the GAVI, the BMGF was the principal donor in the beginning (in 2000), and in several, but not all later years; regarding the WHO, since 2008, the BMGF is either the second (after the U.S.) or the third (after the UK) largest funder. See online: https://vizhub.healthdata.org/fgh/ (accessed July 10, 2019).

corporations.[10] While there are legal ways, such as trust deeds, to try to limit mission drift in the future, it is likely that the mastery experiences of wealth accumulation and empire-building will be less pronounced among the heirs of the self-made billionaires. For the time being, the next step will be to assess how these "super-actors" project power on the global stage.

Individual Agency within the International System

What can billionaires accomplish in a world of states? The general neglect of individual agency in IR, as discussed in Chapter 2, rests largely on the assumption that individuals do not matter, because they cannot compete with the dominant actors in modern world politics. The international system is, above all, based on the interaction between states, as realists argue (Morgenthau 1947, Gilpin 1987, Waltz 1959, 1979). Most IR theorists agree on this, although many liberals and constructivists emphasize more how, under certain circumstances, societal actors and international regimes can affect outcomes with some autonomy. Within the study of transnational actors, arguments against state-centrism are therefore less about whether states are being supplanted by transnational actors. Rather, the objective is to find out when and how transnational actors manage to influence public policy across borders and at the international level, within the broader shift towards global governance (Price 2003: 592, Orenstein & Schmitz 2006: 482ff, Tallberg et al. 2013). A critical question concerns the "private" authority of transnational actors, whether they are acquiring a recognized right to participate in rule-making (Cutler et al. 1999, Hall & Biersteker 2002, Risse 2013, Green 2014).

George Soros, despite being a self-described "stateless statesman," has always been aware of the limits imposed by the international system: "A foundation will never be able to compete with the state, . . . because a state has powers of coercion" (1995: 140). He experienced this power on many occasions, most notably vis-à-vis Russia, where state authorities raided the Moscow offices of his Open Society

---

[10] In 2018, Soros's son Alexander became Deputy Chair on the Global Board of the OSF. In 2019, Murdoch's son Lachlan was co-chairman of News Corp and executive chairman and CEO of Fox Corporation, see online: http://newscorp.com/about/leadership/ and https://www.foxcorporation.com/management/executive-team/. Charles Koch's son Chase seems poised to take over his father's legacy, but with different priorities, see Maggie Severns, "The Next Koch Doesn't Like Politics," *Politico*, December 14, 2018, online: https://www.politico.com/magazine/story/2018/12/14/koch-brothers-chase-charles-next-generation-223099. Sheldon Adelson's wife Miriam, who is twelve years younger than him, became the publisher of *Israel Hayom* in 2018. See Yonatan Kitain, "Miriam Adelson takes reins at Israel Hayom," *Globes*, May 17, 2018, online: https://en.globes.co.il/en/article-miriam-adelson-takes-reins-at-israel-hayom-1001236852 and Christina Binkley, "Meet Dr Miriam Adelson: the record-breaking Republican donor driving Trump's Israel policy," *The Guardian*, January 7, 2019, online: https://www.theguardian.com/us-news/2019/jan/07/meet-dr-miriam-adelson-the-record-breaking-republican-donor-driving-trumps-israel-policy (all accessed July 9, 2019).

Foundations in 2003, and made his foundation's operations outright illegal in 2015. State-related Russian hackers also seem to have been behind the intrusion into the Open Society Foundations intranet, which lead to the publication of more than 2,500 internal documents in 2016. In 2017, the Hungarian government started to shut down Soros's Central European University.[11] Such instances of state control over transnational actors had already been highlighted by Samuel Huntington in an early critique of transnational politics: "The price that a transnational organization has to pay for access to national territory will thus, in part, depend on the extent to which the government controlling that territory perceives those operations as contributing to its purposes" (1973: 356). Since 2000, the number of states that have adopted more restrictive laws for foreign NGOs has risen exponentially, most likely in reaction to the growing influence of these transnational actors (Dupuy et al. 2015: 423, Rutzen 2015). The efforts of Russia and Hungary to repress Soros, while demonstrating state power, indicate at the same time that these governments perceive the billionaire as a threat. If one looks into the archive of the Kremlin's online news service *Sputnik International* (since 2014), a search for "Soros" delivered 360 results, many of them highly critical, whereas "Paul Ryan," the 54th Speaker of the U.S. House of Representatives (since 2015), received 442.[12] In terms of newsworthiness and propaganda efforts, *Sputnik International* apparently viewed the "stateless statesman" as similarly important as the chief legislator in the U.S.

The ability of billionaires to move resources across borders also depends on their home state's permission. Within the context of globalization and neoliberalism, as many states endorse free trade and free movement of capital, the opportunities for transnational transfers have increased. And it is particularly in liberal states with domestic state–society relations characterized by pluralism that we see the greatest freedom for transnationalism (Bloodgood et al. 2014), which, as Huntington (again) put it succinctly,

is the American mode of expansion. It has meant "freedom to operate".... U.S. expansion has been pluralistic expansion in which a variety of organizations,

---

[11] See Berg 2006, Ambrosio 2007, Carothers & Brechenmacher 2014, Shaun Walker, "Russia bans two Soros foundations from disbursing grants," *The Guardian*, November 30, 2015, online: https://www.theguardian.com/world/2015/nov/30/russia-bans-two-george-soros-foundations-from-giving-grants, Ben Chapman, "George Soros documents published 'by Russian hackers' say US security services," *Independent*, August 15, 2016, online: http://www.independent.co.uk/news/business/news/george-soros-emails-published-by-russian-hackers-us-security-services-dcleaks-wikileaks-a7192396.html, and Marc Santora, "George Soros-Founded University Is Forced Out of Hungary," *The New York Times*, December 3, 2018, online: https://www.nytimes.com/2018/12/03/world/europe/soros-hungary-central-european-university.html (all accessed July 3, 2019).

[12] Search executed on July 20, 2017, see online: https://sputniknews.com/search/ (search "all"); one news item concerned Ryan and Soros simultaneously. "Merkel" received 4,783 results (fifteen overlap with Soros), "Obama" 18,518 (sixty-one overlap with Soros), and the President of the European Commission (since 2014), "Juncker" received 1,089 results (three overlap with Soros).

governmental and non-governmental, have attempted to pursue the objectives important to them within the territory of other societies.   (1973: 344)

In the U.S., philanthropy forms an integral part of this pluralism (Zunz 2012, Parmar & Rietzler 2014, Reich 2018). Several critics have pointed out how the U.S. (as well as other states) are encouraging billionaires' transnational engagement by subsidizing their philanthropy through tax incentives (Birn 2014: 2, McGoey 2015: 18f, 228ff, Reich 2018: 74–89, 114–34). While some of this is true, the tax exemptions for nonprofit organizations should not be overstated: if these would not exist, in market economies, nothing prevents billionaires from pursuing their objectives via companies that are for-profit by law, yet, if loss-making, incur very little or even no taxation. Adelson's *Israel Hayom* and Murdoch's *New York Post* are both for-profit businesses that have, reportedly, always incurred high losses. It stands to reason that talented corporate tax lawyers could find ways to organize a billionaire's companies in such a way that the deficits of the "philanthropic" businesses reduce the taxable income of the profitable businesses, which would effectively replicate the tax subsidies granted to nonprofits. In fact, several billionaires, e.g. Marc Zuckerberg and Laurene Powell Jobs, have already created their philanthropic ventures as for-profit limited liability corporations (Reich 2018: 199f).[13]

Seen from this angle, as long as private enterprise is "free," the agentic power of billionaires is primarily constrained by their own choice between business (profit) and politics (power), especially if they own private companies, as the Koch brothers, Soros, and Rajaratnam do. If their source of wealth are shares in a publicly listed corporation, they need to maintain control over it, as Adelson and Murdoch have done. This allowed Adelson to authorize billions of dollars in dividend payments that could be reinvested into political projects, and Murdoch could intervene in his media empire, regarding investments and editorial lines, as he saw fit. Or, billionaires need to give up their business, as Bill Gates has done, transforming shareholder wealth into more liquid financial holdings while transitioning from global software to global health. This is even more critical if the billionaire's business, like Microsoft, is directly exposed to the mass consumer market, where concerns over brand image and loss of consumers make political

---

[13] There are other advantages—and obligations—to incorporating as a nonprofit, e.g. concerning reporting requirements. Also, tax advantages are granted to all the people that donate to the nonprofit organization. While this matters enormously for organizations like Amnesty International, which rely on many small donations from a multitude of donors, it matters much less for a billionaire who often is the only donor to "his" nonprofit organization. Corporate tax laws in many countries, such as the U.S., mainly tax corporate profits. In the U.S., billionaires could use the highly popular form of so-called "pass-through" S-corporations, which are not being taxed, since they transfer their income to their owners, who are then being taxed under the individual income tax (Looney & Krupkin 2017). In such a case, receiving income and then donating it (tax-deductible) is not much different, financially, from owning a loss-making S-corporation that never transfers income (that would then be taxed) in the first place.

exposure risky (Page et al. 2019: 20–2, 32, 41, 91). Adelson, with his main gambling markets in Asia and thus outside the U.S.–Israel–Palestine field, did not have to worry about this, nor was it a concern for the finance billionaires Soros and Rajaratnam. The Koch brothers own some mass market brands, but these are part of a conglomerate and not immediately identifiable with "the Kochs," and major segments of Koch Industries concern business-to-business transactions. A potential civil society backlash, via consumer boycotts, is therefore a negligible risk for the billionaires in my case studies.

Like other states, the U.S. still sets certain limits. A billionaire who would like to send arms to insurgent groups in another country will usually face export restrictions on sensitive equipment, and money transfers are subject to the laws against terrorist financing.[14] Thus, direct funding of the Tamil Tigers was not a legal option for Raj Rajaratnam, even if he had wanted to, because the U.S. government had designated the LTTE as a foreign terrorist organization in 1997. For several years, he could support the Tamil Rehabilitation Organization, but this was also made illegal, in 2007,[15] and Rajaratnam then stopped funding. Transactions, whether for- or nonprofit, with countries that are under a U.S. sanctions regime, such as Cuba or Iran, can be severely circumscribed or outright illegal. For both Iran and Cuba, however, certain democracy- and civil society-promoting transactions have been exempted, because they are in line with the U.S. foreign policy objective of destabilizing the ruling regimes and opening up these countries.[16] Here, the "American mode of expansion" takes on another meaning, namely that of a symbiosis between private transnationalism and a government's foreign policy (Hägel & Peretz 2005). How closely intertwined the two can be has already been shown in studies of the major Gilded Age foundations of Carnegie, Ford, and Rockefeller (Berman 1983, Parmar 2012, Parmar & Rietzler 2014). Huntington, in contrast, arguing against the idea of a neocolonial American empire, emphasized that the inherent pluralism of transnationalism would lead to "parallel and often competing transnational structures" (1973: 347). With this, we encounter a first challenge for assessing the individual agency of billionaires in world politics.

Since all of the billionaires under study are resident U.S. citizens, can we differentiate their transnational politics from U.S. foreign policy, or are they merely agents of Washington, as foreign governments sometimes insinuate?

---

[14] See the U.S. government's export control system: https://www.state.gov/bureaus-offices/under-secretary-for-arms-control-and-international-security-affairs/bureau-of-international-security-and-nonproliferation/office-of-export-control-cooperation/ and the Executive Order 13224 of September 23, 2001 on "Blocking Property and Prohibiting Transactions With Persons Who Commit, Threaten To Commit, or Support Terrorism": https://www.state.gov/executive-order-13224/ (accessed July 3, 2019).

[15] See online: https://www.state.gov/foreign-terrorist-organizations/ and https://www.treasury.gov/resource-center/terrorist-illicit-finance/Pages/protecting-charities_execorder_13224-pp.aspx#tamil (accessed July 3, 2019).

[16] See the U.S. Office of Foreign Assets Control, online: https://www.treasury.gov/resource-center/sanctions/Pages/default.aspx (accessed July 3, 2019), Hufbauer et al. 2011: 17, Katzman 2019: 31ff.

Rajaratnam's support of the Tamil cause clearly went against the aims of U.S. foreign policy, especially once the antiterrorism fight took center stage post-9/11, which is when the government made funding of the Tamil Rehabilitation Organization illegal. While Rajaratnam's agency was in many ways the most limited, Sheldon Adelson's policy vis-à-vis Israel represents the most potent example of how billionaires can play a significant role in international affairs, and not just in so-called "soft" policy areas, but in one of the "hardest" security issues, the Israel–Palestine conflict. At home, Adelson's struggle to shift U.S. foreign policy on Israel via his funding of Republican politicians had little immediate success, as Obama remained president for two terms and pushed for peace negotiations between Israel and Palestine, sticking to the established "two-state solution." But in Israel, by single-handedly putting around US$200 million of his money into the free daily newspaper Israel Hayom, which is unquestioningly and consistently supportive of Benjamin Netanyahu, Adelson provided critical support to help keep a politician in power who shares his "entrenchment-annexationism" stance with regard to Israel–Palestine. Under Obama, Adelson's transnational intervention in Israel ran counter to official U.S. foreign policy. Similarly, the Koch brothers' efforts to prevent climate change mitigation contradicted President Obama, who had wanted the U.S. to retake leadership in the global governance of climate change, especially during his second term.[17] The Kochs' sponsorship of think tanks and Republican politicians that advance a "no mitigation" agenda could not prevent Obama from signing the Paris Agreement on Climate Change in 2015, but their machinations contributed much to divide public opinion on climate change along partisan lines, thus preparing the ground for President Trump's withdrawal from the Paris Agreement in 2017.

In Murdoch's case, the clearest instance of him taking a strong foreign policy position was the 2003 Iraq invasion, when he was fully behind the government of President Bush, trying to prop up public support via hawkish agenda-setting in his news media, notably Fox News in the U.S. and The Sun in the UK, but also in Australia (McKnight & McNair 2012). This example comes closest to the notion of a symbiosis between private transnationalism and U.S. imperialism. With Soros and Gates, while there sometimes exists extensive overlap, the billionaires' political agency appears as largely independent from their government. It is true that U.S. foreign policy exhibits a long (and very checkered) history of supporting democratization and the rule of law (Magen et al. 2009), which is grosso modo consistent with Soros's ambition to create open societies. More specifically, however, Soros concentrated on fostering civil society before this became a central part of U.S. democracy promotion (Carothers 1996). Whereas Soros's insistence on

---

[17] Barack Obama, "Inaugural Address," January 21, 2013, online: https://obamawhitehouse.arch ives.gov/the-press-office/2013/01/21/inaugural-address-president-barack-obama (accessed July 2, 2019) and Obama 2017.

free and fair elections during Georgia's Rose Revolution was in alignment with the U.S., the Georgian actors funded by Soros pursued a more aggressive strategy of regime change, compared to the maneuverings of U.S. diplomacy at the time.[18] Likewise, Gates's reliance on biomedical solutions for global health and his reluctance to fund basic healthcare correspond with how the U.S. has approached global health for decades. Yet, his decision, in 1999, to donate billions and thus make global health a priority for the twenty-first century came prior to any such move by the U.S. government. As a showcase of "compassionate conservatism," President Bush's PEPFAR initiative only started in 2004. Since then, there have been closer relations between the Gates Foundation and the U.S. government, as when President Obama appointed former BMGF executive Rajiv Shah to direct USAID, and Nils Daulaire, also from the BMGF's orbit, as the U.S. representative to the WHO executive board.[19] But all of this looks more like Bill Gates shaping the U.S. agenda for global health, rather than the reverse. In sum, the results from my case studies largely validate Huntington in the full sense of his above citation: we have cases where the objectives and policies of the billionaires coincide and other cases where they conflict with official U.S. foreign policy. The examples confirm the assumption that, besides capitalism,[20] pluralism is at the heart of American politics, its system, and its culture, and that this includes transnationalism, which grants U.S. billionaires relatively high degrees of autonomy in world politics.

Acting transnationally implies another side, too, namely the foreign states or the global governance institutions where billionaires try to pursue their goals. As already shown with the example of Soros in Russia and Hungary, if a state is determined to deny foreign actors access, unless they decide to go underground, billionaires will be not be able to do much. But even if the legal framework is permissive, billionaires need to find ways to project power across borders. Picking up again on my initial discussion of agency, an important enabling condition seems to lie in the very fact that the billionaires come from abroad. Both James Rosenau and Neil Fligstein and Doug McAdam have highlighted this in their

[18] In 2004, Soros was also heavily opposing President Bush on domestic politics and the Iraq War, so it seems unlikely that he let himself be employed by the Bush administration with regard to regime change in Georgia, see Julian Borger, "Financier Soros puts millions into ousting Bush," *The Guardian*, November 12, 2003, online: https://www.theguardian.com/world/2003/nov/12/uselections2004.usa (accessed July 14, 2019) and Soros 2003.

[19] See Robert Fortner, "Malaria eradication: How the Gates Foundation sets global health policy," November 5, 2012, online: http://robertfortner.posthaven.com/malaria-eradication-how-the-gates-foundation, and Mark Landler, "Curing the Ills of America's Top Foreign Aid Agency," *The New York Times*, October 22, 2010, online: http://www.nytimes.com/2010/10/23/world/23shah.html?_r=0 (accessed July 10, 2019).

[20] It is, of course, precisely the combination of capitalism and pluralism that has produced some of the most heated discussions about the U.S. system and its democratic or elitist character (Schattschneider 1960, Dahl 1958, 1967, 1982, Manley 1983). With his notion of "civil oligarchy," Winters sees pluralism and oligarchy as compatible in the U.S. (2011: 208–54, Winters & Page 2009).

discussion of external actors who are "not so immediately bound up by the rules and requirements that collectivities demand of those who occupy roles in them" (Rosenau 1990: 119), and who "are free to bring new definitions of the situation and new forms of action to the field" (Fligstein & McAdam 2012: 99). American entrepreneurs seasoned in creative destruction and disruptive innovation appear to have the right set of experience and skills to take advantage of opportunities in established political structures.[21] And indeed, my case studies provide remarkable examples of billionaires being disruptive: Murdoch switched *The Sun* from pro-Labour to pro-Tory, and he emasculated the powerful Fleet Street unions by secretly setting up new computerized print facilities outside London. Soros imported the "electoral revolution" model and its media staging from Serbia to Georgia. Adelson circumvented Israel's very restrictive political finance laws by creating a free national newspaper, upsetting the national news market (Dahan & Bentham 2017). And Gates surprised the international global health community by suddenly committing sums that surpassed the annual contributions of almost all WHO member states.

Disruptive innovation is one mechanism. In order to be effective, billionaires also need allies abroad that can be employed to realize their goals. This concerns what has been conceptualized as brokerage mechanisms (McAdam et al. 2001: 25ff), when actors broker new relations between previously separate groups; except that billionaires represent the giving side and the intermediary actor simultaneously, at least when the intermediary is in their pocket, the pocket with the wallet. Usually, the brokerage relationship between a billionaire and his allies will be marked by a high degree of resource inequality, which tends to amplify the billionaire's power (Stovel & Shaw 2012). Power does not necessarily need to be exercised, because a billionaire may find allies who are in agreement with him. In this case, he simply has to empower them, whereas reluctant allies will need persuasion through incentives or sanctions. Whether incentives should be seen as a form of power, and whether they are coercive, is a longstanding debate. Unlike Julian Eckl in his discussion of the Gates Foundation, who categorizes all incentives as a form of coercion (Eckl 2014: 96), I follow David Baldwin's framework, who sees an initial promise of incentives, which he calls "positive sanctions," as noncoercive, but argues that once a recipient gets used to the provision of incentives, taking them away becomes a coercive form of power (1971, also 2016: 148ff). A fine example of this is Murdoch using his media's opinion-shaping power in the UK: his collaboration with Margaret Thatcher was grounded in shared interests, whereas his sway over Tony Blair, after he had

---

[21] This relates to the billionaires' business background in the archetypical "liberal market economy," the U.S., where innovation and lobbying usually happen at the firm level, rather than through inter-company collaboration, as in "coordinated market economies" (Hall & Soskice 2001, McMenamin 2013).

promoted his election, was based on the threat that his newspapers could turn against him.

We have seen previously how the fungibility of their wealth allows billionaires to follow Machiavelli's recommendation to remain flexible. The ability to shift their backing quickly from one recipient to another is also one of the main sources of the billionaires' power on foreign territory. When Soros became frustrated with President Shevardnadze's anticorruption efforts in Georgia, he started to promote his opponent Saakashvili, and put a new executive director, the strategic organizer Alexander Lomaia, at the head of his Open Society Georgia Foundation. Noticing that John Major was less accommodating in his regulation of the media than Margaret Thatcher, Murdoch switched his support to the up-and-coming Labour politician Blair. Adelson first tried to buy two established newspapers in Israel, and when this failed, he launched his own. Within the U.S., when the Koch brothers recognized the limitations of the diehard libertarian movement, they refocused on the Republican Party. Furthermore, flexibility implies that power does not necessarily have to be exercised. If recipients of a billionaire's funding know that the money can go elsewhere, they have an incentive to comply with the donor's wishes. This "law of anticipated reactions" (Friedrich 1937: 16–18, Bachrach & Baratz 1962: 952) could also be called the rule of "what would Gates do?" (or Murdoch, or Adelson, or any other generous billionaire providing short-term funding):

> Beyond the financing of the [WHO], the BMGF's influence is evident in the reaction and second-guessing of the foundation's interests and position on a number of health issues. This can be seen in leaked memos, Twitter comments of high-profile global health actors, and personal conversations around the BMGF at global health conferences and seminars that tend to be discussed off record.
> (Harman 2016: 355).

Machiavelli gave the prince another piece of advice on how to uphold conquered foreign territory: "establish settlements" (Machiavelli 1531 [2004]: 9ff). This is different from the flexible handling of allies, because it concerns institution-building. In fact, the two strategies or mechanisms are related, since billionaires will often use their organizations to act as brokers in the recruitment of allies. Their beachheads abroad can either be nominally for-profit companies, like Murdoch's and Adelson's newspapers, or nonprofit foundations or NGOs, such as Soros's Open Society Foundations network, which boasts offices in thirty-eight countries outside the U.S., or the Gates Foundation, which had offices in seven foreign countries in 2019.[22] These institutions will necessarily operate with some

---

[22] See online: https://www.opensocietyfoundations.org/who-we-are/offices-foundations and https://www.gatesfoundation.org/where-we-work (accessed July 10, 2019).

autonomy, but, as discussed in Chapter 7, since they are fully dependent on the billionaire's funding, the employees can be expected to execute their funder's objectives. Being locally present, their staff can provide the billionaire with relevant information about, as well as contacts in the country, which, over time, builds social capital in addition to the financial capital (Burt 2004). The billionaire's institutions abroad can thus help him to identify promising allies, before taking on their more mundane function as channels of influence, either via disbursing money or, in the case of news media, favorable coverage to the billionaire's allies. It is through his control of *The Sun* and *The Times* that Murdoch can influence the opinion of voters during UK elections, just as Adelson uses *Israel Hayom* to boost support for Netanyahu. Via the Open Society Georgia Foundation, Soros was able to empower the opposition movements that would defeat Shevardnadze in the 2003 election. In this case, the OSGF's social network, nurtured over the preceding decade, was more vital for coalition formation than the actual grant-making to opposition forces, which, from what is publicly known, amounted to less than US$1 million. Although working at home, but on the global public policy issue of climate change, it is also their organizations—the party-like advocacy group Americans for Prosperity and libertarian think tanks such as the Mercatus Center and the Cato Institute—that provide the Koch brothers with the capacity to engage allies, to shape public opinion and the policy stances of the Republican Party. In many ways, the role of the billionaires' institutions resembles what IR scholars have identified as "orchestration" in global governance: "[International organizations] engage in orchestration when they enlist intermediary actors on a voluntary basis, by providing them with ideational and material support, to address target actors in pursuit of [the international organization's] governance goals" (Abbott et al. 2015: 3). If one replaces "international organization" with "Soros/Open Society Foundations," or "Murdoch/News Corp," or "Koch brothers/Americans for Prosperity," the definition fits. It is even more appropriate for the Gates Foundation. Whereas the organizations of all the other billionaires remain primarily transnational in the sense that they allow their proprietors to project power across borders, Gates's foundation is also giving him access to global governance.

The Gates Foundation is arguably the most powerful institution built by a billionaire in recent times, equal only to its precursor, the Rockefeller Foundation (Youde 2013, Eckl 2014, Brin 2014). And while all the other billionaires mainly try to influence the actors that hold public authority, the BMGF has been granted authority, the right to participate in the making of rules that govern global health. Gates Foundation representatives have sat on the boards of several public–private partnerships, such as GAVI, which decide about the development and the distribution of vaccines against communicable diseases. Gates and his wife have also been invited three times to address the World Health Assembly, and it was apparently the billionaire who set the agenda for the WHO to implement a "decade of vaccines" in 2012. Bill Gates's "right to rule" is a case of what Jessica Green has called "delegated" authority, as distinct from "entrepreneurial" authority, which appears when private actors establish their own rules in the absence of state regulations (Green 2014: 10–14, 33–6). It is delegated, because the Gates Foundation could not participate in global governance without the explicit approval of the WHO and its member states. In 2017, this relationship has been formalized further, as the BMGF entered into "official relations" with the WHO; a year before, the WHO had adopted a new policy on how to deal with nonstate actors.[23] At the same time, this delegation has been spurred by all the capacities that the BMGF has acquired, entrepreneurially, on its own, and which it is offering to the governance of global health. When Bill Gates makes his donations dependent on "matching grants" by governments, he can effectively restructure state budgets according to his own priorities. Again, this has much to do with the enormous financial resources that the Gates Foundation commands. But the BMGF's expenditure on health research generates another source of authority, too. The BMGF-sponsored Institute for Health Metrics and Evaluation (IHME), for example, has become the top source for global health data, officially partnering with the WHO in 2015.[24] Strikingly, in 2019, the WHO's "Global Health Observatory" only had data on the global health expenditure of its member states up to 2010, whereas the IHME's data included 2018. Over the years, working daily with renowned experts in the context of his foundation and its programs, Bill Gates has accumulated technical expertise in the global health field, and he is regularly being interviewed and publishes op-eds on global health policy in some of the world's most respected media.[25] With such authority comes the question of legitimacy, which will be addressed in the following section of this chapter.

Before, one might like to know exactly how much power billionaires have in world politics. Even within the narrow confines of the six billionaires studied here,

---

[23] See Catherine Saez, "Gates Foundation, KEI Enter Into Official Relations With WHO," *Intellectual Property Watch*, January 31, 2017, online: http://www.ip-watch.org/2017/01/31/gates-foundation-kei-enter-official-relations/, and Natalie Huet and Carmen Paun, "Meet the world's most powerful doctor: Bill Gates," *Politico*, May 4, 2017, online: https://www.politico.eu/article/bill-gates-who-most-powerful-doctor/ (accessed July 5, 2019).

[24] Compare online: http://apps.who.int/gho/data/node.main.A1628?lang=en and https://vizhub.healthdata.org/fgh/ (accessed July 5, 2019). During the early 1990s, in what looks like a typical example of the potential dysfunctions within international organizations, "the sum of deaths claimed by different WHO programmes exceeded the total number of deaths in the world several times" (Murray et al. 2004: 1098, also Barnett & Finnemore 1999: 715ff).

[25] See, for example, Bill Gates, "How to Fight the Next Epidemic," *The New York Times*, March 18, 2015, online: https://www.nytimes.com/2015/03/18/opinion/bill-gates-the-ebola-crisis-was-terrible-but-next-time-could-be-much-worse.html, Gates 2015, 2018. Some of this authority-through-expertise also applies to Soros. Data and reports established by Soros-sponsored organizations such as Human Rights Watch are being treated as authoritative sources by many scholars and international practitioners, and Soros's viewpoints are being published at least as prominently as Gates's (e.g.: George Soros, "Aufgewacht, Europa!," *Frankfurter Allgemeine Zeitung*, October 23, 2014, online: http://www.faz.net/aktuell/politik/ausland/europa/ukraine-krise-aufgewacht-europa-13223706.html, all accessed July 5, 2019). However, Soros has never been granted a public rule-making role.

and looking only at some of the most prominent episodes in which they have tried to exercise power, a precise answer is often impossible. An initial difficulty consists in the fact that some of the billionaires' agency is, hubristic as it may seem, geared towards structural changes. The Koch brothers have promoted economic freedom for decades, just as Soros has funded hundreds if not thousands of human rights groups across the world in order to build open societies. One may try to validate via quantitative analyses whether libertarian values are increasing over time, or whether human rights are becoming more respected. But the usually gradual and incremental nature of structural changes makes it hard to isolate individual contributions, since it is not only the Koch brothers or Soros that are involved in such processes; there are many independent and interdependent variables.[26] The chances to identify a billionaire's power are greater if they try to provoke structural changes during episodes of critical junctures, such as Georgia's Rose Revolution. Still, power analysis remains complicated.

This is, firstly, due to the fact that, as a concept, power is dispositional and relational, and it involves intentions on both sides of the power equation, the billionaire pursuing his goals and the other actor(s) he is trying to influence. The analytical line between collective agency (when a billionaire acts in agreement with someone) and power (when he imposes his will) is thin. The WHO had started to embrace the private sector and the eradication of infectious diseases before Bill Gates arrived with his biomedical focus on vaccines and public–private partnerships, hence it is hard to judge where harmony ends and power begins. Secondly, billionaires often project their power indirectly, by empowering political allies, who may then—or: therefore—win against competitors. The difficult question is about the "therefore": since the allies are not puppets, they also exercise agency and power on their own. Tony Blair had already become very popular without *The Sun*'s endorsements in 1997—so what was Murdoch's contribution to Blair's triumph over Major? This brings us, thirdly, to the fact that politics takes place in a crowded arena, in which many actors pursue goals, which can contradict each other or intersect, and hence multiple causation is normal. Claiming that George Soros is not very powerful, since "[d]espite his gargantuan efforts, 'open society'...is in worldwide decline" (Porter 2015: 201), neglects the complex array of forces that promote and prevent open societies in different nations. These problems of power analysis are not unique to billionaires (Baldwin, D. 2016: 49–90). They are arguably even more pronounced in the study of collective actors such as states, where power struggles already afflict the very constitution of collective agency. While, through its military aid to Israel, the U.S. holds a

---

[26] Bill Gates's attempts to eradicate infectious diseases such as polio or malaria can also be seen as aiming at structural change; measurement in these cases is facilitated by the fact that the ultimate targets are nonhuman organisms.

power resource that is greater than what billionaires can put forward,[27] how much power does "the U.S." really have vis-à-vis Israel? Most observers agree that, under President Obama, not much, with one reason being that "America's dysfunctional political culture has imposed severe constraints on Obama's ability to pursue an even-handed approach towards the... Palestine question" (Gerges 2013: 299, also Allin & Jones 2012: 86ff). Sheldon Adelson was, of course, a significant actor in this domestic politics jam that restrained Obama's foreign policy.

In view of all these complexities, one necessary and fruitful, yet always contestable way of assessing power is counterfactual reasoning (Baldwin, D. 2016: 57, Tetlock & Belkin 1996). It is also at the center of the agency question—did (s)he make a difference? In Raj Rajaratnam's case, probably not. Had the Tamil Tigers had access to the largest sums of money a man of Rajaratnam's wealth could provide, multiplying their annual revenues, the final battle of the LTTE may have turned out differently.[28] But from what we know, his US$10 million donations to the Tamil Rehabilitation Organization amounted to little more than paying the "diaspora tax." With regard to the billionaires that have tried to shape public opinion, counterfactuals indicate significant power. Had Sheldon Adelson not launched *Israel Hayom*, or if the newspaper had promoted the Labor or Kadima parties, rather than Netanyahu, the Israeli political landscape would almost certainly look different. This is not to say that Adelson was responsible for the rightward shift in Israel, which had been ongoing for at least a decade before 2007. But in a political system characterized by relatively high electoral volatility, frequent entry of new parties and complicated coalition formation (Martin 2013: 77–95), having the most read national newspaper staunchly behind you does increase your power. The same logic applies to *The Sun* and Murdoch in the UK, except that additional power derives from the billionaire's flexible handling of who he supports. For the 1992 (against Labour), 1997 and 2005 (pro-Labour) elections, research has shown substantial media persuasion effects for *The Sun*'s endorsements (Ladd & Lenz 2009, Brandenburg & van Egmond 2011, Reeves et al. 2016). If Murdoch's news media would have assumed a more neutral position, election results would not have been the same and politicians like Blair would not have felt the need to accommodate Murdoch's demands.[29] Importantly, there are

---

[27] In 2016, Israel and the U.S. signed a new military aid package worth US$38 billion over a decade. See Emma Green, "Why Does the United States Give So Much Money to Israel?," *The Atlantic*, September 15, 2016, online: https://www.theatlantic.com/international/archive/2016/09/united-states-israel-memorandum-of-understanding-military-aid/500192/ (accessed July 2, 2019).

[28] Even then, this would most likely have been insufficient to counter the massive military aid that China provided to Sri Lanka's government since 2007, see Peter Popham, "How Beijing won Sri Lanka's civil war," *Independent*, May 22, 2010, online: http://www.independent.co.uk/news/world/asia/how-beijing-won-sri-lankas-civil-war-1980492.html (accessed July 2, 2019).

[29] Regarding the Iraq War, the counterfactual assessment is more ambivalent. Since public opinion was already opposed to the UK joining the U.S. invasion, it would have made it much more difficult for Blair if the Murdoch press had vocally condemned the invasion, instead of lending it its full support. However, the findings of the "Chilcot" Iraq Inquiry suggest that, early on, Blair had decided "no matter

no indications of a likely alternative actor that could have done the same as Adelson or Murdoch in the hypothetical absence of the two billionaires. This argument applies less to the Koch brothers, which makes it harder to judge their power in blocking climate change mitigation. The available evidence portrays them, especially via their control of Americans for Prosperity, as the spider in the web of climate change skeptics. Yet, other powerful corporate interests within the U.S. oil, gas, and coal industries would possibly have stepped up their own efforts in the absence of the Koch brothers. Unlike publicly listed companies, however, which, like ExxonMobil,[30] are more exposed to diverse shareholder concerns, the private status of Koch Industries has given Charles and David a greater capacity to engage in politics. Nobody had orchestrated an almost-party as professional as Americans for Prosperity before, and hence it makes sense to qualify them as the leaders of the "no mitigation" coalition, which has so far been winning in the struggle over climate change policy in the U.S. In the case of Soros and Georgia, Shevardnadze's days as president were probably counted independently of Soros's actions. But, in 2002, many observers expected a more gradual power shift with varying scenarios of compromise arrangements between the incumbent and the opposition parties. Without the revolution-staging coordinated by the OSGF, it is unlikely that the 2003 election would have turned into the critical juncture that came to be known as the Rose Revolution. Finally, most pundits agree that Bill Gates's philanthropy marked a turning point in global health (Cohen 2006: 163). Absent his massive injection of funding for vaccination programs and research, it would probably have taken longer for developed states to increase their own contributions. And without his agenda-setting, it is unlikely that there would have been a "Decade of Vaccines."

Overall, several of my cases show that billionaires can indeed be individuals that "carry out independent actions in the global arena that may be consequential for the course of events," as James Rosenau once defined "private actors" in world politics (Rosenau 1990: 118). The above counterfactual reasoning is no hard proof of billionaires' power in world politics. Still, at the very least, it shows that individuals equipped with enormous resources and strong self-efficacy beliefs can intervene decisively in world politics, transnationally, or, less frequently, at the global level. Through disruptive innovation, alliances, brokerage, and institution-building, they can act as orchestrators (or even as conductors), employing, usually with a paycheck, other actors to pursue their goals. Counterfactual thought experiments involve the imagination of alternatives, and

what" to join the U.S., see online: https://webarchive.nationalarchives.gov.uk/20171123123237tf_/ http://www.iraqinquiry.org.uk/ (accessed July 10, 2019).

[30] Diane Cardwell, "Exxon Mobil Shareholders Demand Accounting of Climate Change Policy Risks," *The New York Times*, May 31, 2017, online: https://www.nytimes.com/2017/05/31/business/energy-environment/exxon-shareholders-climate-change.html (accessed July 10, 2019).

hence they also include normative choices (Roese 1997). This will be my final focus.

Global Oligarchy and Democracy

[T]he billionaires club...now constitutes an increasingly powerful plutocracy both within countries and...upon the world stage.   (Harvey 2014: xi)

[P]owerful states pose the most serious threat to accountability in world politics.
(Keohane 2003: 153)

The assessments cited above illustrate the intricacies of power at the global level: the neo-Marxist emphasizes the rule of capital, while the liberal IR scholar points to the rule of force. In the typologies set up by Max Weber, which continue to shape much thinking about power and authority in IR (Weber 1978: 58, 212ff, Hurd 1999, 2007, Bernstein 2011), coercion and economic incentives are, of course, the forms of power that do not rely on legitimacy. As the preceding chapters have shown, much of the power of billionaires is indeed based on their control over financial resources: they can empower other actors whose goals they share, or they can make others defer to their goals by offering monetary induce-ments, appealing to their economic self-interest. Like gunboat diplomacy, such actions are not linked to a recognized right to rule. Does this mean that billionaires are illegitimate actors? And how do their behavior and its consequences fit into the current frameworks of political order? When trying to evaluate the normative implications of billionaires in world politics, the fundamental characteristics of world politics require us to differentiate between the national and the global level. On the one hand, we have the principle of sovereignty, which situates political order within territorial units with a claim to self-determination (Jackson 2007). On the other hand, we have global governance, where rules for relations between states and for the establishment of global public goods are being made. Whereas liberal political theory has furnished a relatively coherent (though far from tension-free) normative framework for politics within states, at the global level, the quest for legitimate order is more complicated (Beitz 1999, Held 1995, Zürn 2018).[31]

On the face of it, billionaires that intervene transnationally in the politics of other states are violating national self-determination. Within states, a polity's understanding of legitimate political action is, first and foremost, enshrined in

---

[31] In the social sciences, the discussion of legitimacy involves both normative inquiry (examining whether a claim to rule can be established on the basis of a normative framework) and social investigation (examining whether those subject to rules accept the rule-makers); I will address both aspects, using liberalism as the normative framework.

its constitution, which defines citizenship with its rights and obligations. Usually, some of the most significant political rights, such as voting, are exclusively reserved for citizens, expressing a nationally bounded understanding of self-determination (Rawls 1971, 1999, Song 2012). To some unmeasurable extent, ethnonational solidarity may be at work when Sheldon Adelson intervenes, as a Jewish U.S. citizen, in Israel. Likewise, Murdoch's domination of the Australian newspaper market seems to be tolerated, to some degree, because he is "home-grown," and if Murdoch would have been German rather than an Oxford-educated native of the Commonwealth, resistance against his electioneering in the UK would probably have been much fiercer. While such identity-based forms of transnational legitimacy should not be ignored, the political economy of rights appears as more important for billionaires. With regard to other civil and political rights besides voting, for example freedom of assembly or speech, as well as economic rights, the liberal principle of nondiscrimination is supposed to apply (with exceptions), and states differ in their in- or exclusion of noncitizens. Much of this corresponds with Kant's outline of *Perpetual Peace*, in which he links a cosmopolitan hospitality vis-à-vis strangers with the "commercial spirit"; in international law, this has become codified within the International Covenant on Civil and Political Rights (ICCPR).[32] The political agency of several billionaires that I have analyzed is situated exactly in the gray zones where civil and economic rights granted to noncitizens clash with the democratic process that is supposed to be the exclusive affair of the national demos. Thus, by law, Murdoch could only set up *Fox News* once he had become a U.S. citizen, and it would be illegal for Adelson to own TV channels in Israel.[33] But both Murdoch in the UK (*The Sun, The Times*) and Adelson in Israel (*Israel Hayom*) are rightful foreign owners of major newspapers, which have expressed partisan political speech that has had signifi-cant effects on public opinion and electoral outcomes. In setting up his Open Society Foundations across the world, George Soros has also benefited from the

---

[32] See Kant 1970 [1795], also Doyle 1986. Within the ICCPR, art. 25 allows for discrimination between citizens and noncitizens by claiming rights to participation in public affairs and access to public service only for citizens. When it comes to freedom of expression and assembly (art. 19, 21, 22), restrictions on the grounds of national security, public order, public health, or morals are allowed vis-à-vis noncitizens. Equality before the law (art. 14–17, 26) is supposed to be discriminating between citizens and noncitizens. See the ICCPR online: http://www.ohchr.org/EN/ProfessionalInterest/Pages/ CCPR.aspx. Regarding investment and trade, treating nationals and foreigners equally is an obligation in all major international treaties, but exceptions, especially on the grounds of national security, are usually granted; for the WTO, see online: https://www.wto.org/english/thewto_e/whatis_e/tif_e/fact2_ e.htm (accessed July 6, 2019).
[33] For a comparative overview of national regulations among OECD member states, see "National treatment for foreign-controlled enterprises in telecommunications," OECD, 2013, online: http://www. oecd.org/sti/broadband/2–5.pdf. In 2017, the U.S. allowed full foreign ownership of broadcasting stations for the first time, see David Oxenford, "FCC Approves for the First Time 100% Foreign Ownership of US Broadcast Stations," *Broadcast Law Blog*, February 24, 2017, online: http://www. broadcastlawblog.com/2017/02/articles/fcc-approves-for-the-first-time-100-foreign-ownership-of-us-broadcast-stations/ (both accessed July 6, 2019).

application of the nondiscrimination principle that grants rights of assembly and speech to foreigners.

Seen from this angle, the political agency of these billionaires appears as legitimate not just in a legalistic sense, but also in terms of liberalism, or at least one side of it—the one that Isaiah Berlin has called negative liberty (Berlin 1969), which is at the heart of the libertarian agenda advocated by the Koch brothers. As argued before in Chapter 3, the rise of neoliberalism has been closely associated with expanding individual freedom, especially in the economic sphere. In this context, the challenge of billionaires for liberal democracy turns out to be very similar at the national and the transnational level: more economic freedom tends to lead to greater income and wealth inequality, at least at the top (Okun 1975, Kwon 2016),[34] and, via liberalization and privatization, it also opens new opportunities to acquire resources that may be used in politics. As Adam Smith noticed long ago, wealth per se confers to its owner only the power of purchasing—in order to transform it into political power, there needs to be a market for goods and services, such as media or lobbying, which can be bought in order to shape public opinion or public policy (Goss 2016). The liberalization of political speech in the U.S., with the Supreme Court's 2010 decisions in Citizens United v. FEC and speechNOW.org v. FEC, is the best example of this logic.[35] Because media ownership already gives some individuals unequal voice, the Supreme Court majority argued, freedom of speech should no longer be restricted by limiting the amount of money that corporations and individuals can put into political speech. Since then, the Koch brothers and other billionaires are free to spend as much as they want on private political campaigns, e.g. to block climate change mitigation, as long as they remain technically detached from official candidates. Through the corporate form, this also opens the door for foreigners to engage in political campaigns in the U.S., which is a consequence of Citizens United that has been noted, but remains unresolved so far within the Federal Election Commission, because benchmarks for what constitutes foreign control over a corporation's political speech are hard to establish objectively.[36]

---

[34] Comparative statistical analysis of the relationship between economic freedom and inequality is difficult and inconclusive so far, because the causal relationship may work both ways, and the analysis is very sensitive to measurement and sample selection, see Bennett & Nikolaev 2017 for a review of the empirical debate (which has been largely shaped by economists with a pro–free market stance).

[35] Several billionaires, notably Betsy DeVos, who became Secretary of Education in the Trump administration in 2017, have heavily sponsored the movement that mounted the legal challenges leading to the Supreme Court decisions (Mayer 2016: 226–39).

[36] Jon Schwarz & Lee Fang, "Cracks in the Dam: Three Paths Citizens United Created for Foreign Money to Pour into U.S. Elections," The Intercept, August 3, 2016, online: https://theintercept.com/2016/08/03/citizens-united-foreign-money-us-elections/ and Karl Evers-Hillstrom and Raymond Arke, "Following Citizens United, foreign-owned corporations funnel millions into US elections," opensecrets.org, March 22, 2019, online: https://www.opensecrets.org/news/2019/03/citizens-united-foreign-owned-corporations-put-millions-in-us-elections/ (accessed July 6, 2019).

Some may say that, in the digital age, media consumption and public opinion formation become ever more complex, so that billionaires controlling individual newspapers or TV channels lose influence. This is doubtful. As electioneering and opinion-shaping depend more and more on privately owned data, software, and professional services, the potential for transnational interventions may actually increase, as illustrated by the controversy over the role of U.S. billionaire Robert Mercer in the UK's Brexit referendum. Mercer was the majority owner of Cambridge Analytica, a now-defunct company that possessed extensive data about voters gained from their activities online (mainly on *Facebook*), which could be used to micro-target people on Facebook with political messages that fit their individual "psychographic" profiles. According to Carole Cadwalladr, Mercer "directed his data analytics firm to provide expert advice to the Leave campaign on how to target swing voters via Facebook."[37] Whether a service provided across borders counts as a legal transaction under the WTO's trade regime, whether it has been provided at no cost, or at a politically motivated discount is difficult to judge for a regulator, because it all takes place within the realm subject to the norm of "economic freedom."

What all of this boils down to is a situation in which the principle of negative liberty and the reality of economic inequality together undermine the chief value of liberal democracy, political equality (Erman & Näsström 2013, Hall 2013, Merkel 2014). The more political participation depends on control over unequally distributed financial resources, the less individuals are politically equal, and the more a polity shifts from democracy to plutocracy (Winters 2011). Aiming for equal political opportunity and collective self-determination are the domain of Berlin's positive liberty, and the proper balance between the two types of freedom is very much contested (Cohen 1995, Sen 1999). The Citizens United decision in the U.S. was reached with a narrow 5–4 majority, and the minority voiced strong disagreement, arguing that "[t]he Court's ruling threatens to undermine the integrity of elected institutions across the Nation."[38] Within Israel, three legislative attempts were made to limit Adelson's influence on public opinion via his *Isarel Hayom* newspaper. In the UK, restrictions on Rupert Murdoch's media holdings were also being contemplated. In both cases, the politicians benefiting from the

---

[37] Carole Cadwalladr, "Revealed: How US billionaire helped to back Brexit," *The Observer*, February 26, 2017, online: https://www.theguardian.com/politics/2017/feb/26/us-billionaire-mercer-helped-back-brexit. See also Carole Cadwalladr, "The great British Brexit robbery: how our democracy was hijacked," *The Observer*, May 7, 2017," online: https://www.theguardian.com/technology/2017/may/07/the-great-british-brexit-robbery-hijacked-democracy?CMP=Share_iOSApp_Other and Jane Mayer, "The reclusive hedge-fund tycoon behind the Trump presidency," *The New Yorker*, March 27, 2017, online: http://www.newyorker.com/magazine/2017/03/27/the-reclusive-hedge-fund-tycoon-behind-the-trump-presidency for Mercer's role in Trump's electoral campaign (all accessed July 6, 2019).

[38] Citizens United v. Federal Election Commission 558 U.S. 310, 396 (2010), online: https://www.supremecourt.gov/opinions/boundvolumes/558bv.pdf (accessed July 6, 2019).

billionaires' political speech—Netanyahu, Thatcher, and Blair—made sure that no restrictions were put in place. In an intriguing extension of John Rawls's *Theory of Justice*, Jeffrey Green has argued that liberal theory should pay as much attention to "the most advantaged" as Rawls did with regard to the least favored:

> liberal societies... have justification to single out and regulate the superrich... as a means of counteracting excessive inequalities that undermine basic liberties (especially those pertaining to... political opportunity), and as redress for the fact that even the most well-ordered liberal societies cannot fully realize liberal norms of free and equal citizenship.   (2013: 125)

Exactly how this could work in practice requires a lot of regulatory creativity, notably in the areas of political finance, political speech, and media law. More fundamentally, it may demand a rethinking of rights, because, at the moment, the mechanisms through which billionaires can affect politics outside (and inside) their home state grow out of, and are protected by, the "negative liberty" laws that have been advanced during decades of neoliberal rule-making. If one wants to guarantee a certain amount of political equality within national democracies, some economic and civil rights of billionaires would need to be curtailed in such a way that they cannot transform their control over relevant resources into outsized political power. As discussed in the previous two sections of this chapter, this has already happened in many states. Unfortunately (for liberal democrats), it is openly anti-liberal rulers, such as Putin in Russia or Orbán in Hungary, who are at the forefront of reclaiming national (more than democratic) self-determination (Dupuy et al. 2015: 422), sometimes with xenophobic undertones. These authoritarian precedents should not detract from efforts aimed at strengthening political equality.

In world politics, questions of legitimacy and accountability are thornier, precisely because thinking about these issues has evolved in bounded polities, be it the city-state of the Ancients or the nation-state of the Moderns. At the global level, the links between the people and the rulers are less clear, since, globalization and cosmopolitanism notwithstanding, few people see themselves primarily as citizens of the world, and, the UN notwithstanding, there is no world government. Instead, global governance comprises an increasingly complex array of actors, institutions, and processes (Avant et al. 2010, Tallberg et al. 2013, Zürn 2018). Within this, the consensus principle, especially at the UN and the WTO, guides the making of international law, which implies a territorial understanding of political equality between sovereign states. Yet, as John Locke argued in Chapter 8 of his *Second Treatise of Civil Government*, consensus is often impractical in large groups. A global demos that would accept Locke's solution, the "consent of the majority," does not exist so far. While there may be ways of finding compromises between territorial sovereignty and representation of the people

(Valentini 2014), the current reality is different: key decision-making power is reserved for a small oligarchy of states, institutionalized with the veto right of the five permanent members of the UN Security Council, and via share-weighted voting inside the World Bank and the IMF, which gives the U.S. substantial veto power. Given the democratic shortcomings of state-based world politics, scholars are looking at the democratizing potential of transnational actors in global governance. This debate revolves around the question whether transnational actors (especially NGOs), even though their participation does not create a democratic global system, at least promote democratic principles, such as repre-sentation, deliberation, and accountability, in global governance (Buchanan & Keohane 2006, Bexell et al. 2010, Erman & Uhlin 2010, Erman & Nasstrom 2013).

The billionaires that I have studied simply have no democratic legitimacy,[39] as exposed in their own understanding of their political agency. The first guiding principle for the Gates Foundation was that "[t]his is a family foundation driven by the interests and passions of the Gates family," and the foundation has only three trustees: Bill and Melinda Gates, and Warren Buffett. A confidential 2015 memo from the Open Society Foundations about "[a] short and medium-term comprehensive strategy for the new Ukraine" was signed "George Soros[, a] self-appointed advocate of the new Ukraine."[40] While individual power runs counter to norms of collective self-determination, other—nondemocratic—forms of legit-imacy may be at work with billionaires. The obvious alternative within the Weberian framework is charisma, and it has recently been employed to discuss the legitimacy of the Gates Foundation, emphasizing Bill Gates's personal cre-dentials as a successful innovator and entrepreneur (Harman 2016: 357ff). However, there seems to be a specific social context that allows the individual characteristics of billionaires to be recognized as constituting charismatic legitim-acy, which brings us back to how billionaires can be seen as the prophets of the neoliberal Zeitgeist. In this sense, their mastery experiences in business not only equip them with political agency in terms of resources and self-efficacy beliefs, but also turn them into idols of neoliberal normativity. Within domestic politics, such

---

[39] Even if one tries to adapt the principles of democratic legitimacy to the complexities of global governance, by focusing on an "equal say principle" that grants those subjected to authority some form of participation in rule-making (Erman 2018), the operations of the Gates Foundation, which are very hierarchical, do not comply with this principle. Soros grants more autonomy to the various national foundations in his network, and the leadership boards of Soros's Open Society Foundations network, with George Soros as chair of the Global Board, represent a greater diversity of people than the board of the Gates Foundation (online: https://www.opensocietyfoundations.org/who-we-are/boards). However, Soros is the chairman and director of the Foundation to Promote Open Society, which acts as the financial backbone of Soros's network (online: https://projects.propublica.org/nonprofits/download-filing?path=2009_12_PF%2F26-3753801_990PF_200812.pdf) (all accessed July 9, 2019).

[40] See online: https://web.archive.org/web/20160831075343/http://soros.dcleaks.com/download/?f=/IRF%20documents/Ukraine%20March%20non%20paper%20%202015%20v14.pdf&t=europe (accessed July 9, 2019).

a logic has accompanied the rise of Silvio Berlusconi in Italy and Donald Trump in the U.S., who both appealed to voters on the basis of their entrepreneurial achievements.[41] At the international level, Soros also has benefited from his reputation as a "master of the universe": in 1988, he was still being laughed at by international officials; after 1992, once known as "the man who broke the bank of England," he had no more problems getting appointments with global leaders (Soros 2011: 21, 26). Likewise, when entering global health, in his public speeches, Bill Gates has often emphasized how his Microsoft experience helps him to address global challenges, and this legacy is part of the reason, besides his donations, why global health policymakers listen to him. He embodies the promise of bringing the virtues of entrepreneurship to an international arena that, in the eyes of many, has suffered from the stalemates of international bureaucracy and consensus-building in the past.

For people not steeped in political theory, another criteria is probably essential for assessing whether billionaires can assume a right to participate in world politics: how much good do they do? In fact, this metric has also entered normative thinking about global governance, with notions such as "comparative benefit" (Buchanan & Keohane 2006: 422), "pragmatic legitimacy" (Koppell 2010: 49f), and, most commonly, "output legitimacy," which is actually something of a misnomer. Since it refers to how those subject to power evaluate the results, an instrumental logic is at work, which is very similar to the *ex-ante* calculation of benefits, except that it works in retrospect: one accepts the ruler, because (s)he has delivered what one had hoped for. Deference is thus not based on recognized rightfulness, but on performance.[42] Empirical survey research indicates that, at least with regard to the UN, such a rationality of expected utility often animates people's support of global governance institutions (Ecker-Ehrhardt 2012, 2016, Dellmuth & Tallberg 2015). Although we have no surveys of how people evaluate Gates or Soros in terms of performance, they may garner quite a lot of support, if only because, in terms of "comparative benefit," states have been shown to be often narrowly self-interested (Lall 2017). If one looks at IMF loan-making, for example, countries that are allies of the IMF's major shareholder, the U.S., systematically receive fewer conditions on their loans (Dreher & Jensen 2007). In development aid, many studies demonstrate that the majority of official development aid, in its quantity and its direction, is not determined by objective need. Instead, historical legacies (colonialism), geopolitical considerations, and

---

[41] For Berlusconi, see Stille 2006: 138ff, 163ff, for Trump, see the survey results in Greenberg Quinlan Rosner 2016: 25 and Hart Research Associates/Public Opinion Strategies 2016: 19.

[42] Seymour Martin Lipset was one of the first to make a systematic link between a regime's legitimacy and its output, but he kept his terminology coherent and called the latter "effectiveness" (1959: 86–98); Fritz Scharpf is usually cited as introducing the—conceptually misleading—input/output "legitimacy" dichotomy, especially in the context of supranational EU governance (1970, 1999, also Schmidt 2013).

commercial interests appear to shape the aid allocation of many donor govern-ments.[43] In contrast, an analysis of private development aid has revealed that it does follow a logic of objective need (Büthe et al. 2012).[44] Soros and Gates may be accused of many things, such as angling for a Nobel Peace Prize, but the suspicion of material self-interest seems weak in the case of philanthropists that give away most of their wealth. Accordingly, both of them justify their actions in terms of output performance. "We pride ourselves...as being a selfless foundation...; I aspire to make the world a better place," Soros has said about his philanthropy (2011: 37f). In the first "Annual Letter" to the world, Gates wrote that "[a] key question for Melinda and me is, Where are foundations uniquely suited to causing positive change?...Foundations are unusual because they don't have to worry about being voted out at the next election or board meeting."[45] The 2017 annual letter, addressed to Warren Buffett, demonstrated with lots of statistical evidence about "lives saved" and other accomplishments that the donations to the BMGF were his "best investment."[46]

Evidently, output justifications of power depend on criteria of what counts as "good performance," which directly leads to questions of accountability and politicization (Koppell 2010: 34–41, Zürn et al. 2012, Erman 2018). In general, accountability involves three stages: one in which information about performance is presented, which is then evaluated (oversight), which results in responses (control), including the possibility of sanctions (Buchanan & Keohane 2006: 426, Schillemans 2013: 13f). Regarding the information phase, the key value is transparency.[47] Most of the billionaires studied here already come short on this criteria. Many of them seem to prefer acting without public exposure, which has been aptly called "stealth politics" (Page et al. 2019). Without investigative jour-nalism and disclosure via legal proceedings, we would know much less about how the Koch brothers influence climate change mitigation, or how Sheldon Adelson supports Netanyahu. While many of George Soros's activities are nowadays publicized via his own publications and those of his foundations, before 2000, information was scarce, and even today, his political strategies and funding channels are not always transparent. This is probably one of the reasons why Soros stimulates as many conspiracy theories among conservatives as the Koch

---

[43] See Alesina & Dollar 2000, Collier & Dollar 2002, Kuziemko & Werker 2006, and Büthe et al. 2012: 574f, Fuchs et al. 2014, and Bush 2015: 24ff for literature reviews.

[44] This does not imply that all NGOs operate only with having the objective needs of the world's most marginalized people in mind. For human rights advocacy groups, for example, it has been shown that their focus is biased by the expectations of their Western audiences and donors (Ron et al. 2005, also Cooley & Ron 2002, Murdie 2014).

[45] Bill Gates, "Annual Letter 2009," online: http://www.gatesfoundation.org/Who-We-Are/Resources-and-Media/Annual-Letters-List/Annual-Letter-2009 (accessed July 9, 2019).

[46] Bill and Melinda Gates, "Warren Buffett's Best Investment," February 14, 2017, online: https://www.gatesnotes.com/2017-Annual-Letter (accessed July 9, 2019).

[47] Transparency is not the master value that can act as a substitute for accountability, but it is a prerequisite. See Fox 2007, Etzioni 2010, Hansen et al. 2015.

brothers do among progressives. In this respect, Bill Gates stands out. After earlier critiques of the Gates Foundation's opaqueness (McCoy et al. 2009, Birn 2014), his foundation was one of the first organizations to join the newly created International Aid Transparency Initiative in 2013, and it now has a policy of transparency about its goals, its investments, and its grant-making. Whereas the Gates Foundation is still less transparent than many international organizations, it has improved significantly between 2013 and 2018.[48] It is also at the forefront of scientific outcome assessment, evaluating the results of most of its grant-making: "[w]e must set big goals and *hold ourselves accountable* every step of the way" [emphasis added], the CEO, Sue Desmond-Hellman, is being cited on the foundation's website.[49] Since Gates, via his foundation, is the billionaire who has been granted the most official rule-making power, in the governance of global health, with his agenda-setting at the WHO and board-level participation in various public–private partnerships, high levels of transparency and performance evaluation seem only appropriate as a minimum standard of accountability. Maximum public transparency about who is funding whom, at least once donations reach a certain threshold, is a minimal first step on the way to greater accountability of transnational actors, especially billionaires.

When it comes to the involvement of those affected by the billionaires' actions, accountability remains weak. Often, the discussion of accountability is based on principal–agent relationships and the logic of delegation, where those who act depend on those who have empowered them (Schillemans 2013, Gent et al. 2015). Billionaires, however, gain their power primarily by using their own money. Thus, as Bill Gates noted, billionaires can't be voted out of "office," and they can't be defunded. The main option available to those who question the impact of billionaires is to refuse their funding, which is what Sophie Harman seems to have in mind when she claims, in her evaluation of the Gates Foundation's legitimacy, that "[t]hose who accept the foundation's money are tacitly consenting to its role in the production of knowledge, policy and projects for global health" (2016: 362). This is not a very strong form of accountability, since it relies on decentralized individual decisions, and, in a world where funds are scarce, billionaires can always look elsewhere for acceptance. If one wants to increase the accountability of billionaires in terms of external oversight and control, one would need to create requirements for the participation of stakeholders or independent experts in the funding decisions of billionaires and their organizations (Birn 2014: 19, McGoey

---

[48] See the Aid Transparency Index, where the Gates Foundation ranked "very poor" in 2013 and "fair" (ranked thirty-first among forty-five international aid organizations evaluated) in 2018, see online: http://www.publishwhatyoufund.org/the-index/2018/ (accessed July 10, 2019).

[49] See online: https://www.gatesfoundation.org/How-We-Work, also on information sharing: https://www.gatesfoundation.org/How-We-Work/General-Information/Information-Sharing-Approach and https://www.gatesfoundation.org/How-We-Work/General-Information/Information-Sharing-Approach/International-Aid-Transparency-Initiative, and on evaluation: https://www.gatesfoundation.org/How-We-Work/General-Information/Evaluation-Policy (all accessed July 10, 2019).

2015: 229ff). This would run against the idea of private property, but it may be justified on the grounds that private foundations affect public policy and receive tax exemptions from the state. If states would impose broader public accountability on private foundations, however, a possible reaction of billionaires could be to use the form of the private company for their politics instead (Reich 2018: 200)

To be sure, in their actions, billionaires are accountable to the rule of law—if they do something illegal, they risk legal sanctions. One potentially strong form of accountability lies in tort law, so that in cases where billionaires' actions cause harm, liability and compensation may be sought (Keohane 2003: 141, Erman 2018). Raj Rajaratnam is currently being sued in the U.S. by a law firm representing the relatives of victims killed by the LTTE during the civil war in Sri Lanka, who claim that the billionaire's indirect financing of the Tamil Tigers makes him liable for civil damages to the plaintiffs.[50] However, many years have passed since the initial deposition of the case, and it has not yet gone past the discovery phase in 2019. The challenge is to establish a link between donations to the Tamil Rehabilitation Organization and lethal bombings carried out by the LTTE in Sri Lanka. Similar difficulties of attribution would probably arise in other cases as well.[51] Since billionaires usually act in world politics by channeling money to others, one would need to prove that they are directing the conduct of the recipients. Yet the recipients may comply with their funder simply because they share the same goal, or because the threat of defunding is so obvious that it does not even need to be spelled out. While this constitutes power in the social scientist's sense, it may not be enough to sustain tort claims.

With billionaires as transnational actors, the tensions inherent in modern liberalism get magnified: individual freedom clashes with collective self-determination, private property subverts the public sphere, and territorially bounded conceptions of the demos conflict with cosmopolitan ideals. Finding the right balances within these tensions has never been straightforward and cannot be a task for political theory alone. To address these challenges, the role of billionaires will require politicization, so that "matters are moved from the realm of necessity or the private sphere to the public sphere" (Zürn et al. 2012: 73).

---

[50] See: KRISHANTHI et al. v. RAJARATNAM et al., No. 2:2009cv05395—Document 161 (D.N.J. 2014), see the 2009 complaint online: https://www.unitedstatescourts.org/doc/?a=c8b6ce99d91 d35d12348eff32c14a28c64a6a042&dl=1, as well as the 2014 court decision to allow the case against Rajaratnam: http://cases.justia.com/federal/district-courts/new-jersey/njdce/2:2009cv05395/233958/ 161/0.pdf?ts=1411594807 (both accessed July 14, 2017).

[51] Linsay McGoey has tried to establish a similar liability case against Bill Gates and his connection to vaccine trials in India, which were conducted by PATH, one of the chief recipients of BMGF funding (McGoey 2015: 160–7). However, the case is baseless, as the vaccine had already been officially approved in several countries, including India and the U.S., and allegations about the vaccine causing the death of children have been rejected by an independent medical panel. See Jon Greenberg, "Anti-vaccination blog revives debunked HPV story," Politifact, December 20, 2016, online: http://www.politifact.com/ global-news/statements/2016/dec/20/blog-posting/anti-vaccination-blog-revives-debunked-hpv-story/ (accessed July 14, 2017).

Over the past decades, processes of politicization have affected many institutions of global governance (Zürn & Ecker-Ehrhardt 2013, Zürn 2018: 138–69), but the legitimacy and accountability of billionaires were not major issues of contention. This has started to change, especially with regard to the Gates Foundation, whose rising power has attracted scrutiny (McGoey 2015, Harman 2016); it was in response to public criticism that the BMGF became more transparent. More recently, the whole complex of elite philanthropy has been subjected to rigorous criticism (Skocpol 2016, Callahan 2017, Giridharadas 2018, Reich 2018). Social science research can contribute to politicization by exposing the power of billionaires. Otherwise, the discussion all too often turns partisan, with people pointing to their favorite billionaires, discounting the larger implications of extreme inequalities for democracy. As democratic values are weakening, notably among younger generations in established democracies (Mounk 2018), the greatest danger may be that it becomes socially acceptable for the rich to rule. Politicization will be inhibited if billionaires continue to be seen as the exemplary prophets of our age. In order to counter sympathies for plutocracy, it will be crucial to understand the consequences of billionaires' empowerment more systematically. Within the domestic context of the U.S., political science has just woken up to investigate the influence of the super-wealthy.[52] As this book has shown, when individuals control extraordinary wealth, their power can also extend to world politics. In times where the twenty-six richest billionaires control as much wealth as the poorest half of the globe's population (Oxfam 2019), the study of IR can no longer ignore the role of extremely wealthy individuals in international affairs.

---

[52] The first quantitative studies for the U.S. indicate that among billionaires' philanthropy, liberal causes (in the American political sense) predominate (Goss 2016: 445), but when it comes to electioneering at the state level, Republican donors have the upper hand (Hertel-Fernandez 2016).

Bibliography

Abbott, Kenneth W., and David Gartner (2012). Reimagining Participation in International Institutions. *Journal of International Law & International Relations* 8: 1–35.

Abbott, Kenneth W., Philipp Genschel, Duncan Snidal, and Bernhard Zangl (eds) (2015). *International Organizations as Orchestrators*. Cambridge: Cambridge University Press.

Abbott, Kenneth W., and Duncan Snidal (2002). Values and Interests: International Legalization in the Fight Against Corruption. *Journal of Legal Studies* 31/2: 141–78.

Abbott, Kenneth W., and Duncan Snidal (2009). The Governance Triangle: Regulatory Standards Institutions and the Shadow of the State. In: Mattli, Walter, and Ngaire Woods (eds). *The Politics of Global Regulation*. Princeton: Princeton University Press, 44–88.

Abdelal, Rawi (2007). *Capital Rules: The Construction of Global Finance*. Cambridge, MA: Harvard University Press.

Abdelal, Rawi, Mark Blyth, and Craig Parsons (eds) (2010). *Constructing the International Economy*. Ithaca, NY: Cornell University Press.

Abrahamsen, Rita, and Michael C. Williams (2010). *Security Beyond the State: Private Security in International Politics*. Cambridge: Cambridge University Press.

Abramson, Yehonatan (2017). Making a Homeland, Constructing a Diaspora: The Case of Taglit-Birthright Israel. *Political Geography* 58: 14–23.

Abramson, Yehonatan (2019). Securing the Diasporic "Self" by Travelling Abroad: Taglit-Birthright and Ontological Security. *Journal of Ethnic and Migration Studies* 45/4: 656–73.

Acemoglu, Daron, and James A. Robinson (2006). *Economic Origins of Dictatorship and Democracy*. Cambridge: Cambridge University Press.

Acemoglu, Daron, and James A. Robinson (2012). *Why Nations Fail: The Origins of Power, Prosperity, and Poverty*. London: Profile Books.

Acosta, Benjamin (2014). The Dynamics of Israel's Democratic Tribalism. *Middle East Journal* 68/2: 268–86.

Adams, Gerry (2003). *Hope and History: Making Peace in Ireland*. London: Brandon.

Aday, Sean (2010). Chasing the Bad News: An Analysis of 2005 Iraq and Afghanistan War Coverage on NBC and Fox News Channel. *Journal of Communication* 60/1: 144–64.

Adler, Emanuel (1997). Seizing the Middle Ground: Constructivism in World Politics. *European Journal of International Relations* 3/3: 319–63.

Adler, Emanuel (2002). Constructivism and International Relations. In: Carlsnaes, Walter, Thomas Risse, and Beth Simmons (eds). *Handbook of International Relations*. London: Sage, 95–119.

Adler, Emanuel, and Peter M. Haas (1992). Conclusion: Epistemic Communities, World Order, and the Creation of a Reflective Research Program. *International Organization* 46/1: 367–90.

Adler, Emanuel, and Vincent Pouliot (eds) (2011). *International Practices*. Cambridge: Cambridge University Press.

Adloff, Frank (2010). *Philanthropisches Handeln: Eine historische Soziologie des Stiftens in Deutschland und den USA*. Frankfurt a.M./New York: Campus.

Adair-Toteff, Christopher (2014). Max Weber's Charismatic Prophets. *History of the Human Sciences* 27/1: 3–20.

Admati, Anat, and Martin Hellwig (2013). *The Bankers' New Clothes—What's Wrong with Banking and What to Do about It.* Princeton: Princeton University Press.

Agnew, John (1994). The Territorial Trap: The Geographical Assumptions of International Relations Theory. *Review of International Political Economy* 1/1: 53–80.

Agnew, John (2009). *Globalization and Sovereignty.* Lanham, MD: Rowman and Littlefield.

Aiken, Sharryn J., and Rudhramoorthy Cheran (2005). *The Impact of International Informal Banking on Canada: A Case Study of Tamil Transnational Money Transfer Networks (Undiyal), Canada/Sri Lanka.* Ontario: Law Commission of Canada/ Government of Canada Publications. Online: http://ssrn.com/abstract=2494357.

Albert, Mathias, and Barry Buzan (2013). International Relations Theory and the "Social Whole": Encounters and Gaps Between IR and Sociology. *International Political Sociology* 7/1: 117–35.

Albert, Mathias, Barry Buzan, and Michael Zürn (2013). *Bringing Sociology to International Relations: World Politics as Differentiation Theory.* Cambridge: Cambridge University Press.

Albert, Mathias, and Peter Lenco (2008). Introduction to the Forum–Foucault and International Political Sociology. *International Political Sociology* 2/3: 265–77.

Alesina, Alberto, and David Dollar (2000). Who Gives Foreign Aid to Whom and Why? *Journal of Economic Growth* 5/1: 33–63.

Alexander, Jeffrey C., Bernhard Giesen, Richard Münch, and Neil J. Smelser (eds) (1987). *The Micro-Macro Link.* Berkeley: University of California Press.

Allee, Todd, and Clint Peinhardt (2014). Evaluating Three Explanations for the Design of Bilateral Investment Treaties. *World Politics* 66/1: 47–87.

Allen, Mike (2012). Sheldon Adelson: Inside the mind of the mega-donor. *Politico*, 23 September 2012, online: http://www.politico.com/story/2012/09/sheldon-adelson-inside-the-mind-of-the-mega-donor-081588#ixzz3nnmoMANQ (accessed July 6, 2019).

Allin, Dana H., and Erik Jones (2012). *Weary Policeman: American Power in an Age of Austerity.* London: International Institute for Strategic Studies.

Allin, Paul, and David J. Hand (2014). *The Wellbeing of Nations: Meaning, Motive and Measurement.* Chichester: John Wilely & Sons.

Allison, Graham T. (1969). Conceptual Models and the Cuban Missile Crisis. *American Political Science Review* 63/3: 689–718.

Allison, Graham T. (1971). *Essence of Decision: Explaining the Cuban Missile Crisis.* Boston: Little, Brown and Co.

Allison, John A. (2013). *The Financial Crisis and the Free Market Cure: How Destructive Banking Reform is Killing the Economy.* New York: McGraw-Hill.

Almond, Gabriel A., and Sidney Verba (1963). *The Civic Culture: Political Attitudes and Democracy in Five Nations.* Princeton: Princeton University Press.

Alstadsæter, Annette, Niels Johannesen, and Gabriel Zucman (2018). Who Owns the Wealth in Tax Havens? Macro Evidence and Implications for Global Inequality. *Journal of Public Economics* 162: 89–100.

Alstadsæter, Annette, Niels Johannesen, and Gabriel Zucman (2019). Tax Evasion and Inequality. *American Economic Review* 109/6: 2073–103.

Alvaredo, Facundo, Lucas Chancel, Thomas Piketty, Emmanuel Saez, and Gabriel Zucman (eds) (2018). *2018 World Inequality Report.* Online: https://wir2018.wid.world/files/ download/wir2018-full-report-english.pdf.

Ambrosio, Thomas (2007). Insulating Russia from a Colour Revolution: How the Kremlin Resists Regional Democratic Trends. *Democratisation* 14/2: 232–52.

Ammann, Daniel (2009). *The King of Oil: The Secret Lives of Marc Rich*. New York: St. Martin's Press.

Anable, David (2006). The Role of Georgia's Media—and Western Aid—in the Rose Revolution. *The Harvard International Journal of Press/Politics* 11/3: 7–43.

Anderson, Scot (2012). *Think Like a Billionaire, Become a Billionaire: As a Man Thinks, So Is He*. Tulsa, OK: Harrison House.

Anderson, Tom (2004). *Becoming a Millionaire God's Way: Getting Money to You, Not from You*. Mesa, AZ: Winword Publishing.

Anderson, Mary R. (2010). Community Psychology, Political Efficacy, and Trust. *Political Psychology* 31/1: 59–84.

Andrews, David M. (1994). Capital Mobility and State Autonomy: Toward a Structural Theory of International Monetary Relations. *International Studies Quarterly* 38/2: 193–218.

Angell, Norman (1910). *The Great Illusion: A Study of the Relation of Military Power in Nations to Their Economic and Social Advantages*. London: Heinemann.

Angley, Robyn E. (2010). *NGOs in Competitive Authoritarian States: The Role of Civil Groups in Georgia's Rose Revolution*. PhD dissertation. Boston: Boston University.

Angley, Robyn E. (2013). Escaping the Kmara Box: Reframing the Role of Civil Society in Georgia's Rose Revolution. *Studies of Transition States and Societies* 5/1: 42–57.

Annan, Kofi (2013). *Interventions: A Life in War and Peace*. New York: Penguin.

Ansolabehere, Stephen, and David M. Konisky (2014). *Cheap and Clean: How Americans Think about Energy in the Age of Global Warming*. Cambridge: MIT Press.

Antilla, Liisa (2005). Climate of Skepticism: US Newspaper Coverage of the Science of Climate Change. *Global Environmental Change* 15/4: 338–52.

Appel, Hilary, and Mitchell A. Orenstein (2013). Ideas versus Resources: Explaining the Flat Tax and Pension Privatization Revolutions in Eastern Europe and the Former Soviet Union. *Comparative Political Studies* 46/2: 123–52.

Appiah, Kwame Anthony (2006). *Cosmopolitanism Ethics in a World of Strangers*. New York: W. W. Norton & Co.

Arceneaux, Kevin, Martin Johnson, René Lindstädt, and Ryan J. Vander Wielen (2016). The Influence of News Media on Political Elites: Investigating Strategic Responsiveness in Congress. *American Journal of Political Science* 60/1: 5–29.

Archer, Margaret (1982). Morphogenesis Versus Structuration: On Combining Structure and Action. *The British Journal of Sociology* 33/4: 455–83.

Archer, Margaret (1988). *Culture and Agency: The Place of Culture in Social Theory*. Cambridge: Cambridge University Press.

Archer, Margaret (1995). *Realist Social Theory: The Morphogenetic Approach*. Cambridge: Cambridge University Press.

Archer, Margaret (2000). *Being Human: The Problem of Agency*. Cambridge: Cambridge University Press.

Archer, Margaret (2003). *Structure, Agency, and the Internal Conversation*. Cambridge: Cambridge University Press.

Archer, Margaret (2007). *Making Our Way through the World: Human Reflexivity and Social Mobility*. Cambridge: Cambridge University Press.

Archer, Margaret (ed.) (2013a). *Social Morphogenesis*. Dordrecht: Springer.

Archer, Margaret (2013b). *Social Morphogenesis and the Prospects of Morphogenetic Society*. In: Archer, Margaret (ed.). *Social Morphogenesis*. Dordrecht: Springer, 1–22.

Archer, Margaret (ed.) (2014). *Late Modernity: Trajectories Towards Morphogenetic Society.* Dordrecht: Springer.

Archer, Margaret (ed.) (2017). *Morphogenesis and the Crisis of Normativity.* Dordrecht: Springer.

ARD (2002). *USAID/Georgia Democracy and Government Assessment of Georgia.* Burlington, VT: ARD.

Arendt, Hannah (1970). *On Violence.* London: Allen Lane.

Areshidze, Irakly (2007). *Democracy and Autocracy in Eurasia: Georgia in Transition.* East Lansing: Michigan State University Press.

Ariely, Dan (2008). *Predictably Irrational: The Hidden Forces that Shape our Decisions.* New York: HarperCollins.

Armstrong, Stephen (2010). *The Super-Rich Shall Inherit the Earth: The New Global Oligarchs and How They're Taking Over Our World.* London: Constable.

Aron, Raymond (1966) [2003]. *Peace & War: A Theory of International Relations.* With a new introduction by Daniel J. Mahoney and Brian C. Anderson. London: Transaction Publishers.

Aronoff, Yael (2014). *The Political Psychology of Israeli Prime Ministers: When Hard-Liners Opt for Peace.* Cambridge: Cambridge University Press.

Arsenault, Amelia, and Manuel Castells (2008). Switching Power: Rupert Murdoch and the Global Business of Media Politics: A Sociological Analysis. *International Sociology* 23/4: 488–513.

Art, Robert J., and Robert Jervis (eds) (2016). *International Politics: Enduring Concepts and Contemporary Issues.* 13th edition. New York: Pearson.

Aslund, Anders (2006). The Ancien Régime: Kuchma and the Oligarchs. In: Aslund, Anders, and Michael McFaul (eds). *Revolution in Orange: The Origins of Ukraine's Democratic Breakthrough.* Washington, D.C.: Carnegie Endowment for International Peace, 9–28.

Aslund, Anders, and Michael McFaul (2006). *Revolution in Orange: The Origins of Ukraine's Democratic Breakthrough.* Washington, D.C.: Carnegie Endowment for International Peace.

Atkinson, Anthony B. (2006). *Concentration among the Rich.* UNU-WIDER Research Paper No. 2006/151. Helsinki: United Nations University, World Institute for Development Economics Research. Online: http://www.wider.unu.edu/publications/working-papers/research-papers/2006/en_GB/rp2006-151/_files/78091824924985647/default/rp2006-151.pdf.

Atkinson, Anthony B., and Thomas Piketty (eds) (2007). *Top Incomes over the Twentieth Century.* Oxford: Oxford University Press.

Atkinson, Anthony B., and Thomas Piketty (eds) (2010). *Top Incomes: A Global Perspective.* Oxford: Oxford University Press.

Atkinson, Anthony B., Thomas Piketty, and Emmanuel Saez (2011). Top Incomes in the Long Run of History. *Journal of Economic Literature* 49/1: 3–71.

Au, Wayne, and Christopher Lubienski (2016). The Role of the Gates Foundation and the Philanthropic Sector in Shaping the Emerging Education Market. In: Verger, Antoni, Christopher Lubienski, and Gita Steiner-Khamsi (eds). *World Yearbook of Education 2016: The Global Education Industry.* New York: Routledge, 27–43.

Auletta, Ken (1995). The Pirate. *The New Yorker,* November 13, 1995, online: http://www.newyorker.com/magazine/1995/11/13/the-pirate.

Auletta, Ken (2001). *World War 3.0: Microsoft, the US Government, and the Battle for the New Economy.* New York: Random House.

Ausderan, Jacob (2014). How Naming and Shaming Affects Human Rights Perceptions in the Shamed Country. *Journal of Peace Research* 51/1: 81–95.

Avant, Deborah D., Martha Finnemore, and Susan K. Sell (eds) (2010). *Who Governs the Globe?* Cambridge: Cambridge University Press.

Azevedo, Jane (1997). *Mapping Reality: An Evolutionary Realist Methodology for the Natural and Social Sciences.* Albany: SUNY Press.

Babb, Sarah (2013). The Washington Consensus as Transnational Policy Paradigm: Its Origins, Trajectory and Likely Successor. *Review of International Political Economy* 20/2: 1–30.

Bachrach, Peter, and Morton S. Baratz (1962). Two Faces of Power. *American Political Science Review* 56/4: 947–52.

Bailleux, Julie, and Antoine Vauchez (eds) (2014). *Exploring the Transnational Circulation of Policy Paradigms: Law Firms, Legal Networks and the Production of Expertise in the Field of Competition Policies.* San Domenico di Fiesole: European University Institute.

Baldwin, David A. (ed.) (1993). *Neorealism and Neoliberalism: The Contemporary Debate.* New York: Columbia University Press.

Baldwin, David A. (1971). The Power of Positive Sanctions. *World Politics* 24/1: 19–38.

Baldwin, David A. (2016). *Power and International Relations: A Conceptual Approach.* Princeton: Princeton University Press.

Baldwin, Richard (2016). *The Great Convergence: Information Technology and the New Globalization.* Cambridge: Harvard University Press.

Ball, Molly (2012). Who Is Sheldon Adelson, the Gingrich Super PAC's Billionaire Backer? *The Atlantic,* January 25, 2012, online: http://www.theatlantic.com/politics/archive/2012/01/who-is-sheldon-adelson-the-gingrich-super-pacs-billionaire-backer/252003/.

Balmas, Meital, Gideon Rahat, Tamir Sheafer, and Shaul R. Shenhav (2014). Two Routes to Personalized Politics: Centralized and Decentralized Personalization. *Party Politics* 20/1: 37–51.

Ban, Cornel (2016). *Ruling Ideas: How Global Neoliberalism Goes Local.* Oxford: Oxford University Press.

Bandura, Albert (1997). *Self-efficacy: The Exercise of Control.* New York: Freeman.

Bandura, Albert (2012). On the Functional Properties of Perceived Self-Efficacy Revisited. *Journal of Management* 38/1: 9–44.

Banerjee, Neela, John H. Cushman Jr., David Hasemyer, and Lisa Long (2015). *Exxon: The Road Not Taken.* New York: InsideClimate News.

Barbour, Emily C. (2010). *The SPEECH Act: The Federal Response to "Libel Tourism."* Washington, D.C.: Congressional Research Service. Online: https://fas.org/sgp/crs/misc/R41417.pdf.

Barkan, Joanne (2011). Got Dough? How Billionaires Rule Our Schools. *Dissent,* Winter 2011, online: http://www.dissentmagazine.org/article/got-dough-how-billionaires-rule-our-schools.

Barkin, Samuel (2009). Realism, Prediction, and Foreign Policy. *Foreign Policy Analysis* 5: 233–46.

Barnes, Amy, and Garrett Wallace Brown (2011). The Global Fund to Fight AIDS, Tuberculosis, and Malaria: Expertise, Accountability, and the Depoliticisation of Global Health Governance. In: Rushton, Simon, and Owain David Williams (eds). *Partnerships and Foundations in Global Health Governance.* London: Palgrave Macmillan, 53–75.

Barnes, Barry (2000). *Understanding Agency: Social Theory and Responsible Action.* London: Sage.

Barnes, Lucy, and Peter A. Hall (2013). Neoliberalism and Social Resilience in the Developed Democracies. In: Hall, Peter A., and Michèle Lamont (eds). *Social Resilience in the Neoliberal Era*. Cambridge: Cambridge University Press, 209–38.

Barnett, Michael N. (2016). *The Star and the Stripes: A History of the Foreign Policies of American Jews*. Princeton: Princeton University Press.

Barnett, Michael, and Raymond Duvall (2005). Power in International Politics. *International organization* 59/1: 39–75.

Barnett, Michael N., and Martha Finnemore (1999). The Politics, Power, and Pathologies of International Organizations. *International Organization* 53/4: 699–732.

Barnett, Steven (2017). Murdoch Has Had too Many Favours. *British Journalism Review* 28/1: 51–6.

Barrows, Samuel (2009). Racing to the Top . . . at last: The Regulation of Safety in Shipping. In: Mattli, Walter, and Ngaire Woods (eds). *The Politics of Global Regulation*. Princeton: Princeton University Press, 189–210.

Barry, Colin M., K. Chad Clay, and Michael E. Flynn (2013). Avoiding the Spotlight: Human Rights Shaming and Foreign Direct Investment. *International Studies Quarterly* 57/3: 532–44.

Bartley, Tim (2007). Institutional Emergence in an Era of Globalization: The Rise of Transnational Private Regulation of Labor and Environmental Conditions. *American Journal of Sociology* 113/2: 297–351.

Bartsch, Sonja (2011). A Critical Appraisal of Global Health Partnerships. In: Rushton, Simon, and Owain David Williams (eds). *Partnerships and Foundations in Global Health Governance*. London: Palgrave Macmillan, 29–52.

Bates, Stephen R. (2010). Re-structuring Power. *Polity* 42/3: 352–76.

Bauman, Zygmunt (2000). *Liquid Modernity*. Cambridge: Polity.

Baumol, William J. (1977). On the Proper Cost Tests for Natural Monopoly in a Multiproduct Industry. *American Economic Review* 67/5: 809–22.

Baylis, John, Steve Smith, and Patricia Owens (eds) (2016). *The Globalization of World Politics: An Introduction to International Relations*. 7th edition. Oxford: Oxford University Press.

Beaumont, Elizabeth (2011). Promoting Political Agency, Addressing Political Inequality: A Multilevel Model of Internal Political Efficacy. *The Journal of Politics* 73/1: 216–31.

Bebchuk, Lucian, and Fried, Jesse (2004). *Pay Without Performance: The Unfulfilled Promise of Executive Compensation*. Cambridge, MA: Harvard University Press.

Beck, Ulrich (2004). *Der kosmopolitische Blick oder: Krieg ist Frieden*. Frankfurt a. M.: Suhrkamp.

Beck, Ulrich, and Elisabeth Beck-Gernsheim (eds) (1994). *Riskante Freiheiten: Individualisierung in modernen Gesellschaften*. Frankfurt a. M.: Suhrkamp.

Beichelt, Timm, Irene Hahn, Frank Schimmelfennig, and Susann Worschech (eds) (2014). *Civil Society and Democracy Promotion*. Basingstoke: Palgrave Macmillan.

Beissinger, Mark R. (2007). Structure and Example in Modular Political Phenomena: The Diffusion of Bulldozer/Rose/Orange/Tulip Revolutions. *Perspectives on Politics* 5/2: 259–76.

Beissinger, Mark R. (2009). An Interrelated Wave. *Journal of Democracy* 20/1: 74–7.

Beitz, Charles R. (1999). *Political Theory and International Relations*. Princeton: Princeton University Press.

Bell, Stephen (2012). The Power of Ideas: The Ideational Shaping of the Structural Power of Business. *International Studies Quarterly* 56: 661–73.

Béland, Daniel, and Robert Henry Cox (eds) (2011a). *Ideas and Politics in Social Science Research*. Oxford: Oxford University Press.

Béland, Daniel, and Robert Henry Cox (2011b). Introduction: Ideas and Politics. In: Béland, Daniel and Robert Henry Cox (eds). *Ideas and Politics in Social Science Research*. Oxford: Oxford University Press, 3–20.

Ben-Ami, Jeremy (2011). *A New Voice for Israel: Fighting for the Survival of the Jewish Nation*. New York: Palgrave Macmillan.

Ben Hagai, Ella, Adam Whitlatch, and Eileen L. Zurbriggen (2018). "We Didn't Talk About the Conflict": The Birthright Trip's Influence on Jewish Americans' Understanding of the Israeli-Palestinian Conflict. *Peace and Conflict: Journal of Peace Psychology* 24/2: 139–49.

Ben Meir, Yehuda (2013). The Israeli Public Debate on Preventing a Nuclear Iran. In: Kurz, Anat, and Shlomo Brom (eds). *Strategic Survey for Israel 2012–2013*. Tel Aviv: Institute for National Security Studies, 231–44.

Bendor, Jonathan, and Thomas H. Hammond (1992). Rethinking Allison's Models. *American Political Science Review* 86/2: 301–22.

Bennett, Daniel L., and Boris Nikolaev (2017). On the Ambiguous Economic Freedom-Inequality Relationship. *Empirical Economics* 53/2: 717–54.

Berg, Andrea (2006). Who's Afraid of George Soros? The Conflict Between Authoritarian Rulers and International Actors in Central Asia. In: Berg, Andrea, and Anna Kreikemeyer (eds). *Realities of Transformation: Democratization Policies in Central Asia Revisited*. Baden-Baden: Nomos, 127–40.

Berger, Peter L., and Thomas Luckmann (1966). *The Social Construction of Reality: A Treatise in the Sociology of Knowledge*. Garden City, NY: Anchor Books.

Berlin, Isaiah (1969). *Four Essays on Liberty*. Oxford: Oxford University Press.

Berman, Edward H. (1983). *The Influence of Carnegie, the Ford and Rockefeller Foundations on American Foreign Policy: The Ideology of Philanthropy*. Albany, NY: State University of New York Press.

Berman, Sheri (2011). Understanding the Origins of Ideology: The Case of European Social Democracy. In: Bèland, Daniel, and Robert Cox (eds). *Ideas and Politics in Social Science Research*. Oxford: Oxford University Press, 105–26.

Berman, Sheri (2013). Ideational Theorizing in the Social Sciences since "Policy Paradigms, Social Learning, and the State." *Governance* 26/2: 217–37.

Bernstein, Steven (2011). Legitimacy in Intergovernmental and Non-state Global Governance. *Review of International Political Economy* 18/1: 17–51.

Best, Jacqueline, and William Walters (2013). "Actor-Network Theory" and International Relationality: Lost (and Found) in Translation—Introduction. *International Political Sociology* 7/3: 332–49.

Bexell, Magdalena, Jonas Tallberg, and Anders Uhlin (2010). Democracy in Global Governance: The Promises and Pitfalls of Transnational Actors. *Global Governance* 16/1: 81–101.

Beyer, Jürgen (2005). Pfadabhängigkeit ist nicht gleich Pfadabhängigkeit! Wider den impliziten Konservatismus eines gängigen Konzepts. *Zeitschrift für Soziologie* 34/1: 5–21.

Bhaskar, Roy (1975) [1997]. *A Realist Theory of Science*. 2nd edition. London: Verso.

Bigo, Didier (2011). Pierre Bourdieu and International Relations: Power of Practices, Practices of Power. *International Political Sociology* 5/3: 225–58.

Bigo, Didier, and Mikael R. Madsen (2011). Introduction to Symposium "A Different Reading of the International": Pierre Bourdieu and International Studies. *International Political Sociology* 5/3: 219–24.

Bill & Melinda Gates Foundation (BMGF) (2000). *1999 Bill & Melinda Gates Foundation Annual Report*. Online: http://www.gatesfoundation.org/~/media/GFO/Documents/Annual-Reports/1999Gates-Foundation-Annual-Report.pdf?la=en.

Bill & Melinda Gates Foundation (BMGF) (2008). *2007 Bill & Melinda Gates Foundation Annual Report*. Online: http://www.gatesfoundation.org/~/media/GFO/Documents/Annual-Reports/2007Gates-Foundation-Annual-Report.pdf?la=en.

Bill & Melinda Gates Foundation (BMGF) (2011). *2010 Bill & Melinda Gates Foundation Annual Report*. Online: http://www.gatesfoundation.org/~/media/GFO/Documents/Annual-Reports/2010Gates-Foundation-Annual-Report.pdf?la=en.

Bill & Melinda Gates Foundation (BMGF) (2012). *2011 Bill & Melinda Gates Foundation Annual Report*. Online: http://www.gatesfoundation.org/~/media/GFO/Documents/Annual-Reports/2011Gates-Foundation-Annual-Report.pdf?la=en.

Bill & Melinda Gates Foundation (BMGF) (2013). *2012 Bill & Melinda Gates Foundation Annual Report*. Online: http://www.gatesfoundation.org/~/media/GFO/Documents/Annual-Reports/2012_Gates_Foundation_Annual_Report.pdf.

Bill & Melinda Gates Foundation (BMGF) (2014). *2013 Bill & Melinda Gates Foundation Annual Report*. Online: http://www.gatesfoundation.org/~/media/GFO/Who-We-Are/Annual-Report-2013/BMGF-2013-Annual-Report.pdf?la=en.

Birn, Anne-Emanuelle (2005). Gates's Grandest Challenge: Transcending Technology as Public Health Ideology. *The Lancet* 366: 514–19.

Birn, Anne-Emanuelle (2014). Philanthrocapitalism, Past and Present: The Rockefeller Foundation, the Gates Foundation, and the Setting(s) of the International/Global Health Agenda. *Hypothesis* 12/1: 1–27.

Birtchnell, Thomas, Satya Savitzky, and John Urry (eds) (2015). *Cargomobilities: Moving Materials in a Global Age*. London: Routledge.

Birthright Israel Foundation (2014). *Annual Report 2014*. Online: https://birthrightisrael.foundation/_docs/2014annual_report_brif.pdf.

Birthright Israel Foundation (2019). *Annual Report 2018*. Online: https://birthrightisrael.foundation/annualreport2018.

Bishop, Matthew, and Michael Green (2008). *Philanthrocapitalism: How the Rich Can Save the World*. New York: Bloomsbury.

Blake, Daniel J. (2013). Thinking Ahead: Government Time Horizons and the Legalization of International Investment Agreements. *International Organization* 67/3: 797–827.

Blanchet, Nathan, Miñan Thomas, Rifat Atun, Dean Jamison, Felicia Knaul, and Robert Hecht (2013). *Global Collective Action in Health: The WDR+ 20 Landscape of Core and Supportive functions*. Commission on Investing in Health Working Paper, online: http://www.globalhealth2035.org/sites/default/files/working-papers/global-collective-action-in-health.pdf.

Bleiker, Roland (2000). *Popular Dissent, Human Agency, and Global Politics*. Cambridge: Cambridge University Press.

Bloodgood, Elizabeth A., Joannie Tremblay-Boire, and Aseem Prakash (2014). National Styles of NGO Regulations. *Nonprofit and Voluntary Sector Quarterly* 43/4: 716–36.

Bloom, William (1993). *Personal Identity, National Identity and International Relations*. Cambridge: Cambridge University Press.

Bluth, Christoph (2004). The British Road to War: Blair, Bush and the Decision to Invade Iraq. *International Affairs* 80/5: 871–92.

Blyth, Mark (2002). *Great Transformations: Economic Ideas and Institutional Change in the Twentieth Century*. Cambridge: Cambridge University Press.

Blyth, Mark (2003). Structures Do Not Come with an Instruction Sheet: Interests, Ideas, and Progress in Political Science. *Perspectives on Politics* 1/4: 695–706.

Bob, Clifford (2002). Globalization and the Social Construction of Human Rights Campaigns. In: Brysk, Alison (ed.). *Globalization and Human Rights*. Berkeley/Los Angeles: University of California Press, 133–47.

Boli, John, and Thomas, George M. (eds) (1999). *Constructing World Culture: International Nongovernmental Organizations Since 1875*. Stanford, CA: Stanford University Press.

Boltanski, Luc, and Eve Chiapello (2007). *The New Spirit of Capitalism*. London: Verso.

Boone, Peter, and Simon Johnson (2010). Will the Politics of Global Moral Hazard Sink us Again? In: Turner, Adair et al. (eds). *The Future of Finance: The LSE Report*. London: London School of Economics and Political Science, 247–88.

Bornstein, David (2004). *How to Change the World: Social Entrepreneurs and the Power of New Ideas*. London: Penguin.

Boulding, Kenneth E. (1964). Toward a Theory of Peace. In: Fisher, Roger (ed.). *International Conflict and Behavioural Science: The Craigville Papers*. New York: Basic Books.

Bourdieu, Pierre (1977). *Outline of a Theory of Practice*. Cambridge: Cambridge University Press.

Bourdieu, Pierre (1983). Ökonomisches Kapital, kulturelles Kapital, soziales Kapital. In: Kreckel, Reinhard (ed.). *Soziale Ungleichheiten* (Soziale Welt: Sonderband 2). Göttingen: Schwartz, 183–98.

Bourdieu, Pierre (1989). Social Space and Symbolic Power. *Sociological Theory* 7/1: 14–25.

Bourdieu, Pierre (1990). *The Logic of Practice*. Stanford, CA: Stanford University Press.

Bourdieu, Pierre, and Loïc Wacquant (1992). *An Invitation to Reflexive Sociology*. Chicago: University of Chicago Press.

Boussalis, Constantine, and Travis G. Coan (2016). Text-mining the Signals of Climate Change Doubt. *Global Environmental Change* 36: 89–100.

Boykoff, Maxwell T. (2011). *Who Speaks for the Climate? Making Sense of Media Reporting on Climate Change*. Cambridge: Cambridge University Press.

Boykoff, Maxwell T., and Jules M. Boykoff (2007). Climate Change and Journalistic Norms: A Case-study of US Mass-media Coverage. *Geoforum* 38/6: 1190–204.

Boylan, Brandon M. (2015). Sponsoring Violence: A Typology of Constituent Support for Terrorist Organizations. *Studies in Conflict & Terrorism* 38/8: 652–70.

Brandenburg, Heinz, and Marcel van Egmond (2011). Pressed into Party Support? Media Influence on Partisan Attitudes During the 2005 UK General Election Campaign. *British Journal of Political Science* 42/2: 441–63.

Branson, Richard (2006). *Screw It, Let's Do It: Lessons in Life and Business*. London: Virgin.

Breuning, Marijke (2011). Role Theory in International Relations: State of the Art and Blind Spots. In: Harnisch, Sebastian, Cornelia Frank, and Hanns W. Maull (eds). *Role Theory in International Relations: Approaches and Analyses*. New York: Routledge, 16–35.

Brewer, Paul R. (2012). Polarisation in the USA: Climate Change, Party Politics, and Public Opinion in the Obama Era. *European Political Science* 11/1: 7–17.

Bröckling, Ulrich (2007). *Das unternehmerische Selbst: Soziologie einer Subjektivierungsform*. Frankfurt a.M.: Suhrkamp.

Broers, Laurence (2005). After the "Revolution": Civil Society and the Challenges of Consolidating Democracy in Georgia. *Central Asian Survey* 24/3: 333–50.

Brooks, Stephen G. (1999). The Globalization of Production and the Changing Benefits of Conquest. *Journal of Conflict Resolution* 43/5:646–70.

Brooks, Stephen G. (2005). *Producing Security: Multinational Corporations, Globalization, and the Changing Calculus of Conflict*. Princeton: Princeton University Press.

Brooks, Stephen G. (2013). Economic Actors' Lobbying Influence on the Prospects for War and Peace. *International Organization* 67/3: 863–88.

Brown, Theodore M., Marcos Cueto, and Elizabeth Fee (2006). The World Health Organization and the Transition from "International" to "Global" Public Health. *American Journal of Public Health* 96/1: 62–72.

Brubaker, Rogers (1996). *Nationalism Reframed: Nationhood and the National Question in the New Europe*. Cambridge: Cambridge University Press.

Bruck, Connie (1995). The World According to Soros. *The New Yorker*, January 23, 1995. Online: http://www.newyorker.com/magazine/1995/01/23/the-world-according-to-soros.

Bruck, Connie (2008). The Brass Ring. *The New Yorker*, June 30, 2008. Online: http://www.newyorker.com/magazine/2008/06/30/the-brass-ring.

Bruck, Connie (2012). The Kingmaker. *The New Yorker*, January 11, 2012. Online: http://www.newyorker.com/news/daily-comment/the-kingmaker.

Bruck, Connie (2014). Friends of Israel. *The New Yorker*, September 1, 2014. Online: http://www.newyorker.com/magazine/2014/09/01/friends-israel.

Brulle, Robert J. (2014). Institutionalizing Delay: Foundation Funding and the Creation of US Climate Change Counter-movement Organizations. *Climatic Change* 122/4: 681–94.

Brulle, Robert J., Jason Carmichael, and J. Craig Jenkins (2012). Shifting Public Opinion on Climate Change: An Empirical Assessment of Factors Influencing Concern Over Climate Change in the US, 2002–2010. *Climatic Change* 114/2: 169–88.

Bruno, Michael, and Jeffrey Sachs (1985). *Economics of Worldwide Stagflation*. Cambridge, MA: Harvard University Press.

Bryant, Ralph C. (1987). *International Financial Intermediation*. Washington, D.C.: The Brookings Institution.

Buchanan, Allen (2002). Political Legitimacy and Democracy. *Ethics* 112/4: 689–719.

Buchanan, Allen, and Robert O. Keohane (2006). The Legitimacy of Global Governance Institutions. *Ethics & International Affairs* 20/4: 405–37.

Buchanan, James M., and Gordon Tullock (1962). *The Calculus of Consent: Logical Foundations of Constitutional Democracy*. Ann Arbor: University of Michigan Press.

Bucher, Bernd (2014). Acting Abstractions: Metaphors, Narrative Structures, and the Eclipse of Agency. *European Journal of International Relations* 20/3: 742–65.

Büthe, Tim, Solomon Major, and André de Mello e Souza (2012). The Politics of Private Foreign Aid: Humanitarian Principles, Economic Development Objectives, and Organizational Interests in NGO Private Aid Allocation. *International Organization* 66/4: 571–607.

Büthe, Tim, and Walter Mattli (2011). *The New Global Rulers: The Privatization of Regulation in the World Economy*. Princeton: Princeton University Press.

Büthe, Tim, and Helen V. Milner (2008). The Politics of Foreign Direct Investment into Developing Countries: Increasing FDI through International Trade Agreements? *American Journal of Political Science* 52/4: 741–62.

Büthe, Tim, and Helen V. Milner (2014). Foreign Direct Investment and Institutional Diversity in Trade Agreements: Credibility, Commitment, and Economic Flows in the Developing World, 1971–2007. *World Politics* 66/1: 88–122.

Bull, Hedley (1977). *The Anarchical Society: A Study of Order in World Politics*. New York: Columbia University Press.

Bunce, Valerie J., and Sharon L. Wolchik (2010). Defeating Dictators: Electoral Change and Stability in Competitive Authoritarian Regimes. *World Politics* 62/1: 43–86.

Bunce, Valerie J., and Sharon L. Wolchik (2011). *Defeating Authoritarian Leaders in Postcommunist Countries*. Cambridge: Cambridge University Press.

Bunce, Valerie J., and Sharon L. Wolchik (2009). Getting Real About "Real Causes." *Journal of Democracy* 20/1: 69–73.

Bunce, Valerie J., and Sharon L. Wolchik (2006). International Diffusion and Postcommunist Electoral Revolutions. *Communist and Post-Communist Studies* 39/3: 283–304.

Burgin, Angus (2012). *The Great Persuasion: Reinventing Free Markets since the Depression*. Cambridge, MA: Harvard University Press.

Burn, Gary (2006). *The Re-Emergence of Global Finance*. Basingstoke: Palgrave Macmillan.

Burt, Ronald S. (2004). Structural Holes and Good Ideas. *American Journal of Sociology* 110/2: 349–99.

Busby, Joshua William (2007). Bono Made Jesse Helms Cry: Jubilee 2000, Debt Relief, and Moral Action in International Politics. *International Studies Quarterly* 51/2: 247–75.

Busemeyer, Marius R. (2009). From Myth to Reality: Globalization and Public Spending in OECD Countries Revisited. *European Journal of Political Research* 48: 455–82.

Bush, George W. (2010). *Decision Points*. New York: Crown Publishers.

Bush, Sarah Sunn (2015). *The Taming of Democracy Assistance*. Cambridge: Cambridge University Press.

Buzan, Barry (1995). The Level of Analysis Problem in International Relations Reconsidered. In: Booth, Ken, and Steve Smith (eds). *International Relations Theory Today*. Cambridge: Polity, 198–216.

Buzan, Barry (2014). *The Societal Approach: An Introduction to the English School of International Relations*. Cambridge: Cambridge University Press.

Buzan, Barry, and Mathias Albert (2010). Differentiation: A Sociological Approach to International Relations Theory. *European Journal of International Relations* 16/3: 315–37.

Buzan, Barry, Ole Wæver, and Jaap De Wilde (1998). *Security: a new framework for analysis*. London: Lynne Rienner Publishers.

Byman, Daniel L., and Kenneth M. Pollack (2001). Let Us Now Praise Great Men: Bringing the Statesmen Back in. *International Security* 25: 107–46.

Cafruny, Alan, and Magnus Ryner (eds) (2003). *A Ruined Fortress? Neoliberal Hegemony and Transformation in Europe*. Lanham: Rowman & Littlefield.

Calhoun, Craig (2007). *Nations Matter: Culture, History and the Cosmopolitan Dream*. New York: Routledge.

Calhoun, Craig J. (2002). The Class Consciousness of Frequent Travelers: Toward a Critique of Actually Existing Cosmopolitanism. *The South Atlantic Quarterly* 101/4: 869–97.

Callahan, David (2017). *The Givers: Wealth, Power, and Philanthropy in a New Gilded Age*. New York: Vintage Books.

Campbell, Alastair, and Bill Hagerty (eds) (2010). *Prelude to Power, 1994–1997. The Alastair Campbell Diaries Vol. 1*. London: Hutchinson.

Campbell, Alastair, and Bill Hagerty (eds) (2011a). *Power and the People, 1997–1999. The Alastair Campbell Diaries Vol. 2*. London: Hutchinson.

Campbell, Alastair, and Bill Hagerty (eds) (2011b). *Power and Responsibility, 1999–2001. The Alastair Campbell Diaries Vol. 3*. London: Hutchinson.

Campbell, Colin (2009). Distinguishing the Power of Agency from Agentic Power: A Note on Weber and the "Black Box" of Personal Agency. *Sociological Theory* 27/4: 407–18.

Capoccia, Giovanni, and R. Daniel Kelemen (2007). The Study of Critical Junctures: Theory, Narrative, and Counterfactuals in Historical Institutionalism. *World Politics* 59/3: 341–69.

Capstick, Stuart, Lorraine Whitmarsh, Wouter Poortinga, Nick Pidgeon, and Paul Upham (2015). International Trends in Public Perceptions of Climate Change Over the Past Quarter Century. *Wiley Interdisciplinary Reviews: Climate Change* 6/1: 35–61.

Carlsnaes, Walter (1992). The Agency-Structure Problem in Foreign Policy Analysis. *International Studies Quarterly* 36/3: 245–70.

Carlsnaes, Walter (2013). Foreign Policy. In: Carlsnaes, Walter, Thomas Risse, and Beth A. Simmons (eds). *Handbook of International Relations.* 2nd edition. Thousand Oaks: Sage Publications, 298–325.

Carlsnaes, Walter, Thomas Risse, and Beth A. Simmons (eds) (2013). *Handbook of International Relations.* 2nd edition. Thousand Oaks: Sage Publications.

Carmichael, Jason T., Robert J. Brulle, and Joanna K. Huxster (2017). The Great Divide: Understanding the Role of Media and Other Drivers of the Partisan Divide in Public Concern Over Climate Change in the USA, 2001–2014. *Climatic Change* 141/4: 599–612.

Carnegie, Andrew (1889). Wealth. *North American Review* 148/391: 653–65.

Carothers, Thomas (1996). Aiding Post-Communist Societies: A Better Way? *Problems of Post-Communism* 43/5:15–24.

Carothers, Thomas (2009). Democracy Assistance: Political vs. Developmental? *Journal of Democracy* 20/1: 5–19.

Carothers, Thomas, and Saskia Brechenmacher (2014). *Closing Space: Democracy and Human Rights Support under Fire.* Washington, D.C.: Carnegie Endowment for International Peace.

Carr, E.H. (1939) [2001]. The Twenty Years' Crisis, 1919–1939. Reissued with a new introduction and additional material by Michael Cox. Basingstoke: Palgrave.

Carroll, Berenice A. (1972). Peace Research: The Cult of Power. *The Journal of Conflict Resolution* 16/4: 585–616.

Carroll, William K. (2010). *The Making of the Transnational Capitalist Class.* London: Zed Books.

Carroll, William K., and Jean Philippe Sapinski (2016). Neoliberalism and the Transnational Capitalist Class. In: Birch, Kean, Julie MacLeavy, and Simon Springer (eds). *The Handbook of Neoliberalism.* London: Routledge, 25–35.

Carroll, William K., and Jean Philippe Sapinski (2010). The Global Corporate Elite and the Transnational Policy Planning Network, 1996–2006: A Structural Analysis. *International Sociology* 25/4: 501–38.

Caselli, Marco (2012). *Trying to Measure Globalization: Experiences, Critical issues and Perspectives.* Dordrecht: Springer.

Castells, Manuel (1996). *The Rise of the Network Society.* Malden, MA: Blackwell Publishers.

Centeno, Miguel A., and Joseph N. Cohen (2012). The Arc of Neoliberalism. *Annual Review of Sociology* 38: 317–40.

Cerny, Philip G. (1990). *The Changing Architecture of Politics: Structure, Agency, and the Future of the State.* London: Sage.

Cerny, Philip G. (1997). Paradoxes of the Competition State: The Dynamics of Political Globalization. *Government and Opposition* 32/2: 251–74.

Cerny, Philip G. (2000). Political Agency in a Globalizing World: Toward a Structurational Approach. *European Journal of International Relations* 6/4: 435–63.

Cerny, Philip G. (2008). Embedding Neoliberalism: The Evolution of a Hegemonic Paradigm. *The Journal of International Trade and Diplomacy* 2/1: 1–46.

Cerny, Philip G. (2010). *Rethinking World Politics: A Theory of Transnational Neopluralism.* Oxford: Oxford University Press.

Chalk, Peter (2008). The Tigers Abroad: How the LTTE Diaspora Supports the Conflict in Sri Lanka. *Georgetown Journal of International Affairs* 9/2: 97–104.

Chapin, Holly (2011). Clarifying Material Support to Terrorists: The Humanitarian Project Litigation and the U.S. Tamil Diaspora. *Journal of International Service* 20/2: 69–82.

Checkel, Jeffrey T. (1998). The Constructivist Turn in International Relations Theory. *World Politics* 50/2: 324–48.

Chenoweth, Neil (2001). *Rupert Murdoch: The Untold Story of the World's Greatest Media Wizard.* New York: Crown Business.

Chernow, Ron (1998). *Titan: The Life of John D. Rockefeller, Sr.* New York: Random House.

Chong, Dennis, and James N. Druckman (2007). Framing Theory. *Annual Review of Political Science* 10: 103–26.

Chorev, Nitsan (2013). Restructuring Neoliberalism at the World Health Organization. *Review of International Political Economy* 20/4: 627–66.

Christensen, Søren, Frank Dobbin, Peter Karnøe, Jesper Strandgaard Pedersen (1997). Actors and Institutions: Editors' Introduction. *American Behavioral Scientist* 40/4: 392–6.

Chwieroth, Jeffrey M. (2010). *Capital Ideas: The IMF and the Rise of Financial Liberalization.* Princeton: Princeton University Press.

Chwieroth, Jeffrey M., and Timothy J. Sinclair (2013). How you Stand Depends on How we See: International Capital Mobility as Social Fact. *Review of International Political Economy* 20/3: 457–85.

Cincotta, Richard P., and Eric Kaufmann (2010). *Uncompromising Demography in a Promised Land.* NIC 2010-05. Washington, D.C.: National Intelligence Council.

Clark, Ann Marie (2010). *Diplomacy of Conscience: Amnesty International and Changing Human Rights Norms.* Princeton: Princeton University Press.

Clark, Ann Marie, and Kathryn Sikkink (2013). Information Effects and Human Rights Data: Is the Good News about Increased Human Rights Information Bad News for Human Rights Measures? *Human Rights Quarterly* 35/3: 539–68.

Clarke, Harold D., David Sanders, Marianne C. Stewart, and Paul F. Whiteley (2009). *Performance Politics and the British Voter.* Cambridge: Cambridge University Press.

Clinton, Joshua D., and Ted Enamorado (2014). The National News Media's Effect on Congress: How Fox News Affected Elites in Congress. *The Journal of Politics* 76/4: 928–43.

Ciută, Felix (2009). Security and the Problem of Context: A Hermeneutical Critique of Securitisation Theory. *Review of International Studies* 35/2: 301–26.

Coase, Ronald H. (1960). The Problem of Social Cost. *The Journal of Law and Economics* 3/1: 1–44.

Cody, Anthony (2014). *The Educator And The Oligarch: A Teacher Challenges The Gates Foundation.* New York: Garn Press.

Cohen, Daniel (2014). *Homo Economicus: The (Lost) Prophet of Modern Times.* Cambridge: Polity.

Cohen, Gerald A. (1995). *Self-ownership, Freedom and Equality.* Cambridge: Cambridge University Press.

Cohen, Jon (2002). Gates Foundation Rearranges Public Health Universe. *Science* 295/5562: 2000.

Cohen, Jon (2005). Gates Foundation Picks Winners in Grand Challenges in Global Health. *Science* 309/5731: 33a–35a.

Cohen, Jon (2014). A Hard Look at Global Health Measures. *Science* 345/6202: 1260–5.

Cohen, Samy (2006). *The Resilience of the State: Democracy and the Challenges of Globalisation.* London: C. Hurst & Co.

Cohen, Steven M., and Gabriel Horenczyk (eds) (1999). *National Variations in Jewish Identity: Implications for Jewish Education*. New York: SUNY Press.

Cohen, Steven M., and Ari Y. Kelman (2007). *Beyond Distancing: Young Adult American Jews and Their Alienation from Israel*. New York: Berman Jewish Policy Archive/New York University, online: http://www.bjpa.org/Publications/details.cfm?PublicationID= 326.

Coleman, Janet (ed.) (1996). *The Individual in Political Theory and Practice*. New York: Oxford University Press.

Coll, Steve (2012). *Private Empire: ExxonMobil and American Power*. New York: Penguin.

Collier, Paul, and David Dollar (2002). Aid Allocation and Poverty Reduction. *European Economic Review* 46/8: 1475–500.

Collier, Ruth Berins (1999). *Paths toward Democracy: The Working Class and Elites in Western Europe and South America*. Cambridge: Cambridge University Press.

Collins, Chuck, Helen Flannery, and Josh Hoxie (2016). *Gilded Giving: Top-heavy Philanthropy in an Age of Extreme Inequality*. Washington, D.C.: Institute for Policy Studies.

Collins, Randall (1981). On the Microfoundations of Macrosociology. *American Journal of Sociology* 86/5: 984–1014.

Collins, Randall (1992). The Romanticism of Agency/Structure versus the Analysis of Micro/Macro. *Current Sociology* 40/1: 77–97.

Commission on Global Governance (1995). *Our Global Neighborhood*. New York: Oxford University Press.

Companjen, Francoise J. (2010). Georgia. In: Beacháin, Donnacha Ó., and Abel Polese (eds). *The Colour Revolutions in the Former Soviet Republics: Successes and Failures*. New York: Routledge, 13–29.

Cook, Fay Lomax, Benjamin I. Page, and Rachel Moskowitz (2014). *Political Participation by Wealthy Americans*. *Political Science Quarterly* 129/3: 381–98.

Cooley, Alexander A., and John Heathershaw (2017). *Dictators without Borders: Power and Money in Central Asia*. New Haven: Yale University Press.

Cooley, Alexander A., and James Ron (2002). The NGO Scramble: Organizational Insecurity and the Political Economy of Transnational Action. *International Security* 27/1: 5–39.

Cortright, David (2008). *Peace: A History of Movements and Ideas*. Cambridge: Cambridge University Press.

Crawford, Neta C. (2014). *U.S. Costs of Wars through 2014: $4.4 Trillion and Counting. Summary of Costs for the U.S. Wars in Iraq, Afghanistan and Pakistan* (June 25, 2014). Providence: Watson Institute for International and Public Affairs. Online: http://watson.brown.edu/costsofwar/files/cow/imce/figures/2014/Costs%20of%20War%20Summary%20Crawford%20June%202014.pdf.

Credit Suisse (2013). *Global Wealth Databook 2013*. Zurich: Credit Suisse Research Institute.

Credit Suisse (2018). *Global Wealth Databook 2018*. Zurich: Credit Suisse Research Institute.

Cringely, Robert X. (1996). *Accidental Empires: How the Boys of Silicon Valley Make Their Millions, Battle Foreign Competition, and Still Can't Get a Date*. 2nd revised and expanded edition. New York: HarperCollins.

Crouch, Colin (2011). *The Strange Non-Death of Neo-Liberalism*. Cambridge: Polity.

Crouch, Colin, and Henry Farrell (2004). Breaking the Path of Institutional Development? Alternatives to the New Determinism. *Rationality and Society* 16/1: 5–43.

Cueto, Marcos (2004). The Origins of Primary Health Care and Selective Primary Health Care. *American Journal of Public Health* 94/11: 1864–74.

Curti, Merle (1963). *American Philanthropy Abroad: A History*. New Brunswick: Rutgers University Press.

Cutler, A. Claire, Virginia Haufler, and Tony Porter (eds) (1999). *Private Authority and International Affairs*. Albany: State University of New York Press.

Cutler, A. Claire (2003). *Private Power and Global Authority: Transnational Merchant Law in the Global Political Economy*. Cambridge: Cambridge University Press.

Czempiel, Ernst O., and James N. Rosenau (eds) (1989). *Global Changes and Theoretical Challenges: Approaches to World Politics for the 1990s*. Lexington, MA: Lexington Books.

da Silva, Anna (2013). *Institutional Innovation in Global Health: Changing Roles of State and Non-State Actors in Governance of Vaccine Preventable Diseases*. PhD dissertation. Rutgers, The State University of New Jersey, online: file:///C:/Users/Peter/Downloads/ETD-2013-5126.pdf.

Daddow, Oliver (2011). *New Labour and the European Union: Blair and Brown's Logic of History*. Manchester: Manchester University Press.

Daddow, Oliver (2012). The UK media and "Europe": From Permissive Consensus to Destructive Dissent. *International Affairs* 88/6: 1219–36.

Dahan, Michael, and Mouli Bentham (2017). The Ripple Effects of a Partisan, Free Newspaper: Israel Hayom as Disruptive Media Actor. *Studies in Communication Sciences* 17/1: 99–106.

Dahl, Robert A. (1957) [1969]. The Concept of Power. *Behavioral Science* 2: 201–15. Reprinted In: Bell, Roderick, David V. Edwards and R. Harrison Wagner (eds) (1969). *Political Power: A Reader in Theory and Research*. New York: The Free Press, 79–83.

Dahl, Robert A. (1958). A Critique of the Ruling Elite Model. *American Political Science Review* 52/2: 463–9.

Dahl, Robert A. (1961). *Who Governs? Democracy and Power in an American City*. New Haven: Yale University Press.

Dahl, Robert A. (1967). *Pluralist Democracy in the United States*. Chicago: Rand McNally.

Dahl, Robert A. (1982). *Dilemmas of Pluralist Democracy*. New Haven: Yale University Press.

Dahrendorf, Ralf (1961). *Gesellschaft und Freiheit: Zur soziologischen Analyse der Gegenwart*. München: Piper.

Dardot, Pierre, and Christian Laval (2013). *The New Way of the World: On Neoliberal Society*. London: Verso.

Daucé, Françoise (2015). The Duality of Coercion in Russia: Cracking Down on "Foreign Agents." *Demokratizatsiya: The Journal of Post-Soviet Democratization* 23/1: 57–75.

Davidson, Roei, Nathaniel Poor, and Ann Williams (2009). Stratification and Global Elite Theory: A Cross-Cultural and Longitudinal Analysis of Public Opinion. *International Journal of Public Opinion Research* 21/2: 165–86.

Davies, James D. (ed.) (2008). *Personal Wealth from a Global Perspective*. Oxford: Oxford University Press.

Davies, James B., Susanna Sandström, Anthony B. Shorrocks, and Edward N. Wolff (2011). The Level and Distribution of Global Household Wealth. *The Economic Journal* 121: 223–54.

Davis, David R., Amanda Murdie, and Coty Garnett Steinmetz (2012). "Makers and Shapers": Human Rights INGOs and Public Opinion. *Human Rights Quarterly* 34/1: 199–224.

De Soto, Hernando (2000). *The Mystery of Capital: Why Capitalism Succeeds in the West and Fails Everywhere Else*. New York: Basic Books.

Dehejia, Vivek H., and Philipp Genschel (1999). Tax Competition in the European Union. *Politics & Society* 27/3: 403–30.

Deibert, Ronald (1997). *Parchment, Printing and Hypermedia: Communication and World Order Transformation*. New York: Columbia University Press.

DellaVigna, Stefano, and Ethan Kaplan (2007). The Fox News Effect: Media Bias and Voting. *The Quarterly Journal of Economics* 122/3: 1187–234.

Dellmuth, Lisa Maria, and Jonas Tallberg (2015). The Social Legitimacy of International Organisations: Interest Representation, Institutional Performance, and Confidence Extrapolation in the United Nations. *Review of International Studies* 41/3: 451–75.

Denemark, Robert A. (ed) (2010). *The International Studies Encyclopedia*. Chichester: Wiley-Blackwell. Also online as The *International Studies Compendium Project*: http://www.isacompendium.com/public/.

Dépelteau, François (2008). Relational Thinking: A Critique of Co-Deterministic Theories of Structure and Agency. *Sociological Theory* 26/1: 51–73.

Desai, Mihir A. (2009). The Decentering of the Global Firm. *The World Economy* 32/9: 1271–90.

Dessler, David (1989). What's at Stake in the Agent-Structure Debate. *International Organization* 43/3: 441–73.

Deudney, Daniel H. (1993). Dividing Realism: Structural Realism versus Security Materialism on Nuclear Security and Proliferation. *Security Studies* 1/1: 7–37.

Deudney, Daniel H. (2000a). Regrounding Realism: Anarchy, Security, and Changing Material Contexts. *Security Studies* 10/1: 1–42.

Deudney, Daniel H. (2000b). Geopolitics as Theory: Historical Security Materialism. *European Journal of International Relations* 6/1: 77–107.

Deudney, Daniel H. (2007). *Bounding Power: Republican Security Theory from the Polis to the Global Village*. Princeton: Princeton University Press.

DeVotta, Neil (2004). *Blowback: Linguistic Nationalism, Institutional Decay, and Ethnic Conflict in Sri Lanka*. Stanford: Stanford University Press.

DeVotta, Neil (2009). The Liberation Tigers of Tamil Eelam and the Lost Quest for Separatism in Sri Lanka. *Asian Survey* 49/6: 1021–51.

Dieleman, Joseph L., Matthew T. Schneider, Annie Haakenstad, Lavanya Singh, Nafis Sadat, Maxwell Birger, Alex Reynolds, Tara Templin, Hannah Hamavid, Abigail Chapin, and Christopher J. L. Murray (2016). Development Assistance for Health: Past Trends, Associations, and the Future of International Financial Flows for Health. *The Lancet* 387/10037: 2536–44.

DiMaggio, P. J. (1988). Interest and Agency in Institutional Theory. In: Zucker, L. G. (ed.). *Institutional Patterns and Organizations*. Cambridge, MA: Ballinger, 3–22.

Dittmar, Helga, Rod Bond, Megan Hurst, and Tim Kasser (2014). The Relationship between Materialism and Personal Well-Being: A Meta-Analysis. *Journal of Personality and Social Psychology* 107/5: 879–924.

Diuk, Nadia (2006). The Triumph of Civil Society. In: Aslund, Anders, and Michael McFaul (eds). *Revolution in Orange: The Origins of Ukraine's Democratic Breakthrough*. Washington, D.C.: Carnegie Endowment for International Peace, 69–83.

Djelic, Marie-Laure (2005). From Local Legislation to Global Structuring Frame: The Story of Antitrust. *Global Social Policy* 5/1: 55–76.

Dobbin, Frank (1994). Cultural Models of Organization: The Social Construction of Rational Organizing Principles. In: Crane, Diana (ed.). *The Sociology of Culture: Emerging Theoretical Perspectives*. Oxford: Basil Blackwell, 117–41.

Donati, Pierpaolo, and Margaret S. Archer (2015). *The Relational Subject*. Cambridge: Cambridge University Press.

Donnelly, Jack (2009). Rethinking Political Structures: From "Ordering Principles" to "Vertical Differentiation"—and Beyond. *International Theory* 1/1: 49–86.

Donnelly, Jack (2012). The Elements of the Structures of International Systems. *International Organization* 66/4: 609–43.

Donnelly, John (2012). The President's Emergency Plan for AIDS Relief: How George W. Bush and Aides Came to "Think Big" on Battling HIV. *Health Affairs* 31/7: 1389–96.

Donnelly, Shawn (2014). Power Politics and the Undersupply of Financial Stability in Europe. *Review of International Political Economy* 21/4: 980–1005.

Dowding, Keith (2008). Power, Capability and Ableness: The Fallacy of the Vehicle Fallacy. *Contemporary Political Theory* 7/3: 238–58.

Dowding, Keith (2011). Agency. In: Dowding, Keith (ed.). *The Encyclopedia of Power*. London: SAGE, 6–10.

Doyle, Michael (1986). Liberalism and World Politics. *American Political Science Review* 80/4: 1151–69.

Dreher, Axel, and Nathan M. Jensen (2007). Independent Actor or Agent? An Empirical Analysis of the Impact of US Interests on International Monetary Fund Conditions. *The Journal of Law and Economics* 50/1: 105–24.

Dreiling, Michael C., and Derek Y. Darves (2016). *Agents of Neoliberal Globalization: Corporate Networks, State Structures, and Trade Policy*. Cambridge: Cambridge University Press.

Drew, Elizabeth (2015). How They Failed to Block the Iran Deal. *The New York Review of Books*, October 22, 2015, online: http://www.nybooks.com/articles/2015/10/22/how-they-failed-block-iran-deal/.

Drezner, Daniel W. (2007). *All Politics is Global: Explaining International Regulatory Regimes*. Princeton: Princeton University Press.

Drezner, Daniel W. (2014). *The System Worked: How the World Stopped Another Great Depression*. Oxford: Oxford University Press.

Druckman, James (2004). Political Preference Formation: Competition, Deliberation, and the (Ir)relevance of Framing Effects. *American Political Science Review* 98/4: 671–86.

Druyen, Thomas (ed.) (2011). *Vermögenskultur: Verantwortung im 21. Jahrhundert*. Wiesbaden: VS.

Duda, Aleksandra (2010). *When "It's Time" To Say "Enough!": Youth Activism Before and During the Rose and Orange Revolutions in Georgia and Ukraine*. PhD thesis. Birmingham: The University of Birmingham.

Duménil, Gérard, and Dominique Lévy (2004). *Capital Resurgent: Roots of the Neoliberal Revolution*. Cambridge, MA: Harvard University Press.

Dupuy, Kendra E., James Ron, and Aseem Prakash (2015). Who Survived? Ethiopia's Regulatory Crackdown on Foreign-funded NGOs. *Review of International Political Economy* 22/2: 419–56.

Dvir-Gvirsman, Shira, R. Kelly Garrett, and Yariv Tsfati (2015). Why Do Partisan Audiences Participate? Perceived Public Opinion as the Mediating Mechanism. *Communication Research*, DOI: https://doi.org/10.1177/0093650215593145.

Ecker-Ehrhardt, Matthias (2012). Cosmopolitan Politicization? Relating Public Perceptions of Interdependence and Expectations in Internationalized Governance. *European Journal of International Relations* 18/3: 481–508.

Ecker-Ehrhardt, Matthias (2016). Why do Citizens Want the UN to Decide? Cosmopolitan Ideas, Particularism and Global Authority. *International Political Science Review* 37/1: 99–114.

Eckl, Julian (2014). The Power of Private Foundations: Rockefeller and Gates in the Struggle against Malaria. *Global Social Policy* 14/1: 91–116.

Eckstein, Harry (1975). Case Studies and Theory in Political Science. In: Greenstein, Fred, and Nelson Polsby (eds). *Handbook of Political Science, Vol. 7*. Reading, Mass.: Addison-Wesley, 79–138.

Edwards, Michael (2010). *Small Change: Why Business Won't Change the World*. San Francisco: Berrett-Koehler.

Ehrenfeld, Rachel (2005). *Funding Evil: How Terrorism is Financed and How to Stop It*. Expanded edition. Chicago: Bonus Books.

Eichengreen, Barry (2008). *Globalizing Capital: A History of the International Monetary System*. 2nd edition. Princeton: Princeton University Press.

Eichengreen, Barry (2018). *The Populist Temptation: Economic Grievance and Political Reaction in the Modern Era*. Oxford: Oxford University Press.

Eisinger, Peter (1973). The Conditions of Protest Behavior in American Cities. *American Political Science Review* 81/1: 11–28.

el Sehity, Tarek, and Anna Schor-Tschudnowskaja (2011). Vermögende in Deutschland—Die Perspektive der Vermögenskulturforschung. In: Lauterbach, Wolfgang, Thomas Druyen, and Thomas Grundmann (eds). *Vermögen in Deutschland—Heterogenität und Verantwortung*. Wiesbaden: VS, 143–202.

Elder-Vass, Dave (2007). Reconciling Archer and Bourdieu in an Emergentist Theory of Action. *Sociological Theory* 25/4: 325–46.

Elias, Norbert (1991). *The Society of Individuals*. Oxford: Basil Blackwell.

Elkins, Zachary, Andrew T. Guzman, and Beth A. Simmons (2006). Competing for Capital: The Diffusion of Bilateral Investment Treaties, 1960–2000. *International Organization* 60/4: 811–46.

Elliott, Kimberly Ann (ed.) (1997). *Corruption and the Global Economy*. Washington, D.C.: Institute for International Economics.

Emirbayer, Mustafa (1997). Manifesto for a Relational Sociology. *American Journal of Sociology* 103/2: 281–317.Emirbayer, Mustafa, and Ann Mische (1998). What is Agency? *American Journal of Sociology* 103: 962–1023.

Epstein, Charlotte (2013). Theorizing Agency in Hobbes's Wake: The Rational Actor, the Self, or the Speaking Subject? *International Organization* 67/2: 287–316.

Erlandson, Dawn (1994). The BTU tax experience: What Happened and Why it Happened. *Pace Environmental Law Review* 12/1: 173–84.

Erman, Eva (2018). The Political Legitimacy of Global Governance and the Proper Role of Civil Society Actors. *Res Publica* 24: 133–55.

Erman, Eva, and Anders Uhlin (eds) (2010). *Legitimacy Beyond the State? Re-examining the Democratic Credentials of Transnational Actors*. London: Palgrave Macmillan.

Erman, Eva, and Sofia Näsström (eds) (2013). *Political Equality in Transnational Democracy*. London: Palgrave Macmillan.

Erskine, Toni (2008). Locating Responsibility: The Problem of Moral Agency in International Relations. In: Reus-Smit, Christian, and Duncan Snidal (eds). *The Oxford Handbook of International Relations*. Oxford: Oxford University Press, 699–707.

Estevadeordal, Antoni, Brian Frantz, and Alan M. Taylor (2003). The Rise and Fall of World Trade, 1870–1939. *Quarterly Journal of Economics* 118/2: 359–407.

Etzioni, Amitai (2010). Is Transparency the Best Disinfectant? *Journal of Political Philosophy* 18/4: 389–404.

European Commission (2019). *Final Report from the Commission to the European Parliament, the Council, the European Economic and Social Committee and the Committee of the*

Regions: Investor Citizenship and Residence Schemes in the European Union. Brussels: European Commission.

Evans, Peter B., and William H. Sewell (2013). Neoliberalism: Policy Regimes, International Regimes, and Social Effects. In: Hall, Peter A. and Michèle Lamont (eds). *Social Resilience in the Neoliberal Era*. Cambridge: Cambridge University Press, 35–68.

Fair, C. Christine (2005). Diaspora Involvement in Insurgencies: Insights from the Khalistan and Tamil Eelam Movements. *Nationalism and Ethnic Politics* 11/1: 125–56.

Fairbanks, Charles H. (2004). Georgia's Rose Revolution. *Journal of Democracy* 15/2: 110–24.

Falguera, Elin, Samuel Jones, and Magnus Ohman (eds) (2014). *Funding of Political Parties and Election Campaigns: A Handbook on Political Finance*. Stockholm: International Institute for Democracy and Electoral Assistance.

Farrell, Justin (2016a). Corporate Funding and Ideological Polarization about Climate Change. *Proceedings of the National Academy of Sciences* 113/1: 92–7.

Farrell, Justin (2016b). Network Structure and Influence of the Climate Change Counter-movement. *Nature Climate Change* 6/4: 370–4.

Fearon, James D. (1994). Domestic Political Audiences and the Escalation of International Dispute. *American Political Science Review* 88/3: 577–92.

Fearon, James D., and David D. Laitin (2003). Ethnicity, Insurgency, and Civil War. *American Political Science Review* 97/1: 75–90.

Featherstone, Mike, Scott Lash, and Roland Robertson (eds) (1995). *Global Modernities*. London: Sage.

Fejerskov, Adam Moe (2015). From Unconventional to Ordinary? The Bill and Melinda Gates Foundation and the Homogenizing Effects of International Development Cooperation. *Journal of International Development* 27/7: 1098–112.

Feldman, Lauren, Edward W. Maibach, Connie Roser-Renouf, and Anthony Leiserowitz (2011). Climate on Cable: The Nature and Impact of Global Warming Coverage on Fox News, CNN, and MSNBC. *The International Journal of Press/Politics* 17: 1–29.

Feldman, Lauren, Teresa A. Myers, Jay D. Hmielowski, and Anthony Leiserowitz (2014). The Mutual Reinforcement of Media Selectivity and Effects: Testing the Reinforcing Spirals Framework in the Context of Global Warming. *Journal of Communication* 64/4: 590–611.

Filc, Dani (2010). *The Political Right in Israel: Different Faces of Jewish Populism*. New York: Routledge.

Financial Stability Board (2014). *Global Shadow Banking Monitoring Report 2014*. Available online: http://www.financialstabilityboard.org/wp-content/uploads/r_141030.pdf.

Findley, Michael G., Daniel L. Nielson, and Jason C. Sharman (2014). *Global Shell Games: Experiments in Transnational Relations, Crime, and Terrorism*. Cambridge: Cambridge University Press.

Finkel, Steven E., Aníbal S. Pérez Liñan, Mitchell A. Seligson (2007). The Effects of U. S. Foreign Assistance on Democracy Building, 1990–2003. *World Politics* 59/3: 404–39.

Finnemore, Martha, and Kathryn Sikkink (1998). International Norm Dynamics and Political Change. *International Organization* 52: 887–917.

Fioretos, Orfeo (2010). Capitalist Diversity and the International Regulation of Hedge Funds. *Review of International Political Economy* 17/4: 696–723.

Fish, M. Steven (2009). Encountering Culture. In: Barany, Zoltan, and Robert G. Moser (eds). *Is Democracy Exportable?* Cambridge: Cambridge University Press, 57–84.

Fishbach, Ayelet, and Melissa F. Ferguson (2007). The Goal Construct in Social Psychology. In: Kruglanski, Arie W. and E. Tory Higgins (eds). *Social Psychology: Handbook of Basic Principles*. 2nd edition. New York: Guilford, 490–515.

Fisher, Dana R., Joseph Waggle, and Philip Leifeld (2013). Where Does Political Polarization Come from? Locating Polarization within the US Climate Change Debate. *American Behavioral Scientist* 57/1: 70–92.

Fleischacker, Samuel (1999). *A Third Concept of Liberty: Judgment and Freedom in Kant and Adam Smith*. Princeton: Princeton University Press.

Fligstein, Neil (2001). Social Skill and the Theory of Fields. *Sociological Theory* 19/2: 105–25.

Fligstein, Neil, and Doug McAdam (2011). Toward a General Theory of Strategic Action Fields. *Sociological Theory* 29/1: 1–26.

Fligstein, Neil and Doug McAdam (2012). *A Theory of Fields*. Oxford: Oxford University Press.

Florini, Ann M. (ed.) (2000). *The Third Force: The Rise of Transnational Civil Society*. Tokyo/Washington, D.C.: Japan Center for International Exchange/Carnegie Endowment for International Peace.

Folkenflik, David (2013). *Murdoch's World: The Last of the Old Media Empires*. New York: PublicAffairs.

Forsythe, David P. (2012). *Human Rights in International Relations*. 3rd edition. Cambridge: Cambridge University Press.

Fortescue, Stephen (2006). *Russia's Oil Barons and Metal Magnates: Oligarchs and the State in Transition*. Basingstoke: Palgrave Macmillan.

Foucault, Michel (1975). *Surveiller et Punir*. Paris: Gallimard.

Foucault, Michel (1982). The Subject and Power. *Critical Inquiry* 8/4: 777–95.

Fougner, Tore (2006). The State, International Competitiveness and Neoliberal Globalisation: Is There a Future Beyond "The Competition State"? *Review of International Studies* 32: 165–85.

Fourcade-Gourinchas, Marion, and Sarah Babb (2002). The Rebirth of the Liberal Creed: Paths to Neoliberalism in Four Countries. *American Journal of Sociology* 108/3: 533–79.

Fowler, James H., and Christopher T. Dawes (2008). Two Genes Predict Voter Turnout. *Journal of Politics* 70/3: 579–94.

Fox, Jonathan (2007). The Uncertain Relationship between Transparency and Accountability. *Development in Practice* 17/4: 663–71.

Frank, Robert (2007). *Richistan: A Journey through the 21st Century Wealth Boom and the Lives of the New Rich*. New York: Crown.

Frank, Robert H., and Philip J. Cook (1995) [2010]. *The Winner-Take-All Society: Why the Few at the Top Get So Much More Than the Rest of Us*. New edition. London: Virgin Books.

Fraser, Nancy, and Axel Honneth (2003). *Redistribution or Recognition? A Political-Philosophical Exchange*. London: Verso.

Freedman, Robert O. (ed.) (2012). *Israel and the United States: Six Decades of US-Israeli Relations*. Boulder, CO: Westview Press.

Freeland, Chrystia (2012). *Plutocrats: The Rise of the New Global Super-Rich and the Fall of Everyone Else*. New York: Penguin.

Freeman, Ben (2012). *The Foreign Policy Auction: Foreign Lobbying in America*. Self-published. Printed by CreateSpace, Charleston.

Freund, Caroline (2016). *Rich People Poor Countries: The Rise of Emerging-Market Tycoons and their Mega Firms*. Washington, D.C.: Peterson Institute for International Economics.

Frieden, Jeffry A. (1991). Invested Interests: The Politics of National Economic Policies in a World of Global Finance. *International Organization* 45/4: 425–51.

Frieden, Jeffry A. (2006). *Global Capitalism: Its Fall and Rise in the Twentieth Century*. New York: W.W. Norton & Company.

Frieden, Jeffry A., David A. Lake, and Kenneth A. Schultz (2018). *World Politics: Interests, Interactions, Institutions*. 4th edition. New York: W. W. Norton & Company.

Friedman, Lawrence J. (2003). Philanthropy in America: Historicism and its Discontents. In: Friedman, Lawrence J., and Mark D. McGarvie (eds). *Charity, Philanthropy, and Civility in American History*. Cambridge: Cambridge University Press, 1–21.

Friedman, Lawrence J., and Mark D. McGarvie (eds) (2003). *Charity, Philanthropy, and Civility in American History*. Cambridge: Cambridge University Press.

Friedman, Milton (1962). *Capitalism and Freedom*. Chicago: University of Chicago Press.

Friedrich, Carl J. (1937). *Constitutional Government and Politics*. New York: Harper and Brothers.

Fuchs, Stephan (2001). Beyond Agency. *Sociological Theory* 19/1: 24–40.

Fuchs, Andreas, Axel Dreher, and Peter Nunnenkamp (2014). Determinants of Donor Generosity: A Survey of the Aid Budget Literature. *World Development* 56: 172–99.

Fukuyama, Francis (1989). The End of History? *The National Interest* 16: 3–18.

Fukuyama, Francis (2012). The Future of History. *Foreign Affairs* 91/1: 53–61.

Gabaix, Xavier, and Augustin Landier (2008). Why has CEO Pay Increased so Much? *Quarterly Journal of Economics* 121/1: 49–100.

Gaddis, John Lewis (2005). *The Cold War: A New History*. London: Penguin.

Galbraith, James K. (2014). Kapital for the Twenty-First Century? *Dissent* (spring 2014), online: http://www.dissentmagazine.org/article/kapital-for-the-twenty-first-century.

Galpin, Charlotte, and Trenz, Hans-Jörg (2018). Die Euroskeptizismus-Spirale: EU-Berichterstattung und Medien-Negativität. *Österreichische Zeitschrift für Soziologie* 43/S1: 147–72.

Gandhi, Gian (2015). Charting the evolution of approaches employed by the Global Alliance for Vaccines and Immunizations (GAVI) to address inequities in access to immunization: A systematic qualitative review of GAVI policies, strategies and resource allocation mechanisms through an equity lens (1999–2014). *BMC Public Health* 15/1: 1, online: http://bmcpublichealth.biomedcentral.com/articles/10.1186/s12889-015-2521-8.

Garrett, Geoffrey (1998). *Partisan Politics in the Global Economy*. Cambridge: Cambridge University Press.

Garrett, Laurie (2007). The Challenge of Global Health. *Foreign Affairs* 86/1: 14–38.

Gartzke, Erik (2007). The Capitalist Peace. *American Journal of Political Science* 51/1: 166–91.

Gat, Azar (2006). *War in Human Civilization*. Oxford: Oxford University Press.

Gat, Azar (2013). Is War Declining–and Why? *Journal of Peace Research* 50/2: 149–57.

Gat, Azar, with Alexander Yakobson (2012). *Nations: The Long History and Deep Roots of Political Ethnicity and Nationalism*. Cambridge: Cambridge University Press.

Gates, Bill (2015). The Next Epidemic—Lessons from Ebola. *New England Journal of Medicine* 372/15: 1381–4.

Gates, Bill (2018). Innovation for Pandemics. *New England Journal of Medicine* 378/22: 2057–60.

Gauchat, Gordon (2012). Politicization of Science in the Public Sphere: A Study of Public Trust in the United States, 1974 to 2010. *American Sociological Review* 77/2: 167–87.

Gavil, Andrew I., and Harry First (2014). *The Microsoft Anti-trust Cases: Competition Policy for the Twenty-first Century*. Cambridge: MIT Press.

Geddes, Barbara (1990). How the Cases you Choose Affect the Answers you Get: Selection Bias in Comparative Politics. *Political Analysis* 2: 131–50.

Gelvin, James L. (2014). *The Israel-Palestine Conflict: One Hundred Years of War*. 3rd edition. Cambridge: Cambridge University Press.

Genschel, Philipp (2002). Globalization, Tax Competition and the Welfare State. *Politics & Society* 30/2: 244–74.

Genschel, Philipp (2004). Globalization and the Welfare State: A Retrospective. *Journal of European Public Policy* 11/4: 613–36.

Genschel, Philipp (2005). Globalization and the Transformation of the "Tax State." *European Review* 13/1: 53–71.

Genschel, Philipp, and Thomas Plümper (1997). Regulatory Competition and International Co-operation. *Journal of European Public Policy* 4/4: 626–42.

Genschel, Philipp, and Peter Schwarz (2011). Tax Competition: A Literature Review. *Socio-Economic Review* 9/2: 339–70.

Gent, Stephen E., Mark JC Crescenzi, Elizabeth J. Menninga, and Lindsay Reid (2015). The Reputation Trap of NGO Accountability. *International Theory* 7/3: 426–63.

George, Alexander L., and Bennett, Andrew (2005). *Case Studies and Theory Development.* Cambridge, MA: MIT Press.

Gerbaudo, Paolo (2017). *The Mask and the Flag: Populism, Citizenism, and Global Protest.* Oxford: Oxford University Press.

Gerber, Alan S., Gergory A. Huber, David Doherty, Conor M. Dowling, Connor Raso, and Shang E. Ha (2011). Personality Traits and Participation in the Political Process. *Journal of Politics* 73/3: 692–706.

Gerber, David (2012). *Global Competition: Law, Markets, and Globalization.* Oxford: Oxford University Press.

Gerges, Fawaz A. (2013). The Obama Approach to the Middle East: The End of America's Moment? *International Affairs* 89/2: 299–323.

Gerharz, Eva (2009). Zwischen Krieg und Frieden: Die Tamil Tigers und ihre Diaspora als Konfliktpartei und Entwicklungsakteur. *SOCIOLOGUS* 59/1: 33–49.

Gerharz, Eva (2014). *The Politics of Reconstruction and Development in Sri Lanka: Transnational Commitments and Social Change.* New York: Routledge.

Gersbach, Hans, and Armin Schmutzler (2014). Does Globalization Create Superstars? A Simple Theory of Managerial Wages. *European Economic Review* 71: 34–51.

Gerring, John (2007). Is There a (Viable) Crucial-case Method? *Comparative Political Studies* 40/3: 231–53.

Gershkoff, Amy, and Shana Kushner (2005). Shaping Public Opinion: The 9/11-Iraq Connection in the Bush Administration's Rhetoric. *Perspectives on Politics* 3/3: 525–37.

Gerstenfeld, Manfred (2015). The Run-Up to Israel's 2013 Elections: A Political History. *Israel Affairs* 21/2: 177–94.

Giddens, Anthony (1979). *Central Problems in Social Theory: Action, Structure and Contradictions in Social Analysis.* London: Macmillan.

Giddens, Anthony (1984). *The Constitution of Society: Outline of the Theory of Structuration.* Cambridge: Polity.

Giddens, Anthony (1989). A Reply to my Critics. In: Held, David, and John B. Thompson (eds). *Social Theory of Modern Societies: Anthony Giddens and his Critics.* Cambridge: Cambridge University Press, 249–301.

Giddens, Anthony (1990). *The Consequences of Modernity.* Stanford: Stanford University Press.

Gilboa, Eytan (2008). The Evolution of Israeli Media. *Middle East Review of International Affairs* 12/3: 88–101.

Gilens, Martin (2012). *Affluence and Influence: Economic Inequality and Political Power in America.* Princeton: Princeton University Press.

Gill, Stephen (1990). *American Hegemony and the Trilateral Commission.* Cambridge: Cambridge University Press.

Gilpin, Robert (1971). The Politics of Transnational Economic Relations. *International Organization* 25/3: 398–419.

Gilpin, Robert (1987). *The Political Economy of International Relations*. Princeton: Princeton University Press.

Gingrich, Newt (2005). Defeat of Terror, Not Roadmap Diplomacy, Will Bring Peace. *Middle East Quarterly* 12/3: 3–13, online: http://www.meforum.org/729/defeat-of-terror-not-roadmap-diplomacy-will-bring.

Giridharadas, Anand (2018). *Winners Take All: The Elite Charade of Changing the World*. New York: Knopf.

Giving USA (2013). *Twenty-Five Years of International Giving: 1987–2012*. Giving USA 2013 Spotlight 2. Chicago: Giving USA Foundation.

Glassman, Amanda, and Miriam Temin (2016). *Millions Saved: New Cases of Proven Success in Global Health*. Washington DC: Center for Global Development/Brookings Institution Press.

Gleditsch, Nils Petter, Steven Pinker, Bradley A. Thayer, Jack S. Levy, and William R. Thompson (2013). The Forum: The Decline of War. *International Studies Review* 15/3: 396–419.

Glick, Caroline (2014). *The Israeli Solution: A One-State Plan for Peace in the Middle East*. New York: Crown Forum.

Goddard, Stacie E. (2009). Brokering Change: Networks and Entrepreneurs in International Politics. *International Theory* 1: 249–81.

Gofas, Andreas, and Colin Hay (eds) (2010a). *The Role of Ideas in Political Analysis: A Portrait of Contemporary Debates*. New York: Routledge.

Gofas, Andreas, and Colin Hay (2010b). Varieties of Ideational Explanation. In: Gofas, Andreas, and Colin Hay (eds). *The Role of Ideas in Political Analysis: A Portrait of Contemporary Debates*. New York: Routledge, 13–55.

Goffman, Erving (1959). *The Presentation of Self in Everyday Life*. Edinburgh: University of Edinburgh Social Sciences Research Centre.

Goklany, Indur M. (2012). *Humanity Unbound: How Fossil Fuels Saved Humanity from Nature and Nature from Humanity*. Policy Analysis no. 715. Washington, D.C.: Cato Institute.

Goldberg, Pinelopi K., and Nina Pavcnik (2016). The Effects of Trade Policy. In: Bagwell, Kyle, and Robert W. Staiger (eds). *Handbook of Commercial Policy*. Vol. 1A. Amsterdam: North-Holland, 161–206.

Goldgeier, James, and Philip Tetlock (2001). Psychology and International Relations Theory. *Annual Review of Political Science* 4/1: 67–92.

Goldstein, Joshua S., and Jon C. Pevehouse (2016). *International Relations*. 11th edition. New York: Pearson.

Goldstein, Judith, and Robert Keohane (eds) (1993a). *Ideas and Foreign Policy: Beliefs, Institutions and Political Change*. Ithaca, N.Y.: Cornell University Press.

Goldstein, Judith, and Robert O. Keohane (1993b). Ideas and Foreign Policy: An Analytical Framework. In: Goldstein, Judith, and Robert Keohane (eds). *Ideas and Foreign Policy: Beliefs, Institutions and Political Change*. Ithaca, N.Y.: Cornell University Press, 3–30.

Goldstein, Judith, Douglas Rivers, and Michael Tomz (2007). Institutions in International Relations: Understanding the Effects of the GATT and the WTO on World Trade. *International Organization* 61/1: 37–67.

Gollwitzer, Peter M. (1993). Goal Achievement: The Role of Intentions. *European Review of Social Psychology* 4: 141–85.

Goodman, John B., and Louis W. Pauly (1993). The Obsolescence of Capital Controls? Economic Management in an Age of Global Markets. *World Politics* 46/1: 50–82.

Goosby, Eric, Mark Dybul, Anthony A. Fauci, Joe Fu, Thomas Walsh, Richard Needle, and Paul Bouey (2012). The United States President's Emergency Plan for AIDS Relief: A Story of Partnerships and Smart Investments to Turn the Tide of the Global AIDS Pandemic. *JAIDS Journal of Acquired Immune Deficiency Syndromes* 60/Supplement 3: S51–S56.

Gorrell, Genevieve, Ian Roberts, Mark A. Greenwood, Mehmet E. Bakir, Benedetta Iavarone, and Kalina Bontcheva (2018). Quantifying Media Influence and Partisan Attention on Twitter during the UK EU Referendum. In: Staab, Steffen, Olessia Koltsova, and Dmitry I. Ignatov (eds). *Social Informatics. 10th International Conference, SocInfo 2018, St. Petersburg, Russia, September 25–28, 2018, Proceedings, Part I.* Cham: Springer, 274–90.

Goss, Kristin A. (2016). Policy Plutocrats: How America's Wealthy Seek to Influence Governance. *PS: Political Science & Politics* 49/3: 442–8.

Gravelle, Jane G. (2013). *Tax Havens: International Tax Avoidance and Evasion.* Congressional Research Service report R40623. Washington, D.C.: Congressional Research Service.

Graz, Jean-Christophe (2003). How Powerful are Transnational Elite Clubs? The Social Myth of the World Economic Forum. *New Political Economy* 8/3: 321–40.

Graz, Jean-Christophe, and Andreas Nölke (2012). The Limits of Transnational Private Governance. In: Guzzini, Stefano, and Iver Neumann (eds). *The Diffusion of Power in Global Governance: International Political Economy Meets Foucault.* Basingstoke: Palgrave Macmillan, 118–40.

Green, Jeffrey Edward (2013). Rawls and the Forgotten Figure of the Most Advantaged: In Defense of Reasonable Envy toward the Superrich. *American Political Science Review* 107/1: 123–38.

Green, Jessica F. (2014). *Rethinking Private Authority: Agents and Entrepreneurs in Global Environmental Governance.* Princeton: Princeton University Press.

Greenberg Quinlan Rosner (2016). *Why? Report from Election Night Survey, November 2016.* Washington, D.C.: Greenberg Quinlan Rosner, online: http://www.wvwvaf. org/wp-content/uploads/2016/12/WVWVAF-Post-Election-Presentation-11.17.2016. pdf.

Greene, Toby (2015). Israel's Two States Debate. *International Affairs* 91/5: 1009–26.

Greenhouse, Carol J. (ed.) (2010). *Ethnographies of Neoliberalism.* Philadelphia: University of Pennsylvania Press.

Greenpeace USA (2010). *Koch Industries Secretly Funding the Climate Denial Machine.* Washington, D.C.: Greenpeace USA.

Grieco, Joseph (1988). Anarchy and the Limits of Cooperation: A Realist Critique of the Newest Liberal Institutionalism. *International Organization* 42: 485–507.

Griffiths, James (2019). *The Great Firewall of China: How to Build and Control an Alternative Version of the Internet.* London: Zed.

Grundmann, Matthias (2011). Nur reich oder auch vermögend? Zum Handlungsvermögen Reicher. In: Lauterbach, Wolfgang, Thomas Druyen and Thomas Grundmann (eds). *Vermögen in Deutschland—Heterogenität und Verantwortung.* Wiesbaden: VS, 205–14.

Grundmann, Reiner, and Mike Scott (2014). Disputed Climate Science in the Media: Do Countries Matter? *Public Understanding of Science* 23/2: 220–35.

Guber, Deborah Lynn (2013). A Cooling Climate for Change? Party Polarization and the Politics of Global Warming. *American Behavioral Scientist* 57/1: 93–115.

Guilhot, Nicolas (2005). *The Democracy Makers: Human Rights and International Order.* New York: Columbia University Press.

Guilhot, Nicolas (2007). Reforming the World: George Soros, Global Capitalism and the Philanthropic Management of the Social Sciences. *Critical Sociology* 33: 447–77.

Guilhot, Nicolas (2008). The Realist Gambit: Postwar American Political Science and the Birth of IR Theory. *International Political Sociology* 2/4: 281–304.

Guriev, Sergei, and Andrei Rachinsky (2005). The Role of Oligarchs in Russian Capitalism. *Journal of Economic Perspectives* 19/1: 131–50.

Guzzini, Stefano (1993). Structural Power: The Limits of Neorealist Power Analysis. *International Organization* 47/3: 443–78.

Guzzini, Stefano (2000). A Reconstruction of Constructivism in International Relations. *European Journal of International Relations* 6/2: 147–82.

Guzzini, Stefano (2005). The Concept of Power: a Constructivist Analysis. *Millennium: Journal of International Studies* 33/3: 495–521.

Guzzini, Stefano (2009). *On the Measure of Power and the Power of Measure in International Relations*. DIIS Working Paper 28. Copenhagen: Danish Institute for International Studies.

Guzzini, Stefano, and Iver Neumann (eds) (2012). *The Diffusion of Power in Global Governance: International Political Economy Meets Foucault*. Basingstoke: Palgrave Macmillan.

Hacker, Jacob S., and Paul Pierson (2010). *Winner-Take-All Politics: How Washington Made the Rich Richer—And Turned Its Back on the Middle Class*. New York: Simon & Schuster.

Hägel, Peter (2009). Standard-Setting for Capital Movements: Reasserting Sovereignty over Transnational Actors? In: Peters, Anne, Till Förster, Lucy Koechlin, Gretta Fenner-Zinkernagel (eds). *Non-State Actors as Standard-Setters*. Cambridge: Cambridge University Press, 351–78.

Hägel, Peter (2012). Billionaires: Oligarchy within Democracy? *Books & Ideas* 26 October 2012, online: http://www.booksandideas.net/Billionaires-Oligarchy-within.html.

Hägel, Peter, and Pauline Peretz (2005). States and Transnational Actors: Who's Influencing Whom? A Case Study in Jewish Diaspora Politics during the Cold War. *European Journal of International Relations* 11/4: 467–93.

Hafner-Burton, Emilie M., Stephan Haggard, David A. Lake, and David G. Victor (2017). The Behavioral Revolution and International Relations. *International Organization* 71/S1: S1–S31.

Hafner-Burton, Emilie M., D. Alex Hughes, and David G. Victor (2013). The Cognitive Revolution and the Political Psychology of Elite Decision Making. *Perspectives on Politics* 11/2: 368–86.

Hafner-Burton, Emilie M., and James Ron (2009). Seeing Double: Human Rights Impact through Qualitative and Quantitative Eyes. *World Politics* 61/2: 360–401.

Hainmueller, Jens, and Michael J. Hiscox (2006). Learning to Love Globalization: Education and Individual Attitudes toward International Trade. *International Organization* 60: 469–98.

Hainmueller, Jens, and Michael J. Hiscox (2010). Attitudes towards Highly Skilled and Low Skilled Immigration: Evidence from a Survey Experiment. *American Political Science Review* 101/4: 61–84.

Halbach, Uwe (2013). *Bilanz einer "Farbrevolution": Georgien im politischen Wandel 2003-2013*. SWP-Studie S24. Berlin: Stiftung Wissenschaft und Politik Deutsches Institut für Internationale.

Hall, Peter A. (ed.) (1989). *The Political Power of Economic Ideas: Keynesianism across Nations*. Princeton, N.J.: Princeton University Press.

Hall, Peter A. (1993). Policy Paradigms, Social Learning and the State: The Case of Economic Policymaking in Britain. *Comparative Politics* 25/3: 275–96.

Hall, Peter A., and Michèle Lamont (eds) (2013a). *Social Resilience in the Neoliberal Era*. Cambridge: Cambridge University Press.

Hall, Peter A., and Michèle Lamont (2013b). Introduction. In: Hall, Peter A., and Michèle Lamont (eds). *Social Resilience in the Neoliberal Era*. Cambridge: Cambridge University Press, 1–31.

Hall, Peter A., and David Soskice (eds) (2001). *Varieties of Capitalism: The Institutional Foundations of Comparative Advantage*. Oxford: Oxford University Press.

Hall, Peter A., and Rosemary C.R. Taylor (1996). Political Science and the Three New Institutionalisms. *Political Studies* 44: 936–57.

Hall, Peter Dobkin (2013). Philanthropy, the Nonprofit Sector & the Democratic Dilemma. *Daedalus* 142/2: 139–58.

Hall, Rodney Bruce (1999). *National Collective Identity: Social Constructs and International Systems*. New York: Columbia University Press.

Hall, Rodney Bruce, and Thomas J. Biersteker (eds) (2002). *The Emergence of Private Authority in Global Governance*. Cambridge: Cambridge University Press.

Halperin, Morton H. (1974). *Bureaucratic Politics and Foreign Policy*. Washington, D.C.: Brookings Institution.

Halperin, Morton H., and Priscilla A. Clapp (2006). *Bureaucratic Politics and Foreign Policy*. 2nd edition. Washington, D.C.: Brookings Institution.

Hamilton, Lawrence C., Joel Hartter, Mary Lemcke-Stampone, David W. Moore, Thomas G. Safford (2015). Tracking Public Beliefs about Anthropogenic Climate Change. *PloS one* 10/9: e0138208, online: https://doi.org/10.1371/journal.pone.0138208.

Hampton, Mark P. (1996). *The Offshore Interface: Tax Havens in the Global Economy*. London: Macmillan.

Handler, Scott P. (ed.) (2013). *International Politics: Classic and Contemporary Readings*. London: Sage.

Hanrieder, Tine (2015a). WHO Orchestrates? Coping with Competitors in Global Health. In: Abbott, Kenneth W., Philipp Genschel, Duncan Snidal, and Bernhard Zangl (eds). *International Organizations as Orchestrators*. Cambridge: Cambridge University Press, 191–213.

Hanrieder, Tine (2015b). *International Organization in Time: Fragmentation and Reform*. Oxford: Oxford University Press.

Hansen, Hans Krause, Lars Thøger Christensen, and Mikkel Flyverbom (2015). Introduction: Logics of Transparency in Late Modernity: Metaphors, Power and Paradoxes. *European Journal of Social Theory* 18/2: 117–31.

Hanson, Elizabeth C. (2008). *The Information Revolution and World Politics*. Lanham: Rowman & Littlefield.

Harley, C. Knick. (1988). Ocean Freight Rates and Productivity, 1740–1913: The Primacy of Mechanical Invention Reaffirmed. *Journal of Economic History* 48: 851–76.

Harman, Sophie (2016). The Bill and Melinda Gates Foundation and Legitimacy in Global Health Governance. *Global Governance* 22/3: 349–68.

Harnisch, Sebastian, Cornelia Frank and Hanns W. Maull (eds) (2011). *Role Theory in International Relations: Approaches and Analyses*. New York: Routledge.

Harrington, Brooke (2016). *Capital without Borders: Wealth Managers and the One Percent*. Cambridge: Harvard University Press.

Hart Research Associates/Public Opinion Strategies (2016). NBC News/Wall Street Journal Survey (Study #16306, May 2016). Washington, D.C.: Hart Research Associates, online: http://www.wsj.com/public/resources/documents/16306NBCWSJMay2016Poll.pdf.

Hartmann, Michael (2007). *The Sociology of Elites*. New York: Routledge.

Harvey, Charles, Mairi Maclean, Jillian Gordon, and Eleanor Shaw (2011). Andrew Carnegie and the Foundations of Contemporary Entrepreneurial Philanthropy. *Business History* 53/3: 425–50.

Harvey, David (1990). *The Condition of Postmodernity*. Oxford: Blackwell.

Harvey, David (2005). *A Brief History of Neoliberalism*. Oxford: Oxford University Press.

Harvey, David (2014). *Seventeen Contradictions and the End of Capitalism*. London: Profile Books.

Hasen, Richard L. (1999). Campaign Finance Laws and the Rupert Murdoch Problem. *Texas Law Review* 77/7: 1627–65.

Hash-Gonzalez, Kelli (2012). *Popular Mobilization and Empowerment in Georgia's Rose Revolution*. New York: Lexington Books.

Haugaard, Mark (ed.) (2002). *Power: A Reader*. Manchester: Manchester University Press.

Hawkins, Benjamin (2012). Nation, Separation and Threat: An Analysis of British Media Discourses on the European Union Treaty Reform Process. *Journal of Common Market Studies* 50/4: 561–77.

Hay, Colin (1999). Crisis and the Structural Transformation of the State: Interrogating the Process of Change. *The British Journal of Politics & International Relations* 1/3: 317–44.

Hay, Colin (2011). Ideas and the Construction of Interests. In: Béland, Daniel, and Robert Henry Cox (eds). *Ideas and Politics in Social Science Research*. Oxford: Oxford University Press, 65–81.

Hay, Colin (2017). Globalization's Impact on States. In: Ravenhill, John (ed.). *Global Political Economy*. 5th edition. Oxford: Oxford University Press, 287–316.

Hay, Iain (ed.) (2013). *Geographies of the Super-Rich*. Cheltenham: Edward Elgar.

Hayek, Friedrich A. (1937). *Monetary Nationalism and International Stability*. London: Longmans, Green.

Hayek, Friedrich A. 1944 [1994]. *The Road to Serfdom*. Fiftieth anniversary edition with a new introduction by Milton Friedman. Chicago: Chicago University Press.

Hayward, Clarissa (2000). *De-Facing Power*. Cambridge: Cambridge University Press.

Hayward, Clarissa, and Steven Lukes (2008). Nobody to Shoot? Power, Structure, and Agency: A Dialogue. *Journal of Power* 1/1: 5–20.

Heemskerk, Eelke M., and Frank W. Takes (2016). The Corporate Elite Community Structure of Global Capitalism. *New Political Economy* 21/1: 90–118.

Heilbrunn, Jacob (2009). *They Knew They Were Right: The Rise of the Neocons*. Anchor. New York: Anchor.

Heilman, Samuel (ed.) (2010). Are Israel and Young American Jews Growing Apart: Debating the Distancing Hypothesis. Special issue of *Contemporary Jewry* 30/2–3.

Held, David (1995). *Democracy and the Global Order: From the Modern State to Cosmopolitan Governance*. Stanford: Stanford University Press.

Held, David (2010). *Cosmopolitanism: Ideals and Realities*. Cambridge: Polity.

Held, David, Anthony McGrew, David Goldblatt, and Jonathan Perraton (1999). *Global Transformations: Politics, Economics and Culture*. Cambridge: Polity.

Held, David, Anthony McGrew, David Goldblatt, and Jonathan Perraton (2006). The Globalization Debate. In: Hall, Stuart, David Held, and Anthony McGrew (eds). *Classic Readings and Contemporary Debates in International Relations*. 3rd edition. Belmont, CA: Wadsworth.

Helleiner, Eric (1994). *States and the Reemergence of Global Finance: From Bretton Woods to the 1990s*. Ithaca, NY: Cornell University Press.

Helleiner, Eric (2014). *The Status Quo Crisis: Global Financial Governance After the 2008 Meltdown*. Oxford: Oxford University Press.

Henderson, Sarah (2003). *Building Democracy in Contemporary Russia: Western Support for Grassroots Organizations.* Ithaca: Cornell University Press.

Hendrix, Cullen S., and Wendy H. Wong (2013). When Is the Pen Truly Mighty? Regime Type and the Efficacy of Naming and Shaming in Curbing Human Rights Abuses. *British Journal of Political Science* 43: 651–72.

Henrekson, Magnus, and Daniel Waldenström (2014). *Inheritance Taxation in Sweden, 1885–2004: The Role of Ideology, Family Firms and Tax Avoidance.* IFN Working Paper No. 1032. Stockholm: Research Institute of Industrial Economics.

Henrekson, Magnus, and Gunnar Du Rietz (2014). The Rise and Fall of Swedish Wealth Taxation. *Nordic Tax Journal* 1/1: 9–35.

Henry, James S. (2012). *The Price of Offshore Revisited: New Estimates for Missing Global Private Wealth, Income, Inequality, and Lost Taxes.* Chesham: Tax Justice Network, online: http://www.taxjustice.net/cms/upload/pdf/Price_of_Offshore_Revisited_120722.pdf.

Hermann, Margaret G. (1980). Explaining Foreign Policy Behavior Using the Personal Characteristics of Political Leaders. *International Studies Quarterly* 24/1: 7–46.

Hertel-Fernandez, Alexander (2016). Explaining Liberal Policy Woes in the States: The Role of Donors. *PS: Political Science & Politics* 49/3: 461–5.

Hertel-Fernandez, Alex (2019). *State Capture: How Conservative Activists, Big Businesses, and Wealthy Donors Reshaped the American States–and the Nation.* Oxford: Oxford University Press.

Herz, John (1960). *International Politics in the Atomic Age.* New York: Columbia University Press.

Herz, John (1968). The Territorial State Revisited: Reflections of the Future of the Nation-State. *Polity* 1/1: 11–34.

Hill, Peter S. (2011). The Alignment Dialogue: GAVI and its Engagement with National Governments in Health System Strengthening. In: Rushton, Simon, and Owain David Williams (eds). *Partnerships and Foundations in Global Health Governance.* London: Palgrave Macmillan, 76–101.

Hintze, Otto (1906) [1975]. *Staatsverfassung und Heeresverfassung.* Speech given at the Gehe-Stiftung zu Dresden on 17 February 1906. Translated as: Military Organization and the Organization of the State. In: Gilbert, Felix (ed.) (1975). *The Historical Essays of Otto Hintze.* New York: Oxford University Press, 178–215.

Hirschman, Albert O. (1970). *Exit, Voice, and Loyalty: Responses to Decline in Firms, Organizations, and States.* Cambridge, MA: Harvard University Press.

Hirschman, Albert O. (1977). *The Passions and the Interests: Political Arguments for Capitalism before its Triumph.* Princeton: Princeton University Press.

Hiscox, Michael J. (2017). The Domestic Sources of Foreign Economic Policies. In: Ravenhill, John (ed.). *Global Political Economy.* 5th edition. Oxford: Oxford University Press, 76–108.

Hitlin, Steven, and Glen H. Elder Jr. (2007). Time, Self, and the Curiously Abstract Concept of Agency. *Sociological Theory* 25/2: 170–91.

Hmielowski, Jay D., Lauren Feldman, Teresa A. Myers, Anthony Leiserowitz, and Edward Maibach (2014). An Attack on Science? Media Use, Trust in Scientists, and Perceptions of Global Warming. *Public Understanding of Science* 23/7: 866–83.

Hobbs, Mitchell, and David McKnight (2014). "Kick this Mob out": The Murdoch Media and the Australian Labor Government (2007 to 2013). *Global Media Journal* (Australian edition) 8/2, online: http://www.hca.westernsydney.edu.au/gmjau/?p=1075.

Hochschild, Jennifer L. (1995). *Facing up to the American Dream: Race, Class, and the Soul of the Nation.* Princeton: Princeton University Press.

Hoffman, David E. (2011). *The Oligarchs: Wealth and Power in the New Russia*. 3rd revised and updated edition. New York: PublicAffairs.

Hollis, Martin, and Steve Smith (1994). Two Stories about Structure and Agency. *Review of International Studies* 20: 241–51.

Holmes, Marcus (2013). The Force of Face-to-Face Diplomacy: Mirror Neurons and the Problem of Intentions. *International Organization* 67/4: 829–61.

Holmes, Marcus (2014). International Politics at the Brain's Edge: Social Neuroscience and a New "Via Media." *International Studies Perspectives* 15: 209–28.

Holsti, Ole (1970). National Role Conceptions in the Study of Foreign Policy. *International Studies Quarterly* 14: 233–309.

Holzinger, Katharina (2003). Common Goods, Matrix Games and Institutional Response. *European Journal of International Relations* 9/2: 173–212.

Honneth, Axel (1994). *Kampf um Anerkennung: Zur moralischen Grammatik sozialer Konflikte*. Mit einem neuen Nachwort. Frankfurt/Main: Suhrkamp.

Honneth, Axel (2003). Redistribution as Recognition: A Response to Nancy Fraser. In: Fraser, Nancy, and Axel Honneth. *Redistribution or Recognition? A Political-Philosophical Exchange*. London: Verso, 110–97.

Hoover, Joseph (2012). Reconstructing Responsibility and Moral Agency in World Politics. *International Theory* 4/2: 233–68.

Hopf, Ted (1998). The Promise of Constructivism in International Relations Theory. *International Security* 23/1: 171–200.

Hopf, Ted (2010). The Logic of Habit in International Relations. *European Journal of International Relations* 16: 539–61.

Hopkins, Daniel J., and Jonathan M. Ladd (2014). The Consequences of Broader Media Choice: Evidence from the Expansion of Fox News. *Quarterly Journal of Political Science* 9/1: 115–35.

Horn, Robert Van, Philip Mirowski, and Thomas A. Stapleford (eds) (2011). *Building Chicago Economics: New Perspectives on the History of America's Most Powerful Economics Program*. Cambridge: Cambridge University Press.

Hornsey, Matthew J., Emily A. Harris, Paul G. Bain, and Kelly S. Fielding (2016). Meta-analyses of the Determinants and Outcomes of Belief in Climate Change. *Nature Climate Change* 6: 622–6.

Horowitz, Donald L. (2000). *Ethnic Groups in Conflict*. Second revised edition. Berkeley and Los Angeles: University of California Press.

Horsfall, Daniel Gary (2011). *From Competition State to Competition States? An Empirical Exploration*. PhD thesis. University of York, online: http://etheses.white rose.ac.uk/1607/.

House of Lords (2008). *Diseases Know No Frontiers: How Effective are Intergovernmental Organisations in Controlling their Spread? Volume I: Report*. House of Lords Select Committee on Intergovernmental Organisations, 1st Report of Session 2007–08. London: The Stationery Office, online: http://www.publications.parliament.uk/pa/ld200708/ldselect/ldintergov/143/143.pdf.

Hovi, Jon, Tora Skodvin, and Steinar Andresen (2003). The Persistence of the Kyoto Protocol: Why Other Annex I Countries Move on Without the United States. *Global Environmental Politics* 3/4: 1–23.

Hudson, Valerie M. (2005). Foreign Policy Analysis: Actor-Specific Theory and the Ground of International Relations. *Foreign Policy Analysis* 1/1: 1–30.

Hudson, Valerie M. (2007). *Foreign Policy Analysis: Classic and Contemporary Theory*. Boulder, Colorado: Rowman & Littlefield.

Hudson Institute (2006). *The Index of Global Philanthropy 2006*. Washington, D.C.: Hudson Institute.

Hudson Institute (2010). *The Index of Global Philanthropy and Remittances 2010*. Washington, D.C.: Hudson Institute.

Hudson Institute (2013). *The Index of Global Philanthropy and Remittances 2013*. Washington, D.C.: Hudson Institute.

Hufbauer, Gary Clyde, Jeffrey J. Schott, Kimberly Ann Elliott, Milica Cosic (2011). *Case Studies in Economic Sanctions and Terrorism: Case 60–3, US v. Cuba*. Washington, D.C.: Peterson Institute for International Economics, online: https://www.piie.com/sites/default/files/publications/papers/sanctions-cuba-60-3.pdf (accessed December 13, 2019).

Huliaras, Asteris, and Nikolaos Tzifakis (2010). Celebrity Activism in International Relations: In Search of a Framework for Analysis. *Global Society* 24/2: 255–74.

Huliaras, Asteris, and Nikolaos Tzifakis (2012). The Fallacy of the Autonomous Celebrity Activist in International Politics: George Clooney and Mia Farrow in Darfur. *Cambridge Review of International Affairs* 25/3: 417–31.

Human Rights Watch (2006). *Funding the "Final War": LTTE Intimidation and Extortion in the Tamil Diaspora*. Human Rights Watch 18/1(C). New York: Human Rights Watch.

Human Security Research Group (2014). *Human Security Report 2013–The Decline in Global Violence: Evidence, Explanation, and Contestation*. Vancouver: Human Security Press.

Hummels, David (2007). Transportation Costs and International Trade in the Second Era of Globalization. *Journal of Economic Perspectives* 21/3: 131–54.

Huntington, Samuel P. (1973). Transnational Organizations in World Politics. *World Politics* 25/3: 333–68.

Huntington, Samuel P. (2004). Dead Souls: The Denationalization of the American Elite. *The National Interest* 75: 5–18.

Hurd, Ian (1999). Legitimacy and Authority in International Politics. *International Organization* 53/2: 379–408.

Hurd, Ian (2007). *After Anarchy: Legitimacy and Power in the UN Security Council*. Princeton: Princeton University Press.

Hussein, Cherine (2015). *The Re-Emergence of the Single State Solution in Palestine/Israel: Countering an Illusion*. New York: Routledge.

Huysmans, Jeff (1998). Security! What Do You Mean? From Concept to Thick Signifier. *European Journal of International Relations* 4/2: 226–55.

Ikenberry, John G. (1993). Creating Yesterday's New World Order: Keynesian "New Thinking" and the Anglo-American Postwar Settlement. In: Goldstein, Judith, and Robert Keohane (eds). *Ideas and Foreign Policy: Beliefs, Institutions and Political Change*. Ithaca, N.Y.: Cornell University Press, 57–86.

Immergut, Ellen M. (1998). The Theoretical Core of the New Institutionalism. *Politics Society* 26/1: 5–34.

Inda, Jonathan Xavier, and Renato Rosaldo (2008). Tracking Global Flows. In: Inda, Jonathan Xavier, and Renato Rosaldo (eds). *The Globalization of Anthropology: A Reader*. 2nd edition. Oxford: Blackwell, 3–46.

Independent Evaluation Group/World Bank Group (2014). *The World Bank's Partnership with the GAVI Alliance* (Global Program Review). Washington DC: World Bank Group, online: http://ieg.worldbank.org/Data/reports/wbp_gavi_alliance2_0.pdf.

Inglehart, Ronald and Christian Welzel (2005). *Modernization, Cultural Change, and Democracy: The Human Development Sequence*. Cambridge: Cambridge University Press.

International Crisis Group (2010). *The Sri Lankan Tamil Diaspora After the LTTE*. Asia Report N°186. Brussels: International Crisis Group.

IPCC [Intergovernmental Panel on Climate Change] (2001). Climate Change 2001: Synthesis Report. Geneva: IPCC.

IPCC [Intergovernmental Panel on Climate Change] (2008). Climate Change 2007: Synthesis Report. Geneva: IPCC.

IPCC [Intergovernmental Panel on Climate Change] (2015). Climate Change 2014: Synthesis Report. Geneva: IPCC.

Iriye, Akira (ed.) (2014). *Global Interdependence: The World After 1945*. Cambridge, MA: Harvard University Press.

Isaacson, Walter (2014). *The Innovators: How a Group of Hackers, Geniuses and Geeks Created the Digital Revolution*. London: Simon & Schuster.

Isrotiuli Memkvidreoba (2009). *Zone Deprived of Rights (Collection of Materials Describing the Cases of Violation of Fundamental Human Rights and Freedoms in Georgia)*. Tbilisi: Isrotiuli Memkvidreoba, online: http://dspace.nplg.gov.ge/bitstream/1234/24076/1/ZoneDeprivedOfRights.pdf.

Iyengar, Shanto, and Kyu S. Hahn (2009). Red Media, Blue Media: Evidence of Ideological Selectivity in Media Use. *Journal of Communication* 59/1: 19–39.

Jackson, Patrick Thaddeus (2010). *The Conduct of Inquiry in International Relations: Philosophy of Science and Its Implications for the Study of World Politics*. London: Routledge.

Jackson, Robert (2007). *Sovereignty: Evolution of an Idea*. Cambridge: Polity.

Jacobson, Gary C. (2010). Perception, Memory, and Partisan Polarization on the Iraq War. *Political Science Quarterly* 125/1: 31–56.

Jaeger, Hans-Martin (2007). "Global Civil Society" and the Political Depoliticization of Global Governance. *International Political Sociology* 1/3: 257–77.

Jamison, Dean T., Lawrence Summers et al. (2013). Global Health 2035: A World Converging Within a Generation. *The Lancet* 382: 1898–955.

Jang, S. Mo, and P. Sol Hart (2015). Polarized frames on "Climate Change" and "Global Warming" Across Countries and States: Evidence from Twitter Big Data. *Global Environmental Change* 32: 11–17.

Jasny, Lorien, Joseph Waggle, and Dana R. Fisher (2015). An Empirical Examination of Echo Chambers in US Climate Policy Networks. *Nature Climate Change* 5/8: 782–6.

Jensen, Michael C., and William H. Meckling (1976). Theory of the Firm: Managerial Behavior, Agency Costs and Ownership Structure. *Journal of Financial Economics* 3/4: 305–60.

Jervis, Robert (1976). *Perception and Misperception in International Politics*. Princeton: Princeton University Press.

Jervis, Robert (1978). Cooperation under the Security Dilemma. *World Politics* 30/2: 167–74.

Jervis, Robert (2013). Do Leaders Matter and How Would We Know? *Security Studies* 22/2: 153–79.

Jesse, Eckhard, and Roland Strum (eds) (2003). *Demokratien des 21. Jahrhunderts im Vergleich: Historische Zugänge, Gegenwartsprobleme, Reformperspektiven*. Opladen: Leske & Budrich.

Joas, Hans (1996). *Die Kreativität des Handelns*. Frankfurt a.M.: Suhrkamp.

Johannesen, Niels, and Gabriel Zucman (2014). The End of Bank Secrecy? An Evaluation of the G20 Tax Haven Crackdown. *American Economic Journal: Economic Policy* 6/1: 65–91.

Johns, Richard Anthony (1983). *Tax Havens and Offshore Finance: A Study of Transnational Economic Development.* London: Frank Pinter.

Johns, Richard Anthony, and Chris M. Le Marchant (1993). *Finance Centres: British Isle Offshore Development since 1979.* London: Pinter.

Johnson, Jesse C., Mark Souva, and Dale L. Smith (2013). Market-Protecting Institutions and the World Trade Organization's Ability to Promote Trade. *International Studies Quarterly* 57/2: 410–17.

Jones, Christopher M. (2010). Bureaucratic Politics and Organizational Process Models. In: Denemark, Robert A. (ed.). *The International Studies Encyclopedia.* Volume 1. London: Blackwell, 151–68.

Jones, Daniel Stedman (2012). *Masters of the Universe: Hayek, Friedman, and the Birth of Neoliberal Politics.* Princeton: Princeton University Press.

Jones, Stephen F. (2006). The Rose Revolution: A Revolution without Revolutionaries? *Cambridge Review of International Affairs* 19/1: 33–48.

Jones, Seth G., and Patrick B. Johnston (2013). The Future of Insurgency. *Studies in Conflict & Terrorism* 36/1: 1–25.

Jonsson, Anna, and Nicolai J. Foss (2011). International Expansion through Flexible Replication: Learning from the Internationalization Experience of IKEA. *Journal of International Business Studies* 42/9: 1079–102.

Joseph, Sarah (2013). *Blame it on the WTO? A Human Rights Critique.* Oxford: Oxford University Press.

Josephson, Matthew (1934). *The Robber Barons: The Great American Capitalists, 1861–1901.* New York: Harcourt, Brace and Company.

Jupille, Joseph, Walter Mattli, and Duncan Snidal (2013). *Institutional Choice and Global Commerce.* Cambridge: Cambridge University Press.

Kahneman, Daniel (2011). *Thinking, Fast and Slow.* New York: Farrar Straus & Giroux.

Kahneman, Daniel, and Angus Deaton (2010). High Income Improves Evaluation of Life But Not Emotional Well-being. *Proceedings of the National Academy of Sciences.* 107/38: 16489–93.

Kaiser, Karl (1969/1972). Transnationale Politik: Zu einer Theorie der multinationalen Politik. *Politische Vierteljahresschrift* 10: 80–109. Revised English version published in 1972 as: Transnational Politics: Toward a Theory of Multinational Politics. *International Organization* 25: 790–817.

Kaldor, Mary (2003). *Global Civil Society: An Answer to War.* Cambridge: Polity Press.

Kaldor, Mary (2012). *New and Old Wars: Organized Violence in a Global Era.* 3rd edition. Cambridge: Polity Press.

Kamat, Sangeeta (2004). The Privatization of Public Interest: Theorizing NGO Discourse in a Neoliberal Era. *Review of International Political Economy* 11/1: 155–76.

Kandelaki, Giorgi (2006). *Georgia's Rose Revolution.* USIP Special Report 167 (July 2006). Washington, D.C.: United States Institute of Peace.

Kandelaki, Giorgi, and Giorgi Meladze (2007). Enough! Kmara and the Rose Revolution in Georgia. In: Demes, Pavol, and Joerg Forbrig (eds). *Reclaiming Democracy: Civil Society and Electoral Change in Central and Eastern Europe.* Washington, D.C.: German Marshall Fund of the United States, 101–25.

Kant, Immanuel (1795) [1970]. *Perpetual Peace: A Philosophical Sketch.* Cambridge: Cambridge University Press.

Kaplan, Morton (1961). Is International Relations a Discipline? *Journal of Politics* 23/3: 462–76.

Kaplan, Robert D. (2012). *The Revenge of Geography: What the Map Tells Us About Coming Conflicts and the Battle Against Fate.* New York: Random House.

Kapstein, Ethan B. (1992). Between Power and Purpose: Central Bankers and the Politics of Regulatory Convergence. *International Organization* 46/1: 265–87.

Karatnycky, Adrian (2006). The Fall and Rise of Ukraine's Political Opposition: From Kuchmagate to the Orange Revolution. In: Aslund, Anders, and Michael McFaul (eds). *Revolution in Orange: The Origins of Ukraine's Democratic Breakthrough*. Washington, D.C.: Carnegie Endowment for International Peace, 29–44.

Karumidze, Zurab, and James V. Wertsch (ed.) (2005). *"Enough!" The Rose Revolution in the Republic of Georgia 2003*. New York: Nova Science Publishers.

Katzenstein, Peter (ed.) (1996). *The Culture of National Security*. Ithaca, NY: Cornell University Press.

Katzman, Kenneth (2019). Iran Sanctions. Washington, D.C.: Congressional Research Service, online: https://fas.org/sgp/crs/mideast/RS20871.pdf (accessed December 13, 2019).

Kaufman, Michael T. (2002). *Soros: The Life and Times of a Messianic Billionaire*. New York: Alfred A. Knopf.

Kaufmann, Chaim (2004). Threat Inflation and the Failure of the Marketplace of Ideas: The Selling of the Iraq War. *International Security* 29/1: 5–48.

Keck, Margaret, and Kathryn Sikkink (1998). *Activists Beyond Borders: Advocacy Networks in International Politics*. Ithaca, NY: Cornell University Press.

Kelemen, R. Daniel, and David Vogel (2010). Trading Places: The Role of the United States and the European Union in International Environmental Politics. *Comparative Political Studies* 43/4: 427–56.

Keller, Suzanne (1963). *Beyond the Ruling Class: Strategic Elites in Modern Society*. New York: Random House.

Kelman, H. C. (1970). The Role of the Individual in International Relations: Some Conceptual and Methodological Considerations. *Journal of International Affairs* 24/1: 1–17.

Kelner, Shaul (2010). *Tours That Bind: Diaspora, Pilgrimage, and Israeli Birthright Tourism*. New York: New York University Press.

Keohane, Robert O. (1984). *After Hegemony: Cooperation and Discord in the World Political Economy*. Princeton: Princeton University Press.

Keohane, Robert O. (2003). Global Governance and Democratic Accountability. In: Held, David, and Mathias Koenig-Archibugi (eds). *Taming Globalization: Frontiers of Governance*. Cambridge: Polity, 130–59.

Keohane, Robert O. (2015). The global politics of climate change: Challenge for political science. *PS: Political Science & Politics* 48/1: 19–26.

Keohane, Robert O., and Helen V. Milner (eds) (1996). *Internationalization and Domestic Politics*. Cambridge: Cambridge University Press.

Keohane, Robert O., and Joseph S. Nye Jr. (eds) (1972). *Transnational Relations and World Politics*. Cambridge: Harvard University Press.

Keynes, John Maynard (1927). *The End of Laissez-Faire*. London: Hogarth.

Keynes, John Maynard (1933). National Self-Sufficiency. *The Yale Review* 22/4: 755–69.

Keynes, John Maynard (1936). *The General Theory of Employment, Interest, and Money*. London: Macmillan.

Khan, Shamus Rahman (2012). The Sociology of Elites. *Annual Review of Sociology* 38: 361–77.

Kiernan, Thomas (1986). *Citizen Murdoch*. New York: Dood, Mead & Company.

Kilz, Hans Werner, and Joachim Preuß (1983). *Flick: Die gekaufte Republik*. Reinbek: Rowohlt.

Kim, Moonhawk (2012). Disguised Protectionism and Linkages to the GATT/WTO. *World Politics* 64/3: 426–75.

Kingston, Christopher, and Gonzalo Caballero (2009). Comparing Theories of Institutional Change. *Journal of Institutional Economics* 5/2: 151–80.

Kinsella, David, Bruce Russett, and Harvey Starr (2013). *World Politics: The Menu for Choice*. 10th edition. Boston: Wadsworth.

Kirshner, Jonathan (1999). Keynes, Capital Mobility and the Crisis of Embedded Liberalism. *Review of International Political Economy* 6/3: 313–37.

Kitschelt, Herbert (1986). Political Opportunity Structures and Political Protest: Anti-Nuclear Movements in Four Democracies. *British Journal of Political Science* 16/1: 57–85.

Klemmensen, Robert, Peter K. Hatemi, Sara Binzer Hobolt, Inge Petersen, Axel Skytthe, and Asbjørn S. Nørgaard (2012). The Genetics of Political Participation, Civic Duty, and Political Efficacy Across Cultures: Denmark and the United States. *Journal of Theoretical Politics* 24/3: 409–27.

Klotz, Audie (2002). Transnational Activism and Global Transformations: The Anti-apartheid and Abolitionist Experiences. *European Journal of International Relations* 8/1: 49–76.

Knight, Kathleen (2006). Transformations in the Concept of Ideology in the Twentieth Century. *American Political Science Review* 100/4: 619–26.

Knobel, Andres, and Markus Meinzer (2014). *"The End of Bank Secrecy"? Bridging the Gap to Effective Automatic Information Exchange: An Evaluation of OECD's Common Reporting Standard (CRS) and its Alternatives*. Preliminary Report. Tax Justice Network. Online: http://www.financialsecrecyindex.com/PDF/TJN2014_AIE-Technical-Report.pdf.

Knox, Paul L., and Peter J. Taylor (eds) (1995). *World Cities in a World-System*. Cambridge: Cambridge University Press.

Koch, Charles G. (2007). *The Science of Success: How Market-Based Management Built the World's Largest Private Company*. Hoboken: John Wiley & Sons.

Koch, Charles G. (2015). *Good Profit: How Creating Value for Others Built One of the World's Most Successful Companies*. New York: Crown Business.

Koesel, Karrie J., and Valerie J. Bunce (2013). Diffusion-proofing: Russian and Chinese Responses to Waves of Popular Mobilizations against Authoritarian Rulers. *Perspectives on Politics* 11/3: 753–68.

Koppell, Jonathan GS (2010). *World Rule: Accountability, Legitimacy, and the Design of Global Governance*. Chicago: University of Chicago Press.

Koremenos, Barbara, Charles Lipson, and Duncan Snidal (2001). The Rational Design of International Institutions. *International Organization* 55/4: 761–99.

Kornprobst, Markus (2011). The Agent's Logics of Action: Defining and Mapping Political Judgement. *International Theory* 3: 70–104.

Kortmann, Klaus (2011). Vermögen in Deutschland—Die methodische Anlage der Untersuchung. In: Lauterbach, Wolfgang, Thomas Druyen, and Thomas Grundmann (eds). *Vermögen in Deutschland—Heterogenität und Verantwortung*. Wiesbaden: VS, 15–28.

Koschut, Simon, and Andrea Oelsner (eds) (2014). *Friendship and International Relations*. Basingstoke: Palgrave Macmillan.

Koslowski, Rey (ed.) (2005). *International Migration and the Globalization of Domestic Politics*. London: Routledge.

Kovacs, Philip E. (ed.) (2011). *The Gates Foundation and the Future of U.S. "Public" Schools*. New York: Routledge.

Kratochwil, Friedrich, and John Ruggie (1986). International Organization: A State of the Art on an Art of the State. *International Organization* 40/4: 753–75.

Krebs, Ronald R., and Jennifer K. Lobasz (2007). Fixing the Meaning of 9/11: Hegemony, Coercion, and the Road to War in Iraq. *Security Studies* 16/3: 409–51.

Krestin, Ruth Viviane (2010). *More Money, More Science? How the Malaria Research Community Responds to Funding Opportunities*. Masters thesis. Cambridge: Massachusetts Institute of Technology. Available online: http://dspace.mit.edu/bit stream/handle/1721.1/59780/671244315-MIT.pdf?sequence=2.

Krisch, Henry (2009). George Soros. In: Forsythe, David P. (ed.). *Encyclopedia of Human Rights*. Oxford: Oxford University Press. Online: http://www.oxfordreference.com/ views/ENTRY.html?subview=Main&entry=t286.e255.

Krysmanski, Hans Jürgen (2012). *0,1 Prozent: Das Imperium der Milliardäre*. Frankfurt a. M.: Westend.

Kull, Steven, Clay Ramsay, and Evan Lewis (2003). Misperceptions, the Media, and the Iraq War. *Political Science Quarterly* 118/4: 569–98.

Kuziemko, Ilyana, and Eric Werker (2006). How Much is a Seat on the Security Council Worth? Foreign Aid and Bribery at the United Nations. *Journal of Political Economy* 114/5: 905–30.

Kuznets, Simon (1953). *Shares of Upper Income Groups in Income and Savings*. Cambridge, MA: National Bureau of Economic Research.

Kuznets, Simon (1955). Economic Growth and Income Inequality. *American Economic Review* 45/1: 1–28.

Kwon, Roy (2016). Can We Have Our Cake and Eat it Too? Liberalization, Economic Growth, and Income Inequality in Advanced Industrial Societies. *Social Forces* 95/2: 469–502.

La, John (2004). Forced Remittances in Canada's Tamil Enclaves. *Peace Review* 16/3: 379–85.

Ladd, Jonathan McDonald, and Gabriel S. Lenz (2009). Exploiting a Rare Communication Shift to Document the Persuasive Power of the News Media. *American Journal of Political Science* 53/2: 394–410.

Lake, David A., and Donald S. Rothchild (eds) (1998). *The International Spread of Ethnic Conflict: Fear, Diffusion, and Escalation*. Princeton, NJ: Princeton University Press.

Lall, Ranjit (2012). From Failure to Failure: The Politics of International Banking Regulation. *Review of International Political Economy* 19/4: 609–38.

Lall, Ranjit (2017). Beyond Institutional Design: Explaining the Performance of International Organizations. *International Organization* 71/2: 245–80.

Lancet (2009). Editorial: What Has the Gates Foundation Done for Global Health? *Lancet* 373: 1577.

Lanskoy, Miriam, and Elspeth Suthers (2013). Outlawing the Opposition. *Journal of Democracy* 24/3: 75–87.

Las Vegas Sands Corporation (2012). *Annual Report 2011*. Las Vegas: Las Vegas Sands Corporation. Online: http://investor.sands.com/files/doc_financials/2011/LVS_2011_ Annual_Report.pdf.

Las Vegas Sands Corporation (2015). *Annual Report 2014*. Las Vegas: Las Vegas Sands Corporation. Online: http://investor.sands.com/files/doc_financials/2014/LVS-2014- Annual- Report.pdf.

Las Vegas Sands Corporation (2017). *Annual Report 2016*. Las Vegas: Las Vegas Sands Corporation. Online: https://s21.q4cdn.com/635845646/files/doc_financials/2016/annual/Las-Vegas-Sands-Annual-Report.pdf (accessed December 13, 2019).

Las Vegas Sands Corporation (2019). *Annual Report 2018*. Las Vegas: Las Vegas Sands Corporation. Online: https://s21.q4cdn.com/635845646/files/doc_financials/2018/annual/Annual-Report-2018.pdf.

Lassen, David Dreyer, and Søren Serritzlew (2011). Jurisdiction Size and Local Democracy: Evidence on Internal Political Efficacy from Large-Scale Municipal Reform. *American Political Science Review* 105/2: 238–58.

Latour, Bruno (1986). The Powers of Association. In: Law, John S. (ed.). *Power, Action and Belief: A New Sociology of Knowledge?* London: Routledge, 264–80.

Latour, Bruno (2005). *Reassembling the Social: An Introduction to Actor-network Theory*. Oxford: Oxford University Press.

Lauterbach, Wolfgang, Thomas Druyen, and Thomas Grundmann (eds) (2011). *Vermögen in Deutschland—Heterogenität und Verantwortung*. Wiesbaden: VS.

Lauterbach, Wolfgang, Melanie Kramer, and Miriam Ströing (2011). Vermögen in Deutschland: Konzept und Durchführung. In: Lauterbach, Wolfgang, Thomas Druyen, and Thomas Grundmann (eds). *Vermögen in Deutschland—Heterogenität und Verantwortung*. Wiesbaden: VS, 29–53.

Lauterbach, Wolfgang, and Alexander Tarvenkorn (2011). Homogenität und Heterogenität von Reichen im Vergleich zur gesellschaftlichen Mitte. In: Lauterbach, Wolfgang, Thomas Druyen, and Thomas Grundmann (eds). *Vermögen in Deutschland—Heterogenität und Verantwortung*. Wiesbaden: VS, 57–94.

Lebow, Richard Ned (2008). *A Cultural Theory of International Relations*. Cambridge: Cambridge University Press.

Lebow, Richard Ned (2010). Motives, Evidence, Identity: Engaging my Critics. *International Theory* 2/3: 486–94.

Lebow, Richard Ned, and Thomas Risse-Kappen (eds) (1994). *The End of the Cold War and International Relations Theory*. New York: Columbia University Press.

Leca, Bernard, Julie Battilana, and Eva Boxenbaum (2008). *Agency and Institutions: A Review of Institutional Entrepreneurship*. Working Paper. Cambridge, MA: Harvard Business School.

Lee, Tien Ming, Ezra M. Markowitz, Peter D. Howe, Chia-Ying Ko, and Anthony A. Leiserowitz (2015). Predictors of Public Climate Change Awareness and Risk Perception Around the World. *Nature Climate Change* 5/11: 1014–20.

Levinson, Marc (2006). *The Box: How the Shipping Container Made the World Smaller and the World Economy Bigger*. Princeton: Princeton University Press.

Levitsky, Steven, and Lucan A. Way (2010). *Competitive Authoritarianism: Hybrid Regimes After the Cold War*. Cambridge: Cambridge University Press.

Levy, David A. L., Billur Aslan, and Diego Bironzo (2016). *UK Press Coverage of the EU Referendum*. Oxford: Reuters Institute for the Study of Journalism/PRIME Research, online: https://reutersinstitute.politics.ox.ac.uk/sites/default/files/2018-11/UK_Press_Coverage_of_the_%20EU_Referendum.pdf (accessed December 13, 2019).

Levy, Jack S. (2013). Psychology and Foreign Policy Decision-Making. In: Huddy, Leonie, David O. Sears, and Jack S. Levy (eds). *The Oxford Handbook of Political Psychology*. 2nd edition. Oxford: Oxford University Press.

Lewandowsky, Stephan, Gilles E. Gignac, and Samuel Vaughan (2013). The Pivotal Role of Perceived Scientific Consensus in Acceptance of Science. *Nature Climate Change* 3/4: 399–404.

Lidén, Jon (2013). *The Grand Decade for Global Health: 1998–2008.* London: Chatham House.

Lieberman, Robert C. (2002). Ideas, Institutions, and Political Order: Explaining Political Change. *American Political Science Review* 96/4: 697–712.

Lijphart, Arend (2012). *Patterns of Democracy: Government Forms and Performance in Thirty-six Countries.* 2nd edition. New Haven: Yale University Press.

Lin, Ken-Hou, and Donald Tomaskovic-Devey (2013). Financialization and U.S. Income Inequality, 1970–2008. *American Journal of Sociology* 118/5: 1284–329.

Lind, Michael (2004). A Tragedy of Errors. *The Nation*, February 5, 2004, online: https://www.thenation.com/article/tragedy-errors/.

Lindblom, Charles (1977). *Politics and Markets.* New York: Basic Books.

Linklater, Andrew (2010). Global Civilizing Processes and the Ambiguities of Human Interconnectedness. *European Journal of International Relations* 16/2: 155–78.

Linklater, Andrew, and Katie Liston (2012). Sociology and International Relations—the Future? *Human Figurations* 1/2, available online: http://hdl.handle.net/2027/spo.11217607.0001.201.

Lipschutz, Ronnie D. (2001). Because People Matter: Studying Global Political Economy. *International Studies Perspectives* 2/4: 321–39.

Lipset, Seymour Martin (1959). Some Social Requisites of Democracy: Economic Development and Political Legitimacy. *American Political Science Review* 53/1: 69–105.

List, Christian, and Kai Spiekermann (2013). Methodological Individualism and Holism in Political Science: A Reconciliation. *American Political Science Review* 107/4: 629–43.

Lloyd, Theresa, and Beth Breeze (2013). *Richer Lives: Why Rich People Give.* London: Directory of Social Change.

Lodge, Martin (2008). Regulation, the Regulatory State and European Politics. *West European Politics* 31/1: 280–301.

Looney, Adam, and Aaron Krupkin (2017). *9 Facts About Pass-through Businesses.* Washington, D.C.: Tax Policy Center, online: http://www.taxpolicycenter.org/publications/9-facts-about-pass-through-businesses/full.

Lorenzoni, Irene, and Nick F. Pidgeon (2006). Public Views on Climate Change: European and USA Perspectives. *Climatic Change* 77/1: 73–95.

Loyal, Steven, and Barry Barnes (2001). "Agency" as a Red Herring. *Philosophy of the Social Sciences* 31/4: 507–24.

Lukes, Steven (1974). *Power: A Radical View.* London: Macmillan.

Lukes, Steven (1977). *Essays in Social Theory.* New York: Columbia University Press.

Lukes, Steven (2005). *Power: A Radical View.* 2nd edition. Basingstoke: Palgrave Macmillan.

Lupovici, Amir (2016). Securitization Climax: Putting the Iranian Nuclear Project at the Top of the Israeli Public Agenda (2009–2012). *Foreign Policy Analysis* 12/3: 413–32.

Lutsevych, Orysia (2013). *How to Finish a Revolution: Civil Society and Democracy in Georgia, Moldova and Ukraine.* Chatham House briefing paper REP BP 2013/01. Online: https://www.chathamhouse.org/sites/files/chathamhouse/public/Research/Russia%20and%20Eurasia/0113bp_lutsevych.pdf.

Lyon, David (2015). *Surveillance after Snowden.* Cambridge: Polity.

Macdonald, Dwight (1956). *The Ford Foundation: The Men and the Millions.* New York: Reynal.

Machiavelli, Niccolo (1531) [2004]. *The Prince.* Translated by George Bull. London: Penguin.

MacKinnon, Mark (2007). *The New Cold War: Revolutions, Rigged Elections and Pipeline Politics in the Former Soviet Union.* Toronto: Random House Canada.

Maclean, Mairi, Charles Harvey, Jillian Gordon, and Eleanor Shaw (2015). Identity, Storytelling and the Philanthropic Journey. *Human Relations* 68/10: 1623–52.

MacLeod, Dag (2004). *Downsizing the State: Privatization and the Limits of Neoliberal Reform*. University Park: Pennsylvania State University Press.

Mäder, Ueli, Ganga Jey Aratnam, and Sarah Schilliger (2010). *Wie Reiche denken und lenken: Reichtum in der Schweiz: Geschichte, Fakten, Gespräche*. Zurich: Rotpunktverlag.

Magen, Amichai, Thomas Risse, and Michael McFaul (eds) (2009). *Promoting Democracy and the Rule of Law: American and European Strategies*. Basingstoke: Palgrave Macmillan.

Mahoney, James (2000). Path Dependence in Historical Sociology. *Theory and Society* 29/4: 507–48.

Mahoney, James, and Kathleen Thelen (2010). A Theory of Gradual Institutional Change. In: Mahoney, James, and Kathleen Thelen (eds). *Explaining Institutional Change: Ambiguity, Agency, and Power*. Cambridge: Cambridge University Press, 1–37.

Maisel, L. Sandy, and Ira N. Forman (eds) (2004). *Jews in American Politics*. Lanham, MD: Rowman & Littlefield.

Majone, Giandomenico (1994). The Rise of the Regulatory State in Europe. *West European Politics* 14/3: 77–101.

Mallaby, Sebastian (2010). *More Money than God: Hedge Funds and the Making of the New Elite*. London: Bloomsbury.

Manger, Mark (2009). *Investing in Protection: The Politics of Preferential Trade Agreements between North and South*. Cambridge: Cambridge University Press.

Manley, John F. (1983). Neo-pluralism: A Class Analysis of Pluralism I and Pluralism II. *American Political Science Review* 77/2: 368–83.

Mann, Michael (1986). *The Sources of Social Power, Vol. 1: A History of Power from the Beginning to A.D. 1760*. Cambridge: Cambridge University Press.

Manners, Ian (2002). Normative Power Europe: A Contradiction in Terms? *Journal of Common Market Studies* 40/2: 235–58.

Mansfield, Edward D., and Diana C. Mutz (2009). Support for Free Trade: Self-Interest, Sociotropic Politics, and Out-group Anxiety. *International Organization* 63: 425–57.

Mansfield, Edward D., and Diana C. Mutz (2013). US Versus Them: Mass Attitudes toward Offshore Outsourcing. *World Politics* 65/4: 571–608.

Manzetti, Luigi (2010). Are You Being Served? The Consequences of Telmex Monopolistic Privatization. *Law & Business Review of the Americas* 16/4: 781–802.

March, James G., and Johan P. Olsen (1984). The New Institutionalism: Organizational Factors in Political Life. *American Political Science Review* 78/3: 734–49.

March, James G., and Johan P. Olsen (1998). The Institutional Dynamics of International Political Orders. *International Organization* 52/4: 943–69.

Marcuzzo, Maria Cristina (2010). Whose Welfare State? Beveridge versus Keynes. In: Backhouse, Roger E., and Tamotsu Nishizawa (eds). *No Wealth but Life: Welfare Economics and the Welfare State in Britain, 1880–1945*. Cambridge: Cambridge University Press, 189–206.

Marquart-Pyatt, Sandra T., Aaron M. McCright, Thomas Dietz, and Riley E. Dunlap (2014). Politics Eclipses Climate Extremes for Climate Change Perceptions. *Global Environmental Change* 29: 246–57.

Marshall, T H. (1950). *Citizenship and Social Class: And Other Essays*. Cambridge: Cambridge University Press.

Martell, Luke (2010). *The Sociology of Globalization*. Cambridge: Polity.

Martin, James R. Jr. (2013). *Cause and Consequence: Electoral Volatility in the Modern Democractic Polity*. PhD dissertation. Tallahassee: Florida State University, online: http://diginole.lib.fsu.edu/islandora/object/fsu:183814/datastream/PDF/view.

Martin, John Levi (2003). What Is Field Theory? *American Journal of Sociology* 109/1: 1–49.

Martin, Lisa L., and Beth A. Simmons (1998). Theories and Empirical Studies of International Institutions. *International Organization* 52/4: 729–57.

Marx, Karl (1859) [2002]. *A Contribution to the Critique of Political Economy*. In: Sitton, John F. (ed.). *Marx Today*. Basingstoke: Palgrave Macmillan, 91–4.

Mathews, Jessica T. (1997). Power Shift. *Foreign Affairs* 76/1: 50–66.

Matthews, Kirstin R.W. and Vivian Ho (2008). The Grand Impact of the Gates Foundation: Sixty Billion Dollars and One Famous Person Can Affect the Spending and Research Focus of Public Agencies. *EMBO Reports* 9/5: 409–12, online: http://www.ncbi.nlm.nih.gov/pmc/articles/PMC2373372/pdf/embor200852.pdf.

Mattli, Walter, and Ngaire Woods (eds) (2009). *The Politics of Global Regulation*. Princeton: Princeton University Press.

Mauss, Marcel (1967). *The Gift: Forms and Functions of Exchange in Archaic Societies*. With an introduction by E. E. Evands-Pritchard. London: W. W. Norton & Company.

Mayer, Jane (2010). Covert Operations. *The New Yorker*, August 30, 2010, online: http://www.newyorker.com/magazine/2010/08/30/covert-operations.

Mayer, Jane (2016). *Dark Money: The Hidden History of the Billionaires behind the Rise of the Radical Right*. New York: Penguin Random House.

McAdam, Doug (1996). Political Opportunities: Conceptual Origins, Current Problems, Future Directions. In: McAdam, Doug, John D. McCarthy, and Mayer Zald (eds). *Comparative Perspectives on Social Movements*. Cambridge: Cambridge University Press, 23–40.

McAdam, Doug, Sidney Tarrow, and Charles Tilly (2001). *Dynamics of Contention*. Cambridge: Cambridge University Press.

McCoy, David, Gayatri Kembhavi, Jinesh Patel, and Akish Luintel (2009). The Bill & Melinda Gates Foundation's Grant-Making Programme for Global Health. *Lancet* 373: 1645–53.

McCoy, David, and Linsey McGoey (2011). Global Health and the Gates Foundation–In Perspective. In: Williams, Owain Davi, and Simon Rushton (eds). *Partnerships and Foundations in Global Health Governance*. Basingstoke: Palgrave Macmillan, 143–63.

McCright, Aaron M., and Riley E. Dunlap (2000). Challenging Global Warming as a Social Problem: An Analysis of the Conservative Movement's Counter-claims. *Social Problems* 47/4: 499–522.

McCright, Aaron M., and Riley E. Dunlap (2003). Defeating Kyoto: The Conservative Movement's Impact on US Climate Change Policy. *Social Problems* 50/3: 348–73.

McCright, Aaron M., and Riley E. Dunlap (2011). The Politicization of Climate Change and Polarization in the American Public's Views of Global Warming, 2001–2010. *The Sociological Quarterly* 52/2: 155–94.

McCrone, David, and Frank Bechhofer (2015). *Understanding National Identity*. Cambridge: Cambridge University Press.

McDermott, Rose (2004). *Political Psychology in International Relations*. Ann Arbor: University of Michigan Press.

McGoey, Linsey (2014). The Philanthropic State: Market–State Hybrids in the Philanthrocapitalist Turn. *Third World Quarterly* 35/1: 109–25.

McGoey, Linsey (2015). *No Such Thing as a Free Gift: The Gates Foundation and the Price of Philanthropy*. London: Verso.

McInnes, Colin, Adam Kamradt-Scott, Kelley Lee, Anne Roemer-Mahler, Simon Rushton, and Owain David Williams (2014). *The Transformation of Global Health Governance*. Basingstoke: Palgrave Macmillan.

McKnight, David (2003). "A World Hungry for a New Philosophy": Rupert Murdoch and the Rise of Neo-liberalism. *Journalism Studies* 4/3: 347–58.

McKnight, David (2010). Rupert Murdoch's News Corporation: A Media Institution with a Mission. *Historical Journal of Film. Radio and Television* 30/3: 303–16.

McKnight, David (2013). *Murdoch's Politics: How One Man's Thirst for Wealth and Power Shapes our World*. London: Pluto.

McKnight, David, and Brian McNair (2012). The Empire Goes to War: News Corporation and Iraq. *Australian Journalism Review* 34/2: 7–17.

McMenamin, Iain (2013). *If Money Talks, What Does it Say? Corruption and Business Financing of Political Parties*. Oxford: Oxford University Press.

McSweeney, Bill (1999). *Security, Identity and Interests: A Sociology of International Relations*. Cambridge: Cambridge University Press.

Mead, George H. (1934). *Mind, Self, and Society*. Chicago: University of Chicago Press.

Mearsheimer, John J. (2001). *The Tragedy of Great Power Politics*. New York: W. W. Norton and Company.

Mearsheimer, John J., and Stephen M. Walt (2007). *The Israel Lobby and U.S. Foreign Policy*. New York: Farrar, Straus & Giroux.

Mehta, Suketu (2011). The Outsider. *Newsweek* 158/18: 46–51.

Mellman, Mark, Aaron Strauss, and Kenneth D. Wald. (2012). *Jewish American Voting Behavior 1972–2008*. Washington, D.C.: The Solomon Project.

Mercer, Jonathan (2010). Emotional Beliefs. *International Organization* 64/1: 1–31.

Merkel, Wolfgang (2014). Is Capitalism Compatible with Democracy? *Zeitschrift für Vergleichende Politikwissenschaft* 8/2: 109–28.

Merlingen, Michael (2003). Governmentality: Towards a Foucauldian Framework for the Study of IGOs. *Cooperation and Conflict* 38/4: 361–84.

Merton, Robert K. (1936). The Unanticipated Consequences of Purposive Social Action. *American Sociological Review* 1/6: 894–904.

Merton, Robert K. (1957). Patterns of Influence: Local and Cosmopolitan Influentials. In: *Social Theory and Social Structure*. Revised and enlarged 2nd edition. New York: The Free Press, 387–420.

Migration Policy Group (2013). *Migrant Political Participation*. Brussels: European Web Site on Immigration, online: https://www.migpolgroup.com/_old/wp-content/uploads/2013/05/EWSI_SF-2013-01_Migrant-Political-Participation_layout.pdf (accessed December 13, 2019).

Milanovic, Branko (2016). *Global Inequality: A New Approach for the Age of Globalization*. Cambridge: Harvard University Press.

Mildenberger, Matto, and Anthony Leiserowitz (2017). Public Opinion on Climate Change: Is there an Economy-Environment Tradeoff? *Environmental Politics* 26/5: 801–24.

Mill, John Stuart (1859) [1974]. *On Liberty*. London: Penguin.

Mills, C. Wright (1956). *The Power Elite*. Oxford: Oxford University Press.

Milner, Helen V. (2014). Introduction: The Global Economy, FDI, and the Regime for Investment. *World Politics* 66/1: 1–11.

Mingst, Karen A., Jack L. Snyder, and Heather Elko McKibben (eds) (2019). *Essential Readings in World Politics*. 7th edition. New York: W. W. Norton and Company.

Mintz, A., Redd, S., and Vedlitz, A. (2006). Can we Generalize from Student Experiments to the Real World in Political Science, Military Affairs, and International Relations? *Journal of Conict Resolution* 50/5: 757–76.

Mirowski, Philip, and Dieter Plehwe (eds) (2009). *The Road from Mont Pèlerin: The Making of the Neoliberal Thought Collective*. Cambridge, MA: Harvard University Press.

Mitchell, Katharyne, and Matthew Sparke (2016). The New Washington Consensus: Millennial Philanthropy and the Making of Global Market Subjects. *Antipode* 48/3: 724–49.

Mitchell, Lincoln A. (2004). Georgia's Rose Revolution. *Current History* 103: 342–8.

Mitchell, Lincoln A. (2009). *Uncertain Democracy: U.S. Foreign Policy and Georgia's Rose Revolution*. Philadelphia: University of Pennsylvania Press.

Mitchell, Lincoln A. (2012). *The Color Revolutions*. Philadelphia: University of Pennsylvania Press.

Monson, Gabriel C. (ed.) (2009). *Georgia after the Rose Revolution*. New York: Nova Science Publishers.

Monteiro, Nuno P., and Keven G. Ruby (2009). IR and the False Promise of Philosophical Foundations. *International Theory* 1/1: 15–48.

Moody, Michael (2008). "Building a Culture": The Construction and Evolution of Venture Philanthropy as a New Organizational Field. *Nonprofit and Voluntary Sector Quarterly* 37/2: 324–52.

Moorcraft, Paul (2012). *Total Destruction of the Tamil Tigers: The Rare Victory of Sri Lanka's Long War*. Barnsley: Pen & Sword Military.

MOPAN (Multilateral Organisation Performance Assessment Network) (2012). *Organisational Effectiveness Assessment GAVI 2012, Volume I*. Online: http://www.mopanonline.org/assessments/gavi2012/MOPAN_2012_GAVI_Final_Vol_1_Issued_December_2012.pdf.

MOPAN (Multilateral Organisation Performance Assessment Network) (2013). *Institutional Report World Health Organization (WHO), Volume I, 2013*. Online: http://www.mopanonline.org/assessments/who2013/MOPAN_2013-_WHO_Vol._I.pdf

MOPAN (Multilateral Organisation Performance Assessment Network) (2017). *Global Fund to Fight AIDS, Tuberculosis and Malaria (The Global Fund) Institutional Assessment Report*. Online: http://www.mopanonline.org/assessments/globalfund2015-16/Mopan%20Global%20Fund%20report%20[interactive]%20[final].pdf.

Moran, Michael, and Michael Stevenson (2013). Illumination and Innovation: What Philanthropic Foundations Bring to Global Health Governance. *Global Society* 27/2: 117–37.

Moravcsik, Andrew (1997). Taking Preferences Seriously: A Liberal Theory of International Relations. *International Organization* 51: 513–53.

Moravcsik, Andrew (1999). A New Statecraft? Supranational Entrepreneurs and International Cooperation. *International Organization* 53/2: 267–306.

Morgenthau, Hans J. (1947). *Politics Among Nations*. New York: Knopf.

Morgenthau, Hans J. (1951). *In Defence of the National Interest: A Critical Examination of American Foreign Policy*. New York: Alfred A. Knopf.

Morgenthau, Hans J. (1964). The Four Paradoxes of Nuclear Strategy. *American Political Science Review* 58/1: 22–35.

Morriss, Peter (1987). *Power: A Philosophical Analysis*. Manchester: Manchester University Press.

Morriss, Peter (2002). *Power: A Philosophical Analysis*. 2nd edition. Manchester: Manchester University Press.

Morvaridi, Behrooz (2012). Capitalist Philanthropy and Hegemonic Partnerships. *Third World Quarterly* 33/7: 1191–210.

Mounk, Yascha (2018). *The People vs. Democracy: Why Our Freedom Is in Danger and How to Save It*. Cambridge, MA: Harvard University Press.

Mount, Ferdinand (2012). *The New Few or a Very British Oligarchy: Power and Inequality in Britain Now*. London: Simon & Schuster.

Mousseau, Michael (2009). The Social Market Roots of the Democratic Peace. *International Security* 33/4: 52–86.

Mügge, Daniel (2013). The Political Economy of Europeanized Financial Regulation. *Journal of European Public Policy* 20/3: 458–70.

Müller, Hans-Peter (2007). *Max Weber: Eine Einführung*. Köln/Weimar/Wien: Böhlau.

Mueller, John (2010). *Atomic Obsession: Nuclear Alarmism from Hiroshima to Al-Qaeda*. Oxford: Oxford University Press.

Münkler, Herfried (2002). *Die neuen Kriege*. Reinbek bei Hamburg: Rowohlt.

Munck, Ronaldo (2005). Neoliberalism and Politics, and the Politics of Neoliberalism. In: Saad Filho, Alfredo, and Deborah Johnston (eds). *Neoliberalism: A Critical Reader*. London: Pluto Press, 60–9.

Muraskin, William (2002). The Last Years of the CVI and the Birth of GAVI. In: Reich, Michael M. (ed.). *Public-Private Partnerships for Public Health*. Cambridge, MA: Harvard University/Harvard Centre for Population & Development Studies, 115–68.

Muraskin, William (2005). *Crusade to Immunize the World's Children*. Los Angeles: USC Marshall Global BioBusiness Initiative.

Murdie, Amanda (2014). *Help or Harm: The Human Security Effects of International NGOs*. Stanford: Stanford University Press.

Murdie, Amanda, and Tavishi Bhasin (2011). Aiding and Abetting: Human Rights INGOs and Domestic Protest. *Journal of Conflict Resolution* 55/2: 163–91.

Murdie, Amanda, and Alexander Hicks (2013). Can International Nongovernmental Organizations Boost Government Services? The Case of Health. *International Organization* 67/3: 541–73.

Murdie, Amanda, and Dursun Peksen (2013a). The Impact of Human Rights INGO Shaming on Humanitarian Interventions. *The Journal of Politics* 76/1: 215–28.

Murdie, Amanda, and Dursun Peksen (2013b). The Impact of Human Rights INGO Activities on Economic Sanctions. *The Review of International Organizations* 8/1: 33–53.

Murray, Christopher JL, Alan D. Lopez, and Suwit Wibulpolprasert (2004). Monitoring Global Health: Time for New Solutions. *BMJ* 329: 1096–100.

Muskhelishvili, Marina, and Gia Jorjoliani (2009). Georgia's Ongoing Struggle for a Better Future Continued: Democracy Promotion through Civil Society Development. *Democratization* 16/4: 682–708.

Mutch, Robert E. (2014). *Buying the Vote: A History of Campaign Finance Reform*. Oxford: Oxford University Press.

Myres, Graham (2012). Investing in the Market of Violence: Toward a Micro-Theory of Terrorist Financing. *Studies in Conflict & Terrorism* 35/10: 693–711.

Naim, Moisés (2005). *Illicit: How Smugglers, Traffickers and Copycats are Hijacking the Global Economy*. London: Heinemann.

Naimoli, J. F. (2009). Global Health Partnerships in Practice: Taking Stock of the GAVI Alliance's New Investment in Health Systems Strengthening. *International Journal of Health Planning and Management* 24/1: 3–25.

Nasaw, David (2006). *Andrew Carnegie*. New York: Penguin.

Negroponte, Nicholas (1996). *Being Digital*. New York: Alfred A. Knopf.

Neier, Aryeh (2003). *Taking Liberties: Four Decades in the Struggle for Rights*. New York: PublicAffairs.

Neier, Aryeh (2011). Afterword. In: Sudetic, Chuck. *The Philanthropy of George Soros*. New York: PublicAffairs, 335–41.

Netanyahu, Benjamin (1993). *A Place Among Nations: Israel and the World*. New York: Bantam Press.

Neumayer, Eric (2004). The Super-Rich in Global Perspective: A Quantitative Analysis of the Forbes List of Billionaires. *Applied Economics Letters* 11: 793–6.

Niemi, Richard G., Stephen C. Craig, and Franco Mattei (1991). Measuring Internal Political Efficacy in the 1988 National Election Study. *American Political Science Review* 85/4: 1407–13.

Nisbet, Matthew C., and Teresa Myers (2007). The Polls—Trends: Twenty Years of Public Opinion about Global Warming. *Public Opinion Quarterly* 71/3: 444–70.

Nodia, Ghia (2005). *Civil Society Development in Georgia: Achievements and Challenges*. Tbilisi: Caucasus Institute for Peace, Development, and Democracy (CIPDD).

Nordstrom, Carolyn (2007). *Global Outlaws: Crime, Money, and Power in the Contemporary World*. Berkeley: University of California Press.

Norris, Pippa, John Curtice, David Sanders, Margaret Scammell, and Holli Semetko (1999). *On Message: Communicating the Campaign*. London: Sage.

North, Douglass C. (1990). *Institutions, Institutional Change and Economic Performance*. Cambridge: Cambridge University Press.

North, Douglass C., John Joseph Wallis, and Barry R. Weingast (2009). *Violence and Social Orders: A Conceptual Framework for Interpreting Recorded Human History*. Cambridge: Cambridge University Press.

Nussbaum, Martha C. (2019). *The Cosmopolitan Tradition: A Noble but Flawed Ideal*. Cambridge: Belknap Press.

Nye, Joseph (2004). *Soft Power: The Means to Success in World Politics*. New York: PublicAffairs.

Nye, Joseph S. Jr., and Robert O. Keohane (1971a). Transnational Relations and World Politics: An Introduction. *International Organization* 25/3: 329–49.

Nye, Joseph S. Jr., and Robert O. Keohane (1971b). Transnational Relations and World Politics: A Conclusion. *International Organization* 25/3: 721–48.

Obama, Barack (2017). The Irreversible Momentum of Clean Energy. *Science* 355/6321: 126–9.

Obinger, Herbert, Carina Schmitt, and Reimut Zohlnhöfer (2014). Partisan Politics and Privatization in OECD Countries. *Comparative Political Studies* 47/9: 1294–323.

O'Brien, Richard, Anne Marie Goetz, Jan Aart Scholte, and Marc Williams (eds) (2000). *Contesting Global Governance: Multilateral Economic Institutions and Global Social Movements*. Cambridge: Cambridge University Press.

O'Clery, Conor (2007). *The Billionaire Who Wasn't: How Chuck Feeney Secretly Made and Gave Away a Fortune*. New York: PublicAffairs.

Odell, John S. (2013). Negotiation and Bargaining. In: Carlsnaes, Walter, Thomas Risse, and Beth A. Simmons (eds). *Handbook of International Relations*. 2nd edition. Thousand Oaks: Sage Publications, 379–400.

OECD (2008). *Growing Unequal? Income Distribution and Poverty in OECD Countries*. Paris: OECD Publishing.

OECD (2011a). *Divided We Stand: Why Inequality Keeps Rising*. Paris: OECD Publishing.

OECD (2011b). *Tackling Aggressive Tax Planning through Improved Transparency and Disclosure*. Paris: OECD Publishing.

OECD (2011c). *Society at a Glance 2011: OECD Social Indicators*. Paris: OECD Publishing, online: http://dx.doi.org/10.1787/soc_glance-2011-en.

OECD (2013). *Addressing Base Erosion and Profit Shifting*. Paris: OECD Publishing.

OECD (2014). *Standard for Automatic Exchange of Financial Information in Tax Matters*. Paris: OECD Publishing.

OECD (2015). In It Together: Why Less Inequality Benefits All. Paris: OECD Publishing.

OECD (2018). *The Role and Design of Net Wealth Taxes in the OECD*. Paris: OECD Publishing.

OECD (2019). *OECD/G20 Inclusive Framework on BEPS: Progress Report July 2018–May 2019*. Paris: OECD Publishing.

Okun, Arthur M. (1975). *Equality and Efficiency: The Big Tradeoff*. Washington, D.C.: Brookings Institution Press.

Olopade, Dayo (2010). Gatekeepers: Is Giving Away Money—and Lots of It—Really the Best Way to Change the World? *The American Prospect* 21/8, online: http://prospect.org/article/gatekeepers-0.

Olson, Mancur (1965). *The Logic of Collective Action: Public Goods and the Theory of Groups*. Cambridge, MA: Harvard University Press.

Onuf, Nicholas (1989). *World of Our Making: Rules and Rule in Social Theory and International relations*. Columbia, SC: University of South California Press.

Onuf, Nicholas (1995). Levels. *European Journal of International Relations* 1/1: 35–58.

Ooms, Gorik, Wim Van Damme, Brook Baker, Paul Zeitz, and Ted Schrecker (2008). The "Diagonal" Approach to Global Fund Financing: A Cure for the Broader Malaise of Health Systems? *Globalization and Health* 4/1: 1–7.

Open Society Institute (2001). *Building Open Societies: Soros Foundations Network 2000 Report*. New York: Open Society Institute. Online: https://www.opensocietyfoundations.org/uploads/5e4f2b5f-075a-4190-ad2f-25bc95f64255/a_complete_8.pdf.

Open Society Institute (2003). *Building Open Societies: Soros Foundations Network 2002 Report*. New York: Open Society Institute. Online: https://www.opensocietyfoundations.org/uploads/569ceb5a-5a08-472e-ac5f-00b0c0595cf2/a_complete_report_0.pdf.

Open Society Institute (2004). *Building Open Societies: Soros Foundations Network 2003 Report*. New York: Open Society Institute. Online: https://www.issuelab.org/resources/8009/8009.pdf.

Open Society Institute (2006). *Building Open Societies: Soros Foundations Network 2005 Report*. New York: Open Society Institute. Online: https://www.opensocietyfoundations.org/uploads/d5ba8428-a284-4b67-87d4-af66fb93aeff/a_complete_2.pdf.

Orenstein, Mitchell A., and Hans Peter Schmitz (2006). The New Transnationalism and Comparative Politics. *Comparative Politics* 38: 479–500.

O'Rourke, Kevin H., and Jeffrey G. Williamson (1999). *Globalization and History: The Evolution of a Nineteenth-Century Atlantic Economy*. Cambridge, MA: MIT Press.

O'Rourke, Kevin H., and Jeffrey G. Williamson (2002). When Did Globalization Begin? *European Review of Economic History* 6: 23–50.

O'Rourke, Kevin H., and Jeffrey G. Williamson (2004). Once More: When Did Globalization Begin? *European Review of Economic History* 8: 109–17.

O'Rourke, Kevin H., and Jeffrey G. Williamson (2005). From Malthus to Ohlin: Trade, Industrialisation and Distribution Since 1500. *Journal of Economic Growth* 10: 5–34.

OSGF (Open Society Georgia Foundation) (2004). *Annual Report 2003*. Tbilisi: Open Society Georgia Foundation. Online: http://www.osgf.ge/files/wliuri_angarishi/Annual_Report_2003_Eng_NiJ750oTBG.doc.

OSGF (Open Society Georgia Foundation) (2014). *The Story of Open Society Georgia Foundation*. Tbilisi: Open Society Georgia Foundation. Online: http://www.osgf.ge/files/2014/20th%20anniversary/Report_by_infographs_20_years.pdf.

Ostrower, Francie (1995). *Why the Wealthy Give: The Culture of Elite Philanthropy.* Princeton: Princeton University Press.

Ottaway, Marina, and Thomas Carothers (eds) (2000). *Funding Virtue: Civil Society Aid and Democracy Promotion.* Washington DC: Carnegie Endowment.

Overesch, Michael, and Johannes Rincke (2009). Competition from Low-wage Countries and the Decline of Corporate Tax Rates–Evidence from European Integration. *World Economy* 32/9: 1348–64.

Oxfam (2019). *Public Good or Private Wealth?.* Oxford: Oxfam, online: https:// oxfamilibrary.openrepository.com/bitstream/handle/10546/620599/bp-public-good-or-private-wealth-210119-en.pdf.

Page, Benjamin I., Larry M. Bartels, and Jason Seawright (2011). Interviewing Wealthy Americans. Paper presented at the annual meeting of the Midwest Political Science Association, Chicago, March 30–April 3. Available as WP-11-07, Institute for Policy Research, Northwestern University.

Page, Benjamin I., Larry M. Bartels, and Jason Seawright (2013). Democracy and the Policy Preferences of Wealthy Americans. *Perspectives on Politics* 11/1: 51–73.

Page, Benjamin I., and Lawrence R. Jacobs (2009). *Class War? What Americans Really Think about Economic Inequality.* Chicago: University of Chicago Press.

Page, Benjamin I., and Jason Seawright (2014). *What Do United States Billionaires Want from Government?* Working paper WP-14-05, Institute for Policy Research, Northwestern University.

Page, Benjamin I., Jason Seawright, and Matthew J. Lacombe (2019). *Billionaires and Stealth Politics.* Chicago: The University of Chicago Press.

Page, Bruce (2003). *The Murdoch Archipelago.* London: Simon & Schuster.

Page, Scott E. (2006). Path Dependence. *Quarterly Journal of Political Science* 1/1: 87–115.

Page, William H., and John E. Lopatka (2007). *The Microsoft Case: Antitrust, High Technology, and Consumer Welfare.* Chicago: University of Chicago Press.

Painter, James, and Teresa Ashe (2012). Cross-national Comparison of the Presence of Climate Scepticism in the Print Media in Six Countries, 2007–10. *Environmental Research Letters* 7/4: 044005.

Palan, Ronen (1998). Trying to Have Your Cake and Eating It: How and Why the State System Has Created Offshore. *International Studies Quarterly* 42/4: 625–44.

Palan, Ronen (2002). Tax Havens and the Commercialization of State Sovereignty. *International Organization* 56/1: 151–76.

Palan, Ronen (2003). *The Offshore World: Sovereign Markets, Virtual Places, and Nomad Millionaires.* Ithaca: Cornell University Press.

Palan, Ronen, Richard Murphy, and Christian Chavagneux (2010). *Tax Havens: How Globalization Really Works.* Ithaca: Cornell University Press.

Palan, Ronen, and Duncan Wigan (2014). Herding Cats and Taming Tax Havens: The US Strategy of "Not In My Backyard." *Global Policy* 5/3: 334–43.

Pallas, Christopher L. (2012). Identity, Individualism, and Activism beyond the State: Examining the Impacts of Global Citizenship. *Global Society* 26/2: 169–89.

Paris, Roland (2001). Human Security: Paradigm Shift or Hot Air? *International Security* 26/2: 87–102.

Parmar, Inderjeet (2012). *Foundations of the American Century: The Ford, Carnegie, and Rockefeller Foundations in the Rise of American Power.* New York: Columbia University Press.

Parmar, Inderjeet, and Katharina Rietzler (2014). American Philanthropy and the Hard, Smart and Soft Power of the United States. *Global Society* 28/1: 3–7.

Parsons, Talcott (1963). On the Concept of Political Power. *Proceedings of the American Philosophical Society* 107/3: 232–62.

Payton, Robert L., and Michael P. Moody (2008). *Understanding Philanthropy: Its Meaning and Mission*. Bloomington: Indiana University Press.

Pedahzur, Ami (2012). *The Triumph of Israel's Radical Right*. Oxford: Oxford University Press.

People's Health Movement (2008). *Global Health Watch 2*. London: Zed Books.

Peri, Yoram (2004). *Telepopulism: Media and Politics in Israel*. Stanford: Stanford University Press.

Perliger, Arie, and Eran Zaidise (2015). The Peculiar Victory of the National Camp in the 2013 Israeli Election. *Israel Affairs* 21/2: 195–208.

Peters, B. Guy, Jon Pierre, and Desmond S. King (2005). The Politics of Path Dependency: Political Conflict in Historical Institutionalism. *Journal of Politics* 67/4: 1275–300.

Peterson, Timothy M., Amanda Murdie and Victor Asal (2018). Human Rights, NGO Shaming and the Exports of Abusive States. *British Journal of Political Science* 48/3: 767–86.

Petras, James (2008). Global Ruling Class: Billionaires and How They "Make It." *Journal of Contemporary Asia* 38/2: 319–29.

Pew Research Center (2012). *The Global Religious Landscape: A Report on the Size and Distribution of the World's Major Religious Groups as of 2010*. Washington, D.C.: Pew Research Center.

Pew Research Center (2013). *A Portrait of Jewish Americans Findings from a Pew Research Center Survey of U.S. Jews*. Washington, D.C.: Pew Research Center.

Pew Research Center (2016). *The Politics of Climate*. Washington, D.C.: Pew Research Center, online: http://assets.pewresearch.org/wp-content/uploads/sites/14/2016/10/14080900/PS_2016.10.04_Politics-of-Climate_FINAL.pdf.

Pfeffer, Jeffrey, and Gerald Salancik (1978). *The External Control of Organizations: A Resource Dependence Perspective*. New York: Harper & Row.

Philippon, Thomas, and Ariell Reshef (2012). Wages and Human Capital in the U.S. Finance Industry: 1909–2006. *Quarterly Journal of Economics* 127/4: 1551–609.

Philipsen, Dirk (2015). *The Little Big Number: How GDP Came to Rule the World and What to Do about It*. Princeton: Princeton University Press.

Pierson, Paul (1996). The New Politics of the Welfare State. *World Politics* 48/2: 143–79.

Pierson, Paul (2000). Path Dependence, Increasing Returns, and the Study of Politics. *American Political Science Review* 94/2: 251–67.

Pierson, Paul (2004). *Politics in Time: History, Institutions, and Social Analysis*. Princeton: Princeton University Press.

Piketty, Thomas (2014). *Capital in the Twenty-First Century*. Cambridge, MA: The Belknap Press of Harvard University Press.

Piketty, Thomas, and Emmanuel Saez (2014). Inequality in the long run. *Science* 344/6186: 838–43.

Piketty, Thomas, Emmanuel Saez, and Gabriel Zucman (2018). Distributional National Accounts: Methods and Estimates for the United States. *The Quarterly Journal of Economics* 133/2: 553–609.

Piiroinen, Tero (2014). For "Central Conflation": A Critique of Archerian Dualism. *Sociological Theory* 32/2: 79–99.

Pinker, Steven (2011). *The Better Angels of Our Nature: The Decline of Violence in History and its Causes*. New York: Viking.

Pitofsky, Robert (ed.) (2008). *How the Chicago School Overshot the Mark: The Effect of Conservative Economic Analysis on U.S. Antitrust.* Oxford: Oxford University Press.

Plant, Raymond (2010). *The Neoliberal State.* Oxford: Oxford University Press.

Plattner, Marc F. (2009). Introduction. In: Barany, Zoltan, and Robert G. Moser (eds). *Is Democracy Exportable?* Cambridge: Cambridge University Press, 1–12.

Pleasants, Nigel (1999). *Wittgenstein and the Idea of a Critical Social Theory: A Critique of Giddens, Habermas and Bhaskar.* New York: Routledge.

Plehwe, Dieter, and Bernhard Walpen (2006). Between Network and Complex Organization. In: Plehwe, Dieter, Bernhard Walpen, and Gisela Neunhöffer (eds). *Neoliberal Hegemony: A Global Critique.* New York: Routledge, 27–50.

Plehwe, Dieter, Bernhard Walpen, and Gisela Neunhöffer (eds) (2006a). *Neoliberal Hegemony: A Global Critique.* New York: Routledge.

Plehwe, Dieter, Bernhard Walpen, and Gisela Neunhöffer (2006b). Introduction: Reconsidering Neoliberal Hegemony. In: Plehwe, Dieter, Bernhard Walpen, and Gisela Neunhöffer (eds). *Neoliberal Hegemony: A Global Critique.* New York: Routledge, 1–24.

Polanyi, Karl (1944) [1957]. *The Great Transformation: The Political and Economic Origins of Our Time.* Boston: Beacon.

Popper, Karl (1935). *Logik der Forschung.* Vienna: Julius Springer Verlag.

Popper, Karl (1945). *The Open Society and Its Enemies* (2 Volumes). London: Routledge.

Popper, Karl (1963). *Conjectures and Refutations: The Growth of Scientific Knowledge.* London: Routledge.

Porter, Anna (2015). *Buying a Better World: George Soros and Billionaire Philanthropy.* Toronto: TAP Books.

Posner, Elliot, and Véron, Nicolas (2010). The EU and Financial Regulation: Power without Purpose? *Journal of European Public Policy* 17/3: 400–15.

Potoski, Matthew, and Aseem Prakash (eds) (2009). *Voluntary Programs: A Club Theory Perspective.* Cambridge, MA: MIT Press.

Potter, Philip B. K., and Matthew A. Baum (2014). Looking for Audience Costs in all the Wrong Places: Electoral Institutions, Media Access, and Democratic Constraint. In: *The Journal of Politics* 76/1: 167–81.

Pouliot, Vincent (2008). The Logic of Practicality: A Theory of Practice of Security Communities. *International Organization* 62: 257–88.

Pouliot, Vincent (2016). *International Pecking Orders: The Politics and Practice of Multilateral Diplomacy.* Cambridge: Cambridge University Press.

Poulsen, Lauge N. Skovgaard, and Emma Aisbett (2013). When the Claim Hits: Bilateral Investment Treaties and Bounded Rational Learning. *World Politics* 65/2: 273–313.

Powell, Frederick (2007). *The Politics of Civil Society: Neoliberalism or Social Left.* Bristol: Policy Press.

Powell, Christopher, and François Dépelteau (eds) (2013). *Conceptualizing Relational Sociology: Ontological and Theoretical Issues.* New York: Palgrave Macmillan.

Pragasam, Nirad (2012). *"Tigers On The Mind": An Interrogation of Conflict Diasporas and Long Distance Nationalism. A Study of the Sri Lankan Tamil Diaspora in London.* Doctoral thesis submitted to the Department of International Development of the London School of Economics. London: London School of Economics.

Price, Richard (2003). Transnational Civil Society and Advocacy in World Politics. *World Politics* 55: 579–606.

Putnam, Robert D. (1993). *Making Democracy Work.* Princeton, NJ: Princeton University Press.

Putnam, Robert D. (2000). *Bowling Alone: The Collapse and Revival of American Community*. New York: Simon & Schuster.

Radnitz, Scott (2010). *Weapons of the Wealthy: Predatory Regimes and Elite-Led Protests in Central Asia*. Ithaca: Cornell University Press.

Radtke, Katrin (2009). *Mobilisierung der Diaspora: Die moralische Ökonomie der Bürgerkriege in Sri Lanka und Eritrea*. Frankfurt a.M.: Campus.

Raghavan, Anita (2013). *The Billionaire's Apprentice: The Rise of the Indian-American Elite and the Fall of the Galleon Hedge Fund*. New York: Business Plus.

Ravenhill, John (2017). Regional Trade Agreements. In: Ravenhill, John (ed.). *Global Political Economy*. 5th edition. Oxford: Oxford University Press, 141–73.

Rawls, John (1971). *A Theory of Justice*. Cambridge, MA: Harvard University Press.

Rawls, John (1999). *The Law of Peoples*. Cambridge, MA: Harvard University Press.

Reeves, Aaron, Martin McKee, and David Stuckler (2016). "It's The Sun Wot Won It": Evidence of Media Influence on Political Attitudes and Voting from a UK Quasi-natural Experiment. *Social Science Research* 56: 44–57.

Regan, Donald H. (1972). The Problem of Social Cost Revisited. *The Journal of Law and Economics* 15/2: 427–37.

Reich, Michael R. (ed.) (2002). *Public-Private Partnerships for Public Health*. Cambridge: Harvard Center for Population and Development Studies.

Reich, Rob (2016). Repugnant to the Whole Idea of Democracy? On the Role of Foundations in Democratic Societies. *PS: Political Science & Politics* 49/3: 466–72.

Reich, Rob (2018). *Just Giving: Why Philanthropy is Failing Democracy and How It Can Do Better*. Princeton: Princeton University Press.

Rengger, Nicholas (2010). Remember the Aeneid? Why International Theory Should Beware Greek Gifts. *International Theory* 2/3: 454–60.

Renshon, Jonathan (2015). Losing Face and Sinking Costs: Experimental Evidence on the Judgment of Political and Military Leaders. *International Organization* 69/3: 659–95.

Reus-Smit, Christian (2002). Imagining Society: Constructivism and the English School. *The British Journal of Politics & International Relations* 4/3: 487–509.

Reus-Smit, Christian, and Duncan Snidal (eds) (2008). *The Oxford Handbook of International Relations*. Oxford: Oxford University Press.

Riesebrodt, Max (2001). Ethische und exemplarische Prophetie. In: Kippenberg, Hans G., and Martin Riesebrodt (eds). *Max Weber's "Religionssystematik."* Tübingen: Mohr Siebeck, 193–208.

Rinscheid, Adrian, Burkard Eberlein, Patrick Emmenegger, and Volker Schneider (2019). Why do Junctures Become Critical? Political Discourse, Agency, and Joint Belief Shifts in Comparative Perspective. *Regulation & Governance*, https://doi.org/10.1111/rego.12238.

Risse, Thomas (2013). Transnational Actors and World Politics. In: Carlsnaes, Walter, Thomas Risse, and Beth A. Simmons (eds). *Handbook of International Relations*. 2nd edition. Thousand Oaks: Sage Publications, 426–52.

Risse, Thomas, Steven C. Ropp, and Kathryn Sikkink (eds) (1999). *The Power of Human Rights: International Norms and Domestic Change*. Cambridge: Cambridge University Press.

Risse, Thomas, Stephen C. Ropp, and Kathryn Sikkink (eds) (2013). *The Persistent Power of Human Rights: From Commitment to Compliance*. Cambridge: Cambridge University Press.

Risse-Kappen, Thomas (ed.) (1995). *Bringing Transnational Relations Back In: Non-State Actors, Domestic Structures, and International Institutions*. Cambridge: Cambridge University Press.

Rixen, Thomas (2011). From Double Tax Avoidance to Tax Competition: Explaining the Institutional Trajectory of International Tax Governance. *Review of International Political Economy* 18/2: 197–227.

Roach, Stephen C. (ed.) (2009). *Governance, Order, and the International Criminal Court: Between Realpolitik and a Cosmopolitan Court*. Oxford: Oxford University Press.

Robinson, William I. (2012). Global Capitalism Theory and the Emergence of Transnational Elites. *Critical Sociology* 38/3: 349–63.

Robinson, William I., and Jerry Harris (2000). Towards a Global Ruling Class? Globalization and the Transnational Capitalist Class. *Science & Society* 64/1: 11–54.

Roese, Neal J. (1997). Counterfactual Thinking. *Psychological Bulletin* 121/1: 133–48.

Roger, Charles, and Peter Dauvergne (2016). The Rise of Transnational Governance as a Field of Study. *International Studies Review* 18/3: 415–37.

Rognlie, Matthew (2015). *Deciphering the Fall and Rise in the Net Capital Share: Accumulation or Scarcity?* Brookings Papers on Economic Activity, Spring 2015. Washington, D.C.: Brookings, online: https://www.brookings.edu/wp-content/uploads/2016/07/2015a_rognlie.pdf.

Roine, Jesper, Jonas Vlachos, and Daniel Waldenström (2009). The Long-Run Determinants of Inequality: What Can We Learn from Top Income Data? *Journal of Public Economics* 93: 974–88.

Roland, Gérard (ed.) (2008). *Privatization: Successes and Failures*. New York: Columbia University Press.

Ron, James, Archana Pandya, and David Crow (2016). Universal Values, Foreign Money: Funding Local Human Rights Organizations in the Global South. *Review of International Political Economy* 23/1: 29–64.

Ron, James, Howard Ramos, and Kathleen Rodgers (2005). Transnational Information Politics: Human Rights NGO Reporting, 1986–2000. *International Studies Quarterly* 49: 557–87.

Rose, Andrew K. (2004). Do We Really Know that the WTO Increases Trade?. *American Economic Review* 94/1: 98–115.

Rose, David (2011). Crouching Tiger, Hidden Raj. *Vanity Fair*, September 2011, online: http://web.archive.org/web/20140105134746/http://www.vanityfair.com/politics/features/2011/09/tamil-and-raj-201109.

Rose, Gideon (1998). Neoclassical Realism and Theories of Foreign Policy. *World Politics* 51/1: 144–72.

Rose-Ackerman, Susan, and Bonnie J. Palifka (2016). *Corruption and Government: Causes, Consequences, and Reform*. 2nd edition. Cambridge: Cambridge University Press.

Rosecrance, Richard (1986). *The Rise of the Trading State: Conquest and Commerce in the Modern World*. New York: Basic Books.

Rosen, Sherwin (1981). The Economics of Superstars. *American Economic Review* 71: 845–58.

Rosenau, James N. (1961). *Public Opinion and Foreign Policy: An Operational Formulation*. New York: Random House.

Rosenau, James N. (1968). *The Attentive Public and Foreign Policy: A Theory of Growth and Some New Evidence*. Princeton: Center of International Studies, Princeton University.

Rosenau, James N. (ed.) (1969). *Linkage Politics: Essays on the Convergence of National and International Systems*. New York: The Free Press.

Rosenau, James N. (1971). *The Scientific Study of Foreign Policy*. New York: The Free Press.

Rosenau, James N. (ed.) (1974). *Comparing Foreign Policies: Theories, Findings, and Methods*. New York: Wiley.

Rosenau, James N. (ed.) (1980). *The Study of Global Interdependence: Essays on the Transnationalization of World Affairs*. New York: Nichols.

Rosenau, James N. (1990). *Turbulence in World Politics: A Theory of Change and Continuity*. Princeton: Princeton University Press.

Rosenau, James N. (1995). Governance in the Twenty-First Century. *Global Governance* 1/1: 13–43.

Rosenau, James M. (1997). *Along the Domestic-Foreign Frontier: Exploring Governance in a Turbulent World*. Cambridge: Cambridge University Press.

Rosenau, James N. (2003). *Distant Proximities: Dynamics Beyond Globalization*. Princeton: Princeton University Press.

Rosenau, James N. (2008). *People Count! Networked Individuals in Global Politics*. Boulder, CO: Paradigm.

Rosenau, James N., and Ernst-Otto Czempiel (eds) (1992). *Governance without Government: Order and Change in World Politics*. Cambridge: Cambridge University Press.

Rosenberg, Emily S. (ed.) (2012). *A World Connecting, 1870–1945*. Cambridge, MA: Harvard University Press.

Rosenberg, Justin (1992). *The Empire of Civil Society: A Critique of the Realist Theory of International Relations*. London: Verso.

Roth, Anat (2015). "Something new begins"—Religious Zionism in the 2013 Elections: From Decline to Political Recovery. *Israel Affairs* 21/2: 209–29.

Rothkopf, David (2008). *Superclass: How the Rich Ruined our World*. New York: Farrar, Straus and Grioux.

Rowinski, Paul (2017). *Evolving Euroscepticisms in the British and Italian Press: Selling the Public Short*. Cham: Palgrave Macmillan,

Rubin, Neil (2012). The Relationship Between American Evangelical Christians and the State of Israel. In: Freedman, Robert O. (ed.). *Israel and the United States: Six Decades of US-Israeli Relations*. Boulder, CO: Westview Press, 232–56.

Rueschemeyer, Dietrich, Evelyne Huber Stephens, and John D. Stephens (1992). *Capitalist Development and Democracy*. Chicago: University Of Chicago Press.

Ruggie, John G. (1982). International Regimes, Transactions, and Change: Embedded Liberalism in the Postwar Economic Order. *International Organization* 36/1: 379–415.

Ruggie, John Gerard (1998). What Makes the World Hang Together? Neo-utilitarianism and the Social Constructivist Challenge. *International Organization* 52/4: 855–85.

Rummel, Rudolph J. (1976). *Understanding Conflict and War: The Conflict Helix, vol. 2*. Beverly Hills, CA: Sage.

Rummel, Rudolph J. (1983). Libertarianism and International Violence. *Journal of Conflict Resolution* 27/1: 27–71.

Rushton, Simon (2011). *AIDS: Five Neglected Questions for Global Health Strategies*. Briefing Paper GH BP 2011/03. London: Chatham House. Online: https://www.chathamhouse.org/sites/files/chathamhouse/public/Research/Global%20Health/bp1111_rushton.pdf.

Rushton, Simon, and Owain David Williams (2012). Frames, Paradigms and Power: Global Health Policy-Making under Neoliberalism. *Global Society* 26/2: 147–67.

Russell, Bertrand (1938). *Power: A New Social Analysis*. London: George Allen and Unwin.

Russell Sage Foundation (2016). *What We Know About Economic Inequality and Social Mobility in the United States*. New York: Russell Sage Foundation, online: https://www.russellsage.org/sites/default/files/RSFissuebriefs_0.pdf.

Russett, Bruce, and John R. Oneal (2001). *Triangulating Peace: Democracy, Interdependence, and International Organizations.* New York: W. W. Norton & Company.

Rustow, Dankwart A. (1970). Transitions to Democracy: Toward a Dynamic Model. *Comparative Politics* 2/3: 337–63.

Rutzen, Douglas (2015). Aid Barriers and the Rise of Philanthropic Protectionism. *International Journal of Not-for-profit Law* 17/1: 1–41.

Rynhold, Jonathan (2015). *The Arab-Israeli Conflict in American Political Culture.* Cambridge: Cambridge University Press.

Rynhold, Jonathan, and Dov Waxman (2008). Ideological Change and Israel's Disengagement from Gaza. *Political Science Quarterly* 123/1: 1–27.

Saad Filho, Alfredo, and Deborah Johnston (eds) (2005). *Neoliberalism: A Critical Reader.* London: Pluto Press.

Sacerdoti, Giorgio (2008). The Proliferation of BITs: Conflict of Treaties, Proceedings and Awards, in Appeals Mechanism. In: Sauvant, Karl P. (ed.). *Appeals Mechanism in International Investment Disputes.* Oxford: Oxford University Press, 127–36.

Sadeh, Jana, Mirco Tonin, and Michael Vlassopoulos (2014). *Why Give Away your Wealth? An Analysis of the Billionaires' View.* Discussion Papers in Economics and Econometrics no. 1417. Southampton: University of Southampton.

Saideman, Stephen M. (2001). *The Ties That Divide: Ethnic Politics, Foreign Policy, and International Conflict.* New York: Columbia University Press.

Sanandaji, Tino (2012). *The International Mobility of the Super-Rich.* IFN Working Paper No. 904. Stockholm: Research Institute of Industrial Economics.

Sandberg, Kristin Ingstad, Steinar Andresen, and Gunnar Bjune (2010). A New Approach to Global Health Institutions? A Case Study of New Vaccine Introduction and the Formation of the GAVI Alliance. *Social Science & Medicine* 71/7: 1349–56.

Sassen, Saskia (1991). *The Global City.* Princeton: Princeton University Press.

Sasson, Theodore (2014). *The New American Zionism.* New York: NYU Press.

Sasson, Theodore, Michelle Shain, Shahar Hecht, Graham Wright, and Leonard Saxe (2014). Does Taglit-Birthright Israel Foster Long-Distance Nationalism? *Nationalism and Ethnic Politics* 20/4: 438–54.

Sauvant, Karl P., and Lisa E. Sachs (eds) (2009). *The Effect of Treaties on Foreign Direct Investment: Bilateral Investment Treaties, Double Taxation Treaties, and Investment Flows.* Oxford: Oxford University Press.

Saxe, Leonard, and Barry Chazan (2008). *Ten Days of Birthright Israel: A Journey in Young Adult Identity.* Waltham, MA: Brandeis University Press.

Saxe, Leonard, Shira Fishman, Michelle Shain, Graham Wright, and Shahar Hecht (2013). *Young Adults and Jewish Engagement: The Impact of Taglit-Birthright Israel.* Waltham, MA: Brandeis University/Maurice and Marilyn Cohen Center for Modern Jewish Studies.

Saxe, Leonard, Benjamin Phillips, Theodore Sasson, Shahar Hecht, Michelle Shain, Graham Wright, and Charles Kadushin (2009). *Generation Birthright Israel: The Impact of an Israel Experience on Jewish Identity and Choices.* Waltham, MA: Brandeis University/Maurice and Marilyn Cohen Center for Modern Jewish Studies.

Saxe, Leonard, Michelle Shain, Graham Wright, Shahar Hecht, and Theodore Sasson (2017). *Beyond 10 Days: Parents, Gender, Marriage, and the Long-Term Impact of Birthright Israel.* Waltham, MA: Brandeis University/Maurice and Marilyn Cohen Center for Modern Jewish Studies.

Scharpf, Fritz W. (1970). *Demokratietheorie zwischen Utopie und Anpassung*. Konstanz: Universitätsverlag.

Scharpf, Fritz W. (1999). *Governing in Europe*. Oxford: Oxford University Press.

Schattschneider, Elmer E. (1960). *The Semi-Sovereign People: A Realist's View of Democracy in America*. New York: Holt, Rinehart & Wilson.

Scheidel, Walter (2017). *The Great Leveler: Violence and the History of Inequality from the Stone Age to the Twenty-First Century*. Princeton: Princeton University Press.

Schervish, Paul G. (2003). *Hyperagency and High-Tech Donors: A New Theory of the New Philanthropists*. Boston College, Social Welfare Research Institute, mimeo.

Schervish, Paul G. (2006). The Moral Biography of Wealth: Philosophical Reflections on the Foundation of Philanthropy. *Nonprofit and Voluntary Sector Quarterly* 35/3: 477–92.

Schervish, Paul G. (2014a). Beyond Altruism: Philanthropy as Moral Biography and Moral Citizenship of Care. In: Jeffries, Vincent (ed.). *The Palgrave Handbook of Altruism, Morality and Social Solidarity: Formulating a Field Study*. New York: Palgrave Macmillan, 389–405.

Schervish, Paul G. (2014b). High-Tech Donors and Their Impact Philanthropy: The Conventional, Novel and Strategic Traits of Agent-Animated Wealth and Philanthropy. In: Taylor, Marilyn L., Robert J. Strom, and David O. Renz (eds). *Handbook of Research on Entrepreneurs' Engagement in Philanthropy: Perspectives*. Northampton: Edward Elgar Publishing, 148–82.

Schervish, Paul G., and John J. Havens (2001). The Mind of the Millionaire: Findings from a National Survey on Wealth with Responsibility. *New Directions in Philanthropic Fundraising* 32 (Summer 2001): 75–107.

Scheve, Kenneth, and David Stasavage (2009). Institutions, Partisanship, and Inequality in the Long Run. *World Politics* 61/2: 215–53.

Scheve, Kenneth, and David Stasavage (2010). The Conscription of Wealth: Mass Warfare and the Demand for Progressive Taxation. *International Organization* 64: 529–61.

Scheve, Kenneth, and David Stasavage (2012). Democracy, War, and Wealth: Lessons from Two Centuries of Inheritance Taxation. *American Political Science Review* 106/1: 81–102.

Schill, Stefan (2009). *The Multilateralization of International Investment Law*. Cambridge: Cambridge University Press.

Schillemans, Thomas (2013). *The Public Accountability Review: A Meta-analysis of Public Accountability Research in Six Academic Disciplines*. Working paper. Utrecht: Utrecht University School of Governance. Online: https://dspace.library.uu.nl/bitstream/handle/1874/275784/2013+The+Public+Accountability+Review_Schillemans.pdf?sequence=1.

Schiller, Dan (1999). *Digital Capitalism: Networking the Global Market System*. Cambridge, MA: MIT Press.

Schmid-Petri, Hannah, Silke Adam, Ivo Schmucki, and Thomas Häussler (2017). A Changing Climate of Skepticism? The Factors Shaping Climate Change Coverage in the US Press. *Public Understanding of Science* 26/4: 498–513.

Schmidt, Brian C. (1998). *The Political Discourse of Anarchy: A Disciplinary History of International Relations*. Albany: State University of New York Press.

Schmidt, Steffen (2011). *Mitgliedschaft und Aktivitäten in Parteien und Verbänden*, available online: http://www.bpb.de/system/files/pdf/FNFYZU.pdf.

Schmidt, Vivien A. (2013). Democracy and Legitimacy in the European Union Revisited: Input, Output and "Throughput." *Political Studies* 61/1: 2–22.

Schneider, Gerald, and Nils Petter Gleditsch (2010). The Capitalist Peace: The Origins and Prospects of a Liberal Idea. *International Interactions* 36/2: 107–14.

Schneider, Volker, Simon Fink, and Marc Tenbücken (2005). Buying out the State: A Comparative Perspective on the Privatization of Infrastructures. *Comparative Political Studies* 38/6: 704–27.

Schneider, Volker, and Häge, F. M. (2008). Europeanization and the Retreat of the State. *Journal of European Public Policy* 15: 1–19.

Schneiderman, David (2008). *Constitutionalizing Economic Globalization: Investment Rules and Democracy's Promise*. Cambridge: Cambridge University Press.

Scholte, Jan Aart (2005). *Globalization: A Critical Introduction*. 2nd edition. Basingstoke: Palgrave.

Schulman, Daniel (2014). *Sons of Wichita: How the Koch Brothers Became America's Most Powerful and Private Dynasty*. New York: Grand Central Publishing.

Schumpeter, Joseph A. (1912). *Theorie der wirtschaftlichen Entwicklung*. Leipzig: Duncker & Humblot.

Schumpeter, Joseph A. (1919). Zur Soziologie der Imperialismen. *Archiv für Sozialwissenschaft und Sozialpolitik* 46: 1–39, 275–310.

Schuyler, Glen T. (1997). Power to the People: Allowing Private Parties to Raise Claims before the WTO Dispute Resolution System. *Fordham Law Review* 65: 2275–311.

Sclar, Jason, Alexander Hertel-Fernandez, Theda Skocpol, and Vanessa Williamson (2016). *Donor Consortia on the Left and Right: Comparing the Membership, Activities, and Impact of the Democracy Alliance and the Koch Seminars*. Presented at the 2016 Meetings of the Midwest Political Science Association, Chicago IL.

Scruggs, Lyle, and Salil Benegal (2012). Declining Public Concern About Climate Change: Can we Blame the Great Recession? *Global Environmental Change* 22/2: 505–15.

Seabrooke, Leonard, and Lasse Folke Henriksen (eds) (2017a). *Professional Networks in Transnational Governance*. Cambridge: Cambridge University Press.

Seabrooke, Leonard, and Lasse Folke Henriksen (2017b). Issue Control in Transnational Professional and Organizational Networks. In: Seabrooke, Leonard, and Lasse Folke Henriksen (eds). *Professional Networks in Transnational Governance*. Cambridge: Cambridge University Press, 3–24.

Seabrooke, Leonard, and Duncan Wigan (2017). The Governance of Global Wealth Chains. *Review of International Political Economy* 24/1: 1–29.

Searle, John R. (2005). What is an Institution? *Journal of Institutional Economics* 1/1: 1–22.

Searle, John R. (2010). *Making the Social World*. Oxford: Oxford University Press.

Sears, David O. (1986). College Sophomores in the Laboratory: Influences of a Narrow Data Base on Social Psychology's View of Human Nature. *Journal of Personality and Social Psychology* 51/3: 515–30.

Sen, Amartya (1985). Well-Being, Agency and Freedom: The Dewey Lectures. *The Journal of Philosophy* 82/4: 169–221.

Sen, Amartya (1999). *Development as Freedom*. New York: Knopf.

Service, Robert (2015). *The End of the Cold War: 1985–1991*. London: Macmillan.

Sewell, William H., Jr. (1985). Ideologies and Social Revolutions: Reflections on the French Case. *The Journal of Modern History* 57/1: 57–85.

Sewell, William H., Jr. (1992). A Theory of Structure: Duality, Agency, and Transformation. *American Journal of Sociology* 98/1: 1–29.

Sewell, William H. (1996). Historical Events as Transformations of Structures: Inventing Revolution at the Bastille. *Theory and Society* 25/6: 841–81.

Shachar, Ayelet (2009). *The Birthright Lottery: Citizenship and Global Inequality*. Cambridge: Harvard University Press.

Shachar, Ayelet (2014). Dangerous Liaisons: Money and Citizenship. In: Shachar, Ayelet, and Rainer Bauböck (eds). *Should Citizenship be for Sale?* EUI Working Paper RSCAS 2014/01. San Domenico di Fiesole: European University Institute, 3–8.

Shachar, Ayelet, and Rainer Bauböck (eds) (2014). *Should Citizenship be for Sale?* EUI Working Paper RSCAS 2014/01. San Domenico di Fiesole: European University Institute.

Shain, Yossi (2007). *Kinship and Diasporas in International Affairs.* Ann Arbor: University of Michigan Press.

Shain, Yossi, and Neil Rogachevsky (2014). Between JDate and J Street: US Foreign Policy and the Liberal Jewish Dilemma in America. In: DeWind, Josh, and Renata Segura (eds). *Diaspora Lobbies and the US Government: Convergence and Divergence in Making Foreign Policy.* New York: Social Science Research Council & New York University.

Shani, Giorgio, and David Chandler (2010). Assessing the Impact of Foucault on International Relations—Introduction. *International Political Sociology* 4/2: 196–215.

Sharman, Jason C. (2006). *Havens in a Storm: The Struggle for Global Tax Regulation.* Ithaca, NY: Cornell University Press.

Sharman, Jason C. (2011). Testing the Global Financial Transparency Regime. *International Studies Quarterly* 55: 981–1001.

Shawcross, William (1997). *Murdoch: The Making of a Media Empire.* Revised and updated 2nd edition. New York: Simon & Schuster.

Shaxson, Nicholas (2016). *Treasure Islands: Tax Havens and the Men who Stole the World.* 2nd edition. London: Vintage.

Sheffer, Gabriel (2003). *Diaspora Politics: At Home Abroad.* Cambridge, UK: Cambridge University Press.

Sheffer, Lior, Peter John Loewen, Stuart Soroka, Stefaan Walgrave, and Tamir Sheafer (2018). Nonrepresentative Representatives: An Experimental Study of the Decision Making of Elected Politicians. *American Political Science Review* 112/2: 302–21.

Shelley, Louise I. (2018). *Dark Commerce: How a New Illicit Economy Is Threatening Our Future.* Princeton: Princeton University Press.

Shlaim, Avi (2014). *The Iron Wall: Israel and the Arab World.* 2nd updated edition. New York: W.W. Norton & Company.

Sil, Rudra (2000). The Foundations of Eclecticism: The Epistemological Status of Agency, Culture, and Structure in Social Theory. *Journal of Theoretical Politics* 12/3: 353–87.

Silk, Roger D., James W. Lintott, Andrew R. Stephens, and Christine M. Silk (2003). *Creating a Private Foundation: The Essential Guide for Donors and Their Advisers.* Princeton: Bloomberg.

Simmons, Beth A. (2001). The International Politics of Harmonization: The Case of Capital Market Regulation. *International Organization* 55/3: 589–620.

Simmons, Beth A. (2009). *Mobilizing for Human Rights: International Law in Domestic Politics.* Cambridge: Cambridge University Press.

Simmons, Beth A. (2014). Bargaining over BITs, Arbitrating Awards: The Regime for Protection and Promotion of International Investment. *World Politics* 66/1: 12–46.

Simmons, Beth, Frank Dobbin, and Geoffrey Garrett (eds) (2008a). *The Global Diffusion of Markets and Democracy.* Cambridge: Cambridge University Press.

Simmons, Beth, Frank Dobbin, and Geoffrey Garrett (2008b). Introduction: The Diffusion of Liberalization. In: Simmons, Beth, Frank Dobbin, and Geoffrey Garrett (eds). *The Global Diffusion of Markets and Democracy.* Cambridge: Cambridge University Press, 1–63.

Sinclair, John (2016). Political Economy and Discourse in Murdoch's Flagship Newspaper, *The Australian*. *The Political Economy of Communication* 4/2: 3–17.

Singer, David Andrew (2007). *Regulating Capital: Setting Standards for the International Financial System*. Ithaca, NY: Cornell University Press.

Singer, J. David (1960). International Conflict: Three Levels of Analysis. *World Politics* 12/3: 453–61.

Singer, J. David (1961). The Level-of-Analysis Problem in International Relations. *World Politics* 14/1: 77–92.

Singer, Peter (2010). *The Life You Can Save: Now to Do Your Part to End World Poverty*. New York: Random House.

Singer, Peter (2015). *The Most Good You Can Do: How Effective Altruism is Changing Ideas About Living Ethically*. New Haven: Yale University Press.

Singer, Peter W. (2007). *Corporate Warriors: The Rise of Privatized Military Industry*. 2nd revised edition. Ithaca, NY: Cornell University Press.

Sklair, Leslie (1995). *Sociology of the Global System*. 2nd edition. Hemel Hempstead: Prentice Hall/Harvester Hweatsheaf.

Sklair, Leslie (2001). *The Transnational Capitalist Class*. Malden: Blackwell.

Sklair, Leslie (2006). Capitalist Globalization: Fatal Flaws and the Necessity for Alternatives. *Brown Journal of World Affairs* 13/1: 29–37.

Skocpol, Theda (1979). *States and Social Revolutions: A Comparative Analysis of France, Russia, and China*. Cambridge: Cambridge University Press.

Skocpol, Theda (1985). Cultural Idioms and Political Ideologies in the Revolutionary Reconstruction of State Power: A Rejoinder to Sewell. *The Journal of Modern History* 57/1: 86–96.

Skocpol, Theda (2016). Why Political Scientists Should Study Organized Philanthropy. *PS: Political Science & Politics* 49/3: 433–6.

Skocpol, Theda, and Alexander Hertel-Fernandez (2016). The Koch Network and Republican Party Extremism. *Perspectives on Politics* 14/3: 681–99.

Skocpol, Theda, and Vanessa Williamson (2012). *The Tea Party and the Remaking of Republican Conservatism*. Oxford: Oxford University Press.

Slater, Robert (2009). *Soros: The World's Most Famous Investor*. 2nd edition. New York: McGraw-Hill.

Slobodian, Quinn (2018). *The Globalists: The End of Empire and the Birth of Neoliberalism*. Cambridge, MA: Harvard University Press.

Smith, Charles D. (2013). *Palestine and the Arab-Israeli Conflict: A History with Documents*. 8th edition. New York: St. Martin's Press.

Smith, Hazel, and Paul Stares (eds) (2007). *Diasporas in Conflict: Peace-Makers or Peace-Wreckers?* Tokyo: United Nations University Press.

Smith, Steve, Amelia Hadfield, and Tim Dunne (eds) (2016). *Foreign Policy: Theories, Actors, Cases*. 3rd edition. Oxford: Oxford University Press.

Snyder, Richard C., H. W. Bruck, and Burton Sapin (1962). Decision-Making: An Approach to the Study of International Politics. In: Snyder, Richard C., H. W. Bruck, and Burton Sapin (eds). *Foreign Policy Decision-Making: An Approach to the Study Of International Politics*. Glencoe: Free Press.

Soederberg, Susanne, Georg Menz, and Philip G. Cerny (2005). *Internalizing Globalization: The Rise of Neoliberalism and the Decline of National Varieties of Capitalism*. Basingstoke: Palgrave Macmillan.

Soifer, Hillel David (2012). The Causal Logic of Critical Junctures. *Comparative Political Studies* 45/12: 1572–97.

Solomon, John, and B. C. Tan (2007). Feeding the Tiger: How Sri Lankan Insurgents Fund Their War. *Jane's Intelligence Review* (August 2007): 16–20.

Song, Sarah (2012). The Boundary Problem in Democratic Theory: Why the Demos Should be Bounded by the State. *International Theory* 4/1: 39–68.

Soros Foundations Network (2000). *Soros Foundations Network 1999 Annual Report*. New York: Open Society Institute, online: https://www.opensocietyfoundations.org/sites/default/files/a_a_complete_99_0.pdf.

Soros, George (1987). *The Alchemy of Finance*. Hoboken, NJ: Wiley & Sons.

Soros, George (1991). *Underwriting Democracy*. New York: Free Press.

Soros, George (1995). *Soros on Soros: Staying Ahead of the Curve*. New York: John Wiley & Sons.

Soros, George (2000). *Open Society: The Crisis of Global Capitalism Reconsidered*. London: Little, Brown & Company.

Soros, George (2004). *The Bubble of American Supremacy*. New York: PublicAffairs.

Soros, George (2006a). The Pursuit of Truth: A Talk with George Soros. *World Policy Journal* 23/3: 59–63.

Soros, George (2006b). *The Age of Fallibility: The Consequences of the War on Terror*. New York: PublicAffairs.

Soros, George (2011). My Philanthropy. In: Sudetic, Chuck. *The Philanthropy of George Soros*. New York: PublicAffairs, 1–57.

Soros, George (2013). Fallibility, Reflexivity, and the Human Uncertainty Principle. *Journal of Economic Methodology* 20/4: 309–29.

Spier, Tim (2011). Wie aktiv sind die Mitglieder der Parteien? In: Spier, Tim, Markus Klein, Ulrich von Alemann, Hanna Hoffmann, Annika Laux, Alexandra Nonnenmacher, and Katharina Rohrbach (eds). *Parteimitglieder in Deutschland*. Wiesbaden: Verlag für Sozialwissenschaften, 97–119.

Spina, Nicholas, and Christopher Raymond (2014). Civil Society Aid to Post-communist Countries. *Political Studies* 62/4: 878–94.

Sprout, Harold, and Margaret Sprout (1965). *The Ecological Perspective in Human Affairs*. Princeton, NJ: Princeton University Press.

Sriskandarajah, Dhananjayan (2005). Tamil Diaspora Politics. In: Ember, Melvin, Carol Ember, and Ian Skoggard (eds). *The Encyclopedia of Diasporas*. New Haven, CT: Yale University Press/Kluwer, 493–501.

Staniland, Paul (2012). Organizing Insurgency: Networks, Resources, and Rebellion in South Asia. *International Security* 37/1: 142–77.

Staniland, Paul (2014). *Networks of Rebellion: Explaining Insurgent Cohesion and Collapse*. Ithaca: Cornell University Press.

Starling, Mary, Ruairi Brugha, Gill Walt, Annie Heaton, and Regina Keith (2002). *New Products into Old Systems: The Global Alliance for Vaccines and Immunizations (GAVI) from a Country Perspective*. London: Save the Children Fund.

Starrs, Sean (2013). American Economic Power Hasn't Declined—It Globalized! Summoning the Data and Taking Globalization Seriously. *International Studies Quarterly* 57/4: 817–30.

Stebbins, Robert A. (2001). *Exploratory Research in the Social Sciences*. London: Sage.

Steen, Jennifer A. (2006). *Self-Financed Candidates in Congressional Elections*. Ann Arbor: University of Michigan Press.

Stein, Janice Gross (2013). Psychological Explanations of International Decision Making and Collective Behavior. In: Carlsnaes, Walter, Thomas Risse, and Beth A. Simmons (eds). *Handbook of International Relations*. 2nd edition. Thousand Oaks: Sage Publications, 195–219.

Stenebo, Johan (2010). *The Truth about IKEA: The Secret Behind the World's Fifth Richest Man and the Success of the Flatpack Giant.* London: Gibson Square.

Stewart, Susan (ed.) (2009). Special Issue: Democracy Promotion Before and After the "Colour Revolutions." *Democratization* 16/4.

Stewart, Susan (2009). The Interplay of Domestic Contexts and External Democracy Promotion: Lessons from Eastern Europe and the South Caucasus. *Democratization* 16/4: 804–24.

Stigler, George J. (1975). *The Citizen and the State: Essays on Regulation.* Chicago: University of Chicago Press.

Stiglitz, Joseph E., Amartya Sen, and Jean-Paul Fitoussi (2010). *Mismeasuring Our Lives: Why GDP Doesn't Add Up.* New York: The New Press.

Stille, Alexander (2006). *The Sack of Rome: How a Beautiful European Country with a Fabled History and a Storied Culture Was taken Over by a Man Named Silvio Berlusconi.* New York: Penguin.

Stokke, Kristian (2006). Building the Tamil Eelam State: Emerging State Institutions and Forms of Governance in LTTE-controlled Areas in Sri Lanka. *Third World Quarterly* 27/6: 1021–40.

Stone, Diane (2008). *Transnational Philanthropy, Policy Transfer Networks and the Open Society Institute.* Centre for the Study of Globalisation and Regionalisation Working Paper 238/08 (March 2008). Warwick: University of Warwick.

Stone, Diane (2010). Transnational Philanthropy or Policy Transfer? The Transnational Norms of the Open Society Institute. *Policy and Politics* 38/2: 269–87.

Stones, Rob (1991). Strategic Context Analysis: A New Research Strategy for Structuration Theory. *Sociology* 25/4: 673–95.

Storeng, Katerini T. (2014). The GAVI Alliance and the "Gates Approach" to Health System Strengthening. *Global Public Health* 9/8: 865–79.

Stovel, Katherine, and Lynette Shaw (2012). Brokerage. *Annual Review of Sociology* 38: 139–58.

Strand, Håvard, Siri Aas Rustad, Henrik Urdal, and Håvard Mokleiv Nygård (2019). Trends in Armed Conflict, 1946–2018. *Conflict Trends* 3/2019. Oslo: PRIO. Online: https://www.prio.org/utility/DownloadFile.ashx?id=1830&type=publicationfile.

Strange, Susan (1988). The Future of the American Empire. *Journal of International Affairs*: 1–17.

Strange, Susan (1996). *The Retreat of the State: The Diffusion of Power in the World Economy.* Cambridge: Cambridge University Press.

Strecker, David (2012). *Logik der Macht: Zum Ort der Kritik zwischen Theorie und Praxis.* Weilerswist: Velbrück Wissenschaft.

Streeck, Wolfgang (2013). *Gekaufte Zeit: Die vertagte Krise des demokratischen Kapitalismus.* Berlin: Suhrkamp.

Streeck, Wolfgang, and Kathleen Thelen (eds) (2005). *Beyond Continuity: Institutional Change in Advanced Political Economies.* Oxford: Oxford University Press.

Ströing, Miriam, and Melanie Kramer (2011). Reichtum und die Übernahme sozialer Verantwortung. In: Lauterbach, Wolfgang, Thomas Druyen, and Thomas Grundmann (eds). *Vermögen in Deutschland—Heterogenität und Verantwortung.* Wiesbaden: VS, 95–142.

Stuart, Douglas T. (2008). Foreign Policy Decision-Making. In: Reus-Smit, Christian, and Duncan Snidal (eds). *The Oxford Handbook of International Relations.* Oxford: Oxford University Press, 576–93.

Sudetic, Chuck (2011). *The Philanthropy of George Soros.* New York: PublicAffairs.

Sumption, Madeleine, and Kate Hooper (2014). *Selling Visas and Citizenship: Policy Questions from the Global Boom in Investor Immigration*. Washington, D.C.: Migration Policy Institute.

Sussman, Gerald, and Sascha Krader (2008). Template Revolutions: Marketing U.S. Regime Change in Eastern Europe. *Westminster Papers in Communication and Culture* 5/3: 91–112.

Swank, Duane (2002). *Global Capital, Political Institutions and Policy Change in Developed Welfare States*. Cambridge: Cambridge University Press.

Swank, Duane (2006). Tax Policy in an Era of Internationalization: Explaining the Spread of Neoliberalism. *International Organization* 60/4: 847–82.

Swank, Duane (2016). Taxing Choices: International Competition, Domestic Institutions and the Transformation of Corporate Tax Policy. *Journal of European Public Policy* 23/4: 571–603.

Swidler, Ann (1986). Culture in Action: Symbols and Strategies. *American Sociological Review* 51: 273–86.

Tallberg, Jonas, Thomas Sommerer, Theresa Squatrito, and Christer Jönsson (2013). *The Opening Up of International Organizations: Transnational Access in Global Governance*. Cambridge: Cambridge University Press.

Tarrow, Sidney (1994). *Power in Movement*. Cambridge: Cambridge University Press.

Tarrow, Sidney (2001). Transnational Politics: Contention and Institutions in International Politics. *Annual Review of Political Science* 4: 1–20.

Tarrow, Sidney (2005). *The New Transnational Activism*. Cambridge: Cambridge University Press.

Tarrow, Sidney, and Charles Tilly (2007). Contentious Politics and Social Movements. In: Stokes, Susan, and Charles Boix (eds). *The Oxford Handbook of Comparative Politics*. Oxford: Oxford University Press.

Tatzel, Miriam (ed.) (2013). *Consumption and Well-Being in the Material World*. New York: Springer.

Taylor, Marilyn L., Robert J. Strom, and David O. Renz (eds) (2014). *Handbook of Research on Entrepreneurs' Engagement in Philanthropy*: Perspectives. Northampton: Edward Elgar Publishing.

Taylor, Peter J., Pengfei Ni, Ben Derudder, Michael Hoyler, Jin Huang, and Frank Witlox (eds) (2011). *Global Urban Analysis: A Study of Cities in Globalization*. London: Earthscan.

Teachout, Zephyr (2009). Extraterritorial Electioneering and the Globalization of American Elections. *Berkeley Journal of International Law* 27/1: 162–91.

Teles, Steven M. (2016). Foundations, Organizational Maintenance, and Partisan Asymmetry. *PS: Political Science & Politics* 49/3: 455–60.

Testerman, Matthew (2015). Removing the Crutch: External Support and the Dynamics of Armed Conflict. *Studies in Conflict & Terrorism* 38/7: 529–42.

Tetlock, Philip E., and Aaron Belkin (eds) (1996). *Counterfactual Thought Experiments in World Politics: Logical, Methodological, and Psychological Perspectives*. Princeton: Princeton University Press.

Therborn, Göran (1977). The Rule of Capital and the Rise of Democracy. *New Left Review* 103: 3–41.

Thiemann, Matthias (2014). In the shadow of Basel: how competitive politics bred the crisis. *Review of International Political Economy* 21/6: 1203–39.

Thiemann, Matthias (2018). *The Growth of Shadow Banking: A Comparative Institutional Analysis*. Cambridge: Cambridge University Press.

Thies, Cameron G., and Marijke Breuning (2012). Integrating Foreign Policy Analysis and International Relations through Role Theory. *Foreign Policy Analysis* 8/1: 1–4.

Thun, Eric (2017). The Globalization of Production. In: Ravenhill, John (ed.). *Global Political Economy*. 5th edition. Oxford: Oxford University Press, 174–96.

Tiffen, Rodney (2014). *Rupert Murdoch: A Reassessment*. Sydney: NewSouth.

Tilly, Charles, and Sidney Tarrow (2006). *Contentious Politics*. Boulder: Paradigm Publishers.

Tomz, Michael (2007). Domestic Audience Costs in International Relations: An Experimental Approach. *International Organization* 61/4: 821–40.

Tooze, Adam (2018). *Crashed: How a Decade of Financial Crises Changed the World*. London: Allen Lane.

Torgler, Benno, and Marco Piatti (2013). Extraordinary Wealth, Globalization, and Corruption. *Review of Income and Wealth* 59/2: 341–59.

Transparency International, and Global Witness (2018). *European Getaway: Inside the Murky World of Golden Visas*. Online: http://files.transparency.org/content/download/2321/14306/file/2018_report_GoldenVisas_English.pdf.

Treverton, Gregory F., and Seth G. Jones (2005). *Measuring National Power*. Santa Monica: RAND Corporation.

Tsaliki, Liza, Christos Frangonikolopoulos, and Asteris Huliaras (eds) (2011). *Transnational Celebrity Activism in Global Politics: Changing the World ?* London/Chicago: Intellect/Chicago University Press.

Tsfati, Yariv, and Adi Chotiner (2016). Testing the Selective Exposure—Polarization Hypothesis in Israel Using Three Indicators of Ideological News Exposure and Testing for Mediating Mechanisms. *International Journal of Public Opinion Research* 28/1: 1–24.

Tsingou, Eleni (2015). Club Governance and the Making of Global Financial Rules. *Review of International Political Economy* 22/2: 225–56.

Tucker, Joshua A. (2007). Enough! Electoral Fraud, Collective Action Problems and Post-Communist Colored Revolutions. *Perspectives on Politics* 5/3: 535–51.

Turner, Rachel S. (2008). *Neo-liberal Ideology: History, Concepts and Policies*. Edinburgh: Edinburgh University Press.

Turner, Ted, with Bill Burke (2008). *Call Me Ted*. New York: Grand Central Publishing.

Tyrangiel, Josh (2005). The Constant Charmer. *Time* 166/26 (December 26): 46–62.

UNCTAD (United Nations Conference on Trade and Development) (2018). *World Investment Report: Investment and New Industrial Policies*. New York/Geneva: United Nations.

UNDP (United Nations Development Programme) (1994). *Human Development Report 1994*. New York: United Nations Development Programme/Oxford University Press.

United for a Fair Economy (2012). *Born on Third Base: What the Forbes 400 Really Says About Economic Equality & Opportunity In America*. Boston: United for a Fair Economy, online: http://faireconomy.org/sites/default/files/BornOnThirdBase_2012.pdf (accessed December 13, 2019).

USAID (2005). *Democracy Rising*. Washington, D.C.: USAID. Online: http://pdf.usaid.gov/pdf_docs/Pdacf571.pdf.

Vaïsse, Justin (2010). *Neoconservatism: The Biography of a Movement*. Cambridge: Harvard University Press.

Valentini, Laura (2014). No Global Demos, No Global Democracy? A Systematization and Critique. *Perspectives on Politics* 12/4: 789–807.

Vallier, Ivan (1971). The Roman Catholic Church: A Transnational Actor. In: *International Organization* 25/3: 479–502.

Varmus, H., R. Klausner, E. Zerhouni, T. Acharya, A. S. Daar, and P. A. Singer (2003). Grand Challenges in Global Health. *Science* 302/5644: 398–9.

van Creveld, Martin L. (1991). *The Transformation of War*. New York: The Free Press.

van der Pijl, Kees (1998). *Transnational Classes and International Relations*. London: Routledge.

van Dyck, Marcus (2015). *Private philanthropische Stiftungen in der Global Health Governance*. Masters thesis. Munich: Geschwister-Scholl-Institut für Politikwissenschaft/Ludwig-Maximilians-Universität München. Online: https://epub.ub.uni-muenchen.de/24565/1/94_M%C3%BCnchner%20Beitr%C3%A4ge%20zur%20Politikwissenschaft_Marcus%20van%20Dyck.pdf.

van Harten, Gus (2005). Private Authority and Transnational Governance: The Contours of the International System of Investor Protection. *Review of International Political Economy* 12/4: 600–23.

Varmus, Harold (2013). Making PEPFAR: A Triumph of Medical Diplomacy. *Science & Diplomacy* 2, online: http://www.sciencediplomacy.org/article/2013/making-pepfar.

Veblen, Thorstein (1899) [1994]. *The Theory of the Leisure Class: An Economic Study of Institutions*. New York: Penguin.

Victor, David G. (2011). *Global Warming Gridlock: Creating More Effective Strategies for Protecting the Planet*. Cambridge: Cambridge University Press.

Vogel, David (2009). The Private Regulation of Global Corporate Conduct. In: Mattli, Walter, and Ngaire Woods (eds). *The Politics of Global Regulation*. Princeton: Princeton University Press, 151–88.

Vogel, David (2012). *The Politics of Precaution: Regulating Health, Safety, and Environmental Risks in Europe and the United States*. Princeton: Princeton University Press.

Vogel, Kenneth P. (2014). *Big Money: 2.5 Billion Dollars, One Suspicious Vehicle, and a Pimp—On the Trail of the Ultra-Rich Hijacking American Politics*. New York: PublicAffairs.

Vogel, Steven K. (1996). *Freer Markets, More Rules: Regulatory Reform in Advanced Industrial Countries*. Ithaca, NY: Cornell University Press.

Voigt, Stefan (2013). How (Not) to Measure Institutions. *Journal of Institutional Economics* 9/1: 1–26.

Volodarsky, Sasha, Hecht, Shahar, Shain, Michelle, and Saxe, Leonard (2019). *The Impact of Taglit-Birthright Israel on Participants from Russia, Ukraine, Belarus, and Germany*. Waltham, MA: Brandeis University, Maurice and Marilyn Cohen Center for Modern Jewish Studies, online: http://bir.brandeis.edu/bitstream/handle/10192/36852/impact_bri_fsu_043019.pdf.

Wæver, Ole (2011). *Securitization*. London: Routledge.

Walker, R. B. J. (1993). *Inside/Outside: International Relations as Political Theory*. Cambridge: Cambridge University Press.

Wallace, James, and James Erickson (1993). *Hard Drive: Bill Gates and the Making of the Microsoft Empire*. New York: Harper Business.

Wallerstein, Immanuel (1974). *The Modern World System: Capitalist Agriculture and the Origins of the European World Economy in the Sixteenth Century*. New York: Academic Press.

Wallerstein, Immanuel (2004). *World-Systems Analysis: An Introduction*. Chapel Hill: Duke University Press.

Walpen, Bernhard (2004). *Die offenen Feinde und ihre Gesellschaft: Eine hegemonietheoretische Studie zur Mont Pèlerin Society*. Hamburg: VSA.

Walt, Stephen M. (1987). *The Origins of Alliances*. Ithaca: Cornell University Press.

Walter, Andrew (2001). NGOs, Business, and International Investment: The Multilateral Agreement on Investment, Seattle, and beyond. *Global Governance* 7: 51.

Waltz, Kenneth N. (1959). *Man, the State and War: A Theoretical Analysis*. New York: Columbia University Press.

Waltz, Kenneth N. (1979). *Theory of International Politics*. Reading, Mass: Addison-Wesley.

Waltz, Kenneth N. (1990). Nuclear Myths and Political Realities. *American Political Science Review* 84/3: 731.

Watson, Tom, and Martin Hickman (2012). *Dial M for Murdoch: News Corporation and the Corruption of Britain*. London: Penguin.

Waxman, Dov (2012). The Pro-Israel Lobby in the United States: Past, Present, and Future. In: Freedman, Robert O. (ed.). *Israel and the United States: Six Decades of US-Israeli Relations*. Boulder, CO: Westview Press, 79–99.

Waxman, Dov (2016). *Trouble in the Tribe: The American Jewish Conflict over Israel*. Princeton: Princeton University Press.

Waxman, Dov (2017). American Jews and the Israeli-Palestinian Conflict: Part of the Problem or Part of the Solution?. *Political Science Quarterly* 132/2: 313–40.

Way, Lucan (2008). The Real Causes of the Color Revolutions. *Journal of Democracy* 19/3: 55–69.

Way, Lucan (2009). A Reply to my Critics. *Journal of Democracy* 20/1: 90–7.

Wayland, Sarah (2004). Ethnonationalist Networks and Transnational Opportunities: The Sri Lankan Tamil Diaspora. *Review of International Studies* 30/3: 405–26.

Wealth-X (2014). *WEALTH-X and UBS Billionaire Census 2014*. New York/London/Singapore: Wealth-X.

Wealth-X (2016a). *WEALTH-X Billionaire Census 2015–16*. New York/London/Singapore: Wealth-X.

Wealth-X (2016b). *Changing Philanthropy: Trend Shifts In Ultra Wealthy Giving*. New York/London/Singapore: Wealth-X, online: https://www.wealthx.com/wp-content/uploads/2016/12/WealthXArtonPhilanthropyReport2016wxcomfinal.pdf.

Wealth-X (2017). *Billionaire Census 2017*. New York/London/Singapore: Wealth-X, online: http://www.wealthx.com/wp-content/uploads/2017/07/Wealth-X-Billionaire-Census-2017.pdf.

Wealth-X (2018). *Billionaire Census 2018*. New York/London/Singapore: Wealth-X, online: https://www.wealthx.com/wp-content/uploads/2018/05/Wealth-X_Billionaire_Census_2018.pdf.

Wealth-X (2019). *Billionaire Census 2019*. New York/London/Singapore: Wealth-X, online: https://www.wealthx.com/wp-content/uploads/2019/05/Wealth-X-Billionaire-Census-2019.pdf.

Weber, Max (1904) [2002]. *The Protestant Ethic and the "Spirit" of Capitalism and Other Writings*. London: Penguin.

Weber, Max (1918) [2004]. Politics as a Vocation. In: Owen, David, and Tracy B. Strong (eds). *The Vocation Lectures*. Indianapolis: Hackett, 32–94.

Weber, Max (1921–1922) [1980]. *Wirtschaft und Gesellschaft. Grundriß der verstehenden Soziologie*. 5. revidierte Auflage. Besorgt von Johannes Winckelmann. Tübingen: J. C. B. Mohr (Paul Siebeck).

Weber, Max (1978). *Economy and Society*. Guenther Roth and Claus Wittich (eds). Berkeley/Los Angeles: University of California Press.

Weeks, Jessica L. (2008). Autocratic Audience Costs: Regime Type and Signaling Resolve. *International Organization* 62/1: 35–64.

Weinberg, David Andrew (2014). Israel and the United States: An Alliance like None Other. In: Shindler, Colin (ed.). *Israel and the World Powers: Diplomatic Alliances and International Relations beyond the Middle East*. London: I.B.Tauris, 61–91.

Weisberg, Herbert F. (2014). Tradition! Tradition? Jewish Voting in the 2012 Election. *PS: Political Science & Politics* 47/3: 629–35.

Weiss, Linda (ed.) (2003). *States in the Global Economy: Bringing Domestic Institutions Back in*. Cambridge: Cambridge University Press.

Welch, Claude E. (2001). Amnesty International and Human Rights Watch: A Comparison. In: Welch, Claude E. (ed.). *NGOs and Human Rights: Promise and Performance*. Philadelphia: University of Pennsylvania Press, 85–118.

Welt, Cory (2006). *Georgia's Rose Revolution: From Regime Weakness to Regime Collapse*. Paper prepared for the "Waves and Troughs of Post Communist Transitions" workshop, Center on Democracy, Development, and the Rule of Law, Stanford University, April 28–29, 2006. Stanford, CA: Center of Democracy, Development, and the Rule of Law, online: http://www18.georgetown.edu/data/people/cdw33/publication-32608.pdf.

Wendt, Alexander (1987). The Agent-Structure Problem in International Relations. *International Organization* 41/1: 335–70.

Wendt, Alexander (1992). Anarchy is What States Make of It: The Social Construction of Power Politics. *International Organization* 46/2: 391–425.

Wendt, Alexander (1999). *Social Theory of International Politics*. Cambridge: Cambridge University Press.

Wendt, Alexander (2004). The State as Person in International Theory. *Review of International Studies* 30: 289–316.

Wendt, Alexander (2015). *Quantum Mind and Social Science: Unifying Physical and Social Ontology*. Cambridge: Cambridge University Press.

West, Darrell M. (2014). *Billionaires: Reflections on the Upper Crust*. Washington, D.C.: The Brookings Institution.

White, Harrison (2008). *Identity and Control: How Social Formations Emerge*. 2nd edition. Princeton, NJ: Princeton University Press.

White, Stephen, and Ian McAllister (2009). Rethinking the "Orange Revolution." *Journal of Communist Studies and Transition Politics* 25/2–3: 227–54.

Whitman, Richard G (ed.) (2011). *Normative Power Europe: Empirical and Theoretical Perspectives*. Basingstoke: Palgrave Macmillan.

WHO (2010). *World Health Report 2010: Health Systems Financing: The Path to Universal Coverage*. Geneva: World Health Organization.

WHO (2018). Public Spending on Health: A Closer Look at Global Trends. Geneva: World Health Organization. Online: https://apps.who.int/iris/bitstream/handle/10665/276728/WHO-HIS-HGF-HF-WorkingPaper-18.3-eng.pdf?ua=1.

Wight, Colin (2006). *Agents, Structures and International Relations: Politics as Ontology*. Cambridge: Cambridge University Press.

Wight, Colin (2013). Morphogenesis, Continuity and Change in the International Political System. In: Archer, Margaret (ed.). *Social Morphogenesis*. Dordrecht: Springer, 85–101.

Wight, Colin (2014). Morphogenesis and Cooperation in the International Political System. In: Archer, Margaret (ed.). *Late Modernity: Trajectories towards Morphogenetic Society*. Dordrecht: Springer, 221–40.

Wight, Martin (1977). *Systems of States*. Leicester: Leicester University Press.

Williams, Owain David, and Simon Rushton (2011). Private Actors in Global Health Governance. In: Williams, Owain David, and Simon Rushton (eds). *Partnerships and Foundations in Global Health Governance*. Basingstoke: Palgrave Macmillan, 1–25.

Williamson, John (1990). What Washington Means by Policy Reform. In: Williamson, John (ed.). *Latin American Adjustment: How Much Has Happened?* Washington, D.C.: Institute for International Economics, 5–20.

Williamson, John (2003). From Reform Agenda to Damaged Brand Name: A Short History of the Washington Consensus and Suggestions for What to Do Next. *Finance and Development* 40/3: 10–13.

Wilson, A. Jeyaratnam (2000). *Sri Lankan Tamil Nationalism: Its Origins and Development in the Nineteenth and Twentieth Centuries*. Vancouver: University of British Columbia Press.

Wilson, Andrew (2006). Ukraine's Orange Revolution, NGOs and the Role of the West. *Cambridge Review of International Affairs* 19/1: 21–32.

Winter, Brian (2007). How Slim Got Huge. *Foreign Policy*, October 11, 2007, available online: http://www.foreignpolicy.com/articles/2007/10/11/how_slim_got_huge.

Winters, Jeffrey A. (2011). *Oligarchy*. Cambridge: Cambridge University Press.

Winters, Jeffrey A., and Benjamin I. Page (2009). Oligarchy in the United States? *Perspectives on Politics* 7/4: 731–51.

Wolfe, Tom (1987). *The Bonfire of the Vanities*. New York: Farrar Straus Giroux.

Wolfers, Arnold (1952). "National Security" as an Ambiguous Symbol. *Political Science Quarterly* 67/4: 481–502.

Wolfers, Arnold (1959). The Actors in International Politics. In: Fox, William T. R. (ed.). *Theoretical Aspects of International Relations*. Notre Dame: University of Notre Dame Press.

Wolff, Michael (2010). *The Man Who Owns the News: Inside the Secret World of Rupert Murdoch*. London: Vintage.

Wolff, Stefan (2005). *Ethnic Conflict: A Global Perspective*. Oxford: Oxford University Press.

Woll, Cornelia (2011). *Beyond Ideological Battles: A Strategic Analysis of Hedge Fund Regulation in Europe*. Les Cahiers européens de Sciences Po, 02/2011. Available online: http://www.cee.sciences-po.fr/fr/publications/les-cahiers-europeens/2011.html.

WTO (2019). *Global Trade Growth Loses Momentum as Trade Tensions Persist*. Press Release 837, April 2, 2019. Geneva: WTO.

Wu, Tim (2018). *The Curse of Bigness: Antitrust in the New Gilded Age*. New York: Columbia Global Reports.

Youde, Jeremy (2013). The Rockefeller and Gates Foundations in Global Health Governance. *Global Society* 27/2: 139–58.

Young, Kevin L. (2012). Transnational Regulatory Capture? An Empirical Examination of the Transnational Lobbying of the Basel Committee on Banking Supervision. *Review of International Political Economy* 19/4: 663–88.

Young, Oran R. (1972). The Actors in World Politics. In: Rosenau, James N., Vincent Davis, and Maurice A. East (eds). *The Analysis of International Politics: Essays in Honor of Harold and Margaret Sprout*. New York: The Free Press, 125–44.

Zengerle, Jason (2015). Sheldon Adelson Is Ready to Buy the Presidency. *New York Magazine*, September 7, 2015. Online: http://nymag.com/daily/intelligencer/2015/09/sheldon-adelson-is-ready-to-buy-the-presidency.html.

Zitelmann, Rainer (2017). *Psychologie der Superreichen: Das verborgene Wissen der Vermögenselite*. Munich: FinanzBuch Verlag.

Zitelmann, Rainer (2019). *Die Gesellschaft und ihre Reichen: Vorurteile über eine beneidete Minderheit*. Munich: FinanzBuch Verlag.

Žižek, Slavoj (2006). Nobody has to be vile. *London Review of Books* 28/7 (April 6), online: https://www.lrb.co.uk/v28/n07/slavoj-zizek/nobody-has-to-be-vile.

Zucman, Gabriel (2013). *La Richesse Caché des Nations: Enquête sur les Paradis Fiscaux*. Paris: Seuil.

Zucman, Gabriel (2014). Taxing across Borders: Tracking Personal Wealth and Corporate Profits. *Journal of Economic Perspectives* 28/4: 121–48.

Zucman, Gabriel (2019). Global wealth inequality. *Annual Review of Economics* 11: 109–38.

Zürn, Michael (2018). *A Theory of Global Governance: Authority, Legitimacy, and Contestation*. Oxford: Oxford University Press.

Zürn, Michael, Martin Binder, and Matthias Ecker-Ehrhardt (2012). International Authority and Its Politicization. *International Theory* 4/1: 69–106.

Zürn, Michael, and Matthias Ecker-Ehrhardt (2013). *Die Politisierung der Weltpolitik*. Berlin: Suhrkamp.

Zunz, Olivier (2012). *Philanthropy in America: A History*. Princeton: Princeton University Press.

Index